University of Nebraska Press, Lincoln and London

Frederick E. Hoxie

A Final Promise: The Campaign to Assimilate the Indians, 1880–1920

With a new preface by the author

Preface to the Bison Books
Edition © 2001 by the
University of Nebraska Press

© 1984 by the
University of Nebraska Press
All rights reserved
Manufactured in the
United States of America

First Bison Books printing: 2001

Library of Congress Cataloging
in Publication Data

Hoxie, Frederick, E., 1947–
A final promise : the campaign to
assimilate the Indians, 1880–1920 /
Frederick E. Hoxie ; with a new preface
by the author.
p.   cm.
Originally published: c1984.
Includes bibliographical references
and index.
ISBN 0-8032-7327-4 (pbk.:
alk. paper)
1. Indians of North America—
Cultural assimilation.   2. Indians
of North America—Government
relations—1869–1934.
I. Title.
E98.C89 H68 2001
323.1'197073'09034—dc21
2001045002

For Elizabeth

Contents

Preface to the Bison Books Edition

A Final Promise has been a very lucky book. Not only did it find an audience that has sustained it for nearly two decades, but it also caught the attention of thoughtful reviewers who have helped identify and illuminate the text's central themes. Upon publication of this new edition of *A Final Promise* it seems fitting to focus readers' attention on those themes.

The three aspects of the historical analysis in *A Final Promise* that have attracted the most attention from reviewers and that have stimulated the most discussion are (1) the precise origins of late nineteenth-century Indian policy, (2) the shifting definition of the term "assimilation" used by policymakers from 1880 to 1920, and (3) the relationship of Indian people to this "assimilation era." Each of these topics has generated questions, both for me, the author, and for other historians who have written about them since the book first appeared.

The first significant theme identified by reviewers is the contention that the new Indian policies of the 1880s—allotment, Indian education, and the effort to extend citizenship to Native Americans— were not primarily the product of policy experts or reformer lobbyists. Instead I argue that the policies of the 1880s had complex cultural and political origins. Their foundations included Republican party ideology, anthropological social theories, and the popular desire to incorporate "alien" peoples into a homogenous social whole. The book explores the extent to which racial and ethnic tensions, arising from the end of Reconstruction and the onset of mass immigration from Europe, have influenced the political sponsors of allotment and Indian education. *A Final Promise* also examines the intellectual currents and popular ideas surrounding the study of Native Americans themselves and how these ideas have influenced political leaders and government officials who address policy questions. In this book I argue, in short, that policy decisions affecting Native people were the product of a wide array of forces, some emanating from the relatively small number of people directly involved in Indian affairs and others coming from the larger cultural and political discourse of the day.

Running through the book's discussion of political movements, anthropological theories, and popular attitudes is the unspoken argument that the racial and cultural attitudes expressed by Indian policymakers resembled—sometimes vaguely, sometimes explicitly— attitudes expressed elsewhere in government and the culture at large toward African Americans, new immigrants, and the populations of America's new overseas colonies. Indian policymaking was part of the political culture of the time; it was not something that took place in a vacuum. Assimilation-era policies reflected shifting national cultural styles and priorities, and they influenced those broader currents in return. While this view is certainly my own, it does reflect the profound influence that the work of my graduate school mentor, Morton Keller, has had on my thinking. Keller published *Affairs of State* while I was writing *A Final Promise*, and his style and insights certainly have inspired my own work.

A number of reviewers have professed that they were not persuaded by the argument that Indian policymaking had its origins in the political cultural and intellectual climate of Gilded Age America. One reviewer put his position this way:

While the book is an imaginative attempt to present the making of policy towards Indians in a framework that includes other minorities, one finds little evidence to support that view. Indeed, racism and ethnocentrism were characteristics of the dominant white Protestant majority who made policy, but that does not mean that they perceived Indians as being part of a larger problem of dealing with minority races and white ethnics. No evidence is presented to support the thesis that assimilation of Indians provided a model for dealing with blacks, Asians, and Catholic Europeans. (*Journal of American History*, September 1985)

In this reviewer's opinion, my argument that anthropologists at the Smithsonian supported allotment (albeit in many cases with doubts), for example, or my assertion that politicians, such as Massachusetts senator Henry Dawes, supported Indian reform for short-term political reasons rather than out of a particular commitment to Native Americans did not rise to the level of "evidence." Moreover, my assertions concerning the atmosphere of the early twentieth century, when the deepening public pessimism regarding the ability of African Americans and new European immigrants to become part of American society seemed to be reflected in a similar pessimism among Indian policymakers, were not convincing.

Reflecting on the shifting nature of racial discussions in America after 1900, I have been struck by the remarkably different political atmosphere that existed in Congress as a growing number of new western states entered the Union and sent senators to Washington, D.C. It seemed evident that over time Indians were viewed as a peculiarly "western" problem in much the same way African Americans were viewed as a "southern" responsibility. The hardening attitudes toward Indians after 1900 and the rising power of western politicians who were unapologetic boosters of western "progress" seemed to confirm this shift. The concordance between Indian policy and larger currents of racial thinking and racially charged political debate continues to persuade me even as some readers and reviewers continue to be skeptical. It should not be surprising to learn that the late C.

Vann Woodward's *The Strange Career of Jim Crow* hovered in my mind as I was writing about these issues.

The second theme reviewers identified was less a "theme" than a central historical judgment. In the early twentieth century, *A Final Promise* argues, "total assimilation was no longer the central concern of policy makers and the public." While attitudes toward Native Americans had always been ambivalent, there was a profound shift away from "optimistic" programs such as universal education, citizenship, and the protection of Indian resources. In their place Congress and the Bureau of Indian Affairs emphasized vocational training, delayed or limited citizenship, and the transfer of control over Native resources from Indians to whites. Again not everyone was convinced of this assertion. One thoughtful reviewer put it this way:

I am unpersuaded by Hoxie's revisionist argument as a whole. It rests on a comparison that puts Hoxie in the position of defending the first phase of assimilation in order to attack the second. . . . Reformers and administrators in the period 1880–1900 were committed to the elimination of a distinctive native cultural presence in America; so were their successors after 1900. . . . To praise the earlier reformers for more benign intentions and greater sincerity is to praise Carlisle's Richard Pratt for agreeing that the only good Indian is a dead Indian, therefore kill the Indian and save the man. (*Great Plains Quarterly*, winter 1986)

Continuities in policymaking were more striking to this reviewer than the shift I had described. Certainly I would concede that those continuities are evident. Moreover, while I can understand this reviewer's reading of the book, it was not my intention to describe the first phase of this reform era as a "model" period for later policymakers. Nevertheless it is difficult to escape the fact that the impulse to assimilate Native Americans—the "final promise"—reflects an expansive view of American society and citizenship, an expansive view that quickly disappeared after the turn of the new century. Coupled with constitutional protection of Native religion, respect for treaties, and tribal property, these early reforms, while not necessarily "better," would certainly have produced a different result. The point of my argument, however, was not to rehabilitate the memory of Henry Dawes or Richard Pratt. Rather it was to show the extent to which Native Americans in the early twentieth century shifted in both the public mind and in the minds of policymakers from the category of potential citizens to something resembling the station occupied by colonized people.

Some would argue that the policy shifts I describe in *A Final Promise* are distinctions that do not define a difference. White people had their way; Indians were marginalized, abandoned, and forgotten. Perhaps. That single sentence may tell the story better than my three-hundred-page monograph. On the other hand, when one casts an eye forward and asks why has the economic status of Native Americans improved so little despite more than a half-century of "enlightened" policymaking, it seems vital that historians should look closely at the attitudes and relationships that have locked Indian people into the position they too often occupy in the modern United States (casinos aside). The "problems" Indian people face are not simply prejudice, infringements on civil liberties, and poor education. They are all of those things, certainly, but the problems are also defined by a set of attitudes and economic relationships that have placed Native communities and their resources under the control of outsiders. Of course any conscious person must also recognize that "decolonization" alone is not a total solution, but it is a start. My response to reviewers who doubt the shifts I describe in the early twentieth century, or the significance I ascribe to those shifts, is to ask a question of my own: How else can one explain the economic and political powerlessness of Indian people in the half-century following the end of World War I?

Finally, a number of reviewers have asked for a discussion of an assertion I had made in the final pages of the book but did not develop. "The assimilation effort," I wrote, "helped create its antithesis—a plural society." I speculated that the "lowered expectations" of government officials and bureaucrats had enabled Indian cultural practices to survive: "Tribal members could take advantage of their peripheral status, replenish their supplies of belief and value, and carry on their war with homogeneity." Several reviewers questioned the optimism implied by that sentence, "Anyone who has lived on a reservation might dispute that point since life on the periphery seldom provides a group with much leverage" (*Nevada Historical Society Quarterly*, fall 1985), and nearly all asked at least for an elaboration. One wrote: "[The book] would have been strengthened . . . by an analysis of how Indians reacted to the promise of assimilation and citizenship. We need to know if Indian attitudes about assimilation and allotment and their capacities as farmers and students were directly linked to the changing white perceptions about the possibility of rapid Indian assimilation into the mainstream of society" (*American Indian Culture and Research Journal* 9, no. 2 [1985]).

Having acknowledged at the outset that the focus of *A Final Promise* would be on non-Indian politicians and policymakers, there was little I could say in response to these comments except to agree with them. In fact the final pages of *A Final Promise* and the reactions to them has launched new projects. *Parading through History: The Making of the Crow Nation in America, 1805–1935* (New York: Cambridge University Press, 1995) began with those final pages. This book traces the political evolution of one tribal group and pays special attention to the tribe's self-transformation in the early twentieth century. In addition, a recent edited collection, *Talking Back to Civilization: Indian Voices from the Progressive Era* (Boston: Bedford/St. Martins, 2001), examines the words of Native American leaders and intellectuals who endured the government's new policies. This is a theme I expect to be puzzling over for many years to come.

I never hoped that *A Final Promise* would be the "last word" on the assimilation era. There were too many unexplored paths in the project, too many unexamined forces, and too many complicated aspects to federal Indian policy that I had not mastered. But I have been gratified that the book has been a "first word" in ongoing discussions about the nature of Indian policy, the role of Indian people in policymaking, and the legacy of allotment, Indian education, and other "reform" policies. Still there are subjects reviewers chose not to address that might prove interesting to new readers. Two strike me as particularly interesting.

First, *A Final Promise* takes a fairly conventional approach to "public attitudes" toward Native Americans by culling newspaper and magazine articles for evidence of non-Indian thinking. But this was one arena where whites did not dominate. During the early twentieth century the first generation of popular Native American writers began to win an audience. These included Charles Eastman, Gertrude Bonnin (Zitkala-Ša), Mourning Dove, and Luther Standing Bear. This emergence of Native people was also evident in the new hobbyist movement and in the beginnings of a commercially viable Indian art movement. Public attitudes toward Native Americans might well have been shaped by these people as well as by the non-Indians mentioned in *A Final Promise*. It may also be the case that Native Americans collaborated in the popularization of romantic ideas about Indian culture that stressed its simplicity. Ideas about Native people deserve a deeper and more complex history than they receive here.

Second, few reviewers discussed the legal history in *A Final Promise*. Chapter 7, "Redefining Indian Citizenship," traces the idea of limited citizenship for Indians in the early twentieth century. Based on a reading of a series of court decisions that so far have received very little attention elsewhere, the chapter describes how the grant of federal citizenship created problems for whites seeking to "protect" Indians from exploitation even as it threatened local political arrangements in western states. The role of the law, both as an instrument of control over tribes and individuals and as one of the "levers" Native Americans could use to improve their situations, deserves far more attention from historians than it has received to date.

I wish to express my sincere thanks to the staff of the University of Nebraska Press for its interest in publishing this paperback edition of *A Final Promise*. Frank Smith and his colleagues at Cambridge University Press also have my continuing gratitude for their faith in me and in this book over many years. I owe a particular debt of gratitude to Gary Dunham for his sustained interest in this work. Finally I am deeply appreciative of the efforts of the reviewers of this book over the past seventeen years. These "reviewers" include those who produced the originally published reviews as well as the many others who have communicated their reactions in other ways. In the midst of rapid change, it is reassuring to know that the phrase "community of scholars" continues to have meaning.

*The conviction tat everything that happens
on earth must be comprehensible to man can
lead to interpreting history by commonplaces.
Comprehension does not mean denying the
outrageous, deducing the unprecedented from
precedents, or explaining phenomena by such
analogies and generalities that the impact of
reality and the shock of experience are no longer
felt. It means, rather, examining and bearing
consciously the burden which our century has
placed on us—neither denying its existence nor
submitting meekly to its weight. Comprehension,
in short, means the unpremeditated, attentive
facing up to, and resisting of reality,—what ever
that may be.*

Hannah Arendt, *The Origins of Totalitarianism*

Preface

From the time of the nation's founding, American politicians, missionaries, and reformers protested to their critics that warfare with the country's native inhabitants was only the regrettable first step in a process of assimilation. While others gloried in the annihilation of tribal peoples, pious leaders from Thomas Jefferson to William Lloyd Garrison asserted that the Indians, once "freed" from their "savage" heritage, would participate fully in the nation's institutions. This final promise rested on two assumptions. The first was clear: motives were savages. Whether "noble" or "godless," Native Americans existed outside the white man's world and were by definition ineligible for automatic membership in "civilized" society. Second, national leaders expected that the destruction of "savagery" and the expansion of Christian "civilization" would convert individual natives into docile believers in American progress. With these ideas in hand, the future appeared predictable. On some future day, the

Indians would be surrounded, defeated, and somehow rendered eager to join the dominant culture.

Between 1860 and 1880, it became obvious that this old assimilationist commitment was about to be tested for the last time. With shocking speed, the Indians who had previously avoided American domination suffered complete military defeat. Every tribe and band was now encircled by a rising tide of farmers, miners, and entrepreneurs. That "future day" when "savagery" would meet its end was at hand.

What follows is an investigation of the effort to fulfill the Americans' final promise to the Indians. I will describe the process by which political leaders and their constituents adjusted to the reality that all natives would now live within the borders of the nation. This period of adjustment—during which Indians became an internal American minority group—is usually presented as an era of assimilation. According to the traditional view, the government in the late nineteenth century embarked on a wrong-headed but persistent campaign to push Native Americans into American citizenship and force them to adopt Anglo-American standards of land ownership, dress, and behavior. Such an interpretation fails to recognize that the assimilation campaign consisted of two distinct phases.

In the first phase there was widespread interest in transforming Indians into "civilized" citizens. Fueled by the memory of the Civil War and a self-serving desire to dismantle the tribal domains, politicians and reformers fashioned an elaborate program to incorporate native Americans into the nation. In the second phase, Americans altered much of that original program. Reacting to new, more pessimistic assessments of Indian abilities, as well as to the rising power of western politicians, policy makers redefined their objectives and altered the federal effort. They continued to work for the incorporation of native Americans into the majority society, but they no longer sought to transform the Indians or to guarantee their equality. By 1920 a new, more pessimistic spirit governed federal action.

Understanding that the assimilation campaign passed through two stages-each marked by its own set of assumptions, expectations, and programmatic emphases—helps clarify the last century of the Native American experience. In the eighteenth and nineteenth centuries, those who conquered tribal lands and fought native peoples defended their actions with a promise to compensate their victims with full membership in a "civilized" nation. But as the assimilation programs got underway, it became apparent that such compensation would be impossible. Not only did Indians resist the process, but complete acceptance of them demanded more of the nation's institutions, social values, and cultural life than the citizenry was willing to grant.

And so American leaders altered the terms of their pledge. As a consequence, modern Indians found themselves defined and treated as peripheral people—partial members of the commonwealth—and a web of attitudes, beliefs, and practices soon appeared to bind them in a state of economic dependence and political powerlessness. To be sure, Native Americans were incorporated into the nation, but their new status bore a grater resemblance to the position of the United States' other nonwhite peoples than it did to the "full membership" envisioned by nineteenth-century reformers. By 1920 they had become an American minority group, experiencing life on the fringes of what had come to be regarded as a "white man" land." The assimilation campaign was complete.

Today the dependence and powerlessness cultivated by the assimilation campaign continues to be a major theme in the life of native American communities. Despite the reforms of the new Deal era and the legal victories of recent decades, federal actions continue to betray and ambivalence toward Indian equality. Educational programs regularly join poor curricula with low expectations, while legal protection and resource management occur in an atmosphere highly charged by economic pressure and fears of political backlash. Doubts concerning the abilities of native people and resistance from state and local governments undermine federal efforts. Policy goals are rarely clear or long-lasting. In this sense, the assimilation campaign as produced a legacy of racial distrust and exploitation we have thus far been unable to set aside.

There are two ways to illuminate the shifting history of the government's assimilation campaign in the late nineteenth and early twentieth centuries. The first is to concentrate on the administration of government policies. Native resistance, economic development, political realignment, and shifts in cultural perception affected the implementation of specific programs; these particular events deserve description and analysis.

But on must also take into account important changes that were occurring in the nation's larger political culture. In the early nineteenth century, most Americans envisioned their society as homogeneous. People were either "citizens" (member of society) or "savages" (those ineligible for citizenship). Although the United States was relatively open to immigration from overseas, the country's leaders usually insisted that newcomers adhere to Protestant, Anglo-Saxon standards of conduct. Blacks and Asians, like Indians, were for the most part barred from this society while most European immigrants were admitted.

In the 1880s, as the nation was evolving into an industrial state and the stream of immigrants was growing in diversity, the old model of society seemed inappropriate. Policy makers began to imagine a new category of membership. They modified the old division between external "savages" and domestic citizens, for in their eyes homogeneity was no longer possible and groups of people could no longer be wholly included or wholly excluded from the country's institutions. In place of the old ideas, politicians and intellectuals began thinking that nonwhite minorities could be granted *partial* membership in the nation. In a complex, modern country, with its hierarchy of experts, managers, and workers, "aliens" could most easily and efficiently be incorporated into society's bottom ranks. In this way minorities could serve the dominant culture without qualifying for social and political equality. Not surprisingly, the new, more limited interpretation of Indian assimilation gained popularity during the first two decades of the new century, at the some time that the thoroughgoing segregation of blacks, the exclusion of Japanese immigrants, and the virtual suspension of immigration from southern and eastern Europe were winning popular approval. Clearly, a study of the Indian assimilation campaign should look beyond specific government programs and the problem of their administration to consider their relationship to broader changes in the United States' political culture.

My objective, then, is dual. First, I will describe the sources and effects of the campaign to bring all Indians inside the boundaries of the United States. That campaign produced the social and economic suffering that has been a central feature of Native American life in this century. Second, I will explain how the assimilation campaign was itself a reflection of America's move beyond a preoccupation with the Indians' "savagery" and toward the more complex outlook of our own time. When intellectuals and policy makers searched beyond the old certainty that Indians were savages, they initiated a lengthy process of reexamination and adjustment that is still underway.

Before proceeding, three disclaimers are in order. First, because I have focused on the behavior of white leaders, I have followed there interests and prejudices. Most thinkers and policy makers of the late nineteenth and early twentieth centuries assumed that the "Indian question" involved the trans-Mississippi West, and I have accepted this tendency to define national policy in terms of that region. I have therefore paid little attention to the many eastern tribes that my subjects ignored, and—like them—have treated Oklahoma as a special case with limited significance for national policy formulation.

Second, more that two-thirds of the text is devoted to the years after 1900, This is a function of the extensive secondary literature that already exists on the earlier period as well as a measure of the importance of the early twentieth century. In the years after 1900 the assimilation campaign of the 1880s was fundamentally altered. During that process relationships between Indians and whites became fixed in ways that have persisted down to the present.

And third, I should make clear what this book is and is not. Native American history has traditionally been the province of two groups of scholars. Ethnohistorians have produced studies of tribal groups. Many of the best of these detail the impact of European cultures on native American cultures. Such work has done a great deal to make native behavior understandable in non-Indian terms. Recently these efforts have gone further, to reveal the tribes' positive influence on white society. Nevertheless, such studies often fail to view the Indians' relations with whites as a clash of two complex cultures. Rather, their chief concern is with the process of native action in the face of a relentless and impersonal American expansion.

To understand the motives of non-Indians, one must look to a second body o historians, who describe the government's policies in a particular region or period. The fundamental concern of this group is usually the guilt or innocence of their subjects in the annihilation of Native American communities. The literature is filled with good and evil actors alternately winning and losing the day for the Indians, bringing on either the "final defeat" or a "new dawn." Very few students of white society have gone beyond this scenario to attempt to view Indian affairs in a broader, national context, and to ask, How did *this society*, at *this time*, produce *these ideas* and *these actions*?

It is as much a comment on the historical profession as on native American historiography itself to point out that it is time for non-Indian historians to do for their own society what the anthropologists and ethnohistorians have been so eager to do for tribal peoples: to attempt to see attitudes and actions as expressions of a complex culture confronting an alien people in a rapidly changing environment. This effort carries my study beyond the sources typically employed in policy analysis — to popular literature, anthropological theory, and the history of education. Although the connections between these topics and specific programs might appear obscure, they are crucial to an understanding of the assimilation campaign. They indicate the nature of the environment politicians and bureaucrats inhabited and reveal the extent to which that environment shaped both the formulation and the administration of federal policy.

Because my primary focus is federal policy as a reflection of changes in white society, much of the influence of Native Americans has been slighted. The effect of Indian communities on policy formulation during these years must await other much-needed studies. Until those studies appear, every history — including this one — will be incomplete.

The assimilation campaign was a product of specific ideas and programs as well as of the United States' political culture. Thus, my study is a work of history: I discuss individual events, particular ideas, certain pieces of legislation, and important actors. But the point of the discussion is to place the assimilation campaign in the context of a national experience. This political history, but only if politics is broadly defined as the interplay of ideas and interests with changing perceptions of both the problems and the solutions in Indian affairs. With this work we should be able to move away from accusations of guilt and professions of innocence and begin to understand better both the actions of the inscrutable white man and the responses of Native Americans.

One of the most pleasant aspects of completing this project is the opportunity it provides to thank publicly the many people and institutions that had a hand in its preparation. I first heard the expression "community of scholars" long ago, but it was not until I wrote this book that I understood what it could mean.

The staffs of the Boston Public Library, Harvard University's Widener and Langdell Libraries, the Goldfarb Library at Brandeis University, the Newberry Library in Chicago, Illinois, and the Library of Congress assisted me regularly and reliably during the research. Moreover, I have enjoyed the aid and hospitality of archivists at the Beinecke Rare Book and Manuscript Library at Yale, the Houghton Library at Harvard, the Harvard University Archives, the Manuscripts Division of the Library of Congress, the National Archives, the National Anthropological Archives, and the Wisconsin State Historical Society. And my friends at Antioch's Olive Kettering Library always responded promptly to my requests for books and citations; their enclave of quiet efficiency requires a special acknowledgment.

I am grateful for the financial support of the Irving and Rose Crown Fellowship in American Studies at Brandeis University, a predoctoral fellowship at the Newberry Library Center for the History of the American Indian, and a grant from the Antioch College Faculty Fund.

The list of friends and colleagues who have helped enliven my prose, verify my conclusions, and keep me out of the briar patch should include Robert Bieder, Hugh Donahue, Robert Fogarty, David Gould, Michael Grossberg, Dirk Hartog, Mark Higbee, Curtis Hinslay, Joan Mark, and David Reed. In addition, I have received both advice and encouragement from a number of persons whose openness and generosity are a measure of what is right with American academic life. These include Robert Berkhoffer, Helen Codere, John Demos, Lawrence Kelly, Howard Lamar, Richard Metcalf, Marvin

Meyers, Paul Prucha, and Helen Tanner. It is not difficult for one who is a teacher to thank *his* teachers, for he knows how much goes into the job and how uncertain are its consequences. No. Gordon Levin's ideas and enthusiasm propelled me into the project, while the wit, curiosity, and matchless energy of Morton Keller got me out. While everyone mentioned should share whatever credit accrues to this project, I alone am responsible for what I have written.

Parents and spouse come last—not because of sentimentality, bur because at the end one wonders, "Why did I do this?" Catherine, John, and Elizabeth Hoxie convinced me that it mattered.

A Final Promise

Chapter 1

The Appeal of Assimilation

On the morning of January 15, 1879, a front-page story in the *Boston Post* carried its readers far from their New England homes. An exclusive dispatch reported that a group of Cheyenne Indians had escaped from Fort Robinson, Nebraska: "Out into the night and frozen snow [the Indians] leaped and on the discovery of their escape they were pursued and slaughtered." The article evoked scenes of warriors plunging through deep snow, pursued by soldiers who fired into the night. For a few days newspapers from California to Georgia covered the story with similar enthusiasm. A headline in St. Louis, despite its ignorance of winter conditions in western Nebraska, was typical: "Several Soldiers Killed and Many Indians Made to Bite the Dust."[1]

The excitement following the Cheyenne outbreak did not continue. The incident was confined to a small area; and as more details of the fighting became known, pride in the cavalry's skill turned to disgust. The conflict had pitted mounted troops against 150 men, women, and children. The Indians—members of Dull Knife's band of Northern Cheyenne—had been confined to Fort Robinson after they refused to return to their bleak reservation in Indian Territory (present-day Oklahoma). The camp commander cut off the group's food and water. On the fifth night of their confinement the Indians gathered weapons they had hidden under the floorboards of the barracks and staged their pitiful breakout. This was not Kit Carson opening the southern plains or Custer battling for the inland empire. It was a shabby police action carried out by a well-equipped garrison force against a starving band of refugees. "The affair was a brutal and inhuman massacre," proclaimed the *Atlanta Constitution,* "a dastardly outrage upon humanity and a lasting disgrace to our boasted civilization."[2]

But the cruelty of the Fort Robinson incident was only partially responsible for the public outrage. The fighting in Nebraska seemed to be the harbinger of a new, repugnant form of Indian warfare. The Cheyennes were wards of the government, a people long since defeated in battle. Their purpose in leaving Indian Territory—and escaping from the army post—was similar to that of other racial groups in the late nineteenth century. Like their black and Asian contemporaries in the South and Far West, they were seeking a place for themselves in a changing and unsettled society. The confrontation with the cavalry suggested that their search was doomed.

Before the Civil War it had been possible to imagine that Indians and whites could remain permanently separate from one another. A series of policies, beginning in the eighteenth century with the adoption of the first Trade and Intercourse Acts and continuing through the removal and early reservation eras, were aimed at keeping the two races apart. That goal satisfied a number of interests. Humanitarians believed that separation would reduce the level of violence on the frontier and provide Indians with enough time to become "civilized." Expansionists thought that designating specific areas as "Indian country" allowed remaining lands to be settled more rapidly. And for many tribes, reservations were the only way to retain a portion of their national autonomy.

After 1865, the Grant and Hayes administrations tried to revitalize this separation strategy with their celebrated peace policy. For a decade the Indian Office endeavored to consolidate agencies, end corruption in the federal bureaucracy, and replace tribal agents with men approved by the nation's religious leaders. Government officials hoped that an efficient evangelical Indian service could successfully "civilize" the Native American population before it was completely overrun by white settlement.

The peace policy was a praiseworthy effort. A product of the idealism of the reconstruction era, it won enthusiastic backing from both politicians and reformers. Unfortunately, like so many ambitious schemes of the postwar period, it did not work. President Grant assigned most of the agency openings to Protestants, thereby alienating the one group—the Catholics—with the most experience in the West. Many of his appointees were Methodists and Quakers who were ill prepared for the responsibility. Appropriations for schools and farming implements were almost nonexistent. Because administrators had difficulty deciding on the location of the new consolidated agencies, tribes were repeatedly moved or asked to accommodate themselves to white encroachment. And an extended struggle over whether to locate the Indian Office in the War or the Interior Department undermined the government's efforts.[3]

For many, the Northern Cheyenne incident typified the failure of the peace policy. That tribe had been moved from its traditional home in the northern plains to a "consolidated" reservation in Indian Territory. The Indians hated the relocation; there they found food supplies low and medical care unavailable. And so they escaped, forcing the army to hunt them down and return them to their reservation. After a decade of effort, the government seemed incapable of producing anything but more bloody headlines.

The outcry surrounding the Fort Robinson tragedy subsided in a few weeks. After all, Indian affairs were a relatively minor feature of national life and the natives themselves represented only a tiny percentage of the American population. But the issues raised by the fighting did not disappear, for the Cheyenne escape proved to be only the first in a year-long succession of disastrous encounters between the government and Native Americans. Additional incidents captured public attention and brought the failure of both the peace policy and the entire separation strategy home to the American people.

The first of these incidents began to unfold in late January 1879, when the Cheyennes were burying their dead outside Fort Robinson. Standing Bear and a small band of his fellow Poncas escaped from Indian Territory. Following the same general trail that Dull Knife had used the previous fall, the group headed north toward their homes along the Niobrara River. In March, army units detained the chief and ordered him to return to his agency. While the Indian Office prepared transportation, he was confined at Fort Omaha, Nebraska.

Despite their similar predicaments, the Poncas did not share the fate of the Northern Cheyennes. Standing Bear's arrest came less than two months after the January massacre, and the memory of that night was not far from the minds of the public or the officials handling the new case. What is more, the Poncas were an agricultural people who had never warred on the United States. Before long a committee of local ministers had formed to petition for the chief's release. Even the military wanted to set him free. General George Crook, the local commander who would later distinguish himself as the captor of Geronimo, cooperated in this effort by encouraging a habeas corpus suit to test the legality of Standing Bear's imprisonment. Crook had no special love for Native Americans—he called the Apaches the "tiger of the human species"—but he saw no reason to damage the army's reputation further by repeating the heavy-handed tactics used at Fort Robinson.[4]

Two Omaha attorneys (one of whom normally served the Union Pacific Railroad) volunteered to handle Standing Bear's case. They based their brief on the old man's constitutional rights, arguing, "In time of peace, no authority, civil or military, exists for transporting Indians from one section of the country to another . . . nor to confine them to any particular reservation against their will." Thomas Henry Tibbles, an editor for the *Omaha Herald*, offered to publicize the case and together with the ministers' committee he soon succeeded in turning the prisoner of Fort Omaha into the "celebrated Chief Standing Bear." By April 30, when U.S. District Court Judge Elmer Dundy heard oral arguments in *Standing Bear* v. *Crook*, the plight of the Poncas had become familiar to newspaper readers across the country.[5]

Dundy announced his decision to release the chief on May 12, and editorial writers greeted the news with uniform enthusiasm. San

Francisco's *Alta California* referred to the ruling as the "only case now recollected where a court of this country [had] rendered justice to the Indian as if he were a human being." The *Chicago Tribune* agreed, pointing out that the court's action foretold a new era in Indian affairs: "Means should be devised by which an Indian, when he has attained the necessary degree of civilization, shall be released from the arbitrary control of the Indian Bureau and allowed all the rights and immunities of a free man." Standing Bear's release encouraged critics of the government's programs. The decision effectively removed the legal basis for the entire separation strategy. It appeared that the Indian Office was no longer able to confine tribes to reservations and force "civilization" on them.[6]

The *Standing Bear* decision was a blow to the government's power to create reservations; the "Ute War" that broke out four months later raised fundamental questions about the reasons for maintaining such enclaves. Nathan C. Meeker, an honest, humanitarian Indian agent, was killed by members of the tribe entrusted to his care. The Utes resented Meeker's insistence that they forsake their old ways and become farmers. And they mistrusted him for suggesting that they give up their mountain hunting grounds and content themselves with small homesteads.[7]

Despite his inexperience, Meeker had struck his superiors as the perfect peace policy agent. He was an ardent Christian and an agricultural expert who had long been interested in social reform. He helped found the farming community of Greeley, Colorado, and had served for years as the agricultural editor of the *New York Tribune*. Responding to his editor's famous admonition, he had indeed gone west to grow up with the country, and had devoted himself to making the frontier a more humane and prosperous place. But Meeker had no diplomatic skill. He did not understand the Utes' fear of Colorado's booming white population. Prospectors and other adventurers were appearing on the tribe's lands in growing numbers, and the agent made little attempt to remove them. He concentrated instead on farming instruction. In early September 1879, after a heated argument with some headmen, Meeker became nervous and called for the cavalry. The Utes grew fearful and tensions rose. As the troops drew near, fighting broke out and Meeker was killed. On October 2 the *Chicago Tribune* announced its view of the tragedy in a dramatic headline: "Massacred By Utes!"[8]

The officer in charge of the cavalry detachment was also killed, along with twelve soldiers, several agency employees, and thirty-seven members of the tribe. The nation's press was uniform in its sympathy for Meeker and the other white victims, but (as had been the case in January) descriptions of the fighting were soon buried under an avalanche of editorials condemning the reservation system. Within two days of its initial headline, the *Chicago Tribune* observed, "There are two sides to every question, even an Indian question." The editorial went on to list the problems that had plagued the Ute agency and to conclude that the tribe had turned to violence because it had been so "exasperated" by the agent's stubbornness. Even western papers shared this view. The *Virginia City* (Nev.) *Territorial Enterprise* noted on October 30, "It is daily growing more and more certain that there was no occasion for trouble with the Utes; that, if justice had been done them, there would have been no outbreak." The *Alta California* made this argument even more forcefully. It denounced the reservation policy as a "murderous system": "[It] is starvation for the savage, it is oppression by the lawless white pioneer; it is death to our gallant officers and men." Meeker's honesty and good intentions were irrelevant. "One thing is certain," the San Francisco editors observed, "and that is that our whole Indian policy is a miserable one and a failure."[9]

Two events at the end of 1879 amplified the papers' criticisms. First, Standing Bear made an extensive tour of the East Coast. Appearing before large audiences in Chicago, Boston, New York, Philadelphia, and Washington, the newly freed Ponca chief condemned the reservation system and called for the extension of constitutional guarantees to Indians. Second, in December a well-publicized dispute arose between the secretary of the interior and critics of the government's Indian policy. This controversy reached its climax in late January 1880, when the commissioner of Indian affairs resigned after being charged with corruption. Both the Standing Bear tour and the mounting attacks on the Indian Office galvanized criticism of the government's programs. Indian policy reform became a national issue, and groups emerged to lead the critics and lobby the politicians.

Standing Bear was not the first Native American leader to argue his case before crowds of eastern sympathizers, nor would he be the last. John Ross, Black Hawk, and Red Cloud had preceded him, and Geronimo and Sitting Bull would follow. Officials often brought chiefs and headmen to Washington to be cowed by the splendor of the Great White Father's dusty city, interviewed by his scientists, and cooed over by the press. But the Ponca's tour was unique. His visit was not official—it was organized as a political campaign rather than as a state visit. The reason for this difference (and the primary cause of the trip's dramatic success) was the work and showmanship of Thomas Tibbles.

Tibbles was an experienced agitator. Born in Ohio in 1840, he had moved west as a young man, first to Illinois with his parents, and then (at the age of sixteen) to Kansas to ride with John Brown. Tibbles served briefly in the Civil War, but soon returned to the Middle Border, where he spent the Reconstruction era promoting evangelical Methodism and greenback reform. During the depression of the 1870s he moved to Omaha and began a career in journalism. Following the Ponca crusade Tibbles married an Indian woman and lived for a time on her reservation. Later, he would turn to homesteading, fiction writing, and, finally, politics. He ended his public career as Tom Watson's running mate on the Populist ticket in the 1904 presidential election.[10]

In the spring of 1879 Tibbles found himself at the center of a cause with national appeal. The Standing Bear case promised to raise the eccentric journalist from frontier obscurity, and Tibbles was determined to make the most of the opportunity. Within a few days of his first interviews with General Crook and the chief, the newspaperman was sending stories over the wire to Chicago and New York. In July, after Standing Bear was released, Tibbles traveled east to arrange a fall tour. The purpose of the trip would be to publicize the evils of the reservation system and raise money for future court action.

Standing Bear made his Chicago debut in October. Each of the chief's appearances was carefully orchestrated. Tibbles selected two young, well-educated Omaha Indians to accompany the elderly Ponca: Susette LaFlesche and her brother Joseph. While on stage Susette obscured the memory of her French and English grandfathers and bore an English version of her tribal name: Bright Eyes. She appeared in buckskin, translated the chief's speech, and delivered a brief appeal of her own. The effect of her mannered Indianness was electric. "This," exclaimed Longfellow upon meeting her, "is Minnehaha." Susette's brother Joe appeared on the platform in "civilized" attire and acted as the chief's interpreter. Tibbles also chose his audiences carefully. In Chicago, where the newspapers were filled with stories about "murderous Utes," the group's stay was brief. In cities like Boston, where they found allies among both press and public, they settled in for several weeks.[11]

But showmanship alone was not responsible for the success of the tour. Tibbles cast the chief's appeal in constitutional terms. He began each appearance with a description of the government's hated programs. The reservation, he declared, created "a horde of minor but absolute monarchs over a helpless race." Standing Bear and Bright Eyes would repeat these charges. The Indian woman would tell of corruption and plead for support, saying that her people "ask you for their liberty." And the famous Ponca would bring the message home: "We are bound, we ask you to set us free." Indian citizenship, education, and the abolition of the reservation system were all identified as solutions for the present injustice.[12]

The audiences who flocked to hear Standing Bear found him irresistible. While political expediency had long since emasculated the ambitious programs of the immediate postwar era, the antislavery crusade still evoked pleasant memories. The Union's great victory was trotted out each election eve, praised at every patriotic celebration, and preserved by all the Republican hacks who could commandeer platforms large enough to accommodate a delegation of veterans. Tibbles's tour played on this nostalgia by giving people an opportunity to reaffirm their symbolic attachment to constitutional principles. "I think I feel as you must have in the old abolition days," wrote one such person to Thomas Wentworth Higginson a few days after she had heard Standing Bear. Helen Hunt Jackson continued those sentiments: "I cannot think of anything else from morning to night."[13]

By mid-November it was clear that the tour was a triumph. Five hundred Bostonians representing the city's business and political establishment attended a noon meeting at the Mercantile Exchange a few days before Thanksgiving. By a voice vote they approved a resolution calling for Indian citizenship, and they created an executive body to investigate the plight of the Poncas. This group, later named the Boston Indian Citizenship Committee, sponsored the remainder of Standing Bear's trip. December and January were spent in New York, and the following three months in Philadelphia, Washington, and Baltimore. Everywhere the chief and his entourage appeared before friendly audiences and won the support of local Republicans and Protestant ministers.[14]

The final crisis of 1879 occurred while Standing Bear was filling lecture halls in New York and Brooklyn. In mid-December Commissioner of Indian Affairs Ezra A. Hayt was accused of covering up wrongdoing on an Arizona reservation so as to protect the business interests of his friends; six weeks later he resigned. Before his departure, the commissioner was defended by the man who appointed him, Interior Secretary Carl Schurz. The sudden resignation attracted the attention of the government's critics and confirmed again their belief in the evils of the reservation system.

Though he was an efficient administrator, Schurz had done little during his two years in office to please those who had a stake in the operations of his department. White westerners were angered by his attacks on agency corruption as well as his reluctance to use force to subdue unruly tribes. The army resented his opposition to their proposal to transfer the Indian Office to the War Department. And the churches felt betrayed by his decision to suspend their control over agency appointments. At the end of 1879 all of these groups—now joined by Standing Bear's excited supporters—trained their fire on the secretary.

Schurz's most outspoken critic was Helen Hunt Jackson. A popular author of children's books who first discovered the plight of the Indians at one of Standing Bear's Boston appearances, Jackson leveled both barrels at the secretary on December 15. In columns appearing first in the *New York Tribune* and later reprinted across the country, she attacked Schurz for his actions in the Northern Cheyenne and Ponca cases and called on him to end the "tyranny" of the reservations. Surprised and hurt by these appeals, the secretary gave way to anger, writing that his critics' efforts were "in danger of being wasted on the unattainable." Horace Greeley at the *Tribune* responded for the critics and raised the verbal stakes. The "despotic power" of the agents, he wrote, was "a more direct denial of human rights than was slavery."[15]

When Commissioner Hayt resigned and left Washington at the end of January, Jackson and her fellow critics felt vindicated. One editor hooted that the secretary had "no more conception of his duties than a wild Zulu has of the magnetic telegraph." But even Schurz's supporters saw more than a grain of truth in a Chicago editorial: "The temptation to steal is so great and the opportunities so abundant that no Secretary of the Interior, no matter how competent and honest he may be himself, . . . will be able to put a stop to corrupt practices. . . . The only remedy for abuses in the management of Indian affairs is to abandon the present system of supporting and coddling the Indians."[16]

In the past the impact of disasters like those of 1879 had quickly dissipated. Massacres or revelations of corruption had shocked, then bored the public. But as the 1880s began, a central truth was becoming self-evident: the government's policy was unworkable. The crisis of 1879 was conceptual as well as political. Not only were the Indian Office's specific actions unpopular, but each misstep called forth attacks on an entire approach to policy making. Critics everywhere demanded an end to the "despotic" and "corrupt" reservation system.

What was the alternative? The angry public and the activists mobilized by the Ponca tour were beginning to agree on an answer: total assimilation. They promised that dismantling the reservation system (and the separation strategy that lay behind it) would end frontier violence, stop agency corruption, and "civilize" the Indians while demonstrating the power and vitality of America's institutions. Such expectations were most common among the eastern Protestants and Republicans who had flocked to hear Standing Bear and Bright Eyes. These groups most clearly articulated the assimilation argument and formed the core of the organizations that began to lobby for its adoption.

Three reform associations emerged in the 1880s to tap the growing public interest in Indian assimilation. The first, the Boston Indian

Citizenship Committee, was organized in the aftermath of the Standing Bear tour. The committee exploited its connections with the state's prominent Republican politicians and helped publicize the attacks on Schurz. It included Governor John Davis Long; Boston mayor Frederick Prince (a Democrat); Protestant minister Rufus Ellis; old abolitionists Dr. Oliver Wendell Holmes and Wendell Phillips; and—significantly—the city's postmaster, Edward S. Tobey, whose political patron was the state's senior U.S. senator, Henry L. Dawes.[17]

Efforts to organize what was to become the Women's National Indian Association began in 1879. Reviving the old abolitionist tactic of presenting petitions to Congress, Amelia Stone Quinton and Mary Bonney of Philadelphia began circulating statements urging the government to "keep faith" with the tribes. The first of these was submitted during Standing Bear's visit to Washington in early 1880. The group soon established branches in a number of eastern cities, urging each of them to call for the "civilization, Christianization and enfranchisement" of the tribes. Separate branches also undertook individual acts of charity such as supporting schools, providing funds for farm equipment, and marketing Indian handicrafts.[18]

For three years the Women's National Indian Association and the Boston Committee were the only voices advocating total assimilation as a remedy for the failures of the reservation system. They were amply reinforced, however, in 1882, when Herbert Welsh organized the Indian Rights Association following a trip to Sioux country. A member of a prominent Philadelphia family, Welsh was a nephew of one of the principal architects of Grant's peace policy. But his energies were devoted to abolishing the older program. The reservations, he wrote, "are islands, and about them a sea of civilization, vast and irresistible, surges." The leader of the new association argued that the government should "educate the Indian race and so prepare it for gradual absorption into ours." Welsh's association pursued these goals by maintaining a permanent lobbyist in Washington, conducting its own investigations of Indian affairs, and publishing a long list of reports and pamphlets.[19]

Each new reform organization bore a surface similarity to the antislavery groups of the 1840s and 1850s and to the previous decade's peace policy advocates. Like their predecessors they campaigned for "equal rights" for Native Americans and declared that they were driven by a sense of Christian mission. But the reformers of the 1880s also wanted to dismantle the reservations. Muting their sectarian differences, they acted with greater political sophistication. Their annual conferences at Lake Mohonk, New York, bespoke a more modern approach. Begun in 1883, the meetings attracted dozens of religious leaders, politicians, and reformers to an upstate resort for a weekend of speeches, reports on legislation, and debate. Each year the Mohonk delegates would fashion a platform to guide the next year's efforts. While Catholics were not welcome, and the number of participating politicians soon declined, the Lake Mohonk Conferences of the Friends of the Indian were marked by a minimum of factionalism and a general willingness to shape contrasting interests into common proposals.

But organization alone could not create support for the assimilation remedy. Like all agitators, the reformers became successful only when they linked their agenda to the wider concerns and aspirations of the American public. The late nineteenth century was a time when growing social diversity and shrinking social space threatened many Americans' sense of national identity. In the past, the country's communities had been intensely local and homogeneous. Cultural differences were tolerated, but the white Protestant majority continued to imagine that its values and the nation's were identical. Suddenly, amid unprecedented industrial expansion and dramatic increases in the rate of immigration, this majority found itself surrounded by people who did not share their cultural heritage or their definition of Americanism. At the same time, tremendous technological changes brought social groups closer together. The city became a metropolis, towns entered the orbit of industrial centers, and villages became crossroads for rail lines stretching across the continent. Even isolated farmers were drawn into an expanding web of commercial exchange. The Indian reformers of the 1880s responded to those conditions as well as to the specific suffering of Native Americans.

Before the Civil War, American social life had followed a pattern reminiscent of the Indian Office's separation strategy. The majority believed that minority ethnic groups were deviants from the national norm who should maintain a separate existence. Separation was more attractive than group conflict. Just as the government maintained tribes in cultural enclaves, so the white Protestant majority found it easier to deal with blacks or Irishmen as discrete units. Slavery was the most obvious example of this tendency, but the pattern was apparent in other areas. Farming communities and small towns often had distinct ethnic identities. Cities divided themselves into neighborhoods that functioned independently from the whole. In this compartmentalized society, minority groups welcomed the opportunity to be socially isolated and culturally autonomous. But the decades following the Civil War demonstrated that most Americans —like the Indians—would soon have to live nearer than ever before to people quite different from themselves. The new environment would require a new pattern of social relationships and a new set of social values. The Indian reformers provided an attractive model for those new relationships.

The political and economic expansion of the postwar era undermined America's "island communities." Americans—especially the white Protestant majority—felt the need to define more precisely the meaning of national citizenship. In this respect they shared a number of the Indian reformers' concerns. Like Herbert Welsh and Amelia Quinton they wondered how minority cultures could become integral parts of a modern nation. Like the Boston merchants they asserted that legal citizenship would promote cultural unity. And like Helen Hunt Jackson, they tried to specify the proper role of national institutions in hastening the assimilation process.

Herbert Welsh had condemned the reservations for being "islands" in the midst of civilization, but in a sense white Protestants could say the same thing about American ethnic groups who felt the "sea" of a new industrial world surging around them. And of course discomfort arose because leaders could not foresee the exact shape of that new world or the effect it would have on their way of life. By discussing the Indians' future, the white majority could also explore its own.

Newspaper editorials in 1879 provide a more precise measure of the reformers' attitudes, for they show that despite its sympathy, the public had no interest in delaying or diverting America's westward march to accommodate Native Americans. Every editor agreed that the problem was not how to keep whites away from tribal lands, but how to manage Indians so that American "progress" could continue. The *New Orleans Times-Picayune,* for example, argued that the Indian could not "any longer be permitted to usurp for the purpose of barbarism, the fertile lands, the products of mines, the broad valleys and wooded mountain slopes, which organized society regards as magazines of those forces which civilization requires for its maintenance and development." Expansionists dwelled in every camp. Even the ardent reformers on the *New York Tribune* pointed out that the destruction of reservations would provide a "powerful impetus" for the development of the nation's resources.[20]

As they condemned the Indians for failing to "develop" their lands and called for more "civilization," editors added that the nation had a special obligation to the tribes. "The sins committed by Americans upon Indians . . . are a perpetual stain upon our history" the *Virginia City Territorial Enterprise* declared, adding that these transgressions "should be continued no longer." At the same time the editors made it clear that help for Native Americans did not require white Protestants to abandon their sense of racial superiority. Journals that vilified the Chinese "rat-eaters," denounced the new immigrants as the "off-scouring of European prisons," condemned the "Roman church," or warned of the imminent arrival of "Negro paupers" in the North did not find it difficult to express sympathy for Indians.[21]

Whatever the motives of reformers like Thomas Tibbles and Helen Hunt Jackson, the campaign that began in 1879 did not threaten prevailing racial and cultural attitudes. The San Francisco *Alta California,* for example, juxtaposed attacks on Secretary Schurz with a public declaration that it had "never employed Chinese in any department." The *Atlanta Constitution* condemned the Fort Robinson massacre while it defended the "contentment" of southern blacks. And the *Boston Daily Advertiser,* edited by a member of the Boston Indian Citizenship Committee, was aggressively anti-Catholic.

Clearly the total assimilation being offered the Indians would require conformity to the standards of the white Protestant majority
culture.[22]

Total assimilation was a goal that combined concern for native
suffering with faith in the promise of America. Once the tribes were
brought into "civilized" society there would be no reason for them to
"usurp" vast tracts of "underdeveloped" land. And membership in a
booming nation would be ample compensation for the dispossession
they had suffered. But most important, the extension of citizenship
and other symbols of membership in American society would reaffirm the power of the nation's institutions to mold all people to a
common standard. Success in assimilating Indians would reaffirm
the dominance of the white Protestant majority, for such an achievement would extend the reach of the majority's cultural norms. As the
New York Tribune put it in February 1880, "The original owner of
the soil, the man from whom we have taken the country in order that
we may make of it the refuge of the world, where all men should be
free if not equal, is the only man in it who is not recognized as entitled to the rights of a human being." The force of the statement was
clear: extend the "rights of a human being" to the Indians, expand
the American "refuge," and prove that when the pioneers had "taken
the country" they had served a higher good. Moreover, the editorials' implications were quite satisfying: traditional American values
continued to represent the best foundation for the nation's future.[23]

Like the sweep of a search light, the events of 1879 momentarily
illuminated the weakness and unpopularity of the separation strategy. Not only were reservations the provinces of corrupt and cruel
administrators, but they didn't work: they had not "civilized" anyone. Nevertheless, it would take more than exposure and the cries of
the outraged to overturn so long-standing a policy. Once the bright
light of crisis had passed, legislators and bureaucrats were bound to
descend into their traditional ruts. If the general desire for a new policy of rapid assimilation was to be translated into specific programs,
a fresh blueprint for government action would have to be adopted by
the nation's leaders. American policy makers had long viewed the
strategy of racial separation as both humanitarian and practical. If

they were to reject that strategy, the nation's leaders would need a new guide for their actions.

In March 1879, while Standing Bear was confined at Fort Omaha, two events occurred in Washington, D.C., that focused attention on an important source of ideas about the Indians' future. On March 3 Congress passed the annual civil appropriations bill. It authorized an appropriation of twenty thousand dollars to establish a bureau of ethnology within the Smithsonian Institution. On the following day the recently organized Anthropological Society of Washington met to hear its first paper, "Relic Hunting," by Frank Cushing. The founding of the Bureau of Ethnology (after 1893, the Bureau of American Ethnology) and the Anthropological Society of Washington mark the emergence of professional anthropology in the United States. The Bureau was the nation's first institution committed exclusively to ethnological inquiry, and the society the first scholarly association in the field. Together they represented anthropology's passage from individual, privately financed research to large coordinated studies conducted by teams of trained experts. After 1879 the discipline was led by a group of scientists with stable institutional affiliations and a common interest in the scholarly examination of human society.[24]

The most interesting societies available for ethnological research were the Indian tribes of North America. There were several reasons for this. Indians were accessible—militarily defeated, marvelously exotic, and relatively close at hand. They were also diverse, having produced varied cultures in every section of the continent. And perhaps most significant, Native Americans were "safe" subjects for scrutiny. Unlike European immigrants, blacks, or Asians, Indians still were living outside "civilized" society; in the 1880s it was unlikely that investigations of native cultures would offend any political constituencies or disrupt a settled community. White southerners would certainly have seen research in their region as Yankee "meddling," westerners would have balked at the prospect of Washington experts arriving to study Asians, but aside from a few missionaries who wanted to erase the memory of the race's "heathen" past, few white men protested the anthropologists' preoccupation with

Indians. By 1879 the bond between scientists and Native Americans was well established.[25]

But the anthropologists of the late nineteenth century had more in common than an incipient professionalism and their fascination with Indians. The men and women who staffed the new bureau and participated in the anthropological society also shared a common intellectual heritage. They came from widely different backgrounds—some had very little advanced training—but they all accepted social evolution as the general explanation of human development. Lewis Henry Morgan (1818–81) was the chief American proponent of this point of view. Even though his career (which began in 1851 with the publication of *The League of the Iroquois*) was drawing to a close in 1879, he was easily the country's most respected anthropologist. His Iroquois volume pioneered the use of field observations in tribal studies, and *Systems of Consanguinity and Affinity of the Human Family* (1871) introduced comparative kinship studies to ethnology. Morgan's most important work was *Ancient Society*, which received an enthusiastic reception when it appeared in 1877. The book traced the development of intelligence, the family government, and the idea of property through all of human history. The historian and philosopher Henry Adams wrote that *Ancient Society* "must be the foundation of all future works in American historical science." Major John Wesley Powell, the founding director of the Bureau of Ethnology was even more enthusiastic. After receiving his advance copy of the book he reported, "The first night I read until two o'clock. I shall take it into the field and in my leisure hours study it carefully reading it many times."[26]

Throughout the nineteenth century scientific social theorists had described human history in terms of movement from simplicity to complexity. Building on this tradition, Morgan taught that societal development occurred in three stages—savagery, barbarism, and civilization—and that all people could be placed at one of these levels. The order and clarity of this perspective appealed to students of Indian life, but it was also attractive because it combined sympathy for the "savage" tribes with a justification for "civilization's" conquest. A century ago it seemed clear to most Americans that native people fit into a lower stage of culture. One could hope that Indians would rise to a "higher" plane, while finding comfort in the idea that cruel policies such as removal or punitive warfare were unavoidable steps along the road to progress.[27]

On one level Morgan typified the sympathy and resignation that coexisted in social evolutionary thinking. He classified most tribes as savage or barbarian, and feared that the Indians would be unable to shift to higher levels of development before they were swept away by their civilized conquerors. But the author of *Ancient Society* believed the process could produce positive results. In fact, his great work had a distinctly optimistic quality for it attempted to turn evolutionary thinking on its head. Morgan argued that the study of cultural inequality could produce guidelines for human advancement.

Morgan grew up in central New York state in the early nineteenth century. As a young man he witnessed the displacement of the Iroquois tribes by American settlement and recognized the drastic changes that occurred whenever "civilized" societies came into contact with Indians. The Indians' habits, he reported, were "perishing daily and [had] been perishing for upwards of three centuries." Could the consequences of this upheaval be positive? For Morgan, the answer was certain. "It can now be asserted," he wrote, "that savagery preceded barbarism in all the tribes of mankind, as barbarism is known to have preceded civilization. The history of the human race is one in source, one in experience, one in progress."[28]

Since civilization was the ultimate consequence of social change, it was logical to assert that change itself was part of a universal progressive process. Morgan conceded that some groups advanced more rapidly than others, but he asserted that everyone was bound to rise. What was more, he added, progress occurred at an accelerating rate: "Human progress, from first to last, has been in a ratio not rigorously but essentially geometrical. This is plain on the face of the facts; and it could not, theoretically have occurred in any other way. Every item of absolute knowledge gained became a factor in further acquisitions, until the present complexity of knowledge was attained. Consequently . . . progress was slowest in time in the first period, and most rapid in the last." Morgan rejected racial explanations of human differences, preferring theories of environmental influences or the working of chance. He argued, for example, that even though the "Aryan and Semitic races" represented "the main streams of human progress," they began as part "of the indistinguishable mass of barbarians." Thus, "the distinction of *normal* and abnormal races falls to the ground." While he continued to believe in distinct levels of culture, the American scientist saw potential progress in all societies.[29]

For Morgan the chief measure of a society's achievements, as well as the principal instrument for its advancement, was the private ownership of property. Actually each stage of societal development corresponded to a particular economic system. Savages were disorganized foragers who owned nothing but tools and weapons. Barbarians (the discoverers of agriculture) owned their farms in common and had no commercial activity. Civilized people prospered through individual acquisition of land, complex machinery and domestic animals. Their wealth produced nuclear families that were flexible yet capable of maintaining rules of inheritance. Thus private property promoted both economic prosperity and social sophistication:

> Property, as it increased in variety and amount, exercised a steady and constantly augmenting influence in the direction of monogamy. It is impossible to overestimate the influence of property in the civilization of mankind. It was the power that brought Aryan and Semitic nations out of barbarism into civilization. . . . Governments and laws are instituted with primary reference to its creation, protection and enjoyment. . . . With the establishment of the inheritance of property in the children of its owner, came the first possibility of the strict monogamian family.[30]

Morgan's emphasis on private property suggested that economic arrangements were more than badges of cultural development. The impact of a particular system could be far-reaching. Logically the introduction of a more "advanced" method of landownership could inspire progress in an entire society.

By emphasizing the uniformity of progress and the accelerating speed with which it occurred, Morgan called attention to the dynamic potential of social evolutionism. Cultures were not prisoners of their stage of development. They could expect change to occur in a "positive" direction, and the principal source of these changes would be a new economic system. Shifting property relationships were the engines that produced improvements in other areas of life.

Morgan's position was ambiguous on a number of crucial points. How quickly could a people move from one stage to another? How wide was the gap between the "civilized" and "uncivilized" world? How long would it take for "barbarians" to adopt private property? Could the "civilization" process be accelerated? In a world beset by racial animosity, economic uncertainty, and national chauvinism, the idea of social evolution could become a tool for defending "advanced" peoples and exploiting those considered "backward." Morgan's predecessors—and his successors—argued that "uncivilized" peoples were destined to remain where they were. But that was not Morgan's world. He published *Ancient Society* amid a growing demand that the United States' "uncivilized" natives be "improved" and incorporated into the nation. In this environment Morgan could become an apostle of progress and hope. He rejected racial determinism and taught that social change inevitably wrought improvements in human society. Moreover, he identified one factor, private property, as the key to movement from one stage to another. Societies were not fixed; they could advance up the evolutionary scale in response to human effort.

Lewis Henry Morgan's dynamic vision influenced all the professional anthropologists of the late nineteenth century but his impact was most striking on two who became directly involved in the formulation of Indian policy. Both John Wesley Powell (1834–1902) and Alice Cunningham Fletcher (1838–1923) applied *Ancient Society* to contemporary problems. Powell, the director of the nonpartisan Bureau of Ethnology was quite circumspect. His efforts were largely confined to written comments and private lobbying. Fletcher was an activist. She advocated specific legislation, maintained ties to prominent reformers, and worked as a special agent for the Indian Office. Together they succeeded in fashioning a scientific defense of Indian assimilation. Their contributions were crucial, for they established the context within which politicians and reformers would act.

Soon after Morgan's death in 1881, his student and protégé Adolph Bandelier wrote that John Wesley Powell was the "direct successor to Mr. Morgan in the study of Indian life."[31] This was no exaggeration. For the next two decades Powell dominated anthropological thinking in the United States. Equally important, the Bureau of Ethnology expanded under his direction to become the chief sponsor of scholarly research in the discipline.

Powell was a unique and engaging character. Ever the eclectic and the organizer, the major never shrank from bold new theories or dramatic actions. He was a one-armed veteran of Shiloh who, before assuming control of the ethnology bureau, had already dug for fossils in the trenches before Vicksburg, taught at Illinois Normal University, made the first recorded descent of the Colorado River, organized and led the Rocky Mountain Survey, and written a pioneering study of western land management. And all the while—as he mingled with the spoilsmen and politicos of Chester Arthur's Washington—he maintained his native curiosity and optimism. While the tragic events of 1879 were unfolding in the West, he predicted confidently, "When society shall have passed to complete integration in the unification of all nations, and differentiation is perfected in universal liberty, then the sole philosophy will be science."[32]

For Powell the teachings of "that sole philosophy" were unambiguous: "In all the succession of phenomena with which anthropologists deal, . . . there is always some observable change in the direction of progress." In fact, he believed so firmly in this axiom that he set about "improving" Morgan's scheme by reducing its ambiguities and emphasizing its optimism. He added a fourth stage of cultural development—enlightenment—to account for modern industrialization. Modern nation states contained large bureaucracies and giant corporations. He argued that these institutions made people interdependent. They raised people above competition and hastened the age of enlightenment. "To the extent that culture has progressed beyond the plane occupied by the brute," the major argued, "man has ceased to work directly for himself." Powell dwelled on the positive consequences of progress. He was confident that the extension of modernity would produce a single world language, international peace, and the rule of benevolent associations.[33]

When it came to Indian assimilation, the major spoke from first-hand experience. He had traveled throughout the West and was familiar with a number of native culture areas. His most direct encounter had come in 1873, when he visited several Great Basin tribes, recording their languages and observing their customs. These contacts only confirmed Powell's belief in social evolution. He argued that the process would be neither simple nor quick, but, like many social scientists, he had great faith in his assumptions. He reported in 1874 that the Numic peoples were nomads who should be forced to a higher stage of culture. "The sooner this country is entered by white people and the game destroyed so that the Indians will be compelled to gain a subsistence by some other means than hunting," he told the House Indian Affairs Committee, "the better it will be for them." He closed with an invitation: "Let the influx of population and the slow progress of civilization . . . settle the question."[34]

According to Powell, the Bureau of Ethnology would "organize anthropological research in America." Its projects would follow Morgan's teachings. "Primitive" Indians would be their subject. The scientists hoped to record the habits and ideas of people before the forces of progress raised them to civilization and forever changed their ways of life. Powell assumed this change would come quickly and that the Bureau should therefore be prompt. At the end of its first year, he asked Congress for a 100 percent increase in the bureau's budget, warning, "If the ethnology of our Indians is ever to receive proper scientific study and treatment the work must be done at once."[35]

Social evolutionary theories also influenced Powell's view of specific findings. For example, an extensive study of the eastern mound builders proved to him that these people were at "about the same culture-status" as historic tribes and not the remnants of some lost golden civilization. The bureau's first project in South America in 1894 revealed "that the aborigines [there] like those of the North American continent, [were] partly in the higher stages of savagery and the lower stages of barbarism." The most striking example of the major's insistence on conceptual purity came in 1896, when he criticized the young ethnologist James Mooney for comparing the ghost dance religion to Christian revivalism. "The movements are not homologous," the Methodist major wrote, for the gap between civilized and uncivilized peoples was "so broad and deep that few representatives of either race [were] ever able clearly to see its further side." Progress followed a single, predictable path. The stages of culture were universal and affected every aspect of a people's way of life.[36]

Powell and the Bureau of Ethnology made two contributions to the growing interest in Indian assimilation. First, the major and his employees dominated professional anthropology. They founded the Anthropological Society of Washington and were instrumental in the organization of the American Anthropological Association in 1902. William John McGee, Powell's chief assistant, was the latter association's first president. The American Association for the Advancement of Science established a section of anthropology in 1876. Powell headed that group in 1879 and for the remainder of the century Washington scientists were the leading contributors to its survival and growth. Powell's version of social evolution—the notion of culture stages, continuous progress, and the inevitable transformation of Indian life—became dominant within the discipline. In short, he set the terms for informed discussions of Indian affairs in the 1880s.

Powell's other contribution was his direct influence on reformers and policy makers. The major was careful not to expose his new bureau to political controversy. He recognized that while powerful friends like Speaker of the House James Garfield had created his office, powerful enemies could easily destroy it. Originally Powell had hoped that the bureau would serve Congress as a source of objective information. C. C. Royce began his work on native land cessions in 1879 and the major promised that his was only the first of many projects that would illuminate "the effect of the presence of civilization upon savagery." But Congress expressed little interest in such studies and other tasks quickly forced them into the background.[37]

Powell's personal lobbying was more extensive—and more subtle. He maintained close contact with key committeemen and Interior Department officials. His published works, from the famous *Report on the Lands of the Arid Region* (1878) to the annual reports of the bureau, were liberally sprinkled with comments on the present condition of the tribes. And the major responded willingly to individual requests for advice. In 1880, for example, Senator Henry Teller asked for information concerning a Ute agreement then before Congress. Debate over the issue was being used as a sounding board for a number of new policy proposals, and Powell took the opportunity of Teller's note to write a wide-ranging essay in which he argued that three principles should guide all future government actions.

First, since a tribe's traditional lands represented "everything most sacred to Indian society," the anthropologist urged that the "removal of the Indians [was] the first step to be taken in their civilization." Second, he noted that "ownership of lands in severalty should be looked forward to as the ultimate settlement of our Indian problems." Individual land tenure would undermine both the clan system and "traditional modes of inheritance." Finally, the major recommended that citizenship and total assimilation should be the twin goals of all legislation. Enforcing treaties and maintaining reservations, he wrote, discharged "but a minor part of the debt" that the government owed the Indians: "The major portion of that debt can be paid only by giving to the Indians Anglo-Saxon civilization, that they may also have prosperity and happiness under the new civilization of this continent." Here was a chilling condensation of the social evolutionist blueprint: separate Indians from their homes and their past, divide their land into individual parcels, make them citizens, and draw them into American society. Powell's suggestions carried an air of scientific precision. Who could doubt that they were reasonable and practical?[38]

John Wesley Powell remained a firm advocate of Indian assimilation throughout the 1880s. He looked on the mounting collection of artifacts in the Smithsonian Institution not as evidence for the irreducible differences between Native Americans and "civilized" societies, but as a sure indication that the forces of assimilation were gaining the upper hand. The major believed "a new phase of Aryan civilization [was] being developed in the western half of America," and his efforts as an anthropologist were bent to the service of that vision.[39]

Alice Fletcher had none of the constraints that hampered Powell's involvement in Indian policy making. A private student of Frederick Ward Putnam at Harvard's Peabody Museum, she had concentrated most of her energy in archaeology until she heard Standing

Bear and Bright Eyes in a Boston lecture hall in 1879. After that evening, she turned to ethnology. She visited Thomas Tibbles and his Omaha assistants in the West, later collaborating with Francis LaFlesche on a number of monographs. In fact, she spent most of the next forty years in field research and writing. Throughout her career, Fletcher alternated between scholarship and policy reform. She believed her work was "for the student . . . [and] for men and women who [would] be wiser and kinder by knowing their fellow countryman, the Indian as he [was] at home and in peace." As a result she was an outspoken advocate of both Indian education and the individual allotment of native lands. Perhaps more important, she served as a link between the anthropological community and the politicians who made policy.[40] Indian education in her view did not require an elaborate justification. "The task of converting the American Indian into the Indian American," she told the commissioner of Indian affairs in 1890, "belongs to the Indian student." Not surprisingly, then, when Captain Richard Henry Pratt established the Carlisle Industrial Training School—where conversion to "civilization" was the central objective—he found in Alice Fletcher an energetic ally and supporter. She cultivated congressmen, testified in support of larger appropriations for the school, and organized vip tours of the campus. Fletcher's activity in education reform was recognized in 1888, when Henry Dawes' Senate Indian Affairs Committee commissioned her to conduct a nationwide survey of the government's Indian school system. Her seven-hundred-page report ended with an appeal for an expansion of the program. "More . . . and better equipped schools," she wrote, were "a national need."[41]

On the question of land allotment, Fletcher rejected Powell's cautious recommendations. She urged Congress to begin assigning Indians individual tracts of land as soon as possible. The major's principal contact had been with the gathering tribes of the Great Basin. His observations of these people led him to conclude that individual landownership—while desirable—should not be forced on unwilling subjects until after they had begun to live communally. Both Fletcher's experience and her attitude were quite different. On her first trip to the West, in September 1881, she visited the Omahas and was the guest of a leading mixed-blood family. Her hosts were among the most acculturated members of an agricultural tribe that had long been in contact with white settlers. Fletcher found many Omahas upset over the recent Ponca removal and fearful that they too would be marched to Indian Territory. The local white community seemed eager for them to leave. The anthropologist was certain that the division of this tribe's lands into individual homesteads would protect the Indians from removal and dispossession while it spurred them on to "civilization." By December 1881 she was back in Washington lobbying for a special law to accomplish this goal. She supported her case with a petition (it contained signatures from 53 of the tribe's 1,121 members) and the claim that she had a special understanding of the Omahas' plight. "I have not learned from the outer, but from the inner circles," she told Massachusetts senator Henry Dawes, adding, "because I thus know them, see their needs, see their possibilities, see their limitations, I plead for them."[42]

Fletcher's Omaha proposal called for the sale of fifty thousand acres of the reservation to finance the development of individual homesteads. Not surprisingly, Nebraska's congressional delegation was quick to support her. Charles Manderson managed the bill through the Senate and the state's lone congressman, Edward Valentine, was one of its principal backers in the House. With Nebraska's representatives agreeing that "everybody [was] satisfied to have a bill of this kind passed," the Omaha Severalty Act became law on August 7, 1882.[43]

The Omaha tribe was now ready for civilization. "They are on the eve of a new life," Fletcher wrote a friend. "Soon their farms will be staked out and the beautiful lands along the Logan opened up, and the foundations of new homes laid. The future whence they must prosper or perish is at hand."[44] A few weeks after these words were written a new phase of the anthropologist's career began. The commissioner of Indian affairs appointed her a special agent charged with carrying out the survey and allotment of the Omaha lands.

The Omaha assignment was the first of three allotting projects Alice Fletcher would undertake during the next decade. Her work with the Omahas lasted until 1884. Between 1887 and 1889 she supervised the allotment of the Winnebagos, who lived on a reservation adjoining the Omahas. Finally, from 1889 to 1893, she served as the allotting agent for the Nez Perce tribe of Idaho.

Both the Omaha and Winnebago allotments involved small agricultural tribes occupying relatively productive farmland. Whether out of fear of the alternatives or a conviction that they had no choice, many of these Indians were willing to accept their allotments. Alice Fletcher reported that her charges "carefully treasure[d]" their deeds, and that groups within the tribe who opposed the new law were "steadily losing ground." She was not discouraged by opposition. After all, she told students at the Carlisle school, "severalty [meant] pioneering." Neither was she dismayed when complications arose following the end of her work. In 1887, for example, drought threatened the Omahas' crops and disputes over finances and the handling of the remaining tribal land divided the tribe. After a visit to the troubled agency Alice Fletcher reported, "Although I saw thriftlessness, yet manliness was astir; . . . the disintegration process is at work all over the reservation [and] has made the incoming of new life possible. . . . The Omaha afforded me a glimpse into the workshop into which every true Indian worker must enter and labor with a wisdom, patience, and prudence such as was never before demanded of him."[45]

Alice Fletcher's career offers a clear example of the power of social evolutionary theory in late nineteenth-century America. She believed the nation's expansion and industrialization created an entirely new set of circumstances for native people. "The fact is," she wrote in 1889, "the Indian is caught in the rush of our modern life, and there is no time for him to dally with the serious questions that are upon him." Such conditions required a sharp break with the past. Thus she rejected the gradualism of the reservation system. As Morgan and Powell had taught, the forces undermining the old ways also were shaping the future. "Civilization" was sure to sweep across the West, and those who understood its impact had an obligation to minister to its victims. Fletcher argued that Native Americans should embrace individual landownership, literacy, and exclusive monogamy. She was aware of at least some of the difficulties of the task, but her studies convinced her there was no alternative.

The individual Indian was "doomed to suffer and all that the best of friends [could] do [was] to give him every chance by means of education and a common sense training of his religious nature to meet the dangers that beset him."[46]

In the midst of her allotting work, Fletcher once confessed that she was "burdened with the future of this people." Nevertheless she persisted, spurred on by her convictions: change brought progress; progress ended in civilization; civilization was a singular condition that did not recognize cultural variety. The logic both of abstract principle and historical reality was compelling: one must conform to the demand of civilization—that is, assimilate—or disappear. This demand had been familiar in the removal and reservation eras, when pessimists stressed the second alternative—disappearance—but in the 1880s the emphasis had changed. Scholars now taught that assimilation was possible.[47]

The impact of anthropologists on Indian policy making was cumulative and indirect. It consisted of the influence of Morgan's dynamic social theory on discussions of progress, the weight of Powell's optimism and expertise, and the specific contributions of Alice Fletcher. By the mid-1880s, the public had a specific blueprint for interpreting and shaping events and a cadre of experts to inspire them. Powell might emphasize the positive potential of social evolution, and Fletcher could demonstrate the kind of action the new discipline required, but critics of the Indian Office did not have to rely on these anthropologists. They now had a coherent explanation of the government's failures and a practical scheme for reform. The science of man taught that the rapid incorporation of American Indians into "civilized" society was both possible and desirable. Total assimilation would exemplify and encourage the irresistible march of progress.

But the attractiveness of total assimilation rested on more than a convenient marriage of public outrage and scientific theory. The idea also drew support from politicians. Legislators and bureaucrats were attracted to the notion of bringing Indians into American society because they believed it would be both practical and popular. Total assimilation promised to refurbish the policy makers' view of them-

selves without alienating any constituents. Like reformers, newspapermen, and scientists, people in government believed that the
successful assimilation of the nation's aboriginal population would
demonstrate the United States' virtue and wisdom.

Amid the crises of 1879, it is unlikely that anyone would have
predicted that Henry Dawes would soon come to dominate Indian
policy making. He was not attached to a reform group, and he had
shown only a passing interest in Indian affairs during his two decades
in Washington, D.C. The senator had been in politics for nearly
thirty years, first serving his western Massachusetts constituents in
a series of local offices, then going to Washington in 1857 as one of
the state's first Republican congressmen. When Charles Sumner died
in 1874, party leaders chose Dawes to take his place.

In 1879 the veteran politician's chief concern was winning renomination to the Senate. This was a new experience for Dawes because
he had always been a party regular. In the House he had been reluctant to challenge gop leaders, and for his faithful service had been
rewarded with patronage appointments and the chairmanship of the
appropriations committee. His behavior in the Senate was similar.
He cooperated with his colleagues and benefited from his amiabil-
ity. Dawes had no personal ideology that overrode his loyalty to the
party. And for him, the party's principles were constant: a strong
central government, racial equality, sound money, and a high tariff.
While his stalwart allegiances continued to serve him well, they also
made Dawes increasingly vulnerable to a group of younger Republicans who became active during the 1870s. This new group (often
called "halfbreeds" by their stalwart opponents) contained men from
a number of ideological camps; they shared only a common antipa-
thy to the party's aging leadership. Their chief in Massachusetts was
John Davis Long, who, after being elected governor in 1879, immediately began campaigning to unseat Dawes at the following year's
GOP convention.

Dawes had reason to be worried by Long's challenge. The governor
was younger and more articulate. His recent campaign had involved
a number of modern techniques: extensive newspaper advertising,
effective organization, and concentration on the growing industrial
areas around Boston. It would not be enough for Dawes to repeat

the party's slogans and await the verdict of the bosses. He was sixty-two, and, despite his long career, little more than a rural loyalist. His home in Pittsfield was far from the center of power in Boston, and he seemed incapable—despite his patronage power—of overcoming the distance.

But Dawes was not defeated. He was renominated and reelected in 1880 and again in 1886. The young halfbreeds did not win their victory until 1892, when the senator retired and Henry Cabot Lodge took his place. Even more remarkable, Dawes ended his career as a kind of Victorian saint, universally acclaimed as the Indians' truest friend and therefore (however illogically) one of Massachusetts's great senators. It would seem that the senator's sudden involvement in Indian affairs in late 1879 saved his career. In the ensuing months and years, the issue provided Dawes with a platform for national leadership; it made his reputation as a lawmaker; and it bathed his political activities in the glow of a popular cause. Indian assimilation's appeal to both Dawes and his backers is a good measure of its meaning in the political life of the 1880s.

Henry Dawes never thought of himself as simply an office seeker or party reliable. Rather, he held so strongly to the stalwart wing of the gop precisely because it seemed to represent a principled approach to government. One cannot read his speeches and letters without concluding that here was a true believer. Political contests were not competitions between interest or ethnic groups; they were confrontations between opposing philosophies. "The next election," he told a group of Republicans in 1882, "will determine not only with whom the political power shall hereafter rest, but also questions of government, grave and vital, involving the very future of the institutions under which we live." He continued:

First, and before all else in importance, it will be decided: whether under the Constitution, the Nation or the State is sovereign and whether there is power in one to maintain its life and authority in the other, with or without its consent. Whether the Nation shall protect its citizen, whoever and wherever he may be in a free and honest ballot for national officers or shall surrender him to the State. Whether or not the peace of the United

States shall abide with its humble citizens, however humble and wherever he may go or dwell within the limits of the broad Union.[48]

For a man who had left the Whigs over slavery, sat in Congress during the Civil War, served as one of Lincoln's pallbearers, and joined the radical rebellion against Andrew Johnson, such talk represented more than the flapping of the bloody shirt. The supremacy of national institutions, cautious attempts at racial justice, the use of federal power—these were themes that stretched back a quarter-century for Dawes and his constituents.

Yet it was apparent that there was a great difference between the Washington of Lincoln and the capital city presided over by a succession of anonymous, bearded leaders and their battalions of placemen. For these people, the protection of national sovereignty had devolved into defending large railroads and their clients with government contracts. The defense of racial equality had been reduced to the defense of the Republican party in the South and the hope that *private* philanthropy might somehow alter the caste system there. New, divisive issues—such as the efforts to stop Chinese immigration—failed to arouse the party or its leaders to defend their principles in a new environment. Increasingly in the 1870s and 1880s, Republicans were on the defensive. They could unite on subjects of traditional concern, but they divided over the specific role of the party in shaping the nation's future.

Thus the piety of Dawes's campaign rhetoric had become something of a lie. After visiting the prim Republican White House of Rutherford B. Hayes, where, as one wag put it, "the water flowed like champagne," the senator wrote his wife: "I called on Mrs. Hayes Friday night. She 'Brother Dawes-ed' me and I 'Sister Hayes-ed' her back again, and that was pretty much all." The old Republican morality had become an uncomfortable pose, something to feel uneasy over or to joke about. In a sense, of course, this had always been the case: there had never been a time when Republican truth unhampered by interests and tensions had marched forth to do battle with its foe.[49] But by 1879 Republicans felt the need to affirm their "principled" approach to politics. This was especially true in states like Massachusetts, where the events of the 1860s had faded into mythology while the need to galvanize support and beat back young insurgents had increased.

Just as Dawes, who occupied Sumner's old desk in the Senate, took pride in showing visitors the unrepaired marks left by "Bully" Brooks's cane in 1856, so did he seek to retain his connections with the gop's ideals. It was in this atmosphere of both nostalgia and unease that the senator first embraced the campaign for total assimilation. Indian affairs raised again the possibility that the government could "deliver" an embattled minority from tyrannical rule; it evoked an echo of the old crusade.

As a congressman Dawes had led the movement in 1870 to stop the practice of dealing with the tribes by treaty. At that time his chief concern had been government economy. Treaties enabled senators and bureaucrats to appropriate money without proper congressional review. While he occasionally commented on Indian affairs during the 1870s, he did not become a prominent public spokesman for policy reform until after Standing Bear captured Boston audiences in 1879. At the request of the Boston Indian Citizenship Committee (via its chairman, John Davis Long), Dawes joined in the attack on Secretary Schurz and his "halfbreed policies." These actions were not lost on Massachusetts Republicans, who trumpeted Dawes's statements on the Poncas and—in his son's words—overturned the "Boston prejudices" of the gop leadership. With their backing, the senator defeated Long and won renomination in 1880.[50]

In 1881, safely reelected and impressed with the appeal of his Indian policy statements, Dawes joined the Senate Indian Affairs Committee. Despite the fact that he was a new member, he immediately became its chairman. For the next twelve years he used his position to advocate Indian assimilation. He was principally responsible for the expansion of appropriations for Indian education; the passage of the General Allotment Act that bore his name; and the approval of a number of large land cessions, among them the Crow and Blackfoot agreements and the Great Sioux agreement of 1889.

But despite its importance in Dawes's career, the wider attractiveness of Indian assimilation seems somewhat incongruous in the context of the 1880s. While Standing Bear was inciting the merchants of Boston, Southern redeemers were busily rebuilding their white supremacist state governments with the tacit approval of federal authorities. Westerners, assisted by Congress, succeeded in placing a ban on all Chinese immigration. And anti-Catholicism was a regular feature of life in most major cities. Clearly, the call for the incorporation of natives into white society ran counter to these movements. But this incongruity should not be confusing, for it illuminates the appeal of the Indian assimilation issue.

The singularity of Indian assimilation is less striking when one recalls that the goal of men like Dawes was not a blending of Indian and white societies but Anglo conformity: the alteration of native culture to fit a "civilized" model. Reformers insisted that Indians should follow the "white man's road." The expression is significant, for it indicates the kind of future being planned for Native Americans. Here was an important link between Dawes and the new anthropologists. Like them, the senator believed in a single standard of civilization and expected that Indians—like other minority groups—could be made to conform to it. Moreover, both scholars and politicians believed the incorporation process could occur quickly and contribute to the general good.[51]

A comparison of the Indians with other minorities of the period shows that Native Americans posed the smallest threat to existing social relationships. In 1879 most tribes lived in federal territories such as Washington, Arizona, the Dakotas, and what would later become Oklahoma. Most of their white neighbors had no voice in Congress. In addition, once they had been defeated militarily, the majority culture took little notice of the Indians' activities. It appeared that incorporating native people into the larger society would displace no one; it would carry few political costs. Politicians such as Dawes assumed that their programs would provoke only mild resistance from whites. Consequently they stood a good chance of succeeding.

The successful civilization of the Indians also would demonstrate the wisdom of accommodation. Native Americans might require extensive federal assistance, but that aid would simply give the Indians opportunities that were already available (at least theoretically) to other groups: jobs, schools, and citizenship. In the end Indian "advancement" would be a salutary model to hold before other minority communities. Assimilated natives would be proof positive that America was an open society where obedience and accommodation to the wishes of the majority would be rewarded with social equality.

Thus Henry Dawes and his colleagues did not invent the appeal of total assimilation; they simply exploited it. They believed Congress could afford to take the steps necessary to introduce Native Americans to a universal process of assimilation through conformity. Positive results would advertise and encourage that process. In an essay written after his retirement, the senator emphasized these goals.

It is true that we have not yet assimilated the Indians, but it is also true that we have already absorbed the Indian. The State can only bring the Indian into the environment of civilization, and he is 'absorbed' wherever and whenever that occurs. The rest is the work of time and contact, of individual effort and social force, of education and religion. The Bohemians in Chicago, the Polish Jews in New York, are absorbed into our civilization, though they speak no English or live in squalor. Assimilation is another and a better thing, but it is the step that follows absorption.[52]

While it constituted an important acceleration of the government's assimilation efforts and produced an extraordinary degree of federal activity, the campaign to assimilate America's natives by forcing them to conform to the majority's culture was not inconsistent with contemporary attitudes toward other racial and ethnic minorities. The nation would make Native Americans the same offer it extended to other groups: membership in society in exchange for adaptation to existing cultural standards. The major difference would be that federal officials would initiate and carry out this program. They could afford to do so, for the Indian assimilation campaign promised to be popular, safe, and therapeutic.

The total assimilation theme had such a wide appeal that Henry Dawes was able to rely on a substantial group of his fellow lawmakers to support his proposals. It was Dawes's legislative influence that was the key to his success. Between 1880 and 1885, for example, nineteen roll call votes affecting Indians were held in the Senate.

Table 1. The Dawes Loyalists, 1880–85 *

Name	Years in Senate	Mean Agreement Score
Henry W. Blair (R–N.H.)	1880–91	68
Edward Rollins (R–N.H.)	1877–83	67
William B. Allison (R–Iowa)	1872–1908	64
Benjamin Harrison (R–Ind.)	1881–87	63
Omar Conger (R–Mich.)	1881–87	60
George F. Hoar (R–Mass.)	1887–1904	59
William Windom (R–Minn.)	1871–81, 1881–83	57
William Frye (R–Maine)	1881–1911	55
Joseph Hawley (R–Conn.)	1881–1905	55
Henry Dawes (R–Mass.)	1874–1893	53
John I. Mitchell (R–Pa.)	1881–87	52
Austin Pike (R–N.H.)	1883–86	52
Elbridge Lapham (R–N.Y.)	1881–85	51

* See votes 1–19, Appendix 1. Mean agreement scores represent the average rate of agreement between Senator Dawes and his colleagues.

A dozen senators who served during this period and responded to at least five of these votes can be identified as "Dawes loyalists." These men, who are listed in Table 1, followed the Massachusetts senator's lead—voting yea, nay or abstaining—50 percent of the time or more.

In 1880 there were seventy-six people in the Senate. It would be difficult to argue that thirteen men could "dictate" policy to the entire group. Nevertheless, the Dawes faction was extremely powerful. It was led by a committee chairman to whom people naturally deferred, and it was active in a relatively unimportant field where an average thirty-two votes were all that were needed to carry a particular measure. Thus, with Dawes's support a particular position could be assured of a substantial proportion of the votes necessary for it to prevail. As a result, when the group united it usually won. In 1880, for example, an attempt was made to cut off funds for the Board of Indian Commissioners, a group set up under the peace policy to monitor Indian Office purchasing, and provide reformers with a role in policy making. All of the Dawes loyalists opposed the proposal and it was defeated. In 1882 a motion to more than double the annual appropriation for Indian education was supported unanimously by the group; it passed, twenty-nine to eighteen. In the nineteen votes taken before 1885, a majority of the men in Table 1 voted with the winning side fourteen times.

All of the Dawes loyalists were Republicans. Two were from west of the Mississippi, but only one of these—William Windom of Minnesota—represented a state with a significant Indian population. A majority of the Dawes group was from New England. Their average age in 1880 was fifty-four. Here was the core of the Massachusetts senator's support: men who were party loyalists from traditionally Republican states who had lived through the heady victories of the Civil War and shared Dawes's proclivity for a pious, "principled" approach to politics. Only William Boyd Allison of Iowa, who became influential in the 1890s, could be called a party leader.

Dawes's opponents in the Senate came chiefly from two regions. Westerners opposed any "meddling" in their states' affairs. They saw federal programs to aid Indians as unnecessary intrusions on the domestic life of their region. The second center of opposition to Dawes and his followers was in the South. Uniformly Democratic and resentful of Republican social engineering, men like Wade Hampton of South Carolina were quick to line up against the pious reformers. Significantly, the men who represented the states surrounding Indian Territory (Kansas, Missouri, Arkansas, and Texas) were linked to both areas of opposition. They were easily Dawes's most vocal critics. Pushed by large constituencies of "sooners" eager to bypass the Indians, largely Democratic, and led by George Vest of Missouri and Richard Coke of Texas, this group called for the abolition of reservations without any concern for assimilation. Open the land to white homesteaders, they cried, and let nature take its course.

An angry exchange recorded in the House in 1884 typified the disputes between Dawes and his critics. The lower house appears to have been divided in much the same way as the Senate, with eastern Republicans leading the reform effort over the opposition of a few westerners and some southerners. In the midst of the debate over the 1885 Indian appropriations bill, James Belford (whose Colorado

admirers called him the "Red Headed Rooster of the Rockies") delivered a long speech attacking the government's attempts to civilize the Indians. "If we are going to appropriate every year millions
of money for the support of an idle, vagrant, malevolent, malicious
race, then let us go to work and take on our hands all the paupers of
the United States," he told his colleagues. "Who can tell us where a
distinction should exist between the white pauper who can not obtain employment and the Indian who will not work?" Belford and his
allies from the West and South opposed "paternalistic" policies of education and federal assistance. They argued that such programs were
naïve and constituted unwarranted expansions of federal authority.
The reforms singled out Indians for benefits they did not deserve.[53]

John Kasson, an Iowan who had begun his political career as a
delegate to the Buffalo Free Soil convention in 1848, was quick to
respond. Kasson argued, "A moral obligation rests upon the United
States to change by proper and humane methods the system by
which the Indians formerly lived, a system of which we deprived
them, into the system of the white man which we are urging upon
them." Like Henry Dawes, Kasson was comfortable with the use of
federal power for his "moral obligation." And like the Massachusetts
senator his goal was to bring the "system of the white man" to
the tribes.[54]

Congressional support for Dawes's ideas was ideological; his opposition was largely sectional. Most of his supporters were men from
the East who appeared motivated by the rhetoric of national action
and racial uplift. They took few political risks, operating with the
confidence of those who know their idealism is cheap and profitable.
Critics of the reformers were relatively weak. Few states besides the
ones bordering Indian Territory were directly affected by the government's policies—even unreconstructed southerners found the connections between Indian reform and their own past tenuous. In the
early 1880s there was little to unite these skeptics; the appeal of assimilation overrode their objections.

In the late nineteenth century Indian assimilation represented but a
small piece of a much larger issue. Every section of the country had
significant numbers of the people who stood outside the majority

culture. These groups were themselves quite varied. Some—most prominently the European immigrants and newly freed slaves—demanded social acceptance. Others—like the Chinese and Native Americans—held themselves aloof but were forced to accommodate themselves because of their circumstances. Nevertheless, all of these minority communities raised disturbing questions for the white Protestant majority. How would shrinking the geographic and social space that separated Americans affect the nation's social order? What kinds of new relationships would develop between minorities and the majority culture? And what would be the cost of these new relationships?

Fear of diversity was not new in America. The persistence of movements such as anti-Catholicism proved this, as did more recent events—attempts to limit immigration and the government's retreat from Reconstruction. But the 1880s produced something unique. Minority cultures confronted the majority in several areas simultaneously. And the future of one ethnic community—the Indians—was primarily in the hands of federal authorities. Thus, precisely when the issue of pluralism impressed itself with new urgency upon the nation, prominent politicians acquired an opportunity to test their solutions on a politically neutral group. Their response would measure both the country's plans for the Indians and its general attitude toward the social fact of cultural diversity.

A generation ago John Higham called the 1880s an "Age of Confidence." While historians since have refined that image by describing in greater detail the tension and cruelty of the period, the phrase remains essentially accurate. At least among the articulate leaders of the majority culture, there was a uniform conviction that economic expansion, political freedom, and the widening influence of institutions such as the home, the school, and the church would hold the country's social fabric together. Powerful white Americans reasoned that the future could be an extension of the present. Culturally homogeneous communities could distribute themselves across the landscape, and the concurrent growth of social and political institutions would ensure that uniform structures would give shape to American society These institutions would mold the diverse—but malleable—population of the United States into a society that believed in individualism, free enterprise, the nuclear family, the common school, and the promise of prosperity.[55]

It was this deeply traditional vision that lay behind the appeal of Indian assimilation. White journalists, social scientists, and politicians believed that the "uplift" of the red man would confirm their own definition of America. In their view other groups might not be as successful as Native Americans—the Irish might be too numerous, the Chinese might be persecuted by their white neighbors, blacks might not be capable of rapid progress—but the Indians would demonstrate that a "civilized" nation could accommodate nonwhite people by encouraging them to give up their traditional lifeways. The assimilation campaign promised to destroy the Indians' ancient cultures, but that destruction would serve what reformers believed was a greater good: the expansion of "civilized" society.

Chapter 2

The Campaign Begins

Unprecedented reform activity followed the disasters of 1879. In the ensuing decade, legislators and bureaucrats worked to replace the reservation system with a program to incorporate Native Americans into the larger society. While a variety of motives—from narrow self-interest to airy idealism—lay behind this new policy the federal government sustained a remarkable level of activity. During the 1880s federal officials became involved in the details of Indian land tenure, education, and citizenship. Appropriations expanded to support a growing bureaucracy that operated throughout the country. And a cadre of professionals emerged to operate the system. By 1890 the nation had adopted a new approach to Indian affairs and created the machinery for effecting a campaign of total assimilation.

In the wake of the Cheyenne Massacre, an exasperated Henry Dawes told his colleagues, "We appropriate from the treasury at the least $2,700,000 and . . . in the meantime the great Indian question remains unsettled; we have made no advance toward it; we have not even touched it; but we have aggravated it." Sixteen years later the senator was more sanguine. All the necessary legislation had been enacted; the task had become one of implementation. The Indian, he wrote, "is today civilized in the elemental sense of that term. He is 'surrounded everywhere by white civilization'; all his race wear civilized clothes; more than two-thirds of them cultivate the ground, live in houses, ride in Studebaker wagons, sends his children to school, drinks whiskey, may if he likes own property. What he needs is individual help." The Indian problem, he concluded, was now "no different from the Bohemian problem or the German problem."[1]

Having been exposed to the influence of "white civilization," the Indians were now expected to evolve into facsimiles of their white mentors. The "Indian problem" had not been completely solved, but the nation's lawmakers believed they had found answers to the issues that had tormented them in the 1870s. The new programs focused on three areas: Indian landholding, education, and citizenship. In each of these, divergent party and sectional interests acted together in the belief that total assimilation was both practical and possible in a relatively short time. Everyone agreed that the success of the new policies would ensure that the embarrassing incidents of 1879 would not happen again.

In 1880 the United States still recognized the existence of a substantial Indian empire. An area one and a half times the size of California lay under tribal control. Tribes maintained their own political and legal systems and for the most part were economically self-sufficient. Although scattered across the country, these pockets of native sovereignty guaranteed the Indians' continued independence. They allowed Native Americans to separate themselves from the white majority and maintain many of their traditional lifeways. Because they formed a cultural barricade, the tribes considered their reservations to be their most important possessions. For the same reason, the architects of the assimilation policy believed that any program designed to bring natives into the majority culture would require a drastic reduction in Indian landownership.

After 1879 a fundamental change in the government's Indian land policies was a certainty. The reservation system was under attack from a number of directions. The army wanted to shed its distasteful police responsibilities. Reformers who had applauded Grant's peace policies were now disenchanted. The nation's anthropologists, committed to both a version of human progress and a vision of themselves as experts, attacked the idea of permanent enclaves. And government officials, aware of the political costs of maintaining the reservation system, were ready to act.

But even without this constellation of attitudes, the tribal empire was doomed, for the nation's shrinking reservoir of "vacant" land made a new Indian land policy inescapable. West of the Mississippi the population was exploding: it rose from seven to more than eleven million in the 1870s. And much of the increase of that ten-year period took place in areas with large numbers of Indians: the population doubled in Montana and Idaho, tripled in Nebraska and Washington, and quadrupled in Arizona and Colorado. In 1870, Dakota Territory had contained almost twice as many Indians as whites. By 1880 the tribes were outnumbered by white settlers by a ratio of better than six to one. The non-Indian population in the territory had increased tenfold in a single decade.

Expansion of the nation's rail system accompanied this growth in population. In 1870 the Union Pacific was the nation's only transcontinental line. It concentrated on cross-country service and maintained few branches to western towns. But by 1880 three rival lines snaked their way to the coast and dozens of smaller regional companies were pushing into the interior, uniting the West with intersecting bands of steel.

Thus the central issue of the 1880s was not *whether* the reservation system would be changed, but *when* and *how*. Would it be nibbled to death by special interests who first attacked the choicest lands and then moved to marginal areas as these rose in value? Or would the end come swiftly with policy makers adopting a comprehensive program aimed simultaneously at all reservations? While events never corresponded exactly to either, these two models are useful illustrations of an important aspect of the era that has often been overlooked in the historian's search for heroes and villains: laws governing Indian lands changed in the 1880s because policy makers linked the economic development of the West to the goal of total assimilation. Businessmen were often divided over the disposition of lands. What is more, Westerners were relatively weak in Congress; they were not capable of determining policy alone, no matter how vital their imagined stake in any decision. In the same way reformers could not arouse Congress with simple rhetoric. The goal of total assimilation galvanized support for a new land policy among a wide range of political interests. Consequently both ideas and interests lay behind the events of the 1880s; neither was dominant. It is no more accurate to concentrate on western venality than on the reformers' sweet promises. Self-interest meshed with idealism, for public policy makers siezed on a plan they felt would reconcile the goals of Native Americans and whites.

In the fifteen years after Standing Bear's tour nearly half of "Indian country" was opened to white settlement. Between 1880 and 1895 tribes lost 60 percent of the amount that would be taken in the next century. The Dawes Act, often cited as the principal source of land loss in this period, accounted for far less. The massive reduction in Indian landholdings that occurred in the 1880s derived primarily from seven major land cessions. These affected Ute lands in Colorado (1880), the Columbia and Colville Reservation in Washington Territory (1884 and 1892), Oklahoma (1889), the Great Sioux Reservation (1889), the Blackfoot and Crow lands in Montana (1889), and the Bannock-Shoshone reserve at Fort Hall, Idaho (1889). Some of these reservations had existed for only a few years at the time of their dissolution. Others, such as the Crow, Sioux, and Ojibwa lands, had been set aside for over twenty years. Oklahoma had been a part of Indian Territory for over a half-century when the first sections were opened to non-Indians in 1889.[2]

Business interests in the West and elsewhere played a significant role in winning approval of these land cessions. The Ute Treaty of 1880, for example, which required the White River Utes to cede all 12 million acres of their land in a mineral-rich section of Colorado, was enthusiastically supported by local businessmen and speculators. On the southern plains, the pressure to open first Oklahoma (the "unassigned lands") and then the other parts of the Indian Territory could also be traced to economic forces. The "boomers" led by

David Payne, who pestered federal authorities and helped undermine the Five Civilized Tribes, were regularly supported by railroads and local merchants. One convention of these businessmen proclaimed, "The highest obligation of a government towards a helpless, conquered people, penned in a tract of country . . . is to teach them the arts by which they alone can endure, and to infuse into them the spirit of self-reliance and industry which underlies all civilization and all permanent prosperity." These people believed that the advent of white settlers and the example of their "arts" would be the best teachers of "self-reliance and industry." Like similar groups throughout the West, they argued that the destruction of this tribal preserve would be "uplifting" because it would mean "permanent prosperity" for the region.[3]

On the northern plains railroad companies were actively involved in the destruction of several large reservations. Three lines—the Northern Pacific, the Chicago, Milwaukee and St. Paul, and the Great Northern—undertook ambitious expansion programs that promised to make them rivals of the Union Pacific. Early in their growth, however, they each found themselves confronted with a basic fact of railroad life: long-distance traffic cannot support a long-distance road. As the industry's leading journal, the *Railroad Gazette,* observed in 1881, "It is one of our commonest errors to exaggerate the amount and still more the profitableness of the through traffic of very long lines. . . . Lines across the continent, like most other lines, have to draw their chief support from their local traffic."[4]

When the Northern Pacific inaugurated its transcontinental service in 1883 it was already in deep trouble. The final link in its construction program had saddled the company with a huge debt; it would take more than frontier optimism to keep its creditors at bay. For three years, the railroad survived by selling off its land grant in northern Dakota Territory and Montana. In 1885, for example, freight charges earned a profit of only $91,960. With fixed interest payments of $265,000 due on January 1, 1886, the company would have faced a severe crisis had its land department not earned over $1.6 million during the same period. Each of the companies might have survived these precarious years if their supplies of land had been unlimited and they had enjoyed a monopoly over the western trade. Instead, the amount of available land was dwindling rapidly and there was intense competition between lines.

During the 1880s, the major western railroads were faced with a financial version of Hobson's notorious choice. They were committed to expansion, but their rising fixed costs could not be met by transcontinental freight revenues or (for very long) by land sales. The single alternative available to them was spelled out by the editors of the *Railroad Gazette*. Commenting on the Northern Pacific, these observers wrote that earnings would increase only by a growth of local traffic: "This is the foundation on which the future prosperity of the company must be built." Turning to the Chicago, Milwaukee and St. Paul, which purchased and built over twenty-two hundred miles of track on the Plains between 1879 and 1881, the journal added that "nothing could justify this course but the conviction that this country was on the eve of a great growth in population and production."[5]

Thus as Senator Dawes and his colleagues began to discuss the reform of the reservation system, the most powerful businesses in the West were becoming convinced that they had a direct stake in the expansion of agricultural production. As a result they were increasingly interested in both gaining entry to and reducing the size of tribal holdings. The Northern Pacific completed its original cross-country line with rights of way through the Crow and Flathead reservations. But in the 1880s the company acquired branch lines that tapped new mines and towns and led it into the Coeur d'Alene and Nez Perce preserves. The Milwaukee road won access to the Great Sioux Reservation and the Union Pacific (through its subsidiary, the Utah and Northern) pushed north from Salt Lake after acquiring rights to Bannock and Shoshone lands near Fort Hall. It was the Great Northern, however, that was most dependent on tribal lands. The 17.5-million-acre Crow-Blackfoot cession of 1888 enabled the recently reorganized line to cross Montana and reach the Pacific. What is more, these lands also served as the basis for the company's ambitious program of attracting settlers to the northern plains. Indeed, the success of the Great Northern must be attributed in large part to the massive subsidy it received from the Indians.[6]

Of course railroad executives and businessmen did not act alone. Most settlers living near reservations saw these lands as barriers to local economic growth. In Washington Territory for example, where the population increased nearly 500 percent during the 1880s, the demand for a reduction in the area controlled by the Colvilles was deafening. The House Indian Affairs Committee observed that there was "no room for so vast an area of unemployed land as that in the Colville Reservation and its continuance as such [was] no less an injustice to the Indians themselves than a menace to the progress of the surrounding commonwealth." The committee report was accepted without opposition and the reservation quickly opened to non-Indian settlers.[7]

In every major land cession there were specific economic interests who were bound to profit by a reduction of the reservations. Whether they were merchants, railroad executives, or simple farmers, their cry was the same: tribal lands were a barrier to prosperity. Nevertheless, the lure of profits does not in itself explain the passage of these huge land cessions. If the Kansas City merchants were strident in their declaration of 1888 it was because they had been lobbying for an opening of Indian Territory for ten years. The first "boomer" invasion of the area took place in April 1879; the land was not opened to settlement until 1889. Throughout that decade railroads with special privileges in the territory and cattlemen holding profitable leases joined the tribes in opposing the settlers' demands. One marvels not at the power of the "boomers" and their allies, but at their persistence in the face of such strong opposition.

Similarly the railroads were neither unified nor omnipotent. Congress' failure to approve rights of way across reservations was a notorious roadblock to construction. The Utah and Northern, for example, waited seven years for lands at Pocatello to be ceded by the Indians at Fort Hall. What is more, small lines backed by individual legislators were often more successful in winning access to tribal land than were the giant transcontinentals. The result was often legalized extortion, as tiny companies with no assets other than their rights of way demanded huge sums to lease their roadbeds. And finally, companies sometimes opposed a particular reservation opening. During much of the 1880s, for example, the Northern Pacific and the Chicago, Milwaukee and St. Paul resisted settlers' demands that the Great Sioux Reservation be opened. The Northern Pacific feared a reduction in land prices that was sure to follow any increase in the number of available homesteads, while the Milwaukee felt unprepared to build on its right of way through the area. As long as the reservation remained closed, the company's exclusive rights could be protected.[8]

Settlers and railroad men were intimately involved in the great land cessions of the 1880s, but these occurred only after westerners joined forces with other political factions and succeeded in tying their self-interest to the broader goal of Indian assimilation and American progress. In Congress, the assistance of two particular groups was crucial. Southerners often lined up to vote with western railroad boomers. Attacks on tribal preserves appealed to men eager to rebuild the economy of the region and acquire their own badge of progress: a railroad to the Pacific. To apostles of the New South, federally administered reservations threatened local enterprise. Indian Territory was their chief concern. It appeared to prevent railroads from connecting ports on the Gulf of Mexico to the West, and it diverted the transcontinentals north to Kansas City and Chicago rather than to New Orleans. The South was laying down hundreds of miles of track in the 1880s; delaying construction of new roads because of treaty rights or past promises was, in one senator's view, "poppycock."[9]

The benefits of an alliance between westerners and southerners were first demonstrated in 1882, when Congress overrode both a half-century of tradition and numerous treaty guarantees and approved a railroad right of way across Indian Territory. The measure promised to benefit not David Payne and his army of merchants and settlers, but the St. Louis and San Francisco Railroad. The Senate vote on the proposal took place in April. Nearly half the thirty-one "yea" votes recorded in the upper house came from men who represented the old confederacy and Kentucky. Another eleven votes came from west of the Mississippi. More than three-quarters of the bill's opponents were easterners.[10]

When the right-of-way bill reached the House, it met with similar support and opposition. An easterner's proposal that the easement be made contingent on tribal ratification went down to defeat. And with Olin Welborn of Texas warning that the reservation threatened to stand "as a Chinese wall between the growing commerce of [the] States and Territories," a chorus of "ayes" rose to approve the measure by a voice vote. The new statute set an important precedent: Congress would now decide both the timing and the terms of reservation entries. Although treaty restrictions would still restrain most legislators, it was clear that particular issues attractive to both southerners and westerners could be approved. As one member of the upper house exclaimed in 1886 during another right-of-way debate, "The interests of these great communities on both sides [of the reservation] being vitally interested, the Territory being inhabited only by a few Indians . . . we can hardly suppose that the company would undertake to build upon any other than the usual terms." A "few Indians" could not be expected to receive more attention than the future of the "great communities" that surrounded them.[11]

Legislators interested in reforming federal land policies gladly linked their concerns to those of the reservations' enemies. By the 1880s the public had become aware of the widespread abuse of the existing homestead laws. Reformers pointed out that an enterprising settler could claim far more than the mythical 160 acres. In addition, false claims and the use of land script allowed—if they did not encourage—speculation and fraud. For this reason, angry farmers and their representatives often favored reducing the size of reservations so as to open new agricultural lands under a fresh set of rules. To them, tribal preserves were little more than land monopolies that prevented honest yeomen from acquiring their American birthright.[12]

Congressman James Weaver, later a founder of the Populist party and its first presidential nominee, was one of those who believed the destruction of the reservations would benefit the cause of agrarian reform. Keeping the reservations intact, he argued, served only to protect railroads with rights of way and cattlemen with rich leases. Weaver was an ardent supporter of the Oklahoma "boomers." To charges that Payne and his followers were simply lazy misfits, Weaver replied, "Cattle syndicates of this country are occupying that Territory." Thus, he noted, "it is no time to denounce as lawless the poor men who were trying to go in there and makes homes for their families." A few years later, William A. Peffer, a Populist senator from Kansas, put the argument more bluntly. "The time for bartering with the Indian for his land is passed," he observed, "We have come to a time when under the operation of natural laws, we need all the land in this country for homes."[13]

Westerners, southerners, and agrarian reformers formed an impressive coalition. Each member of the alliance would benefit from more land cessions. But none of these groups was interested in the future of the tribes. The attention of each was focused on a particular point or region of conflict. They lacked sufficient incentive to cast their grievances in general terms. The theme of assimilation drew these interests together, allowing them to reshape their arguments and broaden their appeal. This process occurred first in 1882, when Alice Fletcher worked with Nebraska's congressional delegation to reduce the size of the Omaha preserve. Her argument—endorsed by both reformers and scientists—was that Indians could not progress until they adopted a system of individual landownership. Her approach was vital to the passage of every major land cession of the 1880s.

Throughout the decade, Indian reform groups and their political allies in Congress were less concerned with the enforcement of existing treaties than with programs to accelerate Indian "progress" by forcing the tribes out of their traditional paths. As Henry Dawes explained in 1882, "We may cry out against the violation of treaties . . . but the fact remains the same and there will come of this outcry, however just, no practical answer to this question . . . these Indians are to be somehow absorbed into and become a part of the 50,000,000 of our people. There does not seem to be any other way to deal with them." As the author of most of the major land cession agreements of the period, Dawes acted on these principles. He believed that reductions in the size of reservations would bring the two races closer together and allow America's institutions—its schools, its political system and its expanding economy—to "raise up" the Indian.[14]

The 1888 Crow and Blackfoot cession, which provided an annual payment of $430,000 in return for nearly 30 million acres of tribal land, typified the Massachusetts senator's approach. When it emerged from the Indian Affairs Committee, the agreement's preamble noted that the reservation was "wholly out of proportion to the number of Indians occupying [it]," and that the natives should dispose of their excess property "to enable them to obtain the means to become self-supporting as a pastoral and agricultural people, and to educate their children in the paths of civilization." The document went on to stipulate that proceeds from the sale would be used for agency supplies, tools, and seed. Similar arrangements soon were pressed on the Sioux and Ojibwas.[15]

Through the efforts of people like Dawes and Fletcher, land cessions became a component of the national assimilation campaign. Many of the new statutes bore Dawes's personal stamp, but his ideas were widely shared. The House Indian Affairs Committee reported the Colville agreement with the explanation that "a lessening of the dimensions of the Colville Reservation, the planting of active, prosperous and well-ordered white communities on every side of the Indians, the building of railroads, the creation of towns and cities, the opening of mines, and the consequent establishment of markets near at hand so that the Indians can realize an income on their industry, would be the greatest blessing [the United States] could bestow upon these children of benighted savagery." These sentiments were echoed even by Westerners like Henry Teller who were eager for the tribes to give way to "progress." The Colorado senator (who corresponded with John Wesley Powell) told his colleagues, "No nation in the history of the world ever came up from savagery to civilization except it was by manual labor and no nation ever will." Teller in fact was the author of the decade's most extreme proposal for achieving rapid assimilation through a land policy. He suggested that the Great Sioux agreement, intended to reduce the size of that tribe's reservation, contain a provision requiring all Indian homesteads to be located on alternate sections of land. By mandating a "checkerboard" pattern of occupancy, the senator intended to ensure the interspersion of Indians and whites. "Isolate them as we have done and they will continue as they are," the veteran Republican cried, and he promised, "If you can put them in the midst of an intelligent community you will have them civilized in a few years."[16]

The assimilation argument was more than window-dressing. It encouraged the modification of a number of land cessions to ensure that changes in Indian lifeways would occur gradually. Congress did not simply throw natives and whites together as Teller had proposed. With the support of Dawes and his eastern allies, the Montana, Minnesota, Colville, and Sioux agreements provided that reservation openings would take place in two stages. First, tribal lands would be taken and whites would be allowed to settle in areas away from principal Indian communities. Funds from the sale of this property would be applied to teaching farming to the tribes. After a period of years, what was left of the reservation would be divided into allotments or individual homesteads. Once every family had received its land, the remaining area would be opened to settlement. Each change in the reservation's borders would have to be approved by the Indians.[17]

During the debate over the Sioux agreement of 1886 (which was intended to reduce the tribe's land base), Dawes expressed his preference for a policy of gradualism. Senator Teller represented an opposing point of view. The Indian, he declared, should be "compelled to enter our civilization whether he will or whether he wills it not." In keeping with this view, the Colorado lawmaker urged his colleagues to open all reservation lands to settlement. Dawes replied that the goal of assimilation required gentler tactics. He explained, "When the time shall come, after the white man has gone in upon this that is opened today and settled there among them . . . and the Indian himself shall have been set up in severalty . . . then negotiations with each of these tribes will be easy and the result which the Senator says ought to come will certainly come." Aided by his legislative allies—and the general assumption that the Indians would accept his plan—Dawes won approval for this version of the Sioux agreement.[18]

Congress succeeded in reducing the native land base during the 1880s because its actions appealed to a remarkably diverse group. Settlers, railroad magnates, small merchants, Populists, southerners, apostles of western expansion, and even the Indians' new "friends" shared a desire to destroy the "Chinese wall" that separated Indians and whites. Each group had its own perspective and its own considerable stake in the land cessions, but they shared a belief that reducing the size of the reservations would promote prosperity and entice the Indians into "civilized" society.

Tribal lands were not treated like the rest of the public domain. Laws dissolving their boundaries provided for native schools and supplies for farming as well as for the gradual introduction of non-Indian settlers. Nor were the tribes perceived as simple squatters to whom the government owed nothing but the right to preempt a quarter-section of land. Amid the confusion and greed, the fraudulent negotiations and the broken promises, a new national Indian land policy was taking form. The policy reflected a belief that total assimilation would be a consequence of economic prosperity. The new program was made possible by the Indians' relative political popularity and the promise that the government's actions would—in Senator Teller's words—"have them civilized in a few years." What to later generations seemed naïve or hypocritical appeared in the 1880s to be self-evident: the Indian of the West would grow up with the country.

Long before the Crisis of 1879 focused the public's attention on Indian assimilation, the education of Native Americans was a federal concern. During the colonial era a number of missionaries and social reformers had advocated the use of schools to "raise" the Native American to civilization. In the early nineteenth century Congress established a "civilization fund" to support these efforts. Treaties with individual tribes often contained pledges that the "Great Father" would educate his wards. The most extravagant of these were made by the 1868 Peace Commission. It promised a schoolhouse and a teacher for every thirty children. But if these vows were ever fulfilled money usually went to missionaries; there were almost no government institutions.[19]

The year 1879 marked the beginning of a new era in federal Indian education. Over the next fifteen years congressional appropriations for native schooling rose from $75,000 to over $2 million. Twenty off-reservation government boarding schools were founded along with dozens of new agency schools. In 1882 a superintendent of Indian education was appointed to oversee the program. Perhaps most significant, instruction evolved from a haphazard affair directed by evangelical missionaries and incompetent placemen to an orderly system run by trained professionals. By the end of the 1880s federal schools operated on every reservation in the country. Native American education became the province of people devoted to applying modern techniques to the job of "civilization," and Indian schools—once an embarrassing rhetorical flourish on treaties and appropriations bills—became an integral part of the government's assimilation program.[20]

Like the supporters of new land policies, educational reformers believed that American progress would create replicas of established communities throughout the West. Each of those communities would surely have a common school. As for the Indians, they would attend institutions designed to imbue them with the habits of the majority and prepare them to participate in "civilized" society. As they prospered on the frontier, Native Americans would grow more eager for education, and more appreciative of Horace Mann's genius.

One may view the growing popularity of native education in the 1880s by tracing the career of Captain Richard Pratt. Pratt founded the Carlisle Industrial Training School in 1879, and thus began the following decade as the nation's most successful educator of Indians. Ten years later he was an embattled reactionary, defending his own brand of schooling against modern experts. His experience measures the shift from an older, evangelical style of Indian education to the reformers' approach, which was devoted to the progress and assimilation of the entire race.

Pratt was a tinsmith from Logansport, Indiana, who—like many small-town Americans—was wrenched from his quiet existence by the Civil War. The conflict gave him his first glimpse of the world beyond the Midwest. Pratt returned to his trade at the close of hostilities, but could no longer content himself with its quiet routine. In 1867 he joined the regular army and was posted immediately to the western frontier. For the next eight years the captain served as a cavalry officer and commander of Indian scouts. He was involved in the Washita River campaign, the Red River War, and a number of smaller skirmishes.

Pratt's battlefield career came to a close in April 1875, when he was ordered to escort seventy-two Kiowa, Comanche, and Southern Cheyenne warriors—the ringleaders of the recent Red River fighting—to Fort Marion, Florida, and once there to supervise their confinement. The captain watched over every aspect of his prisoners' lives. He introduced them to English, to the idea of working for wages, and to his culture's rules of behavior. He guarded them carefully, but prided himself in their increasing independence. Fort Marion was located in St. Augustine, a winter refuge for wealthy northerners. Several tourists became interested in the captain's work and soon two of them were conducting classes for the prisoners. The "civilized" warriors became a town curiosity. By chance, a few vacationers were also leaders in the Indian reform movement. One of them, Episcopal bishop Henry Whipple of Minnesota, who had been involved in missionary work among the Sioux, was deeply impressed. He wrote to Pratt in 1876, "I do not remember to have ever met a person to whom I was drawn more strongly and in whose work I have felt so deep an interest."[21] Ohio's Senator George Pendleton and Spencer Baird of the Smithsonian Institution also praised the captain and encouraged him to expand his "experiment."

As a result of these new contacts, Pratt became more confident and gained a broader view of his work. If his prisoners—some of the most recalcitrant Indians in the country—could be "tamed" by his methods, then why not the entire race? As the captain told an audience in 1878:

The mass of the Indians in our land have with few tribal exceptions remained until very recently in the enjoyment of their savage life, but now a change has come, the advance of our civilized population from the East has reached the heart of the continent. . . . The dawn of a great emergency has opened upon the Indian. . . . He is in childish ignorance of the methods and course best to pursue. We are in possession of the information and help and are able to give the help that he now so much needs.[22]

In 1877 Pratt requested permission to send his charges to Hampton Institute in Virginia. The famous school for freedmen—Booker T. Washington's alma mater—was founded in the aftermath of the Civil War by the American Missionary Association, and was directed by General Samuel Chapman Armstrong. With the general's help, Pratt's proposal was approved by the War Department in August 1878.

The alliance with Armstrong brought Pratt into contact with a still wider circle of reformers. The general had powerful supporters in Congress and easy access to the religious press. But more important, Pratt's stay at Hampton heightened his evangelical view of his work. He came to believe that his instruction not only would educate the Indian, it would transform his as well. A publicity gimmick suggested to Pratt by Armstrong symbolized this dramatic self-image. Writing in the summer of 1878, just before the captain was to leave Fort Marion for Virginia, the general instructed him, "Be sure and have them bring their wild barbarous things. . . . Good pictures of the Indians as they are will be of great use to us." Staged photographs of native children taken before and after their educational "conversions" became a staple of appeals for Indian education in the early 1880s. The viewer could not help but be struck by the contrast between the new arrivals—unkempt and blanketed—and the scrubbed and uniformed students. Only the faces, curious and bewildered, were constant.[23]

Neither Pratt nor Armstrong was satisfied with the Hampton arrangement, so in the summer of 1879 the captain requested permission to establish a boarding school of his own at an abandoned army barracks outside Carlisle, Pennsylvania. He proposed that the new institution provide both a basic common-school education and instruction in manual skills. Interior Secretary Carl Schurz agreed, and authorized an enrollment of 150 students, with more promised if the "experiment" were successful. Pratt was overjoyed. As he wrote to a reformer friend, "If Carlisle can be made a grand success then the wisdom that has existed for ages will be listened to and our poor Indian's children will . . . be trained up as they should go . . . if only we give them a chance."[24]

With Pratt's organizational talent and Armstrong's skill at public relations, the "experiment" at Carlisle was successful. By 1890 the school had nearly one thousand students. As the number of new students increased the two educators widened their appeals. Both Hampton and Carlisle had print shops that published newspapers which they distributed free to senators, congressmen, and cabinet officers. Both men were within a few hours from Washington by train. And both headmasters recognized the value of congressional inspection tours. Aided by Alice Fletcher, whom he had met in Washington, Pratt arranged for excursion trains to bring legislators to Pennsylvania to view his model school. Upon his return from one of these trips, Congressman Nathaniel Deering told his colleagues, "Here, then, is the solution of the vexed Indian problem. When we can educate the Indian children . . . other kindred questions will naturally take care of themselves."[25]

But despite the enthusiasm of their supporters in congress, Pratt and Armstrong recognized that they could not educate all forty thousand Indian children in their eastern boarding schools. They agreed that schools nearer the reservations would have to bear the responsibility of educating what the captain called the "great mass." One way of doing this—while maintaining the evangelical approach of Hampton and Carlisle—was to build duplicates of their schools in the West. Unfortunately, such a program would require substantial congressional and bureaucratic support. In 1879 that support was not in evidence—only $64,000 was allotted to the general education fund. Monies from other sources raised the total amount for Indian schools other than Hampton and Carlisle to nearly $188,000; that amount provided instruction for barely 10 percent of school-age Indian children. In addition, despite increases in the amount of money available for native schools, the Indian Office had no administrative personnel assigned to education. There was no systematic supervision of existing schools nor was there any bureaucratic machinery for identifying specific needs and planning for the future.[26]

With the successful founding of Carlisle, Indian reformers and their congressional allies began calling for an expansion of the boarding-school concept. Massachusetts' two senators, George Frisbie Hoar and Henry Dawes, led a drive to raise funds for new off-reservation institutions. Speaking of the task of civilization that stood before them, Hoar asked, "Could we not accomplish it with the present instrumentality if we had money enough?" In the House men like Michigan's Byron Cutcheson (who had recently visited Carlisle) were equally vocal. Somewhat surprisingly however, the creation of a new group of boarding schools was primarily the achievement of a retired major general in the Colorado Militia: Secretary of the Interior Henry Teller.[27]

When Henry Teller was first mentioned as a candidate to head the Interior Department, a missionary friend of Richard Pratt noted that the choice would be "extremely absurd." The Colorado senator had opposed the reformers since 1879, when the Ute outbreak in his home state had made him a spokesman for outraged white settlers. He argued that easterners did not understand the Indian problem and should not meddle in the affairs of the frontier. Nevertheless, when President Arthur appointed him to the cabinet in 1882, Teller quickly became a champion of boarding-school education. After his first visit to Carlisle in August 1882, the new secretary wrote to Alice Fletcher, "I want to fill Pratt's school as full as it will bear." He did more than that. Not only did enrollments at Hampton and Carlisle increase during his three-year administration, but six new schools were also founded: Fort Stevenson, Dakota; Genoa, Nebraska; Fort Yuma, Arizona; Haskell Institute, Kansas; Fort Hall, Idaho; and Chilocco Training School in Indian Territory. And Indian school attendance doubled.[28]

Teller defended the new schools in coldly practical terms. In his first annual report he estimated that the expenditure of five or six million dollars for education over a fifteen-year period would make the Indian, "if not a valuable citizen, at least one from whom danger need not be apprehended." The Indian would thus "cease to be a tax on the government." Better to "civilize" the tribes than dispute with them over boundaries and property. Better also to establish new schools under a Republican administration so that contracts and jobs might be distributed for the greatest political benefit.[29]

But despite the fact that Teller had no sympathy for eastern reformers, his expansion of the boarding-school program relied on them for its support. The following list of senators shows their responses to two measures that would have expanded the government's support for Indian education.

Senators *supporting* both proposals	Senators *opposing* both proposals
William B. Allison (R–Iowa)	Francis M. Cockrell (D–Mo.)
Henry B. Anthony (R–R.I.)	Richard Coke (D–Tex.)
Henry W. Blair (R–N.H.)	James T. Farley (D–Calif.)
Matthew C. Butler (D–S.C.)	Augustus H. Garland (D–Ark.)

Senators *supporting* both proposals	Senators *opposing* both proposals
Angus Cameron (R–Wis.)	James B. Groome (D–Md.)
David Davis (D–Ill.)	Isham G. Harris (D–Tenn.)
Henry L. Dawes (R–Mass.)	Benjamin F. Jonas (D–La.)
Nathaniel P. Hill (R–Colo.)	John T. Morgan (D–Ala.)
George H. Pendleton (D–Ohio)	Preston B. Plumb (R–Kans.)
Edward H. Rollins (R–N.H.)	James L. Pugh (D–Ala.)
Alvin Saunders (R–Nebr.)	Daniel W. Voorhes (D–Md.)
William Windom (R–Minn.)	

The first was an amendment offered in 1881 to appropriate one thousand dollars annually to supplement Richard Pratt's military salary. This amount would enable the captain to continue at Carlisle rather than return to his cavalry regiment, and the vote was seen as a referendum on the man's efforts. The second was a motion offered the following year by Massachusetts senator Hoar to raise the annual Indian education appropriation by 85 percent.[30] Three-quarters of the senators supporting both proposals were Republicans. The same percentage represented states east of the Mississippi. Nearly all the opponents of both measures were Democrats, and none came from the northeast.

The remarkable alliance between a Colorado firebrand and eastern humanitarians is vivid evidence of the extent to which Captain Pratt's evangelical view of Indian assimilation was supported by his contemporaries. Like the headmaster of Carlisle, Senator Teller believed that a period of intense "civilization" would transform the Indians into self-sufficient people. In 1884, at the end of Teller's reign at the Interior Department, Commissioner of Indian Affairs Homer Price observed that "an impartial view" of the government's recent efforts would warrant "the belief that some time in the near future . . . with the aid of such industrial, agricultural, and mechanical schools as [were] now being carried on, the Indian [would] be able to care for himself, and be no longer a burden but a help to the Government." Schools were symbols of a common faith in education's ability to convert native children to "civilization." During the remainder of the decade, this evangelical vision fueled the creation of a national Indian educational system on the model of the country's public schools.[31]

The popularity of boarding schools as the preferred means of educating Indians was relatively short-lived. Three groups undermined the original program. First, Democratic legislators argued that boarding schools for all forty thousand Native American children would be prohibitively expensive. Providing such facilities would require that congress double the entire Indian Office budget. Second, southeners and others hostile to the idea of federal aid for nonwhite minorities asserted that native children should not receive such elaborate training. And finally, the growing interest in Indian schools attracted a cadre of professional educators who began to dominate educational policy making. These people admired men like Armstrong and Pratt but were eager to introduce modern methods to the task of "civilization."

Budgetary arguments against boarding schools made themselves felt after the Democratic landslide of 1884. For the first time since the Civil War the party of Calhoun and Jeff Davis controlled both the presidency and the House of Representatives. The Democrats' election slogans had been "Retrenchment and Reform" and once in office the party's leaders began a widespread effort to cut federal spending. Riding what one observer called a "sweet and aromatic wave of economy," they turned their attention to the Indian Office. In 1885 the House took the unprecedented action of cutting the general education appropriation. But the Senate, still controlled by Republicans and the Dawes supporters on the Indian Affairs Committee, restored these cuts and provided for a 10 percent increase.[32]

Even though Captain Pratt—who had lobbied in person for the 1885 budget—celebrated this victory over the Democrats, it was obvious that a turning point had been reached. Between their inception in 1877 and 1885, general appropriations for Indian education had increased an average of 75 percent per year. For the ten years after 1885 the average increase was 10 percent and the largest, 35 percent, came in 1891. "Our people," the Democratic chairman of the House Indian Affairs Committee warned, "are growing tired of being taxed and taxed almost out of existence to enrich a few manufacturers in this country and to support these lazy Indians in dirt and idleness." Throughout the next two decades the budget cutters kept to this rhetorical high ground—and in the process forced their adversaries across the aisle to follow suit. Republican Henry Johnson, for example, told his House colleagues that if the Indians who met Columbus had been able to see into the future, none of the infamous events of American history would have appalled them "until they saw the apparition of the gentlemen from Indiana [Appropriations Committee chairman Richard Holman] in the noonday of the nineteenth century standing up in the American House of Commons with his well-known face begrimed all over with the war paint of economy holding in one hand his scalping knife and in the other that instrument of still worse torture, his contemptible, penurious Indian appropriations bill." Neither party had the congressional strength to overcome the other on this issue and both refused to moderate their positions. The result was an end to federal largesse and a corresponding modification of the Indian Office's plans for the future.[33]

For southerners and some particularly hostile westerners, these emotional budgetary arguments were often linked to doubts concerning the Native American's ability to learn. Grover Cleveland's commissioner of Indian affairs was a Tennessean who typified the attitude. John Atkins wrote that as far as he was concerned Indians should be taught the English language only. "The English language as taught in America," he added, "is good enough for all her people of all her races." Kansas senator Preston Plumb expanded on this theme. An opponent of boarding schools, Plumb declared, "It is not possible to take an Indian and by the mere process of school education put him upon the plane of the white people." Plumb's fellow Kansan John J. Ingalls was even more direct. He argued that boarding schools were "as absurd" and "futile" as going "among a herd of Texas broadhorn steers and endeavoring to turn them into Durhams and thoroughbreds by reading Alexander's herd book in their cattle-pens at Dodge City or Wichita."[34]

Despite this hostility, few politicians wanted to abandon the government's education program altogether. Everyone involved, legislators, bureaucrats, and private reformers, agreed that the "uncivilized" Indians ought somehow to be "raised" to the "plane of white people." The cruel rhetoric of Ingalls and Plumb attested to their rejection of Pratt and his new schools, but even these men assumed that the government should educate its wards. They were willing to support programs that were more closely tied to the reservations. Consequently, in the mid-1880s the Indian Office began to accommodate itself to skeptical politicians by shifting its attention away from off-reservation boarding schools and toward the creation of a more comprehensive system.

In 1881, Alfred Riggs, a Presbyterian missionary among the Sioux, sketched out his solution to the problem of Indian education for the readers of the *Journal of Education*. Writing for a professional audience, he urged the government "to organize and operate a school system for the whole Indian country which [would] do for the Indian what the public school systems of Massachusetts, or New York, or Ohio, [did] for every son and daughter of these commonwealths." Riggs's advice summarized the approach of most modern educators. They argued that the government's obligation to the now-defeated Indians required it to replace the older boarding schools with newer, more practical facilities. Their proposals were more attractive to politicians and matched the new ideas that were beginning to percolate to the surface from the Indian Office bureaucracy.[35]

J. J. Haworth became the government's first inspector of Indian education in 1882. He was responsible for overseeing school supply contracts and making personnel recommendations. The title of the position was changed in 1885 to Indian school superintendent. Now there was a bureaucratic structure charged with supervising the entire school program and making recommendations for future growth. While this "structure" first consisted of no more than an administrator and a clerk, the people involved in it were experienced educators who argued that a modern education should be the basis for the Indians' assimilation. "The position of Supervisor," wrote William Hailmann, who served from 1894 to 1898, "is not at first glance a very attractive one, [it] calls for a high degree of missionary spirit and enthusiasm in order to be successful."[36]

The meaning of the evolution from the older Pratt approach to a newer, more professional style first became clear in 1884, when Inspector Haworth spoke before the annual meeting of the National Education Association's Department of Superintendence. With the founders of Hampton and Carlisle in the audience, Haworth attacked eastern boarding schools for their expense and their "errors in teaching." These institutions kept Indians in an artificial environment and prevented them from adapting the lessons they learned to their surroundings. Pratt responded immediately from the floor. "It is not practicable to educate them *on* the reservation," he cried, "if we desire them to be anything else than Indians." But the captain's protests found few supporters. If his experiment had been successful, and if it was politically impossible to bring all forty thousand children to the East, then was it not logical to duplicate his techniques in the West? As an editorial in the *Journal of Education* argued, "Good as is the work done at Carlisle, there is little glory in that fact if it is only a show school for the civilization of a few while the multitude remain outside pleading in vain for admittance." Pratt was not being attacked by his critics, but by followers who were seeking a politically practical way of building on his achievements.[37]

John Oberly, an Indian school superintendent (and later Indian commissioner) in the Cleveland administration, was the first to sketch out a proposal for a national educational system for Native Americans. He recommended beginning with the construction of boarding schools on each reservation. These facilities would put the lessons of Hampton and Carlisle to work for every tribe while they "reflect[ed] some of the light of civilization into the Indian camp."[38] He called also for centralizing school administration in his office. Hiring, construction, teacher training, and even the disposition of "incorrigible" students would best be handled from Washington. Finally he suggested that Indian Office experts prepare a special series of textbooks for use in Indian schools. His immediate successors added requests for a compulsory attendance law and the delineation of grade levels in all institutions. These loyal Democrats were as interested in centralizing patronage as they were in reforming the education program, but their efforts also went a long way towards systematizing the government's attempts and placing them in the hands of specialists.

Under Benjamin Harrison such specialists moved to center stage. Between 1889 and 1893 the commissioner of Indian affairs was Thomas Jefferson Morgan, a man whose career is best understandable to the late twentieth century only by analogy. Like modern economists and lawyers who glide silently between universities, government agencies, and private foundations, Morgan had skills that were valued in several of the nineteenth century's most prestigious professions. He had been a commander of black troops in the Civil War, a Baptist minister, a professor of theology, the principal of the New York State Normal School at Potsdam, and an officer in the National Education Association. While the connections between the battlefield, the pulpit, and the classroom may seem obscure a century later, they were clear to Morgan and his contemporaries. The new commissioner was captivated by the potential for moral uplift within the public schools and eager to focus their power on the job of "civilizing" the Indians.

Morgan's superintendent of Indian education was the Reverend Daniel Dorchester. Like his superior, Dorchester had been both a minister and an educational reformer before coming to Washington. The new team's faith in the schools was revealed in a special pamphlet issued with Morgan's first annual report: "Education is to be the medium through which the rising generation of Indians are to be brought into fraternal and harmonious relationship with their white fellow-citizens, and with them enjoy the sweets of refined homes, the delight of social intercourse, the emoluments of commerce and trade, the advantages of travel, together with the pleasures that come from literature, science and philosophy, and the solace and stimulus afforded by a true religion." The commissioner went on to describe how "the condition of this whole people [could] be radically improved in a single generation." First, every Indian community or village should have a day school for its children. These institutions would provide an "impressive object lesson" in the virtues of civilized living and serve as a center for funneling students into a second tier of facilities, the primary schools. The primary schools would provide boarding and be located at most agencies and population centers. Their mission was to lay the "foundation work of native education." For this reason, Morgan wrote, the primary schools had to take students "at as early an age as possible, before camp life [had] made an indelible stamp on them." At about age ten, students would advance to grammar schools, which would "accustom pupils to systematic habits" by making them adhere to a rigid daily schedule and begin learning a trade. Finally, at about fifteen, academically inclined Indians would enter government high schools, which, Morgan wrote, "should uplift the Indian students on to so high a plane of thought and aspiration as to render the life of the camp intolerable." He added that this fourth level of school would thus serve as "a gateway out from the desolation of the reservation into assimilation with natural life."[39]

The editors of the *Journal of Education* applauded Morgan's proposal, calling it "the key-note so long desired by all thoughtful well-wishers of the Indian."[40] Congress was not so enthusiastic, and lagging appropriations left many of the commissioner's proposals on the drawing board. Nevertheless, he and Dorchester accomplished a great deal of the "systemization" envisioned in his first report. Grades were established in all government schools and a uniform series of textbooks was adopted for each level of instruction. In 1891 all school personnel came under the provisions of the Civil Service Act, and "professional" employees began attending federally sponsored summer institutes to sharpen their skills and hear lectures by prominent educators. Finally Congress adopted a compulsory attendance law that gave Indian agents and policemen the power to force children into Morgan's new system.

While hailed by progressive educators and most Indian reformers, Morgan's program was not universally popular among policy makers. His harshest critic was the celebrated headmaster of Carlisle. Richard Pratt argued that schools like his own, which were self-contained and far away from the Indians' traditional surroundings, were the only institutions that could "civilize" native children. "Morgan's Public School for the Indian craze," Pratt told Alice Fletcher in 1893, "is in my judgment worse than no school at all." He felt that the new civil service rules prevented him from selecting a compatible staff and that grading the government schools would reduce Carlisle itself to a trade school. The carloads of bereft children would soon be replaced by shipments of students who already had received a basic education near their homes. (A law passed in

1893 required all off-reservation students to complete three years at agency schools before going elsewhere.) "I despise the plans of my good friend Gen. Morgan more than I can tell you," Pratt wrote.[41]

But it is the symbolism of this conflict rather than its size that is significant. By the early 1890s Pratt's opinions had little influence in policy making. Commissioner Morgan's successor at the Indian Office left Daniel Dorchester in charge of the Indian schools for a full year before replacing him with a Democrat, and that man, William Hailmann, shared his predecessor's preference for a modern national school system. As Hailmann told the National Education Association in 1895, the day when "the few philanthropic men and women missionaries" guided the Indians' progress were past. In recent years, "they gradually stepped aside and the schoolmaster stepped in." In keeping with this trend, Hailmann proposed a final step in the government's program: the integration of native children into local public schools.[42]

There was of course a practical aspect to Hailmann's proposal. The Democrats continued to oppose increases in the Indian budget (cuts were made in 1894, 1895, and 1896), and the economic crisis of the 1890s made larger expenditures unthinkable. Still, the superintendent believed his plan was "in line with the enlightened policy that labor[ed] to do away with tribal life, reservations, agencies, and military posts among the Indians." A small number of Indian students had been attending public schools during Morgan's term. In 1892 the commissioner had seen "no insuperable obstacles" to expanding the practice, so when Hailmann took office in 1894 he proposed to place as many children as possible in public schools.[43]

To facilitate this process, Hailmann drew up a general contract that spelled out the responsibilities of both the Indian Office and the receiving institutions. It committed the government to pay county school boards ten dollars per quarter for each child; it required local authorities to give native students the same education they gave the children of tax-paying citizens; and it called on teachers and administrators "to protect the pupils included in this contract from ridicule, insult and other improper conduct at the hands of their fellow pupils, and to encourage them . . . to perform their duties with the same degree of interest and industry as their fellow pupils, the children of white citizens." This remarkable document made explicit what professional Indian educators in the late nineteenth century believed was the logical extension of their efforts: the complete absorption of Indian children into white society. Emulating the nation's modern common schools rather than the lonely missionary outposts of the past, policy makers envisioned a comprehensive system that would admit "savages," expose them to the nation's most powerful assimilating institution, and graduate "civilized" men and women who would be treated with respect by their white peers.[44]

In 1892 Commissioner Morgan wrote of Indian education, "I doubt if there is a question before the public in which there is more general consensus of opinion. Even the Western States and Territories, where the feeling against the Indians has been exceedingly bitter, show a surprising and most gratifying change in public sentiment." This certainly appeared to be true. The haphazard arrangments of the previous decade, based as they were on a revivalistic notion of immediate conversion to white ways, had been replaced by an impressive national system of native schools. These institutions were organized by grade level, supplied with special materials, and staffed by nonpolitical professionals. The new system appeared cheap, practical, and up-to-date. While politicians continued to differ over the extent of the commitment that should be made to Indian education, most of them endorsed the new approach and embraced its assimilationist goals. "If every Indian child could be in school for five years," the *Journal of Education* predicted in 1893, "savagery would cease and the government support of Indians would be a thing of the past."[45]

The national Indian school system was an integral part of the new assimilation campaign. It sought to extend the institutions of the majority culture so that they could surround and absorb Indian communities. It was designed explicitly to incorporate native people into the larger society and to "raise" them to a common standard of civilization. In this sense, Native American education bore a striking resemblance to the urban school reforms then underway in many parts of the United States. People like Thomas Jefferson Morgan and William Hailmann moved from public to Indian education, and the two systems shared a number of concepts and expectations.

Michael Katz has argued that in late-nineteenth-century America, urban school systems emerged that were "universal, tax-supported, free, compulsory, bureaucratic, racist and class biased." These characteristics may not have been as universal (or as self-consciously repressive) as Katz asserts, but they summarize accurately the goals (and much of the reality) of the new government schools for both Indians and whites. The comprehensive program of the Indian Office was universal. The new facilities were supported by tribal funds and congressional appropriations ("tax supported"), and were "free" to native children. Attendance was compulsory. Finally, Indian schools were "racist" and "class biased" in the sense that their explicit goal was the overthrow of traditional cultures and the imposition of "civilized" lifeways. Neither Indian nor white children were to be exposed to haphazard, personalized learning. Rather, they were to be introduced systematically to a common version of life in modern America.[46]

Many of the Indian Office's educational programs also ran parallel to those being instituted in the public schools. The trend toward a centralized nonpolitical hiring system was common to both systems, as was the popularity of summer teachers' institutes. Carlisle became famous both because of its success with Indians and because it was an example of Calvin Woodward's new theories of manual education. From his post at Washington University in St. Louis, Woodward taught that manual instruction should be the basis for all learning. He was interested not in vocational skills but in habits of work and concentration that could be transferred to academic areas. If students received the "symmetrical training" he advocated, Woodward told the National Education Association, "this age of scientific progress and material wealth [would] be also an age of high intellectual and social progress." Pratt adopted these ideas and provided both industrial and academic training. Carlisle offered instruction in a number of trades and established an "outing" program that placed students on nearby farms for several months at a time.[47]

Perhaps the most telling indicators of the similarities between native education and the "modern" public schools were the many differences between the programs offered by the Indian Office and the instruction available to blacks and Asians. While southern blacks saw the promises of Reconstruction reduced to the shabby reality of inadequate segregated schools, and Asians on the Pacific Coast were either ignored or excluded by white educators, Native Americans became the favored focus of a national "civilization" program.

Throughout the late nineteenth century, reformers and humanitarians proposed the extension of a common-school education to blacks. These proposals usually relied on private philanthropy, but during the 1880s congressional Republicans, led by New Hampshire senator Henry Blair, suggested federal assistance. The Blair bill promised to aid all poor school districts, but its supporters believed blacks would be its principal beneficiaries. Congress approved geometrical increases in the annual Indian school budget during the same years that the Blair bill floundered and died. Asians met a similar fate. When anti-Chinese rioting occurred in a number of western towns, federal authorities took little or no action. Ultimately, in 1882, Congress responded to its white constituents rather than the embattled minority by passing the Chinese Exclusion Act.[48]

It would be misleading to overstate the differences between white attitudes toward Indians and other racial minorities in the late nineteenth century. Native Americans were considered less than civilized, and a number of officials expressed doubt over their ability to adapt to modern living. Nevertheless, the Indian education program constituted a unique level of federal activism on behalf of a nonwhite minority. There were several reasons for this. First, the advocates of Indian education did not arouse local opposition. Many southerners viewed the Blair bill as a federal intrusion into state politics and southern race relations. An attempt by Washington to aid Asians on the Pacific Coast would have met a similar reaction. Most Indian groups lived in areas that were still federal territories in the 1880s; interests that might have objected to the government's programs were unrepresented in Congress. And the sparsely settled West often welcomed federal spending as a prop to the region's fragile economy. Thus, men like Dawes could succeed in Indian affairs where they had failed with the Blair bill or the Chinese Exclusion Act. Indian reform allowed whites to adopt "principled positions" while taking few political risks.

But there was more at work in this area than a political calculus. Indians were a relatively small group. They numbered roughly

250,000 in 1900, compared to 4 million blacks and 100,000 Asians. And they were scattered across several states and territories. For these reasons, and because of the special hold they had on the white imagination, politicians and educators could argue that, unlike other nonwhite peoples, Native Americans might be absorbed by the majority. Captain Pratt imagined that 40,000 young people would be educated and employed by the country's booming new industries. Secretary Teller fashioned a federal school system to accommodate them. And William Hailmann planned for their eventual incorporation into the nation's public schools.

Thomas Morgan was right: there was a "general consensus of opinion" regarding Indian education. Building on the assumption that schooling was an essential component of assimilation, policy makers worked within the political boundaries of the 1880s to erect a national program. The new institutions were patterned after common schools; they were run by professionals, opened to all, and designed to spread the values of the majority culture. They profited by the Native American's dearth of political enemies in Congress, as well as the educators' expectations that systematic instruction would produce rapid "progress." By the end of the decade this aspect of the government's assimilation policy was fixed. Policy makers now waited for the Indians to respond as the experts had predicted.

Henry Dawes's General Allotment Act was the final part of the government's new assimilation campaign. The law, which was approved in February 1887, established a pathway for the legal, economic, and social integration of Native Americans into the United States. It was the first piece of legislation intended for the general regulation of Indian affairs to be passed in half a century, and it remained the keystone of federal action until 1934, when the Indian Reorganization Act replaced it.

Because supporters of the Dawes Act hailed it as the "Indians' Magna Carta," and because it governed Indian affairs for nearly fifty years, historians have treated its passage as an event that produced drastic shifts in policy. This was not the case. Congress passed the allotment law toward the end of a decade of reform activity. Consequently its provisions embodied a number of ideas and expectations that already had gained acceptance and become a part of government action. In addition, the new severalty statute was a remarkably plastic document; it required no immediate action and gave administrators considerable discretionary power. The law set general goals and ignored many of the problems of implementation. It is properly viewed as a statement of its sponsors' common assumptions about the Indians' place in American society rather than as a technical prescription for prompt change.[49]

In January 1881, Democratic senator Richard Coke of Texas, Dawes's predecessor as chairman of the Indian Affairs Committee, introduced the first general allotment bill of the decade. Although Congress never approved Coke's proposal, the bill initiated a six-year public debate, during which three major allotment schemes were considered. By 1887 this debate produced a document that had such wide support that it passed both the House and Senate on a voice vote. In its final form, the severalty law represented the consensus view of policy makers. It set out general plans for Indian land administration, Indian education, and Indian citizenship. And in each area it proposed actions that promised to hasten native assimilation.

As we have seen, virtually all policy makers endorsed the idea of reducing the size of the reservations. Differences arose over how— and how quickly—to proceed. Prospective settlers cared little for legal niceties. As one of their leaders in congress explained, the westward movement could not be delayed. "Its march," he added, was as "irrestible as that of Sherman's to the sea." Thus, "no Indian treaties, no Interior Department regulations, no Indian Bureau contrivances [could] stop the onward flow of white emigration." A number of reformers also accepted this expansionist perspective; they believed the swift replacement of reservations with individual homesteads would end the rule of corrupt agents and hasten the civilization process. Lyman Abbott, editor of the *Christian Union* in New York, was the most outspoken of this group. The reservation system, he wrote, was "hopelessly wrong" and could not be reformed. "It can only be uprooted, root and branch and leaf, and a new system put in its place."[50]

Two dissimilar groups opposed Abbott and the expansionists. Senator Dawes and his congressional supporters argued that any plan to put Indians on individual tracts of land should be implemented gradually. In addition, he pointed out that allotment had to be accompanied by continued federal support and protection. "If we are to set an Indian up in severalty," he told his fellow senators, "we must throw some protection over him and around him and aid him for awhile in this effort; we must countenance the effort; we must hold up his hand." This gradualist position was shared by other legislators who were pessimistic about the ability of Native Americans to survive as individual farmers. John Tyler Morgan of Alabama, for example, saw forced allotment as an attempt "to substitute in place of the traditional and simple and ancient form of government obtaining among these various tribes the proud and magnificent system which has been built up to accommodate itself to the most enterprising and enlightened nation in the world." In the House, Charles Hooker of Mississippi echoed Morgan as he called for the establishment of permanent tribal homelands in the West.[51]

The original Coke bill emphasized the gradual approach to allotments. It gave each tribe the right to choose—by a two-thirds vote—between allotment and the issuance of patent that would guarantee common ownership of a specific tract of land (presumably of a size approximating 160 acres per person). Thus, no group would be allotted until they became "civilized" enough to ask for individual lands. A revised version of the Coke bill that Senators Dawes and Coke sponsored jointly in 1884 also contained this tribal consent provision. The Coke-Dawes proposal passed the Senate, but opponents prevented it from reaching the floor of the House. The resulting stalemate continued until 1886, when a third proposal eliminated the consent clause in favor of two other forms of protection. This third proposal became the Dawes Act. It stated that allotment would occur only at the president's direction—"whenever in his opinion" the Indians were ready for it. In addition, the new statute retained a provision of the earlier bills which stipulated that allotments would be "inalienable" for twenty-five years. An Indian's land would thus be exempt from taxation and ineligible for sale for a generation. Finally, the Dawes Act stated that it did not apply to the Five Civilized Tribes of Indian Territory or to the New York Indians. Thus the debate over severalty was separated from the more complicated argument over how to reduce the size of those older reservations.[52]

Western expansionists and the more aggressive reformers could now look forward to a succession of presidential proclamations initiating the allotment of attractive reservations. But those with a gradualist view could assume that most of the Indians' white neighbors were politically impotent and unlikely to influence the chief executive. Further, the inalienable title would prevent surrounding non-Indian communities from raiding the allottees' new property. Senator Dawes's law also required that any future sale of "surplus" lands (lands not needed for allotment purposes) would require the approval of the tribes. The Dawes Act contained no timetable for the dismantling of the reservations and the creation of individual Indian homesteads. The issue was neatly blurred and tossed into the hands of future presidents.

In addition to disputes over the administration of tribal lands, the Dawes Act also revealed—and compromised—disagreements over Indian citizenship. Policy makers endorsed the ultimate goal of total assimilation but differed over its timing, as they had in the case of the reservation lands. Many of the same factions were involved in the two disputes. Just as the pious Lyman Abbott and David Payne's rabid Oklahoma "boomers" agreed that reservations should be abolished immediately, so the Reverend William J. Harsha, chairman of the Omaha Citizenship Committee, found his allies among Colorado miners and Dakota sodbusters when he called for the immediate extension of the Fourteenth Amendment to Native Americans. Their opponents—southerners concerned with an invasion of state's rights and reformers uncomfortable with eliminating all federal protection for the tribes—also tended to speak out against rapid allotment. Both Florida's Senator Wilkinson Call and Secretary Carl Schurz, for example, opposed an immediate granting of the franchise.[53]

The original Coke bill proposed placing allotted Indians under state law without granting them citizenship. The bill's author defended this unique arrangement by saying that it would allow the Interior Department to continue to "aid the Indian in his attempts to become civilized." The effect of Coke's proposal was to put Indians in a position comparable to that of blacks, whose national citizenship had been voided in the years since the Civil War. That process in fact reached its logical end in the *Civil Rights* cases, decided in the midst of the debates over the severalty law. In its 1883 decision the Supreme Court had promised that national standards of citizenship would not be enforced in the South. Under the Coke bill, Indians, like southern blacks, would be unable to appeal to federal courts for protection. Not surprisingly, therefore, the measure called forth support in Congress from the New South.[54]

But southerners like Coke were not the only opponents of rapid citizenship. The Ponca controversy in 1879 indicated that there were deep divisions even among the Indians' "friends" on this issue. Carl Schurz opposed Judge Dundy's order to release Standing Bear because he believed an immediate grant of citizenship would destroy the government's ability to aid the tribes. John Wesley Powell also endorsed gradual citizenship, arguing that Indians needed "a period of probation prior to assuming the responsibilities and obtaining the privileges of citizenship." Apparently a majority of the Senate shared this view, for when a proposal to grant Indians immediate citizenship was brought up in January 1881, it was defeated by a vote of twenty-nine to twelve.[55]

Other reformers divided over the question of how rapidly to grant citizenship. The *Nation* and the *American Law Review* (defenders of Schurz in the *Standing Bear* case) continued to advocate gradualism. George F. Canfield, a Columbia University law professor, was an outspoken member of this group. He pointed out that the franchise would expose the Indians to a variety of risks. They "would be withdrawn from the power of Congress to keep them exempt from taxation, to prevent the introduction and sale of liquor among them, and, in general, to regulate and control our intercourse with them." Supporters of immediate citizenship—the Boston Indian Citizenship Committee, the Indian Rights Association, and others— thus faced "humanitarian" justifications for limiting citizenship as well as cynical ones. Schurz and his supporters asserted that the status quo should continue until the Indians themselves gave up their old ways and demonstrated individually their readiness for the franchise.[56]

The debate over citizenship changed dramatically in 1884, when the Supreme Court decided the case of *Elk* v. *Wilkins*. The case grew out of an attempt by John Elk, a "civilized Indian," to vote in Omaha, Nebraska. Local election officials argued that Elk was not a citizen and therefore was ineligible for the franchise. The Supreme Court agreed, stating that Indians were not born within the jurisdictional boundaries of the United States and that Congress had never established a naturalization process for them. The justices declared that it was up to the legislative branch to decide the issue: "The question whether any Indian tribes, or any members thereof have become so far advanced in civilization that they should be let out of the state of pupilage, and admitted to the privileges and responsibilities of citizenship, is a question to be decided by the nation whose wards they are and whose citizens they seek to become; and not by each Indian for himself."[57] Those who had supported Schurz's benign notion of gradual citizenship or Powell's concept of a "probation" period now were on the spot. They could leave the Indians without federal guarantees, as the Coke bill had proposed, or they could suggest a substitute. Without new legislation the Indians would continue under the absolute control of the Indian Office; the "tyranny of the reservation" would be absolute.

Faced with an explicit choice between leaving the Indians in limbo and providing for their legal assimilation, policy makers chose the latter. Both the Dawes-Coke bill of 1884 and the final Dawes Act declared that all allottees would be granted citizenship. There were many reasons for this. In the face of the *Elk* decision reformers who had advocated gradualism could no longer argue that individual natives would become citizens as they rose to "civilization." Again, the group's relatively small numbers and generally positive public image worked in favor of "humanitarian" treatment. And finally, the alternative of *not* granting citizenship was unacceptable. A denial of the franchise would maintain the Indians' wardship indefinitely and embarrass those who saw total assimilation as a vindication of the universality of American institutions.

Despite its commitment to citizenship, the Dawes Act continued to satisfy a wide variety of interests. Under the new law Indians would not become citizens until after they received allotments. And allotment presumably would not occur before they had demonstrated the ability to manage their own farms. As Senator Dawes explained shortly before his bill passed the upper house in 1886, the franchise was granted "in order to encourage any Indian who [had] started upon the life of a civilized man and [was] making the effort to be one of the body-politic in which he live[d], giving the encouragement that if he so maintain[ed] himself he [would] be a citizen of the United States." The extent of congressional support for this position was demonstrated soon after Dawes spoke. Samuel Bell Maxey of Texas proposed an amendment to strike the citizenship provision. He argued that there was ample precedent for barring natives from membership in the polity. "Look at your Chinamen," he cried, "are they not specifically excepted from the naturalization laws?" But Maxey's colleagues would not extend the Chinese Exclusion Act to the Indians. They rejected his proposal by a voice vote and sent the severalty bill to the House. There the section was approved without significant opposition.[58]

In a commentary on the new law published early in 1887, the Indian Rights Association observed that the Dawes Act had "thrown wide open the door to Indian citizenship. . . . The native [was] invited and even urged to enter whatever places he [might] choose to occupy as a citizen of this free Republic." The law provided a general procedure for enfranchising Indians but—as in the sections on dividing up the reservation lands—it contained no specific timetable or regulations. Instead, policy makers had seized on—and been satisfied with—a general commitment to Indian citizenship.[59]

Indian education was the final policy area affected by the new severalty law. While the Dawes Act did not refer directly to the native school system, it assumed that Indians should become citizens and that they would adopt the habits of the white majority. Allotment, the House Indian Affairs committee observed in 1885, would "be such an incentive to labor that the Indian [would] gradually but surely abandon his nomadic habits and settle down to a life of comparative industry."[60] But there was considerable disagreement over what the government should do to foster the process.

Supporters of the growing Indian school system believed that allotment would require a new level of government activity. As Alice

Fletcher observed, the reservations "reduced . . . mental life to a minimum" and Indian farmers therefore would need both training and support. Otherwise, Carlisle's Captain Pratt warned, the allottee's land would "remain like himself, barren and waste." Simply dividing the land among tribal members would not create "civilized" natives. Olin Welborn of Texas told his House colleagues that while allotment was the "great goal" of government action, assigning lands in severalty was "the final step, and before it [was] taken the Indians [had to] be prepared for it."[61]

But critics of the new education programs had a very different view of allotment. They welcomed the severalty law because it promised to end decades of government "coddling," and they urged the Indian Office to reach the goal of Indian self-sufficiency as rapidly as possible. Senator John Ingalls of Kansas typified this position. He endorsed the original Coke bill because it meant a reduction in the annual budget. "I am not an advocate of butchery," he explained, "I am in favor of some humane policy that shall relieve the Treasury from the annual imposition of millions of dollars to support these people in unproductive idleness, and I assented to the reporting of this bill in the hope that something might be done in that direction."[62] The final Dawes bill did not specifically endorse either view of education. Nowhere was the government's future role in fostering "civilization" spelled out; everything passed by implication.

Despite the power it exerted over Indian-white relations for nearly half a century, the Dawes Act was little more than a statement of intent. It contained no timetables and few instructions as to how it would be implemented. At its core, the law was an assertion that the gap between the two races would be overcome and that Indians would be incorporated into American society. They would farm, participate in government, and adopt "higher" standards of behavior. The statute assumed that landownership, citizenship, and education would alter traditional cultures, bringing them to "civilization." What is more, the new law was made possible by the belief that Indians did not have the "deficiencies" of other groups: they were fewer in number, the beneficiaries of a public sympathy and pity, and capable of advancement.

The passage of the General Allotment Act completed the organization of the new campaign to assimilate the Indians, but its immediate impact was unclear. Ambiguous provisions echoed the proposals of dozens of reformers and reform groups; thus the law left a number of important issues unresolved. When would the president "direct" allotment to begin? How much power would tribes have when they "negotiated" for the sale of their surplus lands? Furthermore, who would decide which tribal lands were surplus and which were needed for future allotments? How would the Indians' citizenship rights be enforced? And how much assistance could the new allottees expect from the government schools? While answers to these questions would change dramatically during the years ahead, the first decade of the Dawes Act's existence was marked by a clear pattern: the new law was implemented slowly and in a manner consistent with the assimilationist assumptions that inspired it. Lands were opened to settlement at a relatively slow pace, native citizenship rights were generally protected, and the Indian Office continued to accept responsibility for fostering Indian "progress."

Most students of the severalty era have concluded that "the application of allotment to the reservations was above all characterized by extreme haste."[63] While in the long run this was the case, it was not true of the period immediately following the passage of the act. During those early years, most administrators and lawmakers were willing to allow allotment to proceed slowly and selectively. By 1895 only twenty-four reservations had been surveyed and allotted. Of these, fifteen required more than two hundred parcels of lands to accommodate the entire tribe, and but ten required more than three hundred. Most groups allotted in this period were quite small (allotments went to every tribal member—men, women, and children). What is more, with the exception of the Cheyenne and Arapaho reservation in Oklahoma, most of the allotted tribes were living in areas that had long since been settled by whites. Of course the Indian Office was usually acting unilaterally, but it was not proceeding precipitately.

John Atkins, the first Indian commissioner to administer the severalty law, established guidelines for allotment that appear to have been followed by both his Republican and Democratic successors for the next decade. Commenting on the new law in 1887, he wrote, "Too great haste in the matter should be avoided, and if the work proceeds less rapidly than was expected the public must not be impatient. . . . Character, habits, and antecedents cannot be changed by an enactment." To his general statement Atkins appended a list of twenty-four reservations that the president believed were "generally favorable" to allotment. Nineteen of those were allotted in the next eight years. In 1895 the original nineteen accounted for three-quarters of all allotted reservations. In other words, despite the tragedies it produced, the severalty law was not applied initially in the "feverish hurry" many historians have observed.[64]

The Indian Office followed a general plan. Commissioner Thomas Morgan, for example, reported in 1892 that, with the exception of the Sioux, "the allotment of land to all of the Indians to whom application of the severalty law would be for their interest [could] be made and completed within the next three or four years." Morgan's statement was based on a comprehensive review of the allotment process. He was aware that large areas in Utah, southern Colorado, Arizona, Montana, and Indian Territory were as yet untouched. In 1887 the Indian Rights Association suggested, "Reservations should be taken first which are ripest for the work, where the way is clear, the risks small, the complications few." During its first decade of administering the Dawes Act, the Indian Office generally took that advice.[65]

Few allotments were leased before 1895. An amendment to allow Indians to lease their individual holdings had been rejected in the Senate in 1881 and was not reintroduced. The Dawes Act therefore contained no provisions for leasing allotments. But in 1891 Congress gave those Indians who for reasons of "age or disability" could not work their land the right to rent it with the approval of their agent. Only 2 such leases were approved in 1892; 4 were granted in 1893. The following year Congress added a new, elastic category—"inability"—to the list of reasons that justified leasing. That year the number of approved rentals rose to 296, although 223 of them took place on a single reservation. The following year the secretary of the interior approved 328 leases. While this figure represented a substantial increase, it amounted to barely 2 percent of all allotments.

Leasing was not yet the great evil it was to become in the twentieth century. The Indian Office generally opposed the practice, viewing it primarily as an administrative convenience that enabled agents to maximize production on native lands. Reformers like Captain Pratt also justified it as an instrument for freeing "progressive" Indians from their farms. Such people, "who have the disposition to build themselves up out of and away from the tribal connection," he wrote Senator Dawes, "ought not to be discouraged by any governmental hindrances whatsoever."[66]

The early allotment years also were marked by a continuation of federal protection for the tribes, despite the grant of citizenship. In Nebraska, the Omaha and Winnebago agent ordered squatters and unapproved lessees who had insinuated themselves on newly allotted land to leave the reservation. When the affected people resisted and threatened violence the commissioner proceeded against them with the aid of the army and the federal courts. Reformers continued to advocate federal protection for Indians. The most vocal among them was Harvard Law School professor James Bradley Thayer, who wrote a series of articles on the subject for the *Atlantic Monthly* in 1891. Thayer's thesis was that Native Americans "need, and [would] need for a good while, the very careful and exceptional protection of the nation." While Dawes pointed out to Thayer that such protection already existed, there was little dissent from the idea that assimilation would result from the judicious application of the severalty law. This was not to be an era of termination; federal guardianship would continue until the Indians appeared ready to stand on their own.[67]

Finally, it should be noted that the period immediately following the passage of the Dawes Act saw the rapid expansion of the native school system and the first extension of civil service reform to the Indian Office. The innovations of school superintendents Oberly and Hailmann and Commissioner Morgan occurred in the context of concern over the success of allotment. "Preparation for citizenship" and "education for the future" were common themes of their administrations. Increasing emphasis was placed on the quality of federal employees. "Right intentions, experience, and sound judgment . . . on the part of the resident agent," Herbert Welsh wrote in 1892, "are most necessary to a successful operation of the severalty law." Not only would the local agents oversee the assignment of homesteads but they would also direct various "civilization" programs and mediate between tribesmen and local non-Indian settlers. While the struggle over civil service classifications continued into the twentieth century, the reformer's initial victories came in the early 1890s. President Harrison placed the Indian Service under civil service regulations in 1891. And two years later Congress empowered the Indian Office to make school superintendents the agents for their reservations. Since these people already came under the civil service laws, that step seemed to signal the eventual end of patronage appointments in the Indian Service.[68]

Both the formulation and the initial administration of the General Allotment Act reflected a broad popular interest in total Indian assimilation. The law promised to achieve goals that policy makers agreed were appropriate for Native Americans: private landownership, education, and citizenship. In this sense it embodied the attitudes of the public, interested scientists, politicians, and reformers. There would continue to be differences between those who sympathized with the Indians and those who did not, and between those who wanted a gradual process and those who were more impatient. But for the moment there was universal agreement that an assimilation campaign that was both practical and comprehensive was finally underway.

Chapter 3

The Transformation of the Indian Question

Four hundred years after Columbus set sail for the New World, the city of Chicago organized a world's fair to demonstrate the significance of his voyage. The Columbian Exposition mixed an optimistic vision of the future with a nostalgic look backward. For the civic boosters who conceived it, and the millions of tourists it attracted, the Chicago World's Fair was a celebration of the power and promise of a new America. Special trains put the fairgrounds within easy reach of most sections of the country. On the midway, visitors were surrounded by marvels: entertainers arrived from across the globe, a full-scale replica of a steel battleship stood offshore in Lake Michigan, and Alexander Graham Bell conveyed his greetings from New York over the nation's first long-distance telephone line. Humming dynamos drove arc lights that shone on an elaborate collection of fountains and sculpture, providing fairgoers with dramatic nightly "illuminations." By far the most impressive exhibit was the setting itself, a series of mammoth buildings arranged around broad lagoons.

Built in the space of a few months, their plaster facades towered over the displays and cast gleaming reflections across the water. The White City conveyed a vision of the future.

But the exposition also celebrated the past. The White City itself, a wonder of modern construction, was built to resemble a series of Greek temples, and the statues that shimmered under the electric floodlights were executed in the classical style. An evocation of the American past was found on an artificial island in the central lagoon. There the Boone and Crockett Club, an organization of hunters and conservationists led by Theodore Roosevelt and the naturalist George Bird Grinnell, presented a scene from what they called a "typical and peculiar phase of American national development . . . life on the frontier." Like keepers of a shrine, the two men supervised the construction of a display that they believed to be accurate in every detail. As they reported to their fellow members, "The club erected a long, low cabin of unhewn logs . . . of the kind in which the first hunters and frontier settlers dwelt." Inside the building there was "a rough table and settles, with bunks in one corner, and a big, open stone fireplace." To the furniture they added artifacts: "Elk and deer hides were scattered over the floor or tacked to the walls. The bleached skull and antlers of an elk were nailed over the door outside; the head of a buffalo hung from mid-partition . . . and the horns of other game, such as mountain sheep and deer, were scattered about." In front of the cabin stood a "white-capped prairie schooner."[1] Visitors to the island would also see stuffed elk and deer staring unblinkingly at them from behind hastily planted trees.

The Boone and Crockett Club display, standing literally in the shadows of the White City suggests the extent to which Americans of the 1890s were beginning to realize that their cities, telephones, and battleships were purchased with the space and homogeneity of the past. The message of the club's exhibit resembled the one Frederick Jackson Turner brought to a meeting of historians that same summer: the frontier, the "crucible" that had formed the American character, was slipping into history. Like Turner's view of a national past, the island, with its elk hides and prairie schooner, its stone fireplace and animal skulls, was not an accurate representation of the American experience. Nevertheless it captured public attention because it conveyed an attractive, compelling image that offered an alternative to the mechanical whir and bustle of the Chicago midway.

The frontier was taking on new meaning. At the exposition it became an object men like Turner and Roosevelt could grasp as a counterpoise to the present—a model for the American character. Within this context, the public perception of the Indian was bound to undergo a subtle but significant metamorphosis. Like the prairie schooner and the roughhewn cabin, the Indian too would slip into history. The race would become more important for what it represented than for what it might become. As the frontier began to evoke nostalgia rather than dread, Native Americans would cease to be an immediate threat that required bludgeoning or "civilization." The need to eradicate native cultures faded with the memory of the frontier struggle. In the new century, Indians would be redefined as vital players in America's dramatic past. They would become a valued part of a fading, rustic landscape.

In the early twentieth century, these shifts in public image promised to have an important effect on the Indians' future. The laws and policies adopted in the 1880s had been intended to define a new, permanent relationship between Native Americans and the United States. Land, education, and citizenship awaited those who walked the "white man's road." But the reforms of that era were effective only as long as the assimilationist expectations fueling them were widely shared. If the commitment to rapid "civilization" began to fade, federal programs—like the treaties that preceded them—would become mere paper commitments to be altered, avoided, or ignored. An optimistic view of natives was crucial to the implementation of the reformer's agenda. So long as policy makers viewed Indians as people in transition—moving "upward," from one stage of culture to another—the total assimilation campaign would continue uninterrupted. If that perception shifted, the ambiguously worded laws and policies would lose their initial meaning, and the "Indian question" of the 1880s would be transformed.

While public images are as elusive as they are invisible, it is possible to trace their reflections through time. One canvas against which the image of the Indian was projected vividly at the turn of the century was the American world's fair. In the forty years following the

Philadelphia Centennial in 1876, at least ten fairs were staged in the United States. The Philadelphia and Chicago events, the Louisiana Purchase Exposition in St. Louis (1904), and the Panama-Pacific International Exposition in San Francisco (1915) were truly international extravaganzas, while the shows in New Orleans (1884), Atlanta (1895), Nashville (1897), Omaha (1899), Buffalo (1901), and San Diego (1915) were smaller and more regional in focus. Nevertheless, all the fairs were founded on grand expectations. Among those was the hope that the exhibits would be (in one organizer's words) the "university of the masses."[2] An important element in this educational conception was a presentation of Indian life. Every fair devoted space to an exhibition of the Native American's place in American culture. These self-conscious displays are an excellent measure of the public's shifting perception of the Indians.

The Philadelphia exposition was held in honor of the nation's centennial. Between the opening day in March, when President Grant and the Emperor of Brazil trooped through the exhibits, and the rain-drenched closing ceremonies in November, more than 9 million people came to Fairmount Park to marvel at the United States' achievements. Most visitors went first to Machinery Hall to see the amazing new telephone and the massive Corliss steam engine. But close by—and no doubt second on many itineraries—was the barn-like Government Building with its displays organized on the theme "A Century of Progress." The building was a hit. As the *New York Times* correspondent wrote: "It will convince the world that the future of America is based upon a rock and will endure." Fully half of the Government Building was given over to a display of Indian life. Local newspapers reported that the Smithsonian Institution and other federal agencies had collected "all manner of curious things," including totem poles from the Northwest, "Esquimaux artifacts, and a series of plains warriors made from papier-mache."[3]

But the exhibit did not concentrate solely on traditional culture. In keeping with the fair's theme, a large part of the Indian area was devoted to evidence of native "progress." A number of display cases contained descriptions of missionary work, public education efforts, and government programs to encourage farming. The *Philadelphia Bulletin* noted, "The whole [Indian exhibit] is completed by numerous photographs of Indian life . . . representing the progress made in the schools established among the tribes." The effect of this emphasis on Indian advancement was quite striking. As one of the Centennial guidebooks explained, "It is odd to see these pet enemies of the country seated calmly in front of the school-houses . . . Their educational varnish is warranted by those who are applying it to stand, and some of them look as though it might, even under the trying conditions it remains for them to encounter." Former commissioner of Indian affairs Francis A. Walker, who wrote a multivolume summary of the fair, was even more enthusiastic:

This exhibit has contributed much to a solution of the vexed question, "What shall be done with the Indians?" For if not only the Creeks, Choctaws and Cherokees can be tamed and civilized to this degree, but even the savage Modoc, and the fierce Apache, when brought together and held under the civilizing influence of civilizing agencies, have not the friends of humanity gained a powerful argument?

Another observer put it more simply: "We could not but fancy we saw a future in the pleasant and gentle faces of some young Pawnees."[4]

The optimistic tone of the exhibit indicated that its designers believed the Indians' future was a national responsibility. Apparently fairgoers agreed that Native Americans deserved both sympathy and assistance. In the summer of Custer's death at the Little Big Horn, the Indian display summarized both the hopes of the public and the expectations of policy makers. These groups imagined Native Americans were entering a period of rapid change. It seemed that a nation devoted to progress could promise nothing less.

By 1893, when the Columbian Exposition was staged in Chicago, some of the optimism in evidence in Philadelphia had begun to fade. As the Boone and Crockett Club exhibit suggested, new attitudes were reflected in the Midwest's first fair. Actually there were two Indian displays at Chicago. Frederick Putnam, director of Harvard's Peabody Museum, organized one exhibit for the exposition's anthropology department. The second was supervised and designed by Commissioner of Indian Affairs Thomas Morgan, the former preacher who had been widely praised for his reform of the Indian school system. In 1876 the scientists from the Smithsonian and the administrators at the Indian Office had worked together; their exhibits in 1893 were separate. Each group was more intent on presenting its own work than on hewing to a common theme.

According to Professor Putnam, his presentation was "the first bringing together on a grand scale of representatives of the people who were living on the continent when it was first discovered by Columbus." He added that his displays would be arranged chronologically so that "the stages of the development of man on the American continent could be spread out as an open book from which all could read." In this sense the exhibit would follow the theme presented in Philadelphia. But unlike the 1876 exposition, the Chicago showing included a feature rejected by the Centennial's apostles of progress: living natives from Indian reservations. These people included Navajos, Senecas, Kwakiutls, Penobscots, and Pueblos (the last group lived on the midway in plaster replicas of their adobe homes). Smaller groups of Sioux, Apaches, Nez Perces, and others settled along the lake front, demonstrating and selling their handicrafts. Their presence, wrote Hubert Howe Bancroft, demonstrated in "a series of object lessons the development of various phases and adjuncts of civilization."[5]

The Indians' tribal past was no longer to be presented by glass cases filled with implements and clothing. The "object lessons" of the Chicago fair were alive. They could teach something about "the development of man on the American continent" only if the public could imagine them as objects from the past—breathing substitutes for artifacts on a shelf. Peabody and his colleagues were diverting the fairgoer's attention from the future to the past and identifying their Native American contemporaries as relics and throwbacks.

The Indian Office saw the fair as an opportunity to demonstrate the promise of its new assimilation program. Its principal exhibit was a two-story frame schoolhouse. During the fair, delegations from government schools occupied the building; each group spent a few days in the model classrooms, demonstrating "civilized" skills and enduring the stares of the curious. These were considerable, for the school attracted over one hundred thousand visitors a week during the summer. Commissioner Morgan proudly announced that the display vindicated the government's efforts. "It sets forth the future of the Indian," he wrote; "it shows concretely and unmistakably his readiness and ability for the new conditions of civilized life and American citizenship upon which he is entering."[6]

Obviously, dividing the Indian exhibit between the anthropology department and the Indian Office was more than a bureaucratic convenience, for the themes of the two displays were strikingly different. One conveyed the idea that Indians were members of an exotic race with little connection to modern America. The other, by stressing education and native "progress," pointed to the possibility of Indian assimilation. What is more, there seemed to be a good deal of uncertainty—among the organizers of the fair as well as the public—over which focus was more appropriate.

Captain Richard Pratt, still headmaster at Carlisle, was outraged by Putnam's living "object lessons." He viewed them as reminders of the Indians' "barbaric" past, and feared that they would distract the public from the evidence of progress on display in the Indian schoolhouse. In fact, the old cavalryman was so incensed that he demanded a special room for Carlisle in the Liberal Arts Building. He did not want to be associated with the other exhibits. His demand was met, as was a request that Carlisle students be invited to march in the opening day parade. Pratt took that occasion to demonstrate the reality of Indian "progress." Ten platoons of students participated, each representing one of the skills taught at the school. The front row of each platoon carried the tools of a trade while those in the rear held high samples of finished products they had made.[7]

Some of the displays of traditional life produced reactions similar to Pratt's. On seeing a Kwakiutl dance performed during the first week's festivities, a *Chicago Tribune* reporter complained that "right in the midst" of an event "that marks the progress of mankind were these ceremonies of this strange and semi-barbarous race carried on." Similar protests surfaced throughout the summer. An August editorial perhaps epitomized this disapproval: "Those in authority have gone to the farthest extreme and sanctioned a so-called entertainment which may be the height of amusement among the Kwakiutl or the Dahomen cannibals, but which should have no place in the beautiful White City."[8]

The most sustained attack came from Emma Sickles, a Chicagoan who had been fired by Putnam from a position on his staff. She launched a newspaper campaign to shut down all of the "primitive" presentations. "The exhibit of Indian life now given at the fair," she wrote, "is an exhibit of savagery in its most repulsive form." While her campaign ultimately failed, her cries that the Indians should not be viewed as "helpless specimens" were heard—and printed—by newspapers in New York and Chicago.[9]

The unified picture of a people in transition presented at Philadelphia had been altered. "Backward" natives were now an important part of public displays, even though the physical presence of traditional Indians disturbed those who predicted the rapid "civilization" of the race. The government schools attracted large crowds, but so did the native villages and the anthropology building. (Buffalo Bill's Wild West Show played to enthusiastic audiences elsewhere in the city throughout the summer.) The public appeared as interested in exotic "savages" as it was in Indian "advancement."

By 1904, when the Louisiana Purchase Exposition opened in St. Louis, these divergent themes had been resolved. Interest in the Indians' "primitive" character was paramount, and—more important—both the government and the public greeted the exotic displays with enthusiasm.

St. Louis tried to imitate the successes of the White City. The city fathers promised that their displays would be larger and their buildings more elaborate than anything seen in Chicago. Old dreams of becoming the Midwest's chief metropolis revived and were nurtured. Henry Adams described the result in his autobiography:

One saw a third-rate town of half-a-million people without history, education, unity, or art, and with little capital—without even an element of natural interest except the river which it studiously ignored—but doing what London, Paris, or New York would have shrunk from attempting. This new social conglomerate with no tie but its steam-power and not much of that, threw away thirty or forty million dollars on a pageant as ephemeral as a

stage flat. . . . One enjoyed it with iniquitous rapture, not because of the exhibits, but because of their want.[10]

The Indian exhibits in St. Louis were more elaborate than those
in Chicago. As it was in 1893, the major display was the product
of the exposition's department of anthropology. When the Smithsonian's W J. McGee was appointed chairman of this department
in 1901 he quickly set about organizing a "Congress of the Races"
that he promised would be a "comprehensive exhibit of the primitive peoples of the globe." When the fair opened, Ainus from Japan,
African pygmies, Patagonian natives, and several groups of Native
Americans were assembled on a hillside in the center of the anthropology area. McGee wrote that he selected these people because they
were "least removed from the sub-human or quadrumane form" and
would therefore serve as living illustrations of human progress. "In
brief," the chairman declared, "one may learn in the indoor [mu-
seum] exhibit how our prehistoric forebears lived, and then see, outside, people untouched by the march of progress still living in a similar crude manner."[11]

At the top of McGee's hillside exhibit stood a government Indian
schoolhouse, like the one the Indian Office had constructed in Chicago. The scientist explained the significance of its location:

The outdoor exhibit, beginning at the foot of a sloping hill, where the
bearded men and the tattooed women of the Ainu sit outside their thatch-
work huts and carve bits of wood into patterns, employing their toes as well
as their hands, and ending with the Government Indian school at the top
of the hill, where Sioux and Arapaho and Oneida attend kindergarten and
primary and grammar classes, and build things so fitted to modern needs
as farm wagons—this exhibit tells two living stories. It presents the race
narrative of odd peoples who mark time while the world advances, and of
savages, made, by American methods, into civilized workers.

Within the school, students demonstrated their ability to cook, do
laundry, and operate a printing press, as well as their skill at wagon-
making, carpentry, and blacksmithing. A forty-piece Indian band
gave daily concerts, and a battalion of cadets paraded every afternoon

at 5:30. The aim of the exhibit, McGee noted, was to present "a practical illustration of the best way of bearing the white man's burden."[12]

The "Congress of Races" suggested how American scientists and policy makers resolved their disagreements over the proper way to present American Indians to the public. No longer portrayed as both a "people in transition" and a breed of primitive exotics, Native Americans had become members of one of the world's many "backward races." Nearly "subhuman," the Indians of 1904 needed nothing more than simple training to become "civilized workers." Like the Ainus and the pygmies, they were a different order of being, a people who could not be expected to "progress" as far as those from more "civilized" societies.

McGee's hillside exhibit attracted three million visitors; none of them appear to have protested his presentation of traditional Indian life. In fact, the St. Louis newspapers found the encampment thoroughly entertaining. Early in the summer, Joseph Pulitzer's *Post-Dispatch* ran daily photos of the Indians. These staged shots appeared under headlines such as "Real Thing in the TeePee Line" and "Patagonian Giants Start To Run When They See Philippine Midgets." Traditional natives were accepted as anthropological curios: harmless objects to be ridiculed without fear or embarrassment.[13]

Fairgoers also demonstrated their interest in "backward races" by flocking to the exhibit from the United States' new colony in the Philippines. This forty-seven-acre display was the largest at the fair. It included a plaster reproduction of the old walled city of Manila, replicas of native villages, a government school, a military garrison (complete with loyal Philippine soldiers), and eleven hundred natives in traditional dress. The similarity of this exhibit to the Indian encampment was pointed out by Secretary of War William Howard Taft, when he observed at the ribbon-cutting ceremony that the Archipelago's annexation promised Americans a reenactment of the winning of the West. According to Taft, "[America has] reached a period . . . in which we find ourselves burdened with the necessity of aiding another people to stand upon their feet and take a short cut to the freedom and civil liberty which we and our ancestors have hammered out."[14]

Superficially, the Indian exhibits changed only slightly between 1876 and 1904. All three fairs presented Native Americans as "uncivilized," and each of them assumed that members of the race could enter white society only by shedding their traditional cultures. But beyond these similarities, the presentations in Chicago and St. Louis revealed an important shift in popular perceptions. By 1904 the Indian's future—which a Philadelphia observer had seen "in the pleasant and gentle faces of some young Pawnees"—appeared limited. Native Americans now appeared handicapped by their race and limited by their "backwardness." Positioned in the center of a bizarre anthropological curio shop and described as an element of the "white man's burden," the tribesmen seemed best suited for a life of manual labor. In 1876, journalists had dwelt on the Indian's future; a visitor to the Indian exhibit in St. Louis called it "The Last Race Rally of the Indians."[15]

When the Panama-Pacific International Exposition opened in San Francisco in 1915, the metamorphosis of the Indians' public image was complete. At this final American fair before World War I, Native Americans appeared as people whose future was of only marginal concern to the white majority. There was no Indian encampment in San Francisco, nor was there an elaborate anthropological presentation. The only living Indians in evidence were some Zunis hired by the Santa Fe Railroad to grace their Grand Canyon show. The Smithsonian sponsored a modest display in the government pavilion, but it contained only a few archeological artifacts. The model villages of St. Louis and Chicago became plaster dioramas portraying scenes of traditional life under glass. And exhibitions of student work—furniture, canned fruit, needlework—replaced the Indian Office's model schoolhouse.

By far the most popular presentation of native life at the San Francisco fair was in bronze: James Earle Fraser's statue, "The End of the Trail." Fraser's work portrayed a nameless, exhausted Indian slumped in the saddle of a worn-out pony. With remarkable candor, the artist later explained the message of his work: "It was [the] idea of a weaker race being steadily pushed to the wall by a stronger that I wanted to convey."[16] To emphasize its symbolic meaning, Fraser's piece was placed beside a statue of an American frontiersman. "Pioneer" was a symbolic figure who (according to one guide-book) had a "challenge in his face," as he stared "into early morning." The guide added that the pioneer was "typical of the white man and the victorious march of civilization." The effect of this juxtaposition was not lost on fairgoers. One reviewer wrote, "So it has been with the Indian. His trail is now lost and on the edge of a continent he finds himself almost annihilated."[17]

"The End of the Trail" won a gold medal and became a major attraction. At the close of the fair a citizen's group tried to acquire it for a park overlooking the Pacific, but their campaign was cut short by World War I. Years later, Fraser himself said that it was still his dream to find a home for the horse and rider on the California coast. "There he would stand forever," he said, "driven at last to the very edge of the continent." The public message contained in the statue was clear: the pioneer was victorious; the Indian race was on its way to extinction.[18]

The popularity of Fraser's pathetic Indian indicated that despite a generation of reform-inspired optimism, the romantic Indian of Cooper and Longfellow was coming back into vogue. In 1876, the presentation of Native American life had emphasized the changes taking place among the tribes. The public supported this optimistic view, but by the 1890s interest in Indian "progress" was coexisting with curiosity about the tribal past. Exhibitors in Chicago and St. Louis returned to a static, romantic view of the native life and stressed the notion that traditional culture was antithetical to modern civilization. And the "living specimens" put on display raised anew long-standing doubts about the Native American's ability to survive assimilation. By 1915 the public was growing accustomed to viewing Indians as members of one of the world's many "backward races." "Pushed to the wall," they could look forward to little besides manual labor and extinction.

Fair exhibits are historical artifacts, mute displays that might be read differently by different observers. Other areas of the nation's popular culture provide evidence that places the expositions in a broader context. In the press, for example, despite the fact that the level of interest in Indians varied considerably between 1890 and 1920, books and articles dealing with native life appeared regularly and projected a consistent point of view. Moreover, new reform groups and clubs interested in Indian life continued to be organized. Both areas communicated an image of the Indian that was remarkably similar to the one produced by the world's fair displays.

In the 1880s, Helen Hunt Jackson and Alice Fletcher often used the new mass-circulation weeklies to advertise their cause. A generation later, the practice continued, but the reformers' optimism was replaced with darker judgments. For example, in 1907 *World Today*, a picture-filled monthly under the editorial control of the University of Chicago's William Rainey Harper, published an article entitled "Shaping the Future of the Red Man." After surveying conditions on the reservations, the piece concluded that the "crudeness" and "shortcomings" of the Indian were "insuperable deterrents to the success of our new policy of standing [him] upon his feet and teaching him to walk alone." This pessimistic view of the Indians' future was echoed elsewhere. The following year, *Harper's*, in an article entitled "Making Good Indians," argued the Indian was hampered by a "strong streak of childishness," while the *Atlantic Monthly*, once a platform for Senator Dawes and Professor Thayer, promised that "the epic of the American Indian has closed."[19]

Perhaps most surprising, the muckrakers—journalists sympathetic to Jackson and other reformers—shared the popular disenchantment with Indian progress. Ray Stannard Baker, whose *Following the Color Line* revealed the evils of segregation and questioned the accuracy of many Jim Crow stereotypes, exemplified the change of heart. His description of the allotment of the Fort Hall reservation in Idaho, written for *Century Magazine* in 1903, observed, "It is the fate of the Anglo-Saxon that he go forever forward without resting; he stands for civilization, improved roads and cities." As for the Indians, they were invulnerable to the government's good intentions. Following their allotment at Fort Hall, he noted that the tribesmen there went on "exactly as before, looking on imperturbably, eating, sleeping, idling, with no more thought of the future than a white man's child."[20]

Fiction writers developed a similar theme. Helen Fitzgerald Sanders, for example, a Montanan who traveled widely in the West, published "The Red Bond" in San Francisco's *Overland Monthly* in 1911. The short story described Judith, a mixed-blood woman who had attended eastern boarding schools before settling in a small town on the plains. In the hands of a Helen Hunt Jackson, Judith would have resembled Ramona, the lacemaking heroine of her 1884 reform novel. But in Sanders' story Judith abandoned her education after witnessing the arrest of a young Indian for the drunken murder of a white man. The young woman helped the boy escape and then followed him into the hills. "The red bond of her forefathers," Sanders wrote, "held her as relentlessly as though she had never left the blanket and the teepee." The implications of this reversion were unsettling. Sanders wrote that Judith "had clung to those newer teachings of the adopted race, but at last the old, old yearnings surged up, and she forgot all but the crooning songs her mother used to sing and the spell of the wilderness." *The Virginian,* Owen Wister's immensely popular portrait of a gallant cowboy contained similar observations, as did his short story "Little Big Horn Medicine," Elliot Flower's "Law and the Indians" (which appeared in the *Atlantic Monthly),* and Honore Willsie's novel, *Still Jim.*[21]

When they imagined the Indian's place in contemporary society, popular writers concluded that Native Americans were destined to live on the fringes of civilization. The successful Indians of the early twentieth century were not the teachers, ministers, or yeomen farmers promised by the nineteenth-century reformers. Now the highest praise was saved for hired hands and construction laborers. Such Indians, *Munsey's Magazine* reported in 1901 (in an article entitled "Making the Warrior a Worker"), were "learning the gospel of work." In her novel *Still Jim,* Honore Willsie put it more poetically. She praised the Apaches who wielded picks and shovels on modern road crews: "The last of Geronimo's race was building new trails for a new people." Just as the organizers of the St. Louis fair had found it most appropriate for Indian students to be carpenters and blacksmiths, so the popular writers of the early twentieth century matched their pessimistic view of Indian capabilities with a call for Native Americans to pursue a life of unskilled labor.[22]

Hamlin Garland made this modern view of Native Americans a central theme in *Captain of the Grey Horse Troop,* by far the most popular Indian book of the early twentieth century. Based on extensive research on the Tongue River Reservation and a great deal of genuine sympathy, the novel was serialized in the *Saturday Evening Post* before its publication by Harper and Brothers in 1902. It described that experiences of Captain George Curtis during his tenure as an Indian agent for the imaginary "Tetongs" of Montana. Garland's hero started his charges on the road to "civilization" while combatting corruption in Washington, greed in a nearby cattle town, and the indifference of the beautiful Elsie Brisbane. In the end, everyone was overwhelmed by the captain's courage and charm. While hardly great literature, the story provided Garland with a vehicle for discussing the Indians' future.

The "Tetongs," Curtis explained, were good-hearted but backward. "I like these people," the captain announced. "It touches me deeply to have them come and put their palms on me reverently—as though I were superhuman in wisdom—and say: 'Little Father, we are blind . . . Lead us and we will go.' " A scientist visiting the reservation agreed, reminding Garland's hero that "fifty thousand years of life proceeding in a certain way results in a certain arrangement of brain-cells which can't be changed in a day, even in a generation." People with such handicaps required a protector; they could not survive on their own because education had no impact on them and citizenship had no meaning. Captain Curtis, with his benevolent control over their reservation, would save them. Garland wrote that the cavalryman "felt himself in some sense their chosen friend—their Moses, to lead them out of the desolation in which they sat bewildered and despairing."[23]

Garland's vision of the solution to the tribe's plight appeared in the novel's closing scene. Having defeated his foes and won young Elsie's promise to marry, Curtis took his fiancée and his sister Jennie on a walk through a "Tetong" village. He passed among them like an antebellum overseer; the reservation had become his plantation.

Everywhere they went Curtis and his friends met with hearty greeting. "Hoh—hoh! The Little Father!" the old men cried and came to shake hands, and the women smiled, looking up from their work. The little children, though they ran away at first, came out again when they knew that it was the Captain who called. Jennie gave hints about the cooking and praised the neat teepees and the pretty dresses. . . . Here was a little kingdom over which Curtis reigned, a despotic monarch, and [Elsie] if she did her duty, would reign by his side. . . .

There were tears in Elsie's eyes as she looked up at Curtis. "They have so far to go, poor things! They can't realize how long the road to civilization is."

"I do not care whether they reach what you call civilization or not; the road to happiness and peace is not long, it is short; they are even now entering upon it. They can be happy right here."

Landownership, citizenship, and adequate schools do not complicate the tableau. Rather than a racial group "rising" to civilization and joining white society, Garland's natives defined a western version of the plantation Sambo. They were "happy right here."[24]

Garland repeated his attack on total assimilation in his short stories and an essay in the *North American Review*. There he argued that government schools separated children from their parents and that allotment destroyed tribal life and sentenced inept farmers to lonely starvation. Significantly, he pointed out that Indians—because of their backwardness—deserved the same pity and concern as blacks: "We are all answerable for them, just as we are answerable for the black man's future," he wrote. "As the dominant race we have dispossessed them, we have pushed them to the last ditch which will be their grave, unless we lay aside greed and religious prejudice and go to them as men and brothers; and help them to understand themselves and their problems; and only when we give our best to these red brethren of ours, do we justify ourselves as the dominant race of the Western continent." Garland's writings present a vivid example of the modern view of Indians. He ascribed the cultural differences that separated the Native American from the rest of society to racial backwardness, expressed sympathy for the tribesmen's poverty and called on whites to guide their less fortunate brethren with Captain Curtis's mosaic leadership. His position mixed compassion with ethnocentrism; it suggested that Indians must understand their own shortcomings before they could rise from their poverty. And while he spoke of progress, Garland clearly rejected the evangelical optimism of Henry Dawes and Alice Fletcher.[25]

There was more to the popular view of Indians than pity. Harsh racial judgments coexisted with fascination and sympathy in literature as they had in the exhibition hall. Not suprisingly, then, in the early twentieth century tribal mythology and handicrafts gained in popularity even as the Indian was being indicted for childishness and ignorance. As the symbol of America's heroic history, Native Americans represented virtues the nation risked forgetting in the headlong pursuit of wealth and power. Safely confined in the past, Indians could be a tonic for the country's old age, a living remnant of a younger America. As one journalist wrote in 1917, "Many of us cannot help regretting the fact that we are witnessing the effacement of what we have known as the real American red man, the wild Indian."[26]

George Bird Grinnell and Charles Lummis were among the most outspoken of those who viewed the passing of the Indians' traditional lifeways with regret. The attitude of both men arose—at least in part—as a consequence of personal experience. Lummis and Grinnell were members of the last generation to have experienced life on the American frontier. Grinnell, whose New York boyhood had included a friendship with the famous Audubons, accompanied his Yale mentor, Othniel C. Marsh, on the first paleontological expedition to the Dakotas in 1870. And Lummis, a Massachusetts native, "discovered" the Southwest in 1884, when he walked from Ohio to California. Both men became journalists—Grinnell edited *Forest and Stream* and Lummis owned a California magazine called, successively, *Out West* and *Land of Sunshine*—and their early adventures remained central to their work. Grinnell was an eager advocate of forest and game preservation, while Lummis used his magazine to promote the beauties of the Southwest and to campaign for the protection of the region's historic sites. The two men were captivated by Indian culture and eager to insulate Native Americans from the press of modernity. Unlike the reformers of the previous generation, they viewed the Indian as a victim of progress, not its beneficiary. Lummis believed that "the Indian, poor devil, will presently die off." Grinnell agreed, writing that the Indian's way of life had "passed away and will not return."[27]

To Grinnell and Lummis the Indians were doomed because, like the redwoods and the buffalo, they could neither resist the white man's advances nor adapt to his civilization. Echoing Hamlin Garland's captain, the two men believed Indians to be lovable but backward; their outdated way of life was a badge of their primitive nature. Grinnell noted, for example, that the Indian had "the mind and feelings of a child with the stature of a man," while Lummis observed that one of his favorite tribes, the Hopi, "are ethnically in about the development of a ten year old." The transplanted westerner went on to suggest that whites should abandon their hopes of assimilating the Indians. He called instead for a "modest forbearance" that would "lead us to 'let nature take her course' and not kill [the Indian] before his appointed hour."[28]

In 1902 Lummis and Grinnell joined forces to found the Sequoyah League, a reform organization with chapters in New York and Los Angeles. Their effort was short-lived. The league disappeared by 1907, but their policy suggestions illustrate the implications of their sentimental point of view. Lummis wrote that the Sequoyah League sought "not to have hysterics or to meddle, but to assist the Indian department." This "assistance" usually took the form of attacks in *Out West*. Lummis's chief complaint was that agents and teachers ignored the Indian's inability to change. "Ignorant of government and history," he wrote, "the government insists that the Indian shall civilize as much in twenty years as our own Saxon or Teuton ancestors did in five hundred." Such an effort, he added, tried to "subvert the law of gravitation."[29]

The Sequoyah League focused on two areas: education and land policy. Grinnell wrote that government schools were not necessarily a blessing. "In many cases," he observed, "the attempt to educate the Indian beyond a certain point tends to injure rather than to help him." Lummis was even more direct; he added, "We should not educate [Indians] to death." An institution like Carlisle, charged by nineteenth-century reformers with the "civilization" of native children, was to them a "peon factory" doomed to failure. The Sequoyah League called instead for training in traditional handicrafts. Baskets and pottery for sale to tourists, not land and citizenship, would enable the Indians to be self-supporting. As for allotment, Lummis and Grinnell pointed out it was not a panacea. Referring to the Dawes

Act, Grinnell argued that in the administration of Indian Affairs, "no hard and fast rule of treatment [could] be established."[30]

Undoubtedly the founders of the Sequoyah League shared a genuine concern for the Native American's future. Nevertheless, it is equally true that their interest stemmed from what the Indians represented as well as from their actual condition. For Grinnell and Lummis it was important to protect the first American's picturesque way of life both because the people—being backward—could live no other way and because they represented an important element in the American past. The Indians could not be educated beyond a certain point and, indeed, they should not be; the rapid "civilization" of the Indian would call into question the racial struggle that was basic to the American experience. Lummis and Grinnell believed that conquest of the West represented the triumph of Anglo-Saxon civilization over unbending barbarism. History proved that the races could not intermingle. Thus, the best that could be hoped for in the present was the gradual "improvement" of the defeated inferior races. Lummis wrote in 1904, for example, that the reformer's enthusiasm for education was generous, but naïve. It was absurd, he argued, to "go on butting [their] heads against history and the attraction of gravitation—trying to make Chinaman, darkey and Indian into hand-me-down white men." For these men, it was both practical and altruistic to preserve racial differences.[31]

The Sequoyah League's blending of racism and nationalism surfaced often in the early years of the twentieth century. In 1906, for example, Edward S. Curtis launched his famous forty-volume study, *The North American Indian.* With the financial backing of J. P. Morgan and the technical assistance of the Bureau of American Ethnology, Curtis spent twenty-five years recording the habits and costume of dozens of tribes. The finished books were an artistic triumph, but they were also a monument to Indian extinction. From the opening photograph, labeled "The Vanishing Race," through scores of images of old warriors, young maidens, and Indian encampments, Curtis demonstrated both the beauty and the transience of the old ways. Theodore Roosevelt added the expected note of patriotism in the "foreward" he wrote for the first volume. The president told Curtis his books were a "good thing for the whole American people." He welcomed the project because the Indian's life had "been lived under conditions through which our own race passed so many years ago that not a vestige of their memory remains. It would be a calamity if a vivid and truthful record of these conditions were not kept."[32]

In the years before World War I other Americans expressed a similar interest in vivid—if not entirely accurate—records of the Indian's role in the national past by supporting a number of projects as monuments to the race. Among these was a campaign organized by the president of Stanford University and the leader of the Boy Scouts to preserve a bison herd on part of Montana's Flathead reservation. Another project was completed in 1912, when Chicago sculptor Lorado Taft unveiled a 50-foot-high cement statue of Black Hawk on the banks of the Rock River in Illinois. Monuments also appeared in Minnesota, Colorado, Oregon, and Massachusetts. But the grandest plan of all was conceived by department store executive Rodman Wanamaker. At a New York banquet honoring Buffalo Bill Cody, Wanamaker announced that he intended to erect a bronze statue of a young Indian at the entrance to the city's harbor. The figure would be 165 feet high, posed with his hand raised in a sign of peace. The monument to the "departed race" would be 15 feet taller than the Statue of Liberty and built entirely with private funds. All that was needed was land for a site. Congress obliged in 1911, setting aside a section of Fort Wadsworth on Staten Island.

That a monument to a vanishing race would be a source of national pride might seem ironic, but there was no irony intended when Wanamaker selected February 22, 1913—George Washington's birthday—for the groundbreaking ceremony. At the appointed hour thirty-two aging chiefs gathered to watch President Taft break ground for the project and to hear him say that the statue "tells the story of the march of empire and the progress of Christian civilization to the uttermost limits." That the public Indian had become a national treasure was made more explicit at the close of the morning's festivities, for the U.S. Mint had chosen the occasion to begin distributing the new Indian-head nickel. The shiny coins, with an Indian profile on the front and a buffalo on the reverse, were passed with great ceremony to Taft, Wanamaker, and the assembled Indians.[33]

James Baldwin once asked a white audience, "Why do you need a nigger?" He spoke with the anger and frustration of someone who felt that America refused to recognize his humanity and his past. Native Americans must have had similar feelings in the early twentieth century as they witnessed the emergence of a new public image of themselves. Apparently, white artists and writers needed to see the Indian as someone burdened by his race and limited by his "backwardness." And the white public needed to preserve a vestige of the vanishing race as a symbol of the nation's past victories. As one reporter wrote of the New York Indian memorial, it would be a reminder of the people "to whom we are indebted for the great, free gift of a continent." But Baldwin's question remains: Why was the new image needed? Why did the optimism of the reform era fade so quickly? What made racial explanations of Indian behavior so attractive? And why should Americans equate patriotism with a bronze memorial? To answer these questions fully, one must turn from art to politics.[34]

When told of President McKinley's assassination, so the famous story goes, Republican boss Mark Hanna exclaimed that the White House now belonged to "that damned cowboy." Whether apocryphal or not, the incident reveals that in his brief political career Theodore Roosevelt had successfully identified himself as a roughrider, a man of the West. While he had spent less than three years ranching in the Dakotas, the new president studiously cultivated his frontiersman image. Every schoolboy knew that Teddy was a big-game hunter and a cowpuncher.[35]

Roosevelt brought a westerner's perspective to the administration of Indian affairs and supported the nostalgic version of Indian life that was emerging in the public press. What is more, throughout his time in office, the young president drew on the advice of an informal "cowboy cabinet" he had gathered around him. The "cabinet" had six members: Hamlin Garland, George Bird Grinnell, Charles Lummis, Frederic Remington, Owen Wister, and Francis Leupp. With the possible exception of Garland, none of the men were native-born westerners, but like Roosevelt they had all discovered the region on trips across the plains during their youth. They shared a paternalistic concern for the Indians and believed they should protect the Native American from the naïve reformers who preached total assimilation.[36]

Like other cabinets, the president's cowboy advisers were not always crucial to policy making. In his second term, as his confidence in his own judgments increased, TR relied less on the group. But in his first years, Roosevelt called on them often. They were old friends. He had known Lummis and Wister at Harvard; Grinnell, Garland, and Remington he had met in New York in the 1880s and 1890s; and he had worked with Leupp in Washington while Roosevelt was serving on the civil service commission. They were also loyal. Soon after TR's inauguration Lummis had written, "I am glad you are in the saddle when the hard days come." All the men visited him in Washington; Grinnell, Wister, and Remington arrived within the first few weeks after he took office.[37]

Roosevelt consulted with his friends over appointments and policy decisions, but the significance of the group lay in what it reveals about the president's approach to Indian affairs. For the first time since 1880, an administration saw the assimilation effort as a regional concern rather than a national obligation. Grinnell spoke for the group when he urged the president to appoint someone familiar with the West to head the Indian Office. He argued that such a person "would do more to transform the Indians into working, earning people than anything else that could be devised." Grinnell and others also called for a reorientation of federal programs and a new, more cautious approach to Indian "uplift."[38]

Less than a year after taking office Roosevelt discussed the problem of selecting Indian agents with one of his advisers. While observing that the best agents were often men who were *not* from the areas adjoining a reservation, he pointed out that "in the long run the success of a governmental policy . . . must depend upon the active good will of those sections of people who take the greatest interest in the matter." Federal meddling in local affairs was ultimately self-defeating. "Wise eastern philanthropists can do a good deal," he added, "but many . . . are anything but wise; and these are in the aggregate very harmful." Under the Rough Rider, government actions would take into account the interests of white westerners

as well as the Indians. The "active good will" of the tribe's neighbors would be more important to policy making than the dictates of
eastern philanthropists.[39]

A regional approach to racial issues was characteristic of both
Theodore Roosevelt and his era. The president told an audience at
all-black Tuskegee Institute in Alabama, for example, "The white
man who can be of most use to the colored man is that colored man's
neighbor. It is the southern people themselves who must and can
solve the difficulties that exist in the South." And he repeated the
theme in reference to the Pacific Coast when he completed the Gen-
tleman's Agreement with Japan in 1907 and wrote that the exclusion
of Asian immigrants was "the only sure way to avoid . . . friction."
With the passing of nineteenth-century reformers and their rhetoric
of equality, and the rise of a politically powerful white population
in the West and South, politicians like Roosevelt began arguing that
accommodation to local prejudices was more realistic than federal
"philanthropy."[40]

Like most westerners, the president's chief concern was the economic development of the frontier. His *Winning of the West* argued
that it was the United States' destiny to "civilize" the continent,
a message Roosevelt repeated in 1903, when he asserted that it had
been the nation's task "to wage war against man, to wage war against
nature for the possession of the vast lonely spaces of the earth which
we have now made the seat of a mighty civilization." TR initiated efforts to establish a national reclamation program, develop a scientific
approach to forest management, and adopt a systematic approach to
mining on the public domain. The purpose of these activities, he
wrote in 1907, was "to promote and foster actual settling, actual
homemaking on the public lands in every possible way. Every effort
of this administration [had] been bent to this end." He replaced the
nineteenth-century idea that the West and the Indians would develop
together with regional boosterism.[41]

But Roosevelt's approach to Indian assimilation was not simply a
product of his deference to regional chauvinism. He also maintained
a pessimistic view of Native American abilities, a view supported
by his cowboy advisors. In 1893 the Rough Rider returned from a
tour of the West with a conclusion that would be echoed in the

writings of Lummis, Grinnell, and Garland: "To train the average Indian as a lawyer or a doctor is in most cases simply to spoil him." While continuing to support universal schooling, Roosevelt called on eastern reformers to lower their expectations.[42]

Roosevelt's views on Indian education were consistent with his advocacy of American imperialism and his support for racial segregation. Roosevelt was an outspoken defender of overseas expansion. He believed that the white races had a duty to raise less powerful non-white nations to a better standard of living. This is what Roosevelt believed Americans had set out to do in the Philippines, despite the fact that the archipelago was a military "heel of Achilles" and the Filipinos would need a "succession of Tafts [to] administer them for the next century." TR believed that participation in world trade and contact with efficient businessmen would teach natives the advantage of civilization and stimulate them to improve themselves.[43]

He also thought American blacks would benefit from an extended period of domination by whites. "Negroes," Roosevelt wrote an English friend, should only have "the largest amount of self-government which they can exercise." With this axiom in mind the president had little difficulty justifying segregation, disenfranchisement, and—a bizarre paradox—the maintenance of the color bar at the 1912 Progressive party convention. "I have the most impatient contempt," he wrote, "for the ridiculous theorists who decline to face facts and who wish to give even to the most utterly undeveloped races of mankind a degree of self-government which only the very highest races have been able to exercise."[44]

And Indians belonged to a nonwhite race. In his speeches and correspondence TR emphasized that the Indian, like his Filipino and black brothers, should learn to labor at the lower echelons of the white man's industrial society. "No race, no nationality ever really raises itself by the exhibition of genius in a few," he told a graduating class of blacks and Indians at Hampton Institute in 1906; "what counts is the character of the average man and average woman." He urged the students to develop "courage, willingness to work, [and] the desire to act decently." When presenting this message to whites, the president was more direct and less benign. Responding to a critic of his imperialistic views, Roosevelt snapped, "If we were morally bound to abandon the Philippines, we were also morally bound to abandon Arizona to the Apaches."[45]

Near the end of his life, TR wrote: "Some Indians can hardly be moved forward at all. Some can be moved both fast and far. . . . A few Indians may be able to turn themselves into ordinary citizens in a dozen years. Give to these exceptional Indians every chance; but remember that the majority must change gradually, and that it will take generations to make the change complete." This analysis reveals how profoundly Roosevelt differed from the evangelical reformers and Republican stalwarts who had fashioned the assimilation campaign of the 1880s. Viewing the Native American's future in the context of twentieth-century political realities, the former president saw no alternative to his pessimistic judgments. Popular writers applauded his "realism," and his cowboy advisers nodded their approval.[46]

The years following Roosevelt's presidency were marked by political turmoil. William Howard Taft, whipsawed between warring factions within his own party, was quickly dumped by the electorate. TR returned from his famous safari and launched the most successful third-party movement of the century. In its aftermath the Democrats placed the first southerner in the White House in over half a century despite his failure to win more than 42 percent of the popular vote in the 1912 election. And the Socialists, gaining strength at every election, hovered on the verge of respectability. Nevertheless the two men who followed Roosevelt into the White House shared his view of the Indian question. The new "realism" of the Rough Rider replaced the assimilationist consensus of the 1880s and 1890s. Backward but beautiful, the Indian stirred little controversy among the leading political warriors of the progressive era.

As TR's hand-picked successor, Taft shared many of his predecessor's attitudes and continued most of his policies. Like Roosevelt he addressed the students at Hampton, praising their instruction in "manual dexterity" and complimenting them for recognizing that "the best home for the negroes [was] on the farm." As a former governor general of the Philippines, Taft was also a firm defender of what he called the "altruistic work" being carried out in the colony. And the new president agreed that Indians, like blacks and Filipinos, should be protected by their more "civilized" countrymen. In what was probably his only appearance before an entirely Indian audience during his four years in office, the president told students at the Haskell Institute, "You are under the guardianship of the United States which is trying in every legitimate way to fit you to meet what you have to meet in future life." Taft added that Indians who received an education should be an example to their tribesmen "in industry, in loyalty to the country, in law abiding character, and in morality."[47]

When Woodrow Wilson took office it was obvious that the total assimilation of the Indians had ceased to be a public concern. Greeting a delegation from the new Society of American Indians in 1914, the president confessed, "Problems have crowded upon me so fast and thick since I became President that this is one of the problems to which I have not as yet been able to give proper study." He dismissed the group with a promise to give their concerns his "very serious consideration." Significantly, however, despite his ignorance, Wilson agreed with Roosevelt that Indian affairs were best administered by westerners. Franklin K. Lane, a San Francisco lawyer endorsed by the Los Angeles Chamber of Commerce and the Asiatic Exclusion League, served as the Democrat's secretary of the interior. Lane's first assistant secretary in charge of the Indian Office was Andrieus Jones of New Mexico, and Cato Sells, a banker and party official from Texas, became commissioner of Indian affairs. Wilson rejected the idea that the federal government had a special responsibility to oversee and encourage Indian progress. The concerns of white westerners were foremost in his administration; little would override their influence in Indian affairs.[48]

Important changes were also taking place in Congress. Once the cost-free plaything of eastern reformers, Indian legislation was becoming the special province of western politicos. The transition began in 1889, when four new states—the Dakotas, Montana, and Washington—began sending representatives to Washington. It continued through the 1890s as Utah, Wyoming, and Idaho received their statehood, and was completed when Oklahoma (1907), Arizona (1912), and New Mexico (1912)—each with a significant Indian population—entered the union. Since most of the new states were sparsely populated, their impact on the House of Representatives was slight. But in the Senate, the arrival of eighteen new senators in an arena where power was already evenly balanced altered that body's treatment of issues affecting the West.

In the first ten years of the twentieth century there was no single senator who dominated policy making in the Senate the way Henry Dawes had in the 1880s. Nevertheless, a study of the voting behavior of senators from 1900 to 1910 reveals a group of fourteen men who voted together at an average rate of more than 65 percent. Twelve of the fourteen were from states west of the Mississippi. While these senators served for varying lengths of time, they all participated in at least five of the eleven roll call votes held on questions affecting Indians during the decade. And they influenced the outcome of those votes; on nine of them a majority of the group voted with the winning side. Lists of voting blocs are inherently artificial—men who voted infrequently may have been influential, and members of the group may have believed they were acting independently—but the list in Table 2 contains most of those who guided Indian policy in the Senate during the Roosevelt era.

Voting behavior during the Wilson administration followed a similar pattern. Eleven roll call votes were held on legislation affecting Indians between 1913 and 1921. Of the fifteen senators who participated in at least five of those votes and voted identically 50 percent of the time or more, nearly half were from the West. The group listed in Table 3 also includes two men who chaired the Senate Indian Affairs Committee: insurgent Republican Moses Clapp (1907–11) of Minnesota and Arizonan Henry Ashurst (1915–19). Perhaps most significant, the Wilson years marked a sharp decline in congressional involvement in Indian affairs. An average of nearly half the Senate was absent during the eleven roll call votes held during the Democrat's two terms, and on *none* of them did more than fifty-five members of the upper house register a vote. Thus no more than twenty-eight senators were needed to carry any issue. Even a moderately cohesive group of fifteen senators could be confident of deciding the important Indian policy issues that arose.[49]

Men from beyond the Mississippi did not snatch control of Indian policy away from their eastern colleagues; it was handed to

Table 2. Indian Policy Makers, c. 1900–10*

Senator	Years in Senate	Mean Agreement Score
Elmer Burkett, R–Nebr.	1905–11	77
Samuel Piles, R–Wash.	1905–11	77
Chester Long, R–Kans.	1903–9	76
Frank Flint, R–Calif.	1905–11	73
Porter J. McCumber, R–N.Dak.	1899–1920	71
George Perkins, R–Calif.	1899–1915	70
Jacob Gallinger, R–N.H.	1891–1918	64
Henry Teller, R, Silver Democrat–Colorado**	1885–1909	64
Henry Burnham, R–N.H.	1901–13	62
Alfred Kittredge, R–S.D.	1901–9	62
Fred T. Dubois, Populist–Idaho	1891–97, 1901–7	59
William Stewart, R–Nev.	1887–1905	58
Robert Gamble, R–S.Dak.	1901–13	56
Clarence Clark, R–Wyo.	1893–1917	52

*Information presented here is based primarily on votes 44–55 in Appendix 1.
**left GOP in 1896

them. As presidential attitudes and the high rate of abstentions on Indian-related roll call votes indicate, lawmakers increasingly were prepared to view Native Americans as the special concern of the westerner. The chairmanship of the Senate's Indian Affairs Committee also became theirs. Between 1893, when Henry Dawes retired, and 1920, nine men held that influential post. All were from states west of the Mississippi, and three were from states that had not existed before 1889. Beset by dozens of pressing issues, and faced with a group that claimed to "know" the Indian better than they, eastern legislators agreed with the New York congressman who responded to the Indian office's proposed budget for 1907 by calling on his colleagues to "approve a bill as a whole without discussion or change of any character." He added that appropriations in this area were "absolutely safe in the hands of the committee."[50]

Table 3. Indian Policy Makers, c. 1913–20*

Senator	Years in Senate	Mean Agreement Score
James Martine, D–N.J.	1911–17	75
Frank White, D–Ala.	1914–15	73
Henry Ashurst, D–Ariz.	1913–41	72
Nathan Bryan, D–Fla.	1911–17	69
Key Pittman, D–Nev.	1913–40	66
Morris Sheppard, D–Tex.	1913–41	65
William Thompson, D–Kans.	1913–19	64
Henry Hollis, D–N.H.	1913–19	64
Ollie James, D–Ky.	1913–18	58
Henry Myers, D–Mont.	1911–23	57
Joseph Ransdell, D–La.	1913–21	56
William Chilton, D–W Va.	1911–17	55
Atlee Pomerane, D–Ohio	1911–23	55
Thomas Walsh, D–Mont.	1913–33	54
Moses Clapp, R–Minn.	1899–1917	53

*The eleven votes taken during the Wilson administration are numbers 57–67 in Appendix 1.

Like the popular writers who dwelt on Native American racial handicaps and the presidential advisers who called for "practicality" rather than "eastern philanthropy," the western legislators who came to dominate policy making were hostile to an elaborate campaign to achieve total assimilation. "The only element that can elevate the Indian," South Dakota's Senator Richard Pettigrew argued, "is that of showing him how to help himself. No assistance can be given him that will advance him one particle in civilization along any other lines." In the opposite wing of the capitol, Democrat John Stephens of Texas preached a similar gospel to the House of Representatives. "We should reverse our Indian policy," he cried, "cease making these great annual appropriations; break up their tribal relations; allot their lands among them, and open up the surplus lands on their reservations for settlement." These lawmakers believed that the Indian's only hope for survival lay in becoming self-sufficient actors in the new communities now dotting the western landscape.[51]

Finally, western politicans acquired a firm control over appointments in the Indian Office. While Roosevelt put Francis Leupp in the commissioner's chair because the former reporter had traveled widely in the West, Wilson found the genuine article in Texan Cato Sells. Sells, who served from 1913 to 1921, was succeeded by Charles Burke, a South Dakota congressman who had chaired the House Indian Affairs Committee. Appointments at the lower levels of the Indian Office were almost entirely controlled by local congressman and senators. "I simply cannot get a man confirmed," Roosevelt wrote in 1903, "unless the senators from that state approve of him."[52]

In the early twentieth century, shifts in popular perceptions reshaped the public image of the Indian and his place in American society. Writers and politicians turned away from the hopeful view they had created a generation before. They began doubting the speed with which the Native American might "rise" to a civilized state and questioning whether total assimilation was desirable at all. For many, the Indians had ceased to represent a challenge to the assimilative capacities of their dynamic industrial society. Instead, the race came to symbolize the country's frontier past. In this new context, traditional lifeways were less disturbing, and the eradication of old habits ceased to be an overriding policy objective.

Sources of attitudinal change are elusive. Political and economic pressures mold—but do not determine—them. And while ideas often gain endorsement on their own merit—even when they run against the logic of events—it is equally true that people do not form perceptions in a social vacuum. Events and ideas interact with one another. In the case of the Indian in the early twentieth century, popular curiosity about native life reinforced a growing nostalgia for the lost frontier. These ideas in turn profited from the rise of westerners to political power. Although each trend produced its own image of Native American life, they all shared and reinforced a common core of beliefs. Among these was the notion that Indians viewed the world differently from whites, that they were not likely to change, and that ambitious assimilation programs could not succeed. In retrospect, the evangelical reformers of the 1880s now seemed both naïve and out of date. The old faith that Native Americans would magically "rise" to civilization struck people like Theodore Roosevelt and Hamlin Garland as praiseworthy, but foolish. And policies based on that faith would not win side support.

White perceptions of the Indian have always been characterized by ambivalence—contempt mixed with admiration, rejection tempered by compassion—but these uncertainties should not obscure important shifts in attitude. Of course the rhetoric of assimilation and the activities of reformers continued, but in the first decade of the twentieth century the balance of opinion appeared to waver and move. Optimism and a desire for rapid incorporation were pushed aside by racism, nostalgia, and disinterest. Total assimilation was no longer the central concern of policy makers and the public. The Indian question had been transformed.

Chapter 4

Frozen in Time and Space

Undergirding the policy reforms of the late nineteenth century was a faith in the immediacy of Indian progress. Policy makers believed that the path from "savagery" to civilization was difficult to traverse, but they set out to mark it and to guide the Indians along its upward track. Shifts in public attitudes were not likely to destroy the faith of America's leaders, for their belief was rooted in science as well as popular intuition. Nevertheless, as the generation of John Wesley Powell and Henry Dawes left the scene, confidence in the Indians' future receded with them. New scientists appeared. They wrestled with new problems and reached new judgments about human history. In the twentieth century, these scholars shattered the old evolutionary orthodoxy and cast aside the view that progress was a natural human condition. Inevitably, this change of heart undermined support for total Native American assimilation. In the 1880s, the Indians had been viewed as a people moving from a lower to a higher stage of development. By 1920 they were frozen in time and space.

Two broad areas of historical change established the context for changes in the scientific perception of Indians. First, during the early twentieth century racial and ethnic differences attracted the attention of a growing number of scholars. Their interest reflected a rising public concern. In the nation's cities, immigrants continued to arrive at unprecedented rates, creating social enclaves that seemed unconnected to the rest of society or to the American past. At the same time southerners were furiously throwing up legal levees to control a flood of social crises that threatened to sweep away a social order founded on white supremacy. They fashioned a universe of segregation statutes to separate the races and buttressed these with demagoguery and violence. Finally, in the West successive rounds of anti-Asian hysteria produced a similar pattern of fear and exclusion. Just as their counterparts in the late nineteenth century were preoccupied with progress—its causes, its virtues, and its future—so the anthropologists and sociologists of the succeeding generation could not escape an obsession with diversity: were the races equal? Should they mix? Could several cultural groups share the same political system?[1]

Within the academic world a second sequence of events was taking place: the social sciences were passing out of the hands of self-taught amateurs. In the twentieth century, university professors would dominate scholarly inquiry. Their rise to dominance brought with it national associations, new academic journals, and the modern graduate school. These institutions in turn fostered and sustained a cadre of intellectuals who valued rigorous inquiry, shunned abstract speculation, and were loyal to their profession rather than to religious or political ideologies. Among modern scientists there was a new emphasis on scientific inquiry and standardized training and a general disenchantment with a priori schemes and assertions.

Rising racial tensions and the professionalism of the social sciences produced disenchantment with social evolutionary thinking. While usually confining nonwhite people to the lower stages of development, evolutionists like Lewis Henry Morgan had explicitly rejected racial classifications; they argued instead that progress was inevitable and that human development followed a single pattern. Modern scientists concerned themselves with the physical differences between groups and criticized their predecessors for minimizing the importance of race. Others argued that too little was known about individual societies to support Morgan's grand theory of human development. They called for detailed investigations and were willing to postpone attempts at synthesis.

Under these pressures the old social evolutionist orthodoxy broke apart and four competing schools of thought took its place. First, a group of anthropologists associated with the Bureau of American Ethnology began to modify evolutionary theory in order to take into account new research and the supposed importance of racial differences. A second party of social scientists concluded that racial differences alone determined social behavior. They believed that non-white peoples had little chance of joining a "civilized" society led by their racial superiors. Third, scholars in the emerging field of sociology looked to the physical and social environments to explain human differences. And finally, in the first two decades of the new century a number of young anthropologists trained by Franz Boas proposed a new concept—culture—to explain the existence of different racial and ethnic traditions. Rather than producing a single new orthodoxy, modern social scientists produced several.

Where politicians concerned with Indian policy had once found unanimity, they now found confusion and disagreement. In the 1880s, the anthropologists' faith in progress had been reflected in a wide array of federal programs; inevitably the erosion of that faith called the programs into question. Doubts about the wisdom of total assimilation gained scientific support, and, when called upon, scientists gave negative advice. The ambitious assimilation campaign was a mistake and should be restrained—of that they were sure. They were less certain about what should take its place.

In the early twentieth century social evolution continued to be the credo of the Bureau of American Ethnology. The scientists who worked there labored to incorporate new data from field research sites and new attitudes toward racial differences into the evolutionary framework that was the legacy of John Wesley Powell. While their modifications of Powell's teachings allowed them to continue to view themselves as his heirs, their efforts produced a significant shift in the office's attitude toward total assimilation.

Political pressure and advancing age forced John Wesley Powell from the U.S. Geological Survey in 1893. He remained chief of the Bureau of American Ethnology until his death in 1902, but he had very little day-to-day contact with it. The administration of the office fell to "Ethnologist in Charge" W. J. McGee (1853–1912), a self-educated geologist with eccentricities to match those of his mentor. Like the major, McGee grew up on the Middle Border and began his scientific career as an energetic collector of "specimens." His Iowa home was filled with cases containing rocks, insects, stuffed animals, and Indian artifacts. McGee also shared Powell's belief in the need for a partnership between science and government. At the age of twenty-four the young amateur organized a geological survey of his home state. He completed the project in four years, in the process winning the attention of the U.S. Census Bureau (for whom he next worked). In 1883 McGee became Powell's assistant at the geological survey; work with the Bureau of Ethnology followed.

It was McGee who took the lead in reconciling Powell's dynamic view of social evolution with the changes taking place in the social sciences. The major's protégé recognized that human progress was not as evident at the turn of the century as it had been when Powell had organized the Bureau of Ethnology twenty years before. McGee explained this predicament in the presidential address he delivered at the founding meeting of the American Anthropological Association. "The Trend of Human Progress" began with the recollection of an incident from his Iowa boyhood. One summer day McGee had walked to the bluffs overlooking the Mississippi and "for the first time looked down upon the broad Father of the Waters." He remembered, "I already knew from the books and the talks of my elders that it was a river." He continued to the water's edge and there came upon a group of boys, lounging on a pile of lumber. "I inquired of these long-time residents on the river bank which way the river ran. The voluble lad with feet nervously dangling from the edge of the lumber-pile answered promptly, 'Huh! it don't run nowhere; it stays right here.' . . . the lesson was not lost; I had learned how hard it is to find which way the current runs." Like the boys in the parable, McGee pointed out that observers with "conviction transcending experience" often misperceived the course of human history. He saw himself and his fellow anthropologists as people who would take seriously the data being gathered by scientists and reject blind allegiance to a theoretical school. "The direction of flow of the Mississippi might have been learned from a practical boatman," he noted, "and it is meet to inquire whether the trend of human progress may not be gained from actual workers in man's experience of Man."[2]

McGee did not reject the evolutionist's faith in ongoing progress. He told the American Association for the Advancement of Science in 1897 that the evolutionary framework tended "to bring order out of that vast chaos of action and thought which [had] so long resisted analysis and synthesis." And his presidential address contained the assertion that "it should be self-evident that motion involves progression." McGee went on to describe that forward movement in the fields of anthropology (or "somatology": McGee also shared Powell's love of new scientific terms), psychology, ethnology ("demonomy"), philology, and the history of ideas ("sophiology"). But as his image of the muddy Mississippi suggested, McGee was also aware that the evolutionist could ignore contradictory evidence and overstate the speed of progress.[3]

McGee suggested that scholars appreciate the distance between stages of culture. Different rates of progress, he noted, produced the "difference in modes of thinking [that] form of the strongest bar against the union of tribes and nations." The anthropologist quickly added that such differences were "the expression of brain rather than blood," but his observation would hardly be encouraging to a government schoolteacher or a defender of land allotment. Even though McGee promised that "thought [was] extending from man to man . . . toward a higher plane than any yet attained," his emphasis on the gaps that separated "tribes and nations" pushed the unification of human society—something Powell had predicted—far into the future.[4]

According to McGee, the existence of racial differences raised additional barriers between stages of culture. He asserted that each of the major races had evolved independently. Polygenesis, with its suggestion that different races constituted different orders of beings, undermined the prospects for rapid progress. "The progenitors of the white man," he observed, "must have been well past the critical point before the progenitors of the red and the black arose from the plane of beastiality to that of humanity." Progress might be "self-evident," but it was neither uniform—whites evolved before blacks—nor steady. The races of the world might be blending into a single entity, he noted, but this was occurring "through the more rapid extinction of lower races" as well as through intermarriage.[5]

Indeed, progress might not come to everyone. McGee defended American imperialism in the early twentieth century—pointing out that the "lamp of civilization" was shining on the "dark-skinned peoples"—but he did not believe all "barbarians" could be saved. As the civilized nations rose in efficiency and size, their rate of advancement quickened; progress was "decidedly slower among civilization's subjects." Although there was a great deal in "The Trend of Human Progress" that echoed Powell and Lewis Henry Morgan, its emphasis on racial and cultural differences offered a variant on the social evolutionist theme that might be exploited in the increasingly tense atmosphere of the early twentieth century.[6]

After 1899, McGee's pessimism deepened. His theoretical writings often returned to the gulf between culture groups and the importance of race as an indicator of civilization. In 1901, for example, his presidential address to the Anthropological Society of Washington noted, "The savage stands strikingly close to sub-human species in every aspect of mentality. . . . The range from the instinct and budding reason of higher animals to the thinking of lowest man seems far less than that separating the zoomimic [animal-like] savage from the engine using inventor." The distance separating civilization from the world of the "zoomimic savage" seemed to be getting greater. Three years later, he was referring to "aliens" of "foreign or ill-starred birth and defective culture" as the "mental and moral beggars of the community." Such people, he added, "may not be trusted on horseback but only in the rear of the wagon."[7]

Powell died in the fall of 1902, and McGee awaited his appointment as chief of the Bureau of Ethnology. When he was passed over in favor of William Henry Holmes, a curator at the Smithsonian's

National Museum, the major's protégé appealed to the Institution's board of trustees. Franz Boas was one of his most outspoken defenders. In a series of letters to the Columbia University anthropologist, McGee spelled out how he intended to organize the bureau's programs should his appeal be successful. His chief interest was to apply scientific methods to problems confronting American society. He suggested developing a "practical branch" to study the different races living within the United States. Examining the physical and psychological make-up of these groups, he argued, would allow the bureau to "discuss race problems on a scientific rather than a sentimental basis." He wished to extend the bureau's research to "mulattoes as well as to Chinese, Japanese, and other peoples," and to take on such specific tasks as "determining the citizenship value of both pure and mixed Indians."[8]

The changing racial composition of the United States suggested to McGee that the simple line of progress laid out by Morgan and Powell was in need of further examination. One could neither expect assimilation to operate automatically nor confidently predict the outcome of the process. "This country has become a melting pot of humanity," McGee wrote his German-Jewish immigrant colleague. "Without definite foresight on anybody's part, we are working out the greatest experiment in all the world's history in the blending of types of both blood and culture; thereby we are introducing half unwittingly, vital alloys whose properties no one can predict with confidence." He hoped that scientists like himself would be able to guide American statesmen, but his appeal was fruitless (the trustees of the Smithsonian wanted to steer clear of political controversy) and he left the bureau in 1903 to direct the "Congress of Races" at the Louisiana Purchase Exposition in St. Louis.[9]

McGee never produced a comprehensive restatement of social evolutionist theory. His dispute with the Smithsonian's board of trustees cut him off from future work with the Institution, and his lack of professional credentials made securing an academic position unlikely. Theodore Roosevelt appointed him vice-chairman of the Inland Waterways Commission in 1907, and he held that office until his premature death in 1913. But the self-taught Iowan was not the only scientist concerned with the effects of racial differences on social progress. William Henry Holmes (1846–1933) continued his predecessor's questioning when he took control of the Bureau of Ethnology.

With a background as a museum curator, Holmes focused most of his attention on the proper form and organization of displays. He advocated arranging exhibits according to an evolutionary plan. "By this method of presentation," he told one gathering of anthropologists, "we teach . . . the succession of peoples and culture and convey a general notion of mutations of fortune and the slow process from lower to higher phases of existence." His comments on the "process" by which American Indians were moving from lower to higher "phases of existence" were most fully developed in an essay published in the *American Anthropologist* in 1910.[10]

Holmes agreed with McGee that each race had evolved separately and the most "primitive" peoples had separated earliest from a central line of development. He speculated that "the African and Asiatic may be the result of the first branching, taking permanent form in well-separated environments, the Caucasian and especially the American developing later." But Holmes moved beyond McGee in his estimation of what polygenesis implied for the future of the individual races.[11]

McGee had acknowledged that some nonwhite races could learn from the "lamp of civilization," but aside from his desire to keep such people in the "back of the wagon," and his observations regarding racial intermarriage, he had made no predictions regarding their assimilation into "civilized" society; Holmes did. "Our people have been witnesses of a hundred years of vain struggle ending with the pathetic present," the government's chief ethnologist wrote. He believed the bureau's researches enabled him to predict the Indian's future: "We are now able to foretell the fading out to total oblivion in the very near future. All that will remain to the world of the fated race will be a few decaying monuments, the minor relics preserved in museums, and something of what has been written." Holmes allowed that some "peaceful amalgamation" might take place, but for the majority "extinction of the weaker by less gentle means will do the work." Like McGee, Holmes believed racial differences raised the barriers between stages of culture. He carried that belief to its logical conclusions. "The final battle of the races for the possession of the world," Holmes warned, "is already on."[12]

Holmes made the issue plain. The only way to accept evolutionist doctrine while at the same time accepting deep differences between the races was to predict the "fading out to total oblivion" of backward peoples like the Indians. The issue of race had always been an ambiguous element in the writings of American evolutionists, but earlier scientists like Morgan and Powell had suggested that the conflict between "civilized" whites and uncivilized nonwhites could mean advancement for the "inferior" races. Holmes, faced with the "pathetic present" and a century of failed government programs, preferred to exclude the Indians from his blueprint for social progress.

On the few occasions when they turned from scientific speculation to contemporary policy, the twentieth-century evolutionists repeated their warnings. In a letter to Carlisle's Captain Pratt, McGee defended himself against charges that he opposed Indian education. The scientist explained that he simply had lower expectations. "By reason of the intimate acquaintance with the Indian mind," he observed, "I may differ from some Indian educators as to the rate at which the old should be put off and the new taken on." Other scholars were more pessimistic. An article appearing in the *American Anthropologist* in 1919, for example, stated that "primitive peoples [could not] stand an enforced civilization." The author contended, "No better example of this can be cited than that of the American Indians, who even on their own soil have resisted civil conditions unto death." A generation earlier, Major Powell had called for a partnership between science and the Indian Office. In 1919, evolutionists had only bad news: "Many proud tribes have perished, one after another, before the march of civilization, and the remainder at times seem surely destined to ultimate extinction." Believers in total assimilation and ambitious federal programs would have to look elsewhere for support.[13]

While McGee and Holmes attempted to reconcile a dynamic view of social evolution with their estimate of the great distances separating racial and cultural groups, other social scientists looked to race as the ultimate source of human diversity. These racial formalists were a varied lot. They ranged from Daniel Garrison Brinton, who never abandoned his faith in social progress, to Madison Grant, whose narrow racism predicted unending conflict among the races. All of them classified American Indians as a single race with specific inherited characteristics. All inveighed against "race mixing" and predicted the imminent extinction of the Indian.

Brinton (1837–99), who in 1886 became the first professor of anthropology in the United States, was one of the nineteenth century's last great amateur scholars. He shared a number of traits with his contemporary, Lewis Henry Morgan. Like Morgan, he put aside a boyhood interest in Indians when he embarked on a professional career. Morgan became a lawyer; Brinton practiced medicine. Both men also retired from those careers at a relatively early age so that they could devote all of their time to anthropological study. Although Brinton held a chair in anthropology at the University of Pennsylvania, he did no teaching. He devoted the last decade of his life to research and writing.

Daniel Garrison Brinton does not fit neatly into the racial formalist category. He considered himself an evolutionist, his principal interest was linguistics, and he devoted relatively little time to theoretical speculation. It would be wrong to group Brinton with the eugenicists of the early twentieth century or to forget that there were a number of other aspects to his career. Nevertheless, his point of view—particularly as expressed in his published lectures—prefigured the more explicitly racial approaches to Indian life that appeared after 1900.[14]

During the 1890s, three themes appeared in Brinton's work and formed the basis for the racial formalists' perspective. He argued first that one's capacity for progress was determined by race. This capacity was inheritable and changed so slowly that it was a virtually permanent characteristic of each racial group. Second, Brinton predicted that the Indians' racial inferiority would bring about their extinction. And finally, he warned against intermarriage. He argued that unions of Indians and Europeans would damage the "white race."

Although he accepted the fact that all humanity was "of one blood by the judgment of a higher court than anatomy can furnish," Brinton believed that environment and the "differentiation of the species man" had produced wide differences within the world's population. "Certain mental traits and faculties are broadly correlated to . . . physical features," he wrote in 1898, "and no amount of sentimentality about the equality of all men can do away with this undeniable truth." According to this view, "ethnic characteristics" were established early in the evolution of the species and were "hence impressed indelibly on its members."[15] Race preceded culture. As a consequence, the "indelible" qualities of a group limited its progress. Naturally, Brinton viewed all Indian tribes as one, regardless of their social complexity or the sophistication of their technology. The Indian race had some strengths: it was not as dark as the African race, and the "average cubical capacity" of their skulls lay about midway between that of whites and blacks. But there were also weaknesses. Most significant was their inability to create complex social organizations. Aztec and Maya civilization, the good doctor wrote, were simply large versions of "the simple and insufficient models of the cruder hunting tribes of the plains."[16]

In isolation, the Native Americans would survive; their limitations would not impair the race's ability to feed and clothe itself. In the presence of civilized folk, however, the "pathological condition" of the Indians' "ethnic mind" doomed the group to extinction. Most destructive, Brinton argued, was the Native American's "ineradicable restlessness." Indians were easily excited. This trait led to "scenes of the wildest riot," as well as to nervous disorders and alcoholism. The physician's ingenious diagnosis turned the cries of reformers like Helen Hunt Jackson on their head. The dishonor was not the white man's—*he* was not the one with the "nervous disorders" that provoked frontier violence, and *he* was not excitable. White men had different "indelible" characteristics.

Finally, the lesson Brinton drew from the past was antithetical to the guilt-ridden sermonizing of Dawes and Fletcher. Native Americans were locked in a downward trajectory that could not be altered. "If he retains his habits he will be exterminated," Brinton wrote; "if he aims to preserve an unmixed descent, he will be crushed out by disease and competition." Of course intermarriage with those from more progressive races might change this fate, but Brinton quickly sealed that exit. He believed that neither pity, sympathy, nor love should divert whites from marrying their own kind: "That philanthropy is false, that religion is rotten which would sanction a white woman enduring the embrace of a colored man."[17]

In the years following Brinton's death in 1899, the use of racial characteristics to explain social and cultural differences became widespread. Most of the writing in this area, however, focused on European ethnic groups and American blacks because of their greater numbers and political significance. William Z. Ripley's *Races of Europe* (1899) and Madison Grant's *The Passing of the Great Race* (1916) were the most popular of these books that called for the preservation of northern European culture in the United States in the face of mounting numbers of newcomers from Italy, Greece, and the Balkans. Ripley and Grant insisted that southern Europeans belonged to inferior races that should be barred from entry into the New World by restrictive immigration laws. Other social scientists carried the theme to the American South, asserting that the inherent inferiority of blacks precluded their participation in the country's political or social institutions. Although Indians, because of their smaller numbers and relative political unimportance, did not attract wide attention, racial formalists like Ripley and Grant referred to Native Americans and repeated Brinton's three themes. These scholars described a world of racial castes in which Indians were fixed in a subordinate position.[18]

Belief in the inheritance of acquired characteristics was fundamental to the racial formalists' position. "Civilized" races had an inborn respect for law, while "savage" peoples naturally passed their "backward" habits on to their children. Versions of this view ran from Madison Grant's belief that race lay at the base of all social phenomena to Franklin Giddings's more moderate conception that racial characteristics were the product of environmental pressure. Nevertheless all formalists agreed that a racial hierarchy existed and would continue unchanged into the future. Grant favored northern Europeans on purely racial grounds. Giddings and others believed climate and social traditions shaped racial characteristics, but they reached similar conclusions. According to Giddings, the "Scotch" were the most "critical intellectual" race while "Negroes and other colored peoples" were largely "instinctive," "imitative," and "emotional."[19]

When scholars like Grant and Giddings turned to contemporary Indian life they continued to wear their formalist blinders. Like Brinton, most of the racial theorists of the early twentieth century were quick to point out that Native Americans were superior to blacks. Some writers, such as Lindley Keasbey of the University of Texas, based their judgment on color. "Arranged in an ascending series," he noted in 1907, "we rank the Negro or Black race lowest; next the American, or Red race; then the Mongolic [sic], or Yellow race, and finally the caucasic [sic] or White race." Others, like Madison Grant, refined the scale by grouping Indians with Mongoloids. This was a step up from the bottom, for "the Mongol is not inferior to the Nordic in intelligence, as is the Negro." The third means of differentiating Indians from blacks was to refer to the achievement of native civilizations. Lothrop Stoddard of the American Museum of Natural History in New York was an advocate of this last view. In *The Rising Tide of Color*, a defense of Anglo-Saxon supremacy published in the aftermath of World War I, the scientist wrote, "There can be no doubt that the Indian is superior to the Negro. The Negro, even when quickened by foreign influences, never built up anything approaching a real civilization; whereas the Indian . . . evolved genuine polities and cultures." Regardless of their base, however, these comparisons between the inherent character of blacks and Native Americans served only to emphasize the supposed permanence of their nature. Scientists like Grant and Stoddard might view the Native Americans more sympathetically than they did blacks, but Indians too were prisoners of their race.[20]

Specifically, racial formalists found America's natives unable to reason in the abstract, lacking in creativity, and less adventuresome than the European "empire builders." These deficiencies produced what Lothrop Stoddard called the Indians' great conservatism. "The Indian possesses notable stability and poise," the scientist wrote, "but the very intensity of these qualities fetters his progress and renders questionable his ability to rise to the modern plane." As a result, the Indian "exhibits dull indifference to alien innovation." More benign than the lurid accounts of black Americans that titillated the white public at the same time, these descriptions of the Indian personality still relegated natives to an inferior station and sanctioned permanent segregation. In their popular textbook, *Applied Eugenics*, Professors Paul Popenoe and Roswell Johnson stated the lesson clearly for all who cared to study it: "We do not mean, of course, to suggest that all natives who have died in the New World since the landing of Columbus have died because the evolution of their race had not proceeded so far in certain directions as that of their conquerors. But the proportion of them who were eliminated for that reason is certainly very large."[21]

Although they opposed all intermarriage (Grant argued that such union produced "a race reverting to the more ancient, generalized and lower type"), formalists were far more concerned about southern European immigrants and American blacks than they were about Indians. Since Native Americans were bound for extinction, they posed no threat. Their passing, noted one theorist, would spare the country "at least one source of racial impoverishment." In the interim, the Indian Office would be wise to tailor its programs to the race's particular characteristics. In the field of education, for example, racial formalists pointed out that "too much must not be expected of one generation." In an essay entitled "On the Education of the Backward Races," Ernest Coffin pointed out that lowered expectations were the key to a successful school program. Educators should teach only what Indians were capable of learning. "Thus will the indigenous capacities be shaped," he concluded, "not in a mold of our fashioning, but in one of indigenous material, purified and enlarged by the touch of the genius of a higher culture." Stripped of its racism, a proposal of this kind might be interpreted as a call for what educators now call bicultural education. But in the early years of the century, Coffin's ideas were intended as a correction to the belief that Indians could be taught the same subjects as whites. Consideration of what one author called the "ethnic factors in education" would help the Indian Office improve "a race that is in its childhood."[22]

Racial formalists seized on the physical differences between native and white Americans to explain their social differences. Race alone, these scholars argued, explained the Indians' slow progress and justified their "speedy extinction." Natives were destined to remain behind and below the white man during whatever time the race remained on earth. Consequently, government policies based

on the assumption that all people might reach a common plane had
no scientific basis. There were no evolutionary promises of assimilation from the racial formalists, only imprisonment in an "ineradicable" past.[23]

During the early twentieth century, America's growing cadre of professional social scientists produced a large body of reliable data about
human societies. The new evidence often raised questions about the
accuracy of social theories. For example, people who were "savages"
but who lived on opposite sides of the globe were found to have relatively little in common. At the same time other groups on different
cultural levels turned out to share a number of values and practices.
The races of the earth, supposedly distinct and bound by their "ineradicable" past, often possessed strikingly similar characteristics.
The new science of anthropometry proved that head sizes and brain
weights varied hardly at all from race to race. Analysts were beginning to conceive of races as complexes of constantly shifting sub-
groups rather than fixed populations. Such discoveries raised doubts
in many minds about the accuracy of social evolutionary theory as
well as the reliability of simple racial formalism. In this atmosphere
of doubt, a new line of research—one that concentrated on the role
of the environment in determining behavior—began to attract wider
attention.[24]

The early social evolutionists of course had been mindful of environmental influences. Both Morgan and Powell had described the
contrasts between the Old World and the new, pointing out, among
other things, that the absence of large domesticated animals had
nudged the Americans away from large permanent settlements and
intensive agriculture. Naturally, then, Otis T. Mason (1838–1908),
the first of the country's anthropologists to discuss the primacy of
the environment, did not set out to destroy evolutionism. In fact
Mason was part of the Washington establishment's stable of self-
made scholars. Originally a high-school teacher, Mason began working in the ethnology department of the National Museum in 1872.
He became curator of ethnology twelve years later and served as head
anthropological curator from 1902 to 1908. Mason also contributed
to the publications of the Bureau of American Ethnology and was

active in the Anthropological Society of Washington. Like Daniel Garrison Brinton, Mason was essentially an evolutionist, but—also like Brinton—he was curious about the importance of factors other than a group's social organization. Brinton became preoccupied with race; Mason turned to the environment.

Curatorial work formed the basis for Mason's ideas about cultural development and the environment. He believed material objects—tools, cookware, and weapons—should form the basis for the organization of exhibits. And Mason carried his thinking a step further; it occurred to him that the "artificialities of human life" also determined a group's social structure. For this reason, he argued in 1908, cultural development should be measured by a people's technical skill. Technological progress required "an appropriation of all the material of which the earth is composed and the domination of the forces of nature for the help of man." The elaborate technology of western societies revealed their high level of cultural development. The crude tools of "backward" societies were a measure of their barbarism. Mason agreed with other evolutionists that culture was singular—there was one standard of progress—but he suggested a new way of gauging a group's achievements.[25]

Mason thus translated social evolutionism into material terms: material culture could be used to determine where a society fit on the scale of human development. Furthermore, to the extent that the products of a society were a function of its physical environment—climate and resources—Mason asserted that a people's surroundings determined their cultural development. "Culture," he concluded, "has had to do from first to last with the physical universe for its resources, environment, and forces, chiefly in the earth, the waters and the air." He recognized that human ingenuity was vital to cultural development (nature is "a servant not a master"), but he continued to recognize the centrality of environmental influences.[26]

When the Bureau of Ethnology prepared its monumental *Handbook of American Indians* in the first decade of the new century, Mason was the obvious choice to prepare an entry on environment. The assignment provided an opportunity to apply his theoretical speculations to North America. Mason wrote that the "natural phenomena" of the continent surrounded the aborigines, "stimulating and conditioning their life and activities." The arrangement of the stars and planets was significant ("since lore and mythology were based on them"), but the most important factors were physical geography, climate, and the dominant plants and animals. He concluded that these factors "determine cultural development." Using this approach, Mason delineated twelve "ethnic environments" and asserted that "in each area there is an ensemble of qualities that impressed themselves on their inhabitants and differentiated them." While he did not throw over the study of social arrangements or reject the significance of racial differences, Mason delineated a position different from that of his colleagues at the bureau. He provided a broad definition of the environment, and suggested that the diversity of Indian cultures could be explained by the diversity of the American landscape itself. These ideas promised an alternative to the rigid orthodoxies of McGee and Madison Grant.[27]

When he turned to contemporary Indian affairs, Mason extended his environmental argument, recommending that the Indian's surroundings be arranged in such a way as to encourage "civilized" habits. An understanding of anthropology, he told the American Association for the Advancement of Science, would "be of practical value in devising methods for the management and evolution of the Indians, Negroes and Chinese within [the United States'] borders." Schools would benefit most from his advice, for scientists like himself could serve as consultants "pointing out the elements of civilization and the order of their normal evolution." Although Mason cautioned that the "middle steps" of development could not be ignored—native schooling must cover each rung in the ladder of progress—he maintained that Indian education could raise Native Americans to civilization.[28]

Like Brinton, Mason developed his ideas in the 1880s and 1890s. His essay presented variants on the dominant evolutionism of his day. Nevertheless, the curator's environmentalism soon attracted scholars who questioned the old orthodox view. The idea that culture is rooted in the physical universe suggested to them a new basis for the study of human history.

Opponents of southern and eastern European immigration often argued that people from these economically less developed areas were unfit for life in the United States. Scholars who supported this position—Franklin Giddings, John Commons, Richmond Mayo-Smith, Sarah Simons, and others—argued that the so-called new immigrants had been molded by different forces than those acting on the peoples of England, Germany, and Scandinavia. Mayo-Smith, for example, a leader among immigration restrictionists, believed that America's educational, political, and legal systems formed a "super-organic environment" that arrivals from feudal and peasant societies would have difficulty understanding. Like Mason, Mayo-Smith and his colleagues held that one's surroundings shaped mental attitudes as well as technological innovations. They agreed with W. I. Thomas, who wrote in the *American Journal of Sociology*, "When society does not furnish the stimulation, or when it has preconceptions which tend to inhibit . . . attention in given lines, then the individual shows no intelligence in these lines."[29]

When it came to modern Indians, scholars like Mayo-Smith had a ready explanation for the tribes' resistance to the assimilation campaign. The Native American was "not like the white man of any class or condition," George Bird Grinnell wrote. The source of the "difference of mind" between the races lay beyond social organization or genetics. The gap between the races indicated that "the Indian, like every other human being, receive[d] his knowledge and his mental training from his surroundings." Grinnell had little contact with academic sociology, but his view of Indian life attracted Fayette McKenzie, a former reservation schoolteacher who in 1906 earned a Ph.D. in sociology at the University of Pennsylvania with a dissertation on Indian assimilation. McKenzie was the only sociologist of his generation to devote most of his attention to Native Americans. His thesis praised Grinnell for properly defining the distance between whites and Indians as "not a fundamental difference in mental constitution, but a difference in tradition—a difference in the social mind."[30]

McKenzie's assertion that the environment shaped a "social mind" that in turn influenced an entire society led him to a relatively optimistic view of Indian assimilation. The young sociologist helped organize the Society of American Indians and worked with educated Native Americans to promote allotment, education, and the enforcement of native citizenship. New conditions, he believed, would surely stimulate a new Indian civilization. McKenzie attacked scholars who were skeptical of federal intervention. "Is culture a product of biology and blood or one of psychology and tradition?" he asked in 1912. "The pessimist and the indifferentist work from the former premise, the optimist from the latter. . . . We have only to effect a considerable change in circumstances (material and psychic) to bring about a corresponding change in ideas and culture." By granting the environment a central role, McKenzie could imagine that "changes in circumstance" would induce social programs. A colleague writing in the American Journal of Sociology put it more succinctly. Because of new conditions "the character of the Indian himself [was] undergoing a change."[31]

McKenzie continued to act on his "optimistic" assumptions throughout his career. He was active in the public recreation and settlement house movements while on the faculty at Ohio State; in 1915 he became president of Fiske University. Following his retirement from Fiske, the sociologist returned to Indian affairs, serving as a member of Lewis Meriam's survey staff that investigated reservation life and government policies in the mid-1920s.

But in the years before World War I few environmentalists were optimists. Grinnell believed the gap between Indians and whites was so great that "the attempt to educate the Indian beyond a certain point tended to injure rather than to help him." Like John Commons and the opponents of immigration, Grinnell believed that social habits, once formed, could not simply be erased by plunging someone into new surroundings. And he was supported in this position by sociologist Frank W. Blackmar, who argued in the American Journal of Sociology that "social and tribal conditions" as well as "biological heredity" produced distinctive "traits and temperaments" in Native Americans. Environmentalism apparently could cut two ways: methodologically it might avoid the rigidities of earlier theories, but it could be used to defend absolute cultural and racial hierarchies.[32]

The great achievement of the environmentalists was their insight that a wide range of external factors could produce traditions that would hold a people's loyalty for generations. These social scientists rejected the one-dimensionality of social evolution and the constraints of racial formalism. Soon other scholars were studying the environmentalists' innovations and trying to devise new ways to express their insights. The culture concept that emerged in the years before World War I was the product of these deliberations. And its rising influence marked the victory of a conceptual framework that could explain the diversity of North American Indian society while remaining free of the preconceptions of social evolution and racial formalism.

The development of the modern concept of culture was intimately linked to the career of Franz Boas (1858–1942). Boas, a German physicist who earned his Ph.D. at the University of Kiel in 1882, was driven from Europe by antisemitism and limited professional opportunities. He first came to America in 1886 to carry out field studies among the Indians of Vancouver Island for the British Association for the Advancement of Science. Between 1886 and 1896 he continued this project; he also worked on the staff of *Science* magazine and taught briefly at G. Stanley Hall's new Clark University. Boas became a professor of anthropology at Columbia University in 1896, a position he held until his death. At Columbia, Boas organized the first comprehensive graduate program in anthropology in the United States. He also published influential studies in the areas of ethnology, linguistics, anthropometry, and folklore. Both his scholarly output and the fact that he trained more anthropologists than any of his contemporaries made him a central figure in the discipline. It was Boas who first suggested that culture alone—not race, evolutionary development, or physical surroundings—shaped the lives of Native Americans. In the years before 1920 he did not explicitly reject the superiority of western culture or repudiate racial inequality, but his fresh approach to anthropological inquiry eventually accomplished both tasks.

Boas brought a physicist's precision to his field. He recognized from the outset that the data rapidly accumulating in museums and libraries disproved widely held racial and evolutionary theories. In response to those theories he suggested the adoption of a more scientific method. "Anthropology has reached the point of development where the careful investigation of facts shakes our firm belief in the far-reaching theories that have been built up," he wrote in 1898. "Before we seek what is common to all culture," he warned, "we must analyze each culture by careful and exact methods." He repeated this position often, telling a correspondent in 1907, for example, that he was "not very much given to speculations relating to things that cannot be investigated, but rather to work backward from the known to the unknown." Thus, while his work in the years before World War I laid the groundwork for ambitious theories, his preoccupation with the specific meant that he would have little immediate impact on public debate or government policy making.[33]

Boas's major statements on race and culture appeared in *The Mind of Primitive Man*, a collection of essays published in 1911. The book approached racial differences statistically. Carefully reviewing the evidence of brain weights and head size that the racial formalists had amassed to defend their hierarchies, Boas demonstrated that most of their conclusions were based on averages derived from widely varying samples. Consequently there was a great deal of overlap between groups and "the differences between different types of men were, on the whole, small as compared to the range of variation in each type."[34]

Boas conceded that it was "probable" that a difference in brain weight "causes increased faculty," but he could find no conclusive evidence that differences in intelligence coincided with racial categories. Referring to the world's population, he argued that "their faculties may be unequally developed but the differences are not sufficient to justify us to ascribe materially lower stages to some peoples, and higher stages to others." Like the environmentalists, Boas would not accept rigid boundaries between groups or place limits on a race's ability to change or progress.[35]

If racial and cultural categories had no precise meaning, how then to account for the staggering diversity of human society? Boas trod lightly here. "It may . . . be," he wrote, "that the organization of the mind is practically identical among all races of men; that mental activity follows the same laws everywhere, but that its manifestations depend upon the character of individual experience." He avoided the word *environment,* for he intended to avoid simple determinism. "Individual experiences" could be shaped by many forces; their common element was their impact on the human mind.

The bulk of the experience of man is gained from oft-repeated impressions. It is one of the fundamental laws of psychology that the repetition of mental processes increases the facility with which these processes are performed, and decreases the degree of consciousness that accompanies them. This law expresses the well-known phenomenon of habit. . . . When a certain stimulus frequently results in a certain action, it will tend to call forth habitually the same action. If a stimulus has often produced a certain emotion, it will tend to reproduce it every time.

Boas stepped beyond environmentalism by suggesting that "oft-repeated impressions" could derive from religion and mythology as well as physical surroundings or social relationships. He asserted that the totality of individual forces acted on individual people and formed their distinctive approach to life. That totality Boas called culture. Moreover, because the world contained many groups, each experiencing a different collection of "impressions," there were many cultures. The evolutionists' faith in a uniform path of cultural development had no foundation.[36]

At this early stage of his career Boas did not explicitly reject the idea that physical differences might influence the achievements of racial groups, but he argued forcefully that culture explained most of the variety evident in the data before him. "The differences between civilized man and primitive man are more apparent than real," he concluded. "Social conditions, on account of their peculiar characteristics, easily convey the impression that the mind of primitive man acts in a way quite different from ours, while in reality the fundamental traits of the mind are the same." Such a view implied that each set of "social conditions"—each culture—was internally consistent and rational. "To the mind of primitive man," Boas wrote in 1904, "only his own associations can be rational. Ours must appear to him just as heterogeneous as his to us." While not saying that all cultures were equally worthy of admiration or protection, Boas recognized, and eloquently defended, their common humanity.[37]

As George Stocking has amply demonstrated, "Boas began his career with a notion of culture that was still within the framework of traditional humanist and contemporary evolutionist usage." Trained at a modern German university and eager to apply scientific methods to the study of man, the young anthropologist could hardly be expected to reject his own definition of civilization. That he stripped away so many preconceptions from the discipline was remarkable; that he continued to speak of "primitive" and "civilized" man was not. Thus, while *The Mind of Primitive Man* rejected a hierarchy of race or physical environment, it continued to view non-Western peoples as lacking the sophistication of those who lived in the industrial world. "There is an undoubted tendency in the advance of civilization," Boas wrote, "to eliminate traditional elements and to gain a clearer and clearer insight into the hypothetical basis of our reasoning. It is therefore not surprising that, with the advance of civilization, reasoning becomes more and more logical." Thus primitive people like the American Indians would have to become more "logical"—more Occidental—in order to become more "civilized." Boas believed the study of anthropology would teach a "higher tolerance" toward other ways of life. He did not assert that it would teach greater respect.[38]

The culture concept gave social scientists a new tool with which to explore tribal societies. It opposed racial formalism and called for an expansion of the environmentalists' framework to include everything that might condition an individual mind. As Boas presented it in 1911, culture served the same function in all societies. Most significant, the concept—together with the scientific approach that produced it—opened countless paths of inquiry for the scholars beginning to emerge from Columbia's graduate school. Three of the scholars, Clark Wissler, Alfred L. Kroeber, and Robert H. Lowie, were particularly interested in how the culture concept might affect the public perception of Indians and other non-western people.

Clark Wissler (1870–1947), the oldest of the three, became Boas's student at Columbia in 1896. Although Wissler never earned a doctoral degree, he lectured at Columbia and assisted his mentor in curatorial work at the American Museum of Natural History. In 1906 Boas decided he could no longer tolerate the museum's indifference to his research proposals, and he resigned; Wissler succeeded him as curator of anthropology. The incident occurred early in both men's careers and it strained relations between them for many years. Nevertheless Wissler had absorbed his professor's devotion to the scientific method and was eager to join in the search for an alternative to the dominant social theories of his day.

The young curator's chief ambition in the period before 1920 was to use Boas's outlook to compile a general classification of American tribes. This was needed, he believed, because of the confusion wrought by the "speculation" of the amateur anthropologists who had preceded him. Wissler argued that the evolutionists' search for a single organizing theme was futile: "The number of social groups in the New World is so large, that no one can hope to hold in mind more than a small portion of them." He also rejected the environmentalists because their preoccupation with physical surroundings was too mechanistic. "The solution of the environment problem," he wrote in 1912, "depends upon our conception of culture. . . . it is difficult to see how the mere external world could be an important factor in determining cultures." Like Boas, Wissler suggested beginning with the experiences that shape individual persons in a community. "The chief explanation of this phenomenon," he wrote in reference to the origins of culture, "lies in man himself. A group of people having once worked out processes like the use of acorns, maize, manioc, etc., establish social habits that resist change. Then the successful adjustment of one tribe to a given locality will be utilized by neighbors." The landscape tended to set boundaries beyond which certain lifeways could not pass, but it did not determine how people would organize their lives.[39]

Wissler presented his cultural approach to Native American life in *The American Indian,* which appeared in 1917. He divided the hemisphere into culture areas—regions where tribes maintained similar institutions and beliefs. Each culture area had a center, where scholars could observe its characteristic traits more clearly. Moving away from that center, tribes exhibited fewer and fewer of those traits, eventually blending into the neighboring culture areas. Using this framework, and taking "all traits into simultaneous consideration," Wissler delineated fifteen culture areas in North and South America.[40]

Scholars have disputed Wissler's culture areas ever since. Boas himself apparently thought they were too narrowly conceived, and several of his students tried to revise or replace them. Despite its alleged faults, however, Wissler's scheme enabled anthropologists to use the culture concept in a comprehensive description of native societies. He thus fixed in his colleagues' minds a picture of the Americas that was sufficiently complex to incorporate the racial, linguistic, environmental, and societal data that had destroyed earlier theories.

In 1901 Columbia University awarded its first doctoral degree in anthropology to Alfred L. Kroeber (1876–1960). The founding chairman of the anthropology department at the University of California, Berkeley, and president of both the American Folklore Society (1906) and the American Anthropological Association (1917, 1918), Kroeber was the most prominent Boas protégé of the period. His long career produced important achievements in several areas, but the chief contribution of his early years was an elaboration of his teacher's attacks on racial formalism and social evolution. In a series of bold essays that appeared between 1915 and 1917, Kroeber defended racial equality and asserted the primary importance of cultural traditions.

Boas had attacked scientific racism with numbers; Kroeber was more direct. He argued that the study of human society was essentially the study of cultures; race was irrelevant to the enterprise. This assertion was one of a list of professional principles—"Eighteen Professions"—he published in the *American Anthropologist* in 1915: *"The absolute equality and identity of all human races and strains as carriers of civilization must be assumed by the Historian. The identity* [of all races] *has not been proved nor has it been disproved. . . . All opinions on this point are only convictions falsely justified by subjectively interpreted evidence."* To ascribe a people's culture to their race, he wrote a year later, was "untenable except on the preconception that social forces as such do not exist and that social phenomena are all ultimately . . . resolvable into organic factors." Kroeber acknowledged many differences between "primitive" and modern peoples, but he viewed those differences as a function of culture, not race.[41]

Kroeber's insistence on cultural explanations of behavior was the central theme of "The Morals of Uncivilized People," another essay published before World War I. There he asserted that all societies share a common set of "instinctive" moral ideas: condemnation of incest and murder, care for elders, and community self-protection. He asked, Why are so many different standards of conduct built on this common core of beliefs? The answer, he noted, was that each culture encourages and prohibits specific acts on the basis of its own needs and dangers. "There is every reason to believe," Kroeber concluded, "that uncivilized and civilized men practice what they respectively regard as virtue to the same degree." Cultures were not uniform; they existed everywhere.[42]

The centrality of culture as an explanatory tool was repeated and emphasized a few years later by another Columbia scientist. In *Culture and Ethnology* Robert H. Lowie (1883–1957) wrote that psychology, race, and geography were all "inadequate for the interpretation of cultural phenomena." The inference is "obvious," he told his fellow scientists: "Culture is a thing *sui generis* which can be explained only in terms of itself. . . . The ethnologist would do well to postulate the principle, *Omnis cultura ex cultura.*" With the boldness that is the special possession of young Ph.D.s Lowie added that believers in social evolution were clinging to a "pseudo-scientific dogmatism."[43]

Boas and his growing band of students brought both rigor and creativity to anthropological inquiry. Although they often disagreed among themselves, they shared an enthusiasm for professionalism (standardized training, scientific research methods, a common code of conduct) and a disenchantment with abstract speculation. Their energy and productivity propelled them to positions of leadership in the discipline. But the supporters of the culture concept were a relatively small group. The Bureau of American Ethnology had a near monopoly on research funds and its leadership was hostile to Boas after he publicly criticized William Henry Holmes's appointment as Powell's successor in 1902. Moreover, during World War I, scientists from the Bureau even led a move to oust the immigrant professor from the American Anthropological Association for making "disloyal statements." This hostility, together with the resentment of colleagues from competing universities, prevented the "scientific students of culture" from attaining a position of dominance until well after the war. Before 1920 the "Boas faction" operated in an arena controlled by others. They operated in the same intellectual milieu as the evolutionists, the racial formalists, and the environmentalists. Like the others, they were concerned primarily with explaining the differences between "primitive" and "civilized" peoples. And when they discussed the government's campaign to assimilate the American Indians, they had similar complaints.[44]

The discovery of Ishi in 1911 provides a vivid example of the cultural anthropologists' attitude toward contemporary issues. Ishi was a California Indian who had lived his entire life in the wild. His appearance in the corral of a slaughterhouse in the foothills of the Sierra Nevada was his entrance into "civilization." A generation before, Alice Fletcher had taken one of her Omaha informants home to Washington. Francis LaFlesche became her adopted son and the coauthor of a number of her books. In 1911 Alfred Kroeber took Ishi to the University Museum in San Francisco. The museum became his new home. Kroeber's affection for his Indian friend was no less than Alice Fletcher's for LaFlesche, but his sense of what was "best" for the man who came under his care was remarkably different. Kroeber believed that Ishi was the physical and intellectual equal of any man, but he also held that there were differences between the "primitive" and "civilized" worlds that could not be overcome quickly. Describing his new friend for a popular magazine, Kroeber asserted, "Ishi has as good a head as the average American; but he is unspeakably ignorant. . . . He has lived in the stone age, as has so often been said." The anthropologist went on to explain that the Indian's ignorance involved "an almost inconceivable difference in education, in opportunity, in a past of many centuries of achievement on which the present can build. Ishi himself is no nearer the 'missing link' or any other antecedent form of human life than we are; but in what his environment, his associates, and his puny native civilization have made him he represents a stage through which our ancestors passed thousands of years ago." Kroeber agreed with those who saw a deep chasm separating natives and whites even as he cautioned that the differences between the two groups were not permanent.[45]

Like Kroeber, most supporters of the culture concept concentrated their energies on refuting racial and evolutionary speculation. They denied the Indians' inferiority by stressing their "primitiveness." In *The Mind of Primitive Man*, for example, Franz Boas insisted that it was European civilization—not the white man—that had conquered the globe. "Several races," he noted, developed lifeways similar to those of Europe. Europeans were successful primarily because conditions on the continent facilitated the spread of innovations. Of these conditions, "common physical appearance, contiguity of habitat, and moderate difference in modes of manufacture were the most potent." He added that as Western culture spread, it destroyed the "promising beginnings" of development in other areas. "In short," Boas concluded, "historical events appear to have been much more potent in leading races to civilization than their faculty." An advanced culture had overwhelmed the peoples of North America. Their fate was not a function of physical weakness or a hostile environment; they were primitives only in relationship to the expanding power of "civilization."[46]

Although Native Americans might have been pleased to learn that modern anthropologists had rejected the idea of a racial hierarchy, they would not have been heartened by the scientists' predictions for their future. Boas believed that the Indian population was so "insignificant" that it would soon disappear through intermarriage. And Livingston Farrand, a colleague in the Columbia University anthropology department, wrote in his textbook on the history of Native Americans, "Gradual absorption by the surrounding whites seems to be the Indian's most probable fate."[47]

In the short term, students of culture urged the government to demonstrate its sensitivity to primitive people by toning down its assimilation program. Farrand, for example, pointed out, "The failure to understand and appreciate the workings of the Indian mind and the nature of many of his customs, . . . has often produced serious disturbance, unrest and revolt." The wisdom of improving the Indian's "mind," or "civilizing" his "customs" was no longer self evident. John Swanton, a Harvard-trained anthropologist who also studied under Boas, agreed. He cautioned that the work of "the historian of human culture—the anthropologist in the broad sense—is an important element in determining future action, lack of which may result in unproductive and ill-considered change." These scholars did not question the ultimate objective of assimilation; they called instead for restraint and patience. Alfred Kroeber typified this ambiguous position when, in 1908, he introduced an old Mojave man to a meeting of Indian reformers and Bureau of Indian Affairs officials. "He is a man I am proud to call my friend," the anthropologist exclaimed, "not only because he is the only person who wears long hair, but also because he is a Christian and a good American." Kroeber was pleased that the man retained a part of his traditional costume *and* that he was adapting to the presence of the majority culture. If the officials would be patient with people like Kroeber's friend, it seemed, they could look forward to a time when all Indians were "Christians and good Americans."[48]

During the 1880s, anthropologists played a vital role in the conception of the assimilation campaign. Government scientists created an atmosphere of support for the reduction of tribal landholdings, the erection of a national Indian school system, and the extension of citizenship. A generation later, their endorsement of a single set of policy goals had vanished. Social scientists no longer spoke with one voice when discussing the future of Native Americans in the United States.

Scientific opinion was divided over the significance of the Indians' race. While formalists viewed racial characteristics as decisive, environmentalists were undecided. Some, like Fayette McKenzie, wanted to discount race entirely. Others, like John Commons, believed both race and physical surroundings shaped character. The evolutionists were also of two minds: they hewed to the doctrine of universal progress while consistently placing nonwhites in the lowest categories of development. Amid this indecision students of culture rejected the influence of race altogether.

Scholars were also unsure of the Indian's future. In the 1880s faith in evolutionary development led to predictions of the imminent "civilization" of the tribes. By the early 1900s that faith contained an element of doubt. Racial formalists joined with evolutionists like William Henry Holmes to predict the disappearance of the Indian race. Boas expected intermarriage to wipe out the natives' separate existence. Fayette McKenzie, the optimistic sociologist, was the only scholar to maintain a buoyant attitude; he called for the transformation of tribal life through the manipulation of the Indians' social environment.

The disarray among American intellectuals dealt a silent blow to the assimilation campaign. Disagreement and doubt replaced certainty and support. Scholars who confidently moved between science and policy making had been succeeded by professional academics, cautious in their prescriptions and skeptical of "ill-considered" federal intervention. If there was any agreement among modern social scientists or any advice they could give, it was reflected in their warnings. The differences between Indians and whites were great. Native societies were not "in transition" to civilization, they were adapting slowly—if at all—to the forces of modernity. Primitive man would cling to his old ways for as long as he could. The lesson of these insights was clear: the assimilation process was an exceedingly problematic enterprise.

While the existence of competing points of view prevented social scientists from advocating specific new legislation, their collective disenchantment encouraged government officials to revise their expectations for the future. The total assimilation envisioned in the late nineteenth century might be desirable, but it would not occur rapidly or automatically. Anthropologists and sociologists agreed that Western European culture represented an improvement over primitive lifeways, and they favored Indian progress towards that standard. But they did not believe that policy reforms—allotment, education, or citizenship—would transform the race. Instead they suggested extending the timetable for Indian advancement and redefining the assimilationist's expectations.

By 1920 it was clear that social scientists had switched sides. No longer cheering the advancement of a people in transition, they now reminded the public that Indians belonged to primitive, static cultures that would require years of instruction and training before they could join a complex industrial society. Modern academic opinion suggested that total assimilation was an unrealistic goal; perhaps partial accommodation to "civilized" standards was all that policy makers should hope for.

Chapter 5

The Emergence of a Colonial Land Policy

On the day after Christmas 1854, Governor Isaac Stevens of Washington Territory and sixty-two headmen representing the Nisqually, Puyallup, and other Puget Sound tribes signed a treaty of friendship and mutual aid. In this agreement, as in dozens of others negotiated in the heady aftermath of the nation's push to the Pacific, the United States committed itself to the maintenance of a reservation. Qui-ee-metl and his fellow tribesmen promised to relinquish all claims to land outside the new preserve, to "exclude from their reservations the use of ardent spirits," to stop trading with the British at Vancouver Island, and "to be friendly" to the Americans. Stevens's promises were few, but among the most important was his assurance that the tribe's new home would be protected by his government for the Indians' "exclusive use." No white man would live among them without their permission.[1]

None of those who gathered that day at Medicine Creek (or three months later in Washington, D.C., when the treaty was ratified) foresaw the changes that were to overtake Qui-ee-metl and his people during the next half-century. No one discussed the government's obligations in the event of a 200-percent population increase in Washington Territory or the arrival of a transcontinental railroad. Nevertheless the Indian Office seemed ready to live up to its commitments. Reservation boundaries were maintained until 1886, when the booming city of Tacoma grew to the edge of Puyallup lands and those Indians were allotted under a provision of the original agreement. Like the people who received their lands under the Dawes Act, the Puyallups acquired trust patents that protected their homesteads and declared that they were now citizens of the United States. The government began providing for the tribe's "civilization" while continuing to preserve an area for is "exclusive use."

Unfortunately for the Puyallups, the Pacific Northwest continued to experience dramatic economic growth. The Northern Pacific Railroad carried crops and raw material to Tacoma from farms and mines a thousand miles inland, and the Pacific steamer trade made the city a global crossroads. Soon after the allotment of the tribe was completed, demands for Indian lands began afresh. This time the Indian's neighbors would not be satisfied with a simple reduction of the tribal domain—they began to argue that the treaty of Medicine Creek had run its course and should be abandoned.

In the early twentieth century, Tacoma's challenge to the Puyallups was repeated in communities across the West. The region was booming. The states beyond the Mississippi, containing 70 percent of all Indians, led the nation in population growth. Between 1890 and 1920 the number of people living in California doubled. During the same time in Arizona the increase was 300 percent, in Washington, 400 percent. Economic expansion accompanied these demographic changes. Single-crop farming, made possible by railroad transportation and the rise of urban markets, stimulated the cultivation of land previously considered marginal or unproductive. As a result, more area came under the plow in the half-century following the Civil War than had been broken in all of the years since the landing at Jamestown. Only rarely did tribal allotment and its accompanying land sales stem the demand for land. "Surplus" areas made available by the Dawes Act served primarily as reminders that with the closing of the frontier, the last untapped source of land in the West would be the areas previously held by Indians.

Responding to their constituents, Washington's state congressional delegation introduced legislation to terminate the trust titles by which the Puyallups held their land and to end the relationship established at Medicine Creek. Their bill came before Congress in 1892, but debate on the measure continued off and on for six years. Although it had little significance beyond Puget Sound, the Puyallup bill focused the lawmakers' attention on the rising demands that the government alter its policy toward the Indian lands.

Now—unlike 1854—the future was clear. Population growth, railroad construction, and urbanization were sure to continue. There would be no more large tracts of free land over which to scatter new settlers. How long, legislators asked, would the Indian Office stand between native landowners and enterprising farmers eager to buy their property? How could the government reconcile its grant of citizenship with its maintenance of federal protection? Were Indian lands private or public; was the Indian a citizen or not?

During the Puyallup debates the bill's sponsors increasingly defined the issue of Indian lands as a regional one. Seattle's congressman, John L. Wilson, charged that federal protection of the Puget Sound tribe was hampering the westward movement. Referring to the residents of Tacoma, he cried, "Here are 40,000 Anglo-Saxons, flesh of your flesh and bone of your bone, your kin and kindred who are seeking to . . . develop their interests and increase their commerce upon the public highways." John B. Allen, the state's senior senator, described the trust patents as a "policy of paternalism" that had been "interposed" between two groups of citizens. In his view that paternalism was both illogical and unfair. "They are regarded as qualified to vote for President," Allen said of the Indians, "but not competent to manage their personal affairs."[2]

Western politicians responded to this appeal. "There is no greater friend of the Indian," Charles Manderson of Nebraska assured his Senate colleagues, "no man who desires his advancement more than the white man who lives by his side." Manderson (who was born in Philadelphia) argued that people like himself had seen the Indians and knew them "for what they [were] worth." And he resented the Indian Office when it ignored white men while aiding their Indian neighbors. "The contrast . . . between the Indian . . . pampered and . . . sustained," he noted, "and the white man who on the very next farm struggles for life is most marked and most significant, and we of the West are growing most tired of it."[3]

Volatile political issues ran just beneath the surface of Manderson's argument. In his speech supporting the Puyallup bill, Nebraska's senator was reminding his colleagues that the Indian Office was tampering with relations between white men and their nonwhite neighbors. Congress had only recently exorcised the spirit of reconstruction, and there was little interest among lawmakers in reviving what they believed were the demons of that era. Republican proposals to aid southern schools and supervise the conduct of federal elections had gone down to defeat and the gop was now eager to cut its losses. If the South knew the Negro best, westerners argued, was it not appropriate that they be granted a similar free hand with the Indians?

Westerners also appropriated the language of assimilation for use in their cause. The Indian Office was breaking up reservations, extending the protection of citizenship, and crowing over the success of its education programs. If Native Americans were truly ready for civilization, why hold their land under federal supervision? If some assimilation was good, was not more better? Oregon's Joseph Dolph pointed out to the Senate that the trust patent could not continue indefinitely. "The sooner the Indians are absorbed in the body politic the better," he exclaimed; "we shall never be able to solve the Indian problem until that is done." Under these attacks the burden of proof began to shift from the opponents to the defenders of federal supervision. Increasingly, advocates of federal protection would be required to defend themselves before a skeptical public.[4]

Congressmen who opposed opening the Puyallup lands insisted that canceling trust patents would produce a riot of speculation and fraud. "Not only would it result in [the Indians'] financial ruin," wrote Indian Commissioner Browning, but it would "tend to their moral destruction." Unfortunately, however, the commissioner's predictions (which turned out to be accurate) had broad—and disturbing—implications. The tribe's "financial ruin" would occur either because the businessmen of Tacoma were grafters and cheats, or because the native landowners were incapable of handling their own affairs. The first explanation insulted the integrity of the Washington delegation and—by extension—the honor of the seven western states that had joined in the fight. To make such an argument was politically disastrous. The alternative challenged the assumptions on which all Indian assimilation programs were based. To adopt it would be self-defeating. Thus the defenders of federal protection over Indian lands found themselves in a box of their own making. Once they supported allotment and assimilation, they could not step in to protect the tribe without provoking cries of federal "tyranny" a slogan the reformers themselves had used when working to overthrow the reservation system a generation earlier.[5]

The Puyallups' defenders were largely holdovers from the reform era of the 1880s. Older senators like John M. Palmer, the Illinois "gold bug," and Arkansas' James K. Jones insisted that the government should honor its obligations to the tribe. They were joined by Henry Dawes (who retired from the Senate in 1893) and Herbert Welsh, the tireless founder of the Indian Rights Association, who told the association that the government should reject "any sudden or arbitrary act" that would upset the "gradual operation" of the allotment law. Together these men were able to hold off the westerners for a time. The Puyallups did not begin to lose their allotments until the late 1890s; attacks on other tribes would come later.[6]

The Puyallup case prefigured the debates over Indian land that were to occur during the next two decades. Western politicians, increasingly restive over federal restrictions on the taxation and sale of allotments, would call for the termination of the Indian Office's protective role and the abolition of old treaties. Defenders of government protection would find it difficult to answer the assertion that they were "coddling" the tribes and blocking the region's economic growth. In the end, officials charged with implementing assimilation programs would find themselves on the defensive, confronted with a growing demand that they limit their activities.

The land policy that emerged from both the Puyallup debate and the dozens of controversies that followed was never summarized in a single statement or law, but its shape could be discerned in administrative decisions and programs for the development and administration of tribal lands. The policy's central theme was consistent and unmistakable: federal authorities no longer had an obligation to encourage Indians to control their property. Surrounded by prosperous white neighbors and hampered by their backwardness, Native Americans would be better off taking economic directions from others. The consequence of this shift in policy was a gradual redefinition of the broader goals of the Indian Office. Total assimilation—the incorporation of independent Indian landowners into American society on an equal footing with their fellow citizens—appeared to be an illusory objective. Instead, partial assimilation—bringing Native Americans into limited contact with the majority society while dropping the goal of equality—seemed a more reasonable alternative. As pressure on tribal holdings mounted and the political costs of continuing the old campaign became more evident, political leaders fashioned a new policy toward Indian lands and launched a new phase in the assimilation effort.

William Jones, who became commissioner of Indian affairs in 1897, was hardly one to make dramatic departures in policy. A willing, round-shouldered cog in William McKinley's political machine, Jones had no qualifications for the office other than his loyalty to the gop. During his eight years in Washington, the former mayor of Mineral Point, Wisconsin, tried to remain a man without enemies. He was equally cordial to western politicians, eastern reformers, powerful railroad executives, and eager white farmers. He had little contact with the Indians, but that was to be expected, for Jones believed his principal duty was to manage the political forces acting on him and to implement the policies he inherited from his predecessors.

There is no better measure of Commissioner Jones's passivity than his approach to the Indian lands. Between 1897 and 1905 he responded to the growing demand for white access to native property by supporting an acceleration in the pace of allotment and working to open the tribal domain through land cessions and changes in Indian Office procedures. By the end of his tenure, hundreds of thousands of acres had passed out of native control. And, perhaps more important, the commissioner's amiable attitude had inspired a new approach to the allotment process. Policy makers no longer talked of a gradual implementation of the severalty law or the civilizing influence of individual landownership. Government assistance and sympathy passed from Native Americans to the white men who "knew them best."

Although poorly administered and ultimately disastrous, the first division of land in severalty at locations such as the Omaha and Winnebago agency in Nebraska and reservations in Wisconsin and Minnesota were at least defensible in terms of allotment's goals. They involved relatively small agricultural areas and affected tribes with long histories of interaction with whites. During the 1890s, however, larger, more isolated preserves became the focus of attention, and westerners began to press the Indian Office to speed up the rate at which these areas were surveyed and divided. The first important departure from the cautious approach to allotment came in Indian Territory. There thousands of settlers gathered on the unassigned lands of Oklahoma—the western portion of the territory—while equally large groups of squatters camped out on unused portions of the area inhabited by the Five Civilized Tribes. Together these "boomers," and the businessmen who supported them, demanded that Washington open the land to white settlement. Although land cessions involving the unoccupied tracts were approved in 1889, 1890, and 1891, it was not until 1891 that the government used the Dawes Act to dispossess a tribe in the territory. For two years, five special agents moved methodically down the roll of the 3,294 people at the Cheyenne and Arapaho agency assigning each of them a piece of western Oklahoma. At noon on April 19, 1892, the signal was given and more than twenty-five thousand new "neighbors" stampeded onto the surplus lands of the old preserve.

When it occurred, the Cheyenne and Arapaho allotment was an anomaly. It involved more than twice as many Indians as had been assigned homesteads at any other agency and it was the first application of the law to a major plains tribe. It also prompted criticism from people who normally supported Henry Dawes's law. General Hugh Scott, the reform-minded commander of Fort Sill, held that the tribe was "degraded" by its contact with the greedy whites who kept arriving from the East. And Dawes himself told a meeting at

Lake Mohonk in 1895 that the government was abandoning its responsibilities at the Cheyenne and Arapaho agency. Allotment, he warned, had "fallen among thieves."[7]

Commissioner Jones shared none of these anxieties. His first year in office coincided with the final push to dissolve the tribal governments in Indian Territory. Congress approved the Curtis Act in June 1898. This new law established a timetable for the eventual allotment of all the Indians in what later became Oklahoma. Many of those who supported the measure worried about its impact, but Jones was not one to equivocate under such circumstances. He welcomed the new law, calling it "the most important piece of legislation . . . that [had] been passed by Congress relative to Indian affairs since the passage of the [Dawes] Act."[8]

The commissioner also demonstrated his indifference to an acceleration of the allotment process during the controversy over the Kiowa and Comanche reservation. That dispute began with the Jerome Agreement, a fraudulent land cession rejected by the Indians in 1892 but approved by Congress in 1900. Samuel Brosius, the Indian Rights Association's Washington lobbyist, described the pact as a "monstrous measure," a "steal and great wrong to the Kiowas." But the Interior Department—acting on the instructions of Congress—began to prepare for the opening of the reservation.[9] Unable to persuade the government to reconsider, the Kiowa's principal chief brought suit in federal court. Lone Wolf asked for an injunction to halt the implementation of the Jerome Agreement. The case moved quickly to the Supreme Court for a decision.

The issue in *Lone Wolf* v. *Hitchcock* was plain: could Congress ignore the provisions of the Treaty of Medicine Lodge Creek (ratified in 1868), which stipulated that all land cessions must be approved by the tribe? George Kennan, a muckraking critic of the Indian Office, warned that a decision in favor of the government would "mark the beginning of a new departure in [U.S.] Indian policy. There [would] be no legal bar to the removal of all the American Indians from their reservations and the banishment of every man, woman and child of them to Alaska or Porto Rico." A defeat for the Kiowas would strike at one of the fundamental assumptions underlying the Dawes Act—that tribal land was the Indian's private property.[10]

The court's unanimous opinion left little doubt as to the extent of Congress' legal prerogatives. "Plenary authority over the tribal relations of the Indians has been exercised by Congress from the beginning," the justices explained, "and the power has always been deemed a political one, not subject to be controlled by the judicial department of the government." After stating the issue in these terms, the Court moved quickly to a decision: "The power exists to abrogate the provisions of an Indian treaty." The outcome should not have been a surprise; after all, the Cherokee removal crisis in the 1830s had established the supremacy of the U.S. government. But the Supreme Court in *Lone Wolf* went much farther than had John Marshall in its defense of congressional power. The modern view of Indian-white relations stressed the legislature's "plenary" power rather than its responsibilities as a guardian or trustee. The safeguards Henry Dawes had inserted into his law—presidential discretion over initiating allotment and the requirement that tribes consent to the sale of their surplus lands—could now be ignored. "The Supreme Court has virtually given Congress full power to take Indian lands without the Indians' consent," George Kennan explained. And he predicted, "Attempts will undoubtedly be made in all parts of the West to get possession of desirable Indian reservations."[11]

William Jones knew better than to buck the tide. "The decision in the *Lone Wolf* case," he told the House Indian Affairs Committee, "will enable you to dispose of [Indian] land without the consent of the Indians. If you wait for their consent in these matters, it will be fifty years before you can do away with the reservations." Henceforth the Indian Office would offer little support for a gradualist interpretation of allotment. To make his position plain, the commissioner employed a revealing analogy: "Supposing you were the guardian or ward of a child 8 or 10 years of age, would you ask the consent of a child as to the investment of its funds? No; you would not." If Indians were children, then there was no need to use caution in the implementation of the Dawes Act or to expect rapid progress among the tribes. There was no reason to put off the task of dividing the reservations into homesteads and opening the "surplus" to white settlement.[12]

In the years ahead, pressure from western politicians, the dissolution of Indian Territory and the devastating consequences of the *Lone Wolf* decision altered the context in which allotment occurred. Land cessions and severalty programs were no longer based on the assumption of native ownership or the goal of quick and total assimilation. Since Congress could now initiate the breakup of a reservation, Washington decision makers would no longer be insulated in their responsibilities as guardians by layers of bureaucracy. The Indians' neighbors would be heard clearly and federal authorities would be unable to ignore their call.

Congress was ready to exercise its new power. As early as 1896 the legislature had expressed its impatience with the Indian Office by adopting a resolution directing a commission to negotiate land cessions with the Crow, Flathead, Northern Cheyenne, Fort Hall, Uintah, and Yakima Indians. But these early efforts were largely stymied by the intransigence of the tribes. The Crow Indians, for example, agreed to sell 1.5 million acres of surplus land, but demanded one dollar per acre in payment. Previous treaties required the tribe's consent in order for the land transfer to be valid. The high fee and the natives' unanimous resistance infuriated the lawmakers. "How," sputtered one apoplectic Congressman, "can [the Indian] have more than a possession of title simply by making moccasin tracks over it with his bow and arrow?" The Crows refused to budge, and the agreement lay unratified until after the Supreme Court's decision.[13]

The first victims of *Lone Wolf* were the Rosebud Sioux, who, like the Crow, had insisted on a fair market price for their land. The tribe signed an agreement to sell four hundred thousand acres for $2.50 an acre in 1901, but Congress balked at their demands. The changing times were typified by Connecticut's aging Senator Orville Platt, who now took the floor to attack the practices he and Henry Dawes had defended twenty years earlier. Like distorted echoes, his old arguments floated into the twentieth century in an inverted form. "I think that when we make an Indian tribe rich," Platt exclaimed, "we delay its civilization." He argued that "the easiest Indians in the country to civilize" were those who had "no money, no funds, no land, no annuities." The seventy-five-year-old lawmaker went on to suggest that Congress should "improve" the Rosebud bill by simply opening the four hundred thousand acres to white settlers and passing their land payments on to the Indians. The Great White Father would become a real estate agent, acting as the tribe's bursar rather than its benefactor. Platt's amendment violated the original agreement, but it was not forgotten, and in February 1904—after the Supreme Court had affirmed the legislature's "plenary power"—his proposal was dusted off and enacted into law.[14]

The 1904 Rosebud Act's proclamation that "the United States shall in no manner be bound to purchase any portion of the land" won the support of Commissioner Jones, despite opposition from the Indians and Herbert Welsh's charge that the law was "the first attempt under the Lone Wolf decision to steal Indian lands." The logjam was now shattered. Within weeks the stalled Crow agreement came to the floor of the House shorn of its purchase provisions and containing new language lifted directly from the Rosebud bill. Again, William Jones blessed the scheme. "It will be noted, he wrote, "that the bill makes no provision for the consent of the Indians." The omission, he added, should not worry the Crow people: "Believing that the bill . . . will fully safeguard and protect the interests of the Indians, it is not believed that such consent will be necessary or need be obtained." A few days after the Crow bill won approval, a similar measure affecting the Devil's Lake Reservation passed the House without debate. In April, Congress opened the Flathead reservation, and in the following session two other land measures were approved.[15]

In the fall of 1905 four large reservations—Uintah, Crow, Flathead and Wind River—were opened to white settlement. Just as Henry Dawes had envisioned, lands were allotted to their Indian occupants while surplus tracts were made available to outsiders. But the methods used to effect these openings revealed that the process at work was not the senator's original scheme. The Rosebud bill had established a new pattern for allotment and staked out a new approach to Indian land policy. The initiative for dividing each reservation into homesteads had come from Congress and had not been delayed by negotiations. The Indian Office did not purchase the unallotted land; it invited whites to come in and promised to pass their payments on to the tribes. Lawmakers now were concerned principally with western development. Typically, Wyoming's congressman, Frank Mondell, told the House that the opening of Wind River was vital to his state's economic future. Passage of the bill, he testified, meant "the development of [his] State . . . its defeat means that a large portion of [the] state [would] for years remain undeveloped."[16]

Commissioner Jones obligingly swung into line: "The pressure for land must diminish the reservations to areas within which [the Indian] can utilize the acres allotted to him, so that the balance may become homes for white farmers who require them." There was no longer the annoying insistence that the government prepare the tribes for landownership. Officials still spoke of assimilation, but the shifts in policy suggested that the term was taking on new meaning.[17]

The Indian Office also adapted to the rising influence of western politicians by adopting new rules for leasing and selling native-owned property. Leasing had begun early in the nineteenth century. Tribes granted rights of way to travelers and railroads and rented pastures to cattlemen and sheepherders. But the early twentieth century brought new customers to the Indians: farmers eager to cultivate and "improve" the land.

The original Dawes Act prohibited the leasing of allotments, and despite a later modification of this restriction few homesteads were rented before 1895. But by the end of the decade the demand for farms—and the willingness of many Indians—began to overcome government resistance. Agents encouraged this process, pointing out that rentals provided their charges with capital for equipment and seed and suggesting that industrious neighbors stimulated Indian advancement. The superintendent of the Sac and Fox agency spoke for a number of his colleagues when he wrote, "Direct contact between these lessees and the Indians will, I am confident, cause the latter to become more industrious and economical, as well as to elevate their moral and social status."[18]

But leasing subverted the original purpose of allotment. Native American landlords had no reason to farm or become self-sufficient. They remained aloof from the non-Indian communities that sprung up around them, and they had few reasons to change their traditional lifeways. "Not one acre of allotted agricultural land should be leased," wrote one agent in 1898. He added that "it would be far better to burn the grass on the allotted lands than to lease them for pastures to the white man." The Indian Rights Association agreed, pointing out that rental agreements often encouraged bribery and corruption.[19]

The ever cooperative commissioner Jones resolved these conflicting points of view by establishing a new procedure that, typically, bowed in both directions at once. In July 1900, he announced that all future leases running for more than a year had to involve payment in the form of permanent improvements to the property. Two years later he added a provision that able-bodied Indians be required to retain forty acres of their allotment for family gardens. In practice, these new regulations facilitated a dramatic increase in the number of allotments that were worked by whites. A succession of renewable one-year leases made it possible for farmers to avoid the first rule, while the second freed unwilling Indians from the necessity of cultivating their land. All they were required to do was keep forty acres for themselves. And the Indian Office's easygoing enforcement of these procedures made it clear that while the form of the original allotment scheme might be retained, its content was changing. "The results," the Indian Rights Association announced, "are disastrous."[20]

The sale of Indian allotments also grew more frequent during the Jones era as both Congress and the commissioner wrote new rules concerning the disposition of property assigned to deceased allottees. Previously, if the fee patent had been issued, the land was automatically disposed of through a will or probate proceeding. But most allottees still held their lands in trust; their wills had no legal force, and according to the Dawes Act the Indian Office had the task of distributing their holdings among the heirs. The result was a massive backlog of intricate heirship cases and subsequent division of land into tiny uneconomical units. With the commissioner's support, Congress attempted to simplify the process in 1902 by allowing inherited lands to be sold. Jones assured the public that "every practicable safeguard" had been included in the new law, but, as had happened in other areas of land administration, he was swept away by the forces of progress. Ownership of these holdings swiftly passed to non-Indians because allottees were still prohibited from including trust lands in their wills and the Indian Office required that all lands be sold for cash at public auction. No assistance was offered to family members wishing to buy a relative's farm. In effect, an allottee's heirs could do anything with their inherited property as long as they sold it—for cash. A letter from Jones's successor to President Roosevelt makes the impact of these new regulations clear. "Under the present system," Francis Leupp reported, "every Indian's land comes into the market at his death, so that it will be but a few years at most before all the Indians' land will have passed into the possession of the settlers."[21]

The 775,000 acres of inherited land sold between 1902 and 1910 represent only a fraction of the total territory lost during those years. But the figure is significant, both because it represents the loss of land specifically allocated to individual Indians and because it reflects the Indian Office's shifting attitude toward allotment and assimilation. Policymakers no longer considered the Indian homestead a vital element in Native American advancement.

A generation earlier, politicians had agreed that assimilation was a natural process. For example, reformers like Henry Dawes fought bitterly with Alabama's Senator John Tyler Morgan over civil rights and the tariff, but Dawes agreed with the white-maned southerner that the government should "draw [the Indians] through their affections, their instincts, and their tastes up to our civilization, and get them to dissolve their relations with the tribe." From this perspective, there was ample time for the tribes to find their way to civilization. Even William Holman, a Democratic congressman from Indiana who was a regular and fierce opponent of the Indian Office's ever mounting budget, called for a "liberal policy" of patience and federal support. "For myself," he wrote in 1894, "I am not anxious for the present that these Indian lands shall be opened to white settlement. I am not willing that the interests of the Indians shall be impaired by the efforts of the white men to get their lands."[22]

While he never repudiated the reformers who preceded him, William Jones clearly followed other voices and responded to different interests. In addition to western politicians, there were impatient young easterners like Henry Cabot Lodge, who wanted to "get away from this business of reservations," and advocates of American

imperialism, who rejected the idea of rapid assimilation. These critics called for a more authoritarian approach to Indian uplift. "Freedom and liberty in every land and in every age has been established
and maintained by spear, sword and bayonet," Congressman Joseph
Sibley asserted during one debate on Indian policy; there was little
reason to delay allotment or to complicate the government's efforts
by consulting the Indians. "We go forth with the plowshare and the
pruning hook; with the Bible and the spelling book," the Pennsylvania Republican continued, "not to stifle liberty but to give nobler
ideas of liberty; not to forge fetters, but to break them."[23]

Jones's willingness to reduce the government's protective role reflected a more pessimistic view of Indian abilities. He wrote in 1903
that Native Americans had two choices. Either they could remain
a "study for the ethnologist, a toy for the tourist, a vagrant at the
mercy of the State and a continual pensioner upon the bounty of
the people," or they could place themselves under the control of the
Indian Office and be "educated to work, live and act as reputable,
moral citizens." The commissioner did not believe that progress was
inevitable or that it came from gentle prodding or the passage of time.
Force and necessity would cause Native Americans to change their
ways; federal largesse would not.[24]

When William Jones left office in 1905 it appeared on the surface
that he had carried out the land policies established in the 1880s.
Allotment continued, and officials repeated their support for assimilation. But the Indian Office had initiated new approaches to both
severalty and assimilation. Congress now played a major role in the
decision to allot reservations and open them to white settlement. Indians lost control over tribal lands as well as individual allotments.
And policymakers increasingly viewed Native Americans as people
whose progress did not require federal protection. The official view
of native property was passing from the idea that it was a birthright
to the notion that it represented a part of the public domain. As
such, Indian lands should foster regional economic growth rather
than serve the narrow needs of their "backward" inhabitants.

In many respects Francis Leupp was an unusual candidate for the
office of Indian commissioner. He had no experience in government

or national politics and was a model of progressive rectitude. The product of an old New York family schooled in public piety by Mark Hopkins at Williams College, Leupp had devoted most of his life to gentlemanly reform. He was a journalist by profession, trained as an editorial assistant by William Cullen Bryant on the *New York Evening Post* and seasoned as the publisher of his own newspaper in Syracuse. Leupp soon tired of management, however, and drifted to Washington, where in 1889 he became the *Post's* bureau chief. The stately pace of government in the nineteenth century left the future Indian commissioner ample time to pursue other interests. He joined the National Civil Service Reform League and before long became editor of the group's newsletter. Friendship with the organization's chief political backer—Theodore Roosevelt—quickly ensued.

Roosevelt and Leupp shared a number of interests besides civil service reform. They came from similar backgrounds, had traveled extensively in the West, and were careful observers of the Indian policy debates that were going on around them. The two men endorsed the government's new assimilation campaign and supported Herbert Welsh's Indian Rights Association. In 1895, when Welsh (who was also active in the Civil Service Reform League) was looking for a new Washington lobbyist for his association, Roosevelt recommended Leupp as the "very man for the job." Alice Fletcher also endorsed the hiring of Leupp.[25]

Leupp proved an enthusiastic employee. Believing that "the Indian question seems to be the most important with which the government is faced from a humanitarian point of view," he spent his three-year term hounding administrators who ignored the civil service rules, appearing at hearings on appropriations, and investigating charges of corruption and mismanagement. In the process Leupp became an expert, called on to carry out special missions for the Indian Office, and in 1896 he was appointed by President Grover Cleveland to the Board of Indian Commissioners. When, a few weeks after the 1904 election, Roosevelt appointed his fellow New Yorker to succeed William Jones, it seemed that the government was about to replace an aging hack with a modern, disinterested administrator. As one reform journal put it, "Mr. Leupp is the first Commissioner of Indian affairs, we believe, since Grant made his first appointment, who was chosen because he was an expert on the subject."[26]

Jones had been a cipher, buffeted by economic and political pressure groups. Leupp anticipated those groups by downplaying the old assimilation agenda and endorsing bold new government policies. Under Jones the Indian Office had been reactive, responding to the demands of western settlers and businessmen. Under Leupp the government became more aggressive. "The commonest mistake made . . . in dealing with the Indian" he wrote in his first *Annual Report,* "is the assumption that he is simply a white man with a red skin." The commissioner went on to argue that it was foolish to expect too much of Native Americans; landownership and citizenship would not produce equality and racial integration. The assimilation program should be less ambitious; it should have "improvement, not transformation" as its goal. According to Leupp, the Indian was a burden the government should bear gracefully; there were no easy solutions to the problem of native backwardness and there should be no expectation of rapid native progress. "The duty of our civilization," he believed, "is not forcibly to uproot his strong traits as an Indian, but to induce him to modify them."[27]

In the 1880s, the Indians' alleged handicaps were used to defend the reservation system. Carl Schurz had argued that Standing Bear and others like him should remain under federal protection because they could not survive on their own. Leupp held a similar view of the Native Americans' capacity for "civilization," but he argued that there was no alternative to severing the government's ties to the Indians. "The question whether to begin setting the Indian free is no longer before us," he wrote in 1899; "that process is now underway." The commissioner added that rapid allotment might even prove a positive benefit. "When the last acre and last dollar are gone," he wrote, "the Indians will be where the Negro freedmen started thirty-five years ago." Unable to progress with government protection, the Indians would be better off on their own.[28]

Leupp's "expert" administration produced land policies to match his "realistic" assessment of the Indians' future. He applauded Congress' growing power over allotment and land openings. Political pressure to dissolve reservations meant farmers were eager to live among the Indians. And, as he wrote about the opening of the Rosebud Reservation, white neighbors were an important source of native progress. They were, he told the Indian Rights Association, "of vastly more real value to the Sioux in their present stage of development than would be all the wealth of the Orient poured into the tribal treasury." To promote the interaction of settlers and allottees, Leupp also called for a reduction of federal protection for Indian homesteads. For those lands that were not allotted or that belonged to people who could not develop them, Leupp proposed an active program of federal management to improve their productivity and tie them more closely to the American economy.[29]

Like his predecessor, Leupp advocated transferring control of native lands from Indians to whites. But unlike William Jones, Leupp articulated a policy that reconciled the goal of assimilation with the Native Americans' dwindling power over their own resources. For him the key to this reconciliation lay in the Indians' backwardness. Since he believed the Indians' racial traits could not be overcome, he proposed that natives accept the control of outsiders in the name of progress. For some that control would come from the local whites who purchased their allotments and directed the local economy. For others it would appear through federal management of their lands. In any event, non-Indians would provide both long-term guidance and a model to emulate. Leupp recast the meaning of assimilation to allow for the expansion of white control over Indian resources. "I have kept steadily in view," the commissioner wrote on leaving office in 1909, "the necessity for turning the Indian into a citizen . . . realizing the importance of his conforming in his own mode of life generally with the mode of life of his fellow countrymen of other races, but never forcing him into such conformity in advance of his natural movement in that direction."[30]

The pace of allotment, which had accelerated after the *Lone Wolf* decision, continued at a rapid rate under Leupp. Major land cessions, such as the May 1908 opening of 2.9 million acres of the Standing Rock and Cheyenne River reservations, now followed a routine. They were proposed by western politicians, approved by a voice vote in Congress, and greeted with cheers from local settlers and

businessmen. "The best that friends of the Indian often hope to secure," an Indian Rights Association official wrote in 1907, "is an adequate price for the lands to be sold." Old hopes of gradual allotment
were overwhelmed by new political alignments and the increasingly
popular notion that Indians would be better off if made to fend for
themselves.[31]

Nevertheless, debate over allotment had not ended. In fact during
the Roosevelt administration policy makers continued to argue over
federal protection. But the focus of their attention was now allotments rather than reservations. How long, they asked, should the
government continue as the guardian of individual landholdings?
The Indian Rights Association declared in 1905 that the "Indian
homestead . . . [was] the one asset that should be most scrupulously
guarded," but this position had a familiar weakness. If the Indian
was to be assimilated, why should he be coddled and protected on
his homestead? And if it was good that Native Americans were on
their own, why limit their freedom by guarding their land? Fayette
McKenzie, the young sociologist who helped organize the Society of
American Indians, put the argument simply. "The Indian who can
speak English and who has been educated by the government should
be free to sell his lands and to sink to the bottom."[32]

Leupp agreed with McKenzie's opinion. Insulating the Indians
from their white neighbors would only retard the economic development of the West and deprive Native Americans of the opportunity
to rub shoulders with a superior race. "Whatever upbuilds the country in which the Indian lives," Leupp asserted, "upbuilds the Indian
with the rest." With these ideas in mind, the commissioner set out to
eliminate the twenty-five-year trust period stipulated by the Dawes
Act. He succeeded in May 1906, when Congress approved the Burke
Act, which amended the allotment law by giving the secretary of the
interior the power to issue fee-simple titles to any allottee "competent and capable of managing his or her affairs." A fee-simple title
meant that "all restrictions as to sale, incumbrance, or taxation of
said land [would] be removed."[33]

In a letter of protest against the new measure the Indian Rights
Association's Washington lobbyist charged that it was unconstitu-
tional because it changed an agreement "without the consent of both

parties to the contract." The protest had no effect. The *Lone Wolf* decision recognized the legislature's plenary power over native lands, and the lawmakers themselves, of course, welcomed the statute. The Senate committee reporting the bill noted that ending the trust period by executive order would place control over allotments in the hands of "the Secretary of the Interior and the Indian Department who [knew] best when an Indian [had] reached such a stage of civilization as to be able and capable of managing his own affairs." The commissioner agreed. "Through such measures," he wrote, "the grand total of the nation's wards will be diminished and at a growing ratio."[34]

During the remainder of his term, Leupp devoted considerable energy to extending the principles of the Burke Act. The law exempted allotments in Indian Territory from its provisions, but the commissioner insisted that restrictions be lifted there as well. Referring to the territory's Indians, he wrote, "Not until the surplus spaces in their country are settled by a thrifty, energetic, law respecting white population, can the red possessors of the soil hope to make any genuine advancement."[35]

In 1907 Congress gave Leupp the power to sell allotments belonging to "noncompetents." Although the language of the new statute implied that it would affect only those with specific disabilities, the commissioner urged that it be interpreted liberally. In a circular sent to all agents, he wrote that it should apply to "special cases where it [was] shown that Indians [were] unable to properly develop their allotments." Such cases would include those who, "through their own mental incompetency and ignorance," chose poor homesteads and were therefore rendered "noncompetent." Such sophistry had a single purpose: the rapid sale of as many homesteads as possible.[36]

Although Leupp's campaign to eliminate trust patents was generally successful, the depth of his commitment to ending federal guardianship was most evident in a proposal that failed to win congressional approval. In 1908 he and Secretary of the Interior James Garfield suggested that fee-simple titles be issued to any Indian "who, after [a] warning in writing by the Commissioner of Indian Affairs . . . persist[ed] in disobedience to the laws of the State in which he reside[d] or of the United States." Landownership, once the goal of the assimilation program, was now to be a punishment. Clearly, Leupp had little expectation that Indian landowners would be the equal of their white neighbors. Their property was no longer a mark of their progress—the endpoint of the civilization program—it had become the ante in an economic contest Native Americans were sure to lose. The Indian Rights Association declared that Leupp's proposal would "reverse the humane policy of a quarter of a century of protecting the allottee in his weakness," but the commissioner was unmoved. He insisted that the efforts of his administration were "directed toward the emancipation of the red man from the shackles fastened upon him by the artificial and misdirected paternalism of our Government." The cries that Tacoma's greedy representatives once had raised against the Puyallups now were being mouthed by the commissioner of Indian affairs.[37]

The proposal to punish disobedient allottees with fee patents died in committee. Leupp's arguments were so crude that the tragic impact of his proposals could not be ignored. Nevertheless, his suggestion was a mark of how far the Indian Office had come from Commissioner John Atkins's statement that "too great haste" in the administration of the Dawes Act "should be avoided." Leupp viewed gradualism and the protection of native control over their own lands as "misdirected paternalism" that would undermine economic growth and hamper Indian "improvement." He not only supported the shift in control over Indian resources that had begun under William Jones, he trumpeted the departure as an innovative contribution to the assimilation campaign.

The philosophy behind Leupp's attacks on the trust patent also was evident in his administration of the tribal lands that remained under federal control. The commissioner facilitated the leasing of these holdings to non-Indian farmers and developed reservations by including them in federal conservation and irrigation projects. His efforts lowered the barriers surrounding Indian property and encouraged the Native American's metamorphosis from rising citizen to dependent subject.

Leupp believed that "all primitive peoples [were], from [the United States'] economic point of view, grossly wasteful of their natural resources." Leasing would provide a remedy for this malady by turning the Indians' lands over to efficient white businessmen. The lessees would use native lands wisely and provide the Indian landlords with an object lesson in civilized behavior. There was no limit to the commissioner's vision. He supported a mineral leasing bill that would allow prospecting on previously closed tribal lands, agreeing with the secretary of the interior that "lands lying dormant" should be opened "on such terms as [would] promote their development." He suggested that the Choctaws develop their large coal holdings by forming a mining corporation. The tribal stockholders could hire white experts to operate the mines and eventually—when their trust protections were lifted—they could sell their shares in the company to non-Indian investors. And Leupp encouraged white businessmen to contract for the "harvesting" of tribal timber.[38]

The commissioner's most successful scheme involved American sugar-beet companies who received long-term leases to tribal lands in exchange for a pledge to employ Indian laborers. Leupp was convinced that field work was the best thing for the Native American. "Our first duty to the Indian is to teach him to work," he wrote in 1906. "In this process the sensible course is to tempt him to the pursuit of a gainful occupation by choosing for him at the outset the sort of work which he finds pleasantest; and the Indian takes to beet farming as naturally as the Italian takes to art or the German to science. . . . Even the little papoose can be taught to weed the rows just as the pickaninny in the South can be used as a cotton picker." Thinning and weeding sugar beets would do more for the nation's wards, he concluded, than "all the governmental supervision and all the schools, and all the philanthropic activities set afoot in his behalf by benevolent whites, if rolled into one and continued for a century." A leasing project was desirable, therefore, because it demanded simple tasks and placed the Indians under the supervision of their white neighbors. By laboring in the fields, Indians would contribute to the economic development of the West while acquiring the habit of working.[39]

In 1908 Congress authorized Leupp to negotiate long-term leases for the Fort Belknap, Uintah, and Wind River reservations. These agreements were to run for up to twenty years and, it was hoped, would provide the incentive for large companies to enter the sugar-beet business. Although these early leases were successful, they did not attract sufficient corporate interest to launch a widespread movement. His proposals for bringing the gospel of conservation to the reservation had a more lasting effect.[40]

Conservationists in the progressive era were as concerned with the efficient use of the wilderness as they were with its preservation. Irrigating arid western lands thus appealed both to reformers and to advocates of regional development. In the nineteenth century, irrigation had been pursued on an ad hoc basis, usually to carry out a pledge made in a treaty. Appropriations for irrigation did not become a regular part of the Indian Office budget until 1894, and did not exceed one hundred thousand dollars until 1901, when the Indian Office hired its first engineer. As the size of the government's programs grew, however, their focus shifted from agricultural reservations to areas that previously had been nonproductive. Water and careful planning, experts like Leupp believed, could spread prosperity into areas that had been beyond the reach of the United States' burgeoning industrial economy.

The Shoshone and Arapaho Indians at Wind River, Wyoming, were the first to experience this new, ambitious version of irrigation-based development. In March 1905, Congress approved the use of money derived from the sale of surplus lands for a system of ditches and canals that would irrigate forty-five thousand acres of the reservation. The lawmakers also stipulated that reservation residents should receive first priority in hiring for the construction crews. The tribe's agent declared the outlook for his charges was "brighter than at any time in their history" and promised that they would soon be able "without much trouble, to raise large crops of grain and hay and vegetables." The popular press looked forward to tangible results. *Outlook* magazine, often a critic of the Indian Office, was certain that the Wind River project would make the Indians "self-helpful and one of the world's workers." Disenchanted by airy promises of equality, policy makers seemed pleased with the practical notion of turning a bleak Wyoming reservation into productive farms.[41]

Apparent success at Wind River led Leupp to repeat the formula elsewhere. In June 1906, the newly opened Uintah reservation in eastern Utah became the site for a two-hundred-thousand-acre irrigation project. Leupp asked that Congress appropriate five hundred thousand dollars of the tribe's money for the project, arguing, "The future of these Indians depends upon a successful irrigation scheme, for without water their lands are valueless, and starvation or extermination will be their fate." Always generous with tribal funds, the lawmakers allocated six hundred thousand dollars. During the same session Congress authorized the Reclamation Service to include the Yakima agency in a large system being built on the Yakima River, and the following year three hundred thousand dollars from the Blackfoot treasury was earmarked for that tribe's reservation water system. In 1908 a similar project was launched for the Flatheads.[42]

Non-Indian enthusiasm for these new irrigation systems overrode all opposition. When the residents of Wind River protested the appropriation of their tribal funds without their consent the chairman of the House Indian Affairs Committee replied, "Under the *Lone Wolf* decision we have ample authority . . . to provide that this money expended for the Indians shall be reimbursed to the treasury. But the rationale for "reimbursing" the government for expenditures made on behalf of the tribe was more than legal. The chairman added, "[The government will] place the Indians in possession of lands now substantially worthless, but which will be worth a million and a quarter dollars." The desert would bloom, and who was to say that this achievement was less important than obedience to old treaties or adhering to the protests of a few "wasteful" Indians? The tribe was to be saved along with its arid homeland. That non-Indian farmers would also benefit was a welcome dividend.[43]

The irrigation projects subsidized the development of new agricultural land, but they also led directly to the leasing and sale of native property. Rather than make the tribes "self-helpful," these ambitious schemes led to greater outside control of Indian resources. The leading cause of Indian land loss in connection with irrigation was the legal doctrine of beneficial use. Early in the history of the West, state governments responded to the frequent inadequacy of the local water supply by dividing the resource among its citizens. Individual persons acquired rights to specific amounts of water, thus assuring themselves of a constant supply for their needs. States usually used the concepts of prior claim and beneficial use as the basis for making their awards. Early applicants took precedence over later ones, and landowners receiving a water right agreed to use the water—make beneficial use of it—within a specific time limit. Settlers could claim water for their homesteads, but they could be certain of maintaining that water only if they actually used it.

Every law providing for the irrigation of reservation lands stipulated that local regulations would govern the Indians' access to water. Beneficial use was sure to control water assignments on the new projects. Thus, reluctant allottees or those unable to farm could lose their water to their "energetic" white neighbors who would begin farming later than the Indians, but who would stand ready to make beneficial use of their water. In addition, all of the projects were constructed with appropriations from tribal accounts. When a group's treasury was inadequate, the Indian Office would advance the money in anticipation of a reimbursement. To ensure the repayment, it was essential that the surplus lands within them—the lands not assigned to allottees—be sold. When water rights were in danger, the value of those surplus lands was nil.

Local water laws forced the Indian Office to develop newly irrigated reservations as quickly as possible. But how was this to be done? The superintendent of the Uintah agency provided an answer in his annual report for 1906. "It will be necessary," he warned, "to make the most persistent efforts in causing all land to be cultivated." Where the Indians themselves would not farm, there was "but one course open, and that [was] to lease all surplus lands at a very reasonable figure." Leupp agreed, and ordered the agent "to make every possible effort to lease all allotted land which could be irrigated, whenever the allottees were making no use of it." He supplemented this order with a request to Congress that the Indian Office be empowered to grant long-term leases at both Wind River and Uintah. The lawmakers responded promptly: ten-year rentals were negotiated at Uintah, and twenty-year agreements were made at Wind River. Similar solutions to the water-rights issue were implemented at Yakima, Flathead, and Blackfoot agencies.[44]

In the years after Leupp left office, disputes over water rights continued to bedevil the irrigation effort. In 1908 the Supreme Court recognized the Indians' prior claim to water in its resolution of a dispute between the Indians at Fort Belknap and their white neighbors on the Milk River. *Winters* v. *U.S.* based its finding that reservations had inherent water rights on the supposition that Congress intended the Indians to farm their lands. "It would be extreme to believe," the justices wrote, "that within a year Congress destroyed the reservation and took from the Indians the consideration of their grant, leaving them a barren waste, took from them the means of continuing their old habits, yet did not leave them the power to change to new ones." Nevertheless, the decision spoke only of water necessary to "change old habits," and said nothing about allottees who refused or were unable to farm. The Court did not recognize a specific tribal share of the river. It also did not clarify the federal government's power over water on the opened portions of the reservations—the portions where sales to non-Indians presumably would subsidize the Indians' dams and ditches. Despite the Indians' victory in *Winters*, their claims to water for future needs and the value of their surplus lands remained in doubt. The Indian Office continued to lease irrigable land on the assumption that the tribes had to prove beneficial use quickly just as white settlers did. This assumption—which a federal court upheld in 1916—was the tool that undermined native control of the newly irrigated lands.[45]

Throughout the irrigation effort the Indian Office blurred the distinction between tribal land and the public domain. Both tribal and federal lands were opened to private development and managed for maximum return; in both, federal experts guided policy. The Roosevelt administration also demonstrated that it perceived the two areas as one when it turned the administration of forest lands on Indian reservations over to the Forest Service in January 1908. Secretary of the Interior James R. Garfield intended the transfer "to improve the forest and yield the full market value of timber cut" as well as to protect the resource for future development. This arrangement foreshadowed the termination movement of the 1950s, as experts in coordinate branches of the federal system were asked to combine Indian affairs with their other responsibilities. Such cooperation,

Commissioner Leupp reported, prevented "much duplication of work" and hastened "the day . . . when the [Indian] Office [might] be abolished as an anomaly which there [was] no longer any excuse for maintaining." The forestry plan succumbed to departmental rivalry after eighteen months, but its demise did not darken the popularity of bureaucratic cooperation. Secretary of the Interior Walter Fisher wrote Leupp's successor that he wanted "to simplify and strengthen in every way practicable the cooperative relations between various bureaus of the department, and also those with the bureaus of other departments doing closely allied work." Sentiments such as these marked a retreat from the old assumption that trust lands were protected vehicles for the Indians' "civilization." Instead, government officials were now suggesting that national goals—efficiency and economic development—should override the specific work of the Indian Office. Accelerated land sales, sophisticated forestry programs, and grand irrigation projects might benefit the Indians, but they also served a larger goal: the rapid development of the western states. In this context, Native Americans were no longer specially protected landowners who gave up part of their property in exchange for equal admission to the "white man's road." They were evolving into a dependent group that lived under the control of their powerful governors.[46]

In a number of areas, then, Leupp articulated the subtle shifts that had been taking place in Indian land policy during the previous decade. The commissioner welcomed reforms that reduced the Indians' role in decision making. Moreover, he advocated the efficient development of tribal lands, either by federal managers or the Indians' white neighbors. Certainly the goal of assimilation—that is, greater contact between the races—remained, but its content continued to change. The new land policies assumed that Indians were peripheral: they would be tolerated if they survived, but they would not be protected as private landowners. It was no longer expected that natives would rise quickly to the level of the white man or that they would be incorporated totally into the majority culture. Leupp imagined that Indians would be only partially assimilated and that they would remain on the fringes of American society—behind and below their enterprising new neighbors:

When only the Indians who are fit to farm and want to farm are farming, when the multitude who take naturally to the mechanic arts are launched in trades, when those whom nature has not bent in any particular direction have entered upon the first stage of normal human development as hewers of wood and drawers of water, and those who are too old or too weak to work are frankly fed, clothed, and sheltered at the public expense, we may look for a more rapid upward movement by the race as a whole than it has ever yet made.[47]

The reformers who gathered at Lake Mohonk in the fall of 1910 had been meeting annually for nearly thirty years. Activists from Henry Dawes to Alice Fletcher had used these occasions to fire their audiences and excoriate the foes of assimilation. But at the end of the first decade of the twentieth century Matthew Sniffen of the Indian Rights Association had a new message for the faithful: "The Indian problem has resolved itself into one of administration." Careful management had become the key to native progress. The years following Leupp's resignation from the commissionership in June 1909 demonstrated the broad appeal of Sniffen's assessment. Policy makers routinely rejected tribal protests when allotting new reservations or opening surplus lands to homesteading. Officials removed trust restrictions on Indian homesteads at a record rate and expanded the leasing program to include mineral rights, timber, and pastureland. Administrators now held Native American resources firmly in their grasp and acted in the interests of efficiency and regional progress. By 1920 this approach had completed the process by which the Indians' lands had devolved from protected property to areas resembling the Unites States' overseas colonies.[48]

Robert Valentine, Leupp's successor, whose officious punctilio ideally suited the executive style of the Taft regime, contributed substantially to the change in the status of Indian lands. He had little training in Indian affairs, but his Harvard education prepared him for public life, and his brief experience as a settlement worker in Greenwich Village convinced him that the Indian Office should be engaged in a "non-political work of social service." He came to the capital from his settlement work to serve as Leupp's personal secretary. In 1908, after three years at that post, he became assistant commissioner. He rose to the commissioner's job with Leupp's blessing soon after Taft's inauguration.

Valentine was a man of order. During his first year in office he reorganized his staff and created a "Methods Division" which was "charged with the betterment of all methods and organization of the Indian Service." The chief concern of this office was how to administer thousands of allotments and millions of acres of tribal land. The new commissioner agreed with Leupp's objectives—maximum use of native property, efficiency, and a minimum of Indian interference—but he wanted the government to adopt regular procedures and cut overhead costs. These efforts consolidated Leupp's many initiatives and fixed his attitudes in policy.

Despite the passage of the Burke Act in 1906, Valentine believed that too many Indians were hiding behind their trust patents. He argued that tribesmen often remained under federal protection so that they could avoid taxes and rent their lands to white farmers. To combat this tendency, he recommended new, more aggressive policies designed "to place each Indian upon a piece of land of his own where he [could] by his own efforts support himself and his family or to give him an equivalent opportunity in industry or trade, to lead him to conserve and utilize his property . . . rather than to have it as an unappreciated heritage."[49] James McLaughlin was an enthusiastic backer of Valentine's ideas. The agent who supervised the arrest of Sitting Bull (an event that set off a tragic chain reaction leading to the Wounded Knee massacre), McLaughlin was the Indian Office's most experienced field officer. Under Jones, Leupp, and Valentine he served as the government spokesman in major land cession negotiations and an inspector of reservations. In a memoir entitled *My Friend the Indian*, published during the second year of Valentine's term, McLaughlin wrote that the government could do the greatest amount of good by "giving to the Indian his portion and turning him adrift to work out his own salvation." In Congress, McLaughlin's position was endorsed by westerners like South Dakota's Charles Burke, who told his colleagues in the House that the Indian could not hope to progress "if the Government for all time keeps its hand on him and assures him that no matter what happens he will be taken care of." Like Senator Platt, who argued that wealth would delay the

Indians' civilization, these men urged Valentine to go ahead with his plans to "set the red man free."[50]

Within his first year in office, Valentine proposed legislation to systematize the issuance of fee patents. "The Indian problems must ultimately be solved by the Indians themselves and the white communities in which they live," the commissioner argued. Valentine's proposal provided for competency commissions to tour the agencies and issue fee patents to qualified allottees. Rather than wait for natives to apply for titles, the government would issue them on its own. The commissioner believed that tribesmen should sell all land they did not cultivate and receive their individual shares of the tribal treasury. His ideas were incorporated into the Omnibus Act, which was passed on the last day of the session, in June 1910.[51]

Beginning in the summer of 1910, competency commissions began making the rounds of the reservations. Many Indians were uncooperative, but the next two years brought over two hundred thousand acres of trust land onto local tax rolls. The commissioner reported that only 30 percent of those who received clear title to their allotments "failed to make good." But conflicts between Native Americans and their white neighbors persisted, and Indian land loss continued. In a letter to the secretary of the interior the superintendent of the Uintah agency explained why this was so: "Full satisfaction to the local people cannot be encompassed, and at the same time protect the interests of the Indians . . . the conflict with settlers [is] almost continuous, due to settlers endeavoring to obtain all sorts of rights over possessions of the Indians."[52]

The Omnibus Act also allowed for the "segregation" of tribal funds: "competent" Indians could receive their portion of the tribal treasury just as they received full title to their land. Like rapid fee patenting, the distribution of tribal funds had wide support among western politicians and bureaucrats like James McLaughlin. McLaughlin wrote that closing out the tribe's accounts would "relieve the government of the care of these funds and build up manhood and individual self-reliance, which [could] never be realized under the present doling out process." Even the reformer-sociologist Fayette McKenzie supported the idea, as did the Indian Rights Association, which announced in 1907 that tribal treasuries delayed the "proper development of the Indian character." The Indian Office was cautious, noting that the distribution of funds often led to "orgies of drink and disease", but it remained confident that dividing the Indians' money would "speed up their competency."[53]

Valentine's systematic approach created two categories of Indians—the competent and the incompetent. "Competent" Indians had received some education or had some experience with whites and therefore could be expected to survive on their own. It was not necessary for a competent Indian to be the equal of his white neighbor, but only to be "healthy" and a "good laborer or other workman." The incompetent were a "mere waste element," requiring constant supervision and support. Protection for the incompetent was justified by their backwardness. In the debate over the status of allotments in the new state of Oklahoma, for example, Senator Porter McCumber argued for a continuation of trust patents to protect individual landholdings. "Our error," he declared, "has been attempting to do something that was impossible in all our history, and that is to make a white man out of an Indian; to so educate him . . . that he could compete in the business or professional enterprises of the world with the white civilization." Because the Indians were not "progressive," he believed they required continued federal supervision. Pessimism and pity were now the principal rationales for federal protection.[54]

Guardianship was no longer intended for those "rising" to the level of the white man; it would be reserved for individual Indians incapable of progress. What had been a trend in the government's land policies was now a central concern. Federal trust protections would be extended to the worst cases; anyone demonstrating the ability to survive would be judged competent and set "free." Nineteenth-century reformers had viewed every Indian as potentially competent. Consequently, protection had been extended to the entire group and was to be withdrawn gradually as the group progressed. Now protection was reserved for the incompetent; the rest could survive on their own. "It may be that we are keeping the Indian in a fool's paradise," one reform journal explained, "as long as we treat him entirely differently from the way we treat any ignorant foreigner who comes to our shores."[55]

Valentine left office to stump for the Bull Moose cause in September 1912, leaving his organizational plans only partially fulfilled. It fell to his successor to define precisely the difference between competent and incompetent Indians. Woodrow Wilson's choice for the job, a Texas banker named Cato Sells, had little knowledge of the field, but he soon heard from those who were eager to instruct him. Sells joined an administration that had minimal interest in racial equality. Constrained by the powerful southern wing of his party and led by a president who traded deference to party bosses for legislative success, the new Democratic commissioner saw no reason to paddle against the political current. In the aftermath of Valentine's reforms, the direction of that current was clear: the new commissioner would be expected to speed up the competency hearings and reduce the level of federal protection over Indian lands.

At the outset of the Wilson administration, a number of lawmakers were calling for the abolition of the Indian Office. A bill introduced in 1912 by Oklahoma's Robert Owen directed the Interior Department to complete the allotment process and end all federal guardianship in ten years. Montana's Henry L. Meyers was typical of those who supported this sort of direct action. "The solution of the Indian problem," he once declared, "lies in throwing Indian reservations open to allotment and settlement." Uninterested even in the "incompetents," he called on the government to encourage white farmers to "mingle with the Indians and show them by example how to farm and conduct their affairs." Owen's bill failed, for his ideas constituted too radical a break with the past and were opposed by the Indian Office, but he succeeded the following year in gaining congressional approval for the Joint Commission to Investigate Indian Affairs. The commission received full subpoena power and a two-year budget of fifty thousand dollars. Senator Joe Robinson of Arkansas became the group's chairman. He was joined by fellow Democrat Harry Lane from Oregon and Michigan's Republican senator, Charles Townsend. The House also named two Democrats, John Stephens of Texas and Charles Carter of Oklahoma, and a Republican, South Dakota's Charles Burke, to serve on the committee.[56]

Franklin K. Lane, the California civic reformer whom Wilson had appointed secretary of the interior, welcomed the creation of the

Joint Commission. In a letter to one of the western congressmen who had advocated it, Lane even suggested that the Indian Office could be dispensed with entirely. "The Indian Bureau should be a vanishing Bureau," he wrote, adding, "Tens of thousands of so-called Indians . . . are as competent to attend to their affairs as any man or woman of the white race," and thousands more "should be given their property and allowed to shift for themselves." Federal guardianship should be reserved only for the "mature full-blood Indian." The secretary accepted the idea that competence, not equality, should be the goal of the government's efforts. "The Indian," Lane wrote in 1915, "is no more entitled to idle land than a white man."[57]

The Joint Commission called for a "material reorganization" of the Indian Office, but its recommendations did little to dampen the termination sentiment in Congress. Harry Lane and others continued to file their bills and to argue that if the Indians were "given their freedom . . . and then they frittered it away and came to poverty, it might be said that they had had a fair chance, and it was up to them." None of Lane's proposals were passed, but they were received with increasing sympathy. "I am not prepared to . . . go at one step to the length which the Senator from Oregon proposes," one western lawmaker warned, "but I do concur . . . that there is a vast amount of needless and worse than needless expenditure of money in the administration of Indian Affairs."[58]

Attacks on the Indian Office did not come from Congress alone. The Indian Rights Association complained that the government was dragging its feet in the distribution of the fee patents. The organization's annual report for 1913 criticized the persistence of wardship on several reservations and called for the distribution of all "communal property" at a fixed time. Two years later, the group was more insistent. "The time has come," the association declared, "for a change." Other reformers such as Warren K. Moorehead, a self-trained anthropologist who served on the association's Board of Directors, and Frederick Abbott of the Board of Indian Commissioners suggested placing Indian affairs in the hands of an expert commission. "Competent men who understand Indians," Moorehead wrote, would be the best ones to create the "broad highway upon which the Red Man [might] safely travel to his ultimate destination—the civilized community." These critics opposed extreme proposals for the termination of all federal assistance because they continued to believe that the government had a special obligation to the tribes, but they agreed that the time had come for "a reformation in our system of Indian administration."[59]

Commissioner Sells responded to his critics with an energetic and highly visible program of liberalized fee patenting. A new competency commission crisscrossed the West, and the Interior Department promised to put more men in the field as soon as Congress appropriated money to support them. By the end of 1916 Sells was predicting that if the current rate of granting fee-simple titles continued, the Indians would be "practically self-supporting" in ten years.[60]

To publicize its efforts, the Indian Office also began the practice of distributing fee-simple titles to allottees at elaborate pageants called last-arrow ceremonies. These proceedings always began with an order to the entire reservation to assemble before a large ceremonial tipi near the agency headquarters. The crowd would look on while their "competent" brethren were summoned individually from inside the lodge. The candidates for land titles were dressed in traditional costume and armed with a bow and arrow. After ordering a candidate to shoot his arrow into the distance, the presiding officer, usually the agent, would announce, "You have shot your last arrow." The arrowless archer would then return to the tipi and reemerge a few minutes later in "civilized" dress. He would be placed before a plow. "Take the handle of this plow," the government's man would say, "this act means that you have chosen to live the life of the white man—and the white man lives by work." The ceremony would close with the new landowner receiving a purse (at which point the presiding officer would announce "This purse will always say to you that the money you gain from your labor must be wisely kept") and an American flag. Secretary Lane presided at the first of these rituals at the Yankton Sioux reservation in the spring of 1916. Through the following summer the press covered similar proceedings at the Crow, Shoshone, Coeur d'Alene, Fort Hall, Sisseton, Fort Berthold, and Devil's Lake agencies.[61]

But Sells's upbeat projections and last-arrow ceremonies did not end congressional impatience. Charges of excessive protection and inefficiency persisted and by early 1917 threatened to bring the government's programs to a halt. In January three western senators—Henry Ashurst of Arizona, Key Pittman of Nevada, and Thomas Walsh of Montana—blocked the passage of the annual appropriations bill, relenting only after their colleagues agreed to appoint a new joint commission. Two months later the Indian Rights Association indicated that it was willing to join the recalcitrant westerners. In a letter to the commissioner, Herbert Welsh observed that there was "formidable opposition to the present policy and management of the Indians," much of which came from "persons with ulterior motives." But the old reformer added, "There are points of weakness in our Indian administration. . . . These disturbing conditions should be closely studied in order that [their] causes may be determined." Throughout this effort, he concluded, one object should remain above the "detail of routine work"; that was a "complete severance of government control of Indians." Welsh added that despite the growing pressure in Congress there was still time to act: "While there is increased agitation of the need of liberating the Indians from Government wardship, we feel that if your Bureau would favor legislation embodying these principles sufficient influence may be brought to bear upon Congress to secure favorable consideration."[62]

Three weeks later, Sells acted. On April 17, 1917, he issued his "Declaration of Policy," which set out the criteria for issuing fee-simple titles in the future. "Broadly speaking," the commissioner announced, "a policy of greater liberalism will henceforth prevail in Indian administration to the end that every Indian, as soon as he has been determined to be as competent to transact his own business as the average white man, shall be given full control of his property." Competence would now be measured by race and years of schooling. Persons who were less than one-half Indian or who had graduated from a government school would receive fee patents immediately. Incompetent Indians (the uneducated and those whose ancestry was more than 50 percent Indian) would continue to hold their property in trust, but they would be "urged to sell that portion of their land which [was] not available for their own uses." Sells promised that his new policy was the "dawn of the new era in Indian administration" and the "beginning of the end of the Indian problem." An Indian Office circular accompanying his memo ordered all agency superintendents to submit a list of candidates for fee patents "at the earliest practicable date."[63]

With his "Declaration," Sells captured the initiative from his critics. The Indian Rights Association's Washington agent admired the tactic. "I guess," he wrote a colleague, "[Sells] has seen the handwriting on the wall." The press was less cynical. *Outlook* magazine, which sported Theodore Roosevelt on its masthead and took pride in a long involvement with Indian reform, quickly endorsed the measure and editorialized, "There is no hope for the Indians as a race if they are forever kept in tutelage as wards of the Nation . . . it is better that some Indians should be lost as the result of a courageous policy than that the whole Indian race should be denied . . . freedom." These sentiments were echoed in Congress and the Indian Office bureaucracy. The termination movement subsided, and agents in the field applauded. "As soon as the nation rids itself of dependents," one superintendent wrote, "the more virile it can become."[64]

In the ensuing months, as the rest of the nation busied itself with the European war, Sells made good on his promise. By the spring of 1918 he revealed that nearly 1 million acres had been patented and "thousands of Indians [had] been given their freedom." In 1919 he declared that more fee-simple patents (10,956) were issued in the previous three years than had been granted during the previous decade. Competent Indians also received title to a share of their tribe's treasury. Under powers granted by Congress in 1918 and 1919 the Indian Office began dividing tribal funds into individual accounts and placing them in local banks. Patented Indians had free access to these accounts, but those owning trust lands made withdrawals only with the permission of the agent. Finally, the commissioner carried out his promise to "urge" noncompetents to sell their unused lands. In the first four years of his administration, more than 155,000 acres of trust lands had been sold; during the second four years (1917–20) that figure more than doubled. The same increase occurred in sales of inherited allotments. By the time he left office, Sells had presided over the sale of more than 1 million acres of trust land.[65]

Although Sells often declared that there "would be no wisdom" in terminating all federal ties with the Indians, his administration of native lands hastened the end of many forms of governmental protection. Congressional critics attacked his "Declaration" by saying "Nothing more will come of this than has come from the promises heretofore made." But the commissioner parried every thrust with new assertions that he was ending his office's guardianship function. His approach mollified western settlers eager to purchase Indian lands, comforted Welsh and those who attacked bureaucratic inefficiency, and promised to fulfill the administration's prediction that it was beginning the "end of the Indian problem."[66]

In the 1890s, during the debates over the Puyallups, western congressmen had asked how the government could maintain its paternal protection over the Indians while sustaining the economic development of their region. The Sells administration provided a conclusive answer. Assimilation would be redefined as the process of setting Native Americans "free" to seek their own destiny in an expanding society. Policy makers now believed that landownership and economic independence were less important to native advancement than daily interaction with white settlers amid a growing economy. Federal protection would be reserved only for those judged unable to function in that setting.

Both groups—the competent who received titles to their lands and the incompetent who remained under federal supervision—lost control of their resources. While specific figures are not available, reports from the agencies indicated that once the last arrow had been fired, tax collectors, auto dealers, and equipment salesmen descended on the newly patented Indians. Pressures of this kind combined with the Indian Office's support for the "law of necessity" to produce a rapid decline in native landownership. Officials witnessed the impoverishment of allottees with sympathy buttressed by the belief that patented Indians had to survive on their own. They agreed with Theodore Roosevelt, who wrote that the suffering of Indian farmers was "their own fault and not that of whites." He added, "Let them suffer the hardships which their own fault brings."[67]

Indians living on trust land faced a similar loss of control over their resources. Cato Sells expanded the Indian Office's leasing program and extended the list of resources available for exploitation by outsiders. Commissioner Valentine extended the limit of agricultural leases to five years and encouraged rental by white farmers, but it was the prosperity associated with World War I that invigorated the program. The war in Europe caused a dramatic rise in commodity prices and made many Indian lands economically attractive. Once the United States entered the war, Sells launched a patriotic campaign to increase the production of all trust lands. By the end of 1917 he announced that his "aggressive steps" had produced a two-hundred-thousand-acre increase in the amount of land under lease. The Indian Office also repeated Leupp's argument that leasing would surround the tribes with energetic white neighbors. The superintendent of the Crow reserve, for example, reported in December 1917, "The introduction of white owners and white lessees with attractive leases will tend to improve the roads, scatter public schools throughout the Reservation and in every way improve the industrial condition of the Reservation." By 1920, 4.5 million acres of trust land were under lease.[68]

The continuing precariousness of the government's irrigation campaign on the reservations also contributed to the growth of agricultural leasing. Enthusiasm for the program continued—one popular magazine called it "Rescuing a People by An Irrigation Ditch"— but it continued to suffer from legal and financial complications. Uncertainty surrounded the Indians' water rights, for westerners refused to recognize that Indians had first call on the water whether or not they had made "beneficial use" of it. The region's lawmakers insisted that individual states retained complete authority over water, and Congress would not overrule them. Idaho's William E. Borah told his colleagues in the Senate, "The Government of the United States has no control over the water rights of the state of Idaho." As for the *Winters* decision, in which the Supreme Court upheld the tribes' first claim to water, Utah's Senator George Sutherland spoke for many others when he dismissed it as "one of those unfortunate statements that sometimes courts, and the highest court, lapse into."[69]

Completion and maintenance of the water projects also required a steady supply of funds. When land sales failed to produce adequate revenues, Congress refused to make up the difference. The Indian

Office believed that both problems could be solved by opening newly irrigated Indian lands to outsiders, as the superintendent at the Fort Hall agency explained: "We will have to resort to quicker means of developing land than is possible through the encouragement of Indian allottees themselves." The result was a change in the law, allowing rentals of irrigated land to run for ten years instead of five, and a new drive to lease as many irrigated tracts as possible was begun. By 1920, nearly 50 percent more land on Indian irrigation projects was cultivated by whites than by natives.[70]

Commissioner Sells also presided over an unprecedented increase in timber leasing. Robert Valentine began the process in 1910, when he succeeded in inserting a section on timber leasing into the Omnibus Act. The law gave the Indian Office full authority to dispose of mature trees on trust lands and stipulated that Indians should receive the proceeds of all timber sales once deductions for maintenance and fire fighting had been made. These rules governed the disposition of the Indians' timber for the remainder of the decade. When a proposal was made in 1914 to give individual tribal councils authority to approve the sale of their own resources, Sells offered what had become a standard response: "I am confident that a successful administration of Indian affairs is dependent upon a maintenance of the principle that the United States has juridiction over tribal property."[71]

The administration maintained a similar attitude toward mineral leasing. Interest in prospecting for minerals was greatest among the congressmen from Arizona and New Mexico, because the large reservations in their states had been created by executive orders and therefore could not be "opened" without federal action. In 1915, Arizona's Henry Ashurst, the new chairman of the Senate Indian Affairs Committee, proposed allowing the secretary of the interior to grant mineral leases on all reservations on the same terms as on public lands. Ashurst's bill died in committee, but the following year his colleague in the House, Carl Hayden, attempted to attach a similar measure to the annual appropriations bill. This second effort failed as well, but the westerners regrouped, and in June 1918 Ashurst introduced a new bill. He defended it as a war measure (he promised that it would increase the government's output of manganese), and it passed the Senate after three days of debate. The House did not act on the measure, but Hayden succeeded in attaching it to an appropriations bill, which carried it into the statute books in 1919.[72]

The new rules allowed twenty-year mineral leases on Indian lands in every state except Utah and Colorado and stipulated that miners pay royalties of at least 5 percent on their net proceeds. Within four months of its passage, the mineral-leasing bill had opened twenty-four reservations—including the vast Navajo and Apache territories—to prospecting. Proposals soon appeared to expand the law to cover oil and gas exploration, but these additions did not come until later in the 1920s.

Despite its greater size, the leasing program under Sells only extended the practices of Leupp and Valentine. Indian Office administrators intended to develop the Indians' trust lands without the direct involvement of their proprietors and with minimal financial return to the tribes. Government officials justified their efforts by pointing out that they were "improving" the Indians' holdings and providing the nation's wards with an income they otherwise might not have. Carl Hayden, the young congressman from Arizona, welcomed this position, for he believed that encouraging the rental of native lands was the government's duty: "To do otherwise is to deny that there shall be advancement by either the red man or the white man in the West."[73]

By 1920 the Indian Office was implementing a land policy that bore only a superficial resemblance to the program spelled out by the Dawes Act a generation earlier. The idea that Native Americans would control their lands and rise to "civilization" with the aid of the federal government now was rejected. Economic and political pressures, together with changes in white perceptions of who the Indians were and what they could accomplish, had produced a new approach to Native American resources. Like an imperial power, the American government would "develop" native property by opening it to white farmers and businessmen, "freeing" the Indians to participate in the process as they could. Natives who adapted quickly might survive under the new regime; those who failed deserved their fate. People who remained under federal wardship would also be managed by others: white leaseholders would develop the Indians' property

and instruct them by example while government officials looked after the "incompetent" tribesmen's basic needs.

A campaign for equality and total assimilation had become a campaign to integrate native resources into the American economy. Assimilation was no longer an optimistic enterprise born of idealism or
faith in universal human progress; the term now referred to the process by which "primitive" people were brought into regular contact
with an "advanced" society. When this process produced exploitation and suffering, it seemed logical to believe that it was teaching
Native Americans the virtues of self-reliance and the evils of backwardness. The land policies of Jones, Leupp, Valentine, and Sells thus
placed the Indians on the outskirts of American life and promised
them a limited future as junior partners in the national enterprise.
The race's relationship to the majority culture was to be far more
tenuous than what Helen Hunt Jackson, Henry Dawes, and Alice
Fletcher had imagined, for in the twentieth century there was to be
a new category of Americans—those who did not share in the dominant culture, but who served it and were expected to benefit from
their peripheral attachment to "civilization."[74]

Chapter 6

Schools for a Dependent People

Indian education remained a vital part of the government's assimilation campaign during the early twentieth century. Public officials
continued to believe that organized instruction would smooth the
Indians' entrance into American society even as they abandoned
their predecessors' optimism and designed lessons more appropriate
to a "backward" race. Professional educators, journalists, and politicians shared the old reformers' faith in the power of federal activism,
but they attacked and changed the school system Richard Pratt and
Thomas Morgan had created. In the modern view, Indians were incapable of rising to the level of their civilized countrymen. The Indian Office therefore should abandon its hopes of bringing the common school to the reservations; realism demanded a more modest
approach.

By 1895 the reform drive of the previous decade had produced
an impressive educational program. The national government was
spending over $2 million annually to support two hundred institu-

tions. Day schools, agency boarding schools, and large nonreservation establishments like Richard Pratt's showplace in Pennsylvania
served more than eighteen thousand students. In the words of the
superintendent of Indian schools, each of these institutions shared
a "common concern" for Indian education and all "had an equally
important share" in the enterprise. The scale of the government's
program was matched by its idealism. The men and women who designed and supervised the system believed they had found a method
of molding people anew. "Education has become a great potency in
our hands," the U.S. commissioner of education told the reformers at
Lake Mohonk in 1895. "Give us your children," he asked the Indian
parents; "we will give them letters and make them acquainted with
the printed page . . . With these comes the great emancipation, and
the school shall give you that."[1]

Two decades after the founding of Carlisle, the Indian Office's
commitment to a national school system appeared intact. In 1894
William Hailmann, a professional educator known nationally for his
advocacy of public kindergartens, took command of the Indian school
system and pledged to continue the work of his evangelical predecessors, Thomas Morgan and Daniel Dorchester. Hailmann promised to
upgrade the curriculum (replacing "schoolroom pedantry" with "really vital work") and to place native children in white public schools
"within a comparatively short time." His goal was civilization, his
emphasis was uplift, and his predictions were upbeat.[2]

But as the turn of the century approached, doubters appeared. The
first critics were those expected to welcome native children into
their previously all-white classrooms. Commissioner Morgan had
launched his integration scheme in 1891 with the assertion that
there were "no insuperable obstacles in the way of blending Indian
children with white children."[3] He was wrong. In 1895 forty-five
school districts were participating in the program; five years later
that number had declined by more than half. Eight years after that
only four districts in the entire country were contracting with the
government to instruct Indian children who lived among them.

The failure of Morgan's program deflated government optimism.
Policy makers and educators could no longer point to integrated
classrooms as representative of their goal: preparing children to live

in a socially integrated society. The assertion that Indian education might raise Native Americans to equality was proven false by whites who wanted to keep the races apart. "It is clearly apparent," William Jones observed in 1899, "that the groundwork at least of Indian education must be laid under government auspices and control."[4] In the future native schools would continue to be self-contained systems that admitted Indian children to segregated classrooms and returned them to segregated lives.

Disillusionment with the grand designs of the nineteenth century soon spread to Congress. When Henry Dawes chaired the Senate Indian Affairs Committee, he knew his proposals to expand the government's educational programs would win widespread support. Disputes might occur over the rate of expansion, but relatively few policy makers questioned the Native American's ability to learn or to "rise to civilization." A generation later the atmosphere was different. Educators, journalists, and even reformers now doubted the appropriateness of common-school training for Indian children. And lawmakers frightened by the ballooning cost of the nineteenth-century programs began to argue that more modest expectations would require a smaller budget. Westerners—particularly Democrats who had been denied the patronage jobs that were the dividends of a growing Indian Office—often led this group, complaining that "civilized" instruction was wasted on "crude minded Indian youth." Arizona's delegate to Congress, for example, charged that the Interior Department was "frittering away . . . money in a humane chase after a dream."[5] But even those who disagreed with this view and supported the government's programs wondered aloud how long the Indians would require federal support.

Congressional critics of Indian education often were aided by interests otherwise not directly involved in the issue. Advocates of the new Jim Crow legislation in the South, for example, saw no reason for federal authorities to be involved in what they viewed as a local problem of race relations. John Stephens, who chaired the House Indian Affairs Committee, pointed out that western states were in the same position as the members of the old confederacy at the close of the Civil War. He noted that in the South "4,000,000 Negroes (who were as much wards of the Government as the Indians are now)" were "turned loose . . . without one cent ever being appropriated by Congress . . . Likewise why should not the red man be cared for in the States where they live?" Permanent, segregated, inferior schools in the Indians' own communities would be more fitting than a continuation of the evangelical policies of the 1880s.[6]

Imperialists in Congress also questioned the wisdom of native schools. They reasoned that Indians should learn the art of survival in the same way as the Puerto Ricans and Filipinos, who had recently become U.S. subjects. If elaborate civilization programs were impractical in the colonies, did they make any more sense on federally administered reservations? The joining of imperialism with criticism of the government's educational program often occurred in the abstract, but in 1903 the link between the two issues was made explicit when the House defeated an administration proposal to bring Puerto Rican and Filipino students to Carlisle. Joe Cannon, the autocratic chairman of the appropriations committee, told his colleagues, "The taking of children and at public expense educating them above the sentiment of the people from whom they sprang and with whom they must live is demoralizing and pauperizing . . . This whole experiment with the Indian children has worked disastrously, and I do not want to inflict an outrage upon the Porto Ricans."[7] In the minds of the majority that supported him, Cannon was right in pointing out that the "sentiment" of both the Indians and the Puerto Ricans made them unfit for Captain Pratt's model boarding school.

Critics of Indian education were not always negative. They shared a common faith in self-reliance, arguing that federal beneficence insulated Indian children from white society and failed to teach them independence. "The American boy," Congressman Theodore Burton exulted, "loves to spend his time in the clear sunlight and is not penned up within the walls of a boarding school. He does not take his bath in a government bathtub; he goes to the running brook and plunges in." The lesson of this image was clear: "If we do our duty to the Indian we will give him something of the selfsame reliance." Critics like Burton were skeptical of the power of institutions to remake a person. "Paternalism," wrote Lyman Abbott, "assumes that civilization can be taught by a primer . . . this is not true." Like the critics of the trust patent, men such as Abbott and Congressman

Burton believed experience—even work at a menial job—was superior to federal assistance. In their eyes the intervention of the Indian Office inevitably led to stagnation.[8]

Pessimism in Congress was matched by a growing feeling among educational experts that Indians and whites were separated by barriers far greater than literacy or dress. The journal of the American Academy of Social and Political Sciences pointed out, "There is a wide gulf between the civilization of the Indian and that of the white race . . . he who attempts to solve the problem of Indian education . . . must recognize that the circumstances surrounding the Indians are so different from those surrounding our own race that the two races may not be placed in the same category." In the first decade of the twentieth century arguments of this kind became common, even among those who earlier had endorsed the government's program. Herbert Welsh, an early supporter of Hampton and Carlisle, wrote in 1902 that the Native American race was "distinctly feebler, more juvenile than ours." Hollis Frissell, the principal of Hampton Institute, told an audience of educators in 1900 that "Indians [were] people of the child races," adding, "In looking forward to their future I believe we should teach them to labor in order that they may be brought to manhood." And the Board of Indian Commissioners, a group established to give the evangelical reformers of the nineteenth century a voice in policy making, announced in 1898 that while a few Native Americans "might push their way into professional life, the great majority must win their living by manual labor."[9]

What could be done? Educators insisted the solution was vocational training. Learning manual skills would help Indian children overcome their racial handicaps. Frissell told the National Education Association, "those of us who have to do with the education and civilization of Indians can learn many things from the dealings of our southern friends with the plantation negro." The plantation system was a "much more successful school for the training of a barbarous race than [was] the reservation." The Hampton educator believed that while "the Indian [could] never be an Anglo-Saxon," he would benefit from a term of labor under strict supervision.[10]

Other experts stressed job-related skills. In 1901 Calvin Woodward, one of the original advocates of manual training, gave a major address at the annual National Education Association convention. He told the gathering that educating Indians in literature or the arts would "sow seeds on stony ground." Woodward also observed that the vocational programs used in eastern cities were entirely inappropriate for native children. "Their very high merit for our use," he explained, "unfits them for the Indian home." He therefore recommended that the Indian Office simplify its vocational lessons. Two years later Hamlin Garland addressed the same association and repeated Woodward's advice: "Our red brethren . . . cannot be transmuted into something other than they are by any fervor or religious experience, or by any attempts to acquire a higher education. They must grow into something different by pressure of their changed conditions."[11]

Beyond the precincts of Congress and the professional societies there appeared to be considerable support for a more modest approach to Indian education. In the West, Charles Lummis, the Ohioan who published his "magazine of the West" in Los Angeles, asserted that the government's schools were run by "easterners who do not understand the frontier." He condemned Carlisle as a "machine for making machines." San Francisco's *Overland Monthly* expressed its disenchantment with federal programs by recommending that Indians and blacks be mustered into the armed forces and shipped overseas. "The military offers the best employment we can give the Indian," a 1901 article argued. Significantly, these suggestions were often echoed by easterners. *Outlook* chastised the Indian Office for offering native children "the same sort of book education . . . as [was] set before white children," and *Harper's* warned that anyone trying to "hurry up" the Indian's transition to civilization surely would "botch the job." A 1902 article entitled "How to Educate the Indians" probably summarized the popular view when it noted, "Occupations congenial to the white man can never be successfully undertaken by the savage." Manual training would enable tribesmen to take menial jobs while "the white men at the present engaged in these occupations could turn their attention to more intellectual employments."[12]

Bureaucrats, especially those committed to an established program, often are slow to respond to shifts in public attitudes. The leaders of the Indian school system were no exception. Nevertheless, during the first few years of the twentieth century, while their efforts were being denounced as extravagant, inefficient, and even futile, the government's schoolmen (and women) began to alter their course. The process began in 1898, when Estelle Reel replaced William Hailmann as superintendent of Indian education. In contrast to her predecessor—the Swiss-trained apostle of kindergarten reform—Reel came to Washington from Wyoming, and brought with her a practical rather than theoretical approach to schooling. "The theory of cramming the Indian child with mere book knowledge has been and for generations will be a failure," she wrote, "and that fact is being brought home every day to the workers in the cause of Indian regeneration." She accepted the system she inherited from Hailmann, but during her tenure in office Reel worked to reconcile the government's programs with her estimate of native abilities.[13]

The new school superintendent's chief conviction was that native children were different from white children. "The Indian teacher," she explained, "must deal with the conditions similar to those that confront the teacher of the blind or the deaf. She must exercise infinite patience." Reel agreed with those who used the race's alleged backwardness to justify an emphasis on manual training. In an office circular issued in 1900, she reminded her field personnel that half of each school day should be devoted to work and half to classroom learning. She left little doubt which of these areas should receive the most attention. Children should receive a "thorough groundwork in the English branches," the superintendent noted, warning that any further literary training had to be "by special authority of this office." She emphasized her disapproval of violations of this order a few years later, when she reported to the commissioner that several girls at the Chemawa, Oregon, boarding school were being excused from their chores to practice the piano. "I sincerely hope that the Office will require the superintendents of all Indian schools to see that their large Indian girls become proficient in cooking, sewing and laundry work," she wrote, "before allowing them to spend hours in useless practice upon an expensive instrument which in all probability they will never own."[14]

Under Reel the Indian school system continued to expand, but its curriculum and objectives changed. Although the number of students attending nonreservation boarding schools grew by more than one-third, admission was limited to graduates of other schools. Carlisle would no longer work to transform the children who arrived there; its mission became specialized training in a few manual trades. Teachers were urged to dismiss students who remained in government schools for six or seven years. Such a child, Commissioner Jones wrote in 1901, "had fair opportunity to develop his or her characteristics," and should not be retained any longer.[15]

Most significantly, Superintendent Reel announced a new course of study in 1901 that the commissioner was confident would "bring the Indian into homogeneous relations with the American people." The Indian Office's new curriculum covered twenty-eight subjects. In each area, the superintendent's orders were the same: teach only those subjects that apply directly to the students' experience; focus all learning on skills that will promote self-sufficiency. Under agriculture, for example, she ordered, "Do not attempt anything but what can be successfully raised in the locality." Reel's five-year program of farming instruction began with "light chores"; progressed through learning to "fix broken tools" by the third year; and culminated, in the fifth year, when students learned to plow. "Upon this work more than any other," the superintendent said of the plowing lessons, "depends the advancement of the condition of the Indian." Her program covered additional fields such as baking (every girl should learn to bake bread and "must be taught how to cut bread into dainty thin slices and place [them] on plates in a neat, attractive manner"), blacksmithing, canning, history ("they should know enough about it to be good, patriotic citizens"), hygiene, reading, and upholstering.[16] Hers was a curriculum of low expectations and practical lessons.

George Bird Grinnell, the Indian expert who joined Charles Lummis and Theodore Roosevelt in criticizing earlier evangelical programs, praised the new blueprint. "The average American citizen and legislator is so thoughtless and so little familiar with the operation of natural laws," Grinnell wrote Superintendent Reel, "that he believes it possible to transform the stone age man to the twentieth century man by act of Congress." The cofounder of the Boone and Crockett Club went on to assure the superintendent that her program would surely be appreciated "by those who [were] best acquainted with the Indian and his needs."[17]

Reel's curriculum had one vocal critic. Former commissioner Thomas Jefferson Morgan attacked the plan as an attempt to "discredit the whole Indian school system and to call for its abandonment." The old reformer made his charges at the 1902 meeting of the American Social Science Association. He told his audience of academics that limiting Indian children to a rudimentary education would condemn them to a permanent inequality. "Why should the national government offer to its wards so much less in the way of schooling than is offered by the states to the pupils of the public schools?" Morgan asked. "The Indian child has a right that he shall not be hopelessly handicapped by such an inferior training as from the very beginning dooms him to failure in the struggle for existence." Morgan's outrage revealed the distance between the assimilationist zeal of his administration and the "realism" of Estelle Reel. A five-year course ending with plowing lessons? Baking instruction devoted to "dainty slicing"? Morgan approved of manual training, but he had never conceived of it as a central objective. Like other nineteenth-century reformers, he believed industrial training should teach the "habits" of civilization—punctuality, persistence, and attention to detail; in short, industry. Reel's curriculum seemed to do nothing but prepare students for jobs. To accept her course of study was, in Morgan's eyes, to give up the assimilation effort and to sentence native children to life on the fringes of American society.[18]

Morgan delivered his assault a few weeks before his death. The old reformer's complaints were an echo from an earlier generation; the experts of the new century approved the superintendent's plan. Soon the Indian Office was reporting that every federal school had adopted the new course of study. The curriculum, officials declared, was leading to "increasing progress." The Indian Rights Association, in the person of its Washington lobbyist Samuel Brosius, argued that since manual trades were the "only avenues open," Indians "should be encouraged to take up these in earnest." But the most convincing endorsement came in 1904, when Reel summoned teachers and administrators from government schools across the country to the

Louisiana Purchase Exposition for the "Congress of Indian Education." The delegates were uniform in their praise of her new emphasis on manual training. One educator expressed the sense of the gathering when he urged his colleagues to "make [the Indian] understand that there is dignity in toil and the best thing he [could] do [was] labor in the field." Another speaker pronounced a familiar benediction. The superintendent of the Chilocco, Oklahoma, school was confident that the government's new commitment to practical vocational training "solved the Indian problem."[19]

Despite their conviction that Indian education had improved dramatically in the early twentieth century the delegates at St. Louis could point to few concrete changes in their school system. The curriculum now emphasized manual training, but the structure created a generation before remained intact. Students still traveled to distant boarding schools, and their teachers still stressed the goal of "civilization." Estelle Reel was an energetic advocate of "practical" skills, but her superiors, while sympathetic, did not give school reform a very high priority. It was not until Francis Leupp became commissioner in 1905 that the Indian Office embarked on a comprehensive reorganization of its educational programs. During Leupp's administration, complaints about the naiveté of nineteenth-century schoolmen became the basis for policy.

Roosevelt appointed Leupp commissioner because he believed that the journalist was his kind of expert. If the president had any doubts on this score, they were swiftly allayed by his appointee's first annual report. It called for lowered expectations and attacked those who believed in racial equality. In the area of education, Leupp wrote, "The foundation of everything must be the development of character. Learning is a secondary consideration." Although he allowed that Native Americans should not be "classed indiscriminately with other non-Caucasians, like the negro," he insisted that they occupied a station inferior to that of white Americans. "The Indian is an adult child," he told the National Education Association. "He has the physical attributes of the adult with the mentality of about our fourteen-year-old boy."[20]

Like Reel, Leupp held that teaching Indians was a specialized calling. Instructors in Native American schools were to receive specialized training and realize that the Indian "[would] always remain an Indian." As a result the government schools "should not push him too rapidly into a new social order and a new method of doing things." He noted in his first report, "Nothing is gained by trying to undo nature's work and do it over."[21]

As Leupp took office, respect for "nature's work" was becoming a popular theme among educators and social scientists. The United States' new colonies provided a vast testing ground for the education of "backward races," and the lessons educators were learning overseas seemed to support the commissioner's insights. Charles B. Dyke, for example, taught at Hampton Institute before going to Hawaii to administer Kamehameha, an industrial training school for island natives. In 1909 he reported on his experiences to the National Education Association and offered some general guidelines for educating nonwhites. A "knowledge of the race characteristics" of one's students was fundamental, he explained, and low expectations were essential: "It is absurd to theorize about the propriety of a college education for the mass of negroes, or Indians, or Filipinos or Hawaiians. They lack the intellect to acquire it . . . The races of men feel, think, and act differently not only because of environment, but also because of hereditary impulses. . . . Education does not eliminate these differences." Dyke and the new commissioner looked at Hampton's most famous graduate for confirmation of their views. Booker T. Washington, Leupp wrote in 1902, was successful because "the black man [was] to him a black man, and not merely a white man colored black."[22]

Psychologist C. Stanley Hall translated Leupp's views into scientific terms. Hall argued that the development of races was similar to the development of individual persons; some groups had advanced to "adulthood" while others were less "mature." "It is just as essential," he told a gathering of Indian educators, "that [the Indians] should evolve along the lines of their own heredity and traditions as it is for us to do so." In a paper entitled "On the Education of Backward Races," one of Hall's students extended the argument by pointing out, "If there is a need that the teacher know something of the contents of children's minds on entering school in our cities and towns of the East, there is much greater need that the teacher of the barbarian spend long months in long and intensive study of the aboriginal child-mind." With lessons properly tailored to their limited capacities, Native Americans could reach their appropriate level of development and find their places on the margins of American society.[23]

Unlike Estelle Reel's early efforts to temper the older evangelical approach to Indian education with "practical" concerns, Leupp and his colleagues attempted a thoroughgoing reconstruction of the government's program, based on a belief in Indian backwardness. Some of the new commissioner's proposals were not implemented. For example, his suggestion that wood-frame schoolhouses be replaced by open pavilions because "Indians are little wild creatures accustomed to live in the open air" found few takers. Other innovations were cosmetic. He announced in 1907 that teachers should be tolerant of tribal traditions—"I do not consider that their singing little songs in their native tongue does anybody any harm," he wrote. But the most important of Leupp's reforms occurred in three areas: vocational education, job placement, and a reduction in the number of government schools.[24]

Leupp observed that "most natives [would] try to draw a living out of the soil." Those that did not would "enter the general labor market as lumbermen, ditchers, miners, railroad hands or what not." These observations governed Indian Office planning. Immediately after his appointment, Leupp dispatched Superintendent Reel on an extensive survey of government installations. Throughout her travels Reel made a special effort to—in her words—"eliminate from the curriculum everything of an unpractical nature." She recommended building a model housekeeping cottage at Haskell and instituting a cooking department at Carlisle. And for all the schools she recommended a graduation ceremony patterned after the one at Tuskeegee, where students rejected speeches and songs in favor of rough clothes and demonstrations of their manual skills.[25]

By 1908 vocational instruction had become the central purpose of Indian school curricula and commencement speeches such as "What I Will Do With My Allotment" were commonplace. Like their counterparts in the nation's burgeoning cities, government educators now preached the gospel of practical instruction. Vocational training programs, guidance officers, and testing programs placed students in "appropriate" areas of study and pointed them to a place in the nation's work force. As Marvin Lazerson has pointed out, educators at this time were eager to "integrate the schools into the industrial society." Thus the *Journal of Education* editorialized in 1909, "To give the Indian of today culture without industry is only another way of meting out agency rations and blankets as a premium upon idleness . . . When the red man becomes skilled at bench, lathe, or anvil he is not anchored to a life of toil but he is ballasted for a successful voyage on civilization's sea." In the years ahead, the "ballast" of manual skills would be the white man's gift to his "backward" compatriots.[26]

To complement the government's work in vocational training, Leupp established an Indian employment bureau early in his term. He placed Charles Dagenett, a thirty-three-year-old Carlisle graduate, in charge of the program, instructing him, "Gather up all the able-bodied Indians who . . . have been moved to think that they would like to earn some money and plant them on ranches, on railroads, in mines—wherever in the outer world, in short, there is an opening for a dollar to be gotten for a day's work." In its first year (1905–6) Leupp asserted that the employment office was the area where he had placed "greatest stress," and he pointed with pride to the five thousand tribesmen who had recently found work in Colorado sugar-beet fields, on southwestern sheep ranches, and on government building projects.[27]

The employment bureau specialized in migrant labor. Employers contracted for a specific task or time period and agreed to provide transportation and a place to camp. Wage rates varied, but they generally fell below the pay scale for whites doing similar work. One gang spent six weeks in a Colorado sugar-beet field in 1906 and returned home with an average of eighty-nine cents a day to show for their toil. "Indians are employed," the superintendent of the Pima school reported in 1908, "because they are cheaper than the same grade of white help."[28]

The success of the employment bureau confirmed Leupp's estimate: "[The Indian] does not know anything and will not attempt anything but to do as he is shown." Unskilled labor taught Native Americans to follow a daily routine and to survive in a cash economy. These rudimentary lessons, the commissioner noted, would make the race a "very valuable industrial factor in our frontier economy." Leupp was confident that the sight of Indians working patiently on their farms and ranches would convince whites that the tribesmen could be used "for the upbuilding of the country" and should not be dismissed "as nuisances."[29]

According to Leupp, manual labor promised to be a popular way to bring Indians into American society. The employment bureau would reduce the need for federal handouts and foster learning outside the "artificial" environment of the boarding and training schools. Naturally the program won wide support in Congress and among western employers. It spread to the northern plains in 1907 and the following year the board of trade in California's rich Imperial Valley requested crews to harvest cantaloupes and other fruit. By 1909 the employment bureau was operating in Wisconsin as well. "The experiment has proved a marked success," Leupp reported, "because it recognized certain racial traits of the Indian, such as his lack of initiative, his hereditary lack of competition, etc., and wooed him into the labor mart."[30]

The third phase of Leupp's effort to restructure Indian education was his campaign to replace all boarding schools with day schools. The commissioner believed that the local school was the logical place to teach the government's wards the habits necessary for self-sufficiency. Training that was more elaborate, or that drew children away from the realities they would encounter after graduation, created unhealthy distinctions between tribesmen and their white neighbors and alienated Indian children from their homes. The boarding schools, in short, taught "false, undemocratic, and demoralizing ideas."[31]

Leupp of course realized that he could not close all boarding schools immediately. But he began to undermine their position by ordering his agents to stop sending day school graduates on for further schooling. "Day schools are to be maintained," he wrote, "without any reference to their effect on the boarding school attendance." In 1908 he took another step by prohibiting all nonreservation schools from recruiting students at the agencies. "When parents or guardians wish to give their children the advantages of a term of training in a nonreservation school," he told the agency employees, "they will make their wishes known to you." Later that year in a magazine article, the commissioner reported that he was "getting rid of the boarding schools as fast as practicable." He made good on the pledge by eliminating four of the off-reservation installations from his 1909 budget request. "The abandonment of these four schools," he told Congress, "is preliminary to a gradual obliteration of an expensive system which has outgrown its usefulness."[32]

Congressional reaction to Leupp's requests reflected broad sympathy for his point of view. Westerners opposed boarding schools, both because they were "extravagant" and because they diverted federal dollars to eastern communities. Arizona's territorial delegate, for example, placed a rider on the 1908 Indian appropriations bill that would have prohibited the transportation of students more than one hundred miles from their homes to attend school. The amendment was defeated, but it won considerable support. William Hepburn, the progressive Republican who chaired the House Interstate Commerce Committee, spoke for men on both sides of the aisle when he charged that boarding schools served "no purpose in lifting up the great mass of Indians." Another colleague suggested that a better alternative would be "to give all the Indians a proper education instead of giving to a few a pampered education." Fueled by these sentiments, boarding-school attendance declined between 1905 and 1910 by over 10 percent while day school attendance rose by more than 47 percent.[33]

Attacks on the boarding institutions also breathed new life into Thomas Morgan's long forgotten scheme of placing Indian students in public schools. Morgan had commended native children to the public schools in the name of social integration; Leupp was far more practical. His nineteenth-century predecessor insisted on guarantees of equal treatment and complete mixing of the races; Leupp did not. "The enforcement of such stipulations," he noted in 1906, "caused the school authorities to give up their contracts." In the twentieth century no stipulations were required. Moreover, recent innovations in public education such as the introduction of vocational and commercial training made it possible to segregate students by ability and interest. In the 1890s, bringing Native Americans into common schools meant introducing them to a single curriculum. A decade later Indian children could be insulated in the lower branches of a compartmentalized program. Modern schools reserved a special place for the unskilled, unlettered Native American.[34]

Francis Leupp left office in 1909. But in the decade that followed his successors pursued his vision of practical education. Vocational training continued to attract government schoolmen. When Robert Valentine succeeded Leupp, he observed in his first annual report, "The Indian Service is primarily educational. It is a great indoor-outdoor school with the emphasis on the outdoors." Cato Sells was equally forthright. He called for a "happy correlation" between the lessons learned in native schools and the Indian's daily environment. "Our aim at our schools," Sells wrote, "is not the perfect farmer or the perfect housewife, but the development of character and industrial efficiency." Both men agreed that the reforms of the nineteenth century had been well-meaning but naïve, and that "improvement," not transformation, should be the government's goal.[35]

Largely because he had served as Leupp's private secretary, Valentine was devoted to his predecessor's reforms. In 1910—his first full year in office—Valentine divided the school department into six districts and assigned a superintendent to each. The superintendents were to consult with local educators, facilitate curricular reforms, and upgrade their professional staffs. The former settlement-house worker also directed his teachers to devise new courses of study that would reduce the differences between Indian schools and local public institutions as well as to continue work in industrial training.[36]

Cato Sells expanded on these developments by ordering that non-reservation schools become specialized institutions offering training in specific trades (Carlisle was to prepare students for the mechanical trades and apprentice them to Ford Motor Company) and overseeing the development of still another course of study. Unveiled in 1916, his model curriculum promised to respond to a "vital deficiency" in the government's program. "There has been a chasm," Sells wrote, "between the completion of a course in school and the selection of a vocation in life." The new program would "provide a safe and substantial passage from school life to success in real life."[37]

The 1916 course of study went beyond the description of new courses. It divided Indian schools into three categories: primary, pre-vocational, and vocational. During their first three years the students' time would be divided between rudimentary English and arithmetic and "industrial work." A second three-year period would include more specific lessons (such as geography and hygiene) and an introduction to a trade. The final stage, consisting of four years, would be devoted chiefly to "industrial training," with one hour per day spent in "military and gymnastic drills," and occasional periods devoted to "vocational arithmetic," "industrial geography," and "farm and household physics." Sells observed: "The course has been planned with the vocational aim very clearly and positively dominant, with especial emphasis on agriculture and home making. The character and amount of academic work has been determined by its relative value and importance as a means of solution of the problem of the farmer, mechanic, and housewife." He assumed that the Indians' future had sharp limits and that the government should work to "improve" its wards by "training Indian boys and girls for efficient and useful lives under the conditions which they must meet after leaving school."[38]

But the new curriculum signified more than a victory for vocational training. It also marked an important shift in the management and direction of the government's schools. Throughout the nineteenth century, missionaries and politicians had approached the Indian Service with proposals to "save" Native Americans from barbarism and "raise" them to "civilization." Congress responded. By the end of the nineteenth century the reformers and their allies had laid the foundations of a federal educational bureaucracy. By 1916 that bureaucracy had acquired a life of its own. Experts in Indian education defined the goals of the system and generated reforms themselves. In contrast to Thomas Morgan's grand design—in large part a projection of ideas about public education onto the Indians—modern reforms like the 1916 course of study were internal documents. The architects of the new program were employees of the Indian Office who believed that great "gaps" separated the races and gradual "improvement" was the only practical mission for the Indian schools. The bureaucratization of the Indian schools was also reflected in the backgrounds of the people who became superintendents of the system. When Estelle Reel retired in 1910 she was replaced by Harvey Peairs, a veteran teacher and administrator from the Chilocco Training School in Oklahoma. Peairs left in 1917. His successor was Oscar Lipps, who had served as one of Peairs's assistants. The government's schools generated their own leaders as well as their own reforms.

In the second decade of the twentieth century Leupp's employment bureau became a fixture in the Indian Office. Commissioner Valentine believed that the bureau could assist in the "bridging over of that critical period in a boy's life when he leaves school and starts to work," and that its success would mean the "economic and moral salvation of many boys and young men." Sells agreed. During their administrations the two men worked to expand the number of jobs available through Charles Dagenett's office. Most of the program's clients continued to be offered work as low-paid migrant laborers (the exception to this pattern was the scheme to place Carlisle graduates in automobile plants during World War I). Valentine reminded a dissatisfied Colorado beet farmer in 1909, "If you were hiring white labor to do this work, in all probability you would have to pay them more wages than you do the Indians." The "happy correlation" between the Native Americans' schools and the "lives they must lead" was being achieved.[39]

Robert Valentine and Cato Sells also continued to direct attention away from boarding schools and toward day schools. They shared their predecessor's disenchantment with off-reservation institutions and were encouraged in their beliefs by congressional budget cutters. Texan John Stephens, who chaired the House Indian Affairs Committee, was particularly vocal on this issue. He observed in 1910 that federal funds "would be better spent in industrial and day schools, teaching the children . . . how to make a living by farming and stock raising than in any other way." Stephens fought to end the practice of sending native children to Virginia's Hampton Institute. Carlisle also was a target for congressional attacks. The school's alumni and the eastern reformers who had long supported it rallied to the institution's defense, but in 1918, when the army repossessed the Carlisle plant for use as a hospital, there was little interest in saving it. Cato Sells did not believe the matter was worth discussing. "The educational system of the Indian Department will not suffer because of the abolishment of the Carlisle School," he wrote.[40]

Finally, Robert Valentine and Cato Sells implemented Leupp's suggestion that native children attend public schools without the bothersome "stipulations" Thomas Morgan had insisted on in the 1890s. In his first annual report, Valentine issued an open invitation to local educators to apply for subsidies for Indian students. "Whenever application [was] made for government aid," he promised, the Indian Office would "enter into a contract for the Indian pupils at the same rate per capita as that allowed by the State or county for white children." The agreement with the government was to be strictly a business proposition. On reservations such as Walker River, Nevada, where (according to the local agent) whites were "almost entirely lacking in sympathy for the Indian," the Indian Office made no effort to alter local prejudices by insisting that Native American students attend public schools. And where placements did occur, such as at the Cheyenne and Arapaho agency in Oklahoma, officials made sure that students did not arouse white protests. Children "against whom complaint was made" were returned immediately to agency schools. An incident in Montana illustrated the pervasiveness of this pattern.[41]

Early in 1911 the agent for the newly allotted Crow tribe learned that white communities near the reservation were organizing public schools. He requested permission for Indian children (dependents of people who were now citizens) to attend. When the attorney general of Montana refused, asserting that the Indians were neither citizens nor taxpayers, the agent appealed to Washington. Robert Valentine responded in August with an extensive review of the tribe's legal status, but no support for the agent. The commissioner conceded that Crow children had the right to attend local schools, but he observed, "It is not the intention or desire of this Office to force the attendance of children of Indians in the public schools . . . in direct opposition to the manifest wishes of the people." Valentine urged the agent to plead again with state authorities, but without federal action little could be expected. Montana's segregationist policies continued. In 1913 the Crows' agent reported, "There is practically no intercourse between the public and the Indian schools."[42]

The principal reason local authorities accepted Native American children in their schools was financial. At Fort Lapwai, Idaho, for example, a growing community of white landowners and lessees living on the old Nez Perce reservation took advantage of federal support by converting the agency boarding school to a community high school. To make the conversion feasible, two government teachers were retained, their salaries paid by the Indian Office. Indians were eligible to attend the new high school, but were barred from the local grammar schools. Consequently the number of Nez Perce students in the upper grades soon declined. The federally funded teachers spent most of their time instructing the children of local whites. A similar situation developed at Washington's Yakima agency where the local agent reported in 1913, "It is only by having the revenue derived from the enrollment of Indian children that the county has been able, especially throughout the reservation, to increase the standard of the county school system." And from California came the report that "where the local white people [did] not have enough children of their own to maintain a school they usually let in enough Indian children to make up the required number."[43]

When the children of citizen Indians did attend local schools, little was done to ensure that they received adequate instruction. Commissioner Sells praised public schools as the "trysting place in the winning of the race," but felt no obligation to monitor attendance figures or inspect the facilities provided. Once responsibility for educating native children passed to state and local officials, the commissioner saw no reason to look back. An exchange of correspondence between Sells and one Carl Price was typical. Price, a white man, wrote to Washington in 1916 to complain that his mixed-blood children had been denied admission to the local South Dakota schools. He asserted that he paid taxes and that his children were even enumerated in the school census. Sells's response, conveyed through his assistant, was direct: "This is a matter that depends upon the South Dakota state law."[44]

The Indian Office had no more interest in noncitizens who were admitted to public institutions. Substandard conditions and local prejudices were beyond the concern of an administration eager to set the tribes "free" from federal protection. At the Uintah and Ouray reservation, the superintendent reported in 1915 that only 50 percent of school-age children were attending classes. The agency school was dilapidated and attendance at public institutions was "negligible." He also noted that the Utah compulsory attendance law was "inoperative" for native children and there was "no tie existing between the two school systems." Sells refused the Uintah superintendent's call for help.[45]

Sells and his colleagues equated success with reductions in enrollments at federal schools. The nature of the interaction between Indians and their white neighbors did not interest them. Complaints from the Crow agency that "very few full-blood Indian children [were] enrolled" in public schools and that "prejudice against such enrollment" existed went unanswered. And persistent evidence that state attendance and truancy laws were unenforced throughout the West failed to arouse official interest. If the two groups did not use the opportunity to bring about the kind of total assimilation envisioned by nineteenth-century reformers, federal intervention would not alter the outcome.[46]

By the second decade of the twentieth century, policy makers no longer viewed Indian education as a great lever to raise Native American children to positions of equality in American society. Cato Sells believed that the nation's schools would be "a nursery of one American speech and of the simpler but fundamental lessons of civic virtue, social purity and moral integrity." These institutions would do nothing to alter the Indians' marginal economic existence or to equip tribesmen with skills that might enable them to challenge the political power of their non-Indian neighbors. To modern educators, the Indians were radically handicapped, surrounded by powerful interests, and badly served by the naïve romantics of the nineteenth century. There was a government responsibility to educate native children, but no obligation to hasten their integration into the dominant culture.[47]

Commissioner Sells wrote in 1920 that educational policy makers had "no other choice than to regard the Indian as a fixed component of the white man's civilization." His statement carried a message for both races. He was telling Native Americans that they could look forward to continued domination by the majority culture; they would have a "fixed" role in the "white man's" society. And the former banker was reassuring his non-Indian constituents that they would continue to be on top. For Sells, assimilation did not imply wide-ranging social change; it was simply a label for the process by which aliens fit themselves into their proper places in the "white man's" United States. As they found their slots, Indians would not alter existing social relations or overturn accepted notions of Anglo-Saxon superiority. Instead they would be taught to follow the direction of their "civilized" neighbors and labor patiently on the fringes of "civilization." In the twentieth century schools would not transform the tribesmen; they would train them to live on the periphery of American society.[48]

Chapter 7

Redefining Indian Citizenship

Extending citizenship to Indians was perhaps the first feature of the assimilation campaign to win wide support. The men and women who gathered in Boston and New York to hear Standing Bear tell of his plight believed the law would protect Native Americans far better than agents or missionaries. Westerners agreed, for an expansion of the natives' rights promised to reduce federal interference in their local affairs. Thus there were few objections when the Dawes Act proposed that each allottee should receive all the legal rights and privileges of United States citizens.

But the same environment that altered land and education reforms undermined the appeal of Indian citizenship. In the twentieth century, politicians and judges began to argue that "backward" races were not fit for citizenship: they would either abuse their new freedoms or be victimized by the unscrupulous. Just as the government lowered its expectations in the areas of economic development and education, so did it retreat from the idea that Native Americans could exercise their legal rights effectively. Gradually, Indians saw many of those rights slip back into the hands of federal administrators. By 1920, Indian citizenship had been redefined. The law, like the schools and the economic system, now promised the race a peripheral role in American life.

Soon after the general allotment act took effect, Indian Office administrators began to point out that tribesmen owning valuable property required legal protection. It seemed naïve to expect Indian allottees to defend their property interests without assistance. At the Cheyenne and Arapaho agency in Oklahoma, for example, individual Native Americans acquiring plots of land were quickly surrounded by aggressive settlers who scorned the Indians' property rights and refused to recognize the new allottees as fellow citizens. "It is impractical," the agency superintendent wrote two years after the reservation had been allotted, "nay, more, I respectfully submit that it is impossible to make good citizens of reservation Indians . . . by the simple act of allotting them in severalty." If this agency proved representative, the severalty law guaranteed a future of white encroachments and Indian suffering.[1]

As critics of citizenship grew more outspoken, it became clear that a return to tribal guardianship was impossible. Westerners would resent any reimposition of federal authority in their growing states, and the reformers who had lobbied for assimilation would surely oppose a return to the "anomaly" of separate Indian nations. Convinced that the problems such as those in Oklahoma were temporary and that most injustices could be overcome by legal means, reform groups continued to advocate universal citizenship. The report of the American Bar Association for 1891 contained a typical statement of this optimistic point of view. Demanding that all Indians immediately become subject to the laws of the states and territories they inhabited, it concluded: "Let the fiction be abolished. Let us enact laws suitable for the present situation, and place the legal status of the Indian upon a rational and practical basis." In a similar vein, the Board of Indian Commissioners noted, "We have entire faith that before very many years shall have passed the Indians of the United States will be better off under the general laws of our States and Territories and by incorporation with the great body of our American citizens, than they can possibly be under any system of 'paternal' government and peculiar and separate administration which could be devised." From this perspective there was no alternative to the individual protections guaranteed each person by the law.[2]

The problem, then, for people like the agent at the Cheyenne and Arapaho agency was to devise a means of providing greater federal protection without appearing to retreat from the government's commitment to Indian citizenship. The predicament was a new version of the question that had confronted policy makers involved with the management of Indian lands and the administration of native schools: how to modify early expectations about the ease and speed of Indian "progress" without returning to the federally enforced separatism of the reservation era. Supporters of the Dawes Act wanted to dismantle the reservations while continuing to supervise the management of individual allotments. Their solution had been the trust patent, which continued federal control but confined it to small areas. Similarly, educators argued for universal schooling, but suggested new kinds of training that stressed practical skills and vocational objectives. In short, in the early twentieth century the promise of Indian assimilation had been modified to allow for what were believed to be the Native Americans' "special" characteristics. Homesteads might be owned by Indians, but would be managed by whites; and the school system could expand, even as it narrowed its goals and objectives.

Indian citizenship followed a similar evolutionary path. Abandoning the goal of full equality (articulated in the 1880s as an echo of the abolitionist crusade) federal bureaucrats, lawyers, and judges gradually developed the idea that the government had an obligation to supervise and protect native citizens. The basis for their claim was the doctrine of guardianship. Guardianship provided a justification for federal intervention that did not compromise Indian citizenship. Nevertheless, in the legal arena—as in other areas of policy where federal action was based on a reaffirmation of Native American "backwardness"—the guardianship concept would have distinctly negative consequences. It would justify undermining the civil rights of individual Indians and excuse a wide range of state statutes that limited their legal prerogatives. In the early twentieth century, the guardianship doctrine was the basis for a redefinition of Indian citizenship.

Of course, the application of the law of guardianship to Indians was not new. The Supreme Court first recognized it in 1831 in *Cherokee Nation* v. *Georgia*, when it declared that a tribe was ineligible to sue a state government because Indians did not constitute a "foreign state." Instead, Chief Justice John Marshall wrote, they were a people "in a state of pupilage; their relation to the United States resemble[d] that of a ward to his guardian." For the remainder of the nineteenth century, Marshall's words were used to justify federal control of the tribes and to defend actions that overrode treaty guarantees. His meaning was less clear, however, after the allotment law made individual Indians landowners and U.S. citizens. Was it legal for federal authorities to hold individual Americans in such a unique trust relationship? Could Indians be both political equals and federal wards?[3]

The first answer to these questions came in response to a challenge to the trust patents by which allottees held their land. *U.S.* v. *Mullin* (1895) arose when a white farmer refused to recognize the Indian Office's right to remove him from land he had leased from an allotted member of the Omaha tribe. Mullin's lease was negotiated without the approval of the tribe's agent, who subsequently ordered the enterprising Nebraskan off the allotment. Mullin's lawyer argued that the Indian landlord who made the unauthorized lease was a citizen with complete freedom to handle his property as he chose. The district court denied this claim and held that the trust title was simply an extension of the treaty relationship between the Omahas and the United States. "It has never been held," Judge George Shiras wrote, "that the acquisition of the status of citizenship deprives the individual of his right to insist that the treaty obligations . . . should be observed and fulfilled." His decision also contained an apparent warning to other potential challengers of the trust title: "The United States . . . is yet bound by its treaty stipulation, to protect the Indians, whether citizens or wards of the nation, in the use and occupancy of the reservation lands which have never yet been opened to occupancy by the whites." Regardless of the grant of citizenship, then, federal authorities reserved the right to determine how Indian allotments would be used. At least in the area of land titles, Native American citizens would continue in an "anomalous"—and protected—position.[4]

In the decade after *Mullin* the courts further clarified the Indian Office's power as the sole trustee of native-owned land. Although they defended the Indians' inalienable title to the allotments themselves, judges ruled that federal supervision extended to timber on individual homesteads, proceeds from the sales of that timber, and even to the cattle provided by the government to hasten the tribesmen's "civilization." As this doctrine developed, however, a significant change occurred in the legal reasoning behind it. Judges gradually shifted their justification for guardianship from treaty guarantees to racial backwardness. In 1904, for example, a federal appeals court dismissed a suit by Big Boy, an Ojibwa allottee who sued Secretary of the Interior E. A. Hitchcock in an effort to gain control over the proceeds from the sale of timber on his allotment. Although the lower court had accepted Big Boy's claim that his citizenship entitled him to the cash, the District of Columbia Appeals Court ruled against him. Granting that the plaintiff "might well be a citizen, with all the rights and privileges of citizens," the court asserted that government regulations were "analogous to ordinary trusts wherein it [was] sought, by restricting the right of disposition, to guard the beneficiaries against the results of their own improvidence." Justice Marshall's language of guardianship was applied to an individual person; and the Indian Office was placed in the role of trustee with complete authority to act on behalf of their "improvident" wards. "The matter of citizenship is an entirely extraneous thing," the court concluded in *Hitchcock* v. *Big Boy*, "and has had nothing to do with the case."[5]

Basing federal guardianship on Indian backwardness rather than treaty obligations seemed logical in the first decade of the new century. It was a view consistent with the Burke Act's extension of the trust period and delay of citizenship and with the growing pessimism regarding the Indians' intellectual abilities. Not surprisingly, the courts spoke repeatedly of the nation's obligation to its wards and widened steadily the authority of federal officials to act on the natives' behalf. Rather than refer to treaty obligations, the courts stressed the government's duty to educate and protect its charges.

The leading example of the expansion of federal guardianship in property cases involved Marchie Tiger, a citizen Creek who had inherited an allotment in 1903, which he sold four years later to an Oklahoma real estate company. Aided and encouraged by M. L. Mott, the tribe's attorney, Tiger decided in 1908 that he had been swindled; he sued for return of his property. The Oklahoma Supreme Court denied Tiger's claim, citing a 1901 law that placed a six-year limit on all trust patents in the territory. Tiger appealed to the U.S. Supreme Court, pointing out that Congress had passed a second law in 1906 restricting land sales by full-bloods such as himself. In their May 1911 decision, the justices reversed the Oklahoma court and buttressed their findings with an extended discussion of the power of federal authorities and weakness of citizen Indians. "It may be taken as a settled doctrine of this Court," Justice William R. Day wrote for the majority "that Congress . . . has the right to determine for itself when the guardianship which has been maintained over the Indians shall cease." Congress had every right to pass a second law removing the earlier promise of fee-simple ownership. Echoing *Hitchcock,* the Court insisted that guardianship was not altered by a grant of citizenship: "Incompetent persons, though citizens, may not have the full right to control their persons and properties. . . . [T]here is nothing in citizenship incompatible with this guardianship over the Indians' lands."[6]

The *Tiger* decision quickly became the governing authority in disputes over federal supervisory power. A year after it was announced, a federal appeals court in Utah ordered a white man to return the wool he had purchased from a Ute man without agency approval. "The United States has the power," the judges declared, "to protect the Indians and their property from the force, fraud, cunning and rapacity of the members of the superior race." This guardianship power derived from the trust patent as well as from the government's desire to "teach [Indians] to abandon nomadic habits and become farmers, laborers, clerks and businessmen." The U.S. Supreme Court repeated that theme the same year in yet another Oklahoma land case. Writing for the majority, Justice Charles Evans Hughes declared that federal guardianship "traces its source to the plenary control of Congress in legislating for the protection of the Indians under its care, and *it recognizes no limitations that are inconsistent with the discharge of the national duty.*"[7]

Throughout these legal disputes, a broad definition of the government's "duty" to supervise the property of Indians won general endorsement from reformers and policy makers. Lyman Abbott, an early and active supporter of rapid allotment, noted in 1901 that the law of guardianship provided a humane way of protecting the new citizen. "He should be treated as a ward of the courts," Abbott wrote in *Outlook*. "He is not to be condemned to barbarism because he is not equal to the competitions involved in civilization." With encouragement from Abbott and the Indian Rights Association, government officials were quite willing to act. Every commissioner of Indian affairs between 1900 and 1920 worked for greater federal control of trust lands.[8]

Once the courts had freed the doctrine of guardianship from the idea of treaty obligations and had redefined it as an instrument for defending Indians from members of the "superior race," it could be applied to a wide range of situations. Early in the allotment era, for example, the county governments organized by the Indians' settler neighbors attempted to overturn the tax-exempt status of native-owned property. No one disputed that trust land was tax-exempt, but several of these new western communities taxed the personal holdings of citizen allottees. In its efforts to resist these levies, the Indian Office relied on a broad interpretation of its obligation to protect its wards.

The first defense of Indian tax exemptions came in *U.S.* v. *Rickert* (1903). The Justice Department brought suit against James A. Rickert, the county treasurer of Roberts County, South Dakota, to enjoin him from selling property belonging to allottees on the Sisseton reservation for nonpayment of taxes. Roberts County—which encompassed the Sisseton allotments—had adopted a levy on all farm improvements in 1900 and its lawyers argued that since the tax was not on land, all citizens—Indian as well as white—were obligated to pay up. In rejecting this position, the Supreme Court noted that allotments were the "instrumentality employed by the United States for the benefit and control of this dependent race." Farm improvements, the justices reasoned, were simply an extension of that instrumentality and therefore should also be tax-exempt. "It is evident," Justice John Harlan wrote for the majority, "that Congress expected that the lands . . . allotted would be improved and cultivated by the allottee. . . . that object would be defeated if the improvements could be assessed and sold for taxes." As for the county's claim that all citizens were obligated to support their government through taxes, Harlan responded, "It is for the legislative branch of the Government to say when these Indians shall cease to be dependent and assume the responsibilities attaching to citizenship."[9]

The *Rickert* decision settled disputes over the direct taxation of allottees, but the issue continued to plague the Indian Office because county governments—often strapped for funds—tried to enforce indirect levies. Thurston County, Nebraska, which included the old Omaha and Winnebago reservations, taxed the bank accounts of Indians who had recently inherited land from deceased relatives. While the district court approved the practice, a federal appeals court rejected it in 1906. Even though individual Indians might have funds on deposit in local banks, the court declared, "They are still members of their tribes and of an inferior and dependent race." The government's efforts to protect the tribesmen "from want and despair" meant that they were "not subject to taxation by any state or county."[10]

In the years that followed, the courts declared that property protected by federal authorities, purchased with federal funds, or acquired through federal assistance was tax-exempt. Exemptions extended to the landholdings of citizen Indians in Oklahoma, profits white lessees derived from the oil and gas extracted from native allotments, and supplies delivered annually by government extension agents to Native American farmers. In 1919 the Supreme Court even upheld the right of the Interior Department to set aside property taxes on fee-simple land occupied by citizen Indians if those taxes appeared "arbitrary, grossly excessive, discriminatory, and unfair." A guardian must protect his wards from "spoliation," the justices held, and this duty necessarily included "the right to prevent their being illegally deprived of property rights."[11]

But what of the Indian's personal rights? Federal intervention to protect his property was justified by appeals to native backwardness, federal sovereignty, and the plenary power of Congress. Courts could argue that the guardianship relation simply carried forward from the reservation era, when it had provided protection for tribal lands, to the period of allotment, when it helped individual Indians retain control of their property. In effect the courts had said that allotments were miniature reservations. None of this reasoning was directly applicable to the personal liberties of citizen Indians. The Dawes Act was intended to assimilate Native Americans, to set them free from the control of the Indian Office. In the nineteenth century it had been thought that, like their black contemporaries in the South, tribesmen who took land in severalty would rely on state courts for justice. Thus when the subject changed from property to personal freedoms, it appeared that the Indians were on their own.

The Supreme Court affirmed the rights of the nation's new citizens in 1905, when it overturned the conviction of Albert Heff, a white man accused of selling liquor to a group of allottees in Kansas. The prosecution had argued that Heff's customers were "not citizens of full competence, just as . . . citizens under personal or legal disabilities are not *sui juris* in other respects." But the justices were unmoved. Congress had made the allottees citizens, they noted, and the government was "under no constitutional obligation to perpetually continue the relationship of guardian and ward." To decide otherwise, to consider all natives only partial citizens, as Heff's accusers had suggested, would be to sentence all Indians to a condition of permanent wardship. "Can it be," Justice Brewer wrote, "that because one has Indian, and only Indian blood in his veins, he is to be forever one of a special class over whom the General Government may . . . assume the rights of guardianship . . . whether the State or the individual himself consents?" A decade would pass before the Court answered yes.[12]

The Court's declaration in *Heff* that allotment brought Native Americans to full legal equality alarmed Washington's policy makers. The Indian Office feared it would soon be completely incapable of enforcing its prohibition orders or carrying out other actions that might protect allottees from the evils of modern life. And congressmen predicted that the decision would slow the recently accelerating pace of allotment. Undoubtedly administrators would be reluctant to divide reservation lands if they knew they were thereby ending all forms of federal guardianship. To answer these concerns Charles Burke, the South Dakota Republican who chaired the House Indian Affairs Committee, proposed two amendments to the original severalty act. The first would replace the twenty-five-year trust period with a statement that the secretary of the interior might issue a fee-simple title whenever he saw fit. Burke also suggested that Indians not become citizens until they had received their fee-simple titles to their homesteads. The new regulations, he told his colleagues, would reverse the "demoralization" that had followed the *Heff* ruling and restore the practice of treating allottees as if "they were still wards of the nation and subject to the jurisdiction only of the United States." The congressman wanted to make the prosecution's argument in the *Heff* case the law of the land.[13]

Burke's proposal was immediately endorsed by Commissioner Francis Leupp. Leupp wrote, "Citizenship has been a disadvantage to many Indians. They are not fitted for its duties or able to take advantage of its benefits." Because of their infirmities, the commissioner urged that tribesmen continue as wards of the Indian Office until they were "fitted" for political equality. In his view, the Burke Act removed the legal barriers to federal supervision and allowed the allotment process to continue. Such was the expectation when the Burke Act became law in May 1906.[14]

But the "solution" provided by the new statute soon proved unsatisfactory. Political enemies of the Indian Office and westerners who supported the rapid leasing or sale of Indian lands were suspicious of the law's open-ended promise of federal supervision. Senator Henry Teller, long a critic of government "paternalism" and one of the West's oldest apostles of expansion, opposed the measure because it created the anomaly of a specially protected racial group. "When you depart from the principle that every citizen is the equal of every other citizen under the law," he warned, "there is an end to free government." As they had in the debates over the pace of patenting and allotment, western men like the Colorado senator urged an end to the "distinctions" between the protected Indians and their white neighbors.[15]

Equally outspoken were the eastern reform groups who had long viewed citizenship as the key to Indian progress. In their *Annual Report* for 1906 the Board of Indian Commissioners expressed their "regret" over the passage of the new law. "We think that this prolonged period of exclusion from the duties and rights of citizenship is too heavy a price for the Indians to pay for protection by the Indian Bureau." The Indian Rights Association repeated this criticism, calling the statute "detrimental" to the Indians. In the years after 1906 the association's opposition to the Burke Act underlay its campaign to speed up the patenting process and reduce the size of the Indian Office.[16]

Opposition from westerners and reformers, together with the ongoing pressure to issue fee-simple patents at a rapid rate, doomed whatever long-term protection the Burke Act might have provided the Indians. Delays in granting citizenship could only be a temporary solution; the Indian Office needed a new definition of federal guardianship that would extend the controls already available.

The most pressing need was a way to suppress the liquor traffic. The *Heff* decision left the Indian Office with no way to keep liquor dealers away from citizen Indians. After *Heff*, federal restrictions on Native Americans' behavior were unenforceable among allottees. Prosecution was left to state authorities, who, as one agent put it, took "little interest in the suppression of the liquor traffic among the Indians, and [would] only prosecute when a case [was] presented in such form that the defendant [had] no alternative but to plead guilty." Faced with these handicaps, the Indian Office turned to the courts. In a series of cases decided between 1908 and 1916, the government succeeded in expanding the doctrine of guardianship so that federal officials could restrict liquor sales to both citizen and noncitizen Indians. At the end of this effort, the *Heff* verdict was overturned.[17]

The Supreme Court first modified *Heff* in 1908, when it approved the conviction of George Dick, a Nez Perce Indian, for liquor dealing even though both the defendant and his customers were citizens.

Dick v. *U.S.* pointed out that the severalty law's promise that allottees would "be subject to the laws . . . of the State or Territory in which they may reside" was superseded by a separate agreement the tribe had negotiated with the Indian Office in 1893. That document stated that after the severalty process was complete, all "surplus" lands within the boundaries of the old reservation would be sold, but that they would continue under federal prohibitions against liquor dealing for twenty-five years. Justice John Harlan, writing for the Court, insisted that the conviction of Dick did not undermine the Indians' constitutional rights. Instead, he noted, it was "demanded by the highest considerations of public policy." The following year the Court further amended *Heff* by deciding (in *U.S.* v. *Celestine* and *U.S.* v. *Sutton*) that every allotment would be considered "Indian country" until a fee-simple title was issued for it. Federal officials could forbid the introduction of liquor into those areas and prosecute Native Americans who committed crimes within their boundaries.[18]

The question of limiting liquor consumption by citizen Indians was next addressed in 1911, when the high court reviewed the conviction of Simeon Hallowell, an Omaha allottee. Hallowell had been arrested for bringing whiskey to his farm. The defendant argued that Indian Office personnel had no authority to regulate his behavior since he was a citizen subject to state law. The court disagreed, and the justices reminded Hallowell that the grant of citizenship did "not necessarily end the right or duty of the United States to pass laws in their interest as a dependent people." Hallowell's farm stood on trust land that, while granted to him, remained under federal control. The court ruled that "within its own territory" the national government had the right to "pass laws protecting . . . Indians from the evil results of intoxicating liquors." The trust patent, then, would provide the courts with the necessary means for supervising allottees without appearing to interfere with their rights as citizens. But there was still no clear authority for federal intervention in cases involving citizen Indians on their fee-simple lands.[19]

The high court laid the groundwork for a decision giving the government power to supervise Indian behavior wherever it occurred in *Mosier* v. *U.S.* (1912). A federal appeals court in Oklahoma upheld the conviction of Eugene Mosier for selling liquor to Hazel

Grey, an enfranchised Osage woman. Referring to Grey, the court noted that a grant of citizenship "would not sever the relationship of guardian and ward existing between her and the government" and that Congress "could not delegate the power granted by the Constitution of the United States to exercise guardianship towards her to the state of Oklahoma." While the facts in the case loosely paralleled those in *Hallowell*, the court chose to take its stand on the grounds of guardianship; it avoided any discussion of the trust title.[20]

A year later the Supreme Court followed the same course in a case involving the Santa Clara Pueblo in New Mexico. The Santa Clarans held their land in fee simple under a Spanish grant that preceded the U.S. conquest of the Southwest. They had become citizens under the Treaty of Guadalupe Hidalgo in 1848. In 1913 no other tribe could claim to be freer of federal control. *U.S.* v. *Sandoval* addressed the legality of a federal prohibition statute on Pueblo land. Lawyers for Felipe Sandoval pointed out that the tribe had never been a ward of the U.S. government and had no formal ties to Washington. Unable to tie their case to trust lands, the attorneys for the Indian Office turned to the argument presented in *Mosier:* the nation's duty to act in the best interest of a "backward people." Without dissent, the Court accepted this plea. "The people of the pueblos," Justice Willis Van Devanter wrote, "although sedentary rather than nomadic . . . and disposed to peace and industry, are nevertheless Indians in race, customs and domestic government. . . . they are essentially a simple, uninformed, inferior people." Once the people of Santa Clara were portrayed in these terms, the decision could follow in rapid order, despite the precedent of *Heff:* "Not only does the Constitution expressly authorize Congress to regulate commerce with the Indian tribes, but long continued legislative and executive usage and an unbroken current of judicial decisions have attributed to the United States as a superior and civilized nation the power and the duty of exercising a fostering care and protection over all dependent Indian communities within its borders." The *Sandoval* decision did not specifically endorse *Mosier,* but it made clear that in the future officials would not have to show that the government retained a trust title to the Indians' lands in order to prosecute liquor dealers. As long as the individual Indians involved were shown to be "simple, uninformed and inferior people," federal authorities could take whatever steps they deemed appropriate to exercise their control.[21] But despite the government's victories in *Hallowell* and *Sandoval*, the *Heff* decision stood. It applied to the actions of those who had become citizens under the Dawes Act; the later rulings were based on agreements affecting single tribes. Thus they were all considered exceptions to the *Heff* ruling. A categorical reversal of *Heff* did not come until 1916, in *U.S.* v. *Nice*, a case involving the sale of liquor to a group of allottees on the Rosebud Sioux reservation. Citing a number of recent precedents, including *Dick* v. *U.S.*, *Tiger* v. *Western Investment Co.*, *Hallowell*, and *Sandoval*, the Court held that since guardianship and citizenship were compatible, the government's general responsibility to protect Indians continued after the granting of the franchise. According to Justice Van Devanter, it was "obvious" that the Dawes Act's provisions placing Indian allottees under the control of state laws "were to be taken with some implied limitations, and not literally." The severalty law was hereafter to be interpreted in this light. "The Constitution invested Congress with the power to regulate traffic in intoxicating liquors with the Indian tribes *meaning the individuals composing them*," the Court declared. It went on to warn that the government "could not divest itself" of this responsibility.[22]

However benevolent in intent, the effort to prohibit liquor sales among Indians limited their rights as citizens. The Supreme Court's announcement that guardianship over "backward" Native Americans could not be limited or terminated helped stem the destructive flow of alcohol into Indian communities, but it raised the specter of federal control over other aspects of life. If individual liberties could be circumscribed in an area in which the Indian Office felt Native Americans did not measure up to their fellow citizens, they could surely be limited in others. In the first two decades of the twentieth century federal involvement in criminal cases affecting citizen Indians followed the pattern established in disputes over liquor sales. Here too, the guardians' role expanded, and the rights of their newly enfranchised wards contracted.

The Major Crimes Act of 1885 had established the federal courts' exclusive jurisdiction over serious crimes committed by Indians on reservations. In the late nineteenth century allotment altered this absolute control. The Dawes Act provided that "upon the completion of . . . allotment and the patenting of the lands to said allottees," Indians would "have the benefit of and be subject to the laws, both civil and criminal of the State or Territory" in which they resided. Under this statute most early criminal cases involving allotted Indians were taken directly to state courts. Attempts to continue treating allottees like their kinsmen on unallotted reservations were rebuffed, as was the argument that state jurisdiction should begin only after fee-simple titles had been granted.[23]

At first judges and lawyers welcomed this new trend. The supreme court of Kansas observed that whites who settled on newly opened reservations should be protected against Indian lawbreakers by state laws. "We are not to presume," the justices declared, "that Congress would encourage the white man to go with his family among . . . the Indian . . . and not protect him, his family, and his property against the depredations and lawlessness of the Indian." The American Bar Association's Committee on Indian Legislation agreed. In the first years of allotment the association—largely at the urging of Harvard's James Bradley Thayer—had advocated continued federal jurisdiction, but by 1903 attitudes had changed and the association called for an expansion of state power. The Indian, the committee's report noted, was an "object of pity," and their belief was that "he would meet with justice, and often with favor and indulgence, before the juries of the neighborhood." As in the area of liquor sales, the prevailing belief was that, for better or worse, citizen allottees must be free from federal control.[24]

But despite this optimism, there continued to be a significant undercurrent of doubt over the wisdom of transferring Native Americans to the "juries of the neighborhood." Reports of police apathy and discrimination were unsettling. Typically, once allotment had taken place, a tribe's own law enforcement apparatus was disbanded and the group forced to rely on the county sheriff. In this situation Indians frequently suffered the fate of other politically powerless racial minorities. In 1898, for example, two Oklahoma Seminoles suspected of murder were burned at the stake by a white mob. The case was investigated by U.S. marshals and the tribe paid an indemnity, but territorial officials took no action against the murderers.[25]

The tribesmen's new neighbors often exhibited less "favor and indulgence" than the bar association had predicted. The agent for the newly allotted Kiowas reported a typical sequence of events that might occur when a white man filed a suit against an allottee for nonpayment of a debt. "A warrant is served," the agent noted, "and [the defendant], not having understood a word read to him, fails to appear and the case goes against him, by default. His property is ordered sold to cover costs and the amount of the debt claimed."[26] As reports of this kind multiplied, the Indian Office began to question the wisdom of abandoning its jurisdiction over citizen Indians. Despite enfranchisement, it appeared that many tribesmen would continue to require the protection of their former guardian.

The 1906 Burke Act reversed the trend toward rapid citizenship for allottees. Although the new law did not address the issue of criminal jurisdiction directly it promised to extend federal guardianship beyond the point when Indians received their homesteads. It was this pledge that the Indian Office intended to honor. But there were those who criticized the new statute. The Indian Rights Association believed Burke's law would undermine the civilization effort, declaring in its *Annual Report* for 1906 that the new act was "detrimental" to the nation's wards. The association's opposition soon became quite strident, however, for Leupp began acting in a way that confirmed the reformers' long-standing fear that an increase in the commissioner's power would encourage authoritarianism and produce a repetition of the tragedies of 1879.[27]

In late 1906, Leupp severely punished a group of Hopi parents who refused to send their children to the government's schools. The following year he publicly defended an agent at the Crow reservation who was being accused of corruption by the Indian Rights Association and defended by the leaders of the Montana gop. In 1908, relations between the commissioner and his old comrades reached the breaking point.

Leupp had ordered a group of recalcitrant Navajos, led by one Bai-a-lil-le, to be jailed for repeatedly refusing orders to disband and return to their homes. The Indian Rights Association leadership, already angry at the commissioner for his handling of the Hopi and Crow cases, criticized Leupp for holding the Indians without formal charges. Secretary of the Interior James Garfield responded in April by asking General Hugh Scott, an old cavalryman respected by both reformers and Indians, to investigate the Navajo affair. Scott's report, which exonerated Leupp, only added to the association's suspicions. Its officers continued to protest.

The association believed that the Bai-a-lil-le case would be a good vehicle for expressing its opposition to the renewed popularity of federal guardianship. "If the Indians can be stilled by such injustice," Samuel Brosius wrote about Bai-a-lil-le's warrantless arrest, "there is no hope for bringing them out of their slavery . . . The Navajo case is the golden opportunity to teach the Indian Commissioner a lesson." The association's Washington agent set out on his own tour of the Southwest and in the fall of 1908 began preparations for a habeas corpus proceeding in the Arizona courts. Leupp remained unmoved, though certainly he was exasperated. "If you understood fully the situation," he wrote an old friend in the association, "you could appreciate the difficulties encountered in dealing with these uncivilized Indians."[28]

Bai-a-lil-le's arrest brought sharply into focus the issue of criminal jurisdiction over Indians. Leupp, insisting that federal control should remain absolute, refused the Indian Rights Association's demand for a formal hearing of the charges against the renegade Navajos. He argued that the reformers were "painfully uninformed concerning the Indian and his traits." To the association's leadership, Bai-a-lil-le was a modern Standing Bear, and they intended to revive the case they had ridden to glory thirty years before. Significantly, the dispute brought the Boston Indian Citizenship Committee—founded during the Ponca crisis and long since moribund—briefly back to life. With aging figures such as John Davis Long presiding, the Bostonians met and published a circular asserting that the Navajos were "entitled to a fair hearing."[29]

The Boston Committee's reappearance brought a quick response from Theodore Roosevelt. In a letter to the group's leaders, the president repeated his commissioner's assertion that Indians could not be governed like white men. "Devoutly as all of us may look forward to the day when the most backward Indian shall have been brought to the point where he can be governed just as the ignorant white man is governed in one of our civilized communities," the Rough Rider observed, "that day has not yet arrived." TR and Leupp rejected the assumption of the 1880s—the Indians would become a part of white society as soon as they gained their legal rights—and replaced it with a more pessimistic view. Like the modern scientists who taught that racial and ethnic minorities possessed limited abilities, these policy makers argued that "wild" Indians would inevitably occupy an inferior place in the social order. Presumably the group's station might improve as society advanced, but its members would continue to be imprisoned by their racial heritage. To believe anything else was naïve. In this sense, the Navajo's "uncivilized behavior" justified new criminal procedures no less than the *Heff* case had demanded new liquor regulations. In 1880, *Standing Bear* had demonstrated the need for bringing Indians into the white legal system. The *Heff* decision and the Bai-a-lil-le episode proved (at least to Leupp and Roosevelt) the need to exclude them from it.[30]

Although the Indian Rights Association won its legal argument (Bai-a-lil-le was freed in March 1909), it failed to reverse the trend toward greater federal control. Even the judge who released the Navajo leader agreed that increased supervision might be justified on practical—if not legal—grounds. "However salutary in its results and desirable such a method of dealing with recalcitrant Indians may be," he wrote of the commissioner's action, "it cannot be sanctioned." In the years after 1909, the notion that wider guardianship in criminal matters would be "salutary" and "desirable" helped expand the power of federal guardians. The authority for this expansion came not from Congress, but from two important decisions of the Supreme Court.[31]

U.S. v. *Celestine*, decided in the same year that Bai-a-lil-le was set free, was a review of the conviction of a citizen Indian who had committed a murder on the allotted Tulalip reservation in Washington. Bob Celestine's lawyers argued that since the *Heff* decision had removed federal jurisdiction over citizen Indians who violated federal statutes, their client should be set free from federal jurisdiction and retried in a state court. The justices disagreed, noting that the Major Crimes Act gave the national government exclusive jurisdiction over Indians on reservations. "Notwithstanding the gift of citizenship," they wrote, "both the defendant and the murdered woman remain Indians by race, and the crime was committed . . . within the limits of the reservation. . . . It cannot be said to be clear that congress intended by the mere grant of citizenship to renounce entirely its jurisdiction over the individual members of this dependent race."[32]

The second decision, *U.S.* v. *Pelican* (1913), broadened the application of *Celestine.* In the wake of the *Sandoval* decision—which held that federal liquor prohibitions were enforceable on fee-simple Pueblo lands—the Court was asked to review the convictions of two citizen-Indian murderers. The crimes had been committed on allotted land, and the defendants cited the Dawes Act's provision that allottees were subject to the laws of the state in their attempt to have federal charges dropped. Citing the growing body of decisions supporting liquor prohibitions on trust lands, and apparently reversing several lower-court rulings, the justices declared that all allotments held in trust remained under federal jurisdiction. The old reformers' argument—that allotment would set Native Americans free from federal control and incorporate them into the larger society— was now explicitly rejected. Allotments, the Court announced, "remained Indian lands set apart for Indians under governmental care; and [the Court was] unable to find ground for the conclusion that they became other than Indian country through their distribution into separate holdings." Justice Hughes declared, "The fundamental consideration is the protection of a dependent people."[33]

By the second decade of the twentieth century it was clear that federal guardianship would not be terminated. While native landowners were receiving their fee patents and being "set free" to compete with their non-Indian neighbors, the authorities in Washington were completing their redefinition of Indian citizenship. The popularity of this new—if contradictory—policy was revealed in a study of Indian life commissioned during Robert Valentine's term. The commissioner asked Arthur Luddington, a Columbia University political scientist, to investigate conditions at each of the nation's 105 Indian agencies. Luddington designed a detailed questionnaire, which he sent to every superintendent. One question referred to the enforcement of liquor laws. Only 11 agencies reported that state authorities enforced the prohibition statutes adequately. "There is little, if any sentiment in favor of enforcing such laws," the agent at Fond du Lac, Wisconsin, reported. In response to another item, 42 superintendents conceded that state courts protected the interests of allotted Indians in some areas, but indicated that the quality of this protection was often uncertain. The superintendent at Neah Bay, Washington, noted, "There is prejudice, and always will be, against individual Indians . . . and it is right that this prejudice should continue, as it makes for the improvement of the Indian."[34]

Not surprisingly, when asked if it would be "wise to grant citizenship during the trust period to the allotted noncitizen Indians," only 21 of the 105 superintendents answered in the affirmative. Citing the need for federal supervision of the liquor traffic, as well as the laxity of state courts, the majority of the respondents urged the Indian Office to delay the grant of citizenship. Their position became a central element in Luddington's final report. Noting that recent court decisions allowed the "Federal Government to limit citizenship in almost any way which [could] be shown to be important for the welfare of the Indians," the government's expert analyst concluded: "As a general principle, the Federal Government should retain the legal right to exercise certain kinds of control or obtain for the Indians certain kinds of exceptions to existing laws."[35]

The Indian Office no longer based its obligations on treaty commitments or the need to protect new landowners. The Indians' "unfitness" for modern life—their susceptibility to alcoholism and their ignorance—made them "dependent" people whose personal freedoms might legitimately be curbed by their guardians. These limitations redefined Indian citizenship, replacing the nineteenth-century notion of full equality with the idea that political liberties were contingent on one's "civilization." Skepticism concerning the Indians' ability to adapt to American society had produced a new category of partial citizenship.

The redefinition of Indian citizenship proceeded on more than the federal level. State and local authorities shared the pessimism of the Supreme Court and the Indian Office, and they joined those institutions in fashioning an appropriate legal status for what they believed were backward, dependent people. And local lawmakers had an additional incentive: to maintain their control over a minority whose freedom might disrupt the racial status quo within their communities. State officials were most active in the areas of voting rights, laws affecting school attendance, and regulation of interracial marriage.

Indian voting received little attention in the early twentieth century. The Indian Office never made voting a part of its "civilization" campaign, and Native Americans did not vote in large numbers. In 1919 it was estimated that only 25,000 of the nation's 336,000 Indians cast ballots. Even the most fervent reformers argued that suffrage was a privilege the Indian might forego. Fayette McKenzie, an energetic founder of the Society of American Indians, assured those who might feel threatened by the extension of citizenship to Native Americans by noting, "If there be any considerable danger in giving the franchise to the illiterate Indian, every state is still free to exercise its duty to enact an educational qualification for the franchise." The sociologist and his allies appeared to agree with the supreme court of Oklahoma when it defended that state's famous grandfather clause by asserting that "suffrage [was] purely a political right granted by the sovereign power to those worthy and competent to participate in governmental affairs."[36]

The universal belief that individual states could set discriminatory eligibility requirements of course lay behind much of the disinterest in Indian voting. The Supreme Court had demonstrated in the *Civil Rights* cases and *Plessy* v. *Ferguson* that federal police powers could not affect local social arrangements, and the successful disfranchisement movement in the South during the 1890s confirmed the power of state authorities to control access to the voting booth. If individual states were as eager to bar Indians from the polls as they were to exclude blacks, they were legally capable of accomplishing their objective.[37]

Every state with a significant Indian population had voting regulations that limited Native American participation in elections. These limitations fell into four categories. Colorado, Montana, Nebraska, Oregon, South Dakota, and Wyoming had the sole restriction that electors be citizens of the United States. Tribes such as the Oregon

Umatillas and the Omahas of Nebraska, who had been admitted to citizenship en masse when their reservations were allotted, thus had access to the polls. In an 1893 decision that seemed to settle the issue for a number of these states, the Nebraska Supreme Court declared citizen allottees eligible to vote. But in Wyoming, South Dakota, Colorado, and Montana, where most Indians remained on undivided reservations or were allotted after the Burke Act had delayed the granting of citizenship, the impact of the requirement was probably different. In Corson County, South Dakota, for example (which covered a substantial part of the Standing Rock Sioux reservation) the 1910 census revealed there were 503 Indian and 591 white males of voting age. In that fall's election, 545 ballots were cast. With voter turnout customarily high in the early twentieth century, it is likely that almost all of those 545 voters were non-Indians.[38]

A decision in the California Supreme Court issued in 1917 endorsed the practice of barring noncitizens from the polls and gave voice to the argument—which had not been heard since *Elk* v. *Wilkins* in 1884—that Indians could not participate in politics until they were naturalized "Ordinarily," the California justices wrote in *Anderson* v. *Matthews*, "every person residing in the United States . . . if born here is, by that fact a citizen. The only exceptions to this rule are persons . . . who . . . are subject to the jurisdiction of some other country or political community." Echoing the leaders whom the reformers of 1879 had villified, the state tribunal concluded that Indians could be prevented from voting because they were "under the control and protection of the United States." The court noted, however, that because the plaintiff in *Anderson* v. *Matthews* belonged to a group of "wild and uncivilized Indians" and had never been a part of a recognized tribal group, he had no apparent ties to the United States and should be allowed to vote in California. Nevertheless, it is significant that in 1917 few people refuted the court's assertion that tribesmen could be barred from the polls. In 1884, when the *Elk* decision was announced, the reformers in Congress had responded quickly with the grant of citizenship contained in the Dawes Act. Thirty-three years later, policy makers were moving in the opposite direction, expanding the government's guardianship role and delaying the extension of full citizenship to allottees.[39]

In another method of limiting Indian participation in elections, Minnesota, North Dakota, California, Oklahoma, and Wisconsin declared that all voters must be "civilized." Oklahoma and California required electors to be both "civilized" and citizens; the others allowed one's "civilization" to substitute for citizenship. In California literacy was the test of a person's "civilization," but in Minnesota, North Dakota, and Wisconsin, voters were expected to have "adopted the language, customs and habits of civilization." In Oklahoma Indians came under the state's infamous grandfather clause. Descendants of the Five Civilized Tribes were eligible to vote, but all others—whose ancestors were viewed as "blanket" Indians—were restricted.[40]

The stipulation that voters be "civilized" gave states the power to qualify native citizenship. Just as southern states could set their own definitions of what constituted literacy, so westerners could say—as one agent reported—that Indians had "not adopted to a sufficient degree the pursuits and habiliments of civilization." The Minnesota Supreme Court outlined how the rule would be used in a decision handed down in 1917. "Tribal Indians," the court announced, "have not adopted the customs and habits of civilization . . . until they have adopted that custom and habit which all other inhabitants must needs adopt when they come into the state . . . This the Indian may do by taking up his abode outside the reservation and there pursuing the customs and habits of civilization." Residency in an Indian community—even on an allotted reservation—created the presumption that a person was not civilized and therefore could not vote.[41]

A third means of keeping Native Americans from the polls was the provision in the constitutions of three states—Idaho, New Mexico, and Washington—that Indians "not taxed" were excluded from suffrage. Because Indians did not contribute to the support of the government, these states reasoned, they did not belong to the polity. The taxation test also was incorporated into the regulations of the most restrictive states—Arizona, Nevada, and Utah. This final group required all voters to be taxpayers, residents of the state (not reservations), and citizens. The effect of these restrictions can be seen in Apache County, Arizona, where the 1910 census reported a potential electorate of 2,075, roughly half of whom were Indians. Only 253 ballots were cast in the 1912 elections. If Apache County, with the largest concentration of Indians in the state, is any indication, Indian participation in the political life of the more restrictive states was probably nil.[42]

Arizona defended its policies on Indian voting by arguing that Native Americans were people "under guardianship" and therefore like prison inmates or patients in an asylum. The state's supreme court declared in 1928, "So long as the federal government insists that . . . [the Indians] may be regulated . . . in any manner different from that which may be used in the regulation of white citizens, they are within the meaning of our constitutional provision 'persons under guardianship,' and not entitled to vote." The doctrine of guardianship was being used here as it had been when it was applied to criminal law and liquor regulation: to delay rather than to hasten the day when Indians might enjoy full membership in American society.[43]

States with significant Indian populations maintained an ambiguous policy toward native children in their public schools. Decisions by courts in Oregon, California, and North Carolina indicated that local officials would use perceived racial handicaps to segregate Native American children from the rest of the population. The California Supreme Court relied on this type of reasoning in 1924, when it declared, "It is not in violation of the organic law of the state or nation . . . to require Indian children or others in whom racial differences exist, to attend separate schools, provided such schools are equal in every substantial respect with those furnished for children of the white race." And the U.S. Congress agreed, setting up segregated schools in Alaska in 1905. On the other hand, most states were willing to tolerate a limited amount of integrated schooling. Federal subsidies made accepting those students possible, and there was usually the option of returning undesirable children to Bureau of Indian Affairs institutions. Once again federal guardianship was turned against the Indian population; it provided a rationale for state limitations on their personal freedom.[44]

Miscegenation, like public school attendance, produced mixed reactions in states with large Indian populations. Only four states—Arizona, Nevada, North Carolina, and Oregon—had statutes forbidding sexual relations between Indians and whites. But, as in the case of education, there was general agreement that the states could limit Indian freedom if they wished. The Arizona and Oregon laws were tested and upheld in their state supreme courts; three of the states continued their restrictions until well after 1920.[45]

By 1920, the redefinition of Indian citizenship was complete. A version of federal guardianship had been applied to Native Americans that protected them from exploitation by limiting their freedom. Guardianship allowed federal controls on land to continue after allotment, perpetuated the regulation of the Indians' personal life, and allowed states to discriminate against their native populations.

In the nineteenth century, the United States had considered itself the guardian of tribes. In the *Crow Dog* decision, the Supreme Court decreed that the murder of one Indian by another was beyond the reach of federal authorities; the tribes were separate entities whose internal affairs were their own concern. In the twentieth century, as the government worked to destroy tribal life, the meaning of guardianship changed. Rather than being a device to protect the interests of a group, guardianship was now applied to individual Indians. In its modern form, guardianship enabled the government to oversee the behavior of members of a "backward" race.

Shifting the impact of guardianship from tribes to individual Indians won the support of those who called for universal allotment and the abolition of the Indian Office. Nineteenth-century reformers had expected federal officials to supervise native progress and to intervene on the Indians' behalf when they were victimized. But in the twentieth century—after Indian citizenship was redefined—there was less call for interference from Washington. The Indian Office might still administer the remaining trust lands and regulate the liquor traffic, but most property would be "set free" from control and the Indians urged to adapt to local conditions. Questions concerning legal rights would be settled in the courts. Ironically, as individual persons under guardianship Indians required less supervision than they would have if the ambitious campaign of the 1880s had continued uninterrupted. As wards, Indians were a static group. They posed no threat to their non-Indian neighbors. Their peripheral role in American society was clear, and potential disputes with local officials over voting rights, liquor laws, criminal jurisdiction, and school admissions were defused. The modern definition of guardianship fit neatly into the process of peripheralization that was occurring in all areas of federal Indian policy. As the natives' power over their own lands was reduced and their "place" in white society defined, their political rights were altered and the list of their freedoms was shortened. Their legal status, like their economic and social position, became fixed on the fringes of American society.

A final measure of the impact of the new meaning of guardianship on the Native American's "place" in twentieth-century society was the response of legal commentators to Congress' decision in 1924 to grant citizenship to all Indians. Scholars have traditionally considered that action the instrument by which white America finally admitted Native Americans to political equality, but two essays written in the late 1920s suggest that this view falls short of the truth. The authors of these commentaries did not focus on the rights of the newly enfranchised natives. Instead, they reminded the public of what by then was settled legal doctrine: that the extension of citizenship to Indians did not alter their status as legal wards of the government. And the existence of the guardianship relation could limit their rights as citizens.

Chauncey Shafter Goodrich, a San Francisco lawyer, explained the legal status of California Indians in the 1926 *California Law Review*. "It was assumed in the past," he wrote, "that the grant of citizenship to an Indian would make him, politically speaking, as other men." But this was no longer true: "The court gradually came to take the definite position that the guardianship continued in force, regardless of citizenship, until expressly surrendered by Congress." Goodrich observed that "this curious combination of citizenship and tutelage . . . naturally called forth criticism," but he pointed out that "each new case presented to the Supreme Court . . . resulted in a stronger statement of the doctrine." As for the 1924 citizenship act, the lawyer argued that it "[did] not seriously affect the status of the Indians concerned, save, perhaps, further to confuse confusion." Goodrich saw no necessary conflict between native citizenship and a continuation of the limitations imposed on individual Indians by guardianship.[46]

Guardianship was the focus of a second *California Law Review* essay that appeared in 1930. Citing the recent Arizona case of *Porter v. Hall,* in which disfranchisement of the state's Indians was upheld on the grounds that natives were federal wards, Professor N. D. Houghton of the University of Arizona noted, "There appears to be ample ground for similar discrimination by the state government whenever it may be deemed to be necessary or desirable." Houghton agreed with Goodrich's interpretation of the 1924 law. The political scientist asserted that "unless specific provision were made for termination of the conditions of 'guardianship,' that condition, in all its vigor, would attach to the newly made citizen Indians." Both men held that guardianship was the key to the Native American's legal identity and would remain so until Congress specifically repealed all of the laws and treaties that had created their status in the first place.[47]

In the early twentieth century, federal officials became the guardians of individual Indians. The original grant of citizenship in the 1880s had proved inadequate; it had not brought Native Americans to political equality, nor had it removed the necessity of federal intervention to protect them from exploitation. Unwilling to guarantee Indians the rights promised under the Dawes Act, federal policy makers chose a different tack: the extension of guardianship to individual members of a "backward" race.

With the new century came a rise in racial tension in the South and Far West, ethnic pressures in dozens of urban centers, and demands for the creation of a new American empire. The nation altered its view of itself. Policy makers and reformers no longer spoke of incorporating disparate groups into American society by exposing them to the schoolroom and the ballot box and trusting progress. Faced with the job of managing overseas possessions, deluged by a seemingly endless stream of exotic immigrants, they devised a new solution. American society seemed incapable of assimilating its alien populations or of overcoming class divisions. Conditions made a mockery of the confident expectations that had been the gospel a generation before. In this anxious environment, lawyers and politicians began to describe their society hierarchically. They reasoned that each racial and ethnic group had specific strengths and weaknesses.

Consequently assimilation became equated with locating each group in a discrete place within the social structure. Each should have a role in the life of the whole nation, yet each had a natural limit as to what it could achieve and contribute. Guardianship would define the proper "place" for Indians. It would hold them in a spot appropriate to their racial characteristics, at once protecting them from exploitation and limiting their progress. Policy makers could now declare that the campaign for assimilation was complete.

Chapter 8

The Irony of Assimilation

In June 1920, Walter M. Camp, a railroad engineer and self-taught authority on the Indian wars of the late nineteenth century, submitted a brief report to the U.S. Board of Indian Commissioners. Entitled "The Condition of Reservation Indians," Camp's statement was based both on information gathered during seventeen years in the West and data supplied by "hundreds of intelligent and honorable people."[1] The contents of this document serve as a fitting coda to the Indian assimilation campaign.

While Camp admitted that his evidence came primarily from Montana and the Dakotas, he argued that his conclusions were applicable to Native Americans throughout the country. He concluded that the Indians' fundamental problem was their inability to become self-sufficient. Native Americans were notoriously poor farmers, stockraisers, and businessmen. They lacked the drive and talent necessary for moneymaking. The source of these shortcomings, Camp wrote, was not the economic, social, or legal arrangements that had been forged in the previous half-century. Instead, the natives' failures could be traced to their personal weaknesses:

Right here I am minded to express, as pertinent to my subject, my own conclusion as to the fundamental difference between the so-called 'civilized' man and the so-called 'savage,' for the latter of whom 'primitive man' is, I think, a better designation. The savage is concerned only with the immediate necessities of life, while the civilized man looks not only to the future, but beyond mere subsistence. In other words, the Indian is not a capitalist. It matters not which way this fact is stated. One might say that he is lacking in industry, and that the dearth of capital is an effect and not the cause of his poverty. Whichever way one puts it, the fact remains that it has not been in the nature of the Indian to accumulate either property or stores of goods as a reserve against adverse conditions. It has not been the way of the Indian to fortify himself against temporary failure of effort, as is the habit of the more sagacious element of civilized peoples. We thus see a difference of mental attitude as between the two races that, fundamentally, accounts for all of the industrial differences.[2]

Like the anthropologists and popular writers of the early twentieth century who became obsessed with the wide "gap" between Indian and white societies, Camp explained contemporary social conditions by referring to the Indians' racial "traits." It was the Indians' characteristic "mental attitude" and not the government's policies or their own cultural traditions that kept them in poverty.

Because he believed that the Indians' failures were the "natural" result of their "primitive" mind, Camp cautioned the members of the board to lower their expectations for native "progress." To expect "very considerable industrial advance in the short space of one generation," he wrote, would be a mistake. Indians suffered from "communistic ideas" that led them to share their resources unwisely. And their habit of traveling and visiting revealed an "excess of hospitality." These habits, Camp noted, created great "obstacles to progress" that could only be overcome by years of effort. Federal guidance was also required if natives were to "grow out of" their present habits. Echoing contemporary policy makers who defended leasing, vocational education, and qualified citizenship, Camp asserted that most

Indians were incapable of speedy adaptation to western habits. In his view it would not be harmful—indeed, it would be beneficial—if Native Americans served extended terms as menial laborers in a society dominated by whites.[3]

Walter Camp was confident that the future would bring gradual progress. After all, he wrote, "the effect of school education, association with white people, living with white neighbors and of much intermarriage of the races [was] beginning to tell in the social and economic status of these people." These influences would slowly raise the level of "civilization" among Indians. On this point, Camp agreed with the progressive politicians and bureaucrats who believed that native "advancement" could only be secured if the Indians remained under the guidance of whites. Even though the "mental attitudes" of the subject group were "primitive," a persistent policy of education and increased "white association" was bound to show results. Camp concluded, "We should do all that is within our power to elevate him!"[4]

"The Condition of Reservation Indians" illustrates the extent to which Indians had come to be perceived as peripheral members of the nation. The optimistic expectations of the 1880s by now were long forgotten. Assimilation no longer meant full citizenship and equality. Instead, the term now implied that Indians would remain on the periphery of American society, ruled by outsiders who promised to guide them toward "civilization." "Primitive" customs would be tolerated while Indian lands were leased or sold, Indian children were taught manual skills, and limitations were placed on Indian citizenship. The United States' natives were being assimilated, but the modern redefinition of that term meant that they were not expected to participate in American life as the equals of their conquerors.

The redefinition of Indian assimilation in the early twentieth century reflects a fundamental shift in American social values. In the two decades before World War I, politicians and intellectuals rejected the notion that national institutions would dissolve cultural differences and foster equality and cohesion. The optimism and confidence of the Gilded Age faded to doubt and defensiveness. In place of the old ideals appeared a new hierarchical view of society that emphasized the coexistence and interaction of diverse groups.

Confronted with growing ethnic diversity, badgered by malcontents protesting economic inequality, and chastened by the apparent failure of their programs, policy makers rejected the old goal of complete homogeneity and equality. They came to believe instead that each racial and ethnic group—and each class—possessed specific skills and characteristics; a group's "nature" could not be erased by exhortation or government action.

In the twentieth century American leaders argued that each group should play its proper role and work with others to preserve the social order. Blacks should take on manual tasks and keep to themselves in the rural South. Eastern Europeans should be small merchants and tradesmen. Native-born whites should be professionals and political leaders. Each group should contribute to the maintenance of the whole. The key to assimilation was no longer the act of becoming part of an undifferentiated, "civilized" society; instead, assimilation had come to mean knowing one's place and fulfilling one's role. In this sense, the Indian assimilation campaign had succeeded by 1920, for the Native Americans' place in the United States had been fixed and policies devised for holding the race to its duties.

The extent of the human suffering that was the chief feature of tribal life in the early twentieth century became known in stark detail when the Institute for Government Reseach published *The Problem of Indian Administration* in 1928. Commonly known as the Meriam Report, this document described an infant mortality rate double that of the general population, a death rate from tuberculosis seven times the national average, and an illiteracy rate that ran as high as 67 percent in one state. Finally, the institute's field workers estimated that two-thirds of all Indians earned less than one hundred dollars per year. Here was the reality that awaited a people "set free" from government "paternalism."[5]

One feels uncomfortable dwelling on the ironies of the assimilation campaign, for what is ironic to a well-fed historian was disastrous for the Indian people subjected to the government's policies. To shift attention from their plight seems both insensitive and sophistic. Nevertheless, the ironies are significant—both of them. First, the "assimilation" that whites advocated in 1920 was an inversion of what the policy makers of the 1880s had intended. Cynics might assert that the inversion was intentional (Dawes and Fletcher were not serious, they would say), but the early reformers were not so far-sighted or so clever. They organized a campaign to incorporate Indians into American life, and their goal—total assimilation—was a mirror of what they believed was possible. By 1920 their campaign was over. Like generals who claim victory while retreating, men like Walter Camp accepted the marginal place that scientists, educators, and politicians had assigned to native people and announced themselves satisfied. Assimilation had come to mean its opposite.

The second irony is more interesting. The assimilation effort, a campaign to draw Native Americans into a homogeneous society, helped create its antithesis—a plural society. Despite Walter Camp's smug assurance that education and association with civilized citizens was "beginning to tell," the decades following his report were marked by the persistence, rather than the disappearance, of tribal cultures. First in the buoyant days of the Indian New Deal and again in the activism of the 1960s and 1970s, a renewed tribal spirit moved to the center of Indian life. In the process, those native traditions that endured taught the non-Indian world that humanity is not divided into "civilized" and "primitive" camps.

Although the history of the tribal revivals is complex and largely unwritten, its basic outlines are clear. Missionaries and schoolteachers failed to stamp out tribal languages and ceremonies. Those features of Indian culture continued to serve tribal members and provide invisible storehouses for values and traditions. Economic and political pressure produced new generations of native leaders who defended the interests of the group. Family ties continued to insulate individual Indians from alien cultures and provide a source of history and identity. And the land—assaulted, stolen, leased, bulldozed, and flooded—continued as a source of group cohesion and an inspiration for continued activism. Each of these aspects of cultural reorganization was encouraged by the government's decision in the early twentieth century to "lower" its expectations and relegate the Indians to a peripheral role in American life.[6]

Because they believed that Native Americans would take generations to "appreciate" modern ways, politicians and policy makers grew more tolerant of traditional practices. And as long as tribal traditions survived, they could encourage the retention of tribal values, make possible the rise of a new generation of Indian leaders, and provide the cultural space necessary for individual Native Americans to chart their course through the twentieth century. The transformation of the assimilation campaign thus contributed to the survival of native communities and the emergence of modern incarnations of traditional cultures.

Other groups traveled this path to cultural survival. Blacks experienced a new form of rejection in the "nadir" of the early twentieth century, but reemerged as a cultural force in the vibrancy and genius of the Harlem renaissance. Jews reinvented their traditions in the urban ghetto, and Catholics forged a potent political interest group amid the nativist hysteria of the 1920s. Rejection and exclusion—confinement in their "proper station" in the social hierarchy—bred self-consciousness, resourcefulness, and aggressive pride.

The campaign to assimilate the Indians reveals both the burden and the promise of the Native American experience in our own time. Walter Camp's summary demonstrates how satisfied white Americans could be as they relegated Native Americans to the outer ring of Society. But his report also suggests how Indian people survived the suffering and exploitation that has characterized so much of their recent history. Defined as marginal Americans, tribal members could take advantage of their peripheral status, replenish their supplies of belief and value, and carry on their war with homogeneity. We should be thankful that this is a conflict the Indians are winning.

Appendixes

Appendix 1

Senate Roll Call Votes Affecting Indians, 1880–1920

The following list is a compendium of all roll call votes taken in the U.S. Senate between 1880 and 1920 that pertained to Indian affairs. The list includes a statement of the subject of each vote, followed by an indication of the congress and session during which the vote was held, the page of the *Congressional Record* on which the vote was recorded, the date of the vote, and the outcome of the vote.

In the notation of the outcome of each vote, "Y" represents yea votes; "N," nay votes; and "A," abstentions. For example, vote number one occurred during the 46th Congress, Second Session, and was recorded on page 2199 of the *Congressional Record* of that session. The vote was taken on April 7, 1880, and the measure was passed, 35 to 11. There were thirty abstentions.

1. To add to the Ute Treaty that it will not take effect until "the President shall be satisfied that the guilty parties are no longer living

or have fled beyond the limits of the U.S." Amendment to S.1509. 46–2, 2199; April 7, 1880; Y35, N11, A30.

2. An amendment to S.1509 to establish a boarding school for Ute Indians. 46–2, 2258; April 9, 1880; Y44, N8, A24.

3. An amendment to S.1509 that would eliminate tax exemptions for Indian lands guaranteed by treaty. 46–2, 2309–10; April 12, 1880; Y5, N40, A31.

4. An amendment to S.1509 calling for the removal of all Indians from Colorado. 46–2, 2312; April 12, 1880; Y9, N41, A26.

5. An amendment to S.1509 reducing treaty guaranteed annuities to Utes in order to pay damages to white settlers in Colorado. 46–2, 2312; April 12, 1880; Y15, N33, A28.

6. An amendment to S.1509 proposing to limit annuity payments to Indians to five years so as "not to confirm them in their idleness." 46–2, 2316; April 12, 1880; Y15, N33, A28.

7. Final vote on Ute Bill—S.1509—which altered the government's role in the tribe's affairs. Indians were allotted, given special inalienable titles, and exempted from taxation. 46–2, 2320; April 12, 1880; Y37, N16, A23.

8. An amendment to H.R. 4212 calling for the retention of the Board of Indian Commissioners. 46–2, 2829; April 28, 1880; Y37, N21, A18.

9. An amendment to H.R. 6730 appropriating $1,000 annually as supplemental pay for Captain Pratt of the Carlisle Indian school. 46–3, 821; January 21, 1881; Y27, N29, A35.

10. An amendment to S.1773 granting citizenship to all Indians who took land in severalty. 46–3, 939; January 26, 1881; Y12, N29, A35.

11. An amendment to S.1773 to eliminate the requirement that tribal consent be obtained before allotment took place. 46–3, 1064; January 31, 1881, Y10, N40, A26.

12. An amendment to H.R. 4185 to appropriate $250,000 for Indian education. 47–1, 2463–64; March 31, 1882; Y29, N18, A29.

13. Final vote on S.60, a right-of-way permit allowing the St. Louis and San Francisco Railroad to build across Indian Territory. 47–1, 2856; April 13, 1882, Y31, N13, A32.

14. An amendment to H.R. 6092 to eliminate the appropriation

for Indian education in Alaska. 48–1, 4105; May 13, 1884; Y10, N30, A36.

15. An amendment to H.R. 3961 that would require the Gulf, Colorado and Santa Fe Railroad to take the "most direct practicable route" through Indian Territory. 28–1, 5445; June 21, 1884; Y16, N25, A35.

16. A motion to take H.R. 4680, a bill granting the Southern Kansas Railroad a right of way through Indian Territory without Indian consent, from the table. 48–1, 5471; June 23, 1884; Y16, N14, A23.

17. An amendment to H.R. 7970 striking out the clause empowering the president to open negotiations for the opening of Indian Territory to white settlement. The first of three votes on this issue. 48–2, 1748; February 16, 1885; Y35, N20, A21.

18. Amendment to appropriations act—H.R. 7970—to authorize the president to negotiate with Creeks, Seminoles, and Cherokees "for the purpose of opening to settlement . . . the unassigned lands in Indian Territory." 48–2, 2395; March 2, 1885; Y18, N24, A34.

19. Same as above. 48–2, 2368; March 2, 1885; Y33, N27, A16.

20. A motion to bring to the floor S.91, a bill extending the time period allowed the St. Louis and San Francisco Railroad for the construction of a line through various reservations in Indian Territory. 49–1, 1593; February 18, 1886; Y31, N13, A32.

21. Final vote on S.1484, a bill granting the Kansas and Arkansas Valley Railroad a right of way through Indian Territory without prior consent of the Indians affected. 49–1, 3250; April 8, 1886; Y36, N8, A31.

22. Vote to refer H.R. 10614, the Oklahoma bill, to the Committee on Territories rather than the Committee on Indian Affairs. 50–2, 1507; February 5, 1889; Y39, N12, A25.

23. To strike out the provision of H.R. 12578 that appropriated $1.9 million for the purchase of 2.1 million acres of Seminole land without the consent of the tribe. 50–2, 2609; March 2, 1889; Y27, N13, A36.

24. To amend S.895 to expand Oklahoma Territory to include "No Man's Land," in violation of the treaty of 1832. 51–1, 1274; February 13, 1890; Y27, N16, A39.

25. To amend S.895 to grant Oklahoma Territory legal jurisdiction

over all cases in "No Man's Land" except those cases involving Indians. All such cases would be tried in tribal courts. 51–1, 3721; April 23, 1890; Y50, N5, A29.

26. To amend H.R. 10726 to strike out appropriations for two Catholic boarding schools. 51–1, 7668; July 24, 1890; Y19, N27, A38.

27. To amend S.8150 by striking out "no claim shall be allowed which is based upon the unsupported testimony of an Indian." 51–1, 2909; February 19, 1891; Y37, N14, A37.

28. To amend H.R. 13388 to appropriate $2.9 million to purchase, without the tribe's consent, the Chickasaw and Choctaw title to lands at that time leased from them. 51–2, 3540; February 28, 1891; Y38, N23, A28.

29. To amend H.R. 5974 to strike out "the President shall detail officers of the United States Army to act as Indian agents at all agencies . . . where vacancies may hereafter occur." 52–1, 2758; March 31, 1893; Y29, N34, A25.

30. Another attempt to strike out provision for army officers as Indian agents. 52–1, 2998; April 6, 1892; Y25, N28, A35.

31. Motion to table Senator Squire's proposal to allow Puyallups to dispose of their land to Tacoma, Washington, residents in advance of the twenty-five-year inalienability limit. 53–2, 7678; July 19, 1894; Y26, N19, A40.

32. Amendment to H.R. 6792 guaranteeing an allotment to all Utes who did not decline one. 53–3, 1454; January 28, 1895; Y12, N32, A41.

33. Amendment to H.R. 6792 which would add, "This act shall take effect only upon the acceptance thereof and consent thereto by a majority of all adult male Indians." 53–3, 1455; January 28, 1895; Y13, N31, A41.

34. Final vote on H.R. 6792, which, without the tribe's consent, reduced the size of the Southern Ute reservation and allotted homesteads to those Indians who might ask for them. 53–3, 1456; January 28, 1895; Y36, N12, A37.

35. Amendment to H.R. 8479 to end appropriations for education contracts with Lincoln and Hampton institutes. 53–3, 2506; February 21, 1895; Y21, N32, A34.

36. Amendment to H.R. 8479 to reduce appropriations for contract schools 20 percent each year for five years. Further to add that "at the end of five years all contracts for such education shall cease." 53–3, 2544; February 22, 1895; Y31, N23, A34.

37. Amendment to H.R. 6249 to add, "And it is hereby declared the settled policy of the government to make no appropriations whatever for the education of Indian children in any sectarian school." 54–1, 4259; April 22, 1896; Y38, N24, A27.

38. Final vote on H.R. 6249 to accept a conference committee report empowering the Dawes Commission to enroll and grant citizenship to Indians in Indian Territory, thereby bypassing the tribal governments and the treaty process. 54–1, 6085; June 4, 1896; Y27, N20, A42.

39. Vote on the conference report on H.R. 6249, which stated, "The Senate will recede from its statement requiring the government to sever connections with contract schools by July 1, 1898." 54–1, 6086; June 4, 1896; Y17, N31, A41.

40. To amend H.R. 10002 by inserting, "All of the Uncompahgre Indian reservation except 10,000 acres of bottom land . . . is hereby opened to public entry." 54–2, 2140; February 23, 1897; Y48, N17, A25.

41. An amendment to H.R. 10002 to extend the jurisdiction of federal courts to all inhabitants of Indian Territory, in violation of treaty agreements. Roll call over whether such an amendment would be in order. 54–2, 2340; February 26, 1897; Y36, N24, A30.

42. To strike from a proviso of H.R. 10002 extending the jurisdiction of U.S. courts to Indian Territory the words *full and exclusive* before the word *jurisdiction. Full and exclusive* would mean that federal judges would have jurisdiction over citizens of the Five Civilized Tribes. Such wording would violate treaty agreements. 54–2, 2345; February 26, 1897; Y8, N40, A42.

43. Amendment to H.R. 15 to open all of the Uncompahgre Indian reservation to settlement, excepting only those tracts that had already been allotted. As of the date of passage of this bill, no allotments had been made on this preserve. 55–1, 725; April 15, 1897; Y33, N13, A41.

44. Amendment to H.R. 7433 to continue appropriations for contract schools in areas where no government schools were available. 56–1, 3919; April 9, 1900; Y16, N30, A41.

45. Amendment to S.2992, the Rosebud Agreement, to guarantee a price of $2.50 per acre for all Indian land sold to settlers. 57–1, 4971; May 2, 1902; Y19, N38, A31.

46. Vote to recommit (in effect, to kill) the Rosebud Agreement. 57–1, 5024; May 5, 1902; Y12, N35, A41.

47. Amendment to H.R. 12684 to pay J. Hale Sypher $25,000 in fees for representing the Choctaw Indians. Charges of corruption surrounded vote. Claim was first made in 1891. 58–2, 3561; March 23, 1904; Y23, N25, A42.

48. Amendment to H.R. 11128, the Devil's Lake Agreement, to allow white settlers to acquire Indian lands for free after five years of settlement. This vote was not binding because the absence of a quorum was later suggested. The amendment was finally rejected on April 18. 58–2, 4925; April 16, 1904; Y5, N31, A54.

49. Amendment to appropriations bill, H.R. 17474, to allow Indians to send children to sectarian schools with their portion of annual annuities. 58–3, 3622; February 28, 1905; Y31, N26, A33.

50. Vote on the chair's decision that a provision in the appropriations bill, H.R. 17474, giving natives who applied for enrollment in the Five Tribes the right to appeal in U.S. courts, was in order. 58–3, 3639; February 28, 1905; Y26, N20, A44.

51. Amendment to H.R. 5676, the Five Tribes bill, to prevent sale of mining rights alone. The proposal required landowners to be responsible for the entire allotment. 59–1, 3208; March 1, 1906; Y8, N38, A43.

52. To lay on the table the section of H.R. 5676 (see vote 51, above) dealing with leasing mineral lands. Mineral lands would thus be reserved under previous arrangements until a study of the area could be made. Previous arrangements required federally supervised leases. 59–1, 3272; March 2, 1906; Y38, N7, A44.

53. Final vote on H.R. 5976, a bill that continued restrictions on the taxation and sale of land by "full-blooded" members of the Five Tribes. Existing leases arrangements also continued. 59–1, 5122; April 12, 1906; Y41, N11, A37.

54. Final vote on H.R. 15331, the annual appropriations bill. Chief objections referred to restrictions on the sale of allotted lands in Oklahoma, payments to residents of the Colville reservation, and payments to tribal lawyers. 59–1, 8264; June 11, 1906; Y30, N16, A42.

55. Amendment to H.R. 22580, the annual appropriations bill, to remove all restrictions on the sale and taxation of Indian lands in Indian Territory. Vote on whether this motion was in order. 59–2, 2414; February 7, 1907; Y22, N31, A36.

56. Final vote on S.109, a bill to allow the government to sell "surplus" lands on the Standing Rock Reservation. Objections were based on the bill's provision directing 25 percent of the revenue from the land sales to be used to build schools in settlements organized by new white homesteaders as well as the absence of a minimum sale price for the Indian land. 62–2, 1483; January 29, 1912; Y17, N30, A44.

57. Vote on a point of order made on an amendment to H.R. 1915, the annual appropriations bill, which directed the allotment of all tribal funds to members of the Choctaw, Chickasaw, and Cherokee tribes. 63–1, 2088; June 18, 1913; Y36, N15, A45.

58. An amendment to H.R. 12579, the annual appropriations bill, appropriating $100 per capita to Choctaw and $15 per capita to Cherokees from their tribal funds. 63–2, 10673; June 18, 1914; Y40, N15, A41.

59. An amendment to an appropriation for irrigation on reservations which read: "Provided, that no part of this appropriation shall be expended unless the Attorney General of the United States shall, after submission to him by the Secretary of the Interior's request for an opinion, hold affirmatively that in his opinion the Indians under existing law, are protected and confirmed in their water rights." 63–2, 11036; June 24, 1914; Y29, N20, A47.

60. Final vote on conference report on H.R. 12579, the annual appropriations bill. The report eliminated the amendment approved on June 24, (see vote 59, above). 63–2, 12610; July 24, 1914; Y27, N26, A43.

61. Amendment to H.R. 20150, an appropriations bill, striking out per capita payments to Choctaw and Chickasaw Indians. 63–3, 5156; March 2, 1915; Y15, N33, A48.

62. Amendment to H.R. 20150, an appropriations bill, allowing appeals of enrollment applications to the Five Tribes only for those whose cases were pending on March 4, 1907. 63–3, 5162; March 2, 1915; Y33, N13, A50.

63. Amendment to H.R. 18453, an appropriations bill, to allow the purchase of automobiles for the Flathead agency. 64–2, 2117; January 27, 1917; Y33, N19, A44.

64. Amendment to H.R. 18453, an appropriations bill, to provide for relief of Seminoles. 64–2, 2123; January 27, 1917; YI4, N26, A56.

65. Amendment to H.R. 18453, an appropriations bill, to reduce the amount appropriated for the relief of the Seminoles. 64–2, 2167; January 29, 1917; Y23, N26, A47.

66. Final vote on H.R. 18453, an appropriations bill, for fiscal year 1918. 64–2, 4321; February 26, 1917; Y33, N22, A41.

67. Amendment to H.R. 8696, an appropriations bill, to provide for an irrigation project for the Flathead reservation. 65–2, 4075; March 26, 1918; Y16, N25, A54.

Appendix 2

Congressional Appropriations for Indian Schools, 1877–1920

Year	Amount (in dollars)	Percent Change	Total Average Attendance in Government Schools	Indian Schoolage Population
1877	20,000		3,598	
1878	30,000	+50	4,142	
1879	60,000	+100	4,448	
1880	75,000	+25	4,651	34,541[1]
1881	75,000	0	4,976	
1882	135,000	+80	4,714	
1883	487,000	+260	5,686	
1884	657,000	+38	6,960	
1885	992,800	+47	8,143	37,123[1]
1886	1,100,000	+10	9,630	
1887	1,211,415	+10	10,520	
1888	1,179,916	−2.6	11,420	
1889	1,348,015	+14	11,552	
1890	1,364,568	+1	12,232	40–50,000[2]
1891	1,842,770	+35	13,588	
1892	2,291,650	+24	15,167	
1893	2,317,612	+1	16,303	
1894	2,243,497	−3.5	17,220	
1895	2,060,695	−8.9	18,188	37,300[3]
1896	2,056,515	−2	19,262	
1897	2,517,265	+22	18,876	
1898	2,631,771	+4.5	19,648	
1899	2,638,390	+0.25	20,522	
1900	2,936,080	+11	21,568	37–40,000[2]

Year	Amount (in dollars)	Percent Change	Total Average Attendance in Government Schools	Indian Schoolage Population
1901	3,080,368	+4.9	23,077	
1902	3,244,250	+5.3	24,120	
1903	3,531,250	+8.8	24,382	
1904	3,522,950	−1.2	25,104	
1905	3,880,740	+10	25,455	42,600[3]
1906	3,777,100	−2.7	25,492	
1907	3,925,830	+3.9	25,802	
1908	4,105,715	+4.6	25,964	
1909	4,008,825	−2.4	25,568	
1910	3,757,909	−6.3	24,945	45,700[3]
1911	3,685,290	−1.9	23,647	
1912	3,757,495	+2	26,281	
1913	4,015,720	+6.9	25,830	
1914	4,403,355	+9.6	26,127	
1915	4,678,628	+6.25	26,128	49,500[3]
1916	4,391,155	−6.1	25,303	
1917	4,701,903	+7.1	25,297	
1918	5,185,290	+10.3	23,822	
1919	4,837,300	−6.75	20,492	
1920	4,992,325	+1.2	23,248	50,500[3]

[1]Government figure in *Annual Report of the U.S. Commissioner of Indian Affairs.*
[2]Government estimate in *Annual Report of the U.S. Commissioner of Indian Affairs.*
[3]Author's estimate, 15 percent of total Indian population.
SOURCE: *Annual Report of the U.S. Commissioner of Indian Affairs* (1913, 1920).

Appendix 3

The Status of the Indians' Personal Rights and Liberties

Questions and responses from Office of Indian Affairs Circular No. 612, dated March 14, 1912, sent by Arthur C. Luddington. Figures represent number of responses in each category.

How effectively are state liquor laws enforced?

not at all	46
occasionally	24
usually	19
strictly	11
no answer	3

Are the rights of the noncitizen Indians under your charge effectively protected by the federal courts?

yes	74
no	4
unclear answer	16
no answer	24

Has the grant of citizenship to Indians proved in any way a failure?

yes	29
"somewhat"	18
no	28
no answer	30

Would it be wise to grant citizenship during the trust period to the allotted noncitizen Indians under your charge?

yes	22
no	44
no answer	39

Has the introduction of white settlers among Indian allottees been on the whole a benefit or a detriment to the Indians?

benefit	62
detriment	11
unclear answer	9
no answer	23

Abbreviations in Notes

AA	American Anthropologist	*N.W.*	Northwest Reporter
AJS	American Journal of Sociology	P.	Pacific Reporter
ANR	Superintendents' Annual Narrative and Statistical Report Entry 960, Records Group 75, National Archives	*Proc. AAAS*	Proceedings of the American Association for the Advancement of Science
		Proc. NEA	Proceedings of the National Education Association
ARCIA	Annual Report of the U.S. Commissioner of Indian Affairs	RG 75, NA	Records Group 75, National Archives
CR,—,.	Congressional Record, Congress–Session, page.	RG 48, NA	Records Group 48, National Archives
		S.E.	Southeast Reporter
F.	Federal Reporter	S.R.	Senate Resolution
H.R.	House Resolution	*S.W.*	Southwest Reporter
IRA	Indian Rights Association	*U.S.*	United States Reports
IRA AR	Indian Rights Association Annual Report	*U.S. Statutes*	United States Statutes at Large

Notes

Chapter 1

1. *Boston Post*, January 15, 1897, p. 1, *St. Louis Post-Dispatch*, January 13, 1879, p. 1.

2. *Atlanta Constitution*, January 16, 1879, p. 2. For a detailed description of the Fort Robinson incident, see Ramon Powers, "Why the Northern Cheyenne Left Indian Territory in 1878: A Cultural Analysis," pp. 72–81.

3. For descriptions of the religious disputes that undermined the administration of the Peace Policy, see Peter A. Rahill, *The Catholic Indian Missions and Grant's Peace Policy, 1870–1884*, passim. See also Robert H. Keller, "The Protestant Churches and Grant's Peace Policy: A Study in Church State Relations," chaps. 7 and 12; and R. Pierce Beaver, *Church, State and the American Indians.* For the Interior-War Department controversy, see Henry G. Waltmann, "The Interior Department, War Department and Indian Policy, 1865–1887"; and Loring Benson Priest, *Uncle Sam's Stepchil-*

dren, pp. 15–28. Special congressional allocations for Indian education did not begin until 1880, when $75,000 was appropriated.

4. George Crook, "The Apache Problem," p. 269.

5. Quoted in *U.S. ex rel. Standing Bear* v. *Crook*, in Henry L. Dawes Papers. For descriptions of the Ponca incident, see J. Stanley Clark, "Ponca Publicity," pp. 495–516; Thomas H. Tibbles, *The Ponca Chiefs*; and Helen Marie Bannon, "Reformers and the Indian Problem, 1878–1887 and 1922–1934," pp. 11–27. According to Tibbles, oral argument began on April 30. Local newspapers reported that the proceedings began on May 1. See Thomas Henry Tibbles, *The Ponca Chiefs: An Account of the Trial of Standing Bear*, ed. Kay Graber (Lincoln: University of Nebraska Press, 1972), p. 140.

6. *Alta California*, May 14, 1879, p. 2; *Chicago Tribune*, May 19, 1879, p. 4. For Dundy's decision, see *U.S. ex rel. Standing Bear* v. *Crook*, 25 *Federal Cases* 695–701.

7. For a popular account of the Ute War, see Marshall Sprague, *Massacre*.

8. *Chicago Tribune*, October 2, 1879, p. 1.

9. *Chicago Tribune*, October 4, 1879, p. 4; *Virginia City* (Nev.) *Territorial Enterprise*, October 30, 1879, p. 2; *Alta California*, October 3, 1879, p. 2; *Alta California*, Oct. 4, 1879, p. 2. Given the violence of the Ute incident, it is somewhat surprising to see such benign responses in the white press. Colorado and western Kansas papers were strongly anti-Indian, but elsewhere condemnations of the tribe were mixed with attacks on government policy. For a discussion of press reactions to Indian fighting, see Roger L. Nichols, "Printer's Ink and Red Skins: Western Newspapers and the Indians," pp. 82–88. Nichols shows that papers in secure areas had a more sympathetic view of Indian-white relations than those on the frontier. Robert G. Athearn, *William Tecumseh Sherman and the Settlement of the West*, pp. 345–46, also discusses this phenomenon. Another study of newspaper reactions to the Ute fighting is found in Omer C. Stewart, *Ethnohistorical Bibliography of the Ute Indians of Colorado*, app. B. Stewart lists negative responses in Colorado, Wyoming, and western Kansas, and more positive editorials in Knoxville, Tennessee; Hartford, Connecticut; and Philadelphia. For a more general discussion of the Indians' "image" at this time, see Robert Winston Mardock, "Irresolvable Enigma?" *Montana*, January, 1957, pp. 36–47; and Robert F. Berkhofer, Jr., *The White Man's Indian*, pt. 4.

10. The basic source for Thomas H. Tibbles's life is his autobiography, *Buckskin and Blanket Days*.

11. Tibbles, *Buckskin and Blanket Days*, p. 218; Clark, "Ponca Publicity," pp. 504, 505; *Chicago Tribune*, October 21, 1879, p. 4.

12. Tibbles, *Buckskin and Blanket Days*, p. 234; ibid., p. 199; and *Boston Daily Advertiser*, Nov. 26, 1879, p. 4.

13. Helen Hunt Jackson to Thomas Wentworth Higginson, quoted in Thomas W. Higginson, *Contemporaries*, p. 155.

14. See, for example, accounts of January meetings in New York in the *New York Times*, December 13, 1879, p. 2, and January 17, 1880, p. 5.

15. Carl Schurz to Helen Hunt Jackson, January 17, 1880, *Speeches, Correspondence and Political Papers of Carl Schurz*, 3: 499; *New York Tribune*, February 13, 1880, p. 4. The Jackson-Schurz Affair is described fully in Robert W. Mardock, *The Reformers and the American Indian*, and its relationship to the entire reform movement is discussed in Francis Paul Prucha, *American Indian Policy in Crisis*, pp. 116–17. An extended statement by Helen Hunt Jackson not discussed in these works is a letter from her to Henry Wadsworth Longfellow, dated March 2, 1881, Manuscript 1340, 2 (2971), Houghton Library, Harvard University. For the Hayt Affair, see Roy W. Meyer, "Ezra A. Hayt," in Robert M. Kvasnicka and Herman J. Viola, eds., *The Commissioners of Indian Affairs*, pp. 161–62.

16. *Virginia City* (Nev.) *Territorial Enterprise*, February 8, 1880, p. 2; *Chicago Tribune*, January 31, 1880, p. 4.

17. See Prucha, *American Indian Policy in Crisis*, pp. 36, 132–68. The *Boston Daily Advertiser* covered the formation of the committee in its November 26, 1879, issue (see p. 4).

18. See Mary E. Dewey, *Historical Sketch of the Formation and Achievements of the Women's National Indian Association in the United States*, pp. 5–12; Mardock, *Reformers and the American Indian*, pp. 199–200; and Amelia S. Quinton to Henry L. Dawes, January 23, 1884, Dawes Papers.

19. Herbert Welsh, "The Indian Problem and What We Must Do to Solve It," pp. 8–9.

20. *New Orleans Times-Picayune*, December 10, 1879, p. 4; *New York Tribune*, March 8, 1880, p. 4.

21. *Virginia City* (Nev.) *Territorial Enterprise*, January 26, 1879, p. 2; ibid., February 9, 1879, p. 2; *New York Tribune*, October 4, 1879, p. 4; *Boston Daily Advertiser*, November 8, 1879, p. 2; *St. Louis Post-Dispatch*, December 1879 and January 1880, passim.

22. *Alta California*, February 26, 1880, p. 2; *Atlanta Constitution*, Jan-

uary 14, 1879, pp. 1, 2; and *Boston Daily Advertiser,* November 8, 1879, p. 2.

23. *New York Tribune,* February 13, 1880, p. 4. For a fuller discussion of the reformers' ideas, see Bannon, "Reformers and the Indian Problem," especially chap. 5.

24. 20 *U.S. Statutes* 297 (1879).

25. See Regna Darnell, "The Development of American Anthropology 1879–1920"; and "The Professionalization of American Anthropology," pp. 83–103. The anthropologist's decision to study Indians is discussed from the perspective of a modern black scholar in William S. Willis, Jr., "Anthropology and Negroes on the Southern Colonial Frontier," in James C. Curtis and Lewis L. Gould, eds., *The Black Experience in America,* pp. 33–50. Curtis M. Hinsley, Jr., discusses earlier studies of Indian communities in *Savages and Scientists,* pp. 34–63.

26. Henry Adams to Lewis Henry Morgan, July 14, 1877, Morgan Papers; John Wesley Powell to Lewis Henry Morgan, May 23, 1877, Morgan Papers. Hinsley notes that many researchers questioned Morgan's scheme, but agrees that social evolutionism was "formally adopted" at the BAE. See Hinsley, *Savages and Scientists,* p. 139.

27. For the role of evolutionary theory in the nineteenth century, see J. W. Burrow, *Evolution and Society;* Robert E. Bieder, "The American Indian and the Development of Anthropological Thought in America, 1780–1851," chap. 5; and the refinements of George Stocking, "Some Problems in the Understanding of Nineteenth-Century Cultural Evolutionism," in Regna Darnell, ed., *Readings in the History of Anthropology,* pp. 407–25. For the place of evolutionary thinking in the United States, see Roy Harvey Pearce, *Savagism and Civilization;* Reginald Horsman, "Scientific Racism and the American Indian in the Mid-Nineteenth Century," pp. 152–68; and Berkhofer, *The White Man's Indian,* pp. 49–55.

28. Lewis Henry Morgan, *Ancient Society,* pp. 5, 7.

29. Morgan, *Ancient Society,* pp. 39, 427–28, emphasis in original.

30. Morgan, *Ancient Society,* p. 426. Despite his success in real estate, Morgan was uncomfortable with the excesses of private wealth he saw around him. Moreover, he did not advocate the rapid, forced allotment of individual homesteads to Indians. Nevertheless, he always viewed individual landownership as a final step in human progress, and he approved of a

gradual, voluntary allotment program. See his "Factory System for Indian Reservations," pp. 58–59.

31. Leslie A. White, ed. *Pioneers in American Anthropology: The Bandelier Morgan Letters*, 2 vols. (Albuquerque: University of New Mexico Press, 1940), 2:249.

32. John Wesley Powell, "Mythologic Philosophy," *Proc. AAAS* (1879): 2788. The major biographies of Powell are William Culp Darrah, *Powell of the Colorado*; and Wallace Stegner, *Beyond the Hundredth Meridian*. For a more cautious assessment of Powell's role in policy making, see Curtis M. Hinsley, Jr., "Anthropology as Science and Politics: The Dilemmas of the Bureau of American Ethnology, 1879–1904," in Walter Goldschmidt, ed., *The Uses of Anthropology*, pp. 15–32.

33. Powell, "From Barbarism to Civilization," p. 97; idem, "From Savagery to Barbarism," p. 195; and for Powell's optimistic predictions, see idem, "Sketch of Lewis Henry Morgan," pp. 114–21; idem, "Introduction," *17th Annual Report of the Bureau of American Ethnology* (Washington: Government Printing Office, 1899), pp. xvii–xviii; idem, "On the Evolution of Language," *1st Annual Report of the Bureau of Ethnology* (Washington: Government Printing Office, 1881), p. 16; idem, "The Use of Some Anthropological Data," ibid., pp. 80–81.

34. "Statement of Major J. W. Powell, made before the House Committee on Indian Affairs as to the condition of the Indian Tribes west of the Rocky Mountains," January 13, 1874, *House Miscellaneous Document*, no. 86, 43d Cong., 1st sess., ser. 1618, pp. 7–8.

35. Powell, "Introduction," *1st Annual Report of the Bureau of Ethnology*, p. xxxii; Powell to Spencer F. Baird, April 2, 1880, National Anthropological Archives #4677. It is important to note that while Powell was convinced that the savage would disappear, he did not assume that individual natives would die off. His was one of the scientific voices raised against the idea of Indian extinction. He expressed this position most clearly in "The North American Indians," an article in Nathaniel S. Shaler, ed., *The United States of America*, 2 vols. (New York: Appleton, 1894), 1:190–272.

36. See Cyrus Thomas, "Report on the Mound Explorations of the Bureau of Ethnology" *12th Annual Report of the Bureau of American Ethnology* (Washington: Government Printing Office, 1894), p. xlvi; Powell, "Introduction," *16th Annual Report of the Bureau of American Ethnology*, lxxxvii;

idem, "Introduction," *14th Annual Report of the Bureau of American Ethnology* (Washington: Government Printing Office, 1896), p. lx.

37. Powell, "Introduction," *1st Annual Report of the Bureau of Ethnology*, p. xxix. For an example of Powell's caution, one might note his reaction to Frank Cushing's exposure of a land swindle at Zuni. When the affair showed signs of embarrassing Illinois Senator John Logan, Powell immediately recalled the young bureau researcher. See Joan Mark, "Frank Hamilton Cushing and an American Science of Anthropology," *Perspectives in American History* 10 (1976): 461. Powell's contacts with policy makers were especially strong between 1885 and 1888, when John Atkins, who as a congressman had been one of the original sponsors of the Bureau of Ethnology, served as commissioner of Indian affairs.

38. Powell to Henry Teller, March 23, 1880, Manuscript #3751, National Anthropological Archives. It is difficult to assess the impact of Powell's letter to Teller. Even though the Colorado Republican did not become a supporter of individual allotments until after 1885, he did endorse severalty plans based on tribal consent. In addition, he was a leading advocate of Indian education, overseeing an unprecedented expansion of the Indian schools during his tenure as secretary of the interior (1882–85).

39. Powell, "The Non-Irrigable Lands of the Arid Region," p. 922.

40. Alice Fletcher to Frederick W. Putnam, March 6, 1890, Putnam Papers. See Nancy Oestreich Lurie, "Women in Early American Anthropology," in June Helm, ed., *Pioneers in American Anthropology*, pp. 29–81; Lurie, "The Lady from Boston and the Omaha Indians," pp. 31–33, 80–85; Walter Hough, "Alice Cunningham Fletcher," pp. 254–58; and Joan Mark, *Four Anthropologists*, chap. 2, for descriptions of Fletcher's career. It is important to note that although Alice Fletcher was the most active, she was not the only bureau employee to speak out on policy. Frank Cushing, for example, complained of reservation corruption and hoped for peaceful assimilation. See Frank Cushing to Spencer F. Baird, December 4, 1881, National Anthropological Archives. Triloki Nath Pandey's "Anthropologists at Zuni," pp. 321–28, indicates that while Cushing was a critic of federal officials, he often supported the government's position before the tribe. Another prominent anthropologist who spoke out in the public debate was Morgan's protegé Adolph Bandelier, whose novel, *The Delightmakers*, popularized the social-evolutionist analysis of Indian life and whose speeches supported assimilation efforts.

41. Alice Fletcher to Thomas J. Morgan, May 26, 1890, Alice Fletcher

Papers, box 3; "Education and Civilization," *Senate Executive Document* no. 95, 48th Cong. 2d sess., p. 173.

42. Tibbles, *Buckskin and Blanket Days*, p. 237; Alice Fletcher to Henry L. Dawes, February 4, 1882, Dawes Papers. See also Alice Fletcher to Henry Dawes, February 8, 1882, and Alice Fletcher to Secretary of the Interior James Kirkwood, same date, Alice Fletcher Papers.

43. *CR*, 47–1, 3027.

44. Alice Fletcher to William J. Harsha of the Omaha Citizenship Committee, April 3, 1883, Fletcher Papers.

45. Letters Received (Entry 79), Alice Fletcher to Hiram Price, December 13, 1883, RG 75, NA; *Red Man*, February 1887; Alice Fletcher to John E. Rhoads, April 7, 1887, Fletcher Papers, Box 1.

46. Alice Fletcher to Isabel Chapin Barrows, Nov. 11, 1894, Barrows Family Papers, Houghton Library, bMS AM1807.1 (175).

47. Alice Fletcher to Isabel Chapin Barrows, Feb. 1, 1888, Barrows Family Papers, Houghton Library, bMS AM1807.1 (175).

48. "Speech to the Massachusetts Republican Convention," 1882, Dawes Papers.

49. Henry L. Dawes to Electa S. Dawes, December 12, 1880, Dawes Papers.

50. See Chester M. Dawes to Henry L. Dawes, January 18, 1881, Dawes Papers.

51. The term *Anglo-Conformity* is taken from Milton Gordon, *Assimilation in American Life* (New York: Oxford U. Press, 1964), chap. 4.

52. Henry L. Dawes, "The Indian Problem in 1895," manuscript, in Dawes Papers.

53. *CR*, 48–1, 2565.

54. Ibid. For a more detailed discussion of Senate alignments on this issue, see Frederick Hoxie, "The End of the Savage: Indian Policy in the U.S. Senate," *Chronicles of Oklahoma* 55 (Summer 1977): 157–80.

55. John Higham, *Strangers in the Land*, chap. 2.

Chapter 2

1. *CR*, 46–2, 2128; Henry Dawes, "The Indian Problem in 1895," typescript in Dawes Papers.

2. For a description of the land cessions of these years, see Imre Sutton, *Indian Land Tenure*, pp. 115–25.

3. *Proceedings of the Convention to Consider the Opening of Indian Territory, Held at Kansas City, Mo. Feb. 8, 1888* (Kansas City, Mo., 1888), pp. 59–60. The most recent discussion of the Indian Territory opening is H. Craig Miner, *The Corporation and the Indian*. A great deal of Professor Miner's book involves what he sees as the surprising amount of Indian participation in the opening of their homeland to white settlement. My analysis differs from the one presented in *The Corporation and the Indian* and has two major themes. First, the destruction of Indian Territory was undertaken by non-Indians to serve non-Indian interests. And second, natives who participated in this destruction in the 1880s by lobbying for coal leases, building railroads, or fencing land were serving two masters—themselves and their white colleagues. Miner discusses Payne on pp. 97–100. For more on Payne and the Oklahoma "boomers," see Carl Coke Rister, *Land Hunger*; pp. 50, 71–75, and passim. For a thorough analysis of the railroads in Indian Territory, see Ira G. Clark, "The Railroads and the Tribal Lands," especially chap. 9.

4. *Railroad Gazette*, July 22, 1881, p. 402.

5. *Railroad Gazette*, ibid., September 24, 1886, p. 657; March 20, 1885, p. 184.

6. Hill's official biographer described the Great Northern's invasion of the Blackfoot and other preserves with great pride. See Joseph Gilpin Pyle, *The Life of James J. Hill*, 1:377–87.

7. *House Report* no. 1035, 52d Cong., 1st sess., p. 4. The Colville and other Washington Territory land acquisitions are discussed in greater detail in Herman J. Deutsch, "Indian and White in the Inland Empire," p. 44.

8. The Northern Pacific was the victim of the "extortion" process in 1888, when it leased the Washington and Idaho's roadbed across the Coeur d'Alene reservation, and in 1889 at Crow, where it bought the Rocky Fork and Cook City. See *Railroad Gazette*, March 30, 1888; May 18, 1888 (for the Washington and Idaho); and January 4, 1889; Feb. 15, 1889; and March 14, 1890 (for the Rocky Fork and Cook City).

9. *CR*, 47–1, 2852.

10. See *CR*, 47–1, 2856.

11. *CR*, 47–1, 6587; *CR*, 49–1, 3248. Joseph Brown (D-Ga.) was commenting on a proposal to grant the Kansas and Arkansas Valley Railroad an east-

west right of way through Indian Territory that promised to link Denver and New Orleans; see *Senate Report* no. 107, 49th Cong. 1st sess.

12. See Paul W Gates, "The Homestead Law in an Incongruous Land System," *American Historical Review*, pp. 652–81; and Roy M. Robbins, *Our Landed Heritage*, pt. 3, for a description of the abuses of the Homestead Act and the rising sentiment for reform in the 1880s.

13. *CR*, 49–1, 2317; *CR*, 52–1, 2690.

14. Henry Dawes to Henry M. Teller, September 19, 1882, Dawes Papers.

15. 25 *U.S. Statutes* 113; 25 *U.S. Statutes* 888, sec. 17; and 25 *U.S. Statutes* 642, sec. 4.

16. *House Report* no. 1035, 52d Cong., 1st sess.; *CR*, 49–1, 812, 1763.

17. The Ute agreement followed this pattern except that the tribe's original home was completely opened up and the Utes moved to the Uintah reservation in Utah. What is more, Indian Territory was also opened to whites in this way. First Oklahoma and the Cherokee Strip were acquired by the federal government, then the Nations themselves were allotted. The fact that whites wanted signed agreements from the tribes, even when the cession was a foregone conclusion, indicates something of their concern for "reforming" the Indians. Whites believed that by agreeing to a land cession, Native Americans were taking the first steps towards individual landownership and "civilization."

18. *CR*, 49–1, 969. Because this study focuses on white behavior, I have not discussed the impact of Indian negotiators on the land cession agreements of the 1880s. Nevertheless, the skill and tenacity of these people deserve mention. Anyone reading the proceedings of the various negotiating sessions between the white and Sioux leaders that led up to the 1886 agreement will bury forever the notion that the tribes were passive victims of the white onslaught. The band leaders had only a few cards left in their deck, but they played each one well, refusing to concede anything without a struggle. Though less dramatic and of shorter duration, the other negotiating sessions often followed a similar course. Whites were usually insistent and impatient, and the Indians, using this impatience and the sympathies of the eastern press to their advantage, usually drove the best bargain possible.

19. For an overview of Indian education, see Martha E. Layman, "A History of Indian Education in the U.S." (Ph.D. diss., University of Minnesota, 1942). One of the few published case studies of Indian education in the nineteenth century—which emphasizes the reforming zeal of the 1880s and

1890s—is Bruce Rubenstein, "To Destroy a Culture," pp. 137–60. The promise of new schoolhouses was attached to treaties made with the Sioux, Navajo, Ute, Kiowa, Commanche, Cheyenne, Arapaho, Crow, Shoshone, and Pawnee. See *ARCIA* (1881): 30 for a description of these agreements.

20. Educational appropriations came from three sources after 1880: general educational appropriations, treaty commitments, and appropriations for contract schools. After 1883, the treaty commitments accounted for a very small part of the total. Contract funds increased at roughly the same rate as general appropriations, but did not directly affect the federal school program. The rise in general appropriations is therefore the best indicator of congressional interest in government schools for Indians. Incidentally, one should not forget that, throughout this period, the Five Civilized Tribes supported and maintained their own school system in Indian Territory.

21. Henry Whipple to Richard H. Pratt, March 24, 1876, Pratt Papers.

22. Draft of a speech, "On Indian Civilization," in Pratt Papers. Delivered c. 1878.

23. Samuel C. Armstrong to Pratt, August 26, 1878, Pratt Papers. Armstrong's request was repeated the next day. Apparently Booker T. Washington served as a dormitory counselor for the new arrivals. See Bannon, "Reformers and the Indian Problem," p. 326.

24. Pratt to Dr. Cornelius Agnew, July 19, 1881, Pratt Papers. The founding of Carlisle was summarized by Commissioner of Indian Affairs Ezra Hayt in a note to Pratt. Hayt wrote: "You are entitled to the credit of establishing the School. You found the empty barracks, you got the consent of the Secretary of War to use them, you fussed around the Interior Department until you got up sufficient steam to propel the enterprise. You got the children together, in fact did everything but get the money." Ezra Hayt to Pratt, July 5, 1880, Pratt Papers.

25. *CR*, 47–1, 6154.

26. Pratt to Henry L. Dawes, April 4, 1881, Pratt Papers.

27. *CR*, 47–1, 2456.

28. Alfred L. Riggs to Pratt, April 14, 1882, Pratt Papers; Henry M. Teller to Alice Fletcher, August 3, 1882, Fletcher Papers. By 1890, eight additional nonreservation schools opened their doors.

29. *House Executive Document* no. 1, pt. 5, 47th Cong., 2d sess., p. xvii.

30. See votes 9 and 12, Appendix 1.

31. *ARCIA* (1884): 1.

32. *CR,* 48–1, 2565.

33. *CR,* 50–1, 2503; *CR,* 53–2, 6300. For a compilation of statistics regarding appropriations for the Indian schools, see Appendix 2.

34. *ARCIA* (1886): 99; *CR,* 50–1, 4802; *CR,* 48–1, 4074. For a fuller explication of the western position, see Senator James H. Kyle, "How Shall the Indians Be Educated?" pp. 434–47.

35. Alfred L. Riggs, "Where Shall Our Indian Brothers Go to School?" p. 200.

36. The school superintendents were J. M. Haworth (1882–85), John Oberly (1885–86), John B. Riley (1886–87), S. H. Albro (1888–89), Daniel Dorchester (1889–94), and William N. Hailmann (1894–98). It is interesting that after 1889, as civil service regulations removed the power to dispense patronage and a professional consensus on policy decreased criticism, the terms of the superintendents began to overlap presidential administrations. The statement by William Hailmann is in a letter to Herbert Welsh, January 27, 1894, IRA Papers. In 1898 Hailmann enlisted the support of Theodore Roosevelt in an attempt to retain his position under William McKinley. See Theodore Roosevelt to F. E. Leupp, January 29, 1898, Series 2, Theodore Roosevelt Papers.

37. "An Outrage," *Journal of Education* 25 (June 2, 1887): 349. The "institutionalization" of educational reform within the Indian Office is a central theme of Paul Stuart, *The Indian Office,* especially chap. 9.

38. *ARCIA* (1885): 113.

39. *ARCIA* (1889): 94, 103–4, 100, 98. For an excellent biographical sketch of Morgan, see Prucha, "Thomas Jefferson Morgan," in Kvasnicka and Viola, *Commissioners of Indian Affairs,* pp. 193–204.

40. "General Morgan's First Report," *Journal of Education* 30 (December 12, 1889): 376.

41. Pratt to Alice Fletcher, July 30, 1893, Pratt Papers; R. H. Pratt to Alice Fletcher, August 7, 1891, Fletcher Papers, Box 1.

42. *Proc. NEA* (1895): 81.

43. *ARCIA* (1894): 341, *ARCIA* (1892): 55.

44. *ARCIA* (1894): 15.

45. *ARCIA* (1892): 46–47; "Indian Education," *Journal of Education* 37 (February 16, 1893): 104.

46. Michael B. Katz, *Class, Bureaucracy, and the Schools,* p. xx. The emphasis on the total transformation of Indian children through education

is also discussed in Jacqueline Fear, "English versus the Vernacular," pp. 13–24.

47. Calvin M. Woodward, "The Function of the Public School," pp. 222, 224. The curriculum at Carlisle never progressed beyond the high-school level, but the captain maintained that his students should not limit their goals. See R. H. Pratt to Alice Fletcher, August 7, 1891, Fletcher Papers.

48. For a discussion of the Blair Bill, see C. Vann Woodward, *The Origins of the New South* (Baton Rouge: Louisiana State University Press, 1951), pp. 63–64. For a description of the passage of the Chinese Exclusion Act, see Alexander Saxton, *The Indispensable Enemy* (Berkeley: University of California Press, 1971), p. 177.

49. For descriptions of the passage of the Dawes Act, see Prucha, *American Indian Policy in Crisis*, chap. 8; Henry Fritz, "The Board of Indian Commissioners and Ethnocentric Reform," in Jane Smith and Robert Kvasnicka, eds., *Indian-White Relations*, pp. 62–71; D. S. Otis, *The Dawes Act and the Allotment of Indian Lands;* and Priest, *Uncle Sam's Stepchildren*. Also helpful are Henry Eugene Fritz, *The Movement for Indian Assimilation;* and Mardock, *The Reformers and the American Indian*. For a description of the law's broad support, see William I. Hagan, "Private Property, the Indian's Door to Civilization," pp. 126–37. Of course, the idea of allotting individual tracts of land to Indians was not new. Prucha *(American Indian Policy in Crisis,* pp. 227–34) and Priest *(Uncle Sam's Stepchildren,* pp. 177–82) summarize the history of the earlier schemes. The significance of the Coke bill was the intention that it would apply generally.

50. William M. Springer (D.-Ill.), *CR,* 46–2, 178; proceedings of the Lake Mohonk Conference printed in *House Executive Document* no. 109, 49th Cong., 1st sess., pp. 95–96. Lyman Abbott's ideas were echoed by William Graham Sumner, "The Indians in 1887," p. 254. The broad consensus behind the allotment "solution" is also described in Berkhofer, *The White Man's Indian,* pp. 170–75.

51. *CR,* 47–1, 3028; *CR,* 46–3, 784; *CR,* 46–2, 499.

52. Dawes discussed his reasons for compromising with his opponents at the 1886 Lake Mohonk Conference. See *ARCIA* (1886): 992. The "President's discretion" phrase was first adopted in 1881, during debate over the Coke severalty bill. See *CR,* 46–3, 1064–67.

53. See William Justin Harsha, "Law for the Indians," p. 272. Harsha also

put his plea in the form of a novel, *A Timid Brave*. For Call's view, see *CR*, 46–3, 908; Schurz's position is described in chap. 1.

54. *CR*, 46–3, 877.

55. Powell quoted in *CR*, 46–3, 911. The vote is number 10, Appendix 1.

56. George F. Canfield, "Carl Schurz on the Indian Problem," p. 457.

57. 112 *U.S.* 648 (1885).

58. *CR*, 49–1, 1632; ibid., 1634.

59. Charles C. Painter, *The Dawes Land in Severalty Bill and Indian Emancipation*, p. 1. The ambiguous quality of citizenship provisions in the Dawes Act was very perceptively analyzed by Harvard Law School professor James Bradley Thayer in "The Dawes Bill and the Indians," pp. 315–22.

60. *House Report* no. 2247, 48th Cong., 2d sess., p. 1.

61. Alice Fletcher to Thomas J. Morgan, May 26, 1890, Fletcher Papers; *Red Man*, December 1886; *CR*, 49–1, 2470.

62. *CR*, 56–3, 1032.

63. See Otis, *The Dawes Act and the Allotment of Indian Land*, p. 82.

64. *ARCIA* (1887): 4; Otis, *The Dawes Act and the Allotment of Indian Land*, pp. 82, 83. Atkins's restraint in administering the Dawes Act is a prominent theme in Gregory C. Thompson, "John D. C. Atkins," in Kvasnicka and Viola, *Commissioners of Indian Affairs*. See pp. 182–83.

65. *ARCIA* (1892): 69–70; Painter, *The Dawes Land in Severalty Bill*, p. 5.

66. See *ARCIA* (1893): 476 and *ARCIA* (1894): 421; Richard Pratt to Henry Dawes, January 22, 1892, Pratt Papers.

67. See *Beck* v. *Flournoy Live-Stock and Real Estate Co.*, 65 F. 30 (1894); Thayer, "A People Without Law," p. 683.

68. Herbert Welsh, *How to Bring the Indian to Citizenship*, pp. 8–9. See Laurence F. Schmeckebier, *The Office of Indian Affairs*, p. 284. In 1892 Congress also gave the president the authority to name army officers to vacant agencies. This was widely regarded as a blow to patronage. See Prucha, *American Indian Policy in Crisis*, pp. 353–72; and Stuart, *The Indian Office*, pp. 145–49.

Chapter 3

1. George Bird Grinnell and Theodore Roosevelt, "The Exhibit at the World's Fair," in *American Big Game Hunting*. The only full-length history

of the Boone and Crockett Club is an uncritical house history: James B. Trefethen, *Crusade for Wildlife*. An excellent pictorial presentation of the fair is Halsey C. Ives, *The Dream City* (St. Louis: N. D. Thompson, 1893).

2. W. J. McGee, quoted in David R. Francis, *The Universal Exposition of 1904*, p. 523. All the fairs stressed the educational benefits of their displays. While much of this was hucksterism, the expositions did provide large numbers of Americans with their first look at the products of an expanding technology, samples of European art (Marcel Duchamps's *Nude Descending a Staircase* was a main attraction at San Francisco), and representatives of foreign cultures.

3. *New York Times*, March 29, 1876; *Philadelphia Bulletin*, May 23, 1876.

4. *Philadelphia Bulletin*, May 23, 1876; Edward C. Bruce, *The Century*, pp. 224–25; Francis A. Walker, ed., *International Exhibition, 1876*, 8:97; Bruce, *The Century*, p. 225.

5. Frederick W. Putnam quoted in Ralph W. Dexter, "Putnam's Problems in Popularizing Anthropology," p. 316; Hubert Howe Bancroft, *The Book of the Fair*, p. 631.

6. *ARCIA* (1893): 21.

7. *ARCIA* (1893): 22.

8. *Chicago Tribune*, May 7, 1893; ibid., August 20, 1893. See also *New York Times*, August 19, 1893.

9. *New York Times*, October 8, 1893. See also Dexter, "Putnam's Problems in Popularizing Anthropology," pp. 327–28.

10. Henry Adams, *The Education of Henry Adams* (Boston: Houghton Mifflin, 1969), pp. 466, 468.

11. W. J. McGee to F. W. Lehman, August 8, 1901, W. J. McGee Papers; W. J. McGee quoted in Francis, *The Universal Exposition of 1904*, p. 524; McGee, "Strange Races of Men," p. 5186.

12. McGee, "Strange Races of Men," pp. 5184, 5188.

13. For typical stories and photos, see *St. Louis Post-Dispatch*, May 1, 2, 4, 5, 16, 22, June 26, and August 13, 1904.

14. For a description of the exhibit, see Alfred C. Newell, "The Philippine Peoples," p. 5129; *St. Louis Post-Dispatch*, May 1, 1904.

15. Charles M. Harvey, "The Last Race Rally of the Indians," p. 4803. For more on the St. Louis fair, see Richard Drinnon, *Facing West*, pp. 333–46.

16. James Fraser quoted in J. Walter McSpadden, *Famous Sculptors of America*, p. 281.

17. Eugen Neuhaus, *The Art of the Exposition*, p. 32; Juliet James, *Sculpture of the Exposition Palaces and Courts*, p. 34.

18. McSpadden, *Famous Sculptors of America*, p. 282.

19. C. H. Forbes-Lindsay, "Shaping the Future of the Indian," p. 292; idem, "Making Good Indians," p. 13; Harvey, "The Red Man's Last Roll Call," p. 330.

20. Ray Stannard Baker, "The Day of the Run," pp. 643–55.

21. Helen Fitzgerald Sanders, "The Red Bond," p. 163. For Sanders's view of native life, see also *The White Quiver*, a romantic novel about the Piegans before the coming of the European. See Owen Wister, *The Virginian*, p. 197; idem, "Little Big Horn Medicine," in *Red Men and White*, p. 5; Elliott Flower, "Law and the Indian," p. 488; Honore Willsie, *Still Jim*. For yet another example of this theme of the "indelible" quality of one's ancestry see Frederic Remington's *John Ermine of the Yellowstone*.

22. A. Decker, "Making the Warrior a Worker," p. 95; Willsie, *Still Jim*, 168.

23. Hamlin Garland, *Captain of the Grey Horse Troop*, pp. 56, 113, 121.

24. Ibid., 406–7, 414–15.

25. Garland, "The Red Man's Present Needs," p. 488. See also the following short stories on contemporary events: "Wahiah—A Spartan Mother" (on agency schools, 1905); "The Story of Howling Wolf" (on westerners' hatred of Indians, 1903); "Drifting Crane," (on the inevitability of white progress, 1890). All these stories were reprinted in Garland, *The Book of the American Indian*. See also "The Red Plowman," pp. 181–82. For a thorough and sympathetic account of Garland's Indian writings, see Lonnie E. Underhill and Daniel F. Littlefield's introduction to *Hamlin Garland's Observations on the American Indian*.

26. Carl Moon, "In Search of the Wild Indian," p. 545. For a discussion of this new twentieth-century attitude toward the West, see G. Edward White, *The Eastern Establishment and the Western Experience*, especially pp. 184–203.

27. Charles F. Lummis, "My Brother's Keeper," pp. 139, 264; George Bird Grinnell, *When Buffalo Ran*, p. 10.

28. Grinnell, *Blackfoot Lodge Tales*, xii; Lummis, "The Sequoyah League," *Out West*, 1903, p. 301; idem, "My Brother's Keeper," p. 264.

29. Lummis to Theodore Roosevelt, May 19, 1904, Series 1, Roosevelt Papers; Lummis, "My Brother's Keeper," p. 145. It should not be surprising

that Lummis considered *Captain of the Grey Horse Troop* a "very accurate" book and recommended it to his readers. See his "Reading List on Indians," *Land of Sunshine,* March 1903, p. 360.

30. Grinnell, *The Indians of Today,* pp. 155, 156; Lummis, "My Brother's Keeper," p. 226; idem, "Sequoyah League," *Out West* 20 (April 1904): 382, 384; Grinnell, *The Indians of Today,* pp. 169, 170.

31. Lummis, "Sequoyah League," *Out West* 20 (April 1904), 384.

32. Roosevelt to Curtis, November 21, 1911, Series 3A, Roosevelt Papers; Roosevelt, Foreword in Edward S. Curtis, *The North American Indian,* 1: xi.

33. The groundbreaking ceremony and Taft's speech were described in the *New York Times* on February 23, 1913. Wanamaker's statue was never completed. Work was postponed by the world war—apparently because of a shortage of bronze—and later abandoned for lack of interest. Wanamaker also sponsored three western expeditions. The first was devoted to the filming of a dramatization of "Hiawatha" on the Blackfoot reservation. The second was for a "last council of the chiefs," a gathering of old warriors that was also filmed. The final trip was a visit to 169 Indian communities by a special railroad car that carried recorded greetings and patriotic messages from President Woodrow Wilson and Secretary of the Interior Franklin K. Lane. The last two of these projects are described in Joseph K. Dixon, *The Vanishing Race.* See also Louis L. Pfaller, *James McLaughlin,* chap. 15.

34. Beverly Buchanan, "A Tribute to the First American," p. 30. See also Rodman Wanamaker to W. H. Taft, July 10, 1909, Case 4006, Taft Papers. The phrase "departed race" was used by General Nelson A. Miles in a letter of support to Wanamaker (dated January 9, 1909) that the businessman enclosed in his July appeal to the president.

35. I agree with William T. Hagan that Roosevelt "deserves better than the occasional references to him as one of the more articulate racists of the late nineteenth century." Nevertheless, unlike Hagan, I am looking beyond TR's career as civil service commissioner and his fragile friendship with Herbert Welsh to his presidency. Consequently my view is somewhat harsher. See Hagan, "Civil Service Commissioner Theodore Roosevelt and the Indian Rights Association," pp. 187–201. For a general study of Roosevelt's racial attitudes that outlines his view of the Indians, see Thomas G. Dyer, *Theodore Roosevelt and the Idea of Race,* pp. 69–88.

36. On Garland and TR, see Hamlin Garland to Theodore Roosevelt, March 17, 1902, Series 1, Roosevelt Papers, and Jean Halloway, *Hamlin Gar-*

land, pp. 130–31. On Grinnell and TR, see George Bird Grinnell to Theodore Roosevelt, September 14, 1903, Series 1, Roosevelt Papers. On Lummis and TR, see Charles F. Lummis to Roosevelt, October 8, 1901, Series 1, Roosevelt Papers. On Remington and TR, see White, *The Eastern Establishment,* passim; and Remington to Roosevelt, September, 1899, Series 1, Roosevelt Papers. On Wister and TR, see Wister, *Roosevelt,* passim. On Leupp and Roosevelt, see discussions of his special missions for the president in Leupp to Roosevelt, June 24, and September 3, 1903, Series 1, Roosevelt Papers; and June 14, 1904, Series 2, Roosevelt Papers.

37. Charles F. Lummis to Roosevelt, October 8, 1901, Series 1; Roosevelt Papers. See Roosevelt to Grinnell, September 27, 1901, Series 2, Roosevelt to Wister, June 7, 1902, Series 2; and Roosevelt to Remington, November 14, 1901, Series 2, all in Roosevelt Papers.

38. George Bird Grinnell to Theodore Roosevelt, September 14, 1903, Series 1, Roosevelt Papers.

39. Roosevelt to Grinnell, June 13, 1902, Series 2, Roosevelt Papers.

40. "Address at Tuskeegee Institute, Tuskeegee, Alabama, October 24, 1905," in Theodore Roosevelt, *Address and Papers,* p. 265; Roosevelt to King Edward VII, February 12, 1908, *Letters of Theodore Roosevelt,* ed. Elting E. Morison, 6:940. For Roosevelt's reasoning on the Japanese exclusion question, see Roosevelt to Frederic Remington, February 7, 1909, Series 2, Roosevelt Papers; and Roosevelt to Theodore Roosevelt, Jr., February 13, 1909, *Letters of Theodore Roosevelt,* 6: 1520–21.

41. "Speech in San Francisco to Native Sons and Daughters of the Golden West," May 13, 1903, Series 5B, Roosevelt Papers; Roosevelt to James Wilson, secretary of agriculture, June 7, 1907, *Letters of Theodore Roosevelt,* 5:682. See also, Roosevelt to Elihu Root, ibid., 4:812.

42. Roosevelt, *Report of Hon. Theodore Roosevelt Made to the U.S. Civil Service Commission, upon a Visit to Certain Indian Reservations and Indian Schools in South Dakota, Nebraska and Kansas,* p. 12. For the progressives' view of minority education in general, see Harvey Wish, "Negro Education and the Progressive Movement," pp. 184–201.

43. Roosevelt to Silas McBee, August 27, 1907, *Letters of Theodore Roosevelt,* 5:775–6. A great deal has been written about Roosevelt's racism. Howard Kennedy Beale, in *Theodore Roosevelt and the Rise of America to World Power,* and Rubin Weston, in *Racism in U.S. Imperialism,* argue for the importance of the president's racial attitudes in determining his for-

eign policy perspective. William Harbaugh, in *Power and Responsibility*, plays down this factor. The truth probably lies somewhere closer to Seth Schiener's statement: "It is not clear if he made his [racial] distinction for sociological or physiological reasons. In his writings, Roosevelt did not distinguish between the two; in fact, both environmental and physical explanations overlap." Seth Schiener, "President Theodore Roosevelt and the Negro, 1901–8," p. 170.

44. Roosevelt to Sir Harry Hamilton Johnson, July 11, 1908, *Letters of Theodore Roosevelt*, 6:1126. For a further discussion of Roosevelt's progressivism and imperialism, see Dewey Grantham, "The Progressive Movement and the Negro," in Charles E. Wynes, ed., *The Negro in the South Since 1865*, pp. 77–78.

45. "Speech at Hampton Institute," May 30, 1906, Series 5A, Roosevelt Papers. The comment about the Apaches is contained in Roosevelt to Charles Bonaparte, March 20, 1901, *Letters of Theodore Roosevelt*, 3:36–37. Roosevelt also defended the United States' suppression of the Philippine insurrection with the statement, "The reasoning which justifies our having made war against Sitting Bull also justifies our having checked the outbreak of Aguinaldo and his followers." Quoted in Weston, *Racism in U.S. Imperialism*, p. 557. For an extended discussion of the links between imperialism and the Indian question, see Walter L. Williams, "United States Indian Policy and the Debate over Philippine Annexation," 810–31.

46. Roosevelt, *A Book Lover's Holidays in the Open*, pp. 51, 74.

47. William Howard Taft, "Southern Democracy and Republican Principles," in *Present Day Problems*, p. 233; "Speech at Hampton Institute," November 20, 1909, Series 9A, Taft Papers; "Address of President Taft at the Indian School, Haskell Institute, Kansas," September 24, 1911, Series 9A, Taft Papers.

48. "Speech to the Society of American Indians at the White House," December 10, 1914, Series 7F, Woodrow Wilson Papers; see Arthur S. Link, *Wilson*, pp. 17–18; and A. E. Yoell to Woodrow Wilson, March 23, 1913, Series 4, Wilson Papers; Franklin K. Lane to Woodrow Wilson, May 22, 1913, Series 4, Wilson Papers; and Cato Sells to Albert S. Burleson, March 17, 1913, Series 2, Wilson Papers.

49. For a list of the votes used in the tabulation of these figures, see Appendix 1. For discussions of regional prerogatives in congressional discus-

sions of reform legislation during this period, see Howard W. Allen, Aage R. Clausen, and Jerome M. Clubb, "Political Reform and Negro Rights in the Senate, 1909–15," pp. 191–212; and James Holt, *Congressional Insurgents and the Party System, 1909–1916*, especially chaps. 6 and 8.

50. *CR*, 59–2, 471. The chairmen of the Senate Indian Affairs Committee were James K. Jones (D-Ark.), 1893–95; Richard Pettigrew (R-S.Dak.), 1895–99; John Thurston (R-Nebr.), 1899–1901; William Stewart (R-Nev.), 1901–7; Moses Clapp (R-Minn.), 1907–11; Robert Gamble (R.-S.Dak.), 1911–13; William J. Stone (D-Mo.), 1913–15; Henry Ashurst (D-Ariz.), 1915–19; and Charles Curtis (R-Kans.), 1919–21.

51. Richard Pettigrew to E. Whittlesey, secretary of the Board of Indian Commissioners, January 25, 1897, RG 75, NA; *CR*, 57–1, 1944.

52. Roosevelt to Lyman Abbott, September 5, 1903, *Letters of Theodore Roosevelt*, 3:590. See also William A. Jones to Theodore Roosevelt, March 20, 1901, Series 1, Roosevelt Papers.

Chapter 4

1. The racial tensions of these years and their effect on social scientists are described in Barbara Miller Solomon, *Ancestors and Immigrants*; Mark Haller, *Eugenics: Hereditarian Attitudes in American Thought* (New Brunswick, N.J.: Rutgers University Press, 1963); I. A. Newby, *Jim Crow's Defense*; George M. Frederickson, *The Black Image in the White Mind*; John S. Haller, *Outcasts from Evolution*; and George W. Stocking, Jr., "American Social Scientists and Race Theory, 1890–1915." A good description of the growing interest in race in a particular area of the social sciences is Ethel Shanas, "The American Journal of Sociology through Fifty Years," pp. 522–33. The article describes a content analysis of the *Journal*; results for 1895–1919 are on page 524. The role of scientific racism in Indian-white relations during these years is also discussed briefly in Berkhofer, *White Man's Indians*, pp. 59–61.

2. McGee, "The Trend of Human Progress," pp. 401–2, 403.

3. McGee, "The Science of Humanity," p. 323; idem, "The Trend of Human Progress," pp. 409, 424, 436, 442, 444.

4. McGee, "The Trend of Human Progress," pp. 429, 435.

5. Ibid., p. 446.

6. Ibid., pp. 446–47. For McGee's association with imperialism and scientific racism, see Edward A. Atkinson to McGee, June 10, 1899, and Hinton Rowan Helper to McGee, August 28, 1899, both in McGee Papers.

7. McGee, "Man's Place in Nature," 12, 13; idem, "Anthropology and Its Larger Problems," in Howard J. Rogers, ed., *Congress of Arts and Sciences*, pp. 461–62.

8. W. J. McGee to Franz Boas, September 18, 1903, Boas Papers.

9. W. J. McGee to Franz Boas, April 2, 1910, Boas Papers. For a description of Powell's and McGee's last years at the BAE, see Franz Boas to Carl Schurz, August 12, 1903, Boas Papers, and Hinsley, *Savages and Scientists*, chap. 8.

10. William Henry Holmes, "Museum Presentation of Anthropology," *Proc. AAAS* (1898): 487. The bureau's contacts with the Indian Office were few once Powell passed from the scene. In an exchange of correspondence with the Board of Indian Commissioners in 1911, Frederick W. Hodge, who succeeded Holmes as chief, noted that there had been only one minor incidence of cooperation in recent years. Hodge pointed out that the bureau had to be careful of its funding, and that it "hesitated to offer its services unless it could be sure they were desired." Nevertheless, he added, "the bureau is anxious to render to the Government any service, economic or otherwise, that may lie in its power, and is willing to make any reasonable sacrifice to promote the proper administration of our Indian affairs." See Frederick Hodge to Merrill Gates, January 28, 1911, and "Memorandum of a Call on F. W. Hodge, . . . May 3, 1912," both in the Board of Indian Commissioners General Correspondence, Entry 1386, RG 75, NA. Hinsley describes Holmes's tenure in *Savages and Scientists*, chap. 9.

11. Holmes, "Some Problems of the American Race," p. 166.

12. Ibid., p. 161.

13. W. J. McGee to Richard H. Pratt, August 25, 1902, Pratt Papers; George S. Painter, "The Future of the American Negro," pp. 410, 411. Painter, who had taught at Tufts and Clark universities, was, at the time this article was published, a professor of philosophy at New York State Teacher's College. For another example of this point of view, see "What Indian Children Are Taught," *Scientific American Supplement*, April 13, 1907, p. 315.

14. The only modern study of Brinton is Regna Darnell, "Daniel Garrison Brinton." In her essay, Darnell emphasizes Brinton's evolutionism and his belief in psychic unity as an important unifying theme in his career. While

I agree with her conclusions, within the context of the 1890s, Brinton's judgments of Indian culture were among the most racially oriented in the academic community. Berkhofer, in his *White Man's Indian*, shares this view; see p. 60. For an example of Brinton's evolutionism and optimism, see Daniel Garrison Brinton, *Races and Peoples*, especially p. 300.

15. Brinton, *The Basis of Social Relations*, p. 20; Brinton, "The Factors of Heredity and Environment in Man," *AA* 11 (September 1898): 273, 275.

16. Brinton, *The American Race*, p. 39; idem, *The Basis of Social Relations*, pp. 70–71.

17. Brinton, *Races and Peoples*, pp. 294–95, 287.

18. William Z. Ripley, *The Races of Europe*; Madison Grant, *The Passing of the Great Race*; Frederick L. Hoffman, "Race Traits and Tendencies of the American Negro," pp. 1–329.

19. Stocking, *Race, Culture and Evolution*, chap. 10; idem, "Social Scientists and Race Theory," chaps. 3 and 7 and app. B; Franklin H. Giddings, "A Provisional Distribution of the Population of the U.S. into Psychological Classes," *Psychology Review* 8 (July 1901): 337–49.

20. Lindley M. Keasbey, "Civology—A Suggestion," *Popular Science Monthly*, April 1907, p. 368; Madison Grant, *The Conquest of a Continent*, p. 24; and Theodore Lothrop Stoddard, *The Rising Tide of Color against White World Supremacy*, pp. 125–26.

21. Stoddard, *Rising Tide of Color*, p. 126; Popenoe and Johnson, *Applied Eugenics*, p. 132.

22. Grant, *Passing of the Great Race*, 15–16; Seth K. Humphrey, *The Racial Prospect*, p. 176; Ernest W. Coffin, "On the Education of Backward Races," p. 56; Edgar L. Hewitt, "Ethnic Factors in Education," p. 10.

23. See Henry F. Suksdorf, *Our Race Problems*, p. 51.

24. For an early attack on social-evolutionist theories in light of new research, see Talcott Williams, "Was Primitive Man a Modern Savage?" p. 548. For the same type of attack on racial formalism, see Albion Small, "The Scope of Sociology," *AJS* 5 (1899–1900): 22–52. The general direction of these critiques is discussed in Stocking, "Social Scientists and Race Theory," pp. 295–319; and his *Race, Culture and Evolution*, pp. 163–69. Also helpful is Frederick W. Preston, "Red, White, Black and Blue," pp. 27–36; and James R. Hayes, "Sociology and Racism," pp. 330–41.

25. Otis T. Mason, "Mind and Matter in Culture," p. 187.

26. Ibid., p. 190.

27. Frederick Webb Hodge, ed., *The Handbook of American Indians North of Mexico*, 1:427.

28. Mason, "The Uncivilized Mind in the Presence of Higher Phases of Civilization," pp. 347, 355, 361.

29. Richmond Mayo-Smith, "Assimilation of Nationalities in the United States," p. 649; William Isaac Thomas, "The Mind of Woman and the Lower Races," p. 452.

30. Grinnell, *The Indians of Today*, p. 7; Fayette A. McKenzie, *The Indian in Relation to the White Population of the United States*, p. 42.

31. McKenzie, "The American Indian of Today and Tomorrow," p. 140; Sarah E. Simons, "Social Assimilation," p. 550. For an account of the Society of American Indians, see Hazel Hertzberg, *The Search for an American Indian Identity*; for a sketch of McKenzie's career, see the Brookings Institution, Institute for Government Research, *The Problem of Indian Administration*, p. 83.

32. Grinnell, *The American Indian Today*, p. 156; Frank W Blackmar, "The Socialization of the American Indian," p. 661.

33. "The Jesup North Pacific Expedition," in George W. Stocking, ed., *The Shaping of American Anthropology*, p. 108. Franz Boas to Warren K. Moorehead, October 7, 1907, Boas Papers.

34. Franz Boas, *The Mind of Primitive Man*, p. 94.

35. Ibid., pp. 28, 122–23.

36. Ibid., pp. 102, 104.

37. Ibid., pp. 114–15; Boas, "Some Traits of Primitive Culture," *Journal of American Folklore* 17 (October–December 1904): 253.

38. Stocking, *Race, Culture and Evolution*, p. 203; Boas, *Mind of Primitive Man*, pp. 203, 206; Ibid., p. 209.

39. Clark Wissler, *The American Indian*, p. 206; idem, "The Psychological Aspects of the Culture-Environment Relation," 224–25; idem, *The American Indian*, pp. 338–39.

40. Wissler, *The American Indian*, p. 208.

41. Alfred L. Kroeber, "Eighteen Professions," p. 285 (emphasis in original); idem, "Inheritance by Magic," p. 37.

42. Kroeber, "The Morals of an Uncivilized People," p. 446.

43. Robert H. Lowie, *Culture and Ethnology*, p. 66; idem, *Primitive Society*, p. 6.

44. See Stocking, "The Scientific Reaction against Cultural Anthropol-

ogy" in *Race, Culture and Evolution*, pp. 270–307, as well as his "Anthropology as Kulturkampf: Science and Politics in the Career of Franz Boas," in Goldschmidt, *The Uses of Anthropology*, pp. 33–50. See also Regna Darnell, "The Development of American Anthropology," pt. 4.

45. Kroeber, "Ishi, the Last Aborigine," p. 308.

46. Boas, *Mind of Primitive Man*, pp. 16–17.

47. Ibid., p. 253; Livingston Farrand, *Basis of American History*, p. 271.

48. Ibid., p. 267; John R. Swanton, pp. 469–70; Alfred Kroeber quoted in "The Spectator," *Outlook*, May 16, 1908, p. 106.

Chapter 5

1. Charles J. Kappler, ed., *U.S. Laws and Statutes; Indian Affairs: Laws and Treaties* (Washington, D.C.: Government Printing Office, 1904), 2:661–63.

2. *CR*, 53–2, 6251; *CR*, 52–1, 2951.

3. *CR*, 53–2, 7685.

4. *CR*, 53–2, 7672–3.

5. Quoted in *CR*, 54–2, 1260.

6. Welsh to members of the Indian Rights Association, January 27, 1894, IRA Papers.

7. Hugh L. Scott to "Major Davis," August 17, 1896, Hugh L. Scott Papers (Scott was the army commander at Fort Sill when he wrote these words); *ARCIA* (1895): 1023. See also the exchange between Dawes and the Cheyenne and Arapaho agent, Major A. E. Woodson, at the 1897 Lake Mohonk Conference. Major Woodson gave the assembled reformers a glowing account of the progress of his charges, while Dawes repeatedly asked skeptical questions from the floor. *ARCIA* (1897): 979–83. For a detailed description of the pace of allotment, which confirms that allotment activity was heaviest after 1899, see Leonard A. Carlson, *Indians, Bureaucrats and Land*, pp. 73–75.

8. *ARCIA* (1898): 75. For the Indian Rights Association's support for the Curtis Act, see Francis Leupp to Herbert Welsh, March 11, 1898, IRA Papers.

9. Samuel Brosius to Herbert Welsh, February 12, 1899, IRA Papers.

10. George Kennan, "Have Reservation Indians Any Vested Rights?" p. 765.

11. 187 *U.S.*, 565–6 (1903); George Kennan, "Indian Lands and Fair Play," p. 501.

12. Quoted in *House Report* no. 443, 58th Cong., 2d sess., pp. 4–5.

13. *CR*, 56–1, 1913.

14. *CR*, 57–1, 4803.

15. Herbert Welsh to Matthew K. Sniffen, February 18, 1904, IRA Papers; *House Report* no. 890, 58th Cong., 2d sess., p. 5; 33 *U.S. Statutes* 321 (Devil's Lake); 33 *U.S. Statutes* 303 (Flathead); 33 *U.S. Statutes* 1069–70 (Uintah); and 33 *U.S. Statutes* 1016 (Wind River).

16. *CR*, 58–2, 1945.

17. *ARCIA* (1903): 3.

18. *ARCIA* (1895): 34; *ARCIA* (1896): 272. For an overview of the government's leasing policies, see Sutton, *Indian Land Tenure*, pp. 125–35.

19. *ARCIA* (1898): 1113.

20. *IRA AR* (1900): 59.

21 *ARCIA* (1902): 66; Francis Leupp to Theodore Roosevelt, June 23, 1905, Series 1, Roosevelt Papers. For a discussion of land sales under the Dawes Act, see David M. Holford, "The Subversion of the Indian Land Allotment System, 1887–1934," pp. 12–21.

22. *CR*, 52–1, 2404; William S. Holman to Herbert Welsh, March 9, 1894, IRA Papers.

23. Henry Cabot Lodge to Herbert Welsh, March 15, 1894, IRA Papers; *CR*, 56–1, 1407, 1408.

24. *ARCIA* (1903): 2.

25. Theodore Roosevelt to Herbert Welsh, January 23, 1895, and Alice Fletcher to Herbert Welsh, February 12, 1895, IRA Papers.

26. Francis Leupp to Herbert Welsh, February 6, 1895, IRA Papers; "Dealing with the Indians Individually," *Independent*, December 14, 1905, p. 1419.

27. *ARCIA* (1905): 1, 8, 9, 7. Leupp's views bear a surface similarity to those of John Collier. Nevertheless, Leupp's assumption that Native Americans belonged to a "backward" race and his commitment to rapid assimilation make the connections between him and FDR's Indian commissioner more complex than most historians have imagined. For an example of the Leupp-to-Collier argument, see Donald L. Parman, "Francis Ellington Leupp," in Kvasnicka and Viola, *Commissioners of Indian Affairs*, pp. 224, 231.

28. Francis Leupp, "A Fresh Phase of the Indian Problem," pp. 367, 368.

29. Francis Leupp to Samuel Bosius, March 2, 1907, IRA Papers.

30. Francis Leupp to James R. Garfield, February 20, 1909, Garfield Papers.

31. Samuel Brosius to Ezra Thayer, June 10, 1907, IRA Papers.

32. *IRA AR* (1905): 72; McKenzie, *The Indian in Relation to the White,* p. 45.

33. Francis Leupp to James R. Garfield, February 20, 1909, Garfield Papers; 34 *U.S. Statutes* 183.

34. Samuel Brosius to Francis Leupp, March 26, 1906, IRA Papers; *Senate Report* no. 198, 59th Cong., 1st sess., p. 2; *ARCIA* (1906): 30.

35. Francis Leupp to Theodore Roosevelt, January 23, 1906, Series 1, Roosevelt Papers.

36. The law covering "noncompetent land sales" is 34 *U.S. Statutes* 1018.

37. The proposal and the Indian Rights Association's reaction are contained in Samuel Brosius to Members of Congress, March 21, 1908, IRA Papers. Leupp's defense of fee patenting is in his article, "A Review of President Roosevelt's Administration," p. 304.

38. Leupp, *The Indian and His Problem,* p. 93; James R. Garfield to the Speaker of the House of Representatives, Feb. 6, 1908, Entry 121, General Service file #013, RG 75, NA; *ARCIA* (1906): 27. See also Leupp, "The Red Man, Incorporated," p. 20; and idem, "The Indian Land Troubles and How to Solve Them," pp. 468–72.

39. *ARCIA* (1906): 4.

40. See 34 *U.S. Statutes* 1015–34 and 35 *U.S. Statutes* 70 for the congressional authorizations to grant long-term leases. Leupp defended his plan in his valedictory letter to James R. Garfield (February 9, 1909, p. 20, Garfield Papers) and in an article written after his retirement, "The Red Man's Burden," p. 750.

41. 33 U.S. Statutes 1016; *ARCIA* (1905): 382; Rev. James B. Funsten, "The Indian as a Worker," p. 878.

42. *ARCIA* (1905): 147; 34 *US. Statutes* 375; for Yakima, see *House Report* no. 1477, 59th Cong., 1st sess.; the Blackfoot agreement was passed on March 1, 1907, as part of the annual appropriations bill—see 34 *U.S. Statutes* 1035; for the Flathead opening, see 35 *U.S. Statutes* 448–49.

43. *CR,* 60–1, 1909.

44. *ARCIA* (1906): 369; *ARCIA* (1907): 54; 34 *US. Statutes,* 53–54 (Yakima); ibid., 1035 (Blackfoot); 35 *U.S. Statutes,* 449 (Flathead).

45. *Winters* v. *U.S.,* 28 *Supreme Court Reporter* 212; *U.S.* v. *Wightman*

230 F 277 (1916). See also *Sowards et al. v. Meagher et al.* 108 P 1112 (1910) and *Skeem* v. *U.S. et al.* 273 F 93 (1921).

46. "Plan for Cooperation Between the Indian Office and the Forest Service," enclosed in James R. Garfield to Secretary of Agriculture, January 22, 1908, Central Classified File 5–25, "Cooperation—Forest Service," pt. 1, RG 48, NA; F. E. Leupp to James R. Garfield, February 20, 1909, Container 143, James R. Garfield Papers; Walter L. Fisher to Commissioner of Indian Affairs, April 10, 1911, Central Classified File 5–25, "Cooperation—General," pt. 1, RG 48, NA. For an account of the Forest Service's handling of its responsibilities, see Gifford Pinchot to Secretary of Agriculture, July 23, 1909, Central Classified File 5–25, "Cooperation—Forest Service," pt. 1, RG 48, NA.

47. F. E. Leupp, "The Red Man's Burden," p. 752.

48. "Speech by Matthew K. Sniffen to the Lake Mohonk Conference," November 1910, copy filed with correspondence in IRA Papers.

49. *ARCIA* (1912): 5–6.

50. James McLaughlin, *My Friend the Indian*, p. 389; *CR*, 61–2, 6081.

51. Robert G. Valentine, "Making Good Indians," pp. 608, 611; for the text of the omnibus act, see 36 *U.S. Statutes* 855–63.

52. Chalmers G. Hill to Walter L. Fisher, May 27, 1911, Walter L. Fisher Papers.

53. McLaughlin, *My Friend the Indian*, pp. 403–4; McKenzie, *The Indian in Relation to the White*, pp. 47–49; Herbert Welsh, "IRA Circular," January 14, 1907, IRA Papers; Frederick H. Abbott to Walter L. Fisher, May 21, 1912, File 5–6, "Competent Indians," Central Classified Files, Office of the Secretary, RG 48, NA.

54. *CR*, 59–1, 3273; *CR*, 59–2, 2344.

55. "Indians as Wards," *Independent*, February 13, 1908, p. 381.

56. For a discussion of Owen's bill (S.6767, 62d Cong. 2d sess.), see Samuel Adams, first assistant secretary of interior, to Robert Gamble, June 1, 1912, Central Files: Legislation, File 1–64, Administrative General (62d Congress), RG 48; Myers's speech is in *CR*, 64–1, 2111–2, and the creation of the commission is described in *CR*, 63–1, 2038.

57. Franklin K. Lane to Scott Ferris, July 14, 1913, Entry 121, File 013, General Service, RG 75; Franklin K. Lane, "From the Warpath to the Plow," p. 87.

58. *Senate Document* no. 984, 63d Cong., 3d sess., p. 10; *CR*, 64–1, 7572; *CR*, 64–2, 2110.

59. *IRA AR* (1913): 52; *IRA AR* (1915): 4; Warren K. Moorehead, *The American Indian in the United States*, p. 434; Frederick H. Abbott to Robert LaFollette, June 17, 1915, LaFollette Papers.

60. *New York Times*, October 29, 1916, sec. v, 10.

61. This description of the ceremony is based on reports in the *Sioux City (Iowa) Tribune*, May 15, 1916, taken from the clippings in File 5–6, "Competent Indians," Central Classified Files, Office of the Secretary, RG 48, NA. The ceremony was also described in Harvey D. Jacobs, "Uncle Sam—The Great White Father," p. 701; "A Ritual of Citizenship," *Outlook*, May 24, 1916, pp. 161–62; and Pfaller, *James McLaughlin*, pp. 333–38.

62. *CR*, 64–2, 2112; Herbert Welsh to Cato Sells, March 23, 1917, Entry 121, General Service Files, File 020, RG 75, NA.

63. Cato Sells, "A Declaration of Policy in the Administration of Indian Affairs," April 17, 1917, reprinted in *ARCIA* (1917): 3–4; ibid., p. 5; Circular, dated April, 1917, copy in Richard H. Pratt Papers.

64. Samuel Brosius to Matthew Sniffen, April 17, 1917, IRA Papers; "A New Step in Our Indian Policy" *Outlook*, May 23, 1917, p. 136; Superintendent of Red Cliff, Wisconsin, Agency to Cato Sells, April 27, 1917, Entry 121, File 020, General Service, RG 75, NA.

65. The one-million-acre figure is from *ARCIA* (1918): 19; Sells, "The First Americans as Loyal Citizens," p. 524; *ARCIA* (1919): 8; see 40 *U.S. Statutes* 591 and 41 *U.S. Statutes* 9, *ARCIA* (1920): 169.

66. *ARCIA* (1920): 9; *CR*, 66–1, 258.

67. Theodore Roosevelt to Francis Leupp, September 4, 1907, Series 1, Roosevelt Papers. For a description of the aftermath of one "Last Arrow" ceremony see Yankton Superintendent A. W. Leech to Franklin K. Lane, June 21, 1916, File 5–6, "Competent Indians," Central Classified Files, Office of the Secretary RG 48, NA. After describing the large number of automobile purchases and land sales completed after the ceremony the agent added, "I regret that I cannot furnish a more favorable report . . . but when the disposition of the Indian and the greed and activity of the white man is taken into consideration, it is no more than could have been expected."

68. *ARCIA* (1917): 26–29; Calvin H. Asbury to Malcom McDowell, secretary of the Board of Indian Commissioners, December 24, 1917, Entry 1386, Officials, 1915–18, RG 75, NA; *ARCIA* (1920): 23.

69. Owen Wilson, "Rescuing a People by an Irrigating Ditch," pp. 14815–17; *CR* 63–2, 10787.

70. *ANR*, Fort Hall (1920), sec. 4, 10; see *House Document* no. 387, 66th Cong., 2d sess., p. 10.

71. Cato Sells to Board of Indian Commissioners, March 16, 1914, Entry 121, File 339, General Service, RG 75, NA.

72. 41 *U.S. Statutes* 31–32. Treaty reservations could be mined under an 1891 law. For a description of the background to the Hayden bill, see Lawrence C. Kelly, *The Navajo Indians and Federal Indian Policy*, pp. 39–42.

73. *CR*, 65–3, 4940. Kelly describes the impact of this attitude on the Navajos in his *Navajo Indians and Federal Policy*, pp. 43–47 and chap. 4.

74. Carlson's *Indians, Bureaucrats and Land* provides striking confirmation of this view. Carlson shows that as the pace of allotment quickened, whites gained readier access to Native American resources. Self-sufficient Indian agriculture gave way to economic dependence and poverty. Carlson argues that this process proves the government failed to act as the guardian of the tribes. It is my contention that policy makers and bureaucrats *redefined* their role as guardians, rejecting the old objective (the Indian as yeoman farmer) and adopting a new one—the Indian as colonial subject.

Chapter 6

1. *ARCIA* (1895): 354; *ARCIA* (1896): 1016.

2. *ARCIA* (1895): 338–39.

3. *ARCIA* (1892): 55

4. *ARCIA* (1899): 15.

5. *CR*, 55–2, 1008; *CR*, 57–2, 1427.

6. *CR*, 58–3, 1147.

7. *CR*, 57–2, 1426.

8. *CR*, 57–2, 1278; Lyman Abbott, "Our Indian Problem," p. 724.

9. Frank W. Blackmar, "Indian Education," pp. 814–15; Herbert Welsh, "Comment on Thomas Morgan's 'Indian Education,'" p. 178; Hollis Burke Frissell, "What is the Relation of the Indian of the Present Decade to the Indian of the Future?" reprinted in *ARCIA* (1900): 470; *ARCIA* (1898): 1096.

10. Frissell, "The Indian Problem," *Proc. NEA* (1901): 628–83, 692.

11. Calvin M. Woodward, "What Shall Be Taught in an Indian School?" *ARCIA* (1901): 471, 472, 473; Garland, "Indian Education," *Proc. NEA* (1903): 397–98.

12. Lummis, "Lame Dancing Masters," pp. 356–57; idem, "A New Indian Policy" *Land of Sunshine,* December, 1901, p. 464; John T. Bramhall, "Red, Black and Yellow," *Overland Monthly,* February, 1901, p. 723; "Indian Industrial Development," *Outlook,* January 12, 1901, p. 101; "Cutting Indians' Hair," *Harper's Weekly,* March 22, 1902, p. 357; Ella H. Cooper, "How to Educate the Indians," p. 454.

13. *ARCIA* (1901): 431. See also Reel's first annual report, *ARCIA* (1898): 334–49.

14. Commissioner of Indian Affairs, Circular #43, September 19, 1900, Entry #718, RG 75, NA; Estelle Reel to William A. Jones, August 20, 1904, Special Series A, Box 8, RG 75, NA.

15. See "Circulars Issued by the Education Division" (no. 85), November 6, 1902, Entry #718, RG 75, NA; ibid., (no. 48), February 18, 1901. For a fuller view of Jones's perspective, see *ARCIA* (1901): 1–5.

16. *ARCIA* (1901): 9, 426, 418–57.

17. George Bird Grinnell to Estelle Reel, April 14, 1902, Entry #173, RG 75, NA.

18. Thomas J. Morgan, "Indian Education," p. 173.

19. *ARCIA* (1903): 381; Samuel Brosius to Herbert Welsh, November 14, 1900, IRA Papers; *Proc. NEA* (1904): 983, 984.

20. *ARCIA* (1905): 1, 3; Leupp, "Indians and Their Education," *Proc. NEA* (1907): 71.

21. Leupp, *The Indian and His Problem,* p. 139; idem, "Back to Nature for the Indian," p. 336; *ARCIA* (1905): 8–9.

22. Charles B. Dyke, "Essential Features in the Education of the Child Races," *Proc. NEA* (1909): 929, 930, 932; Leupp, "Why Booker T. Washington Has Succeeded in His Life Work," p. 327. The role of racial "pessimism" in the development of industrial education is a central theme of Donald Spivey, *Schooling for the New Slavery.* For the impact of these ideas on the administration of the United States' colonies, see Glenn Anthony May, *Social Engineering in the Philippines.*

23. G. Stanley Hall, "How Far Are the Principles of Education along Indigenous Lines Applicable to American Indians?" p. 1163; Coffin, "Education of Backward Races," p. 46. It should be noted that Hall called for greater sensitivity to Indian traditions and respect for tribal lifeways. Coming before the emergence of the concept of cultural pluralism, however, his

pleas were understood as recommendations for a lowering of governmental expectations.

24. *ARCIA* (1908): 24; Commissioner of Indian Affairs Circular #175, December 3, 1907, Entry 718, RG 75, NA.

25. *ARCIA* (1905): 3; *ARCIA* (1906): 407.

26. Marvin Lazerson, *Origins of the Urban School,* p. 245; "The Need for Practical Training for the Indians," *Journal of Education* 69 (March 18, 1909): 300.

27. *ARCIA* (1905): 5; Leupp, *The Indian and His Problem,* p. 156.

28. See *ARCIA* (1906): 9; (forty-nine schoolboys and three adults took home $1,672.56 for six weeks' work); C. W. Goodman to Charles Dagenett, September 7, 1908, Entry 121, General Service File, File #920, RG 75, NA. Goodman went on to say that Indians received $6–$20 per month while whites received $15–$40.

29. *ARCIA* (1906): 8, 15.

30. Herman Charles, secretary of the Imperial Valley Board of Trade, to Charles Dagenett, April 30, 1908, Entry 121, General Service File, File #920, RG 75, NA; F. E. Leupp to James R. Garfield, February 10, 1908, Series 1, Roosevelt Papers.

31. *ARCIA* (1907): 20.

32. School Circular Number 161 (July 1, 1907), Entry 718, RG 75, NA; Circular Number 216, (June 21, 1908), Entry 718, RG 75, NA; Leupp, "Back to Nature for the Indian," p. 337; F. E. Leupp to E. A. Morse, December 30, 1908, Entry 121, File 803 General Service, RG 75, NA; see action on H.R. 26916, 60th Cong., 2d sess. In February 1909, Congress eliminated the four boarding schools and authorized the construction of thirty new day schools.

33. *CR,* 60–1, 1707, 1712. For school attendance figures, see *ARCIA* (1905–10).

34. *ARCIA* (1906): 46; see introduction in Marvin Lazerson and W. Norton Grubb, eds., *American Education and Vocationalism,* especially p. 25.

35. *ARCIA* (1909): 4; *ARCIA* (1915): 7, 8.

36. *ARCIA* (1910): 14–15.

37. *ARCIA* (1916): 9.

38. Ibid., pp. 11–21, 22.

39. *ARCIA* (1910): 8; Robert G. Valentine to D. D. Wiley, December 18, 1909, Entry 121, General Service File #920, RG 75, NA; Valentine also increased the number of Indian employees of the Indian Office. See Diane T.

Putney, "Robert Grosvenor Valentine," in Kvasnicka and Viola, eds., *Commissioners of Indian Affairs*, pp. 235–36.

40. *ARCIA* (1918): 36.

41. *ARCIA* (1909): 20, *ANR, Walker River (1911): 10; ANR*, Cheyenne and Arapaho (1910): 14.

42. Robert C. Valentine to W. W. Scott, August 8, 1911, Entry 121, File 803, Crow Agency, RG 75, NA; *ANR*, Crow (1913), "Schools."

43. See *ANR*, Fort Lapwai (1910), "Education," *ANR*, Fort Lapwai (1912), "Public Schools;" *ANR*, Yakima (1913) 3:2; "Response to Circular #612, March 14, 1912," from Bishop, California, Special Series A, RG 75, NA.

44. *ARCIA* (1914): 7; Carl Price to Cato Sells, January 9, 1916, and Edgar Meritt to Price, January 21, 1916, Entry 121, General Service File, File 803, RG 75, NA.

45. *ANR*, Uintah and Ouray (1915): 15; ibid., (1919): 15, ibid., (1920): 11.

46. Charles H. Asbury to Edgar Meritt, January 29, 1919, Entry 121, File 803, Crow Agency, RG 75, NA.

47. *ARCIA* (1919): 26.

48. *ARCIA* (1920): 11.

Chapter 7

1. *ARCIA* (1895): 249. The agent's fears were repeated in 1899; see *ARCIA* (1899): 283.

2. William B. Hornblower, "The Legal Status of the Indians," *Reports of the Fourteenth Annual meeting of the American Bar Association* 14 (1891), p. 277; Board of Indian Commissioners quoted in *ARCIA* (1899): pt. ii, 236–37.

3. 30 *U.S.* 1 (1831). For a discussion of Marshall's philosophy see Wilcomb E. Washburn, *Red Man's Land/White Man's Law*, pp. 59–74.

4. *U.S.* v. *Mullin*, 71 F. 685, (1895).

5. *Hitchcock* v. *U.S. ex rel Big Boy, 22 Appeals Cases, District of Columbia*, 284–85 (1904). For the development of the doctrine of federal jurisdiction in this area, see also *U.S.* v. *Gardner*, 133 F. 285 (1904); and *McKnight* v. *U.S.*, 130 F. 659 (1904).

6. *Tiger* v. *Western Investment Co.*, 221 U.S. 286 (1911).

7. *U.S.* v. *Fitzgerald*, 201 F. 296 (1912); *Heckman* v. *U.S.*, 224 U.S. 445 (1912), emphasis added.

8. Lyman Abbott, "The Rights of Man," *Outlook*, June 1901, p. 351.

9. *U.S.* v. *Rickert*, 188 *U.S.* 437, 442, 445 (1903).

10. *U.S.* v. *Thurston Co., Nebraska*, 143 *F.* 289, 292 (1906).

11. *U.S.* v. *Schock*, 187 *F.* 862 (1911); *Choate* v. *Trapp*, 224 *U.S.* 665 (1911); *Colman J. Ward et al* v. *Board of County Commissioners of Love County, Oklahoma*, 253, *U.S.* 17 (1920); *Indian Illumination Oil Co.* v. *State of Oklahoma*, 240 *U.S.* 522 (1916); *U.S.* v. *Pearson Co. Treasurer et al*, 231 *F.* 522 (1916); and *U.S.* v. *Board of County Commissioners of Osage Co., Oklahoma*, 251 *U.S.* 130, 133 (1919).

12. *Matter of Heff*, 197 *U.S.* 497, 499, 508 (1905).

13. *House Report* no. 1558, 59th Cong. 1st sess., pp. 2, 1.

14. *Senate Report* no. 1998, 59th Cong., 1st sess., pp. 3–4.

15. *CR*, 59–1, 4655.

16. *ARCIA* (1906): 128, 46; and see Samuel Brosius to Merrill Gates, October 30, 1908, IRA Papers.

17. *ANR*, Cheyenne and Arapaho, 1918, 1, 2.

18. *Dick* v. *U.S.*, 208 *U.S.* 354 (1908); *U.S.* v. *Celestine*, 215 *U.S.* 278 (1909); and *U.S.* v. *Sutton*, 215 *U.S.* 291 (1909).

19. *Hallowell* v. *U.S.*, 221 *U.S.* 324 (1911).

20. *Mosier* v. *U.S.*, 198 *F.* 58, 59 (1912).

21. *U.S.* v. *Sandoval*, 231 *U.S.* 39, 45–46 (1913).

22. *U.S.* v. *Nice*, 241 *U.S.* 600 (1916), emphasis mine. The background of the *Nice* decision and its implications for subsequent litigation are discussed in David H. Getches, et al., *Cases and Materials on Federal Indian Law*, pp. 495–99.

23. 23 *U.S. Statutes*, 385 (1885); 24 *U.S. Statutes* 388–91, sec. 6 (1887); and see *U.S.* v. *Kiya*, 126 *F.* 879 (1903); and *State* v. *Howard*, 74 *Pac.* 382 (1903).

24. *In re Now—Ge-Zhuck*, 76 P. 880 (1904); *Report of the Twenty-Sixth Annual Meeting of the American Bar Association* 26 (1903): 498.

25. *ARCIA* (1898): 96–100 and *ARCIA* (1899): 130–31.

26. *ARCIA* (1902): 288.

27. *IRA AR* (1906): 46. Leupp's falling out with the IRA is described by Donald Parman, "Francis Ellington Leupp," in Kvasnicka and Viola, eds., *Commissioners of Indian Affairs*, pp. 224–30.

28. Samuel Brosius to Matthew Sniffen, June 15, 1908, IRA Papers; Francis Leupp to Charles C. Binney, November 11, 1908, IRA Papers. For a de-

tailed description of the incident, see Parman, "The 'Big Stick' in Indian Affairs: The Bai-a-lil-le Incident in 1909," pp. 343–60.

29. Leupp to George Bird Grinnell, December 26, 1908, James R. Garfield Papers; see also the statement from the Boston Indian Citizenship Committee December 16, 1908, IRA Papers.

30. Theodore Roosevelt to John Davis Long, Edward Henry Clement, and John S. Lockwood, December 29, 1908, *Letters of Theodore Roosevelt* 6:1449, 1450.

31. *Ex Parte Bi-a-lil-le et al.*, 100 P. 451 (1909). The Arizona court used a spelling of the Navajo leader's name that varies from the one adopted by subsequent commentators.

32. 215 *U.S.* 290–91 (1909).

33. 232 *U.S.* 449, 450 (1913).

34. Response to Circular #612, March 14, 1912, from Fond du Lac, Wis., Special Series A, RG 75, NA; ibid., from Neah Bay. For a summary of the responses to Luddington's survey, see Appendix 3.

35. "Rough Draft of an Analysis of Answers Sent by Superintendents to Circular #612," March 14, 1912, Special Series A, RG 75, NA.

36. For voting statistics, see C. F. Hauke to Ruby Bans, March 2, 1919, Entry 121, File 128, General Service, RG 75, NA; McKenzie, *The Indian in Relation to the White*, p. 35; *Cofield* v. *Farrell*, 134 Pac. 409 (1913).

37. For a brief description of the Supreme Court in these years, see Robert G. McCloskey, *The American Supreme Court* (Chicago: University of Chicago Press, 1960), chap. 5 and pp. 208–19; and C. Vann Woodward, *Origins of the New South*, chap. 12.

38. See Colorado Constitution of 1876, Art. 7, Sec. 1; Montana *Laws of 1913*, chap. 1; Nebraska Constitution of 1875; Art. 6, Sec. 1; Oregon Constitution, Art. 2, Sec. 2; South Dakota Constitution of 1889, Art. 7, Sec. 1; and Wyoming Constitution, Art. 6, Sec. 10. The Oklahoma law was struck down by the U.S. Supreme Court in 1915. For the Nebraska decision, see *State* v. *Norris*, 55 N.W., 1086 (1893). For South Dakota statistics, see South Dakota Secretary of State, *Annual Report* (1910); U.S. Bureau of the Census, *Thirteenth Census of the U.S. Population*, Vol. 3 (Washington: Government Printing Office, 1913).

39. *Anderson* v. *Matthews*, 163 P. 905 (1917).

40. California Constitution of 1849, Art. 2, Sec. 1; Minnesota Constitution of 1857, Art. 7, Sec. 1; North Dakota Constitution of 1889, Art. 5, Sec.

121; Oklahoma Constitution of 1907, Art. 3, Sec. 1; and Wisconsin Constitution of 1848, Art. 3, Sec. 1. Oklahoma's reasoning in this instance was revealed in *Atwater* v. *Hassett*, III P. 802 (1910).

41. *ARCIA* (1896): 143; *Opsahl* v. *Johnson*, 163 *N.W.* 988 (1917).

42. Idaho Constitution of 1890, Art. 6, Sec. 3; New Mexico Constitution of 1911, Art. 7, Sec. 1; and Washington Constitution of 1889, Art. 6, Sec. 1. New Mexico allowed Pueblo Indians to vote, however. See *U.S.* v. *Ortez*, 1 *New Mexico Reports* 422; Arizona Constitution of 1912, Art. 7, Sec. 2; Nevada Constitution of 1864, Art. 2, Sec. 1; and Par. 11, Sec. 20-2-14, *Utah Code Annotated, 1953* (first adopted in 1898); Arizona Secretary of State, *Annual Report* (1912), and U.S. Bureau of Census, *Thirteenth Census of the U.S. Population*, II. Nevada's laws were clarified by two attorney general's opinions. The first (issued September 10, 1900) barred "half-breeds" from the polls, and the second, issued October 17, 1912, declared flatly that Indians, because they were not citizens, were not entitled to vote. Utah's restrictions on Indian voting were upheld by that state's Supreme Court in 1956. See *Allen* v. *Merrell*, 305 P 2nd. 490 (1956).

43. *Porter* v. *Hall*, 271 P. 419 (1928). For a discussion of the reversal of this decision in 1948, see Getches, et al., *Federal Indian Law*, pp. 520–21.

44. *Piper et al.* v. *Big Pine School District of Inyo County et al.*, 226 P. 929 (1924). While accepting the legality of separate schools for Indians, the court ordered Piper and the other plaintiffs to be admitted to the local white schools because the district did not provide separate facilities for Native Americans. See also *Crawford* v. *District School Board for District No. 7*, 137 P. 217 (1913) for the Oregon case; and *State* v. *Wolf*, 59 S.E. 40 (1907) for the North Carolina case. See 33 *U.S. Statutes* 619, Sec. 7; *Senate Report* no. 744, 58th Cong. 2d sess.; and the debates on the bill in *CR* 58–2, 3081–82.

45. See Arizona *Statutes* (1913), Sec. 3837; Nevada *Revised Statutes* (1912), Sec. 6515; North Carolina State Constitution, Art. 14, Sec. 8; and Oregon *Laws* (1920), Sec. 2163. For the tests of the Arizona and Oregon laws, see *In re Walker's Estate*, 46 P. 67 (1896), and *In re Pacquet's Estate*, 200 P. 911 (1921).

46. Chauncey Shafter Goodrich, "The Legal Status of the California Indian," pp. 176–77, 178, 178–79.

47. Neal Doyle Houghton, "The Legal Status of Indian Suffrage in the United States," pp. 520, 516.

Chapter 8

1. Walter M. Camp, "The Condition of Reservation Indians," typescript of a report submitted to Malcom McDowell, secretary of the Board of Indian Commissioners, June 8, 1920. Copy in Edward Ayer Collection, the Newberry Library.

2. Ibid., p. 3.

3. Ibid., pp. 6, 6–8, 13–14.

4. Ibid., pp. 5–6, 14.

5. The Brookings Institution, Institute for Government Research, *The Problem of Indian Administration*, pp. 199, 201, 357, 454.

6. For an anthropologist's view of the relationship between external pressure and cultural survival, see Edward H. Spicer, "Persistent Cultural Systems," *Science*, November 19, 1971, pp. 795–800. For a case study of this phenomenon, see Frederick E. Hoxie, "From Prison to Homeland: The Cheyenne River Indian Reservation before World War I," *South Dakota History* 10 (Winter 1979): 1–24.

Bibliography

The notes that follow should guide the reader through the bibliography. A simple strategy lies behind these long lists. For each aspect of the study I began with a central source or cluster of sources: governmental actions and attitudes were found first in the *Congressional Record* and the *Annual Reports* of the commissioners of Indian affairs; for scientific attitudes I consulted the principal professional journals (*American Anthropologist, American Journal of Sociology*); and for popular opinion, the articles and stories about Indians cited in *Poole's Index* and the *Readers' Guides* to magazines. Each basic source formed the center of a series of concentric circles. The *Congressional Record* led me to committee reports and transcripts of hearings. These in turn led to archival collections, contemporary commentaries, and the activities of lobbyists and reformers. In the process new circles were formed; they too generated concentric rings. Before long, the networks began to intersect. Policy overlapped with science, popular attitudes with political philosophy, "expert" opinion with bureaucratic practice. The story became more tangled—and more interesting. One hopes the study produced from such diverse sources is simple enough to be meaningful and complex enough to be true.

Those interested in further research should consult three excellent bibliographical sources that appeared during the course of my work: Francis Paul Prucha, *A Bibliographical Guide to the History of Indian-White Relations in the United States* (Chicago: University of Chicago Press, 1977); Imre Sutton, *Indian Land Tenure: Bibliographical Essays and a Guide to the Literature* (New York: Clearwater, 1975); and the Newberry Library Center for the History of the American Indian Bibliography Series, edited by Francis Jennings and published by Indiana University Press, Bloomington, Indiana. Finally, the National Archives has published a useful guide to their massive holding in the records of the Bureau of Indian Affairs: Edward E. Hill, *Preliminary Inventory of the Records of the Bureau of Indian Affairs* (Record Group 75), 2 vols. (Washington, D.C.: National Archives and Records Service, 1965).

Notes

1. *Archival Sources.* Material was consulted in the areas indicated within Record Group 75 and Record Group 48. Specific cases were traced through the "letters received" and "letters sent" areas, and special topics such as education or citizenship were pursued through the general service files. "Special Cases" contains material removed from the regular files for congressional inquiries or other purposes; it provided information on the implementation of allotment legislation and irrigation projects. For detailed descriptions of each heading, consult the Edward Hill inventory cited above. The National Anthropological Archives at the Smithsonian Institution contain both the Alice Fletcher papers and the best collection available of letters to and from John Wesley Powell.

The personal papers of persons involved in Indian affairs were extremely useful, particularly the often-used Henry Dawes papers, the Pratt papers, and the McGee papers. The Indian Rights Association papers revealed several points at which the activities of one group—reformers—intersected with those of politicians, scientists, and others.

2. *Government Documents.* The records of the debates on legislation affecting Indians for the years 1880 to 1920 were a fundamental resource for

the study. House and Senate documents and related reports were also invaluable. These records provided an illuminating picture of the intersection of political, ideological, and scientific interests in Indian policy making. The published reports of the Bureau of American Ethnology (particularly Powell's introductions to the *Annual Reports*), the Bureau of Education, and the Office of Indian Affairs for the years 1880–1920 were also read systematically.

3. *Newspapers and Other Contemporary Publications.* The newspapers listed were studied carefully for the crisis year of 1879–80, described in Chapter 1. In addition, they constituted a useful measure of public reactions to such important events as the passage of the Burke Act or the opening of the Chicago world's fair.

Specialized publications were consulted for information on specific policy areas. Those listed were examined for the entire 1880–1920 period, except for the *Railroad Gazette,* which was used for the years immediately surrounding the passage of the Dawes Severalty Act.

4. *Primary Sources.* Drawn from *Poole's* and the *Readers' Guide,* as well as the holdings of the Boston Public, Widener, Langdell, Newberry, and Goldfarb libraries and the Library of Congress, this section contains all contemporary materials consulted for the study. Unsigned editorials have been included, alphabetized by title.

1. Archival Sources

American Philosophical Society, Philadelphia
   Franz Boas Papers (microfilm)
Beinecke Rare Book and Manuscript Library, Yale University
   Richard Henry Pratt Papers
Harvard University Archives
   Frederick Ward Putnam Papers
Houghton Library, Harvard University
   Barrows Family Papers
Library of Congress, Washington, D.C., Manuscripts Division
   Henry L. Dawes Papers
   Walter L. Fisher Papers
   James R. Garfield Papers

Joseph Hawley Papers

Robert M. LaFollette Papers

William John McGee Papers

Key Pittman Papers

Hugh L. Scott Papers

Theodore Roosevelt Presidential Papers (microfilm)

William Howard Taft Presidential Papers (microfilm)

Woodrow Wilson Presidential Papers (microfilm)

National Anthropological Archives, Smithsonian Institution, Washington, D.C.

Alice Cunningham Fletcher Papers

John Wesley Powell Letterbook, 1897–1902

National Archives and Records Service, Washington, D.C.

Record Group 75, Records of the Bureau of Indian Affairs. (Both here and in the note citations, entry numbers refer to listings in Hill's *Preliminary Inventory*. The term *File* refers to the decimal classification used in Entry 121.)

Board of Indian Commissioners General Correspondence (Entry 1386)

Central Classified Files (Entry 121)

Letters Received by the Office of Indian Affairs (Entries 75, 79)

Letters Sent by the Office of Indian Affairs (Entries 80, 84)

Register of Centennial Correspondence (Entry 78)

Special Cases

Superintendents' Annual Narrative Reports (Entry 960)

Record Group 48, Records of the Department of Interior

Office of the Secretary of Interior, Central Classified Files

Pennsylvania Historical Society, Philadelphia

Indian Rights Association Papers

Rochester University Library

Lewis Henry Morgan Papers

2. *Government Documents*

Bureau of American Ethnology Annual Reports

U.S. Bureau of Education, Circulars of Information, Annual Reports of the Commissioner

U.S. Commissioner of Indian Affairs, Annual Reports
U.S. Congress
Congressional Record
House Documents
House Reports
Senate Documents
Senate Reports

3. Newspapers and Other Contemporary Publications

Newspapers
Alta California (San Francisco)
Atlanta Constitution
Boston Daily Advertiser
Boston Evening Transcript
Boston Post
Chicago Tribune
New Orleans Times-Picayune
New York Times
New York Tribune
Philadelphia Bulletin
St. Louis Post-Dispatch
San Francisco Examiner
Virginia City (Nevada) *Territorial Enterprise*
Other
American Bar Association Annual Reports
Journal of Education
National Education Association Proceedings
Railroad Gazette
Red Man (newspaper for the Indian Industrial School, Carlisle, Pa.)

4. Primary Sources

Abbott, L. J. "The Race Question in the Forty-Sixth State." *Independent*,
July 25, 1907, pp. 206–11.

Abbott, Lyman. "Our Indian Problem." *North American Review* 167 (December 1898): 719–29.

———. "The Approaching End of the Indian Problem." *Independent*, October 25, 1902, pp. 2586–87.

Armstrong, S. C. *The Indian Question.* Hampton, Va.: Hampton Normal School Steam Press, 1883.

Austin, Mary. *The Arrow Maker.* New York: Duffield and Co., 1911.

Baker, Frank. "The Ascent of Man." *Annual Report of the Board of Regents of the Smithsonian Institution, 1890.* Washington: Government Printing Office, 1891, pp. 447–466.

Baker, Ray Stannard. "The Day of the Run." *Century*, September 1903, pp. 643–55.

Bancroft, Hubert Howe. *The Book of the Fair.* Chicago: Bancroft, 1894.

Bandelier, Adolph. *The Delightmakers.* New York: Dodd Mead, 1890.

———. *Kin and Clan: An Address before the Historical Society of New Mexico.* Santa Fe, 1882.

Baxter Springs Board of Trade. *Memorial.* Baxter Springs, Kans., November 20, 1888.

Blackmar, Frank W. "The Socialization of the American Indian." *American Journal of Sociology* 34 (January 1929): 653–99.

———. "Indian Education." *Annals of the American Academy of Political and Social Science* 2. (May 1892): 813–37.

Bland, Thomas A. *A History of the Sioux Agreement: Some Facts Which Should Not Be Forgotten.* Washington, 1889.

———. *The Indian—What Shall We Do with Him?* Washington, D.C., 1887.

———. *The Indian Question.* Boston, 1880.

Blue Book of the Panama-Pacific International Exposition at San Francisco, 1915. San Francisco, 1915.

Boas, Franz. "Census of the North American Indians." *Publications of the American Economic Association*, n.s. 2 (March 1899): 49–53.

———. *The Ethnography of Franz Boas.* Ed. Ronald P. Rohner. Chicago: University of Chicago Press, 1969.

———. "The Half Blood Indian: An Anthropometric Study." *Popular Science Monthly*, October 1894, pp. 761–70.

———. *The Mind of Primitive Man.* New York: Macmillan, 1911.

———. "A Review of the Data for the Study of the Prehistoric Chronology of America." *Proceedings of the American Association for the Advancement of Science,* 1887, pp. 283–301.

Brinton, Daniel Garrison. *The American Race: A Linguistic Classification and Ethnographic Description of the Native Tribes of North and South America.* New York: N.D.C. Hodges, 1891.

———. *The Basis of Social Relations: A Study in Ethnic Psychology.* Ed. Livingston Farrand. New York: G. P. Putnam's Sons, 1902.

———. *Races and Peoples: Lectures on the Science of Ethnography.* New York: N.D.C. Hodges, 1890.

Brookings Institution, Institute for Government Research. *The Problem of Indian Administration.* Baltimore: Johns Hopkins University Press, 1928.

Brosius, Samuel. "Turning the Indian Loose." *Case and Comment* 23 (February 1917): 739–41.

Bruce, Edward C. *The Century: Its Fruits and Its Festival.* Philadelphia: Lippincott, 1877.

Bryce, James. *The Relations of the Advanced and the Backward Races of Mankind.* Oxford: Clarendon Press, 1902.

Buchanan, Beverly. "A Tribute to the First American." *World Today,* January 1911, pp. 25–33.

Canfield, George F. "Carl Schurz on the Indian Problem." *Nation,* June 30, 1881, pp. 457–58.

———. "The Legal Position of the Indian." *American Law Review* 15 (January 1881): 21–37.

Carpenter, C. C. *Grand Rush for the Indian Territory.* Independence, Kans.: P.H. Tieman, 1879.

Chapman, Arthur. "Indian Lands for the White Man." *World Today,* September 1905, pp. 980–83.

Chase, O. G. *The Neutral Strip, or No Man's Land: The Cimarron Territory.* Dodge City [?] Kans., 1886.

Coffin, Ernest W. "On the Education of Backward Races." *Pedogogical Seminary* 15 (March 1908): 1–62.

Collins, Mary C. *Practical Suggestions on Indian Affairs.* New York, n.d.

Cook, Joseph. *Frontier Savages, White and Red.* Philadelphia: Indian Rights Association, 1885.

Cook, W. A. "Vocational Training for the Indian." *Vocational Education* 2 (March 1913): 289–98.

Cooper, Ella H. "How to Educate the Indians." *Gunton's Magazine*, May 1902, pp. 452–55.

Crane, Leo. "A Man Ruined by an Idea." *Harper's Weekly*, June 26, 1900, p. 15.

Crook, George. "The Apache Problem." *Journal of the Military Service Institution of the United States* 7 (October 1886): 257–69.

———. *General George Crook: His Autobiography.* Ed. Martin F. Schmitt. Norman: University of Oklahoma Press, 1946.

———. *Letter from George Crook on Giving the Ballot to the Indians.* Philadelphia: Indian Rights Association, 1885.

Curtis, Edward S. *The North American Indian.* 20 vols. Cambridge, Mass.: University Press, 1907–30.

"Cutting Indians' Hair." *Harper's Weekly*, March 22, 1902, p. 357.

Dawes, Henry L. "Have We Failed with the Indian?" *Atlantic Monthly*, August 1899, pp. 280–85.

———. "The Present Crisis." *Lend a Hand* 11 (November 1893): 346–52.

———. "The Indian Territory." *Independent*, October 25, 1900, pp. 2561–65.

Day, Sherman. "Civilizing the Indians of California." *Overland Monthly*, n.s., December 1883, pp. 575–81.

"Dealing with the Indians Individually." *Independent*, December 14, 1905, pp. 1419–20.

Decker, A. "Making the Warrior a Worker." *Munsey's Magazine*, October 1901, pp. 88–95.

Densmore, Francis. "Indian Education in Government Schools." *Overland Monthly*, November 1905, pp. 456–59.

Dewey, John. "Interpretation of Savage Mind." *Psychological Review* 9 (May 1902): 217–30.

Dewey, Mary E. *Historical Sketch of the Formation and Achievements of the Women's National Indian Association in the United States.* Philadelphia: Women's National Indian Association, 1900.

Dixon, Joseph K. "The Indians." *Case and Comment* 23 (February 1917): 712–16.

———. *The Vanishing Race: The Last Great Indian Council.* Garden City, N.Y.: Doubleday, 1913.

[Dodge, Richard I.] *A Living Issue.* Washington, D.C.: F. B. Mohun, 1882.

————. *Our Wild Indians: Thirty Years' Personal Experience among the Red Men of the Great West*. Hartford: A. D. Worthington and Co., 1882.

Dowd, Jerome. "Discussion of 'Leadership in Reform.'" *American Journal of Sociology* 16 (March 1911): 633–35.

Eastman, Elaine Goodale. "The Education of Indians." *Arena*, October 1900, pp. 412–14.

————. "Self-Teaching in the Indian Schools." *Educational Review* 1 (January 1891): 57–59.

Eells, Reverend Myron. *Justice to the Indian*. Portland, Oreg.: G. H. Himes, 1883.

Eggleston, Edward. *The Ultimate Solution of the American Negro Problem*. Boston, R. G. Badger, 1913.

Ellerbe, Rose L. "A School on a 'Ranchita.'" *Journal of Education* 53 (May 16, 1901): 313–14.

Farrand, Livingston. *Basis of American History: 1500–1900*. New York: Harper, 1904.

Fletcher, Alice Cunningham. "Indian Education and Civilization." *Senate Executive Document* no. 95, 48th Cong., 2d sess., ser. 2264.

————. "Preparation of the Indian for Citizenship." *Lend a Hand*, September 1892, pp. 190–98.

Flower, Elliott. "Law and the Indian." *Atlantic Monthly*, October 1910, pp. 488–90.

Flynn, Clinton R. "The Legal Status of the Indians in the United States," *Central Law Journal* 62 (May 25, 1906): 399–404.

Forbes-Lindsey, C. H. "Making Good Indians." *Harper's Weekly* 52 (October 31, 1908): 12–13.

————. "The North American Indian as a Laborer: His Value as a Worker and a Citizen." *Craftsman*, May 1908, pp. 146–57.

————. "Shaping the Future of the Indian." *World Today*, March 1907, pp. 290–92.

Francis, David R. *The Universal Exposition of 1904*. St. Louis: Louisiana Purchase Exposition, 1913.

Funsten, Rev. James B. "The Indian as a Worker." *Outlook*, December 9, 1905, pp. 875–78.

Garland, Hamlin. *The Book of the American Indian*. New York: Harper, 1923.

————. *Captain of the Gray Horse Troop.* New York: Harper, 1902.

————. *Hamlin Garland's Observations on the American Indian, 1895–1905.* Comp. and ed. Lonnie E. Underhill and Daniel F. Littlefield, Jr. Tucson: University of Arizona Press, 1976.

————. "The Red Man as Material." *Booklover's Magazine,* August 1903, pp. 196–98.

————. "The Red Man's Present Needs." *North American Review* 174 (April 1902): 476–88.

————. "The Red Plowman." *Craftsman,* November 1907, pp. 180–82.

Garth, Thomas R. "White, Indian and Negro Work Curves." *Journal of Applied Psychology* 5 (March 1921): 14–25.

Gibbon, John. "Our Indian Question." *Journal of the Military Service Institution of the United States* 2 (1881): 101–20.

Giddings, Franklin H. "The Causes of Race Superiority." In *America's Race Problems.* Philadelphia, 1901.

————. *Democracy and Empire.* New York: Macmillan, 1901.

————. "A Social Marking System." *American Journal of Sociology* 15 (March 11, 1910): 721–40.

Gilman, Samuel C. *The Future Indian: A Brief Treatise on the Indian Question.* Indianapolis: Caron and Hottenbeck, 1891.

Goodrich, Chauncey Shafter. "The Legal Status of the California Indian." *California Law Review* 14 (January 1926): 1–48.

Grafton, B. F. *Argument of B. F. Grafton.* Washington, 1879.

Grant, Madison. *The Conquest of a Continent.* New York: Scribner, 1933. *The Passing of the Great Race.* 4th rev. ed. New York: Scribner, 1922.

Grinnell, George Bird. *Blackfoot Lodge Tales.* New York: Scribner, 1892.

————. *Held Up by the Senate.* Philadelphia: Indian Rights Association, 1896.

————. "The Indian on the Reservation." *Atlantic Monthly,* February 1899, pp. 255–67.

————. *The Indians of Today.* New York: H. S. Stone, 1900.

————. *The Passing of the Great West: Selected Papers of George Bird Grinnell.* Ed. John F. Rieger, New York: Winchester Press, 1972.

————. "Portraits of Indian Types." *Scribner's* 37 (March 1905): 259–73.

————. *The Punishment of the Stingy and Other Stories.* New York: Harper, 1901.

————. *The Story of the Indian.* New York: D. Appleton and Co., 1895.

———. "Tenure of Land Among the Indians." *American Anthropologist*, n.s. 9 (January–March 1907): 1–11.

———. *When Buffalo Ran*. New Haven: Yale University Press, 1920.

———. "The Wild Indian." *Atlantic Monthly*, January 1899, pp. 20–29.

Grinnell, George Bird, and Theodore Roosevelt, eds. *American Big Game Hunting*. New York: Forest and Stream Publishing, 1893.

———. *Hunting at High Altitudes*. New York: Harper, 1913.

Hall, G. Stanley. "How Far Are the Principles of Education Along Indigenous Lines Applicable to American Indians?" *National Education Association Journal of Proceedings and Addresses, 1908*, pp. 1161–64.

Hare, William Hobart. *An Address Delivered by William Hobart Hare, Missionary Bishop of South Dakota, in Calvary Cathedral, Sioux Falls, South Dakota, January 10, 1888*. Sioux Falls, 1888.

Harsha, William Justin. "Law for the Indian." *North American Review* 134 (March 1882): 272–92.

———. *Ploughed Under*. New York: Fords, Howard and Hulbert, 1881.

———. *A Timid Brave*. New York: Funk and Wagnalls, 1886.

Harvey, Charles M. "The Indian of Today and Tomorrow." *American Monthly Review of Reviews*, June 1906, pp. 696–705.

———. "The Last Race Rally of the Indians." *World's Work*, May 1904, pp. 4803–9.

———. "The Red Man's Last Roll Call." *Atlantic Monthly*, March 1906, pp. 323–30.

Hayes, Helen E. *A Teacher's Testimony*. New York, 1888.

Hewitt, Edgar L. "Ethnic Factors in Education." *American Anthropologist*, n.s. 7 (January–March 1905): 1–16.

Hibbitts, J. H. *Peace, Civilization and Citizenship: The Indian Problem*. Topeka, Kans.: G. W. Martin, 1877.

Higginson, Thomas W. *Contemporaries*. Boston: Houghton Mifflin, 1899.

Hodge, Frederick Webb, ed. *The Handbook of American Indians of North of Mexico*. 2 vols. Washington: Government Printing Office, 1907–10.

Hoffman, Frederick L. "Race Traits and Tendencies of the American Negro." *Publications of the American Economic Association* 11 (1896): 1–329.

Holmes, William Henry. "Biographical Memoir of L. H. Morgan, 1818–1881." *National Academy of Science Biographical Memoirs* 6 (1909): 219–39.

———. "Classification and Arrangements of the Exhibits of an Anthropological Museum." *Annual Report of the U.S. National Museum.* Washington, D.C.: Government Printing Office, 1901.

———. "Sketch of the Origin, Development and Probable Destiny of the Races of Men." *American Anthropologist* 4 (July–September 1902): 369–91.

———. "Some Problems of the American Race." *American Anthropologist* 12 (April–June 1910): 149–82.

———. "World's Fair Congress of Anthropology." *American Anthropologist*, o.s. 6 (1893): 423–34.

Houghton, Neal Doyle. "The Legal Status of Indian Suffrage in the United States." *California Law Review* 19 (July 1931): 507–20.

———. "Wards of the United States—Arizona Applications: A Study of the Legal Status of the Indians." *University of Arizona Bulletin* 16 (July 1, 1945): 5–19.

Howard, Oliver Otis. *My Life and Experiences among Our Hostile Indians.* Hartford: A. D. Worthington, 1907.

Humphrey, Seth K. *The Indian Dispossessed.* Boston: Little, Brown, 1905. *The Racial Prospect.* New York: Scribner, 1920.

Hutchinson, Dr. Woods. "The Strength of Races." *World's Work,* May 1908, pp. 10262–68.

"Indians as Wards." *Independent,* February 13, 1908, pp. 380–81.

"The Indian School Blunder." *Independent,* February 9, 1905, p. 333.

"The Indian Schools." *Independent,* April 12, 1906, pp. 883–84.

Jackson, A. P., and E. C. Cole. *Oklahoma!* Kansas City, Mo.: Ramsey, Millett and Hudson, 1885.

Jackson, Helen Hunt. "Wards of the United States Government." *Scribner's Monthly* 19 (March 1880): 775–82.

———. *A Century of Dishonor.* New York: Harper, 1881.

Jacobs, Harvey D. "Uncle Sam—The Great White Father." *Case and Comment* 23 (February 1917): 703–9.

James, Juliet. *Sculpture of the Exposition Palaces and Courts.* San Francisco: H. S. Crocker, 1915.

Johnson, Mrs. Ellen Wadsworth Terry. *Historical Sketch of the Connecticut Indian Association from 1881–1888.* Hartford: Press of the Flower and Miller Co., 1888.

Keasbey, Lindley M. "Civology—A Suggestion." *Popular Science Monthly,* April 1907, pp. 365–71.

Kennan, George. "Have Reservation Indians Any Vested Rights?" *Outlook*, March 29, 1902, pp. 759–65.

———. "Indian Lands and Fair Play." *Outlook*, February 27, 1904, pp. 498–501.

Kroeber, Alfred L. "Eighteen Professions." *American Anthropologist* 17 (April–June 1915): 283–88.

———. "Inheritance by Magic." *American Anthropologist* 18 (January–March 1916): 19–40.

———. "Ishi, the Last Aborigine: The Effects of Civilization on a Genuine Survivor of Stone Age Barbarism." *World's Work*, July 1912, pp. 304–8.

———. "The Morals of an Uncivilized People." *American Anthropologist* 12 (July–September 1910): 437–47.

Kyle, James H. "How Shall the Indians Be Educated?" *North American Review* 159 (October 1894): 434–47.

Lane, Franklin K. "From the Warpath to the Plow." *National Geographic*, January 1915, pp. 73–87.

Leupp, Francis E. "Back to Nature for the Indian." *Charities and the Commons*, June 6, 1908, pp. 336–40.

———. "The Failure of the Educated American Indian." *Appleton's Booklover's Magazine*, May 1906, pp. 594–609.

———. "Four Strenuous Years." *Outlook*, June 5, 1909, pp. 328–33.

———. "A Fresh Phase of the Indian Problem." *Nation*, November 16, 1899, pp. 367–68.

———. *The Indian and His Problem*. New York: Scribner, 1910.

———. "Indian Lands: Their Administration with Reference to Present and Future Use." *Annals of the American Academy of Political and Social Science* 33 (1909): 620–30.

———. "The Indian Land Troubles and How to Solve Them." *American Monthly Review of Reviews*, October 1910, pp. 468–72.

———. *The Latest Phase of the Southern Ute Question: A Report*. Philadelphia: Indian Rights Association, 1895.

———. "The Red Man, Incorporated." *Collier's*, January 9, 1909, p. 20.

———. "The Red Man's Burden." *Hearst's Magazine*, May 1913, pp. 741–52.

———. "A Review of President Roosevelt's Administration." *Outlook*, February 6, 1909, pp. 298–307.

———. "Why Booker T. Washington Has Succeeded in His Life Work." *Outlook*, May 31, 1902, pp. 326–33.

Lowie, Robert. *Culture and Ethnology.* New York: D. C. McMurtrie, 1917.

———. *Primitive Society.* New York: Boni and Liveright, 1920.

———. "Reminiscences of Anthropological Currents in America Half a Century Ago." *American Anthropologist* 58 (December 1956): 995–1016.

Lummis, Charles F. *Bullying the Moqui.* Ed. Robert Easton and Mackenzie Brown. Prescott, Ariz.: Prescott College Press, 1968.

———. "Lame Dancing Masters: An Indian View of Government Schools." *Out West,* May 1900, pp. 356–58.

———. "My Brother's Keeper." *Out West,* August 1899, pp. 139–47; September 1899, pp. 207–13; October 1899, pp. 263–67; November 1899, pp. 333–35, December 1899, pp. 28–30; January 1900, pp. 90–94; February 1900, pp. 178–80.

McGee, William John. "Anthropology and Its Larger Problems." *Congress of Arts and Sciences: Universal Exposition, St. Louis, 1904.* Ed. Howard J. Rogers. Boston: Houghton Mifflin, 1905–7.

———"Man's Place in Nature." *American Anthropologist,* n.s. 3 (January–March 1901): 1–13.

———. "The Science of Humanity." *Proceedings of the American Association for the Advancement of Science* (1897): 296–323.

———"Strange Races of Men." *World's Work,* August 1904, pp. 5185–88.

McKenzie, Fayette A. "Assimilation of the American Indian." *American Journal of Sociology* 19 (May 1914): 761–72.

———. "The American Indian of Today and Tomorrow." *Journal of Race Development* 3 (October 1912): 135–55.

———. *The Indian in Relation to the White Population of the United States.* Columbus, Ohio: Privately printed, 1908.

McLaughlin, James. *My Friend the Indian.* Boston: Houghton Mifflin, 1910.

McSpadden, J. Walter. *Famous Sculptors of America.* New York: Dodd, Mead, 1924.

Manypenny, George W. *Our Indian Wards.* Cincinnati: R. Clarke and Co., 1880.

Mason, Otis T. "Influence of Environment upon Human Industries and Arts." *Annual Report of the Board of Regents of the Smithsonian Institution, 1895.* Washington: Government Printing Office, 1896, pp. 639–65.

———. "Mind and Matter in Culture." *American Anthropologist* 10 (April–June 1908): 187–96.

———. "The Scope and Value of Anthropological Studies." *Proceedings of the American Association for the Advancement of Science,* 1883, pp. 367–83.

———. "Similarities in Culture." *American Anthropologist,* o.s. 8 (April 1895): 101–17.

———. "The Uncivilized Mind in the Presence of Higher Phases of Civilization." *Proceedings of the American Association for the Advancement of Science,* 1883, pp. 367–83.

Mayo-Smith, Richmond. "Assimilation of Nationalities in the United States." *Political Science Quarterly* 9 (December 1894): 649–70.

Meserve, Charles F. *A Tour of Observations among Indians and Indian Schools in Arizona, New Mexico, Oklahoma and Kansas.* Philadelphia: Indian Rights Association, 1894.

Miles, Nelson A. "The Indian Problem," *North American Review* 128 (March 1879): 304–14.

Miller, Joaquin. *Life amongst the Modocs.* London: R. Bentley, 1873.

———. *Shadows of Shasta.* Chicago: Jansen, McClurg and Co., 1881.

Monsen, Frederick. "The Destruction of Our Indians." *Craftsman,* March 1907, pp. 683–91.

Moon, Carl. "In Search of the Wild Indian." *Outing,* February 1917, pp. 533–45.

Moorehead, Warren K. *The American Indian in the United States; 1810–1914.* Andover, Mass.: Andover Press, 1914.

Morgan, Lewis Henry. *Ancient Society.* New York: Henry Holt and Co., 1877.

———. "Factory System for Indian Reservations." *Nation,* July 27, 1876, pp. 58–59.

———. *Houses and House Life of the American Aborigines.* Washington: Government Printing Office, 1881.

———. "The Hue and Cry Against the Indians." *Nation,* July 20, 1876, pp. 40–41.

———. *The Indian Journals of Lewis Henry Morgan, 1859–1862.* Ed. Leslie A. White. Ann Arbor: University of Michigan Press, 1959.

———. *League of the Ho-de-no-sau-nee or Iroquois.* Rochester: Sage and Brother, 1851.

———. "Lewis Henry Morgan's Journal of a Trip to Southwestern Colorado and New Mexico." Ed. Leslie White. *American Antiquity* 8 (July 1942): 1–26.

————. *Systems of Consanguinity and Affinity of the Human Family.* Smithsonian Contributions to Knowledge, vol. 17. Washington: Smithsonian Institution, 1871.

Morgan, Thomas J. "Indian Education." *Journal of Social Science* 40 (December 1902): 165–80.

National Indian Defense Association. *The Sioux Nation and the United States: A Brief History.* Washington: National Indian Defense Association, 1891.

"The Need for Practical Training for the Indians." *Journal of Education* 69 (March 18, 1909): 300.

Neuhaus, Eugen. *The Art of the Exposition.* San Francisco: P. Elder, 1915.

"A New Step in Our Indian Policy." *Outlook,* May 23, 1917, p. 136.

Newell, Alfred C. "The Philippine Peoples." *World's Work,* August 1904, pp. 5128–45.

Newlin, James W. *Proposed Indian Policy.* Philadelphia, 1881.

Oskison, John M. "In Governing the Indian, Use the Indian!" *Case and Comment* 23 (February 1917): 723–33.

Owen, G. W. *The Indian Question.* Ypsilanti, Mich., 1881.

Painter, Charles C. *Civilization by Removal!* Philadelphia: Indian Rights Association, 1889.

————. *The Dawes Land in Severalty Bill and Indian Emancipation.* Philadelphia: Indian Rights Association, 1887.

Painter, George S. "The Future of the American Negro." *American Anthropologist* 21 (October–December 1919): 410–20.

Palladino, Lawrence Benedict, S. J. *Indian and White in the Northwest, or a History of Catholicity in Montana.* Baltimore: J. Murphy and Co., 1894.

Pancoast, Henry S. *The Indian before the Law.* Philadelphia: Indian Rights Association, 1884.

Parker, Arthur C. "The Social Elements of the Indian Problem." *American Journal of Sociology* 22 (September 1916): 252–67.

Peabody, Elizabeth P. *The Piutes.* Cambridge, Mass.: J. Wilson and Son, 1887.

Pope, John. *The Indian Question.* Cincinnati, 1878.

Popenoe, Paul, and Roswell Hill Johnson. *Applied Eugenics.* New York: Macmillan, 1918.

Powell, John Wesley. "Competition as a Factor in Human Evolution." *American Anthropologist,* o.s. 1 (October 1888): 297–324.

———. "Darwin's Contributions to Philosophy." *Proceedings of the Biological Society of Washington,* 1882, pp. 60–71.

———. "Discourse on the Philosophy of the North American Indians." *Bulletin of the American Geographical Society of New York* 2 (1876–77): 46–62.

———. "From Barbarism to Civilization." *American Anthropologist,* o.s. 1 (April 1888): 97–123.

———. "From Savagery to Barbarism." *Transactions of the Anthropological Society of Washington* 3 (1885): 173–96.

———. "Human Evolution." *Transactions of the Anthropological Society of Washington* 2 (1883): 176–208.

———. *Introduction to the Study of Indian Languages.* Washington: Government Printing Office, 1877.

———. "The Non-Irrigable Lands of the Arid Region." *Century,* March 1890, pp. 766–76, 915–22.

———. "The Larger Import of Scientific Education." *Popular Science Monthly,* February 1885, pp. 452–56.

———. "The North American Indians." In *The United States of America: A Study of the American Commonwealth,* ed. Nathanial S. Shaler, 2 vols. New York: Appleton, 1894, 1:190–272.

———. "Outlines of Sociology." *Transactions of the Anthropological Society of Washington* 1 (1882): 106–29.

———. "Proper Training and the Future of the Indians." *Forum,* February 1895, pp. 638–52.

———. "Relation of Primitive Peoples to Environment." *Smithsonian Institution Annual Report,* 1895, pp. 625–37.

———. *Report on Lands of the Arid Region of the United States.* Washington: Government Printing Office, 1878.

———. *Selected Prose of John Wesley Powell.* Ed. George Crosette. Boston: D. R. Godine, 1970.

———. "Sketch of Lewis Henry Morgan." *Popular Science Monthly,* November 1880, pp. 114–21.

———. "Sociology, or the Science of Institutions." *American Anthropologist,* n.s. 1 (July 1899): 475–509; (October 1899): 695–745.

———. "The Three Methods of Evolution." *Bulletin of the Philosophical Society of Washington* 6 (1884): 27–52.

————. "Views of Major Powell on the Propriety of Transferring the Indian Bureau from the War Department to the Interior Department." *House Report* no. 240, 44th Cong., 1st sess., ser. 1708.

Pratt, Richard H. *Address by Captain Pratt before the National Convention of Charities and Correction at Denver, Colorado, June 28, 1892.* Denver, 1892.

————. *Battlefield and Classroom: Four Decades with the American Indian, 1867–1904.* Ed. Robert M. Utley. New Haven: Yale University Press, 1964.

————. *The Indian Industrial School at Carlisle, Pennsylvania.* Carlisle, Pa.: Hamilton Library Association, 1908.

Proceedings of the Convention to Consider the Opening of Indian Territory Held at Kansas City, Mo., February 8, 1888. Kansas City, Mo.: Press of Ramsey, Millet and Hudson, 1888.

Proctor, Edna Dean. *The Son of the Ancient People.* Boston: Houghton Mifflin, 1893.

Reeves, John T. "Probating the Indian Estates." *Case and Comment* 23 (February 1917): 727–29.

Remington, Frederic. *John Ermine of the Yellowstone.* New York: Macmillan, 1902.

Rhoads, Dr. James E. *The Indian Question in the Concrete.* Philadelphia: Women's National Indian Association, 1886.

————. *Our Next Duty to the Indian.* Philadelphia: Indian Rights Association, 1887.

Riggs, Alfred L. "Where Shall Our Indian Brothers Go to School?" *Journal of Education* 14 (September 29, 1881): 199–200.

Ripley, William Z. *The Races of Europe: A Sociological Study.* New York: D. Appleton, 1899.

Roe, Walter C. "The Mohonk Lodge: An Experiment in Indian Work." *Outlook,* May 18, 1901, pp. 176–78.

Rogers, Howard J., ed. *Congress of Arts and Sciences: Universal Exposition, St. Louis, 1904* 8 vols. Boston: Houghton Mifflin, 1905–7.

Roosevelt, Theodore. *Addresses and Papers of Theodore Roosevelt.* Ed. Willis Fletcher Johnson. New York: Sun Dial Classics, 1908.

————. *Addresses and Presidential Messages of Theodore Roosevelt, 1902–1904.* New York: G. P. Putnam's Sons, 1904.

———. *American Ideals and Other Essays, Social and Political.* New York: C. P. Putnam, 1902.

———. *Biological Analogies in History.* Oxford: Clarendon Press, 1910.

———. *A Book Lover's Holidays in the Open.* New York: Scribner, 1919.

———. *Letters of Theodore Roosevelt.* Ed. Elting E. Morison. 8 vols. Cambridge, Mass.: Harvard University Press, 1951–54.

———. *Report of Hon. Theodore Roosevelt Made to the U.S. Civil Service Commission, upon a Visit to Certain Indian Reservations and Indian Schools in South Dakota, Nebraska, and Kansas.* Philadelphia: Indian Rights Association, 1893.

Rowe, E. C. "547 White and 268 Indian Children Tested by the Binet-Simon Test." *Pedagogical Seminary* 21 (September 1914): 454–68.

Russell, Isaac Franklin. "The Indian before the Law." *Yale Law Journal* 18 (March 1909): 328–37.

Sanders, Helen Fitzgerald. "The Opening of the Flathead Reservation." *Overland Monthly,* August 1909, pp. 120–40.

———. "The Red Bond." *Overland Monthly,* August 1911, pp. 161–64.

———. *Trails through Western Woods.* London: Everett and Co., 1911.

———. *The White Quiver.* New York: Duffield and Co., 1913.

Schurz, Carl. "Carl Schurz on Indian Education." *Journal of Education* 13 (April 28, 1881): 283.

———. *Speeches, Correspondence and Political Papers of Carl Schurz.* Ed. Frederic Bancroft. 6 vols. New York: Putnam, 1913.

Seachrest, Effie. "James Earle Fraser." *American Magazine of Art* 8 (May 1917): 276–78.

Seely, O. C. *Oklahoma illustrated: A Book of Practical Information.* Guthrie, Oklahoma Territory; Leader Printing, 1894.

Sells, Cato. "The First Americans as Loyal Citizens." *American Monthly Review of Reviews,* May 1918, pp. 523–24.

Simons, Sarah E. "Social Assimilation." *American Journal of Sociology* 6 (May 1901): 790–822; 7 (January 1902): 539–56.

Skiff, F. J., et al. "An Historical and Descriptive Account of the Field Columbian Museum." *Field Columbian Museum Publications* 1 (1895).

Smith, William Benjamin. *The Color Line: A Brief in Behalf of the Unborn.* New York: McClure, Phillips and Co., 1905.

Stefansson, Vilhjalmar. "The Indian and Civilization." *Independent*, December 28, 1911, pp. 1434–38.

Stoddard, Theodore Lothrop. *The Rising Tide of Color against White World Supremacy.* New York: Scribner, 1920.

Stone, Alfred Holt. *Studies in the American Race Problem.* New York: Doubleday, Page and Co., 1908.

Strong, Josiah. *Our Country: Its Possible Future, and Its Present Crisis.* New York: American Home Missionary Society, 1885.

Suksdorf, Henry F. *Our Race Problems.* New York: Shakespeare Press, 1911.

Sumner, William Graham. "The Indians in 1887." *Forum*, May 1887, pp. 254–62.

Swanton, John R. "Some Anthropological Misconceptions." *American Anthropologist* 19 (October–December 1917): 459–70.

Taft, William Howard. *Present Day Problems.* New York: Dodd, Mead, 1908.

———. *Presidential Addresses and State Papers.* New York: Doubleday, Page and Co., 1910, vol. 1.

Tatum, Lawrie. *Our Red Brothers and the Peace Policy of President U.S. Grant.* Philadelphia: J. C. Winston and Co., 1899.

Thayer, James Bradley, "A People without Law." *Atlantic Monthly*, October–November 1891, pp. 540–51, 676–87.

———. "The Dawes Bill and the Indians." *Atlantic Monthly*, March 1888, pp. 315–22.

Thomas, William Isaac. "The Mind of Woman and the Lower Races." *American Journal of Sociology* 12 (January 1907): 435–69.

Tibbles, Thomas H. *Buckskin and Blanket Days.* Garden City, N.Y.: Doubleday, 1957.

———. *Hidden Power.* New York: G. W. Carleton, 1881.

———. *The Ponca Chiefs.* Boston: Lockwood, Brooks and Co., 1880.

———. *Western Men Defended.* Boston: Lockwood, Brooks and Co., 1880.

Tillinghast, Joseph A. "The Negro in Africa and America." *Publications of the American Economic Association*, 3d Series, 3 (May 1902): 401–638.

"A Trust Not Trustworthy" *Independent* 56 February 25, 1904, pp. 450–501.

Tydings, Thomas J. "Rights of Indians on Public Lands." *Case and Comment* 23 (February 1917): 743–47.

United States Bureau of Census. *Indian Population in the U.S. and Alaska, 1910.* Washington: Government Printing Office, 1915.

U.S. Bureau of Education. *Are the Indians Dying Out? Preliminary Observa-*

tions Relating to Indian Civilization and Education. Washington, D.C.: Government Printing Office, 1877.

Valentine, Robert G. "Making Good Indians." *Sunset,* June 1910, pp. 598–611.

Walker, Francis A. *The Indian Question.* Boston: J. R. Osgood and Co., 1874.

———, ed. *International Exhibition, 1876.* 9 vols. Washington: Government Printing Office, 1880–84.

Ward, Lester F. "Social Differentiation and Integration." *American Journal of Sociology* 8 (May 1903): 721–45.

———. "The Transmission of Culture by the Inheritance of Acquired Characteristics." *Forum,* May 1891, pp. 312–19.

Washington, Booker T. "Inferior and Superior Races." *North American Review* 201 (April 1915): 538–42.

Waterman, T. T. "The Subdivisions of the Human Race and Their Distribution." *American Anthropologist* 26 (October–December 1924): 474–90.

Welsh, Herbert. *Allotment of Lands: Defense of the Dawes Land in Severalty Bill.* Philadelphia: Indian Rights Association, 1887.

———. "Comment on Thomas Morgan's 'Indian Education.'" *Journal of Social Science* 40 (December 1902): 178.

———. *How to Bring the Indian to Citizenship.* Philadelphia: Indian Rights Association, 1892.

———. "The Indian Problem and What We Must Do to Solve It." *Wowapi,* November 7, 1883, pp. 8–9.

———. "The Meaning of the Dakota Outbreak." *Scribner's Magazine,* April 1891, pp. 439–52.

Williams, Talcott. "Was Primitive Man a Modern Savage?" *Annual Report of the Board of Regents of the Smithsonian Institution, 1896.* Washington: Government Printing Office, 1898.

Willsie, Honore. *Lydia of the Pines.* New York: Frederick A. Stokes, 1915.

———. *Still Jim.* New York: Frederick A. Stokes, 1917.

———. "We die! We Die! There Is No Hope!" *Everybody's Magazine,* March 1912, pp. 337–44.

Wilson, Owen. "Rescuing a People by an Irrigation Ditch." *World's Work,* September 1911, pp. 14815–17.

Wissler, Clark. *The American Indian.* New York: D. C. McMurtrie, 1917.

———. "The Psychological Aspects of the Culture-Environment Relation." *American Anthropologist* 14 (April–June 1912): 217–25.

Wister, Owen. *Red Men and White.* New York: Harper, 1895.

―――. *Roosevelt: The Story of a Friendship, 1880–1919.* New York: Macmillan, 1930.

―――. *The Virginian.* New York: Macmillan, 1902.

Wood, C. E. S. "Our Indian Question." *Journal of the Military Service Institution of the United States* 2 (1881): 101–20.

Woodward, Calvin M. "The Function of the Public School." *National Education Association Proceedings*, 1887, pp. 212–24.

Woodworth, R. S. "Racial Differences in Mental Traits." *Science* 31 (February 4, 1910): 171–86.

5. Secondary Sources—Books

Adams, Evelyn C. *American Indian Education: Government Schools and Economic Progress.* New York: King's Crown Press, 1946.

Allen, Robert L. *Reluctant Reformers.* Cambridge, Mass.: Harvard University Press, 1974.

Andrist, Ralph D. *The Long Death: The Last Days of the Plains Indians.* New York: Macmillan, 1964.

Athearn, Robert G. *William Tecumseh Sherman and the Settlement of the West.* Norman: University of Oklahoma Press, 1960.

Bailey, John W. *Pacifying the Plains: General Alfred Terry and the Decline of the Sioux, 1866–1890.* Westport, Conn.: Greenwood Press, 1979.

Bannister, Roger C., Jr. *Ray Stannard Baker: The Mind and Thought of a Progressive.* New Haven: Yale University Press, 1956.

Beale, Howard Kennedy. *Theodore Roosevelt and the Rise of America to World Power.* Baltimore: Johns Hopkins University Press, 1956.

Beatty, Donald R. *History of the Legal Status of the American Indian with Particular Reference to California.* Rand Research Associates Ethnic Studies Series. San Francisco: Rand E. Research Associates, 1974.

Beaver, R. Pierce. *Church, State and the American Indians: Two and a Half Centuries of Partnership in Missions Between Protestant Churches and Government.* St. Louis: Concordia Publishing, 1966.

Benson, Ramsey. *Hill Country: The Story of J. J. Hill and the Awakening West.* New York: Frederick A. Stockes Co., 1928.

Berkhofer, Robert F., Jr. *The White Man's Indian: Images of the American Indian from Columbus to the Present.* New York: Knopf, 1978.

Berry, Brewton. *Almost White.* New York: Macmillan, 1963.

————. *The Education of American Indians.* Washington: Government Printing Office, 1969.

Berthrong, Donald J. *The Cheyenne and Arapaho Ordeal: Reservation and Agency Life in the Indian Territory, 1875–1907.* Norman: University of Oklahoma Press, 1976.

Bremner, Robert Hamlett. *From the Depths: The Discovery of Poverty in the United States.* New York: New York University Press, 1956.

Brimlow, George Francis. *The Bannock Indian War of 1878.* Caldwell, Idaho: Caxton Printers, 1942.

Burg, David F. *Chicago's White City of 1893.* Lexington: University of Kentucky Press, 1976.

Burrow, J. W. *Evolution and Society.* Cambridge: Cambridge University Press, 1966.

Carlson, Leonard A. *Indians, Bureaucrats and Land: The Dawes Act and the Decline of Indian Farming.* Westport, Conn.: Greenwood Press, 1981.

Coan, Otis W., and Richard G. Lillard. *America in Fiction: an Annotated List of Novels that Interpret Aspects of Life in the United States.* 3d ed. Stanford: Stanford University Press, 1949.

Cohen, Felix S. *Handbook of Federal Indian Law.* University of New Mexico edition. Albuquerque: University of New Mexico Press, 1971.

Coletta, Paolo E. *The Presidency of William Howard Taft.* Lawrence, Kans.: Regents Press, 1973.

Chamberlin, J. E. *The Harrowing of Eden.* New York: Seabury, 1975.

Cremin, Lawrence. *The Transformation of the School.* New York: Knopf, 1961.

Danziger, Edmund J. *Indians and Bureaucrats: Administering the Reservation Policy During the Civil War.* Urbana: University of Illinois Press, 1974.

Darnell, Regna, ed. *Readings in the History of Anthropology.* New York: Harper and Row, 1974.

Darrah, William Culp. *Powell of the Colorado.* Princeton: Princeton University Press, 1951.

Debo, Angie. *The Rise and Fall of the Choctaw Republic.* Norman: University of Oklahoma Press, 1934.

Dippie, Brian W. *The Vanishing American: White Attitudes and U.S. Indian Policy.* Middletown, Conn.: Wesleyan University Press, 1982.

Drinnon, Richard. *Facing West: The Metaphysics of Indian Hating and Empire Building.* Minneapolis: University of Minnesota Press, 1980.

Dyer, Thomas G. *Theodore Roosevelt and the Idea of Race.* Baton Rouge: Louisiana State University Press, 1980.

Eastman, Elaine [Goodale]. *Pratt: The Red Man's Moses.* Norman: University of Oklahoma Press, 1935.

Eggan, Fred. "Lewis H. Morgan and the Future of the American Indian." In *The American Indian: Perspectives for the Study of Social Change.* Ed. Fred Eggan. Chicago: Aldine Publishing, 1966.

————, ed. *Social Anthropology of North American Tribes.* 4th ed. Chicago: University of Chicago Press, 1965.

Farb, Peter. *Man's Rise to Civilization: The Cultural Ascent of the Indians of North America.* 2d ed. New York: Dutton, 1978.

Fisher, Berenice M. *Industrial Education: American Ideals and Institutions.* Madison: University of Wisconsin Press, 1967.

Fothergill, Philip. *Historical Aspects of Organic Evolution.* New York: Philosophical Library, 1953.

Fredrickson, George M. *The Black Image in the White Mind.* New York: Harper and Row, 1971.

Friedman, Lawrence J. *The White Savage: Racial Fantasies in the Post Bellum South.* Englewood Cliffs, N.J.: Prentice Hall, 1970.

Fritz, Henry Eugene. *The Movement for Indian Assimilation, 1860–1890.* Philadelphia: University of Pennsylvania Press, 1963.

Frost, O. W. *Joaquin Miller.* New York: Twayne Publishers, 1967.

Furner, Mary O. *Advocacy and Objectivity: A Crisis in the Professionalization of American Social Science, 1865–1905.* Lexington: University of Kentucky Press, 1975.

Gehm, Katherine. *Sarah Winnemuca.* Phoenix: O'Sullivan Woodside, 1975.

Getches, David H., et al. *Cases and Materials on Federal Indian Law.* American Casebook Series. St. Paul: West Publishing, 1979.

Goetzmann, William H. *Exploration and Empire: The Explorer and the Scientist in the Winning of the American West.* New York: Knopf, 1966.

Goldman, Eric. *Charles J. Bonaparte, Patrician Reformer: His Earlier Career.* Johns Hopkins University Studies in Historical and Political Science, series 61, no. 2. Baltimore: Johns Hopkins University Press, 1943.

Goldschmidt, Walter, ed. *The Uses of Anthropology.* Washington, D.C.: American Anthropological Association, 1979.

Gordon, Dudley. *Charles F. Lummis: Crusader in Corduroy.* Los Angeles: Cultural Assets Press, 1972.

Gossett, Thomas F. *Race: The History of an Idea in America.* Dallas: Southern Methodist University Press, 1963.

Green, Norman Kidd. *Iron Eye's Family.* Lincoln, Nebr.: Johnson Publishing, 1969.

Haber, Samuel. *Efficiency and Uplift: Scientific Management in the Progressive Era, 1890–1910.* Chicago: University of Chicago Press, 1964.

Hagan, William T. *United States—Comanche Relations: The Reservation Years.* New Haven: Yale University Press, 1976.

Haller, John S. *Outcasts From Evolution: Scientific Attitudes of Racial Inferiority, 1859–1900.* Urbana: University of Illinois Press, 1971.

Halloway, Jean. *Hamlin Garland: A Biography.* Austin: University of Texas Press, 1960.

Handy, Robert T. *A Christian America: Protestant Hopes and Historical Realities.* New York: Oxford University Press, 1971.

Harbaugh, William. *Power and Responsibility: The Life and Times of Theodore Roosevelt.* New York: Farrar, Straus and Cudahy, 1961.

Harris, Marvin. *The Rise of Anthropological Theory.* New York: Crowell, 1968.

Hellman, Geoffrey. *Bankers, Bones and Beetles: The First Century of the American Museum of Natural History.* New York: Natural History Press, 1968.

Helm, June, ed. *Pioneers in American Anthropology.* Seattle: University of Washington Press, 1966.

Henry Jeanette, ed. *The American Indian Reader: Anthropology.* San Francisco: Indian Historian Press, 1972.

Hertzberg, Hazel. *The Search for an American Indian Identity: Modern Pan-Indian Movements.* Syracuse: Syracuse University Press, 1971.

Higham, John. *Strangers in the Land: Patterns of American Nativism, 1860–1925.* 1955. Reprint. New York: Atheneum, 1970.

Hinsley, Curtis M., Jr. *Savages and Scientists: The Smithsonian Institution and the Development of American Anthropology, 1846–1910.* Washington, D.C.: Smithsonian Institution Press, 1981.

Holt, James. *Congressional Insurgents and the Party System, 1909–1916.* Cambridge, Mass.: Harvard University Press, 1967.

Hunt, Aurora. *Major General James Henry Carlton, 1814–1873; Western Frontier Dragoon.* Glendale, Calif.: Arthur H. Clark, 1958.

Jaher, Frederic Cople. *The Age of Industrialism in America: Essays in Social Structure and Cultural Values.* New York: Free Press, 1968.

Jones, Howard Mumford. *The Age of Energy: Varieties of American Experience, 1865–1915.* New York: Viking, 1971.

Judd, Neil M. *The Bureau of American Ethnology: A Partial History.* Norman: University of Oklahoma Press, 1967.

Katz, Michael B. *Class, Bureaucracy and the Schools: The Illusion of Educational Change in America.* New York: Praeger, 1971.

Keiser, Albert. *The Indian in American Literature.* New York: Oxford University Press, 1933.

Kelly, Lawrence C. *The Navajo Indians and Federal Indian Policy: 1900–1935.* Tucson: University of Arizona Press, 1968.

Kennedy Galleries. *James Earle Fraser: American Sculptor.* New York, 1969.

Kinney, J. P. *A Continent Lost—A Civilization Won.* Baltimore: Johns Hopkins University Press, 1937.

Kirby, Jack Temple. *Darkness at the Dawning: Race and Reform in the Progressive South.* Philadelphia: Lippincott, 1972.

Knight, Oliver. *Following the Indian Wars: The Story of the Newspaper Correspondents among the Indian Campaigns.* Norman: University Oklahoma Press, 1960.

Kvasnicka, Robert M., and Herman J. Viola, eds. *The Commissioners of Indian Affairs, 1824–1977.* Lincoln: University of Nebraska Press, 1979.

Laidlaw, Sally Jean. *Federal Indian Land Policy and the Fort Hall Indians.* Occasional Papers of the Idaho State College Museum, no. 3. Pocatello: Idaho State College, 1960.

Lamar, Howard. *Dakota Territory, 1861–1889: A Study of Frontier Politics.* New Haven: Yale University Press, 1956.

———. *The Far Southwest, 1846–1912; A Territorial History.* New Haven: Yale University Press, 1966.

Lazerson, Marvin. *Origins of the Urban School.* Cambridge, Mass.: Harvard University Press, 1971.

Lazerson, Marvin, and W. Norton Grubb, eds. *American Education and*

Vocationalism; A Documentary History 1870–1970. New York: Teacher's College Press, 1974.

Linderman, Gerald F. *The Mirror of War: American Society and the Spanish American War*. Ann Arbor: University of Michigan Press, 1974.

Link, Arthur S. *Wilson: The New Freedom*. Princeton: Princeton University Press, 1956.

Lubove, Roy. *The Professional Altruist: The Emergence of Social Work as a Career, 1880–1930*. Cambridge, Mass.: Harvard University Press, 1965.

McGee, Emma R. *The Life of W. J. McGee*. Farley, Iowa, 1915.

McNickle, D'Arcy. *Indian Man: The Life of Oliver La Farge*. Bloomington: Indiana University Press, 1971.

McSpadden, J. Walker. *Famous Sculptors of America*. New York: Dodd, Mead, 1924.

Mardock, Robert W. *The Reformers and the American Indian*. Columbia, Mo.: University of Missouri Press, 1971.

Mark, Joan. *Four Anthropologists: An American Science in Its Early Years*. New York: Neale Watson Academic Publications, 1981.

Marty, Martin E. *Righteous Empire: The Protestant Experience in America*. New York: Dial Press, 1970.

May, Glen Anthony. *Social Engineering in the Philippines: The Aims, Execution, and Impact of American Colonial Policy, 1900–1913*. Westport, Conn.: Greenwood Press, 1980.

May, Henry F. *The End of American Innocence*. New York: Knopf, 1959.

Meyer, Roy W. *History of the Santee Sioux: United States Indian Policy on Trial*. Lincoln: University of Nebraska Press, 1968.

Miner, H. Craig. *The Corporation and the Indian: Tribal Sovereignty and Industrial Civilization in Indian Territory, 1866–1907*. Columbia: University of Missouri Press, 1976.

———. *The St. Louis-San Francisco Transcontinental Railroad: The 35th-Parallel Project, 1853–1890*. Lawrence: University Press of Kansas, 1972.

Mott, Frank Luther. *Golden Multitudes: The Story of Best Sellers in the United States*. New York: Macmillan, 1947.

Nash, Roderick, *Wilderness and the American Mind*. New Haven: Yale University Press, 1967.

Newby, I. A. *Jim Crow's Defense*. Baton Rouge: Louisiana State University Press, 1965.

Nohlen, Claude. *The Negro's Image in the South: The Anatomy of Suprem-acy.* Lexington: University of Kentucky Press, 1967.

Odell, Ruth. *Helen Hunt Jackson (H. H.).* New York: D. Appleton-Century, 1939.

Olson, James C. *Red Cloud and the Sioux Problem.* Lincoln: University of Nebraska Press, 1965.

Oswalt, Wendell H. *Other Peoples, Other Customs: World Ethnography and Its History.* New York: Holt, Rinehart and Winston, 1972.

Otis, D. S. *The Dawes Act and the Allotment of Indian Lands,* ed. Francis Paul Prucha. Norman: University of Oklahoma Press, 1973.

Parry, Ellwood. *The Image of the Indian and the Black Man in American Art, 1590–1900.* New York: G. Braziller, 1974.

Pearce, Roy Harvey. *Savagism and Civilization: A Study of the Indian and the American Mind.* Rev. ed. Baltimore: Johns Hopkins University Press, 1967.

Pfaller, Louis L. *James McLaughlin: The Man with an Indian Heart.* New York: Vantage Press, 1978.

Price, Monroe E. *Law and the American Indian: Readings, Notes and Cases.* Indianapolis: Bobbs-Merrill, 1973.

Priest, Loring Benson. *Uncle Sam's Stepchildren: The Reformation of United States Indian Policy, 1865–1887.* New Brunswick, N.J.: Rutgers University Press, 1942.

Prucha, Francis Paul. *American Indian Policy in Crisis: Christian Reform-ers and the Indian, 1865–1900.* Norman: University of Oklahoma Press, 1975.

———. *The Churches and the Indian Schools, 1888–1912.* Lincoln: Univer-sity of Nebraska Press, 1979.

———, ed. *Americanizing the American Indian: Writings by 'Friends of the Indian,' 1865–1900.* Cambridge, Mass.: Harvard University Press, 1973.

Purcell, Edward A., Jr. *The Crisis of Democratic Theory: Scientific Natural-ism and the Problem of Value.* Lexington: University of Kentucky Press, 1973.

Pyle, Joseph Gilpin. *The Life of James J. Hill.* 2 vols. New York: Doubleday Page, 1917.

Rahill, Peter A. *The Catholic Indian Missions and Grant's Peace Policy 1870–1884.* Washington, D.C.: Catholic University of America Press, 1953.

Resek, Carl. *Lewis Henry Morgan: American Scholar.* Chicago: University of Chicago Press, 1960.

Rister, Carl Coke. *Land Hunger: David L. Payne and the Oklahoma Boomers.* Norman: University of Oklahoma Press, 1942.

Robbins, Roy M. *Our Landed Heritage: The Public Domain, 1776–1936.* Princeton: Princeton University Press, 1942.

Ross, Dorothy. *G. Stanley Hall: The Psychologist as Prophet.* Chicago: University of Chicago Press, 1972.

Schmeckebier, Laurence F. *The Office of Indian Affairs: Its History, Activities and Organization.* Baltimore: Johns.Hopkins University Press, 1927.

Schmitt, Peter J. *Back to Nature: The Arcadian Myth in Urban America.* New York: Oxford University Press, 1969.

Service, Elman R. *Cultural Evolutionism: Theory in Practice.* New York: Holt, Rinehart and Winston, 1971.

Smith, Henry Nash. *Virgin Land: The American West as Symbol and Myth.* Cambridge, Mass.: Harvard University Press, 1950.

Smith, Jane, and Robert Kvasnicka, eds. *Indian-White Relations: A Persistent Paradox.* Washington: Howard University Press, 1976.

Solomon, Barbara Miller. *Ancestors and Immigrants: A Changing New England Tradition.* Cambridge: Harvard University Press, 1956.

Spivey, Donald. *Schooling for the New Slavery: Black Industrial Education, 1868–1915.* Westport, Conn.: Greenwood Press, 1978.

Sprague, Marshall. *Massacre: The Tragedy at White River.* Boston: Little Brown, 1957.

Stegner, Wallace. *Beyond the Hundredth Meridian: John Wesley Powell and the Second Opening of the West.* Boston: Houghton Mifflin, 1954.

Stern, Bernard J. *Lewis Henry Morgan: Social Evolutionist.* Chicago: University of Chicago Press, 1931.

Stewart, Omer C. *Ethnohistorical Bibliography of the Ute Indians of Colorado.* University of Colorado Studies Series in Anthropology, no. 18. Boulder: University of Colorado Press, 1971.

Stocking, George W., Jr. *Race, Culture and Evolution: Essays in the History of Anthropology.* New York: Free Press, 1968.

———, ed. *The Shaping of American Anthropology.* New York: Basic Books, 1974.

Stuart, Paul. *The Indian Office: Growth and Development of an Ameri-*

can Institution, 1865–1900. Ann Arbor: University of Michigan Research Press, 1979.

Sutton, Imre. *Indian Land Tenure: Bibliographical Essays and a Guide to the Literature.* New York: Clearwater Publishing, 1975.

Szasz, Margaret. *Education and the American Indian: The Road to Self-Determination, 1928–1973.* Albuquerque: University of New Mexico Press, 1974.

Textor, Lucy E., M. A. *Official Relations between the United States and the Sioux Indians.* Palo Alto: The University, 1896.

Thoreson, Timothy H., ed. *Toward a Science of Man: Essays in the History of Anthropology.* The Hague: Beresford Book Service, 1975.

Trefethen, James B. *Crusade for Wildlife: Highlights in Conservation Progress.* Harrisburg, Pa.: Stackpole, 1961.

Turner, Katharine C. *Red Man Calling on the Great White Father.* Norman: University of Oklahoma Press, 1951.

Washburn, Wilcomb E. *The Assault on Indian Tribalism: The General Allotment Law (Dawes Act) of 1887.* Philadelphia: Lippincott, 1975.

———. *Red Man's Land/White Man's Law: A Study of the Past and Present Status of the American Indian.* New York: Scribner, 1971.

Weigley, Russell F. *The American Way of War: A History of United States Military Strategy and Policy.* New York: Macmillan, 1973

Weinstein, James. *The Corporate Ideal in the Liberal State. 1900–1918.* Boston: Beacon Press, 1968.

Welter, Rush. *Popular Education and Democratic Thought in America.* New York: Columbia University Press, 1962.

Weston, Rubin. *Racism in U.S. Imperialism: The Influence of Racial Assumptions on American Foreign Policy, 1893–1946.* Columbia: University of South Carolina Press, 1972.

White, G. Edward. *The Eastern Establishment and the Western Experience: The West of Frederic Remington, Theodore Roosevelt and Owen Wister.* New Haven: Yale University Press, 1968.

Wilson, Dorothy Clarke. *Bright Eyes: The Story of Susette La Flesche, an Omaha Indian.* New York: McGraw-Hill, 1974.

Wynes, Charles, ed. *The Negro in the South since 1865.* New York: Harper and Row, 1965.

Zolla, Elemire. *The Writer and the Shaman.* New York: Harcourt Brace Jovanovich, 1973.

6. Secondary Sources—Articles

Abrams, Richard M. "Woodrow Wilson and the Southern Congressmen, 1913–1916." *Journal of Southern History* 22 (November 1956): 417–37.

Ahern, Wilbert H. "Assimilationist Racism: The Case of the Friends of the Indian." *Journal of Ethnic Studies* 4 (Summer 1976): 23–34.

Allen, Howard W., Aage R. Clausen, and Jerome M. Clubb. "Political Reform and Negro Rights in the Senate, 1909–1915." *Journal of Southern History* 37 (May 1971): 191–212.

Beatty, Willard W. "The Federal Government and the Education of Indians and Eskimos." *Journal of Negro History* 7 (July 1938): 267–72.

Berens, John F. "Old Campaigners, New Realities: Indian Policy Reform in the Progressive Era, 1900–1912." *Mid-America* 59 (January 1977): 51–64.

Berthrong, Donald J. "Cattlemen on the Cheyenne-Arapaho Reservation." *Arizona and the West* 13 (Spring 1971): 5–32.

———. "White Neighbors Come among the Southern Cheyenne and Arapaho." *Kansas Quarterly* 3 (Fall 1971): 105–15.

Bloom, Paul. "Indian Paramount Rights to Water Use." *Rocky Mountain Mineral Law Review Proceedings* 16 (1969): 669–93.

Blumenthal, Henry "Woodrow Wilson and the Race Question." *Journal of Negro History* 48 (January 1963): 1–21.

Chaput, Donald. "Generals, Indian Agents, Politicians: The Doolittle Survey of 1865." *Western Historical Quarterly* 3 (July 1972): 269–83.

Clark, J. Stanley. "Ponca Publicity" *Mississippi Valley Historical Review* 29 (March 1943): 495–516.

Clubb, Jerome M., and Howard W. Allen. "Party Loyalty in the Progressive Years: The Senate, 1909–1915." *Journal of Politics* 29 (August 1967): 567–84.

Coats, A. W "American Scholarship Comes of Age: The Louisiana Purchase Exposition, 1904." *Journal of the History of Ideas* 22 (July–September 1961): 404–17.

Cohen, Sol. "The Industrial Education Movement, 1906–1917." *American Quarterly* 20 (Spring 1968): 95–110.

Critchlow, Donald T. "Lewis Meriam, Expertise, and Indian Reform." *Historian* 43 (May 1981): 325–44.

Cronin, Morton. "Currier and Ives: A Content Analysis." *American Quarterly* 4 (Winter 1952): 317–30.

Crow, Charles. "Indians and Blacks in White America." In *Four Centuries of Southern Indians*. Ed. Charles M. Hudson. Athens: University of Georgia Press, 1975.

Darnell, Regna. "The Professionalization of American Anthropology." *Social Science Information* 10 (April 1971): 83–103.

Davison, Kenneth E. "President Hayes and the Reform of American Indian Policy." *Ohio History* 82 (Summer–Autumn 1973): 205–14.

Davison, Stanley R. "Hopes and Fancies of the Early Reclamationists." In *The Montana Past: An Anthology*. Ed. Michael P. Malone and Richard B. Roeder. Missoula: University of Montana Press, 1969.

Deutsch, Herman J. "Indian and White in the Inland Empire: The Contest for the Land, 1880–1912." *Pacific Northwest Quarterly* 47 (April 1956): 44–51.

Dexter, Ralph W. "Putnam's Problems in Popularizing Anthropology." *American Scientist* 54 (September 1966): 315–32.

Ellis, Richard. "The Humanitarian Generals." *Western Historical Quarterly* 3 (April 1972): 169–79.

Englund, Donald R. "Indians, Intruders, and the Federal Government." *Journal of the West* 13 (April 1974): 97–105.

Ewing, Douglas. "The North American Indian in Forty Volumes." *Art in America* 60 (July 1972): 84–88.

Fear, Jacqueline M. "English versus the Vernacular: The Suppression of Indian Languages in Reservation Schools at the End of the Nineteenth Century" *Revue Francaise d'Etudes Americaines* 5 (April 1980): 13–24.

Fritz, Henry E. "George Manypenny and Our Indian Wards." *Kansas Quarterly* 3 (Fall 1971): 100–105.

———"The Making of Grant's Peace Policy." *Chronicles of Oklahoma* 37 (Winter 1959–1960): 411–32.

Gates, Paul W. "The Homestead Law in an Incongruous Land System." *American Historical Review* 41 (July 1936): 652–81.

Haan, Richard L. "Another Example of Stereotypes on the Early American Frontier: The Imperialist Historians and the American Indian." *Ethnohistory* 20 (Spring 1973): 143–52.

Hagan, William T. "Civil Service Commissioner Theodore Roosevelt and the Indian Rights Association." *Pacific Historical Review* 44 (May 1975): 187–201.

————. "Private Property, the Indian's Door to Civilization." *Ethnohistory* 3 (Spring 1956): 125–37.

Haller, John S. "Race and the Concept of Progress in Nineteenth-Century American Ethnology." *American Anthropologist* 73 (June 1971): 710–24.

Hallowell, Irving A. "The Beginnings of Anthropology in America." In *Selected Papers from the American Anthropologist*. Ed. Frederica De Laguna. Evanston, Ill.: Row Peterson, 1960.

————. "The Backwash of the Frontier: The Impact of the Indian on American Culture." In *The Frontier Perspective*. Ed. Walker D. Wyman and Clifton B. Kroeber. Madison: University of Wisconsin Press, 1957.

Haney, James E. "Blacks and the Republican Nomination of 1908." *Ohio History* 84 (Autumn 1975): 207–21.

Hayes, James R. "Sociology and Racism: An Analysis of the First Era of American Sociology." *Phylon* 34 (December 1973): 330–41.

Hayter, Earl W. "The Ponca Removal." *North Dakota Historical Review* 6 (July 1932): 262–75.

Holford, David M. "The Subversion of the Indian Land Allotment System, 1887–1934." *Indian Historian* 8 (Spring 1975): 11–21.

Horsman, Reginald. "Scientific Racism and the American Indian in the Mid-Nineteenth Century." *American Quarterly* 27 (May 1975): 152–68.

Hough, Walter. "Alice Cunningham Fletcher." *American Anthropologist* 25 (April–June 1923): 254–58.

Johnson, Ronald M. "Schooling and the Savage: Andrew S. Draper and Indian Education." *Phylon* 35 (March 1974): 74–82.

Kaestle, Carl F. "Social Reform in the Urban School." *History of Education Quarterly* 12 (Summer 1972): 211–28.

Keller, Robert H., Jr. "American Indian Education: An Historical Context." *Journal of the West* 13 (April 1974): 75–82.

King, James T. "A Better Way: General George Crook and the Ponca Indians." *Nebraska History* 50 (Fall 1969): 239–57.

————. "General Crook: Indian Fighter and Humanitarian." *Arizona and the West* 9 (Winter 1967): 333–48.

Knepler, Abraham E. "Education in the Cherokee Nation." *Chronicles of Oklahoma* 21 (December 1943): 378–401.

La Flesche, Francis. "Alice C. Fletcher." *Science*, August 17, 1923, p. 115.

Lowie, Robert H. "Evolution in Cultural Anthropology: A Reply to Leslie White." *American Anthropologist* 48 (January–March 1946): 223–33.

Lurie, Nancy Oestreich. "The Lady from Boston and the Omaha Indians." *American West* 3 (Fall 1966): 31–33, 80–85.

Mardock, Robert W. "Irresolvable Enigma? Strange Concepts of the American Indian Since the Civil War." *Montana* 7 (January 1957): 36–47.

Meyer, Roy W. "Hamlin Garland and the American Indian." *Western American Literature* 2 (Summer 1967): 109–25.

Mintz, Sidney. *Afro-American Anthropology.* Foreword. Ed. Norman E. Whitten, Jr., and John F. Szwed. New York: Free Press, 1970.

Murphee, Idus L. "The Evolutionary Anthropologist: The Progress of Mankind. The Concepts of Progress and Culture in the Thought of John Lubbock, Edward B. Bylor and Lewis Henry Morgan." *Proceedings of the American Philosophical Society* 105 (June 1961): 265–300.

Nash, Roderick. "The American Cult of the Primitive," *American Quarterly* 18 (Fall 1966): 517–39.

Nichols, Roger L. "Printer's Ink and Red Skins: Western Newspapermen and the Indians." *Kansas Quarterly* 3 (Fall 1971): 82–88.

Pandey, TriLoki Nath. "Anthropologists at Zuni." *Proceedings of the American Philosophical Society* 116 (August 1972): 321–28.

Parman, Donald L. "The 'Big Stick' in Indian Affairs: The Bai-a-lil-le Incident in 1909." *Arizona and the West* 20 (Winter 1978): 343–60.

Peterson, Robert L. "The Completion of the Northern Pacific Railroad System in Montana." In *The Montana Past: An Anthology.* Ed. Michael P. Malone and Richard B. Roeder. Missoula, Mont.: 1969.

Powers, Ramon. "Why the Northern Cheyenne Left Indian Territory in 1878: A Cultural Analysis." *Kansas Quarterly* 3 (Fall 1971): 72–81.

Prucha, Francis Paul. "Indian Policy Reform and American Protestantism." In *People of the Plains and of the Mountains.* Ed. Ray Billington. Westport, Conn.: Greenwood Press, 1973.

Quandt, Jean B. "Religion and Social Thought: The Secularization of Post-Millenialism." *American Quarterly* 25 (October 1973): 390–409.

Radin, Paul. "The Mind of Primitive Man." *New Republic* 98 (April 19, 1939): 300–303.

Roberts, Gary L. "Conditions of the Tribes, 1865: The Report of General McCook." *Montana,* December 1974, pp. 14–25.

Rogin, Michael Paul. "Liberal Society and the Indian Question." *Politics and Society* 1 (May 1971): 269–312.

Rubenstein, Bruce. "To Destroy a Culture: Indian Education in Michigan, 1855–1900." *Michigan History* 60 (Summer 1976): 137–60.

Schiener, Seth N. "President Theodore Roosevelt and the Negro, 1901–1908." *Journal of Negro History* 47 (July 1962): 169–82.

Shanas, Ethel. "The American Journal of Sociology through Fifty Years." *American Journal of Sociology* 50 (March 1950): 522–33.

Sievers, Harry J. "The Catholic Indian School Issue and the Presidential Election of 1892." *Catholic Historical Review* 38 (July 1952): 129–55.

Taber, Ronald W. "Sacagawea and the Suffragettes: An Interpretation of a Myth." *Pacific Northwest Quarterly* 28 (January 1967): 7–13.

Unrau, William. "The Civilian as Indian Agent: Villain or Victim?" *Western Historical Quarterly* 3 (October 1972): 405–20.

Utley, Robert. "The Celebrated Peace Policy of General Grant." *North Dakota History* 20 (July 1953): 121–42.

Voget, Fred W. "Progress, Science, History and Evolution in Eighteenth- and Nineteenth-Century Evolution." *Journal of the History of the Behavioral Sciences* 3 (April 1967): 132–55.

Waltmann, Henry G. "Circumstantial Reformer: President Grant and the Indian Problem." *Arizona and the West* 13 (Winter 1971): 323–42.

White, Leslie A. "Evolution in Cultural Anthropology: A Rejoinder." *American Anthropologist* 49 (July–September 1947): 400–411.

Willis, William S., Jr. "Anthropology and Negroes on the Southern Colonial Frontier." In *The Black Experience in America: Selected Essays.* Ed. James C. Curtis and Lewis L. Gould. Austin: University of Texas Press, 1970.

———. "Divide and Rule: Red, White and Black in the Southeast." *Journal of Negro History* 48 (July 1963): 157–76.

Williams, Walter L. "United States Indian Policy and the Debate over Philippine Annexation: Implications for the Origins of American Imperialism." *Journal of American History* 66 (March 1980): 810–31.

Wiebe, Robert H. "The Social Functions of Public Education." *American Quarterly* 21 (Summer 1969): 147–64.

Wish, Harvey. "Negro Education and the Progressive Movement." *Journal of Negro History* 49 (July 1964): 184–201.

7. *Dissertations and Theses*

Bannon, Helen Marie. "Reformers and the Indian Problem, 1878–1887 and 1922–1934." Ph.D. dissertation, Syracuse University, 1976.

Bieder, Robert E. "The American Indian and the Development of Anthropological Thought in America, 1780–1851." Ph.D. dissertation, University of Minnesota, 1972.

Burgess, Larry E. "The Lake Mohonk Conference on the Indian, 1883–1916." Ph.D. dissertation, Claremont Graduate School, 1972.

Cauthers, Janet Helen. "The North American Indian as Portrayed by American and Canadian Historians, 1830–1930." Ph.D. dissertation, University of Washington, 1974.

Clark, Ira G. "The Railroads and the Tribal Lands: Indian Territory, 1838–1890." Ph.D. dissertation, University of California, Berkeley, 1947.

Coen, Rena Neumann. "The Indian as the Noble Savage in Nineteenth-Century American Art." Ph.D. dissertation, University of Minnesota, 1969.

Darnell, Regna. "Daniel Garrison Brinton: An Intellectual Biography." M.A. thesis, University of Pennsylvania, 1967.

————. "The Development of American Anthropology, 1879–1920: From the Bureau of American Ethnology to Franz Boas." Ph.D. dissertation, University of Pennsylvania, 1969.

Fear, Jacqueline M. "American Indian Education: The Reservation Schools, 1870–1900." Ph.D. dissertation, University College, London, 1978.

Gilcreast, Everett Arthur. "Richard Henry Pratt and the American Indian Policy, 1877–1906." Ph.D. dissertation, Yale University, 1967.

Hazen, Don C. "The Awakening of Puno: Government Policy and the Indian Problem in Southern Peru, 1900–1955." Ph.D. dissertation, Yale University, 1974.

Hinsley, Curtis M., Jr. "The Development of a Profession: Anthropology in Washington, D.C., 1846–1903." Ph.D. dissertation, University of Wisconsin, 1976.

Keller, Robert H. "Protestant Churches and Grant's Peace Policy: A Study in Church State Relations." Ph.D. dissertation, University of Chicago Divinity School, 1967.

Layman, Martha E. "A History of the Board of Indian Commissioners and

Its Relation to the Administration of Indian Affairs, 1869–1900." M.A. thesis, American University, 1951.

Nicklason, Fred H. "The Early Career of Henry L. Dawes." Ph.D. dissertation, Yale University, 1967.

Preston, Frederick William. "Red, White, Black and Blue: The Concept of Race in American Sociology: An Exploration in the Sociology of Knowledge." Ph.D. dissertation, Ohio State University, 1970.

Rieger, John F. "George Bird Grinnell and the Development of American Conservation, 1870–1901." Ph.D. dissertation, Northwestern University, 1970.

Stocking, George W., Jr. "American Social Scientists and Race Theory, 1890–1915." Ph.D. dissertation, University of Pennsylvania, 1960.

Trosper, Ronald L. "The Economic Impact of the Allotment Policy on the Flathead Indian Reservation." Ph.D. dissertation, Harvard University, 1975.

Walker-McNeil, Pearl Lee. "The Carlisle Indian School: A Study of Acculturation." Ph.D. dissertation, American University, 1979.

Waltmann, Henry George. "The Interior Department, War Department and Indian Policy, 1865–1887." Ph.D. dissertation, University of Nebraska, 1962.

Winer, Lilian Rosenbaum. "Federal Legislation on Indian Education, 1819–1970." Ph.D. dissertation, University of Maryland, 1972.

Wolfson, Harry. "The History of Indian Education under the Federal Government, 1871–1930." M.A. thesis, City University of New York, 1932.

TESTIMONIALS

✪ ✪ ✪

"This true story is one of our military justice system turned upside down. That it occurred threatens the reputation of all our services.

As you read this well written first person story you can't help but become outraged; It is hard to put down. It begs the question of accountability at the highest levels. The book should be required reading to assure nothing like this is allowed to happen again. The families of Lt. Allen and Capt. Esposito deserve nothing less, as do our country and the finest service men and women in the world."

RADM H. Denny Wisely USN Ret

Admiral Wisely background: Flew 350 missions in F–4 Phantom in Vietnam; first to shoot down 2 airplanes. He was shot down and rescued over N. Vietnam; Commanded Fighter Squadron from Carrier based in Japan; Lead Blue Angels: Ran Legislative Affairs Office in Washington: Commanded USS Sylvania (Supply Ship) and John F. Kennedy (aircraft carrier). Hosted Bush–Gorbachev Summit aboard 6th Fleet Flagship in Malta. After Navy, retired as VP Business Development from General Dynamics.

"*Front Toward Enemy*, resonates because it goes beyond an exploration of our military and judicial system; it's also about motherhood, love, loss, and the American spirit which drives us to seek triumph against all odds. There is a humanity to the author's lens that makes the narrative so compelling."

Kimberly Guilfoyle

Guilfoyle served as an Assistant District Attorney at the San Francisco District Attorney's Office from 2000 to 2004. She is currently a regular contributor on *Geraldo at Large*, a weekend show that airs on the *Fox News Channel*, as well as host of an internet–only crime–related program for Fox News.

"Barbara Allen has written a heart rendering documentary of her three and a half years of her frustrating struggle for bringing justice to the criminal, premeditated explosion resulting in the death of her husband, First Lieutenant Louis Allen, and his friend, Captain Phillip Esposito. Regrettably, prolonged military justice resulted in "butchered justice," emphasizing the clarion need for the reform of military justice in cases of this nature."

Benjamin A. Gilman, *CEO The Gilman Group*
Former Congressman and Former Chairman of the
House International Relations Committee

FRONT TOWARD ENEMY

★ ★ ★

A SLAIN SOLDIER'S WIDOW DETAILS
HER HUSBAND'S **MURDER** AND
HOW MILITARY COURTS ALLOWED
THE KILLER TO ESCAPE JUSTICE

BARBARA ALLEN

NEW YORK

FRONT TOWARD ENEMY

A SLAIN SOLDIER'S WIDOW DETAILS HER HUSBAND'S MURDER
AND HOW MILITARY COURTS ALLOWED THE KILLER TO ESCAPE JUSTICE

by BARBARA ALLEN

ISBN 978-1-60037-829-4 (paperback)
Library of Congress Control Number: 2010931844

Published by:
Morgan James Publishing
The Entrepreneurial Publisher
5 Penn Plaza, 23rd Floor
New York City, New York 10001
(212) 655-5470 Office
(516) 908-4496 Fax
www.MorganJamesPublishing.com

Cover Design by:
Rachel Lopez
rachel@r2design.com

Interior Design by:
Bonnie Bushman
bbushman@bresnan.net

A portion of the author's proceeds from FRONT TOWARD E N E M Y will be donated to Camp Better America. Camp Better America is a 501(c)(3) foundation whose mission is to reconnect military families, giving them the tools they need to create, build and achieve their dreams. To make a donation or to find out more about Camp Better America, please visit www.CampBetterAmerica.org

In an effort to support local communities, raise awareness and funds, Morgan James Publishing donates one percent of all book sales for the life of each book to Habitat for Humanity.
Get involved today, visit **www.HelpHabitatForHumanity.org.**

DEDICATION

✪ ✪ ✪

To Lou, for crossing your heart and never letting go. It was my honor and blessing to be your wife, and I am a better person because of you.

To Phillip Esposito, for taking Lou under your wing and helping him become that soldier he wanted to be. He was proud to know you and call you his friend, as I am proud to have come to know you through the ones you left behind. Your deaths were senseless, but your lives were extraordinary.

ACKNOWLEDGEMENTS

✪ ✪ ✪

I would not have come through these years as I have without the enormous support of countless people. The steadfast presence of family and friends has been invaluable. To my parents and family, thank you for putting up with me and always being ready to help. To Lou's family, thank you for welcoming me as you did, and working through the pain to reestablish a place in my life.

To Siobhan Esposito, thank you for the times you pulled me through and lead the way. To Steven Raiser, thank you for peeling me off the floor and never refusing my call. Meg Foreman, thank you for trailblazing the communication between us and the government, and for sticking with us long after the government tucked tail. To John Benson, thank you for fighting the way you did.

This book would never have come to be without the assistance of a talented support group. Paul von Zielbauer, thanks for pushing me until I saw the light. You are inspirational. Corinne Jacob, thanks for grabbing on and running with it. Kathleen Gagg, Jim Preston, and William "Monsoon" Mimiaga, thank you for spreading the word and opening doors for me, as well as calling me your friend. To those who provided off–the–record support and guidance, thank you. Bill Eastwick, thank you for the time and energy spent helping me on this, and for minimizing the amount of potentially dull moments in our lives. Joyce Bone, Margo Toulouse, and the Morgan James team, thank you for making my work a reality.

To Terri Seifert, thank you for reaching out to me, and helping me navigate the world we have been thrust into. To Roy White, Virginia Link, Dan Barto, Phil and Lisa Taylor, and Mike Kerr, thank you for being part of experiences that have impacted my boys and I tremendously. To the countless others who have done so, please know my thanks extends to you.

Jason Lamphier, thank you for seeing something special in me. I am excited about life again because of you. And to Trevor, Colin, Sean and Jeremy, thank you for the privilege of being your mom. You are everything that is good in this world.

TABLE OF CONTENTS

✪ ✪ ✪

CHAPTER ONE

JUNE 8, 2005

✪ ✪ ✪

"Lou is offline." The same message greeted me each time I checked the computer screen in our bedroom. I knew I had the computer volume cranked as high as it would go, but I checked anyway. When Lou came online and pinged me, I didn't want to miss the beep. Unable to sleep, I snuggled up on the bed with Cassie, our black Lab mix. The four boys were still asleep upstairs. The windows were open wide, welcoming the warm June breeze as it filtered through the trees. The sun had yet to rise as I lay in anxious stillness.

Lou had been in Iraq for four days. We'd managed a video chat the previous morning, and he'd promised to call again but hadn't. There was no way to sleep while imagining the worst.

Eyes closed, mind racing, I let myself breathe the scent of freshly cut grass curling through the window screen. I constantly replayed my memory from ten days ago; Lou in his desert camouflage uniform at Fort Drum, kissing me good bye and promising he'd be okay. How I had tried to believe him.

The sound of heavy footsteps on our front steps jolted me upright. The clock blinked 6 A.M. Our bedroom window was next to the front door and it sounded like a football team was out there. Cassie gave an uninterested grunt when I shifted her off me to leap out of bed as the doorbell rang.

Oblivious of my threadbare blue tank top and shorts, I ran down the short hallway into the living room entry. Looking as shocked by my frantic entrance as I was at their unexpected appearance were three men on my steps. They were in Class As, the formal military uniform. Behind them on my lawn I had a glimpse of a man I thought was in a

1

white t–shirt, studying the ground. The three soldiers gaped at me through my screen door for a moment while I gaped back.

A sickening surge of fear coursed through me as the worry I'd felt all night about Lou, the shock of the doorbell at dawn, and the realization of what these men signified collided within me. I launched back from the door, smacking into the corner where the living room wall meets the front entryway. One of the men was talking through the screen. "Mrs. Allen? Mrs. Louis Allen?" came to me through the screams now bursting in my head. I was grabbing the wall and had my face turned into it, trying to avoid this scene, avoid what it meant. I couldn't find the strength to answer the soldier who insistently called my name. I was desperate to stop him from saying what I already knew.

I was aware the soldiers had opened my screen door and were cautiously approaching me as I clung to that wall. "Ma'am why don't you sit down?" one of them asked softly. "Ma'am, do you want to sit?" I didn't want to sit. I didn't want to look at them. I didn't want them to be here. My throat was closing up. My chest felt like it was ripping apart, and when I opened my eyes, the three men were spinning around with the rest of the room.

They would not go away, I knew, until they carried out their mission. That mission was to tell me Lou was dead. The pre–deployment meeting Lou and I attended covered the procedure and made it abundantly clear that the only reason a military detail would show up at our door would be in the worst case scenario.

The five minutes since my doorbell rang seemed like an hour. I was still clinging to the wall, and the soldiers' voices registered an increased level of concern as they suggested I sit down. I was yelling at them, "Say it. Just say it!" so they would get it over with and leave. It wasn't until one of the men's shaved heads was in front of me, angling in to catch my words that I knew I was barely whispering. He finally understood what I was trying to say and stepped back. I saw only two men now when I cracked my eye open. They were silhouetted against the light coming in from the door and I could not see their faces. But I could see they were ramrod straight at attention as one of them read from a paper before him.

I caught the words, "We regret to inform you" before I slipped back into a pathetic shell against the wall. Determined to convey the message, the soldier's voice continued. I heard phrases like "mortar attack" an officer "had positively identified the body." Most of the rest was lost on me. All I could think was that "the body" these men were referring to could not be Lou. He'd only been there a few days, and I had just seen him so alive in our video chat yesterday morning. He could not possibly be dead. This cannot be happening because I cannot handle it. *Not Lou. Not us. Not our family. Please, God, not us.*

I slowly opened my eyes to see the two soldiers standing close to me now, hands at their sides, a mixture of empathy and concern on their faces. I looked at these two men, so young and so serious, and I had no idea what to do. I managed to stammer out the question "What happened?" In unison they snapped back and one of them read from that paper again. "Ma'am, …killed in his sleep" is all I grasped of that announcement. I was seized then by the vision of Lou lying in bed, and his world exploding around him. Of him exploding with it. So innocently lying there asleep. But something about that didn't seem right, in addition to the news itself.

It came to me that Lou would not have been asleep when this happened, because he hadn't called me. I knew he'd meant his promise to call me before he went to sleep, and the only thing that would have prevented him from doing so was if he was killed or injured before he went to bed. Which meant perhaps they were wrong. Maybe it was some other poor guy who was killed, and Lou was lying injured in a hospital somewhere. Because if he is dead, I prayed, please let me die, too. Right here. Right now. This pain is more than I can take. I am not strong enough to want to live through this.

As I look back now, I am ashamed at how weak I was. Ashamed at being the kind of mom who would rather die than see her children through the devastation that awaited them. It was not the only time those thoughts would cross my mind, that I would wish to die so I could escape my world—escape the pain of what was happening around me. It is something I have since been trying to make up to my kids, and have asked God to forgive me for.

One of the soldiers asked me if there was someone I could call. Someone to come here and help me. My first instinct was to reach for my husband, so this question seemed cruel. But I knew I had to think of someone who could physically arrive in my home in the next few minutes, and my friend Claire popped into my head. I needed to get her here before the kids woke up because I was unable to get through this morning's routine alone.

I was shaking uncontrollably, and grabbed one of Lou's big shirts to cover up. The guy in the white t–shirt turned out to be a security guard from our private lake community. He'd escorted the soldiers to my house earlier, and said he would take the men to Claire's. I asked one soldier to guard my house while my kids slept and had the others drive me to Claire's house around the corner. I rang her doorbell while pounding on her door. Claire's husband, Mark, came down, wiping the sleep from his confused eyes as he noticed the military uniform standing behind me. I fell into the house, landing in a heap on the carpet at the bottom of their stairs, whispering, "Lou is dead." Then I sat with my head on my knees, rocking back and forth, sort of gasping. He ran upstairs and I heard Claire scream.

She came to me and I asked her to come help me get the kids off to school while I figured out what to do. She said she'd be right up, and I let the military guy drive me home. My kids were still asleep. It had been twenty minutes since my doorbell rang.

The soldier duo accompanied me into my kitchen, where I thudded gracelessly into a chair at our table. The chaplain, as I learned the tallest, third uniformed guy was, maintained a discreet distance while I called Chris Protsko. She was a friend whose husband was in Lou's original unit currently serving in Iraq. She's the head of the Family Support Group and I was sure she would say she'd been in touch with people, that this was all a mistake. Instead, she was stunned when I told her the news. One of the soldiers took the phone I extended. I could hear him quietly explaining, "Ma'am, …killed in his sleep."

Claire arrived then, a light, wrinkled t–shirt and shorts combo on her short frame. Her eyes were rimming with tears, and I noticed then I hadn't yet been able to let any tears of my own loose. *Why aren't I crying?* I wondered. Claire flipped her wavy dark hair away from her face and gave me a hug. I asked her to stay inside, get the kids as they woke, while I went outside to let the notification crew leave.

I stood outside in a patch of early morning sunlight in our front yard, talking with the soldiers and the chaplain. One of them told me he was going to Afghanistan soon, and I told him to be careful. One of them was fighting back tears. Another had vivid blue eyes but that is all I remember of them. They gave me their cards—If there is anything we can do… As the chaplain maneuvered his card into my trembling hand, I saw and felt the first of my tears splash onto my arm.

I don't remember in which order the boys woke or who greeted them. I do remember telling them I wasn't feeling well so Claire would be driving them to school and preschool today. While Claire fed the boys breakfast, I went to my room to make the phone calls. Realizing Lou's parents were in Maine, I called his sister Jen and choked on the words, "Lou is dead. The military was here—said he was killed last night." She screamed, said, "I'm coming." And we hung up. Then I called my parents. Same conversation.

The next hour was my first experience of attempting to be a mom in spite of wanting to curl up and die. I made the kids' lunches and packed their backpacks in a state of disbelief and panic. Our oldest son, six–year old Trevor, was all smiles as he proclaimed how wonderful life was now because it's almost summertime, and summertime is always fun. And, he said, it is one day closer to Daddy coming home. I could only hold my breath and stare at him as Claire nudged them out the door past their Aunt Jen and Uncle Tom as they were arriving. Five–year–old Colin asked why Aunt Jen and Uncle Tom were here and I said we had work to do. I gripped the stair railing and the pain hit as I watched all four of my kids being driven away. I realized their days of being innocent, secure children were over. In a few hours I would have to tell them their father is dead.

My parents arrived, hoping I was mistaken. Lou's parents had been called by my brother–in–law and were making the drive from Maine to our Milford, Pennsylvania home. I couldn't stand to say the words anymore, so Jen was telling everyone. Family trickled in and we were all so helpless. What do we do now? There had been no army seminar about this part.

Finally, Lou's parents arrived. I watched them pull up in front of the house and slowly emerge from the car. They walked around to each other, and Lou's mom, a short Italian woman dwarfed by the height of his six–foot–tall dad, leaned into her husband. That picture of husband and wife literally leaning on each other was the first, lasting visual glimpse I had of what would never be for me again. The sound of my mother–in–law's sobs preceded them across the yard as they made their way over and gave me a miserable hug.

It had now been about seven hours since my doorbell rang, and I was as ready as I would ever be to tell the boys. My mom drove me first to kindergarten. I was a mess in the office, blabbering to the openmouthed woman at the desk that I needed to get Trevor right now. Soon, he was walking toward me, his big blue eyes looking warily up at my teary ones as I leaned over to pick him up. I carried him to the nurse's office and told him something really, really bad happened. I told him a bad guy killed daddy. Daddy's body died, so Daddy had to leave it and go to heaven. We would never see him again here on earth. Trevor clung to me and we were both crying. I just held him tight and prayed for the strength and courage to get us through this. I told Trevor when he was ready, we had to go tell his brothers. He said, "Let's go."

Mom drove and I sat in back holding Trevor. I had called ahead and the kids' preschool teachers were waiting with Colin. I sat in the parking lot with him on my lap, and Trevor standing with his arm on my shoulder. Colin's normally over–expressive face was as blank as I'd ever seen it. It was as though the news froze him from the inside out and I could not stop the tears now pouring down my face. Panic filled me as Seanie, our three–year–old, walked out. How can I say this again? Am I doing this right?

I squeezed Sean onto my lap with Colin and told him Daddy died. We would never get to see him again. His little face, which looks so much like Lou's, crumpled. The damage to my children seemed enormous and cruel. Their childhoods were now over. One–year–old Jeremy would never know his father. Lou would miss his youngest son's first sentence, and his children's whole lives. The boys worshipped Lou. He wasn't a perfect dad, but pretty close. He was so proud of them and looking forward to being their dad forever.

Gone.

I sat on a log in the parking lot with all three boys now on my lap. Jeremy was napping inside. We would come back for him later. For now I focused on telling Trevor, Colin, and Sean what happened as best as I could. I held on to them and promised them I would spend the rest of my life taking care of them, and their dad would help me from heaven. I assured them he would never have left if he knew he wouldn't get to come back, and that he had tried really, really hard to stay in his body so he could come back home to us. But his body was too broken for him to be able to stay in it, so God let him come to heaven. I told them daddy would be able to watch over us from heaven, and sometimes we would see or feel something beautiful or happy. That would be Daddy's new way of hugging us.

I just sat in the shade with them and talked. They asked me some questions like "Did it hurt Daddy?" Every nerve in my body shrieked in pain when Trevor asked me that. I answered their questions and did my best to reassure all of us we would be okay. I would get the answers I didn't have now and we would all learn how to be happy again one day. "But for now," I told them, "It's okay to cry."

Once we ran out of things to say and the boys were ready to go, my mom drove us home. Eventually, darkness crept over the house. The military never reappeared. We had been told from someone in Arlington that another official notification detail would come to see Lou's parents, but by 10 p.m. we gave up. Lou's parents were understandably upset to be overlooked by the military. That would soon become a common feeling from then and a common practice of the military.

Gradually, the mass of family and friends at my house began to leave for the day. After Lou's parents left to drive the hour to their home, it was just Lou's sisters Vicki and Jen staying that night with me. I sat up on the glider swing out front. Lou gave it to me for Mother's Day one year. I loved that swing. Once, when I was alone, I was suddenly aware of a comfortingly burning warmth swelling from within me. It was as though Lou were wrapped around me, sending love and strength from a place I could feel, but not see. Afraid to lose him, I froze and concentrated on nothing but the warmth. I wanted so badly to believe it was real. The front door creaked open as Lou's sisters came out to check on me. The warmth ebbed away, but the comfort lingered for a while. We talked and cried for a few minutes before they went back in. I remained out on the swing, rocking the rest of the night away.

The display on my cell phone read 4:32 when crunching gravel and two headlight beams sliced through the dark stillness of the early morning. I was still on the swing, wrapped in our comforter as I watched the delivery guy lean out his car window and slide the local paper into our box by the driveway. I waited for the guy to drive away, then walked slowly to the box.

My heart was pounding as I unrolled the paper and saw us on the front page. I looked like some washed–up, stringy–haired blonde crack addict with four morose children, on the swing in front of the one patch of chipped paint on our house. "TEACHER, FATHER OF FOUR, KILLED IN IRAQ" screamed out the headline above the picture. It was the first of several stories that would run in papers all over. Lou's death and the circumstances surrounding it would soon become one of the most notorious cases in the United States military. It would introduce us to the world of the military justice system, and mire us down in the role of victims. But not yet. For the time being, we were under the impression an Iraqi had killed Lou. We could not fathom how this could get worse and, had we been told what was to come, probably wouldn't have believed it anyway.

CHAPTER TWO

NINE MONTHS BEFORE THE DOORBELL RANG

✪ ✪ ✪

My thirty–second birthday arrived in September 2004, and Lou announced he'd booked our babysitter for the evening so we could go out for dinner. Settling into the subtly lit booth, we unwound with drinks and appetizers. I was enjoying the occasion, feeling the same pull to my husband now as I had the night we met, until I grasped what he'd just said to me, "I'm going to Iraq."

The evening ruined with this announcement, I struggled to refrain from screaming at him for ambushing me with the pretense of a romantic dinner so he could deliver this news. I knew he'd regretted being ineligible to deploy with his unit. I just hadn't realized how much this bothered him until this moment. Having recently completed his last requirement, he was now eligible to deploy. Mistaking my silence for approval, he happily told me of a potential opening in the 42nd Infantry Division Headquarters Company, under the command of his friend Captain Phillip Esposito.

Listening as he told me about his friend and former commander, I sorted through past conversations with Lou, recalling what I knew of Phil.

Lou and Phil developed a friendship and mutual respect for each other in the time Phil held command of the 101 Cavalry unit in Newburgh, New York. Neither wanted to lose this with Phil's transfer to his new command of the 42nd, but that unit's location would mean more time away from home. Knowing I needed him with me, Lou reluctantly turned down Phil's offer to transfer with him. Instead, Phil left and Lou remained at the 101, but the two kept in touch.

May 2004 brought an announcement from Phil; the 42nd's original peacekeeping mission to Kosovo had changed. For the first time since World War II, the famed New York National Guard unit was deploying to a combat zone; Phil was going to Iraq. I knew Phil and his wife, Siobhan, had a new baby daughter. Lou and I had discussed how difficult it must be for Phil to leave. A few months previously, Phil and Siobhan had met Lou for dinner. I'd been unable to make it to that dinner, so had missed the chance to meet the man Lou now seemed so determined to join in Iraq.

Lou was becoming more animated as he spoke, telling me about Phil's leadership style and how well they worked together. I just stared at him, trying hard not to say anything I would regret. Now recognizing my silence for fury rather than acquiescence, Lou changed tactics. He locked his hazel eyes on mine, cracked his impish smile he knew I found sexy, and drew upon all his charm to convince me this was a good thing.

Deployment was inevitable, he reasoned. If he skipped this opportunity, he no doubt would be attached to a unit where he knew no one, which could be sent anywhere for the full twelve to eighteen months of a regular deployment term. In Iraq since June, the 42nd was four months into its deployment. By the time Lou's orders were cut and his boots were on the ground in Iraq, the unit would be in the second half of its mission. Lou could work out some supply problems Phil had said he wanted Lou to come fix in time for the bulk of the unit to redeploy home. He would likely stay in Iraq a little after the bulk redeployment to wrap things up, but would still be gone less time than most soldiers. He would meet the minimum length of deployment requirement, help Phil with an important mission Lou sensed was worrying his friend, and contribute to the country's war on terror. A win–win situation.

Right now, no official action was being taken to get Lou orders, and Phil had told Lou to stand by for further details. As I watched Lou's expression and listened to his voice, I knew he wasn't asking me for permission to deploy. I knew the decision had already been made and he was just breaking the news to me. I was furious with him, and we spent the short ride home in silence as I thought back to how this had all started when he'd joined the National Guard.

Soon after we learned we were expecting our first baby, Lou had announced he was "considering" joining the Guard. He had been an MP once and had always regretted his honorable discharge after struggling to meet the demands of the army. He was not a big man—a smidge under my roughly 5 "10" height. At age eighteen he had not been as physically developed as the other soldiers. Born with a condition called pectus excavatum, his chest had a sunken shape and he could exert himself far less than other kids before becoming winded. Corrective surgery improved that condition but did not erase it. He was still left with a small dish in his chest he hated to have touched, and a diminished ability to endure excessive cardiovascular activity. Physical challenges aside, the rigors of military life forced Lou to acknowledge he wasn't mentally or physically prepared for that life. These factors led him to request and receive an honorable discharge. He left the military but never lost his desire to serve. Now he saw the National Guard as a means to fulfill that desire while earning some extra money.

I vividly remember our argument that summer day. Standing in the heat of the afternoon, not sure if I was burning hot because of the weather or my anger as Lou told me of a decision he'd already made, assuring me the National Guard was a good idea. Besides, he'd said, it is one weekend a month and two weeks a year. That's it. It was 1998 and our country was not at war. The Guard hadn't been deployed since World War II and at most he would have to go help out upstate in an ice storm or something. I looked at him and said, "That isn't the way things go for us." I had a bad feeling about it. I half joked that if he joined the Guard, he would guarantee our country would soon be at war, the National Guard would be deployed to fight this war, and he would die in some freak manner in that war. That made him laugh and dissipated the brewing argument. We'd gone inside laughing together.

By the end of that conversation I knew he was doing it. Part of me was proud of how hard he worked and how he wanted to serve in uniform. The other part of me was seething in jealousy over this institution my husband wanted to join. I had always felt lucky to have Lou in my life. Ruthlessly bullied in school, I'd grown up convinced I didn't deserve someone like him. I was older now, a married woman expecting a baby, but the insecure child was still a part of me and I hated the thought of competing with anything for Lou.

I was an extremely selfish woman when it came to my husband. I genuinely supported and admired his devotion to his job as a high school physics and earth science teacher. I bit my tongue instead of complaining about the nights, weekends, and afternoons spent coaching a soccer or softball team or participating in a school play with the students. I encouraged him in his pursuit of a Masters degree. But I didn't like sharing any of the limited time he had to be home with us, and I didn't want to acknowledge the reality that he'd be deploying.

I'd known I was going to have to share Lou with our country from the moment I watched the Twin Towers fall on TV. As I sat with our newborn and one and two year–old sons, watching Lou dash into our newly acquired apartment and change into his battle dress uniform (BDUs) I'd realized we were at war and he would be a part of it. He spent weeks on and around the pile, and it changed him. Sifting through the debris in the frantic search for survivors, finding personal belongings or remains of victims was the one experience he would not talk about with me. I noticed he became more eager to spend time with us, more tolerant of the sleepless nights of parenthood, more aware of life. I was proud of him, but I never told him, because there was a part of me that had been living in fear of this day when a force greater than I would take Lou away from me, from our family. Now it seemed that day had come.

We didn't speak that night in 2004 until Lou had returned from driving the sitter home. I was sulking in the kitchen, and Lou looked at me for a minute before shaking his head and allowing a smile to ease over his face. The combination of his regulation–style dark hair, his playful smile, and the way he softly pulled me to him was impossible to resist, no matter how mad I was. I leaned into him and inhaled his smell I loved, as he assured me it would be okay. He laughed a little and told me I was crazy for not thinking I could handle things, since I was already doing such an amazing job as a wife and a mom, and he was proud of me for managing my own career while running things during his absences. Meant to be comforting, his words made me feel worse for my tantrum and wonder how he could be so calm about this. Looking back, I believe he just knew he wouldn't have been able to focus on his mission if he entertained the possibility of never coming home.

We spent the next few months in a state of limbo, knowing Lou would deploy. The only questions remaining were when, where, with whom, and for how long. Lou was further fueled to go after he attended services for two young soldiers killed in Iraq. One was from the 42nd and one was from the 101.

Following the service in Albany for the first soldier, Lou came home miserable, barely able to muster a smile for the boys as he tucked them in, and told me how emotional it had been; the enormous flags hanging from firemen's ladders as the procession passed underneath, crowds of people lining the streets, the ceremony. The second soldier killed was new to Lou's original unit and Lou had met him on a handful of occasions. That soldier's death made it all more personal.

Lou and I were sitting in candlelight that January evening, courtesy of a winter storm that knocked out power. A call from Major Reilly, one of Lou's superior officers, interrupted our quiet time. After speaking with the major, Lou told me about the death.

The story of this latest casualty would be on the 10:00 news. I sat close to him on the couch as we talked about that guy's poor family and what they must be going through. I was thankful he was here with me—that I wasn't the one left alone.

Lou presented the flag to the soldier's widow at the cemetery, and told me later how devastated she'd looked. I attended the wake with him. Looking across the packed room at a young girl stoically battling tears as she greeted people next to her husband's casket, I grabbed Lou's hand, leaned over and whispered to him, "Don't you *ever* put me through this. If I lose you my life is over." He looked at me and said, "No way toots. This is terrible." I met Major Reilly there, and the three of us moved into a back room of the funeral parlor to talk. The new widow's Casualty Assistance Officer, or CAO, assigned to every primary next of kin on the fallen soldier's paperwork, joined us. We stood next to an empty gray casket and talked about the family, how the widow was doing. I'd felt awful for her but thought, since I was a stranger, it would be wrong for me to approach her. That I would be intruding. Instead I'd bowed my head, said a prayer for her.

Standing in that room, with a younger than expected, freckle faced Major Reilly and the widow's CAO, looking at Lou across the top of that gray casket, disturbed me. I excused myself and returned to the crowded hallway, where I could not avoid seeing the room full of people, the casket up front, and the widow seated close to it. I knew that could be me up there one day, and I'd be far less stoic than the widow there that night.

Soon after that night, Lou emailed his friend Phil about the two men's services. "… They are horribly depressing. I can't imagine what the families are going through." The following day, January 14, Lou showed me an email from Phil. It read:

"What is your SSN. I need a HQ platoon leader." Two little sentences that changed everything.

Lou began working extra hours after that email. In addition to helping the school prepare for his anticipated absence, he was rear commander of the 101, and had been tasked with full inventory of his unit's supply. This was a large responsibility for "millions of dollars of equipment" he told me, and he was determined to complete that task before deploying. One night after reading the boys their bedtime story and collapsing on the couch, he gave a long, tired sigh. He didn't say anything and neither did I. We just sat there gazing in an exhausted stare at the TV, each of us lost in our thoughts and concerns. We hadn't been talking about much lately. I was busy with my real estate job and the care of our kids. Lou was busy with his life. We had lost much of the closeness to each other and this bothered him as much as it bothered me, I knew. We were just too tired to do anything about it.

Emails from Phil trickled in with references to a supply problem he needed help with. An obsessively organized person, Lou excelled in areas like supply. Keeping track of equipment from pens and pencils to sensitive items like weapons and night vision goggles

(NVGs), ensuring each soldier was properly issued necessary items, and accounting for all materials in and out of the supply room was a perfect outlet for his organizing compulsions. He was excited to get to Iraq and begin his mission.

The weeks ticked by and still Lou did not receive orders. In the meantime, things opened up a little between us as we celebrated Trevor's sixth birthday and Colin's fifth birthday a few weeks apart that February 2005. I watched Lou watching each of the boys blow out the candles on their cakes, and I could see he was as happy as I that he was home for this.

Lou and Phil exchanged a series of emails over the next few months. Lou would check in on the status of orders, and Phil would reply that he was doing everything he could, but people were dying over there, and Lou's orders may not be a high priority for those charged with approving them. When Lou expressed concern over leaving his family for so long, Phil reminded him that they had been away from their families for ten months and that Lou would be fine. In response to Lou's inquiry about the 42nd's mission, Phil relayed their Forward Operating base (FOB) was located in Tikrit, and their mission was to, "basically support/command the division headquarters company." He'd described FOB Danger and the water palace he resided in as a nice place on a lake. It didn't sound so bad, and we began to be more comfortable with the assignment.

These emails at once eased our minds about the deployment and made us more aware it was real. He would be leaving. Lou and I had just marked our ninth wedding anniversary that March. We'd always had it in our minds to celebrate our tenth anniversary with a second honeymoon. During our first dance at our wedding reception we had talked about the anniversaries to come. I said for our tenth we'd have a romantic getaway. He'd responded that he'd go out for drinks with his friends that night while I stayed home, tended to our ten kids, and cooked him dinner, and it became a standing joke between us. Now, with each of us stressed about his imminent deployment, Lou surprised me with tickets for an April getaway to Jekyll Island, Georgia, as an anniversary gift. It was perfect timing since we wanted a chance to be together, away from life, both to recover from the past few months of strain and to squeeze in each moment we could before he left.

The next set of emails between Lou and Phil announced official approval for Lou's assignment had been granted. Phil's plan was to start by bringing Lou to Troy, NY, for a couple of weeks, to straighten out discrepancies with the property book there, before joining the 42nd in Iraq to be the company supply/property book officer. Phil said he needed "quite a bit of help in that area." This mild–toned email drastically downplayed the reality of the situation. A reality I didn't learn for almost a year—that high dollar, sensitive items were missing. Sometime between the 42nd landing in Kuwait and arriving on the FOB, several pairs of NVGs had disappeared. The value was in the tens of thousands. The supply sergeant, Alberto Martinez, blamed Phil, claiming he'd sent someone to take the goggles from the tent Martinez had them in, and Phil blamed Martinez for losing them. An inquiry from official channels had determined both soldiers were at fault, and docked them each a month's pay. Martinez was enraged. But Lou knew none of this as he prepared to deploy.

Finally, on April 19, 2005, Lou received his orders to report to Fort Drum on May 1. We were relieved to know what would be happening, and scared as hell that it was. Me more so than Lou. He was able to pour himself into a multitude of other things: last minute projects around the house, end of the year stuff at work—students preparing for finals and graduation—finishing up his inventory at the 101, arranging to continue his Masters online from Iraq, and the deployment preparations themselves. For me, every moment was now a struggle to quell my inner fears about something happening to him without letting Lou know how terrified I was. I did my best to put on a brave face around him and the boys, who knew only that Daddy had to go again.

This impacted Trevor and Colin the most at first, as they were better able to understand what it meant to see Daddy packing his uniforms. Eventually it dawned on three–year old Sean that Daddy was leaving again, but Sean seemed more comfortable about it. Sean was born in July immediately preceding 9/11. His entire life had been with a dad constantly leaving for some training course, mission, or drill. He was used to life with Mommy here and Daddy coming and going, and had adapted beautifully by maximizing his time with Lou when possible. He seemed content with things the way they were and enjoyed watching Mom battle the challenges of doing things at home. He trusted in me to take care of things while Dad was gone, and he trusted that Daddy would come back. That's just the way life was. I didn't want to ruin that sense of peace for him.

Time passed, customarily indifferent to my silent pleas for it to stop, and the morning of Lou's departure was upon us. Lou loved taking the kids to Perkins and we managed breakfast there that morning. Returning home, the three oldest went inside to play while I stood holding Jeremy in the driveway. Watching Lou load the van, I bit back tears, telling myself to hold it together until he left so he wouldn't have an even tougher time going. The three big guys could not grasp the significance of the moment; Dad left a lot but always came home. They said a casual good bye and I knew that in a few days they would realize the enormity of this deployment. I tied a yellow ribbon on our front tree, telling Lou he could cut it off himself when he returned. Lou gave Jeremy and me a hug and a kiss. We said "I love you" and he strode to the van. He wasn't crying and I was determined to follow suit. As he drove away, I took a few deep breaths and gave myself a pep talk about being strong. Then the van was coming back, kicking up freshly laid gravel in its wake as Lou braked hard and leapt out with the engine still on and the door wide open. He ran across the yard and pulled Jeremy and me to him in a fierce hug. Now he was crying as he said, "I don't know how I'm going to leave you guys." I held on to him as my courage abandoned me in a flood of tears that mixed with his. It was perhaps the most intense moment of our lives together and one that will stay with me forever. Jeremy was confused and his hair was wet with our tears. I wanted to beg Lou to stay but instead assured him I love him and we will be okay. Reluctantly, we let each other go and once again he drove off as I stood in the yard with our little boy.

Lou called me several times most days, and I was grateful he'd kept his promise to keep me updated. He'd be leaving for Kuwait on Memorial Day weekend. Emails between Lou and the executive officer (XO) Lieutenant Luis Badillo, informed Lou they'd be sharing a room and were comfortably set up. Badillo would be home on leave when Lou arrived but would return shortly after.

Those emails made it sound like Lou would be in a decent place with a nice enough guy as a roommate. It helped me relax a little and I hoped it would turn out to be as easy as that guy made it sound. Lou was hopeful he'd be able to hook the webcam up right in his room, and we'd be able to chat frequently.

Lou's mission there became clearer upon receipt of Phil's next email on April 25. He sent Lou a chart outlining Lou's "proposed spot in the HQ platoon" along with a "draft rundown of your duties and responsibilities." The attached chart displayed a neat plan of Lou's arrival and his presence there as rear detachment once the bulk of the 42nd redeployed home. It seemed organized, and I began to think it would be okay. One more email from Badillo made Lou's destination and mission less scary in my mind:

> …*Our room is inside the Water Palace, Building 313. The Water Palace is one of the many palaces located on this FOB. Trust me when I say that I, soon to be we, have the best room in the division… Your (sic) probably going to be doing my job most of the time since I'll be tied up on redeployment, making sure that all our equipment gets out of here on time with no hold ups (sic). I don't want to keep anyone at Drum longer than they have to after this deployment is over with…*

I teased Lou about this now. How he would be going to Palace Land and the boys and I would be here. He was pleased to hear he would not be living out of a tent. I was looking forward to his arriving on the FOB, so we could chat via webcam. Lou had little patience for speaking with the boys on the phone. They were so young they mostly just replied

"What?" to him, or each told him the same story. Except Jeremy, who wasn't talking yet, but I still made Lou talk to him so Jeremy could hear his voice. This would produce a smile from Jeremy, but Lou couldn't see it. We usually hung up annoyed with each other—me at him for getting cranky about talking with the boys, and him at me for insisting he do so in spite of how difficult it was.

His last visit home from Drum was the weekend of Mothers' Day. We had been pleasantly surprised he was given leave to come back that weekend. That morning he dressed and fed the boys, and I interrupted him wrapping a case of my favorite wine in the kitchen. Grinning as he chided me for ruining his surprise, he handed me a Mothers' Day card. Then we left for a gathering at his family's house. Too soon, it was time for him to leave for the armory and catch a ride back to Drum. We all knew it was his last time here before deploying. Not wanting to say good bye in front of the family, Lou walked me out to the car for a private good bye, and I drove around for a while before returning to scoop up the kids and drive home alone. It was the last time his family and our children would ever see him alive. Half a world away, Alberto Martinez was preparing to kill Lou and Phil.

CHAPTER THREE
STAFF SERGEANT
ALBERTO MARTINEZ

✪ ✪ ✪

A May 18th, 2005, email from Phil to Colonel Mereness, his superior officer, was devoid of any illusions that he'd be able to work out his problems with Alberto Martinez:

Sir, I am letting you know what I think I need to get better in my supply room. I need help, and I should have asked for it sooner. I thought I was making progress in my attempts to teach, coach, and mentor the team in the right direction, but it didn't work...

He'd then offered names of soldiers he'd like to have brought in for another inventory, as he was "uncomfortable with the last inventory." Once the problems were straightened out, the team could be scaled back. But for the moment, he needed Martinez gone;

...I also realize now that I was getting the relief for cause NCOER confused with just getting rid of him. I still intend to do both, but I clearly need to pull him first.

Phil's emails to Lou did not mention his procedural confusion between removing a non commissioned officer on the grounds of poor or inappropriate performance, and removing that person entirely as per his discretion. Phil had a full plate with running the division, and counted on having time to fill Lou in when he arrived. Therefore the emails Lou received were still brief and understated, shedding little light on the details. Only after Lou arrived on FOB Danger did he realize the depth of the dysfunctional unit and the mess he was tasked with cleaning up.

Lou had managed to find his way through numerous challenges at the 101, as evidenced on 9/11 when he organized his unit and got them to Ground Zero. Since Phil had been in

Manhattan when the planes hit, it had been up to Lou to coordinate with his commander on the phone, get the men to the armory, and meet Phil down in the city. The 101 had been the first National Guard unit on the scene. Recently, Lou had dug his heels in and had applied himself to the responsibility of accounting for the 101's inventory. Worried about that task, he'd poured an enormous amount of effort into it, but he had not mentioned to me any doubt about his ability to make it so.

That self–confidence changed when he met Staff Sergeant Alberto Martinez and got a firsthand view of the supply unit chaos in the 42nd ID. The concern in Lou's voice when he called me from FOB Danger set off an alarm in my mind.

In a voice lacking his usual lightness, Lou told me what confronted him upon his arrival. The supply unit "was a mess" and the supply sergeant was doing "a terrible job." "No one can find anything" in the supply room. It was no wonder Phil was so stressed about this, Lou said, because this guy (Martinez) should never have been there. With unmasked doubt, Lou admitted for the first time he might be in over his head. Coming from a man with an obsession for organization and a natural ability to create order from disarray, this surprised me to hear. I was worried for Lou—I knew he tended to take his responsibilities seriously and it wasn't normal to hear him so discouraged. I told him I was sure he was up to whatever he was faced with, and encouraged him to take time to think it through. I had faith in him, and knew he could do this.

Curious about the man Lou spoke of with such unusual disdain, I asked about the supply guy. Lou reiterated the man's complete lack of organization, and told me things were so bad the guy was being disciplined with something. I was focused on the fatigue and concern in his voice, and I remember Lou saying whatever action was being taken against the guy was "a really big deal." The guy was "f— pissed" about it. It has always bothered me that I didn't pay more attention when he told me about this. Instead, the conversation had turned to Lou's flight there, and the stunning view of snow–topped mountains en route.

I was in the kitchen, out of range of Lou's family who had come for a barbeque that day, and straining to hear each word Lou was saying. The connection was faint, and listening to Lou's distant voice so notably affected by the beauty of those mountains, with the sun shimmering off them, unexpectedly caused a surge of panic within me; I leaned on the counter, overcome with a sudden notion that I was being weaned from him, that he was describing a scene so incredible it could only be from heaven, and I would not be able to reach him there. I was aware of how unbalanced that seemed, but helpless to stifle the thought. It would be months before I realized the significance of this conversation, and exactly how the supply sergeant would impact our lives.

As supply sergeant for Division Headquarters, Alberto Martinez held a highly demanding position since the mobilization and deployment of the unit. But prior to May 2004, the job had been fairly undemanding. In a non–mobilized status, the atmosphere in the supply unit was relaxed. Martinez set his own pace and whiled away empty hours constructing model airplanes. There was little demanded from him by Captain Werzbowski, the commander of the 42nd Infantry Division's Headquarters Company (HHC 42nd ID).

Martinez was known as a good–natured if unorganized supply sergeant. But the lack of organization did not prevent him from carrying out his duty, and when someone asked him for something, it was always produced. It was simply not always hand receipted or otherwise accounted for.

By most accounts, Martinez was easy to get along with. As a supervisor, he felt he worked with others, not over them. It was not uncommon for Martinez to request a soldier beneath him to perform a task and have that soldier ignore the request. He had a reputation for allowing this behavior by performing the task himself rather than demanding that his order be carried out. Some who know him speculated this meek attitude was due in part to Martinez's nature and in part due to his background.

The bulk of Martinez's childhood was spent in his native Puerto Rico. In his early teens, his parents moved him and his sister to the Troy, New York area. "Al" as Martinez was referred to, entered high school as a shy, awkward teenager with a minimal grasp of the English language. He was befriended by a small group of fellow students who found it entertaining to teach him how to curse in English, and to learn from him how to curse in Spanish. Gradually, the friendships deepened and the group was together more often than they were not. Martinez was soon comfortably ensconced in his social circle and deemed the jokester of the group. Frequent foul language and his Spanish accent made him endearing to his friends, and he added his own brand of humor to this. He would say whatever was on his mind, no matter how inappropriate. But he maintained a shyness around those he did not know well. His lean frame, olive complexion, glasses, and accent all made him stand out from the rest of the kids.

His friends and family stated that Martinez was a hard working guy who always had a job of some kind. While some of his bosses described him as lacking maturity and being unwilling to abide by rules he didn't like, for the most part he was described as a person who worked hard but liked to joke around. Martinez was just a goofy guy who ran his mouth while he worked.

Not everyone was charmed by him, though. Martinez's attempts to enlist in the Navy Reserve and the Army Reserve were met with rejection. Finally, he turned to the New

York National Guard. Failing to meet the required test standards in this institution as well, Martinez applied for and received a Mental Category IV waiver, allowing him to join in spite of low test scores. He began his career in December of 1990 as a light wheel mechanic in the motor pool, working his one weekend a month and two weeks a year as a soldier, and steadily through the week at UPS.

While some of his National Guard records reflect positively on his performance, Martinez's UPS records are far from flattering. He was chastised for stealing company time by idling in his UPS vehicle, driving on personal errands, and failing to meet his delivery schedule. The Beanie Baby craze was in full swing. Demand for these stuffed animals was skyrocketing and constituted a large portion of his deliveries. Martinez's supervisors noted an unusual number of losses of these items reported by him, and suspected him of working with store owners to report the deliveries as lost while accepting kickbacks from reimbursement payments paid by UPS to the store owners. Out of patience and unable to prove the kickback scheme, UPS finally fired Martinez for stealing company time.

Martinez fired back at UPS by filing a union complaint against them for terminating his employment. He won this argument and UPS rehired him, only to fire him again in 1999 on the same charges. This time, Martinez hired an attorney and filed a racial discrimination suit against UPS. Dodging the headache of a lawsuit, UPS caved and awarded Martinez his unemployment benefits. He was now emboldened by outmaneuvering this company twice and believed he was above the laws the rest of society adhered to. Smarter than the rest of us.

While struggling to keep one step ahead of trouble in his professional life, Martinez was working through a difficult time in his personal life, too. He and his girlfriend Tammy conceived a baby they felt ill equipped to care for, and Tammy aborted the baby. But she chose not to terminate her next pregnancy, and the couple had a baby boy. By the time Martinez and Tammy became man and wife, they were living with his parents, and Tammy was pregnant again.

Things began to look up in 1994, and the Martinezes purchased their first home in Cohoes, New York. Martinez went to college part–time and earned a degree in electrical engineering, impressing his professors with his inventive mind and ability to solve problems. All seemed to be going well for him and his family until the second time he was fired from UPS in 1999, and he fell behind on mortgage payments.

Martinez continued his part–time National Guard duties, and supplemented his hours with the Active Duty Special Work program, which brings in available Guard members to work extra days. These jobs can last any period of time from days to weeks and provided him with enough work to stay afloat. He used this foot in the door to win a civilian technician position at the Troy NY Waterlivet Arsenal. A job requiring a uniform even though it is a civilian position, a federal technician must be a National Guard member to qualify.

Martinez's duty was as a floor worker in the warehouse providing supplies to units, and he fit in smoothly enough to be promoted to floor supervisor. But then he began receiving negative ratings for sloppy work, and learned his supervisor was preparing to fire him. Anxious to avoid losing his job, Martinez agreed to receive a deduction in pay and return to his floor worker position.

Unhappy with this development, Martinez looked again for a way to circumvent his situation. The technician job was okay, but had its downsides: The pay wasn't great, there was no vacation time, he had to pay into his health care, and was required to wait until age sixty–five to collect retirement. This wasn't good enough for him, so he set his sights on an AGR position with the NY National Guard. Unlike a technician job, the AGR program came with full benefits, including a pension after twenty years, and the salary was better. It seemed much more worthy of his time, and Martinez perused the openings to determine which one best suited him.

By now, he had fallen so far behind in his mortgage payments that foreclosure proceedings had been initiated. He needed that AGR job to catch up. He tested for the supply position in August 2002. He failed that test and was denied entry into the program.

After failing the test, Martinez was sent by his arsenal friend, Sergeant Lynn Currier, to her sister, Captain Lisa Currier, who was responsible for administering the Armed Forces Vocational Aptitude Battery test. She also helped soldiers who failed or scored low on the test study for a retake and improve their scores. Protocol mandates a waiting period of six months between taking the ASVAB, but the Currier sisters felt bad for this poor struggling guy, and Captain Lisa Currier got him into the October 2002 session to retake the test. He failed again, and this time he had to wait the regulated period before trying again.

With the looming threat of foreclosure and his failure to enter the AGR program, the now desperate Martinez vented his worry to his friends. He talked about needing to sell his house, with the caveat that if he couldn't sell it, he may as well burn it down. Five months past due on his mortgage, Martinez somehow found the means to spend $5,000 on a family vacation to Disney. In October 2002, Martinez increased the insurance policy on his home from $112,000 to $226,000.

On the morning of December 18, 2002, Martinez woke with a "huge headache" according to a statement he later issued to the Cohoes fire investigators. He called in sick to work and took something for his headache. About an hour later, the headache was better and he decided to spend the day with his friend. The two of them caught a matinee of The Lord of the Rings and enjoyed a relaxed day off from work, while Martinez's house burned.

The Cohoes fire department extinguished the flames, and a routine investigation deemed the fire resulted from faulty electrical wiring. Martinez took that report and included it with a claim to Liberty Mutual, his homeowners' insurance company.

Liberty Mutual sent its own investigator to the scene. This investigator strongly disputed the accidental cause findings of the Cohoes fire chief, and the company refused the claim. The company suspected arson, and Martinez was their primary suspect. With the fire chief unyielding in his determination that the fire was accidental, the two sides locked horns and Martinez hired an attorney. The Spada Law Firm sued Liberty Mutual on behalf of their client for two separate amounts totaling over $200,000.

With their home in foreclosure and uninhabitable due to the fire, the Martinez family remained with relatives. Martinez finally exceeded the minimum score for the AGR position on April 3, 2003—his third attempt at the test, and was hired full time. It was a waiting game now for him, and he was confident he'd soon win his case against Liberty Mutual. He'd beaten UPS, and he had no doubt he'd beat Liberty Mutual, too. Then he'd collect his prize and build his dream home.

Biding his time while waiting out his lawsuit, Martinez settled into his AGR job. He'd made it. Successfully landed in a cushy full–time job with part–time supervision. From Monday through Friday, Martinez was free to do what he liked in the vast periods of downtime in the supply unit. Captain Werzbowski, his commander, was a part–timer, sporadically present and not a problem. The 42nd HQ Division was an administrative one. Most of the supply demands revolved around printer cartridges and other office supplies that came in at a snail's pace. It was an idiot–proof position requiring no solid work ethic and with no one overseeing him on a daily basis. Martinez was essentially unaccountable to anyone, and this suited him just fine. As a result, most of his military records reflected a soldier performing well with no discipline problems. On paper, he was an asset to the National Guard.

In the spring of 2004, Captain Werzbowski received notice the 42nd would be deploying to Kosovo on a peacekeeping mission. But before the captain had time to prepare for that mission, the 42nd's destiny was altered; for the first time since WWII this National Guard Unit would deploy to a war zone. And this was not the only change of plans. Captain

Werzbowski learned his first sergeant, a captain's right–hand–man, would be replaced by First Sergeant Lance Willsey, as per orders of CSM Fearnside, command sergeant major of the 42nd. Fearnside felt Willsey was a stronger soldier than the current first sergeant was for deployment to a combat zone. Adding further injury to insult, Fearnside took things a step further, and asked the new first sergeant for recommendations of a more experienced and able commander to lead the 42nd to Iraq. Having worked with Phil previously in Troy, New York, with the Bravo 101, Willsey needed no time to think before recommending him to Fearnside. Captain Werzbowski's command of the 42nd Infantry Division's Headquarters Company had come to an end.

This abrupt change of command startled many in the 42nd. Most upset was Captain Werzbowski, who felt betrayed by superiors. When he inquired to his superior officer about this development, he was told the unit would be bringing its best team forward to Iraq. The clear implication was that Captain Werzbowski did not belong on this team. Others in the 42nd were resentful of this last–minute change, and attributed it to the Good Ol' Boys Club mentality of those in positions of power recruiting their own favorites for coveted slots. Phil's reception from the unit ranged from welcome, to lukewarm, to outright hostile.

Unphased by this resentment and hostility, Phil accepted the assignment and set about learning the nuances of his new command, and the five sections in it. The maintenance, motor pool, medics, food service, and supply sections all needed to amp up their games for the mobilization and deployment. While the application of his West Point standards to this National Guard unit was met with a blanket of resistance, no section resisted more than supply. Staff Sergeant Alberto Martinez had his own method of running things and was not about to be steamrolled by a commander he and his cronies described as "overeager" and "by the book." The other sections gradually adjusted to Phil's command and rose to the challenge. But supply continued to sink.

The mobilization process created a tsunami–like wave of new soldiers and expensive equipment crashing over the supply unit. Keeping up with this pace would be challenging for the most competent, disciplined soldier. Martinez was neither. Phil's determination to teach the soldier quickly gave way to frustrated exchanges with Martinez. These exchanges then turned heated, with both commander and supply sergeant expressing open animosity for each other. While Phil restricted his comments to the supply sergeant's ineptness and possibilities for either "fixing the soldier" or processing him out, Martinez was ranting about wishing Phil would die, and ways he could make that happen.

Lieutenant Luis Badillo, executive officer of the company, had survived the leadership overhaul and was acclimating as best as he could to the new command. Martinez liked

Badillo, and the two got along well. Badillo began acting as a buffer between his friend and the overbearing, "micromanaging" new commander.

While mobilizing at Fort Drum, Martinez would catch the ear of people venturing into supply and lambast the new commander. He'd curse him out and let everyone know what a pain the commander was. How he expected impossible things and made his job unbearable. Most of his rants about Phil involved the foul language that was inexorably entwined in his vocabulary.

Badillo would listen to his friend and try to calm him down. He'd agree that Phil was demanding but urge Martinez to just do what he said, and it would be okay. Phil held daily sync meetings in the evenings. The head of each section was required to attend, and they would all update each other on the status of things. No one enjoyed these meetings, and complaints abounded about having to continue working while others were done for the day.

With his work cut out for him, Phil's focus was not achieving popularity among the soldiers. He cared only about bringing them up to speed, preparing for their mission, and getting everyone home alive. Some soldiers fell into step, and others didn't. For those who needed help and were willing to work, Phil was there with encouraging words and support. He would check in on soldiers pulling overnight shifts to see how they were doing, talk with them about how they felt the unit was running, and see if he could get them anything. But Phil came down hard on Martinez as the supply sergeant continued to resist his command.

The sync meetings became known as a stage for showdowns between Phil and Martinez. In defense of his friend Martinez, Badillo opined that Phil used these meetings as an excuse to berate Martinez in front of the others, publicly humiliating him. How Martinez could "do nothing right" for Phil, and Phil would "set him up for failure."

An advance detail, referred to as a torch party, was scheduled to lead the 42nd to Kuwait before moving on to the FOB in Iraq. Claiming he wanted to escape from Phil's heavy hand, Martinez pleaded with Major John Andonie, who was tasked with overseeing the torch party, to be permitted to join, but was told he'd need the commander's approval. Martinez then unleashed a string of profanities joined with more threats to harm Phil, and Andonie sent Martinez away without reporting him. Knowing Phil would never approve the request, Martinez returned to the supply room cursing out the commander. By the time the bulk of the 42nd deployed in January, Martinez was openly badmouthing the commander to anyone within earshot, and the ill will between the two of them was well known throughout the unit.

The dysfunctional relationship between Phil and Martinez disintegrated irreparably when the unit arrived in Kuwait. NVG's were missing. Martinez blamed Phil, saying Ash Thimmaiah, the Readiness NCO, had taken them from the tent without consulting him and had never returned them. According to Martinez, Ash had been acting on the commander's orders. Phil blamed Martinez, angrily pointing out he was the commander and didn't need Martinez's approval to use Night Vision Goggles or anything else. He also stated the equipment had been returned and thought Martinez had not signed for them. The loss added up to more than ten thousand dollars and resulted in an official inquiry. Martinez, though furious, consoled himself with the thought that such a serious mishap would cost Phil his command, and he'd soon be free of his nemesis. Each soldier continued to Iraq denouncing the other. The inquiry led to dual accountability. Phil and Martinez were both docked one month's pay. He planned on ensuring this would be the last time Martinez caused him any trouble.

Martinez did not take it quite so well. Furious with the ruling, he blamed everyone else for the loss. He'd left another soldier in charge of guarding the tent that night and blamed him for letting Ash Thimmaiah take the equipment. He blamed Phil for losing the equipment and setting him up to take the fall. He blamed the investigator for not placing full responsibility with Phil. He declared he'd be damned if he took the blame for something someone else did. His anger escalating, he began voicing his desire to see Phil get killed by a roadside bomb. Wishing his commander would die in different ways. He was not happy about Lou coming in to oversee him, complaining about how "one of Esposito's boys" was going to add to his misery. To one captain, Carl Prober, he yelled, "I'm going to frag that f—!"

While countless soldiers heard Martinez threaten his commander, no one thought to report him. Unaware his staff sergeant was threatening his life, Phil began the process of removing Martinez from the supply position. He coordinated with Lou to have him come over, take the situation in his hands, and help fix it. He visited the Inspector General and asked for advice on having Martinez disciplined and replaced. He confided his suspicions that Martinez was stealing SINCGARs (Single Channel Ground and Airborne Radio Systems), including the Audio Net Control Devices (ANCDs) that are components of SINCGARs, NVGs and gas masks. He was told to begin by restricting Martinez's access to supply, and this he did. Martinez was notified he was not to enter supply unaccompanied by himself or Badillo but was still responsible for carrying out his duties.

Badillo tried to calm his friend down, but Martinez was beyond that. An Article 15 was being filed against him. Only a commander can initiate an Article 15. This non-judicial punishment allows the commander to inquire into allegations of minor offenses committed by a member in his command. The soldier facing an Article 15 is entitled to a hearing. The commander has the power to dismiss all charges, impose punishment, or, in more serious cases, refer the case for a court martial.

Martinez knew Captain Esposito was determined to remove him. This meant he was in danger of losing his AGR position at home. He swore he wouldn't sign that damned paper acknowledging the charges and told Badillo not to worry, he'd take care of it.

Badillo departed for his scheduled leave, cautioning Martinez to think of his family at home before doing anything stupid. Martinez visited his friend Amy Harlan in the 350 PSYOPS unit. The unit was preparing to redeploy home, and she was tasked with clearing up her supply before leaving.

Sergeant Harlan told Martinez of some leftover claymore mines and grenades. Her unit had inherited them from the previous one, and they were not on the books. Claymores were not even authorized on the FOB. These small, rectangular devices are filled with seven hundred steel ball bearings similar to .22 bullets. The mine is mounted on four metal legs. A wire of about one hundred feet leads to a clacker that must be depressed to detonate the mine. When the pound–and–a–half layer of composition C–4 explosive is ignited, the resulting explosion is tremendous. The area is sprayed with a wall of lethal shrapnel and the kill zone for fifty meters in front is unsurvivable. The casualty zone extends one hundred meters forward, and within one hundred meters to the side and back of the mine any individual not sheltered is subject to casualty. Each mine is labeled clearly on the front side, reading FRONT TOWARD ENEMY. This anti–personnel mine is an ambush weapon, one that is effective only if the enemy's location is known with enough advance notice to mount the weapon, unroll the wire, and take cover—all undetected—before detonating.

After choosing random equipment for his supply room, Martinez said he'd like to take some grenades and the claymores. Sergeant Harlan packed three claymores in one box, and loaded another with grenades. Martinez thanked her, saying they'd be put to good use.

Returning to his supply room, Martinez stowed the boxes under his desk, telling his subordinate, Specialist Diana Portella, not to bother putting them on the books. Portella liked Martinez. She trusted him, and he always looked out for her. Shrugging off the procedural deviation, she threw out the form she'd begun filling out, and forgot all about it.

A few weeks later Lou arrived. Three days after that, he and Phil were killed when a claymore mine was detonated just feet away from them, followed by three grenades in the surrounding area.

CHAPTER FOUR
MILITARY HONORS

✪ ✪ ✪

I watched the sun rise on my first full day in hell, the newspaper on the lawn where I had dropped it. Vicki and Jen helped me with the boys, who were so confused. It was hard for them to understand what had happened. Six–year–old Trevor and three year old Sean would snuggle on any available lap, sniffling, and ask again what happened to Dad. Jeremy reacted to the tears around him at first by reaching out to me, then avoiding me entirely when I dissolved in a pool of my own misery, unable to reassure him. Five–year–old Colin was the only one who would not allow himself to cry. He named himself man of the house and was trying to comfort everyone else. I was most worried about him.

A caller from Mortuary Affairs in Virginia informed me I had been assigned my very own Casualty Assistance Officer, who would arrive later in the day. Family members returned. Reporters called. I could not speak to anyone.

About an hour after the call from Virginia, a government vehicle parked in front of the house and produced another green, Class A clad soldier. I remained in my perch on the glider swing as he approached, beret on his regulation–style brown haircut, white gloves glaringly bright, polished black shoes and medals pinned on his uniform harshly calling attention to the man. I rose to greet him, guardedly accepting his handshake as I looked up into his brown eyes. Captain Letizia offered condolences and announced he was my CAO, here for whatever I wished and to help me through the upcoming events. Anger was building in me as he spoke. I didn't want insincere condolences from a stranger. I didn't want a CAO, and I did not want my husband to be dead. I nodded up at him and rudely gestured for him to follow me inside as I spun abruptly away. Forgetting his name within minutes, I snidely announced to the gathered family "Hey guys, this is my new best friend, Captain" and left his last name dangling. The captain introduced himself to my

29

family. Lou's parents accompanied us to the back porch. He talked about what we've been told. What would happen now? It was Thursday and it would be several days before Lou would be brought home. The first of military procedures we would hear about. I was sitting next to the CAO, mind swirling with doubts about the facts as told. I still did not believe Lou would have gone to bed without calling me, and I said as much to the captain. He responded in a manner I found to be condescending, with a tight smile and reassurances he would look into it. I didn't trust him, and asked if I could please speak with Phil. I knew Phil would tell me the truth.

My CAO's face drained of color. He asked "Esposito? Captain Phil Esposito?" I said "Yes, Phil Esposito!" He seemed upset, trying to say something, sputtering out, "I don't know how to say this. I don't want to say this the wrong way." I was about to get into this guy's face, sure he was about to tell me I was not allowed to speak to Phil. Lou's parents and I, jointly bewildered, awaited an explanation.

"I believe Captain Esposito was the other soldier killed in the attack."

This news overloaded my already over–wrought system and I dropped my head to the table, arms crossed over top, eyes squeezed shut, blocking out my surroundings. I could hear Lou's father demanding answers, asking why we hadn't been told previously. Not Phil, too, I silently pleaded, as the image of a video chat with Lou the previous Sunday—just four days ago—flashed into my mind. Phil had been showing Lou around the FOB and leaned in over Lou's shoulder to smile and wave at me. Phil's eyes glittered behind his glasses, and his somewhat bashful smile amused me, coming from the company commander. I heard him say, "Tell her I say hi" to Lou, before Lou called Phil a dummy because there was a microphone and I had heard him. They had looked happy, and I was relieved to see the two of them together. Now what? How can they both be gone?

Captain Letizia looked as though he would rather be anywhere than in that moment with us. He said he didn't know I knew Phil and, until then, wasn't aware Lou and Phil were friends. He seemed sincere, but I remained distrustful. I could not shake the impression things were not as they had been relayed to us, and I did not know if my CAO knew more than he was sharing. With no further information available, we shifted the conversation to Lou, and family members joined us. Captain Letizia lost some of the stiffness over those hours, as we sat in the sun and I swallowed too many gin and tonics.

Less than an hour after bidding us good night, Captain Letizia unexpectedly returned. He needed to speak to me. Privately. I followed him to his car and leaned on the trunk. I noticed this man, so collected and professional this afternoon, now paced before me with a clenched jaw and furrowed brow. Something was not right. I waited as he stumbled over his words, telling me the Army had opened a criminal investigation into Lou's and Phil's deaths. Officials suspected they were murdered by someone other than the enemy. This made no sense to me, for who would do such a thing, and why? Captain Letizia was still professional but far from collected. He seemed more rattled by this than I. I was more numb than anything. He was fussing with a pack of cigarettes now, and I told him to go ahead and smoke. He wasn't allowed to do so in front of me, he told me. I replied, "Well from here on the rules seem to have changed, haven't they—Frank." And that he better start calling me Barbara instead of Mrs. Allen, at least in private, and ditch the formalities. I needed a human being beside me, not a robot. He seemed taken aback by this but laughed. It was the first genuine smile I got out of him and it altered him completely. He had his cigarette while we speculated about what could possibly be going on, then went back inside to tell everyone else.

The following day was the official condolence call from Lou's superiors. Seeing Major Reilly and Colonel Mallon walk toward me was another moment I could have lived without. We went through the formalities and settled on the back porch. I don't remember too many particulars of the visit. I do remember asking them if they thought it possible Lou had actually been murdered by an American soldier, and the way they hesitated before responding yes.

I dashed a quick note to Siobhan Esposito, and Major Reilly promised to deliver it to her later that day. I wanted her to know how sorry I was and to see if she would mind my attending Phil's wake. But moments after they left, Siobhan called me. I told her I'd just sent a letter for her, and we offered condolences to each other. We had been strangers but now were a team, and we would help each other through this nightmare.

The announcement of a criminal investigation had piqued national media interest, and reporters had begun circling our home. One of these evenings Frank, my sisters, and other family were gathered on the porch. I answered a call from a reporter, who asked me if he could get a feel for the kind of day I was having—What did I do that morning? Did I get up and take care of the kids? "No!" I snapped. "I left them in their filthy diapers and told them to fend for themselves!" Silence descended on the porch and I watched Frank's face turn white. It was the first time I thought he was going to pass out. It was the first time I was able to laugh.

My family—I consider the two families my one big family—was my lifeline. They came and went over these days. They comforted my kids when I could not. They tolerated my moods, angry, standoffish, devastated, sarcastic, and zombielike. They gave me room to be alone when I needed to be, and were right with me when I needed company. Someone was helping me 24/7. Without them, I would not have made it through those first days. I have begun to count my blessings.

The next few day's yielded scraps of information on the investigation. It was definitely not a mortar attack. Lou was not asleep. He was in Phil's room with him, probably planning the next day's activities. I was right. He had not gone to bed without calling me.

We didn't know if it was the work of an American soldier or an Iraqi national. An American would be the ultimate betrayal. It was inconceivable. No way. I asked to speak with whoever got to Lou after the explosion. We'd been told Lou was unconscious immediately and never regained consciousness, but with the amount of confusion surrounding the events, I still needed to confirm this. In the meantime, I spent the days playing back the time since I last kissed Lou goodbye and the time he was killed. He emailed me when he got to Forward Operating Base Danger:

> *Hi Babs, I got into FOB Danger (our base in Tikrit) just a bit ago. It was an uneventful convoy here, but very nerve-racking. You think the worst whenever you pass Iraqis. My room isn't bad. The XO is messy though and never swept the floor I suppose. Also, I cannot hook the webcam to the computer and I can't hook up my laptop in here. It isn't very far to a webcam here on base so we could still chat with the kids and stuff. I will call you in a little while when I get to a phone. Meanwhile I must continue my cleaning spree.*

> *Love ya, Lou*

It was his first time in a combat zone. It was my first time worrying about my husband in a combat zone. I was scared silly. But he was on base now. Division Headquarters, away from the real bad stuff. He would be staying on base until a week or so later, when he was planning a helicopter ride to Baghdad to see one of the guys from the 101. I figured I would worry then, when that time came. For now, I was secure in his location. He sent pictures of the palace and I laughed at his description of his filthy room and his cleaning spree. He had a lakeside view from his window. There were pictures of a gleaming bathroom complete with bidet, and a picture of himself in desert camouflage uniform self-labeled "Assault Teacher." We had no idea that last picture would soon be broadcast to the entire country on every news station.

He called me Sunday, June 6, at four P.M. our time. Midnight there. He was exhausted and pretty pissed. A sandstorm had hit as he was about to go to bed, blasting sand into his room and obliterating his cleaning efforts. After all his work, he now had to sleep on the floor outside his room. Once again I was reassured. He could call me from his room. I loved to hear his voice, and I was glad a sandstorm was his biggest problem.

On it went through my mind. Each moment mentally replaying events, trying to make some sense of this. Killing time before Lou was brought back. My mind was continually churning over information and processing my life, but I couldn't allow myself to vanish entirely in my thoughts; I still had four little boys who were looking to me for guidance, and I had to show them our lives would go on.

Saturday, June 12, was the last day of our kids' Little League, and Trevor and Colin were looking forward to getting their trophies. I decided not to rob the boys of this day. After all, I told myself, this is exactly what I am supposed to do now. Protect their childhoods the best I can. Show them the way to continue to live. At the fields, we were greeted with concern. I appreciated it but tried to think only about the kids and the day for them. It was a perfect summer day with plenty of sunshine. Mom, Vicki, and Jen accompanied us. It was a relief to see the boy's smile and play. *Maybe I can pull this off,* I thought. But then every game came to a halt, and I saw people bowing their heads, coaches and players removing their hats, as the strains of a trumpet replaced the sounds of baseball, and the flag across the field made a slow descent to half–mast. A touching tribute to Lou, and I tucked my head down, trying to hide the onslaught of tears until the games resumed and I could sneak away.

Proceeding to the trophy awards, we came upon a table displaying framed pictures of Lou in his DCUs and the front page of the paper with our story. Next to these pictures was a sign and a collection can for the boys' fund. I panicked. The boys were right behind me. I didn't want them to see this. Not that day. Vicki saw it too and leapt across the crowd to swipe the items out of view. The astonished woman at the table apologized as we explained, and we walked the kids past without seeing the pictures.

I took a last look around knowing I wouldn't return. There is the snack stand Lou took Sean to while the game was on. There is the spot Lou sat with Sean on his lap while they watched the activity. I could see them there in my mind. I knew I would have to find a way to come to terms with the fact we would never do that again.

●   ●   ●   ●   ●

A week after my doorbell rang was Trevor's last day of kindergarten. He'd been excited about the party and I was planning to go. Now, instead, we would be at Lou's wakes. Wanting Trevor to have one last good day at school, I called his teacher and got permission to bring cupcakes to his class that Monday. We walked into his classroom and his friend ran over. "Trevor, I heard your dad got blown up by a grenade!" the little boy yelled. Trevor crumpled. I picked him up, kissed him, and told him I was sorry. He somehow pulled himself together and had a few last laughs with his friends. His strength humbled me.

That afternoon, I attended Phil's wake and met Siobhan. She looked like I felt. I met her family and noticed they wore their pain and grief much like our family. I saw pictures of Phil, noting the enthusiasm and smiles on his and Siobhan's faces as they posed with their baby daughter. The Siobhan in those pictures was not there that day. I paused at the open casket and gazed at Phil's face, offering a prayer for him before making my way past Siobhan and out the door with Frank. It was time to get to the funeral home in our county. Lou was being brought back.

We drove directly to the large white Victorian style funeral home and I waited on the wraparound porch. I'd been on that same porch a few months ago attending the wake for Lou's grandfather. Lou was with me, holding my hand. But that was a different life, and I stood there now, on the porch, freezing in spite of the humid June weather. I'd been freezing for days, unable to shake the chill.

Family arrived but I could not bring myself to speak to them, or even look over to them. I was focused on the road, looking for my husband. The Color Guard was in position as an unnatural silence pervaded the town. A slight breeze lifted the American flag hanging from the porch, but that was the only sound until a procession of vehicles inched down the street toward us. Panic rooted me to that spot, the ever-present tremors in my body passing through me to shake Frank's arm, too. This cannot be happening.

The hearse was opened and a gray casket was eased out. My eyes were glued to that casket. The soldiers began their march or whatever it is called. The casket was carried past me and into the funeral home.

Inside I was screaming, but the only sounds I actually made were soft sobs. Frank guided me into the home and the door shut behind us. What do I do? He brought me to a chair and told me to wait—he would come get me in a minute. He, Major Reilly, and some others went into the next room and I heard some banging around. Caught the sound of latches popping open before someone groaned. Then the only sounds I heard were shuffling and movement.

The minutes passed and I was still sitting there. The panic intensified as I was torn between the need to see Lou and the need to get the hell out of there. I felt my tentative poise slipping, and anxiously watched Frank return. He was handing me a small black pouch. He was saying something but I didn't hear him. I opened the pouch, and Lou's wedding band slid onto my palm. His wedding band. I stared at that ring as the memory of our trip to Georgia just a few months past flooded my mind. It was a new wedding band Lou had surprised me with on that trip. I closed my eyes, shutting out Frank and my surroundings and letting the memory in; the joy of walking on the chilly beach, hand in hand, smelling the salty air, tasting the spray. My delight with Lou's sand dollar discoveries, and Lou's childlike happiness with the blue conch shell I found. Returning to our rooms with our nautical treasures, and Lou slipping two brand new wedding bands in the conch shell for me to discover. How we'd slid them on each other's fingers, and I'd buried my face in his neck as he squeezed me tightly against him. The smell of the beach still on us, and the grains of sand stubbornly clinging to his neck, laughing as I kissed him and tasted that sand.

Now, in my palm, was that new ring. It was chipped. A visible reminder of the fact he was wearing it when he was hurt and when he died. As I processed this, Frank asked, "Are you ready?" He and Major Reilly each took one of my arms and led me into the next room. Half dragged into the room and nearing the casket, I could no longer deny reality; it was Lou. My knees gave out. Frank and the Major held me up, escorting me to the casket and gently helping me kneel in front of Lou.

"What did they do to you?" I cried. He was in his Class As. The sight of him assailed me; putty–filled holes in his neck, his swollen body, makeup sloppily smeared across his nose. His eyes—his long eyelashes were glued shut. I could see a ball of glue in his left eyelash.

I was sobbing. "I love you. I will always love you." I searched for a familiar place to touch, finding nothing familiar about the sight of my husband lying dead before me. His hands were encased in white gloves, velcroed together. Reaching out wobbly fingers, I gently touched his left hand. It felt as if his fingers were separated, unattached to him. Horrified, I leaned back, away from the casket, before steeling myself to lean in one more time. His dimpled chin was smeared with makeup. I ran my fingers through his newly cut hair, searching for the renegade gray strands I'd teased him about when he left. "How could you leave me?" I punched the casket, stood and turned, at a loss as to what to do now. I thought I was alone in the room but I saw Major Reilly had been standing in the back corner. He rushed over and guided me out the back door. Each time I thought it couldn't get worse it did. This cannot be happening. *Not my Lou. He is the strong one. He taught me what love is. He is my world. What do I do now? How can I possibly live without him?*

I needed to get the hell out of there. Now. Chris Protsko materialized and drove me home. I still could not believe this was real. He cannot be dead. He did not suffer this horrible death. My kids do not have to go through this trauma. We had a great life. It simply cannot be gone. We pulled into my street, and I took in the sight of our home. Saw the flags from the candlelight vigil. There was the yellow ribbon I had tied on the tree the day he left, and the Christmas lights still hanging on the pine tree. We never took them down, just plugged them in every year. I walked up the front steps, through our door, into our ghost house.

I spent the night sitting on my glider swing, the dawn watching the sunrise as I braced myself for the day ahead. I was attending Phil's service in the morning and Lou's wake later in the day. Frank pulled into my driveway, and I willed myself into his car. I'd grown familiar with Frank in the past few days. These were intense times conducive to creating fast bonds, and I could now relax in his company. He seemed to be taking his assignment seriously and he put up with my sarcasm. I knew he was becoming comfortable, too, since he began to display his own sarcastic side. He even managed to make me laugh in the midst of this mess.

We made the drive to Rockland County, where Phil's family was gathered at the funeral home for the last time before the funeral. A long line snaked out the door. Frank and I tagged on the end but then decided to jump ahead. Widows first.

Phil's family chose to have an open casket, unlike my decision to close Lou's. I didn't really care about too many details for Lou's services but I did insist on a closed casket for public viewing. I didn't want our little guys seeing him like that, and I didn't want him on display.

We walked past the curious people on line and into the parlor. Siobhan was up front. I walked up to Phil, said a quick prayer, and walked out. Nodded to Siobhan on my way. Frank and I took our places outside with the military. I saw the funeral detail prepare for the exit, and a man and a woman walking toward me. The man was supporting the woman, who could barely walk. I knew that feeling. They introduced themselves as Phil's parents and thanked me for coming, then slowly walked away. I watched as Phil's casket was loaded into the hearse. Frank and I did not join the procession of cars, instead heading back for Lou's wake.

Frank told me I would be able to speak with the surgeon who cared for Lou, and asked when the best time would be. Figuring I'd need time to catch my breath from the wake and prepare a list of questions for her, I said ten PM.

My kids were scheduled to ride over with my in-laws. I couldn't believe my little boys would soon be standing in front of their daddy's casket. And for what? What purpose did Lou's death serve? I asked Frank to take me directly to the funeral home. I needed some time alone with Lou. I felt the familiar tightening in my chest as the fear swept through me. Kneeling by the casket, embracing it, I laid my head over the top, where I thought Lou's head was positioned inside. The volume of pain I was in continued to amaze me. I hadn't realized grief was such a physical emotion. Remembering the boys were due to arrive, I reluctantly left Lou to wait outside for them.

The cars pulled up and my boys tumbled out. Dressed in suits and ties, bearing 101 Cavalry pins, they looked like little men, and I thought Lou would be impressed with them. I hugged them as their chatter about tomorrow's limo ride bounced off me. Reentering the funeral parlor, I was assaulted by the overwhelming floral smell and the sight of pictures of us in happy times. Needing to look away from the pictures, I crossed to the room that held Lou's casket, the boys behind me. Sean asked if Daddy was in the box. I told him the part of Daddy's body that he left behind was in the box but Daddy's spirit is in heaven with God. I told the kids when Daddy's body died God let his spirit into heaven. Now Daddy is watching us, missing us, and trying to send us courage. They nodded vacantly and wandered off to look at the pictures while I wished I had a script to read from when my kids asked me these questions.

I took a seat on one side of the room across from Lou's parents as the first arrivals trickled in. People passed me on the way in and my in-laws on the way out. Suddenly, Frank came plowing in. He is a big guy and he was pushing people out of the way, holding his phone in the air in his left hand and pointing to it with his right. "I have Iraq on the phone." My stomach dropped. "Now? Here?" I hurried out behind Frank as he explained this was the surgeon who had been with Lou until he died. I followed him out to the back of the building, ignoring the hordes of military officials staring at us. We found a semiprivate corner in the shade of a tree close by, and he handed me the phone, leaving me alone.

"Hello" I pushed out. A woman's voice responded, identifying herself as a doctor who was with Lou. She said she understood I had some questions for her. "Yes," I said, "I do." I asked the first thing that came to mind. "Was he conscious?"

"Yes. He was alert and speaking calmly," came the reply. Until then, I'd believed Lou was instantly knocked unconscious and remained so until he died. At least, I'd thought, he hadn't suffered. Wasn't afraid. This new information, combined with everything else, shocked me.

I started to black out but fought it off, needing to hear this. Someone must have noticed my distress, because a chair appeared from nowhere, and I sank onto it. Crazy as it was, I had hoped to hear that Lou was, in fact, not dead. That she had saved him. What

I did not expect to hear was that not only was he not instantly killed, he was talking for hours after the explosion. He felt pain but not in his legs. At first he thought we would live through this. The doctor said he repeatedly told her he had four sons, ages six, five, three, and one. He was taken to another hospital, all the while talking about the boys and me and asking for Phil.

I interrupted her, saying something like, "Why couldn't you save him?" She said something about his having lost a lot of blood, and I interrupted again—"What. There was no blood to give him?" Lou was a regular blood donor and the thought that he died from blood loss seemed cruelly ironic. She tried to explain it gently, saying he was so seriously injured that the blood they gave him wasn't enough. Apparently, with the extent of his injuries, it's amazing he held on for so long. Finally, she told me she'd given Lou his Last Rites before he died.

This information was all so new and sickening, and I was so emotionally and physically weak, that I began to slip back into the pitiable creature who had greeted the notification detail that day. I asked her if he was scared. She replied that if he was, he didn't show it. I was sobbing, heaving for air, and could not muster the strength to speak another word. I was trying to process what I'd just heard. It was as though Lou was dying in front of me. I got out something like "Thank you for taking care of him" and closed the phone. A deep sob wrenched its way from me, and I threw the phone away, not caring if it broke. I began spiraling down into a world of blackness, falling from the chair onto my hands and knees, anxious to escape into oblivion. Again I was begging God to let me die, when a pair of black military dress shoes walked to within a few inches of my face, and stopped. I couldn't raise my head to see who they belonged to. A voice said something about valleys of darkness and light. I was annoyed at the intrusion and wished I could pummel whomever was in those shoes.

But I couldn't breathe, let alone pummel anyone. Someone was lifting me, carrying me away, and voices came through the darkness. "Barbara, it's Kevin (Major Reilly), I'm going to get you through this" and strong arms were on either side of me. Our destination was the church basement, out of sight of spectators. I could do nothing but continue my silent pleas to God to take me, too. Please don't leave me here.

I thought of my husband, and what he went through. How scared he must have been. How I should have at least been able to hold his hand and comfort him in those moments. Struggling to catch my breath, I hoped I'd pass out if God wouldn't let me die. Anything to escape, if even for a moment. When I think back to those moments, I am disgusted with the person I was and the way I handled that.

Realizing I was not going to recover anytime soon, my parents and Frank took me to my parents' house. When I'd collected myself enough to speak, Frank drove me to Lou's parents' house, and I told them of my conversation with the doctor. On the way we passed the Veterans Cemetery where Lou would be buried the following day. This was the same road Lou and I drove thousands of times over the years. This was the way from my house to his. A lot of happy times driving down that road. Those times are history.

Once I destroyed Lou's parents with the information, I was desperate for some alone time with Lou. Frank drove me back to him, and I again kneeled close to him, my head resting on the casket and my arms stretched over the flag on top, my tears leaving a dark spot on it. Some idiot funeral guy told me to relax and I ranked him second place, just behind the chaplain I'd heard was the one in the shoes in front of my face.

I hate my life.

The evening service began, marked again with hundreds of people in line. Family and close friends came in the back. I took my place. After a while, Frank informed me that Siobhan and some of her family members had arrived. I went into the back room. Siobhan entered with her brother, Phil's sister, and some other family. Phil's funeral was just this morning and yet they'd come here to honor Lou and support me. I was again moved at how caring people can be.

Phil's family bore swollen eyes masked in red, contrasted by their drawn, pale faces. A few moments of strained conversation, and everyone but Siobhan left. We sat on the hard chairs in the room, scoping each other out and taking stock of our counterparts. She was an inch or two shorter than my five–ten build. Her deep red hair rolled in tight curls over her shoulders while my limp blond hair just glanced my chin. We didn't know each other well yet but did know we needed each other. I told her again how nice of them it was to come. She said she'd come to the church the following day, and later I asked Frank to be sure she was in the front row with me if she came. An awkward hug good bye, and she left.

I'd missed many of the politicians and military officials earlier due to my collapse, and that night only a few had stayed to offer condolences. A captain of the New York National Guard shook my hand, saying how sorry he was and that he'd tried to think of some way he could help. Handing me four sports cards in plastic cases, he hurried to explain that one day these cards would be quite valuable—He thought I could give one to each of my boys as a little investment. Rationally, I realized this was a nice gesture from a complete stranger. Sadly, the gone crazy part of me took over. Instead of calmly accepting this gift and thanking the captain, I went nuts. My futile attempt to mask my laughter only succeeded in making my face turn red. I could feel my cheeks flushing, and made the mistake of glancing at Frank. His bemused expression triggered a fit of unstemmed, furious laughter loud enough to draw stares from around the room. In an effort to compensate for my rude behavior, I stumbled over an apology to the captain and thanked him for the gifts. The moment was interrupted when a chaplain introduced himself, explaining he was here earlier and tried talking to me outside. It hit me then that this was the "valleys of darkness and light" guy attached to the dress shoes in my face as I was collapsing. "I know" I said. "I recognize your shoes." He didn't get it but Frank, who had witnessed the encounter, did. He choked back a laugh and took my arm, leading me away from the openmouthed group.

We returned to the parlor where Father Eugene, a family friend, was preparing to speak. His prayer signaled the official end time of the wake. I'd had enough, and left. I could see a line of people still waiting to get in as I drove away.

I was alone again that night. Tomorrow night the boys would be back, but for now I was grateful for the solitude. I sat up on the swing again, waiting for the sun to rise. Eventually, it did and it was beautiful but I couldn't appreciate it, because I knew today I had to bury my husband.

●   ●   ●   ●   ●

Arriving at the funeral home, I went directly to Lou. For the last time, I lay my head on the casket and whispered to him through my sobs: "Why did you leave me I love you I love you I love you How could you leave me I'm sorry I'm so sorry for the times I hurt you. Please don't leave me here alone I love you" Voices interrupted me. I jumped up and bolted from the room.

There was Lou's mom crying in a chair. "I have to do it. Please let me." What was she talking about? Then someone explained that she wanted to hug Lou and give him one last good bye kiss. Military protocol required my consent as Primary Next of Kin (PNOK). I was appalled. Tuesday night they'd had to ask my permission to place personal items in with Lou. Now this? This is her son, their brother. They don't have to ask me for any permission. How degrading that is, and how awkward. Nevertheless it is procedure and we mustn't stray. Of course you can. Please understand that I can't see him like that again, but he's your son. You do what you need to. Just let me leave. I ran outside while immediate family gathered in the parlor to file past the casket. Then, I watched a repeat of yesterday's funeral detail performance. Only today it was my husband being carried out. My hopes and dreams and happiness being loaded into a hearse.

I got in the car, and Frank joined me as we pulled away directly behind the hearse leading the procession. My boys were in one of the cars behind me. Lou's mom wanted to drive by their house. En route we passed under an enormous flag hung by the firemen, just as Lou had described for the funerals he'd attended. He was right about how emotional it was to see. We drove on and I saw "our" bar, where we'd met eleven summers ago. It stirred up memories of that night, and I recounted the story to Frank.

My sisters had talked me into going out, and Lou had walked into the bar. Too shy to talk to him, I'd hovered nearby as he chatted with my sisters and their friends. He caught me staring at him and I blushed, then retreated to the jukebox and pretended to pick some songs.

Staring at the choices but not seeing them, I became aware someone was talking to me. I ignored them, hoping they'd go away, but then looked up and it was Lou. He was talking to me. I gave a smile and nod, having not heard a thing he'd said. We picked some songs together and that was that. We were together the rest of the evening.

Wanting to escape the crowds, we found our friends and told them we were leaving. Then we hopped into Lou's car, drove to his nearby neighborhood, past his house, winding up at the elementary school. It was one of those summer nights I dream of each winter, crickets serenading while a warm breeze wrapped itself around us, and the moon lit our way. He led me down one of the trails, and I shyly jammed my hands into my pockets. He said something like "This is a steep hill, you may want to have your hands out in case you fall." Not exactly a smooth line, but it made me smile. Out came my hands and he grabbed my right hand in his left.

Perfection.

We strolled around laughing and swapping stories, and I finally understood what people were talking about when they spoke of moments where time stood still.

Eventually, we wound up outside his house. I was sitting on his car, he was standing in front of me while we talked, and he'd kissed me. What am I doing? I thought. *No way is this going to end well for me. I will probably never hear from him again.* But I ignored these thoughts and took a leap of faith. Best decision I ever made.

But that was literally a lifetime ago. Now, the procession crawled by and Frank was distracting me with idle chatter. He succeeded in getting me to joke with him, and our driver joined in. Giving in to the laughter allowed me to deny my actual feelings. It was a momentary reprieve and I was grateful, because we'd turned onto Lou's street, and every mailbox had a purple and yellow ribbon on it. We passed Lou's house and I didn't look. This was all so unreal. I joked that Lou's mom was trying to kill *me*, too. Maybe we should have started this procession last week in order to make it to the church on time. And so it went all the way to the church. Fits of laughter and tears. *Maybe I'm finally going crazy.*

Along the way we passed people going about their days. Everybody looked. Some looked quickly away and carried on with their business. Some, though, did not. I saw people stop and bow their heads. Others crossed themselves. One look out the window revealed a man whose deep black skin contrasted sharply against the body of the dark green tractor he drove. It seemed as out place to see that tractor on a normally busy road as it felt to be sitting in this procession of death. A straw hat rested on his gray hair, and as we slowly passed each other, I looked up to see him framed by a brilliant blue sky, looking down directly at me. He softly nodded his head, removing his hat and lowering his chin to his chest. The understanding on his face suggested to me he knew something about suffering, and his gaze imparted encouragement. I was strengthened by all those who acknowledged us that day, but in particular by that man.

Finally, we pulled up to the church. The same church we'd baptized Jeremy in. That had been a hectic day that had wreaked havoc on my meager organization skills. I was so flustered, it wasn't until after the Christening that I'd realized I'd put Jeremy's Christening outfit on inside–out. Lou laughed at me, and we all laughed together. Looking at the church now, I could barely remember how good it felt to be so happy.

Lost in my thoughts, I didn't notice the cameras until we stopped. Lots of cameras. It freaked me out. I got out the other side, away from them, and was surrounded by family. Trevor, Colin, and Sean were there. Colin was being held by his aunt. Sean leapt into my arms for a hug before I gave him back to his aunt.

I watched as the casket was unloaded. The funeral detail did their thing and we proceeded up the steps of the church. Standing in the back of the church, Frank offered his arm to me as I looked in at the throngs of people gazing back at us. It was like my wedding day with a sick twist. Instead of my father's arm it was my CAO's. Lou wasn't waiting at the other end of the aisle with a grin and a ring. He was being rolled in front of me in a casket. The casket—they took the drape off and I saw a set of tags dangling. I whimpered, and Frank whispered that they were not the real tags, just a copy. For some reason that helped. I had one arm on Frank. My other arm reached behind me, holding Trevor's hand, as the march up the aisle commenced. We neared the front, and I saw Siobhan there with her brother. I slid into the pew and gave her a hug. Family settled in around us. Father Eugene began the service. The boys rotated amongst us throughout the service. They didn't really understand what was happening. I couldn't fault them for that. I didn't understand much of it, either.

At one point a uniformed guy rushed up and handed Frank a note. Frank read it, his face paled, and he stuffed it into his pocket. I remembered his phone ringing as we arrived at the church. He'd hurriedly whispered to someone to "Fax it to the church." and I'd had no idea what he was talking about. From the shocked expression he wore I thought there was some kind of emergency. I leaned over and whispered, "What's wrong? Do you need to go?" He said no and I figured if something huge had happened, there is no way he'd still be sitting here. But something was definitely up. I couldn't imagine what it could be, and asked again "Do you need to go?" Again he said no. Whatever it was could obviously wait, so I refocused on the service. Lou's friend gave the eulogy, the pastor made a speech, and we rose to go. I took a last look at the Baptism Font where Lou and I had stood with our baby. There was the pew we sat in together, laughing at my careless job dressing Jeremy. Did any of that really happen? *Is this really happening?* We reached the end of the aisle and paused as they lifted the casket.

Once again, I noticed the cameras aimed directly at me. The panic flooded back and the trembling intensified. "Be strong" Frank said. Appreciative of his support but annoyed at the same time, I thought, *who the hell could possibly be strong right now? Are you out of your mind?* We headed down the stairs and Frank held tight until we reached our car, where he deposited me in the backseat. I avoided looking ahead at the hearse, looking instead at the cameras and reporters shooting in our direction, and flipping them the bird through tinted windows. They couldn't see me, but I felt better.

Frank got in and tried to distract me as we pulled away "I didn't know there are still Franciscan priests around," he said, motioning toward Father Eugene. "Apparently there's one," I snapped. Frank looked surprised and the driver stifled a laugh. I was wound tight. Frank tried again. He mentioned something about the Patriot Guard riders escorting us. I told him I didn't care if the freaking Teletubbies led the way, so long as we got the hell out of there. There was a second of surprised silence and then the three of us burst out laughing. Tension eased from my body as the sluggish ride to the cemetery got under way. I could just make out the flags whipping in the breeze as the veterans in the Patriot Guard, maneuvering their motorcycles into position in front of us, set the pace.

We passed the development where I grew up and my parents still lived. In the distance, I saw four Apache helicopters hovering, ready to fly by in the missing–man formation. There was the park Lou and I took the boys to play in. And there, directly across the street, was the Veteran's Cemetery. Another mile–high flag was hanging and more firemen stood at attention.

I was numb now. Earlier, I had told Major Reilly and Frank that I was worried about fainting at the cemetery. I told them that if they saw me start to go down they had two options; catch me so my kids wouldn't see me faint, or point and laugh if I fell so my kids would think it was a joke. We pulled up behind the hearse. Saw a tent set up with chairs underneath. The presence of chairs at least would allow me to sit, and not worry about keeling over in public again. Frank motioned me to come on out. Tired of all this ceremony, I whined that I'd prefer to wait until they carry the casket out and had it all set up. I didn't want to watch them position my husband's coffin over his grave. Frank said something like, "They're doing this for you," and I thought what a joke that was. I didn't want any of this and neither had Lou. He'd wanted a cremation and an Irish wake with drinks, stories, and laughter, not trumpets and tears. I considered arguing but figured it was easier to just be a good widow, and obediently took my place.

The boys were curious, walking up to their dad's grave and leaning over for a peek. I jumped up and grabbed them so they wouldn't fall in. Colin walked around hugging whomever seemed the saddest. Trevor was parked up front next to his cousin Alex. Lou's parents were beside me. Sean rotated laps. I focused on not vomiting. The funeral detail carried Lou's casket up and I watched them struggling with its weight over the open grave. I pictured Lou's body sliding around in it and wanted to scream. Beg them to stop. Wondered why I got out of the car to watch this.

The service began and one stranger after another presented me with a medal I didn't want. The one medal I would have liked to have, the Purple Heart, was not presented. Figuring someone just forgot it, I made a note to myself to find out later who had Lou's Purple Heart. Since he was killed in a war zone, I assumed he merited the award.

Each presentation was another nail in Lou's coffin. My boys received dog tags, and Trevor gave a set to Lou's dad. Seven guns fired three times. In the movies, the widow always jumps at this part. I broke role and just closed my eyes. The helicopters flew over and the boys ran out to watch, Seanie lagging behind and almost missing it. An officer knelt down and helped Sean in place just in time.

"Look, Mom!" Seanie yelled. "Dad is in the big one! They're taking him all the way up to heaven!" I thought I might pass out after all. I caught Frank's eye and he looked the same. "That's right, Seanie," I said, "Daddy is going up to heaven."

Major Reilly was in front of us with another soldier holding a folded flag. *Oh no*, I thought, remembering Lou telling me about his experience presenting the flag. "Duty!" the Major said as he slipped a bullet into the flag. "Honor!" his voice cracked and another bullet went into the flag. "Country!"

The Major walked over to me, and my eyes burned with tears. He leaned in with the flag. I looked up into his eyes and nodded. He nodded back and delivered the flag. Another flag was presented to Lou's parents. TAPS played. It was done. I walked over to the gathered uniforms and shook their hands. Thanked them. People dispersed.

I was ready to get out of there. Away from this. Frank coaxed me to walk by the casket "one last time" so I did, empty inside. I spotted the car and made a beeline for it. People were still milling about but it was peaceful, insulated, in the car. I saw Frank chatting outside and settled in, sure he'd join me in a minute and we could go to Silent Farm for the after–gathering. Lou and I had a lot of great times at that bed and breakfast on an eighty–acre working horse farm, and the owners, John and Mary, were good friends. I was looking forward to a visit and a cocktail or three. But first I needed Frank and what was taking him so long? Our driver asked if I wanted to go and I said yes. He popped out, talked to Frank, and got back in. Frank settled in next to me. Said there'd been a development and he could read me the letter he had been given in church. I asked him if I could just read it myself instead, and he handed it over. My jaw dropped in disbelief as I read an American soldier had been arrested for homicide. It wasn't an Iraqi, after all. Lou and Phil were murdered by *one of us*. This had to be a mistake.

I said I'd tell Lou's parents and we slid back out of the car. *Which one are they in?* I wondered as I gazed at the row of black cars behind us. After a moment, I saw them standing by their vehicle and went to them. Handed Lou's dad the note and promptly crumpled. Major Reilly happened to be the lucky person standing next to me, and had the honors of me crumpling into him. Lou's dad said something like, "I kind of expected this" and he sounded so calm. I felt like an idiot. I didn't know what to feel anymore, so I just hurried back to the car. We drove out, under the giant flag and past the firemen.

Grateful to have arrived at Silent Farm, I basked in the therapeutic presence of the horses, reminisced about Lou, and got down a couple of cocktails before my sister drove the boys and me home. My family took turns staying with me. I was terrified I'd never be ready to be on my own with the boys. The past week had taken a severe toll on me, to put it mildly. One day I had a husband I loved and a great future. Now my husband was dead, murdered by an American soldier. This was national news. Lou's face had been broadcast on CNN and the major networks. I'd held a press conference in my front yard. Our family was hurting beyond belief. I still could neither eat nor sleep, and had begun turning to alcohol for escape. I was unable to care for my children myself. I'd lost all hope and all I truly wanted was to die. Just leave this hell, for surely whatever waited for me on the other side could not be worse than this. But dying was not an option for me. Lou and I loved our boys as intensely as we loved each other. I could never do anything to hurt them. They needed me now more desperately than they ever had before. That night I looked down at my fistful of pills and knew they were not the answer. But what was? Would I be able to find my way through this and be the mother my boys deserved? I needed help—someone who has helped others through where I am now. I need someone who could steer me through this so I could function again.

I got a call on Friday, announcing the counselor I'd been requesting would be arriving. Chaplain Elaine Henderson made her way to me that weekend and was responsible for turning me around. Helping me confront our loss and work through the pain.

After Elaine's visit, I got my kids into their p.j.'s and put them to bed, thinking of Lou reading them their favorite, *Good Night, Moon*. How I loved to sneak up the stairs and watch him. The boys would be on his lap and snuggled into him. Friday nights, if we'd scored a sitter, we'd go out. If not, we would sit at our kitchen table with candlelight, cocktails, and a game of Scrabble. To make it interesting, we would sometimes play "dirty" Scrabble, where foul or offensive words scored double. It would be time for us to savor being together and catch up on our lives. That's what we did his last night home. I couldn't believe we'd never do that again.

I kissed the boys and spent extra time with them that night. There were questions and tears. When I looked into my little boys' faces and listened to them crying for Daddy, my pulse quickened and I was filled with a level of hatred I'd never experienced before. The kind that consumed me, and it was all for Alberto Martinez.

CHAPTER FIVE

FROM MRS. TO MS.

✪ ✪ ✪

The next few weeks were a flurry of events. There was paperwork to be done. Procedures to follow. Frank was extremely thorough and it was easy to allow him to guide me through this. I was so tired and apathetic that I didn't even pay much attention. The first time I signed my name under the word Widow I was choking on tears. It didn't get any better. I felt as though each paper I signed cast me deeper into hell, farther away from Lou.

One day, Lou's Casualty Report arrived. The one page paper for Allen, Louis Edwin, prepared by the Department of the Army in Alexandria, Virginia, listed Lou's status as deceased and the type of incident as non–hostile. That got me going. How can a claymore mine and three hand grenades be deemed non–hostile? It was that non–hostile status which rendered Lou ineligible for the Purple Heart. I could not accept that status, and have been fighting to remedy it ever since that day.

The report also stated Lou's Religious Preference as Baptist. We are Catholic. Lou's parents sent an official request to change the non–hostile status (denied) and the Baptist listing (granted). Next, I had to go to different places to sign various papers. One set of papers required a trip to a branch of the funeral home Lou's service was held in to sign off on the funeral. Frank arrived promptly as always. And he came bearing gifts: He was carrying the display items from the service. As a consolation prize I am now the proud owner of a shiny silver sword, gleaming black boots, and a cavalry hat—none of which were Lou's.

I winced when I saw the stuff and Frank looked apologetic. Then he brandished the sword and said something obnoxious that forced a laugh from me. We stowed the items in Lou's military cabinet in the garage, and set out on our errands. Arriving at the funeral home, I drew upon all my strength to block out the sickening smell of death and flowers, signed the papers, and wondered again when this would end. I wanted our lives back. With the funeral parlor mission completed, Frank and I planned our next adventure to meet the West Point Victim Witness Liaison, and said good bye.

A day off from the widow process provided an opportunity to take the boys to Silent Farm. After a long day outside and a pizza dinner, the kids were ready for bed when I settled the three big guys in the same room.

Minutes ago I had been sitting with three seemingly carefree, happy little farm boys. Sitting with me now were three lost little souls with humongous eyes and a stream of questions;

Why did daddy go to Iraq?

If something bad happens to you, who will take care of us?

Was it a knife in the back, or a bullet?

Why didn't daddy run?

You're not going to join the army, are you mom?

I'd lulled myself into believing they had somehow come to terms with their dad's death on their own, but this new wave of questions proved otherwise, and I was glad I'd found a grief therapist for them to start seeing the following week. Finally, tapped of answers to their questions, I gave up and let them watch Cartoon Network until they fell asleep.

I still had details to take care of. Widow Work. The kids stayed with a sitter each day as Frank whisked me away for these procedures. First order of events, Widow I.D. A reverse process of what I'd done only three months ago with Lou. Now instead of getting my Active Duty Spouse ID, I was with my CAO getting a card identifying me as a widow. Today it was the same drive, same building. It was warm out but I was still freezing as Frank parked the car. Nausea swelling within me, I walked to the door as my CAO—not my husband—adjusted his beret. Down the hall, winding up in front of the chair Lou had sat in playing his phone. Closing my eyes, I visualized him there. The friendly ID guy I remembered from three months ago was chatting away as Frank filled him in. I sat on the same stool, looking to the spot Lou stood last time. He wasn't there smiling at me now. In his spot was Frank, trying his hardest to shoot me a reassuring look.

Finally done, I grabbed my depressing new ID, still warm, and got out of there without looking at it or thanking the ID guy. Made my way back to the car, annoyed that I was shaking again. Frank slid in, looking almost as miserable as I. "You sure know how to show a widow a good time," I teased. We laughed and my nerves began to unwind as he drove me home.

Next mission: JAG office. New WILL. Back to West Point, into a gray stone building, past some plebes being instructed outside. In and up through dreary halls until we reached the JAG office. The lawyer, a kind faced man, looked at Frank and told him to wait outside. The lawyer explained the will procedure and I signed the appropriate places, designating family members as guardians for my children in the event I died, too. We called Frank back in. "Okay Frank, it's official," I said. "If something happens to me, you get my boys." It was the second time I thought he might pass out, and it amused me. Good times.

●   ●   ●   ●   ●

Late one night, the boys were asleep and my quiet time had commenced. Siobhan called and we began our ritual of talking over what we knew. At some point she mentioned that Martinez was the supply sergeant. Hearing the words "Martinez" and "supply sergeant" together brought things into focus for me. In that moment, I knew what had happened. "Lou told me about this guy!" I tripped over my words, spewing out what I knew to Siobhan. "He said the supply guy was doing a terrible job." I explained he was being replaced and disciplined. The supply room was a mess. No one could find anything. The guy was pissed because he was going to be screwed professionally. I shared with Siobhan how Lou had told me, "Oh, yeah, he's f— pissed. It's a really big deal."

I confessed my guilt over not paying more attention when Lou told me about this. How I'd shrugged it off. Did Lou tell me the guy's name? asked Siobhan. Probably. Can I remember? No. I felt as though I let Lou down. If only… But rationally, I know it wouldn't have mattered how much Lou told me. No one could have foreseen this, Siobhan assured me.

Siobhan then told me of her day. She'd met with an agent from the Criminal Investigation Command (CID) at West Point. She received bits of information and learned about the procedures involved in an investigation of this magnitude. I hadn't even thought of doing that yet. But now I could think of nothing other than getting myself there tomorrow with this information and finding out if it corresponded with any information they had. After a lengthy conversation, Siobhan and I said good night, realizing there would be no sleep for either of us. I paced the driveway for a couple of hours. Cassie used to follow me but now she halfheartedly wandered around before lying down to watch me. I was a jumble of nerves and thankful the weather allowed me to spend these sleepless hours outside. It was another warm, clear night. Just like the summer we met. I looked up at the stars and talked to Lou, "You told me about him! Why didn't you know he would do this?! Why did you let this happen?! How could you let him take you from us?!" I was irrationally furious at Lou for not being able to see this coming. Not sensing the danger right before him.

I was beside myself with the need to get to CID. Do they know this? Is this the reason Martinez killed Lou and Phil—because they were working toward having him removed? I could not accept that. What kind of person blows up two human beings over a job? None of it made sense. I continued my crazed pacing. Desperate for the sun to come up, for people to get to work, so I could call Frank and get in to CID.

Later that morning, I'd finally gotten through to the CID agent handling the parts of the case in New York, and was en route to West Point for a meeting. With me was my father–in–law, whom I'd asked to come. Agent John Sweeger had been surprised to hear from me, but assured me he would be happy to discuss my concerns.

Pacing in the miniscule CID waiting area I organized my thoughts and mentally prepared myself for the meeting. Before long a dark–haired head peeked out of the doorway. Agent Lake explained he worked with Agent Sweeger and could take some information from us while we waited, if we'd like. Seated next to my father–in–law I locked on to the agent across the desk from us and launched into what I knew. I laid out everything—my conversation with Lou about the supply sergeant who was being replaced, how pissed the guy was, everything I could remember. Lake listened attentively, surrounded by photos of him and his wife laughing on their wedding day. He suggested I make an official statement about what I knew, so I went through it again while he typed, then reviewed the printout he handed me. Just then the door nudged open and a stocky, smooth–pated man joined the meeting. Agent John Sweeger introduced himself while Agent Lake filled him in. I signed the statement and handed it back, then waited as Agent Sweeger read it. He told me there was a chance the prosecution would ask me to testify to this, which would exclude me from being present at all or part of the trial. Outstanding.

Now Lou's dad and I started with the questions: When will we know about a trial? What is the next step? Can we talk with the surgeon, Colonel Sullivan, again? Did anyone see Martinez do this? Did Lou say anything about what happened before he lost consciousness? How do we get access to the records when the trial is over? Who is running this investigation and when will we speak with them? When do we speak with the prosecutors?

Neither CID man could answer our questions. They nodded at the appropriate times and offered "Yes, ma'am" and "Yes, sir" throughout the meeting. Their expressions serious, they assured us this was the top case in the U.S. military. It was an absolute priority, and they would personally follow through on all of our questions and concerns. They were so sorry for our pain and would be in touch with us the moment they learn anything. We bought it. At least I did. I naively believed I accomplished something by going there that day.

Our families' need to learn the truth about what happened, how it happened, and what to expect from here seemed to be matched by the government's determination to pick and choose what we were told. We'd been as patient as possible waiting for the government to unscramble the details and share them with us. But after the initial announcements of a criminal investigation and an arrest, we'd heard nothing. A gag order had been imposed on the FOB, and contact with our families was forbidden. Even the prosecutors were subject to this order.

By early July, we'd run out of patience and the first shreds of doubt in the government's sincerity began to seep into our minds. Emails and phone calls we made to military officials were met with platitudes and party lines. Eventually, the command in Iraq grew weary of placating us, and communication shut down entirely. In response to the wall of silence, Siobhan began contacting her political representatives while I reached out to military officials in NY. Frank put me in touch with Colonel Fanning, the Public Affairs Officer for the NY National Guard, to help me deal with the unfamiliar world of the media. Colonel Fanning would also be privy to any press releases and act as a backup source of information should the government fail to inform us of events before informing the media.

One of my earliest meetings was with General MacGuire, the Vice Adjutant General of the NYS National Guard. Frank and I spent almost two hours discussing the case with the General, who promised to look into our concerns and offer what help he could. A couple weeks later, I followed up on that meeting with a second meeting, this time with Colonel Ashley, the General's JAG officer and right hand man. Lou's parents joined Frank and me for what turned out to be a review of what we already knew, as opposed to a path for further information. When the pale–faced, gray–haired Colonel had insulted our intelligence enough with his insincere platitudes and ill–concealed agitation over our impertinent need for answers, I let loose. I told him I could not imagine why he was not interested in remedying the mistakes in the system that allowed Martinez to kill Lou and Phil. I asked him why he wasn't concerned with helping us learn the truth about any black market dealings we'd heard Martinez and others were involved in. Why wasn't he angry at the lack of character in any NY National Guard member. Practically hissing at him, I told him he should want to combat the stain this placed on the NY Guard, in particular the 42nd, with a public campaign to raise the standards for these soldiers instead of turning a blind eye to all the soldiers like Martinez who were entrenched in its ranks. At that point, the meeting was abruptly concluded.

•   •   •   •   •

July 20th. What had previously been a special triple birthday shared by Lou, Sean, and Lou's dad, had now become just another event to survive. The stress of the day was compounded by a call from a friend saying she'd heard a radio report about a date being set for the Article 32. Similar to a civilian grand jury hearing, this would be the next step necessary in the process of proffering official charges against Martinez. This was the first I had heard of anything like that and I was annoyed we hadn't been informed before the media. I called John Sweeger, whose receptionist told me he was in a meeting. I then called Colonel Fanning, Frank, General MacGuire, and the Victim Witness Liaison from West Point. No one had heard of any such announcement. John Sweeger called back. What a coincidence, he said. He was "just about to call me." He had been in a meeting with Siobhan. First he assured me that there was not yet a date set for the 32. Next he told me he had been contacted by a Lieutenant Colonel Meg Foreman. She was the lead prosecutor on the case. She had emailed John and asked him to pass along her contact information to Siobhan and me. A letter providing this information was in the mail to each of us, but in her email Meg offered to contact us immediately if we liked. Until now, she had not been granted authorization to do so.

Sweeger continued, saying Colonel Foreman had also answered some of my questions. He said he could forward the email to me or I could meet with him. I asked him to just read it to me. My request was met with a brief pause, laden with the weight of heavy silence. I thought I heard a sigh, and knew what I was about to hear would be worse than I'd prepared for. Slowly, Agent Sweeger's wavering voice relayed the contents of the email.

According to people who were with Lou immediately after the "incident" and stayed with him until he died, Lou had not only been speaking about the boys and me but had expressed feelings of guilt over going to Iraq and sadness about never seeing us again.

I sat down on the grass and tried to take long, deep breaths, anxious to avoid another embarrassing collapse. On the other end of the line, the agent was apologizing for delivering this news over the phone. He continued with more witness statements saying that Lou consistently spoke of his wife and children. This confirmation of his love for me was a mixed blessing. It was at once comforting to know that even under such circumstances he was worrying about us and missing us, while it also rammed home the amount of love we had lost.

What I wouldn't have done to be there with him, holding his hand and talking with him in those moments. I asked Sweeger to email me this information, then hung up and walked inside, past Lou's family and up the stairs to the computer. I logged on but could not access my email. Explaining to everyone that I needed to go home to get something, I made the short drive and was soon holding a copy of the email in my hands. As I read I noticed the date, July 15th. *You have got to be kidding me*, I thought. CID had received the email five days earlier. My steady calls and requests for information about who the prosecutors were, and further details about what Lou talked about as he was dying, left no room to doubt how anxious I was for word from Iraq. Yet for whatever reason, Agent Sweeger had chosen not to share it with me until I called. That's it. I now detested West Point CID. Years later, I would come to realize that Agent Sweeger was far from the inept individual I pegged him as, but for now I let my emotions prevail over logic.

Back at the house, Seanie was waiting to blow out candles on his cake, convinced he wouldn't turn four until then. Ending his wait, I imagined Lou by his side, blowing out the candles together. Sean's grin flashed through the tiny smoke stream from the candles as he happily yelled, "Now I'm four!" I squished him in for a hug before his presents were opened, and then I shared the contents of the email with Lou's parents.

My phone rang as I walked back outside. The weak connection full of static drowned out the woman's voice as she told me her name. Then the static cleared and I heard her say she was from the 101st Airborne Division. "Who?" I asked. "How are you involved in this?" And she explained again. This time the information sank in. It was Terri Seifert. I had requested to speak with her if she was willing. Her husband, Chris, had also served with the military. In the initial days of the war, he was deployed to Iraq. While in Kuwait awaiting orders to cross the border, Chris and another soldier were murdered by Hasan Akbar, an American soldier serving with them. A traitor. It had been national news, and Lou and I had followed the story and trial. We were stunned that someone would do this. Akbar had recently been found guilty and sentenced to death. Who better than Terri, I'd thought, to speak to about what I was now going through? But I hadn't held out much hope that she would call. We spent over an hour talking. United in our experiences. We were laughing and crying, able to speak to each other about things we were unable to say to others. Her call turned my day around, and our ensuing friendship has been a blessing to me.

That night, I read the email from Colonel Foreman again, paying closer attention to things I'd skimmed over earlier, and noticing a comment about one of Lou's friends, a Captain Steven Raiser, who wanted to mail some items to me. I made a mental note to find out more about this guy. The next night, I sent an email to the prosecutor. I thanked her for contacting me. Told her how destroyed I was. Begged her to help us find the answers our families needed. My inbox held a response from her the next morning. She informed me she had just been given permission to contact us, and gave me a brief glimpse of her background. A West Point graduate like Phillip, she had been in the Army for seventeen years and was attached to the 42nd for this deployment. There were two other prosecutors on board. Captain David State had volunteered to remain on active duty past redeployment in order to try the case, and Captain Rob McGovern, an active duty judge advocate normally stationed at Fort Bragg but currently prosecuting detainee abuse cases in Baghdad. Captain McGovern had been one of the prosecutors in the Akbar case. The combination of experience among these three and their seeming dedication to this case alleviated some of my concerns. I added a call to Terri Seifert to my list of things to do, figuring she could give me the skinny on Captain McGovern.

Meg Foreman offered me a meeting with her and David State upon their return, and promised to answer any questions we might have. Then she delved again into more sensitive details about Lou's last hours. How he had been talking only about the boys and me, and had no idea who had gotten him. The rest of her letter mentioned Steven Raiser, and that he had become close to Lou at Fort Drum. That she had provided him my address so he could mail some things to me. That answered my question about him without my having to ask, so I crossed him off my to–do list. Finally, she expressed that the focus of everyone involved was, "to ensure a just result to something that can never be made right. We will make some right of it in the sense of giving our all to Lou and Phil's memory: please rest assured at least with that knowledge." She signed her letter with an informal, "Meg Foreman."

This was the most forthright, down to earth communication I had received from anyone up to this point. There was no tiptoeing around difficult topics. No patronizing condolences. No reluctance to recognize our rights and need for information, and the most assurance I had received that this case was in capable hands. I appreciated her dropping all formalities and talking to me like a person, and opening the door for further discussion. She continued corresponding with me, filling me in on what to expect legally, and reassuring me the case was being investigated thoroughly. Our emails became more and more familiar, and Meg gradually grew into a confidante.

The next order of business was moving into the home I'd decided to rent, closer to my family. Which meant I had to pack up our Milford home. Box up our lives and walk away from the life that had been taken from us. I will never forget the agonizing process of taking Lou's clothes from the closet and placing them in labeled boxes to be stored or given away. Peeling the Scooby Doo stickers from the boys' walls and remembering how they'd laughed while putting them up with Lou. Taking down our wedding pictures, the fridge magnets, removing all the things that created a home and personified our family, packing away our dreams.

My family set up the new house while I headed over to Silent Farm. The once–cozy cottage we'd inhabited for a few weeks now looked like a crime scene. My boys and I had managed to thoroughly trash the place. Short on time, I gathered what I could while casting a guilty look at the blinds Jeremy pulled down, the red stain on the carpet, and promised Mary I'd return to finish cleaning. Before long the truck was empty, boxes unpacked, and the house resembled a home. Lunch was grabbed on the fly, clothes put away, the kitchen unpacked, and the boys were here. Time for our new lives.

The boys and I joined my family at the New Jersey shore that last week in July. I'd booked it last year and found no excuse not to go. The kids deserved the chance to have some fun. It was a difficult week for me, with highs and lows. Taking Trevor on his first log flume was a moment I will always cherish. Watching Trevor, Colin and Sean revel in the waves and cover themselves with sand while laughing at Jeremy's refusal to set foot on the beach at all, nudged me back into life. But then one night in our room, as I lay surrounded by slumbering boys, I heard Jeremy giggling in his playpen. Thinking he was waking up, I leaned over the top for a peek. The giggling came harder, louder, as if he were being tickled. But his eyes were still shut and I realized he was still sleeping. *Must be having a good dream,* I was thinking, and then he yelled "Daddy!" My breath caught, thinking I'd imagined it. But again he called out his dad's name in the midst of his giggling. I wanted to believe it was real—that Lou had somehow managed to be there in that room with us, experiencing the joy of tickling his son. That Jeremy was feeling his dad, and laughing with him. Who wouldn't want to believe that? I spent the rest of that night pondering the mysteries of life, and wishing for some answers to mine.

I returned from the shore with a knot of apprehension; I would be getting Lou's personal effects back in a couple of days. Knowing that is what I would be returning to had hung over me.

Frank had mentioned Lou's thing would be processed at JPED (Joint Personal Effects Depot) in Aberdeen, Maryland. It's where all the items belonging to killed soldiers are processed before being returned to the families. Part of the procedure involves dry cleaning all of his clothes and converting any money into a check. I freaked out over this. My husband is gone. I will never again feel his arms around me, turn my face into him, and inhale his scent. But I could, if given the chance, press my face into his t–shirts or sheets and perhaps be given a final gift of smelling him—feeling him, one last time. No one has the right to take that from me. How dare they try to erase him? Imagine trying to make the Army understand this.

The Army, although comprised of human beings, is essentially one giant body that functions solely by procedure. Any deviation from this procedure, no matter how slight, is cause for alarm. Now here I was trying to get this giant body to pretty please give me back my husband's things dirty. Don't clean them. Don't take money he handled and replace it with a cold check. Don't dehumanize the man I love, the father of my children. He lived. He was a Person. He laughed and cried, smiled and loved. Please recognize that. Let me have this one last piece of him now. Please.

It took an extraordinary combined effort between myself, Frank, and a couple of colonels and generals. We huffed and we puffed, and ultimately I was told that the procedure had been halted. We had won this one small victory. I was at once elated and disgusted.

Tucking the boys in the night before the scheduled delivery took extra strength. Evenings were difficult enough, because as soon as the sun began to dip in the sky and the soft rays of twilight emerged, Trevor suffered anxiety attacks. He would weep and talk about how sunsets made him think of Daddy's soul leaving and going to heaven. It had gotten so bad that I now ushered the kids inside each day well before twilight, closed the curtains to our spectacular view of the sunset, and distracted them all for the hour or so it took to pass through that time of day. Finally succeeding in that evening's ritual, I checked on the sleeping kids and breathed a sigh of relief. Then I came apart.

Curled up on the couch, I remembered going to Siobhan's the day Phil's trunks arrived. How impersonal those two black trunks had seemed, how sad Siobhan had been. Then I thought of Lou's things—strangers had handled them, poked through them, folded them into neat piles and labeled each and every item. Big black trunks with silver latches. I imagined touching the trunks, opening them, and being confronted with the coldly placed belongings that were once important to my husband. Uniforms, things he needed to perform his duties, and things he had taken to keep a slice of home with him. I was embarrassed to know that the softly naughty self–portraits I sent with him had been seen by others. Lou had asked me, each time he'd reported somewhere, to send him with pictures like these. I always refused. But I had made an exception this time. He was going to war for an undetermined amount of time. I thought it would make him laugh to be surprised with these pictures. And it had. We laughed about it together. I had made a card and I wrote on it that if he let anyone else see these pictures, I would break every bone in his body. The joke didn't seem so funny now.

I asked Frank who goes through the boxes. He said once they arrive, he has to go through them to be sure each item is accounted for. I said to him "Hey, Frank. Do *not* go through the boxes, or you and I will never be able to look each other in the eye again." He paused for a moment and then comprehension dawned on his face. He shook his head. Said, "Oh, you didn't! But, yes, of course you did. You are killing me, you know?" And then he promised he would not look at any pictures.

I sat in total darkness, hoping the sleeping pill would kick in, that I would get some rest. But as the night dragged on it became apparent that sleep was not in my immediate future. Instead I was seized by the dread of those trunks and the finality they signified. *Will I be able to smell him? Will I be able to stand the sight of his things coming back instead of him? Do I ask Frank to stay with me or do I wait until he goes?* As these thoughts and emotions swirled through my stressed system I was again overloaded. I had what I can only describe as the mother of all anxiety attacks. I couldn't draw air past the ton of weight I felt on my chest. Gasping for breath, each taste of air seemed to sear my lungs. Blackness toyed with my vision and tortured me with the hint of escape, only to be replaced by the blinding light of consciousness. *Get a grip*, I tried to tell myself. But I was not strong enough. If I could stand, I would have called someone—anyone to come over and stay with me. But my limbs were tingling with the effects of hyperventilation and I worried that if I tried to stand, I might pass out. Finally, the episode subsided. The panic, fear, revulsion, and dread receded and were replaced by an enormous sense of sadness. My breathing returned to normal. The sweat dried and I was cold instead of hot. *Sadness is familiar. I can deal with sadness*, I told myself.

It was almost 4 A.M. I hit the shower and stayed in there until I was on the verge of blistering from the heat. I had a little quiet time to gather myself. Then the boys got up and were on their way to spend the day and have a sleepover with one of my friends.

It was another tauntingly gorgeous day. I pulled up a chair in the sunshine and tried to relax while I waited for Frank. On the plus side, my breakdown the night before had left me emotionally cleansed, I guess. So I was feeling fairly confident that I would be somewhat okay for this shitty visit today. Other than clammy palms, I was not feeling so bad. Now it was more a matter of grim resolve to get this done and put the experience behind me. Cross off one more procedure I have survived.

When Frank arrived, we spent a few minutes catching up before he began working on my computer, trying to fix something for me. I alternated between hanging out with him and wandering outside, trying to bolster my courage and ask him to get Lou's things. On one of my trips out front, I strolled up to his car. There they were. Two ominous black trunks. I figured now was as good a time as any, so on an impulse, I opened the door and eased a trunk out. It was heavier than I'd expected, and I struggled to carry it up to the front door. Entered what I hoped was stealth mode as I snuck upstairs. Placed it on the wood floor. That's one. Back I went for the second and set it on the floor next to its twin.

I crouched down. Took a deep breath. *I can do this*, I told myself. I reached for the latch of one trunk, and realized it was secured by a plastic twisty tie. I looked for the scissors and couldn't find them, so opted for a large knife to hack away at the surprisingly resistant tie. Nothing was going to stop me now. In a moment, I was victorious and the latch was open. I set the knife down. One more breath. *Help me, God. Please.*

The lid was open and I was looking at Lou's things. They were indeed folded precisely and accompanied by an itemized list. Brown t–shirts. Under armor. Military stuff. I reached in and touched the clothes. Gently lifted them out to reach the next layer. Slowly, carefully, I began to sort through until I found his real clothes. Things I recognized. I raised his shirt to my face. Closed my eyes. Inhaled. *There you are, Lou! I have you now!* Mercifully, his scent brought only peace and strength, instead of the pain I'd feared. An affirmation to me that I didn't simply dream him. He was real and he did love me. I could feel him holding me again, one last time. Maybe all of this was really a combination of sleep deprivation and dementia, but I choose to believe it is real. I need to believe.

I opened the second trunk and lay my hands on his things. So familiar and yet so foreign. Could this really be all that was left of him, what his life came down to? Two trunks of disturbingly categorized personal effects? *No*, I told myself. He is more than this so long as I hold on to him. No matter what I wound up doing with the rest of my life I vowed at that moment to do in such a way as to honor Lou and make him proud. Looking down at his things that he carefully and thoughtfully packed, feeling his concern for us and his doubts about leaving, knowing the courage it took for him to go. I was so proud of him. I was so *mad* at him.

After emptying the trunks, I realized there were items missing. Personal items. Change or money he had on him, etc. The pictures. Where were these things? I looked again. Nope. Not there. I headed downstairs. Frank was still on the computer. "We are missing some things," I said. He didn't know what I was talking about. I told him the pictures didn't come back. Then he got it. "You got the trunks out without me?!" he asked. I told him it just felt like that was the way to go. He was laughing and shaking his head while he followed me upstairs. I showed him the trunks and he perused the lists. Where was his wallet, and his watch? This was the beginning of what would turn into a 3–month pursuit of the missing items. Frank got on the phone. Made some calls and put the search in motion.

I felt oddly lighter. Sleepless nights were nothing new, so the fatigue barely registered with me. My in–laws were on standby to come see Lou's things. Frank left and they came over, looking as anxious as I felt. The three of us sat and tried to comprehend the two trunks, and I left them alone to look through his things.

Later, I took his sheets that still held his scent and placed them in ziplocs, hoping to hang on to his presence as long as possible. A few of his favorite t–shirts went into my drawer. His fleece went in my closet with his beret, his dog tags on my dresser.

I spent most of that night outside. I could see the glow of a campfire from next door; the neighbor was hanging out in his backyard again. I had noticed him doing this on several occasions. Other than his four large and louder than life dogs, he was always alone. I wandered up to the backyard in the darkness and made an attempt to enjoy some peace. But I was detected by the dogs, who charged the fence barking at me. A shrill whistle from the neighbor and the pack turned away, blending back into the night, until I saw their silhouettes outlined by his fire. I wished that guy was friendly. It would be nice to have someone to pass these hours with. But I didn't linger there, afraid he would get annoyed at my intrusion. I returned to my front yard and left him to his backyard. Took up my familiar pacing route until I'd walked enough to settle my nerves and sack out on the couch for a while.

Tomorrow came and the boys returned. Life goes on.

CHAPTER SIX

LEARNING TO NAVIGATE THE MILITARY JUDICIAL SYSTEM

✪ ✪ ✪

August 26, more than two months since my doorbell rang, Frank drove me back to West Point. This time it was to meet the two prosecutors on the case. There had been some changes made to the team. Meg was still with us, but Captain John Benson had replaced Rob McGovern. Captain Benson had worked with Rob on the Akbar case. I didn't know much else about him, since all emails from him were clipped, terse. Terri told me she never got the "warm fuzzies" about him, unlike the comfortable rapport she'd developed with Rob. I didn't care so much about liking him as I did about his ability to win our case, and I was happy Meg was still a part of things.

Now Meg and Captain Benson were in from Iraq and awaited us in the small conference room. Siobhan briefed me on her meeting the day before, so I had an idea of what to expect. I arrived early, hoping to have some time alone with the two JAG officers before my in–laws arrived.

I entered the narrow room and saw the two prosecutors rising to greet me. Both small statured, dark haired, officers looked about as apprehensive as I was feeling. Focusing on Meg first, I shook her extended hand and told her it was good to meet her in person. Lively eyes contrasted with her tight dark hair and baleful expression as she took my hand. Turning to Captain Benson, I accepted his handshake, we nodded at each other as he introduced himself first to me and then to Frank, and we all took our seats.

We covered a range of topics in our meeting. By the time we left, I'd confirmed things I'd heard previously, gotten a glimpse into the people we were dealing with, and liked Meg even more than before. Captain Benson was hard to get a handle on. He'd appeared sincere, driven, and focused. He'd met my gaze without looking away as he listened and addressed my questions in what I'd interpreted as a forthright manner. But my overall impression was that Meg was driving this train.

We'd learned the prosecution was pursuing capital charges. We were waiting for the Article 32 Hearing to be scheduled. At this hearing the prosecution must prove to the Investigating Officer (IO) that enough evidence exists to proceed to court martial. The trick would be to accomplish that while presenting the barest minimum of evidence so as not to give away the case strategy to the defense. The IO, Colonel Patrick Reinert, would hear the evidence and make his recommendation to the Convening Authority, in this case General Vines, who would then make the final decision.

Neither Meg nor Captain Benson had any estimate of when the Article 32 would take place. I emphasized my need to be at every proceeding, regardless of the length or significance. My in-laws and Siobhan's family echoed these sentiments. Frustrated to learn the 32 would be in Iraq, we asked about establishing a video feed for the hearing to allow us to witness it. Meg and Captain Benson promised to look into it. Concerned about the two-year span it had taken to try and convict Akbar, we asked if we should be prepared for the same duration. Captain Benson cautioned us that he could not guarantee anything, but felt confident it would be done within a year.

Eventually, we were notified that the 32 was scheduled for late September. Once we confirmed it would be in Iraq we stepped up our pursuit of a live video feed at West Point. We wrote letters to anyone we thought might influence this effort. Congressmen and senators received pleas for help. The Army had denied the live feed, claiming it required too much broadband width and would compromise the military's efforts. Instead we were offered an audio feed. This was unacceptable.

Already disappointed at being denied the opportunity to attend the 32 in person, a live video feed was a compromise for us. The time difference meant we would arrive at West Point at midnight, sit in a conference room, and watch the proceedings on whatever size screen was in place. We felt we could glean some substance at least from that. But arranging to have us stare at a phone all night and rely on the sound quality of that connection was not an appropriate effort to afford us our right to witness the proceeding. No, thank you. We asked again. Denied again.

Siobhan went to her congressman and I went to the media. One day, Siobhan broke her public silence and did an interview with the network news stations. The following day,

I went to CNN studios in Manhattan and did an interview with Soledad O'Brien. Driving in to the city in the car sent by CNN, I could not believe this was my life.

Upon making it to CNN's floor in the building, I was hurried into the hair and makeup room. Two women swooped in on me and transformed me from a harried looking widow to a put together woman. I was expecting a call from Meg with an update on the 32 status, so I carried my phone with me and asked one of the camera crew men to let me know if it rang. Soledad came over and said hi. The petite, dark haired woman with a blinding smile and warm laugh gave off the air of a genuine, down to earth person and it was easy to talk with her about what was going on. I remember catching a glimpse of myself on the monitors during the interview and being unable to look away from the stranger I saw on screen. Thanks to the efforts of the women backstage, I didn't look half as bad as I felt. If I didn't know any better, I'd say the woman on that screen was fairly organized. Finally my spell was broken when someone noticed the distraction and turned the monitors off. I was smiling the whole time—nervously beaming like a madwoman.

The interview took only a few moments and I was on my way back to the car. We'd just pulled away when Meg called. I listened as she asked me how our families felt about a few matters. Did we want to meet with people who knew Lou and Phil? Were we still determined to attend every proceeding? How did we feel about the possibility of a plea deal in this case?

The question about the plea threw me off. I didn't know anything about plea bargains, and my knowledge of military law was limited to what I'd been told to expect in this case. I asked Meg if a plea had been offered. She replied no, but defense counsel was suggesting one may be forthcoming. I had some more questions. Would we be present for any court appearances involving the entering of a plea? Would we be able to speak with people who had been there? Would we find out everything that had happened? Meg could not guarantee me any of those things.

Coming on the heels of months of conflicting, misleading information, frustrated attempts to obtain solid answers to our questions, the unwillingness of the Army to provide a video feed, and the general consensus that things were being kept from us, I was extremely uncomfortable voicing support for a plea. I had been assured the case was ironclad, that it was only a matter of time before Martinez would be sentenced to death. I remembered Lou had been relieved when Akbar received the death penalty because he believed for one soldier to kill another was an act of treason and should be dealt with harshly. I had every reason to believe Martinez would and should receive the death penalty, too, and no reason to trust the government's intention to consider anything less.

I opposed the notion of a plea.

Uneasy about the conversation and now fearful of entrusting the Army to see this through, I knew the time had come for Siobhan and me to step it up. I called Frank and told him I was coming to see him at Camp Smith. "C'mon over" he said, "I'll be here and I can take you home later." I directed the driver over the Bear Mountain Bridge and to the gates of Camp Smith.

Our butts had barely touched our chairs in Frank's office when I said, "I need you to get me to Iraq." Smiling, he shook his head and said, "Of course you do." And we got into it. I explained the audio feed was unacceptable. We were not asking for anything other than to witness the proceedings against the traitor who murdered our husbands. We felt the Army deemed us a nuisance and wanted this entire case to be carried out quietly so as not to draw any negative attention to the military and this war. I had sent out an email to Meg saying that if the president wanted a live feed from FOB Danger, it would be a done deal. But since we were just civilians with no celebrity status or power of our own, our request was not worth the effort a VTC would require. So be it. Then we will go there. If the mountain won't go to Mohammed…

Frank was in a difficult position. Assigned specifically to represent my desires and needs to the Army, he had already been receiving calls about my past actions. The requests he was making on my behalf were extremely unpopular. Worried that he might bear the wrath of unhappy superiors, I apologized for this. He assured me it was okay—he was simply doing the duties that fall within CAO parameters. I teased him that he would either be a private or the president when I was done with him, and we both laughed as he set about drafting my request in email form. I read the final version stating my desire to travel to Iraq to witness the Article 32 Hearing. Siobhan was included in this request. Frank pulled up a list of contacts and clicked away. It wasn't long before his phone began to ring. He calmly took each call and explained that the widows were requesting assistance in a trip to Iraq for the 32 Hearing. Seemed we'd created quite an uproar. Good.

We spent a couple of hours in Frank's office talking through this. Not overly optimistic that the Army would send us to Iraq, I enacted a backup plan. My sister Janice is a full time teacher and part time travel agent. I called and asked her to look into commercial flights for us. I was now hell bent on being there. I needed to be there, look the traitor in the eye, and conquer that dread hanging over me. If the Army thought we would sit back and trust in them, they were mistaken. We did that once and now our husbands were dead. Not likely that we would do it again.

After tucking the boys in that night, I planned the following day with Siobhan. My CNN interview was scheduled to air in the morning. Then Siobhan and I were meeting with Congressman Ingalls and Senator Morahan in Rockland County. They'd called a press conference to announce their support of our request to either watch a live feed of the hearing, or travel to Iraq for the Article 32.

My attempt to watch the CNN piece in the morning was thwarted when Jeremy walked in, whipped off his diaper, and peed on the floor in front of me. He found this to be far funnier than I did, and I was grumbling as I cleaned up the mess. The babysitter handed me the phone I hadn't heard ring, and Siobhan was speaking to me. One of the things we discussed the day before was the possibility that we would be required to have shots for a trip to Iraq. Phil's mom had called a friend who works at a hospital. Free vaccines were available to us that morning. The appointment was in one hour. It is a good forty–five minute drive from here and I was not showered or dressed. But the 32 Hearing was scheduled for three days from now in Iraq. If we succeeded with our request, we would be on a plane that night. Unsure if the shots were necessary, we nevertheless didn't want to provide an ounce of an excuse for the government to deny us. I put myself together as quickly and as best as I could. Kissed the boys good bye and off I went. I arrived at the hospital with Siobhan and we walked in together. I hadn't known Siobhan has an issue with needles. The shots were an ordeal for her. When I saw her struggling with this I was newly angry that we had been placed in this position. Why couldn't we be "normal" Iraq widows who bury their husbands and focus on grieving, putting their lives back together? Why did this have to happen?

As we began the shots, Siobhan mentioned that the congressman had contacted her earlier with news. Once the shots had been done, we thanked the woman and headed to the parking lot. We had one hour before the press conference. My phone rang and it was Meg, relieved she'd caught me before I got on a plane. The 32 had been delayed, she reported. Martinez fired his attorneys and would now have time to acquaint himself with new attorneys. Siobhan then told me that was the news the congressmen shared with her, as well.

Initially disappointed, I soon realized the delay was in our favor because it allowed more time for visas and paperwork to be done. We now stood a better chance of attending. Meeting the congressman and senator at the designated spot for the press conference, we discussed the news and decided to proceed anyway. Our goal was to make it extremely difficult for the Army to deny our request. How ridiculous it seemed to have to go to these extremes, but we had no choice. It was our right to be present and we were exercising that right. Our beef was not with the Army as a whole but rather with the handful of people in the system standing in our way.

The press conference was respectably attended. At its conclusion, we thanked the congressman and senator again and I drove Siobhan back to her in–laws' house. With a smile and assurances to each other that we were doing the right thing, we said good bye and I drove off.

I stopped at Lou's parents' house to fill them in on the shots, the news from Iraq, and the press conference. Lou's dad told me he planned on submitting his own request to attend the hearing. He would work with Representative Sue Kelly on that end. One of the awkward things about this whole mess was that Lou's parents and I had to work as two separate parties. I was on the widow team and they were on the parent team. The military officially recognizes only one next of kin. In this case that is me. Whoever is named in the records, as the soldier's PNOK is the one accorded all the benefits. Everyone else is more or less dependent on their relationship with that person. For example, had I told my CAO that I didn't want any of Lou's family present at the services, they would most likely have been excluded and forced to come and go around my schedule. This is a problem for many families who have broken relationships.

That autumn I sent the kids to their first day of school still not knowing when the 32 would be. I was in steady communication with someone in Iraq, be it Meg, Captain Benson, or Steve Raiser, the captain who had mailed me a stuffed animal for the boys, along with a letter explaining his friendship with Lou. I'd watched the video of the service that was held on FOB Danger for Lou and Phil, and realized Steve was the "Ray" Lou had told me about in several stories from their time at Drum, and one story about how Ray had bequeathed Lou his lieutenant rank when he was promoted to captain ahead of Lou. It had made Lou laugh, and I was grateful he had people to joke around with. Picking up on Lou's relationship with him, I referred to him as Ray when I emailed to thank him. We'd since taken to emailing each other on a regular basis. He seemed to appreciate my need to be in touch with someone over there. Someone who knew Lou and missed him too.

I came to rely on those emails from Ray. The eight–hour time difference between here and Iraq meant he was the only one other than Siobhan who was alert during the long hours each night. His unwavering willingness to correspond was more important to me than he knew. He wasn't assigned to the case but had acquired approval to communicate with me in spite of the gag order still being enforced.

Meg called in early October and told us the Article 32 Hearing was scheduled for October 31 in Kuwait. Fantastic. This meant I would not be here for the boys on Halloween.

I would have to find some way to make that up to them. But for now, my main concern was to be granted approval to attend. Although we were still pushing for a live video feed, we knew it was a losing battle. This rekindled our anger that the Army deemed us to be so unimportant. We were convinced that the live feed (VTC) was not out of the army's grasp to accomplish, and that belief was confirmed soon after our argument. While a VTC for the hearing was "impossible" and "puts our troops at risk," apparently those issues vanished when the president needed a VTC. A live feed between President Bush and troops on FOB Danger was broadcast on the news within a few weeks of the government's explaining to us why it would not be possible for anyone, not even the president. Another lie exposed, and Siobhan and I fumed at the blatant snub. Well then, hell hath no fury like two widows scorned. Bring it on.

We had been told that the hearing is a public procedure. Anyone who was interested would be welcome to attend. But Kuwait is still a hostile environment. Not at the top of the list for two women traveling alone. Nonetheless, my sister honored my request and began sending me information about flights into Kuwait City. We were going to get there with or without the Army's help.

A friend of mine knew someone who knew someone, and I was one day away from meeting with professional bodyguards to hire for this trip. Despite our need to attend the hearing, I believed two American women on their own in Kuwait was an invitation for trouble. Thankfully, we learned the bodyguards were unnecessary. As it turned out, Round One had been a victory for us. Siobhan and I were told to expect Invitational Travel Orders (ITOs) for Kuwait. We didn't know if someone in charge had developed a conscience, or if our public campaign and support was to thank. We were just relieved and pleased with ourselves for not backing down.

We were told we would be met at the airport by soldiers who would take us directly to Camp Arifjan, outside of Kuwait City. This is where the hearing would take place and where we would stay. In our worlds, we had just scored a major victory and it reinforced our belief that we would have to remain poised to act on our own behalf to protect our interests in this case. From that point on, we recognized that the JAG officers, their superiors, and all military personnel involved were representing the United States military. We would have to be the ones to represent our husbands and our families. So be it.

Until we had the orders in hand I didn't believe the Army would keep its word, so it was a relief when they finally arrived. Dad Allen had not been included in this victory, and I was again in a difficult position. Mom and Dad Allen were rightfully outraged when dad's request was denied. I selfishly hoped they would not rock the precarious boat I was in by antagonizing the people who had yet to sign my own ITOs while at the same time I felt guilty that Siobhan and I were the only ones being recognized.

The next few weeks required me to push myself harder than ever. Comforting the boys, trying to convince the media this case was worthy of covering, meeting with politicians and pleading for assistance, and defending ourselves against the Army's accusations that we were jeopardizing the case. I needed to catch a breath of fresh air, do something fun with my boys, and focus on them. But what?

Wanting to make up my absence on Halloween to the kids, I told them we could be in a parade the week before I left. When the box with our Star Wars costumes arrived, the boys tore into the packages and tried them on. Trevor was Darth Vader, Sean was Jenga–Fett, Colin was Qui–Gon–Jin, and Jeremy had a Storm Trooper costume. They pulled out their light sabers, belted out the famous Star Wars music, and whooped it up like the innocent boys they used to be. In the midst of this I snuck down and put on my Chewbacca costume. It was no easy task to see or breathe in the giant hairy outfit and I carefully made my way upstairs to where the boys were playing. Their shocked expressions were priceless. Peals of contagious laughter erupted around me. I was whisked away from the troubles weighing on me and fully in this moment with my boys. That is, until the noise died down and a new sound permeated the costume and my surroundings. Jeremy was crying, scared of the shaggy monster in the living room. I took the head off and poked my face out as I called him. But he would have nothing to do with me until I shed the entire costume, after which he clung to me with a strength I did not know he possessed.

There was one week before the parade and it wouldn't be right if Jeremy didn't join in. I knew what needed to be done. At night the costume hung in the living room where he grew accustomed to passing by and touching it. By day, I wore all or part of the contraption while I made meals, changed his diaper, and played trains with him. By the time the parade came he was fully accustomed to the costume and had a fantastic time. Siobhan and her daughter joined us and it was ridiculously good to enjoy the kids and the day instead of constantly thinking of the hearing.

Meantime, Dad Allen admitted defeat and ordered his own tickets to Kuwait. The government agreed to have an escort for him though it refused to supply him with a ticket or accommodations. Shortly before we were scheduled to go to Kuwait, I got a call from Frank. He wanted to give me a heads up that he would finally be receiving Lou's missing watch and wallet in the mail. After three months of stalking the government for these items, I'd added the unnecessary effort it took to locate and acquire them to my list of aggravations. He cautioned me that the lightweight of the package indicated a strong possibility that I would not be receiving these items back intact. I told Frank I'd drive to Camp Smith and pick the stuff up. It was raining hard and it suited my mood. Giving in to my melancholy, I inserted one of the CDs Lou had made for me and the familiar songs came on. With the music came the memory of Lou smiling as he made these the morning I saw him last. I still loved him so much.

As I walked into Frank's office, he gave me that easy smile of his and offered me a Pepsi. I told him I was not staying long—I'd just get the envelopes and be on my way. But he coaxed me into a chair and we hung out for a few minutes. We started talking about my family, his family, his job. The conversation swung to the trip and upcoming 32 Hearing. Frank was sitting at his computer facing me. I was lounging in his other chair a foot or two away when he mentioned the possibility of there being another witness to the 32. I bolted out of my chair and surprised us both. "His wife!" I yelled. I knew something like this would happen. I understood the part about "innocent until proven guilty," of course. I realized that if the traitor's wife wanted to be there, the Army was obligated to allow her there as well. What I could not fathom is why on earth this woman would want to be there. Could she honestly believe her husband was innocent of these charges? Or did she know he was guilty—maybe even knew of his plan before he did it—and agreed with it? Or worse yet—Could she have even suggested this avenue to her husband? She was either incredibly misled or as evil as her husband. And the thought that he would be allowed to be with his wife after taking our husbands from us was upsetting. Where is our right to be with our husbands? What rights did he afford Lou and Phil? At times, the unfairness of it all created an anger in me I had never experienced before, and I had no outlet other than to scream in Frank's office, cursing out the government, Martinez, his wife, anyone and anything who had wronged us, until I regained some measure of composure.

Frank left the room for a moment and I removed the envelope from my bag. One envelope. The watch, I was told, was en route but that day I had the wallet. Frank was right. By the weight of the envelope there was no way the actual wallet had been returned. I slid my hand in and retrieved a pile of cards—Lou's credit cards, STAR card, license, etc. The contents of his wallet. I knew the wallet was bloodstained and against my wishes they had destroyed it. I replaced the cards in their velvet pouch and returned the entire package to my bag. Frank came back and I took a breath, calmed myself.

What I had intended to be a quick grab–and–go visit had by now stretched into a couple of hours. A glance at the time told me I needed to go get my kids. I stood, and Frank told me the color had returned to my face, that when I'd arrived I was as white as a ghost and looked terrible.

The slow drive in the still–pounding rain allowed time for me to shake off the trip before returning to my boys. The rest of the day was tough. I knew they sensed my sadness and it settled over them. I was ripped apart by the fact that I was robbing them of their surviving parent as well. *One day*, I vowed, *I will be a good mom again.*

A day or so later Frank called again. He had the watch and was bringing it to my house. Here we go again. This is a process designed, it seems, to inflict the maximum amount of torture on the ones left behind. I emailed Ray. Told him about Frank's impending visit. "That's good!" He said. I replied, "Not really—each time I do this is incredibly painful." He was instantly apologetic. "I will be waiting for you in Kuwait," he said. "We will make the best of it." I'd already forgotten the sensation of having one person who is always concerned for me. One person I am a priority for. Ray had recently been assigned to me—it was now his job to escort me while I was in Kuwait. He'd teased me about that once and I went berserk on him. But I felt his sincerity and genuine concern from halfway across the world.

Frank arrived and I told Ray it's go time. I'd be in touch later. As usual, it was a mixed feeling to see my CAO. This was a person I truly liked. That I thought Lou would like. I considered him a friend in spite of his temporary status in my life. But each time we met was for the purpose of something emotionally draining, and this visit was no different. We hung out in the kitchen for a few minutes. Grabbed some cokes. He gave me the envelope and this time I didn't look. Couldn't yet. Then he got serious. Produced his unit's coin from his pocket. "I know I won't be with you in Kuwait, but I will be thinking of you and there in spirit" as he handed me the coin. A sweet gesture. A teddy bear of a man. I looked into his eyes and we smiled. We'd never hugged before. At first I didn't know him well enough and once I did, I figured that if we hugged every time something traumatic happened we'd be locked in a permanent embrace. But this occasion called for a hug and both of us were okay with that. Then I said "Wait here, I'll be right back!" and I hurried downstairs to retrieve something I had for him. While at the shore over the summer I'd had a shirt made for Frank. A solid black t shirt that reads: "I'M STUCK BEING BARB ALLEN'S CAO AND ALL I GET IS THIS SHITTY SHIRT" I hadn't known when I would give it to him, but it made me laugh. I knew the right moment would eventually present itself, and now it had. As his eyes moved across the shirt his face at first registered disbelief and then he erupted in laughter. "You are crazy, you know that, right?" he said. The shirt is completely irreverent but at the same time a good fit for this unique widow—CAO relationship. I knew he'd stash it away in a drawer or box somewhere and forget about it but for the moment it was perfect. I can't imagine how I would have gotten through this with any other person for a CAO. We said our good byes and I watched him go, having no idea it would be the last time I would see or hear from him. Repeated attempts to contact him over the years have been met with silence. I learned he made Major, and wondered if his promotion had anything to do with his decision to write me off. I remain grateful to him for his involvement in those first months, but cannot shake a measure of betrayal and disappointment I feel for the way he excused himself from his duties and walked away without a backwards glance, after convincing me he genuinely cared about our families and this case.

I spent the rest of that day with the kids at Siobhan's house for Madeline's third birthday party. As she blew out her candles I felt a knot in my chest; I was so sorry I was there instead of Phil.

Later that night I got the boys to bed and headed out to the backyard for some fresh air. I was still not sleeping for more than an hour or two at a time and even that was restless. In no hurry for that now, I decided to unwind in the luxuriously hot summer night, and walked up the hill into the back part of the yard. The solitude was comforting. I looked down towards the house. Everything I was living for now was in there. I looked up into the night and talked to Lou, asked him to send me the staying power to make it through this. Suddenly the sound of a pack of dogs was upon me. Barking and howling at ear–splitting levels. *What the*—I wondered. And realized it was my neighbor's dogs. Four big ones. Three hounds and one shepard mix, each making it very clear that I was intruding. It didn't matter that I was in my own yard. They didn't want me there. This sentiment seemed to be shared by my neighbor, who still dismissed me with a turned back. The canine cacophony shattered my peace and I walked away.

Back inside, I sprawled on the couch. By 2 A.M. I decided to check in and see if Ray was there. He was, and I told him about the watch. He suggested having someone there with me when I open it. Well, I figured, Ray is "here" so what the hell. I opened the envelope and stared at the face of a watch with no band attached. Like his wallet, the bloodstained band was destroyed. Then I noticed the face of the watch. It had one time zone. The watch Lou had worn to Iraq had two time zones. I didn't know if the delivery was a mistake or just an attempt to shut me up by sending some random watch, and I still haven't found out.

I continued the back–and–forth with Ray without mentioning the fact that I'd just opened the package. He didn't even know that he'd again helped me through another rough moment. He told me Camp Arifjan is not bad and suggested I bring a bathing suit. Again, he promised that we would make the most of the time there. In an odd sort of way I was looking forward to this trip. Guilt about leaving the boys was tempered with the knowledge they'd be with family, and would have fun on sleepovers.

I'd be partially following in Lou's footsteps and have a sense of what he experienced on his trip there. I hoped it would bring me closer to him. And I would witness the first step of judicial justice being taken. The thought of seeing Martinez in person was constantly on my mind. *What is it like to be with the person who murdered your husband? Will I be afraid of him, will it cause even more pain, will it bring forth all the hatred I have? Will we see his wife, will she be permitted to touch her husband, will I be able to see that without going completely insane?*

The night before the trip, I took the boys to their aunt's house. They'd be splitting time among different family members over the next week. It was a difficult good bye for me as the guilt over leaving them, sadness over the circumstances, and fear for our future burned within me. *Maybe it would be good for the kids to have a break from their basket–case mommy.*

The drive to Siobhan's passed easily in spite of my nerves. I am chronically early for everything and she is chronically late. Today it didn't matter because we had plenty of time before the flight. We settled into the car and stared at each other in disbelief. Neither one of us could fully believe what we were doing. In the military world, a trip to Kuwait is no longer such a big deal. Our troops don't even carry weapons there, we were told. But for a civilian woman—a mom who never intended to travel to hostile territories, it is quite unusual. And forget about the fact that we were headed to face our husbands' murderer.

My sister had contacted the airline and asked about the possibility of bumping us to first class. It hadn't worked, so we trudged to coach with the rest of the herd. Either I grew about a foot since my last flight a few months ago or these were the tiniest seats I have ever seen. Perfect for preschoolers. To make it even better, we were seated in the same row as a young couple with a rambunctious, extremely vocal baby who had been quite the terror at the airport. I had forgotten a bottle of water, and drink service for coach was at least an hour away. Patience not being one of my current virtues, I swallowed two Ambiens dry. One of the best ideas I've had for months and I contorted into a passably comfortable position as Siobhan sang to the crying baby. Night–night, Siobhan.

Almost six hours later I lurched back to consciousness as we approached the airport in Germany for our six–hour layover. The minutes crept by until at last it was time to board for Kuwait. At one point I glanced out the window at a breathtaking view of snow–topped mountains lightly touched with a soft hue of sunlight. My chest constricting, I remembered the last Saturday before Lou died, when he called us from FOB Danger. How he'd talked about seeing the mountains from the flight, and the panic I'd felt listening to him. I couldn't shake the impression that I was being given a heads–up from some higher force that something devastating was going to happen.

Now, as I looked out at perhaps the same mountains Lou spoke of, that memory came careening back to me. I clenched my hands together and bit down hard on some gum. I could not stop staring at the mountains as I imagined I felt Lou with me. *I'm coming*, I told him. *I'm following you and I will never stop searching for answers. I'm so scared. I'm so sorry I didn't pay closer attention. I will never lose you, Lou. Please know that.*

I wasn't aware that I was crying until my tears splashed the window. I imagined Lou crying with me. Siobhan and I spent the rest of the flight talking together and soon descended into Kuwait City.

CHAPTER SEVEN

KUWAIT

✪ ✪ ✪

It felt like we'd landed on another planet instead of another country. Men and women in flowing robes mingled with others dressed like us. Not seeing Meg anywhere, we followed the crowd through some doors. Our carry–on bags went on a belt to be x–rayed before we proceeded to baggage claim. One long, lean box after another moved by and the man next to me commented on the amount of sniper rifles going through. *Of course, I* realized. *Sniper rifles. What else would all these soldiers be waiting for? Did Lou come through these doors; did he stand here and wait for his luggage? Was Ray here with him? How many men and women have stood in this very spot along this leg of their one–way trip to Iraq?*

Grabbing our bags, we emerged through the next set of doors into a walkway with people on either side waiting to greet passengers. I felt their gaze on us and there was a heavy sense of hostility emanating from the men when I dared to look into their eyes. I was relieved to see Meg appear in front of us along with another soldier. We said our hellos and moved out of the spotlight.

On the way to the car, Meg's phone rang a few times. She stopped to read each text message. "Haji messages," she reported with a small smile and a shake of her head. As if we knew what that meant. Catching our confusion, she explained that many of the locals feel it necessary to randomly dial numbers and leave messages like "Go home, American pigs" or other messages along those lines. Meg explained this so calmly that I almost didn't believe her.

The darkness of the hour cloaked much of our surroundings on the trip to base. We spent the drive talking about what had happened to date and what to expect over the next few days. It was Friday night. We'd have Saturday to do as we wished on base and on

Sunday would get a peak at the improvised court room. Monday morning was the hearing, and we should head home either on Tuesday or Wednesday. We would be notified of Mrs. Martinez's whereabouts so as to avoid bumping into her on base.

Approaching the base, Meg called ahead to Major Linda Thorburn, Siobhan's escort, and Ray, who were ready to meet us. I don't know what I expected the base to look like. This one seemed to be a long driveway leading to nowhere and illuminated by stadium lights. We eventually arrived at a booth and security check, where Siobhan and I coughed up our widow IDs. Proceeding, I noticed that short squat buildings reminiscent of my kids' early Lego concoctions appeared to be the design of choice here. We stopped outside one of these buildings and I breathed a sigh of relief. Made it. The air felt like the climate in Arizona. I liked it. Meg had warned us of the "Kuwaiti crud" going around. A congested cough and overall feeling of blah combined with a layer of grit that quickly envelops anything here. But right now I was enjoying the warm break from chilly New York.

A smiling woman in sand colored uniform and chin length graying hair greeted us. Major Linda Thorburn. It was good to see her. We'd exchanged a few light emails over the past weeks and she had been the one to describe our accommodations. Her easygoing manner had made it natural to speak freely with her and she had displayed the sense of humor vital to the survival of all the widow detail members.

I looked around for Ray, but he was nowhere to be seen. I joked about being stood up and Meg called him. He replied that he was en route but having difficulty finding our building. After some time, we gave up and went inside.

We were pleasantly surprised at our rooms. More similar to hotel rooms than the spartan conditions we had anticipated. Two bedrooms with inviting bright comforters. A full bath with a surprisingly large tub, and a wholly equipped kitchen.

Siobhan was wiped out and ready to turn in. I was wired and looking forward to taking a walk. In the absence of my escort, Linda volunteered for duty. Siobhan and I were supposed to be escorted at all times. The Army was not taking any chances of something happening to the widows. That would make for some nasty PR, I suppose.

Linda strode with me, pointing out the sights of the base. I saw the building she and the others were housed in. The cafeteria, pool area, rec hall, and outdoor food court. She explained that this is only one zone, that the base itself extended quite a way. Pointing in the distance, she noted the area containing the building to be used as a courthouse, and we were then again in front of our building. Still keyed up but realizing she must be tired, I thanked her for the tour and said good night. Went inside, grabbed the phone in my room, and called home. I told my mom I was here safely and kept the talk short. Needing to get out of this room, I dialed the number I was given for Ray. He answered quickly. "Ray?" I drawled out. "Yes," he replied. I teased him about standing me up and he defended himself, explaining he couldn't find the building. He was ready for bed, so I told him I was going to take a quick walk and I would see him in the morning. Instead he offered to come meet me, and I went back outside to wait for him.

I watched uncertainly as a man approached. "Barb?" "Ray" he and I said together. I went for the handshake but he pulled me in for a hug. I was instantly comfortable with him. The months of emails made this seem more like meeting an old friend than a stranger. He's taller than my five–ten height and built solidly. I could feel the strength in his arms and chest as we hugged. His smile was genuine and his manner relaxed. We fell into stride together as he gave me a more thorough version of the tour I'd received from Linda. Past the pool and the small group of people congregated there. Into the building that holds the PX, the post office, library, and coffee spot as well as a Subway. We kept the conversation casual, sticking to likes and dislikes, among them coffee. Neither Lou nor I liked coffee but both of us loved the smell. Taking it as a challenge, Ray vowed to have me hooked on coffee before I left.

Walking into the recreational building, we stumbled upon a party. Music, dancing, soft lights. Ray turned to ask if I dance. That was a complicated question. I used to dance. Loved to dance with Lou. Listening to the music reminded me of the fact that I'd do anything for another chance to dance with my husband. I was going to miss dancing. But instead of hammering Ray with all of that I simply replied, "Yes, I dance, but I am not up to it at the moment." He procured a couple of bags of popcorn for us and we moved out to the next room. Ping–pong, pool, and Foozball awaited us in the game room. Ray easily beat me in a Foozball game, and told me about playing ping–pong with Lou.

Re–emerging into the night air, I noticed the temperature had dropped. The cool air felt refreshing as we made our way to the food court, which was fairly well represented. Burger King, a pizza place, a taco place, and a handful of other choices clustered in the middle of the zone. Not bad for the desert. Ray brought two cans of coke to the picnic bench under a streetlight and offered me one with a smile. It was the first look I had of him in good light, and I realized how green his eyes are. I tried not to think about what I must look like, and found myself relaxing in his company. Guiltily chastising myself for keeping him up so late, I thanked him for being there for me as he walked me back to my building. That night I slept peacefully for the first time in months.

●   ●   ●   ●   ●

Friday morning daylight filtered in, and I was stunned to see I'd slept for more than seven hours. I haven't done that since I was a normal person. Siobhan was up and holding a can of Red Bull, her thick auburn hair in a bouncy ponytail and her smile wide. She was also well rested and anxious to go for a run. It was good to see her like this. She left for a run while I lingered in a long shower before waking Ray. I'd hoped to let him sleep in after the late night, but I woke him when I called. He brushed off my apology as unnecessary, and said he'd come over. I stretched in the room before soaking up some sun while I waited for him. We spent that day ambling around the base and getting to know each other. Ray humored my inability to sit still, until I finally dropped on the sand by a bench that night. Sitting together in the cool desert evening, we spent hours talking before he walked me back to my building.

Saturday was more of the same. Breaking only for quick meals, I kept Ray on his feet all day. Occasionally we passed Meg or Linda and Siobhan, but mostly we just walked by ourselves in an endless track around the zone. Before dinner I called home. Lou's dad had started on his trip here. The boys were okay, but sounded sad I wasn't there. I missed them, too, and assured them I'd be back as soon as I could. After dinner we returned to the same sandy spot to kick back and talk. I snuggled up to Ray both for body heat and for comfort. These were unique circumstances and it felt as though I'd known him forever rather than this short period of time. It was uplifting to speak to someone who knew Lou and was willing to talk about the meaning of life and all sorts of other things people talk about in times of great emotion.

We walked back and this time Ray came in. Siobhan was still up and the three of us hung out. This was the first opportunity I had to be with Siobhan outside of our home environments, and she, too, had become a good friend. We are able to joke about things no one else would see humor in, cry about pain no one else can quite understand, and work together to figure out the chaos we'd been thrust into.

At some point Siobhan headed to her room with an Ambien. I was lying face down at the foot of my bed and Ray was sitting at the head. I popped some Ambien myself. He offered to stay until I fell asleep and I didn't argue. Closing my eyes as he sat next to me and gently rubbed my face, I suppressed a giggle, feeling like a child being tucked in. Ray's soothing touch combined with the Ambien, the emotions, and the past months of sleepless nights were enough to torpedo me straight into an oasis of slumber. Even the ever–present disturbing dreams went easy on me that night. The next thing I knew it was morning, Ray was gone, and I'd slept through the night again.

Late Sunday morning I called Ray. He'd been to the gym and was ready to meet. He talked me into attending mass before our scheduled meeting with the prosecutors. Ray's faith had carried me through many long nights of doubt and fear through his reassuring emails. On the day he'd left FOB Danger, I'd asked him to visit the site of the explosion and say a prayer for Lou and Phil. I was mildly disappointed that I would never be able to do so myself and hoped that Ray would be able to stand in for me. As a lapsed Catholic, I'd never lost my faith but had fallen away from the Church. Ray was happy to accommodate my request, he emailed back, and I headed out to the woods with my dogs. While out there, we encountered a herd of loose cows from the neighboring farm. The cows were chaperoned by a very angry, protective bull who didn't appreciate my puppy's challenging bark. I was twenty feet from a snorting bull, faced with the very real threat of having to run for my life less than a week before I was set to go to Kuwait. I'd laughed at the irony. My friends and family were all so concerned for my safety on that trip yet it seemed as though I was in more peril right here at home. Thankfully, the bull decided I wasn't worth the effort of mauling, and the dogs and I arrived safely back home. I checked my email to discover that at the precise moment I was staring at the bull, Ray was bowing his head for Lou and Phil in Phil's room.

Arriving at the building being used for services, I told myself that being in mass does not necessarily mean I will dissolve into tears. Attempted to convince myself that the hymns and rituals will not bring forth the emotions constantly hovering just below my veil of composure. I was wrong.

At home I've gone to countless masses over the years. With a handful of exceptions, those masses had seemed to be attended by people simply fulfilling a Sunday obligation and dreaming about the moment they could escape, enjoy an afternoon off from work. But this mass was different.

Like most people not directly involved in this war, I always kept the troops and families in my thoughts. I'd heard stories of men and women returning home forever altered by their experience and said a quick prayer for them. Yet to be here among these people so close to Iraq was profoundly eye-opening.

Everywhere I went with Ray, we would pass others out walking or at the pool. People at all hours dancing to music, laughing with friends or seemingly enjoying themselves. But there was a tangible element of grief and heaviness emanating from each and every one of the people and a figurative pall hovering over the base. Watch one group for a few minutes and you'd invariably see them laugh together. In the midst of the laughter, at least one of them would abruptly pause, stare into space, and change their entire demeanor. Shoulders sagged, lips drooped, eyes clouded over. The transformation would be quick—a few seconds at most—and the soldier would resume laughing with the group who pretended not to have noticed their friend's episode. Each of them has experienced it themselves and knows that is how they will live the rest of their lives.

Settling into a pew with Ray, I reflected how no one had to be in this room right now. There was no one here to tattle on them for missing a Sunday. They have been to hell and back and have earned the right to doubt in God. Yet they chose to come here, pray with others, sing together, and concentrate on the belief that all is not lost. I could not help but be affected by their faith.

After mass and lunch, we met up with Siobhan and Linda. The four of us headed over to the makeshift courthouse for a preview of the setup. Ray and I, fast walkers, slowed our pace to wait for Siobhan and Linda. Siobhan, ever the classy widow, was dressed in a skirt and heels while I'd opted for comfy shoes and pants. Approaching the courthouse was a reminder of our purpose here, and my nerves began to tingle.

Siobhan mentioned talk she'd heard that this camp has exceptionally nice port–a–potties. We laughed about that and later agreed that the rumor was true; the port–a–potties were very nice. We were then led to the door we'd be using the following day, where we were greeted by two MPs. They searched our bags and nodded us through to a metal detector. Meg joined us and pointed out the entrances to be used by Martinez's wife and the media. Then we were in the room assigned to us, with a couch and table set on the concrete floor next to a little fridge stocked with water bottles. It seemed that care was taken to accommodate us and I appreciated it. We were soon joined by Major Ruzicka and Captain Benson, who along with a few other men whose names escape me. Major Ruzicka was the author of a letter responding to Lou's mom's request for a VTC. In it he'd chastised her for her anger, and urged her to sit back and let them do their jobs. The letter had not been well received, but the man himself appeared to be more restrained.

Formalities were exchanged and inquiries about our accommodations were met with assurance from us that we were grateful for the effort made on our behalf. Time was of the essence that day as everyone was busy with last–minute preparations for the hearing. We were walked into the room where the proceeding would occur. We'd been warned it was a tight room and we would be in close proximity to Martinez. That seemed to have been an understatement.

The room looked to be four hastily assembled walls unattached to any kind of ceiling. Metal folding chairs were arranged in rows facing a u–shaped table. A handful of chairs were set at the tables and two chairs were set at the front of the room. Wires crisscrossed the top of the table and some equipment was set up at the top left. A camera stood in a tripod in a corner of the room. Some of the chairs had names on them. Siobhan and I were sitting up front. Siobhan had the last chair in the row and I was on her left. Next to me was Ray. Behind us were Linda and Dad Allen and Meg. Across the way, a chair was reserved for Martinez's wife Tamara. The remainder of the chairs would be filled with MPs and various military personnel. We inquired about the camera, and someone explained that there would be a live feed shooting down the hall to the media room. The microphone and equipment on the table were for the court reporters to use and for those at home listening to the audio feed at West Point.

The room was small but the occasion was huge. It was a lot to process. One look up at the open air above the room, combined with the noise freely flowing in from beyond the walls, and I knew the audio feed would be terrible. I was glad I came.

Having done what we'd come to do that day, we shook hands and dispersed. I was hepped up now and had no real destination in mind. Back at the room, we changed into shorts and t–shirts. Siobhan went running and I went to find Ray. We checked our emails and spent some time in the sun, walking and talking about the proceeding tomorrow. The rest of the day stretched ahead of us and I was happy to have Ray to help pass the time.

We spent the remainder of the day the same as the others, wandering around the base. Siobhan and I were both getting nervous about tomorrow, and as we passed each other on our travels we shared the concern with a simple look. That evening Ray and I settled into a fairly private spot on the sand near one of the horribly uncomfortable stone benches placed around the zone. These benches seemed designed to discourage hanging out, so after a few attempts to lounge on them we gave up and took to the sand. Leaning our backs on a bench, we snuggled comfortably into each other and talked. Ray had become a close friend, and whether we lost this closeness at home or not, I knew I'd always have a soft spot for him. He'd come into my life at a time when I needed someone like him. His friendship with Lou created the feeling of closeness long before we met. We sat together long into that night talking about life, death, Lou, and whatever else came to mind. For the first time, I cried in front of him. I cried for Lou, for our boys, for myself. The temperature dropped and Ray held me close. I leaned into him as countless visions collided in my mind: Lou when we met, as he laughed, when we danced, when he looked at me. The men at my door, and the boys' faces as I told them what had happened. Lou in the coffin. A life of pain and heartache. Ray extending himself into that life, helping me find my way through.

We sat for a while longer, until I was cried out and we were both exhausted. Like the previous night, he walked me back to my room and stayed until I fell asleep.

Morning. This was it. In a few hours Siobhan and I would be face to face with the individual who'd murdered our husbands. We had each brought several court outfits, unsure how many days this would turn out to be, what the weather would be like here, or what proper attire would be. Short on laughter, we spent some time trying to put ourselves together. Millions of women have hung out with a friend and gotten dressed up together, planning a night out or something fun. A casual observer may have thought the same of us but a closer look would reveal telltale signs of something else. Bags under our eyes, swollen lids. Drooping shoulders, anxious looks, churning stomachs. We were a mess. But we looked at each other and felt our resolve build.

Linda and Ray met us outside and together we walked to the courthouse. Today there were no attempts at humor as we approached the doors. Today I was concentrating on building up as much strength as I had left untapped. Creating a protective wall around my soul for the testimony I knew we would hear.

Through the doors. Bags to the MPs and badges on, we were waved through to the metal detector. Cleared for entry into the hallway and into the holding room. I'd been informed my father–in–law had arrived safely at his hotel the previous evening but neither of us had the other's phone number to call. He was a welcome sight when I saw him as I entered our waiting room. We talked about our trips and accommodations. Introduced Linda and Ray. Then we waited. I was on the couch next to Dad Allen, and Siobhan and Ray were next to each other on the other side. Dad started talking to someone on his other side and I was left undistracted. That one moment of time for my mind to wander was all I needed. Dismayed at the trembling building in me and frantically trying to stem the tears I felt brewing, I bowed my head and lost the fight. Watched the tears soak into my lap. In a flash, Linda was next to me with tissues and a warm hug, whispering soothingly to me. I felt ridiculous. We hadn't even begun and I was already crumpling. Linda has had experience dealing with victims and relatives and took naturally to the role of comfort and support. These people I jokingly dubbed the "Widow Detail" were all instrumental in carrying me through this.

Show time. Someone popped their head into the room and announced that we had to stay inside. Martinez was en route to the court room. Terri had told me about doing that in her trial. Anytime Akbar was led around the building, she and her family had to wait behind a closed door. A few moments later, our turn came. We filed out of our room into the narrow hallway and started the handful of paces to the court room.

I was oddly nervous about seeing him. I wasn't afraid of him, just terrified at what he meant. Here, in flesh and blood, is the man who coldly and maliciously planted a claymore mine in the room where Phil and Lou would be. Here is the man who, fully aware of the effect a claymore mine would have on those in its path, pushed the detonator. He knew Phil and Lou were in that room. He knew a third man, Ash Timmaiaih, might be in there as well. He knew these men had wives and small children. He knew he would cause these men to suffer an excruciating death if they were not instantly killed. And yet he chose to press that clacker. And then he chose to toss a few grenades around to create the illusion of an enemy attack. What is there to be said about such a man? And how can I accept the fact that he is here, breathing, talking, seeing his wife, and being granted all the considerations he denied to so many of us?

Reaching our seats, at first I didn't look at him. I saw compassionate faces turned to us on our way in, and a group of uniforms at the table. Once seated I focused on the man who looked most like the picture from the paper. He had buzzed brown hair, a square face, and dark eyes. All three men, the defense and Martinez, avoided looking our way. To the front left of the table was the court reporter. Ray was on my left, Siobhan on my right. Dad Allen was directly behind me, and Linda was on his right. In a chair across the room sat a disheveled woman who looked as if she were dressed for an outing to Wal Mart. She slouched in the seat, wearing a sloppy t–shirt and jeans suitable for picking up household goods and a day of cleaning or yard work. Her long unkempt hair, black with gray strands running through it, ran in a loose ponytail down her back, and large glasses perched on her nose. It was Tamara Martinez, his wife. As these thoughts raced through my mind, I tried to remind myself to refrain from judging by appearance, but my need to hate this woman overrode all other consideration, and I grasped at any excuse to do so.

Siobhan and I had brought notepads and pens, prepared to take notes. But shortly before the hearing began, we were informed that we would not be permitted to take notes in the court room. This didn't sit well with us, but we figured we'd just hurry during each break to write down what we heard. Now inside the courtroom, we saw Tamara holding a pad and pen, and we were furious. No way, we fumed, will we sit here and allow her to take notes while we are denied that opportunity. Bad enough that Martinez can write and visit with her. If we can't take notes, neither can she! Childish? Absolutely. Do we care? Nope.

An MP walked to her, leaned in and whispered something. Glancing briefly in our direction, she rolled her eyes, emitted an exaggerated sigh, and dramatically shoved her pad and pen under her seat. I felt justified in hating her.

A few moments later someone announced we could take notes. We bolted to the room and grabbed our stuff, came back, and settled again into our hard seats.

"All rise!" was yelled and everyone stood as Colonel Reinert entered the room. Studying him, I thought the colonel had the presence of a man who is serious about his duty yet has retained human qualities. A man who chose not to let his position erase common sense or compassion, yet by the same token will not allow compassion to override the law. Like everyone else, his brown hair was buzzed short, and his eyes reflected experiences he would rather forget. Maybe this was all wishful thinking, but I went with it.

Beyond the walls and open–air ceiling we heard a multitude of voices. People going about their day as if we were not even there. The colonel's voice was hard to hear, and he sent someone to quiet down the racket out there. I was glad we fought to be here. No doubt the people struggling to listen in from West Point would miss key elements of this hearing.

Court was brought to order and the first witness was called. I'd been staring hard at the man I believed to be Martinez. I was wrong: It was Captain Gregory, one of the defense attorneys. Martinez sat next to him, and he looked nothing like his picture that had been splayed across newspapers and TV news shows. I had dismissed Martinez as being the defendant because he seemed so unremarkable. This man, the actual person, appeared meek and resentful. Like a child sent to the corner for reasons he deemed insignificant. He was hollow cheeked, pale faced, spectacled, and pouty. Hardly the image of someone who'd done so much damage to so many lives. Major Cipriano, the other defense attorney, also broke role from the dashing capital defense attorney seen on movie screens. His wan complexion, well–endowed nose and quiet energy rendered him more like the shy quiet kid who passes through high school unnoticed except when the bullies need a victim. I studied our new enemies until the first witness was called.

Captain Carl Prober took the stand and my attention focused on him. In response to the prosecution's questions, the captain answered deliberately, as if concentrating on completely recounting what he knew. His testimony was like a nightmare come true. It started easily enough. This youngish–looking clean–cut guy settled his lanky figure into the witness chair. Swore to tell the truth. His Adam's apple bobbed as he gulped, took a breath, and destroyed me with his words.

Captain Prober was driving back to his building, the Water Palace. There was a sandstorm and it was difficult to see. As he approached his destination, he noticed a wire stretching across the road where he hadn't remembered seeing one before. He filed that away in his mind and chalked it up to some reason that must be authorized yet not in his knowledge. He backed his vehicle up and went inside, up the stairs and to his room. He brushed his teeth, changed out of his uniform, and relaxed on his bed with a book. It was approximately nine–thirty at night. Captain Prober was a few doors down from Lou and Phil. Not long into his reading, he was rocked violently by one deafening explosion, followed on its tail by two more explosions. Silence followed. Then, shattering the silence, he heard Lou yelling.

Oh God Oh God, I prayed, *send me some strength for what I am about to hear*. I was already shaking. Siobhan was stone still.

The captain set his jaw and plowed forward into his memory of those moments. Wanting to cover my ears, I willed myself to listen instead.

Captain Prober reached Phil's door. He heard Lou yelling, "It's Lieutenant Allen! Somebody help me!" He opened the door. Saw Phil lying in a pool of blood, his body broken and unresponsive. Believing Phil to be dead, Captain Prober proceeded to Lou, who was also soaked in blood and very badly injured. But he was talking. Captain Prober held Lou's hand and assured him help was on the way.

I was struggling to hold in a scream. I should have been the one holding Lou's hand. Here he was, in more pain than ever before. Thousands of miles away from home, bleeding, worried for Phil, and looking into the eyes of a stranger. At the very least he should have been with someone who loved him. Inside I was wailing and positively terrified for what Lou and Phil went through. Listening to Captain Prober telling about seeing them, speaking to Lou and listening as Lou talked about me, I gripped the side of my chair in an effort to hold myself in it.

The medics arrived not long after that and took Lou and Phil away. There was a pause in the testimony, and Siobhan and I looked at each other, both of us horrified at what we'd just heard. Ray leaned into me, offering comfort. I was blinded by my tears and helpless to stop them. Colonel Reinert looked at us, sympathy on his face. Captain Prober looked like he needed a hug. Martinez stared ahead vacantly ahead as if he were bored.

The prosecutor asked another question, and Captain Prober replied that he'd heard Martinez speak about Phil before that night. When pressed to be more specific, he leaned into the microphone and said he heard Martinez say he "can't wait to frag that f—." At that he looked apologetic, and I found that I wasn't angry at him when he admitted he hadn't reported the threat. He was so clearly full of remorse for not taking Martinez seriously, and obviously haunted by what he witnessed.

I could feel the anger seeping from Siobhan and Dad, and I was fairly certain they were doing all they could not to jump up and throttle the captain for not doing something. Stopping this from happening.

The prosecutor turned the witness over to the defense, and now the testimony turned absurd. The defense attorney delved into excruciating detail about Captain Prober brushing his teeth that night. We wound up listening to what water was used. The tap water had apparently made several people sick. I think the captain said he used bottled water. How long did he spend brushing his teeth? What toothpaste? It was ridiculous and finally even Colonel Reinert agreed. He told defense to move on.

Another tactic the defense employed was to question the captain's memory. He confessed not remembering which book he was reading that night. He read so many books over there. He had also admitted being sick that night, and the defense insinuated that he was probably so sick that his memory is altered. On and on until finally the witness was excused.

There was a brief lull before the next witness arrived and I tried to lose some tension, let go of what I'd just heard, and focus on the remainder of the hearing.

Staff Sergeant Wentzel took the stand next. The sergeant testified that he was the Unit Driving Instructor. When the prosecution asked him about that night, he said that prior to the explosions, he saw Martinez going up the stairs. Later he heard a series of explosions and saw Martinez standing in the middle of the road. This had struck Wentzel as odd. The base was regularly mortared and common practice was for people to dive for cover in such an event. Yet after these blasts, while others were diving for protection, Martinez was simply standing in the street "as if he knew" there would be no further blasts or any danger to himself. Wentzel had leapt on Martinez and pulled him to cover. He could also hear Lou yelling for help.

I now had the vision of multiple, ground shaking explosions that Lou was immersed in. I could hear him yelling for help. The person who'd done this had stood there listening to Lou's yells. Lou must have been terrified and not yet aware of the fact that any help would prove useless. He was fighting to survive. He was alone and calling for someone to please help him. While this was happening to him, I was driving home, enjoying the sun on my face and thinking about getting back home before Lou called again.

I was brought back to the courtroom, and Siobhan was holding her breath next to me. Wentzel continued his testimony. Prior to that night—I think in March—he heard Martinez talking about Phil. Martinez was complaining about how he hated Phil and saying how he "can't wait for him to get hit." This, too, was incredible to us. It seemed as if that should be proof enough. We were moments into this hearing and any doubt that Martinez is guilty seemed ludicrous. How can he have said such things and not have been reported? This was the second person who heard him threaten Phil.

Finally, Wentzel testified that Martinez had been unofficially relieved of his duties ten days earlier. We sat listening to this testimony and for the first time began to develop a picture of the events leading up to that horrible night. The defense asked a few questions that seemed irrelevant and the witness was excused.

The next witness was called. Staff Sergeant Ash Timmaiaih took the stand. Soft brown eyes flit nervously around in his young face. I didn't know who he is but Siobhan whispered that he was good friends with Phil. Ash testified that he was the Non–Commissioned Readiness Officer, or Readiness NCO. He had grown close to Phil during the deployment. That night, he had been playing a game of RISK with Lou and Phil. This made Siobhan and me laugh for a second. We'd previously speculated that the two men were hard at work when they were killed. In reality, they probably had been planning the next day, relaxing after this day, and managed to unwind with a game the two of them loved. Ash said that at four–thirty that afternoon, Lou left the room to call me. I quickly did the math and realized that was the video chat we'd done with the kids, the last time I saw him.

Ash recounted the day before that night, how he'd been in the room when Martinez came in to talk to Phil. Martinez would have seen the table recently moved adjacent to the window, the board game set up with chairs around. He would have known the entire layout of the room. And then at nine–thirty on the night of the murders, Phil and Lou succeeded in their attempt to gang up on Ash and beat him. He spoke with them good–naturedly and left to take a shower. It was clear why Ash was so shaken up. Just moments before the blasts, he had been sitting with Phil and Lou. Laughing, talking, innocently playing a game. Had he not been beaten, he would have been there and most likely been killed with them.

Siobhan and I cried intermittently throughout Ash's testimony. Ash responded to the prosecutor's questions in a voice filled with strain and emotion, tears brimming under the surface as he relived those moments. He appeared relieved when the topic changed to the days before, when Phil had asked Ash for a list of possible replacements for Martinez. Ash had provided a few names, he said, but there was no further pursuit of the matter.

Defense took their turn with Ash and then he was excused. A break was called and we stepped outside for some fresh air. Upon our return, Martinez and his wife were sitting side by side, nuzzling each other's faces. Outraged, we demanded to the MPs that they immediately separate the two. I asked the Martinezes if they would like us to bring some champagne and candles to the next recess. They ignored me and smiled conspiratorially at each other before moving a couple inches apart. Hatred welled within me. Ray attempted to soothe me, and Siobhan and I spent a few minutes steaming before court was called to order again.

Next up was Specialist Diana Portella. I was surprised that someone as young as this witness appeared to be would hold a supply position. Her black hair in a tight bun, her slightly dark complexion masking the paleness on her woe–is–me face, she spoke sullenly, lacing her speech with "well, um, like" this and that.

Her testimony started out rather low key. Martinez was her supervisor. She testified about a place called the Ammunition Holding Area, or AHA, where she'd go twice monthly as part of her duties. Toward the middle to end of May, Martinez went with her to pick up ammo, including grenades. She then talked about crates, canisters, and numbers on the crates. Martinez told her not to fill out Form 581, the standard procedure accounting for the ammo. She spoke of a place called the vault, where extra weapons and sensitive equipment were stored. Martinez had asked Portella if she would be in the vault, and mentioned that she should stay out of it so she wouldn't "be involved."

Throughout her testimony, Diana Portella was defensive of her friend Martinez, talking about his being a good person. I was annoyed and didn't understand why the prosecution had elicited testimony from someone who championed Martinez. Reviewing things later, I realized she'd established the source of the grenades used in the attack.

Sergeant Major Ciampolillo was the next contestant to come on down. He spoke about stopping in at supply and asking Martinez if he had any grenades. Martinez said yes and then bragged about having access to claymore mines as well. From there the testimony branched out to other areas. A great deal of time was devoted to talk about combat badges, why they are given, what criteria must be met. Hazardous duty was discussed—what qualifies as hazardous duty, talk about the Quick Response Force (QRF), missions that the witness participated in. I was having a difficult time seeing how any of this pertains to the case and grew frustrated at my lack of comprehension.

Captain Benson later explained one this case's aggravating factors, or qualifying characteristics, necessary to proceed as a capital case, was that the crime was committed during a time of war. Prosecution was trying to establish that we are at war, and defense was arguing that this has not been officially labeled a war. Tedious but necessary.

The next witness was called and Colonel Sullivan walked by on her way to the stand. Immediately we placed our pads and pens down on the floor. This was the doctor who had treated Lou and Phil, the woman I spoke to during the wake. This testimony was going to be rough for us and neither one of us tried to pretend we'd be able to take notes. Colonel Reinert saw us put our things down, and I gave a nervous smile as the witness took her seat.

A middle-aged woman with short light hair cut close to her head, Doctor Sullivan wore her uniform comfortably. Her eyes looked through glasses and her overall presence was that of an assured professional. She began her testimony, and the familiar voice brought me back to that phone call. I knew what was coming. Siobhan declined the tissues I offered. "I'm not going to cry," she said. I believed her. She was able to focus more on the anger than the pain so far and had been the one to keep it together much better than I. Having no illusions about my own strength, I clutched a wad of tissues in my hand.

The doctor was attached to the 42nd Infantry Division, and had grown close to many of the troops over there. On that night, she said, she got a call that men were injured. She rushed to the scene and rode in the ambulance with Lou. Behind me I could feel Dad's anguish, and next to me I could feel Siobhan's despair as the doctor recounted the conversation she had with Lou about the boys and me. Wringing my hands together, I leaned toward Siobhan while the doctor told about arriving at the hospital on FOB Speicher, where the hospital Lou and Phil had been transported to was located. Something about that name seemed familiar, but I couldn't recall why.

Since Phil seemed to be more seriously injured than Lou, Dr. Sullivan had turned her attention to him. She told about a tube in his throat and then the words that shattered Siobhan. Phil was on the operating table when the decision was made to crack his chest open in a last-ditch attempt to restore life to him. His heart was massaged. Siobhan began sobbing quietly and unashamedly accepted some tissues. I was stunned. My hand on her shoulder as I tried to comfort her, I knew I wasn't much help. Nothing can possibly comfort a person who has just been given the image of her husband lying there, ripped open with his heart in someone's hands as the life ebbed out of him.

Phil was dead. The doctors and medics now tried everything to save Lou, who had been alert and responsive earlier. Encouraged that someone so seriously injured could carry on a conversation, Dr. Sullivan held hope that he would survive. However, Lou's condition had deteriorated rapidly. Tests and x-ray revealed extensive trauma. He lost consciousness. He was brought into the OR and there he, too, had his chest cracked. As she said those words, my world stopped. My eyes popped in surprise and horror. My body, every inch of me, throbbed violently. Even my teeth were chattering. Ray gripped my hand fiercely in his.

As in my phone conversation with Dr. Sullivan, it was as if Lou were dying before my eyes. The throbbing within me elevated to an all-new level as the room began to spin.

I wanted to scream, to flee the room, to beg the doctor to stop, plead with someone to change the story, make them live again. Come home to us. Please make this stop. Dad Allen's hand reached and rested on my shoulder in the same effort I had just made to comfort Siobhan. I knew he, too, was experiencing unimaginable heartache. I thought about the family members at West Point concentrating on the awful quality audio feed and wondered if they'd been able to hear this. Hoped they hadn't.

Doctor Sullivan was noticeably distraught as she testified. Colonel Reinert had been watching us and I tried to tone it down, afraid he'd have us sent out of the room. But when I looked to him, all I saw was compassion. The doctor was excused, and the colonel called a recess. I dropped my head and Ray had his arm around me as I followed Siobhan out of the room. There was one more witness left.

Back in our waiting room, we were not a pretty sight. Dad, Siobhan, and I were decimated. We stared at one another, not knowing what to do. I was crying now and every ounce of my being was involved in the process. My chest was heaving, and I felt as if my soul, or whatever makes me a person, were mortally wounded. I may physically live for another sixty years but the real part of me had just died. No matter what I managed to do about putting my life back together, I knew the person I was is gone, victim to Martinez as well.

There was talk about ending today's proceedings. There was some technical problem with the audio feed or something and also concern that we would not withstand anything else today. Since there was just one witness remaining, we crossed our fingers and hoped to continue, just get this over with. After what felt like hours, we were called back into the courtroom for the last witness.

I sat and only half listened as the witness testified. I wrote down his name. Paul Comesanas, a CID agent. That is all I remember of him that day.

Before dismissing for the day Colonel Reinert announced we'd reconvene at nine A.M. the following day for his announcement as to his recommendation. This was a surprise. We'd been told this process could take several weeks. Once the colonel announced his recommendation, the ball would be in Colonel Gade's court. He would take Colonel Reinert's recommendation into consideration before passing his own recommendation up the food chain to Lieutenant General Vines, who would make the decision about referring this as a capital or non–capital case.

It was early evening and we were all emotionally and physically drained. I felt as if I'd been hit by an extremely large truck. Returning to our room to change, I went right to sweats. We grabbed some dinner and then split up. Siobhan went for a run, and Ray and I hit the pavement for a walk. After a while we ended up in what we now thought of as our spot and spent the next few hours talking before calling it a night.

Tuesday morning the four of us made our way back to the courthouse. Today didn't seem as bad as yesterday. We knew we'd heard the worst of what we would hear for this part of the judicial process and would be in the building for only a brief time.

I said hello to Dad, who looked as if he had spent a sleepless night. Having originally anticipated a two or three day hearing, we'd all booked return flights home late in the week. But defense had decided not to call any witnesses, thus the hearing took just the one day, and there was no need to remain in Kuwait past this morning for the decision. So his Army escort had brought him back to his hotel and left him there. Dad had then decided to find a travel agency who booked him on an earlier flight home. I was upset that while Siobhan and I were safe on base, my father in law was left to his own devices. Lou was his son, after all, and he was going through his own hell.

We were called into the courtroom and took our seats. Martinez was there looking straight ahead. He refused to meet my eyes.

Colonel Reinert entered and settled into his chair. He began speaking and now I was nervous. What if for some reason he decided not to recommend this as capital to Colonel Gade? What would we do then? But my fears were soon laid to rest when he announced that not only had he decided our way, he'd added a few charges. We listened in relief as he spoke. *There is enough evidence to support a court martial proceeding. A recommendation to add further charges is made. These charges are: larceny and the use of weapons of mass destruction.*

I was staring hard at Martinez now and restraining myself from jumping up and celebrating. But I could not contain the wide smile on my face when I saw him gulp. It was the first time he had shown any emotion, and it was only on his own behalf. He still didn't care about what he had done, only that he might actually be punished for it. Colonel Reinert asked him if he had any questions. Martinez leaned forward to the microphone and said "No." Colonel Reinert left the room and we voiced our happiness out loud. It was a small victory for us. The first time we felt as if he would be held accountable for his actions and the first time we saw him acknowledge his predicament.

We returned to the holding room and waited a few minutes. Put in a call to the people at West Point, and Dad talked to Mom Allen. Meg appeared and we had the chance for a little small talk. I hadn't really seen much of her here, for she'd been pretty busy herself. But each time we ran into each other, she was pleasant and had a smile. Meg mentioned now that Doctor Sullivan was willing to sit down and speak with me if I was interested. My gut did a flip–flop but I pounced on the opportunity. She could fill in the missing moments and I could perhaps get a few precious minutes of Lou's experience brought closer to me. We planned a time that evening, and Meg left to arrange it. Siobhan and Linda left. The prosecutors came out and we thanked them. I said good bye to Dad Allen and wished him a good trip home. Then we walked back toward my room.

Ray told me Captain Prober also indicated a willingness to meet with me, and I leapt on that, too. Who knew if I would have the opportunity again? I asked Ray if he'd sit in on these meetings with me and he agreed. He called Captain Prober and we picked a time in the afternoon, before I was to meet with Doctor Sullivan. Our social calendar was booking quickly.

On our way to meet Captain Carl Prober, we came across Ash Timmaiaih. Up close he appeared even younger than he had in court. He made no effort to avoid us, but instead came directly over and shook my hand. Offered condolences, and then Ray and I continued on to our meeting. We picked a table, got some cokes, and waited for Carl, who arrived a few moments later. He had a quick smile combined with an overall weariness common among the rest of the population there. These people have been through something that few who have not can never fully appreciate.

We started with safe subjects, general information, before I asked him about that night. He paused for a moment to collect his thoughts, much like he had while testifying. His voice wavering, he told me he heard yelling after the explosions and got to the scene in a couple of minutes. The next sentence he spoke frankly and without apology. Indeed, he was brutally honest: "I walked into the room and I saw a dead man on the floor (Phil) and a dead man talking (Lou)." That statement was so powerful it was as if I'd been punched, and I had to struggle to keep from falling over. Ray inched closer. I could feel the color drain from my face as this new image swarmed my senses. Carl was still speaking and it was a while before I was able to refocus on him. He told me he was holding Lou's hand, that Lou seemed calm and mostly concerned for Phil. Carl had seen a lot of injured people in his time, and his instinct was that Lou was not going to make it. But he assured Lou that help was on the way and stayed with him until backup arrived. I tried to take a measure of comfort from that.

When we decided it'd been enough, Carl gave me his email address and told me to feel free to stay in touch. I thanked him and make a mad dash out of there. Ray had the dubious pleasure of spending the next few hours with me.

Filled with dread, I dragged myself to the designated area for our meeting with Doctor Sullivan. I finally understood that any such meetings left me open to the possibility of learning something worse than I anticipated. But I held on to the hope that at some point, I would hear something that helped me to make sense of all this.

The doctor arrived and gave me a hug. We sat in the deserted pool area at a table in the back. It was getting dark and I pulled my fleece tight around me to ward off the chill. Ray was on my left and Doctor Sullivan was to my right, slightly across from me. Her face open and honest, she looked at me and spoke about that night. She told me of getting the call about wounded soldiers, of hurrying to the scene, of riding with Lou. She asked him if he was in pain and he said, "a little." He said his legs were "f— up" and then apologized for saying, "f—" in front of her. She laughed and told him that under the circumstances, he was excused. He said, "Well in that case, my back is f— up, too!" I laughed at this along with her. She was laughing at how remarkable it was for someone to have a sense of humor at a time like that. I was laughing through the heartache because that is the Lou I know and love. We could always, under any circumstances, bring a smile to each other's face. Now he had found a way to do it again. I was proud of him for his courage. I was glad he was able to show the doctor that side of him, to the point that she would remember it so clearly and be affected by it.

Lou had repeatedly told her he had a wife named Barbara and that she was blond. He told her he had four boys, ages six, five, three, and one. She told me that through his expression, tone, and words, he conveyed how much I was on his mind. I know that he loved me. But to hear someone reaffirm that fact was immensely healing. Colonel Sullivan and I were strangers yet I felt strangely connected to her. I took a strong comfort in her and in the fact that she was with Lou throughout his ordeal. I still wish that I had been there with him, that I had been the one comforting him, able to tell him I love him and that I will take care of the boys, that we will hold on to him forever. Or that someone else he loved could have been with him instead of strangers. But as this meeting progressed, something unexpected happened. I felt myself lightened a bit, as if an enormous pressure was being lifted off my chest and I was able to breathe again. I was absolutely certain that Lou was touched by this woman's warmth and compassion and that he was calmed by it. I believed that his fear was greatly subdued and he knew people were there helping him. Compared to everything else I'd heard in the past forty–eight hours, this was like a breath of fresh air.

The meeting over, Dr. Sullivan walked to the food court with us for some cokes and munchies, and spent some time relaxing with us after the long day. Eventually we said good night and I walked away with Ray, back to our spot on the sand. I can't imagine how I would have gotten through this experience without him, and I realized that in twenty–four hours I'd be on a plane headed home. I was looking forward to putting this behind me, to getting back to the boys, recovering. But I knew I'd miss Ray.

Bright and sunny. Our last day in Kuwait. Siobhan and I were up early and packed our bags. Then Siobhan went for a run while Ray and I hung out in the coffee shop. Siobhan and Ray had succeeded in turning me on to coffee and were quite smug about it. Now Ray and I sat in a corner and talked about life at home, what we planned on doing from here, and so on. Later, we met Siobhan and wound up at the recreation hall. There we waged ping–pong war on each other. Some guy there had zeroed in on Ray, challenging him to a game. I was glad to see Ray beat the guy.

Walking to the entrance hall, we talked about what to do for the few hours before leaving for the airport. Linda happened by, and she and Siobhan decided to get some dinner. Ray and I returned to my room, where we kicked back on the bed, leaning against each other in the comfortable way we'd developed. We spent a few moments quietly talking and then just sat in silence, each of us lost in our own thoughts. Siobhan and Linda returned, and Meg arrived. We began a round of goodbye hugs before driving off. I turned to watch Ray and Linda walk away, sorry to see them go. The ride to the airport was quick. We checked in and said good bye to Meg and to the lucky soul chosen to drive us. After making it through the line and checking our bags, we saw that Meg was still there, so we picked up some dinner at a restaurant named something like Mr. Yum Yum. The food was surprisingly good and I enjoyed the chance to hang out with Meg. But then it was really time to go. We said good bye again and Siobhan and I headed to the gate.

On the plane, we had an entire row to ourselves and we stretched out gratefully. The same guy who drove us there picked us up from the airport, in a free limo ride donated by a friend of the family who owned the car company. We got in the limo and I right away popped open a beer. Siobhan tried to join me, but she hates beer. By the time we reached her house, I was seriously buzzed and got in the front seat with the driver to have a conversation. I knew if I sat in back by myself, I'd pass out. Once he dropped me off and drove away, the thought crossed my mind that he thought I was hitting on him. He seemed as if he couldn't drive away fast enough. Ordinarily, that may have bothered me. That day, I simply found it amusing.

Home. In the living room of the empty house. Alone with my thoughts. But I didn't want to think anymore. Didn't want to feel. Didn't want to do anything but sleep. I called Vicki, arranged to get the kids in the morning. Knocked back a couple of sleeping pills and checked out for the night.

CHAPTER EIGHT
LIFE WITHOUT LOU

✪ ✪ ✪

It was an abrupt transition home. Before the trip, I was in close contact with Meg and Ray about the case. Reporters called. Every day presented a situation revolving around Lou's death. Paperwork, meetings, deliveries, phone calls had all become my way of life. Now my meetings with Frank were done. There were no official emails from Iraq. No reporters called. Nothing from the prosecutors or anyone involved in the case.

Siobhan and I agreed that other than the fact that our husbands were still dead, we could almost believe it was all a bad dream. But the glaring absence of Lou and Phil and in our lives grew stronger as the days passed, especially when we attended the homecoming celebration for the 42nd ID HHC. An invitation from General Taluto explained that Lou and Phil would be honored with their own ceremony the day after the unit was welcomed home in a large ceremony. We could not in good conscience skip the torturous welcome home ceremony, and responded we would attend both. We were looking forward to someone in the military finally publicly acknowledging the murders and the needlessness of Lou and Phil's deaths.

Siobhan and I drove to Albany together and filed into the massive gymnasium along with our families. From our seats in the "dead soldiers' families row" we had a close up shot of the politicians on stage, and a panoramic view of the lucky ones packed onto the bleachers behind us. Newly reunited parents bounced kids on their laps, happy to be in the cheap seats instead of next to us. Lifetimes separated us as we all listened to speakers laud the glorious 42nd Infantry Division HHC's heroic deployment. Our families were urged to stand up, and everyone clapped for us in a show of support. Lou's parents and I rose along with Siobhan and Phil's family. We were joined by the family members of another soldier.

No mention of the senseless murders was made at any point in the backslapping speeches. Just assurances to the families that our dead soldiers were heroes.

The following day was a separate, small ceremony in the modest gym of the Waterlivet Arsenal. This ceremony was to be dedicated to Lou and Phil, as well as the other soldier killed. We listened to speeches from General Taluto and Senator Bruno. Each refused to address the murders, or express outrage that such a thing should happen, or assure anyone it would not happen again. Instead, we were trotted up for photo–ops and then sent back to our seats. I literally bumped into Senator Bruno after the ceremony, and he plastered a smile on his face as he encouraged me to contact him if I had questions or concerns. I pounced on that, and asked him why the murders were not addressed, why were Lou and Phil's deaths not confronted? How could they have happened in the first place? He stared at me and allowed a lip to curl up as he half–laughed in my face. His eyebrow raised and he took a step back into his aide's vicinity. His aide then snapped an arm between me and the senator, and followed that with his back as he turned the senator away from me. I had been dismissed.

I found Siobhan and relayed what happened. We made the drive home fuming at how General Taluto's invitation had mislead us into believing Lou and Phil would be directly recognized, and the circumstances of their deaths would be faced.

Once home we attempted to shrug off the cloud of malcontent and adjust to lives as single moms. I grabbed any opportunity to play with the boys, and the five of us made it a point to find something fun to do every day. Thanks to the kids, I managed to push aside the weight of our reality for at least a few minutes each day. Siobhan clung to her daughter, too, and we would often spend time together with our kids, helping each other adjust to our new lives.

Taking advantage of unusually warm weather, I'd been giving the boys rides on an electric scooter. The large hill to one side of our house overpowered the feeble scooter engine and kept us captive on the flat patch of road directly in front of our neighbor's house. He finally began to wave to us, and I considered this progress. We developed a tentative nodding acquaintance and the man I once thought to be snarly and cold turned out to be an actual human being. It was nice to be on friendly terms with him, and I welcomed the opportunity to have adult contact. I was intrigued by a friend of his whom I would see on a regular basis next door. He'd look our way but refuse to return my wave, regardless of the fact that I'd be standing in plain view, waving directly at him. What started out as mild curiosity on my part had developed into a challenge. I was determined to get him to wave back.

Outside one afternoon with a visiting friend, I noticed my neighbor in his yard. He was concentrating on stirring a steamy concoction in a barrel. Curious, I walked over to him, taking in the image of this hulk of a man towering over me, a bandanna wrapped around his head, dirty jeans and t–shirt damp with steam from whatever was brewing in the barrel. He gave me a small smile hello, and I teased him that with the long stick, tall barrel, and volumes of steam coming from the mix, he looked like a warlock stirring a magic potion. Thinking at first I might have offended him, I waited for an angry response. Instead he laughed, and explained what he was doing.

He was a trapper, and he was boiling his steel traps. He'd skin raccoons, fox, and mink to sell their fur. Realizing he wasn't kidding, I tamped down the desire to preach to him about the evils of the fur trade, the unnecessary suffering of animals caught in traps, to attempt to convince him to stop. Instead, I nodded and said "Oh." Told him that I prefer the warlock explanation. He shot me a big grin and it transformed him into a cute country boy. I decided that in the interest of keeping the newfound peace between us, I'd smother my comments about the trapping thing. It was just so good to be able to have an adult conversation right in my own yard. Seeing a friendly face can't hurt. In my other life, I would have argued with him about it, but these days I just didn't care enough. I was still so hurt and weak that the possibility of developing a friendship with someone who apparently knew nothing about me was worth it.

We hung out for a little while and I found myself relaxing, enjoying the conversation with this neighborhood Davy Crockett. It was the first real conversation we'd had, and I finally learned his name, Keith. Excusing myself a while later when one of the boys called for me, I walked back to the house, my step a little lighter. Some sense of me was reawakening, the need to have human contact, be a part of life again.

●　　●　　●　　●　　●

The holiday season was here. Lacking the courage to confront the holidays just yet, I fled to Arizona for Thanksgiving. My sister, Janice, and my brother, Tim, accompanied me while the kids stayed with family members. While I was gone, Vicki and her husband, Rich, took the kids to pick up a Christmas tree and decorate it, and the kids "surprised" me with the decorations when I arrived home.

I knew I was disappointing the kids by leaving. And I was again ashamed at how weak I was. But I could not find the courage to open the boxes with our memories and decorations Lou had packed away last year. I had every intention of helping the kids have a happy Christmas season. I used the trip to Arizona to heal from Kuwait and banish enough fear to find some joy with my kids.

With Thanksgiving behind me, I navigated the first holiday season of the rest of my life. Siobhan and I maintained steady contact, talking each other through bouts of depression and anxiety. Ray, too, continued to be a saving grace for me. His reassurance and steadfast compassion were exactly what I needed. As he and I became closer, and our friendship became independent of the one he had shared with Lou, I began calling him by his real name, Steve, instead of the name Ray that Lou had dubbed him.

I met other widows online, through the Gold Star Wives website. All the women on that site have lost a husband in the military. Some of them were Vietnam widows, others were new like me, and the rest fell in between. I became reliant on these online chats, and several widows and I shared the dark humor that helped me cope. This diverse support group, in addition to my family and friends, was priceless.

A few days after my return from Arizona, Siobhan called me. The day before Thanksgiving she had received a FedEx package with Phil's autopsy report. Caught up in the move and my kids, I hadn't requested Lou's yet. Listening to her relate the experience of opening and reading the report, I could only imagine how traumatizing it had been for her. Hearing what we'd heard in Kuwait had nearly undone us. Now she had read through the autopsy report all by herself. At Thanksgiving.

Knowing how rough it was for Siobhan, we still believed we were better off having that report. There is an insatiable need to uncover every morsel of information available. To arm ourselves with as much knowledge about this as possible in a frantic effort to find a measure of understanding about what our husbands experienced. How this happened. Why it happened. I made the call, faxed the letter, and requested Lou's autopsy report.

I was on the phone with Steve one Friday afternoon when a FedEx truck pulled up to my house. *Oh no. Oh no.* My heart slammed against my chest as the breath rushed out of me. I whimpered into the phone and Steve asked what was wrong. His voice rallied me and I told him a FedEx truck was here. He stayed on the phone as I got the package from Mortuary Affairs. Just like that, the harsh reality of my circumstance careened back. I was holding Lou's autopsy report.

All pride evaporated and I was now literally pleading with Steve to come here tonight. My need to know the contents of the report was outdone by the fear of doing so, and I didn't want to do it alone. I begged him to come tonight, take this report from me. Colonel

Sullivan was up at Drum, and offered to review the report with me. I asked Steve to please come, take it from me tonight, and bring it with him back to Drum.

Steve lived about an hour from me, and had a dinner date that night. But I was so unnerved by this report that I didn't even feel guilty about putting this on him. He said he'd call me later, and I thanked him. I had put the kids to bed and was fresh out of a steamy shower when he called. A few wrong turns and an hour later, he arrived. Mildly cranky about the longer than anticipated drive and visibly tired. But still Steve, and I was happy to see him. A quick hug hello and we settled into the kitchen with a cocktail.

We talked for a while and then, seeing he was tired, I suggested he get some sleep. I still couldn't sleep in bed like a normal person, so I offered him my bedroom while I spread out on the couch and spaced out on TV until morning.

Sunshine found its way past the curtains and into the house. Another night done. I tiptoed upstairs to the kitchen. Started making breakfast as quietly as possible so as not to wake anyone. I had enough time for a cup of coffee in the early morning quiet before one sleepy–eyed boy joined me. This began a trickle of heads until all four boys were with me in the kitchen. A few minutes later, Steve joined us. He hung out for the morning and it was touching to see him with the boys. Normally shy and reserved around strangers, Trevor surprised me by taking an instant liking to Steve. The two of them sat on the couch like old friends, and I wondered if part of Lou was here, watching his friend interact with the kids.

I gave him the report as he stood to go. Told him had I emailed Doc Sullivan and we'd arranged a meeting at Fort Drum that week. He said he'd be able to get together afterwards. A hug goodbye and he was gone.

Later that week, I was in the car, making my way to Watertown. Accustomed to my trips, the kids asked few questions as I left them with family. The last time I made this drive, I was on my way to see Lou, unaware it would be the last time I'd see him. I called him several times en route and we laughed together in anticipation of my arrival. It is a beautiful four–hour drive and I'd absorbed my surroundings that day. I'd been so glad to be going to him. That had been five months ago, and I couldn't believe how life had been spinning ever since.

Today I was driving to the town near Fort Drum. Lou and I ate our last meal together at a restaurant in that town. The Home Depot is there, where we stopped and bought some tile. I still had the receipt in my wallet. Today, however, my husband would not be waiting for me. His autopsy report would. Doc Sullivan would offer compassion and a measure of comfort, but what she shared with me would be sickening. The meeting with Steve was the only bright spot I could expect in this trip.

I tortured myself by listening to CDs Lou had burned for me. Then, like the last time I made this drive, I picked up my cell phone and called him. I knew it was not a healthy thing to do. I knew it was probably a pretty sick thing to do. But I could not stop myself. I have continued paying Lou's cell phone bill because I don't have the heart to turn his phone off. Today I dialed the familiar numbers. Heard his voice, "Hey you've reached Lou. I'm not available to take your call. Leave a message and I'll call you back." So brief. So hard to believe that he would never again answer my call.

Once in the hotel I called Doc. She arrived quickly and faced me from a chair next to the bed. Told me she'd condensed the report to a list. I was bracing myself, deep breaths, gathering my courage. I nodded, and she began.

In as gentle a tone as possible, Doc said things like: His brain was not damaged. His jaw was broken. That surprised her because he was speaking so well. Multiple broken bones on his left hand. I remembered feeling his hand at the funeral home. Cuts, scrapes, bruises here and there. A large amount of fragments throughout his lower body. Extensive liver damage inflicted. And then the fact that a thorough exam proved Lou was in excellent physical condition and would have led a long life had he not been murdered.

My head was bowed, chin to chest. Eyes squeezed shut, I pictured Lou broken, bleeding, suffering. Doc was flipping the page, preparing to itemize the rest of his injuries, but I'd had enough. Asked her to please stop. She set the papers down and moved next to me, arm around my shoulder, and I was crying like a little girl. Again.

When I managed to somewhat compose myself, Doc had a surprise for me. General Taluto was here and would like to meet, offer condolences. I didn't know what to say. Here? Now? I knew he'd been promoted to Adjutant General of the NY National Guard. But normally I prepared for meetings like this. I had questions ready and my thoughts organized. Right now I was about as disheveled as I had ever been—mentally and physically. But knowing I'd regret declining, I agreed to go downstairs and meet him. He knew Phil and had tried to contact Siobhan and me, but the gag order had prohibited him from doing so. Instead, the General's wife sent a letter explaining why her husband had not contacted us. I'd been told General Taluto had been the one taking up our cause in Iraq, pleading our issues with the others, and encouraging the decision makers to accommodate our wish to witness the 32. I was curious to hear what he had to say, and wondering if he would have anything to mention about the disastrous welcome home ceremony we'd attended.

In the hotel lobby, the small–framed, gray haired general offered me a firm handshake coupled with a friendly grin. Having no idea what to say to him, I studied him while he spoke, and asked few questions. I was still reeling from the impact of the autopsy report. Noticing the impromptu meeting, the hotel manager asked if we would prefer a more private room. We accepted and moved to a small office. There we spent about another half hour discussing the case, what had happened and what was yet to happen. The general told me about a day shortly before Lou and Phil were killed. Phil had showed up at the general's office on business and wound up taking a helicopter ride with him. The manner in which General Taluto spoke of Phil suggested a familiarity and respect for him, and a genuine sadness at his loss. I appreciated that he made no attempt to pretend he knew Lou personally or to ingratiate himself with false sincerity. Everything about him seemed up front and candid. Yet I reserved an opinion of him for now. I was still holding a grudge about the ceremony we felt duped into, and I had been introduced to so many officials I wasn't sure I could trust any of them. I later found out the gag order he told me he was complying with had been his own, and he was the one who prevented the trial team from contacting us.

The meeting over, I returned to my room and prepared for the next meeting that night. Captain Dominic Oto had taken over the command of the 42nd HHC for Phil, and he was in town tonight. Steve had supplied Dominic with my phone number, and Dominic called to ask if I'd like him to pick me up. I accepted his offer and was soon seated in the front of Dominic's pickup with the heat vents blasting full force on my face. It was freezing out, and the heat felt great. We arrived at the restaurant and munched on appetizers while waiting for Steve and getting to know each other. The heavyset, soft–faced Captain had a limited acquaintance with Phil, and had never met Lou. But his eyes shimmered with the hint of tears as he spoke of his experience in Iraq and his involvement with Martinez's arrest.

Dominic explained he'd been present when Martinez was arrested. He'd moved into Phil's space after the blood had been washed away and the damage had been repaired. Dominic told me how Martinez spat at him as he was being escorted away, how the soldiers had been shocked to hear one of their own had been arrested.

I made it through a couple of drinks before Steve arrived. Dominic excused himself, and I gladly banished the day's events from my head as Steve turned the night around with his good humor and sense of fun.

I felt different the next morning. More focused. Better able to grasp things, how they were and how they needed to be from this point on. I realized I needed to be alone now.

Decided to use this period in my life to my advantage. Capitalize on the opportunity to do some soul searching, turn the tables on the loneliness and use the time to figure out a new game plan for my life. I felt oddly empowered by the fact that I'd returned to this town, learned what was in the autopsy report, and was still standing. I was here where Lou was, where he should have returned to, and I'd survived the experience. The next order of business was to see my boys through Christmas. I drove home more certain than before that I would be able to turn my life around. Maybe.

CHAPTER NINE

THE NEW YEAR

✪ ✪ ✪

Christmas. This year instead of Lou, I had a Christmas angel. Steve arrived at my house early on the 23rd. That night he came with me to my parents' house. The two rows of Christmas stockings were there, minus Lou's. Just last year Lou was joking about getting bumped up to the head of the second row.

Watching Steve talk with my family, catching his eye as he'd look up to check on me, I wondered how I would have made it through any of this without him. Once the kids opened their presents, we said our good byes to my family, and I had the boys all tucked into bed at home within the hour. Spent the night on the couch, while Steve slept in my bedroom.

After breakfast with Lou's parents the next morning, I walked Steve to his car and he gave me a hug good bye. He'd invited me to spend Christmas Day with him and his mom, and I'd yet to decide what to do. But as he pulled me in for a hug, the decision seemed an easy one, and I told him I'd take him up on his invitation.

Tucking the kids in that night, I studied each of them, thinking about how they were handling this. How I was handling this.

Trevor, whose gigantic blues eyes pierced the faint light in his room. Six years old and yet he was the one who seemed to be guiding me through. He had many of Lou's mannerisms and inherited his dad's natural curiosity. He and Lou were inseparable when Lou was home. I knew Trevor was hurting and still he was determined to squeeze every ounce of enjoyment out of life. He talked about Lou, worried a lot, and sometimes carried himself in such sadness. But I knew he'd be okay in the end. Like Lou, he has an absolute enthusiasm for life. Now, on Christmas Eve, he was nothing but eyes and teeth as he grinned at me.

Colin. Five–years old and already such an old soul. He rarely spoke about Lou, or allowed himself to cry for his father. He worried about protecting me. When this boy smiles, he can capture an entire audience. His outlet is music and he will lose himself in a song. We used to sing, "You are my Sunshine" to each other all the time. I can't remember the last time we'd done that now. A kiss on the cheek, one more hug, and I rubbed his head as he drifted off to his troubled sleep.

Seanie. Four–years old and the family sweetheart. Once his light hair darkens, he will truly resemble Lou. Sean has cheeks a mother has to kiss often. He has a love of puzzles and artwork. He will happily spend hours coloring, drawing, or working out puzzles of any kind. And he'd always agree to a snuggle on my lap. In the car with the boys soon after Lou died, Sean said he saw dad sitting in the van with us, smiling. I'd reached back to take Sean's hand and he'd said, "Oh, mom! Dad is holding your hand!" He wished each night for a magic wand, so he could bring Dad back. I leaned over his bed now, saw he was close to sleep. I kissed his sweet check and he smiled softly. "Best mom ever," he whispered. I closed my eyes and hoped he would always feel that way.

Jeremy. Our baby. One and a half–years old and such a little maniac. His constant antics and wily little grin made it easy to get mad at him but impossible to stay mad at him. He'd take pleasure in being with his brothers, getting into trouble, and stirring things up. I thought back to Lou leaving that day, changing Jeremy's diaper on his way out to the car. "Have this kid potty–trained before I get home," he'd ordered me with a grin. "Wouldn't it be great if this is the last diaper I have to change?" meaning, if Jeremy no longer needed diapers when Lou returned. But the question threw me off guard and gave me the chills. I looked down at Jeremy now and hoped that Lou could see him. Could see all of us and be at peace, trust that I will care for his kids.

My parents and my brother, Tim, were on hand to watch the boys open presents in the morning. Leaving the carnage of wrapping paper behind, the boys and I drove to Long Island and spent the afternoon with Steve and his mom. It took two and a half hours to get there. Jeremy threw up in the car and had a fever when we arrived. But Steve's mom was undaunted by my ragged appearance and Jeremy's vomit–covered clothes, and welcomed us into her home. Our first Christmas was as successful as I could ever have hoped for.

The next day, I took the tree down, relieved to have made it through the season. Dragging it into the woods, I walked out feeling stronger for getting through this, however shakily.

In the woods with the dogs a couple of days later, I ran into Keith. We'd grown friendlier in the past few months so my smile was real as I walked toward him. "Hey how was your Christmas?" he asked. "Over." I replied. Laughing, he said, "Yeah. Same here." We talked as we made our way through the trees and he laughingly told me how it had amused him to see my Christmas tree out there the day after Christmas. The topic of New Year's Eve came up. Still recovering from a disastrously failed marriage, he had no plans for that night. I told him my friend Siobhan was coming over, explained who she was, and said he is welcome to join us. Believing no sane person would willingly spend New Year's Eve with two new widows, I nearly gaped in surprise when he replied, "Okay thanks." with a smile. He did wind up coming, and while Siobhan slept off a cold on my couch, I enjoyed getting to know this stranger next door. Before I knew it, the new year had been rung in.

• • • • •

With the holidays officially over, Siobhan and I returned to business and planned a meeting in DC with the entire prosecution team. We needed to know what was going on. Look all of them in the eye and establish some sort of connection with these people we were forced to rely on. A few weeks ago we'd received notice that Meg was no longer on the trial team but would remain involved with the families. No explanations were given as to why she had either left or been removed from the team, and we were anxious to meet her replacement. While the investigation and case were being conducted and built each day, our families received no word on any developments. We remained uneasy and impatient for updates and resolution.

The night before our meeting, I sat with Keith and relaxed in the nighttime stillness in the house. The boys were long asleep and I was keyed up in anticipation of the meeting tomorrow. Keith and I had grown close over the weeks, and I looked forward to spending time with him. He was planning on moving to Wyoming, where he had a job waiting as a hunting and fishing guide. Neither of us was at a point in life where we were looking for anyone special. I was, though, curious to know how much of life I would be able to reclaim one day. Would I be alone forever? Would a man ever touch me again? Would I ever find someone I could trust, care for, and open the boys up to? I doubted it.

Lou and I had talked about what would happen if one of us died young. He told me we would each recover and find someone else, as difficult as it would be. We were too young to be alone. I was furious with him for saying that. Told him I would come back and haunt him if he ever found someone else. And I was hurt that he thought he could find someone besides me. But I realized later that these thoughts did not mean he didn't love me. I got that now.

It was crazy to be thinking like this only six months after Lou's death. I knew that. I just didn't care. Wasn't thinking clearly, or being fair to anyone. Especially Keith. We sat up on the couch that night, and I told him nothing of what I was thinking. Around four A.M. we dozed off. At 5 A.M. I startled awake. "Get out!" I yelled to Keith. Manners escaped me as I realized the time and all I had to do before getting on the road. He gave me a kiss on the cheek and wished me luck on the trip before closing the door behind himself. I spent the next two hours getting the kids up and dressed and ready to go, delivering them to school and daycare, and then making my way to Siobhan's.

Siobhan is many things but a morning person is not one of them. Harried and running behind schedule, she nevertheless had binders of organized information to bring with us. Between the two of us, we equaled one prepared unit, able to stay focused and on time for meetings, and keep detailed notes of all we learned.

Arriving at Siobhan's by eight–thirty, I harassed her out the door quickly enough to arrive just on time in Arlington for our afternoon meeting. Meg met us downstairs in the designated building, and brought us upstairs to the conference room. There we met Captain Adam Siple for the first time. The compact man with bashful blue eyes and almost yellow hair was new to the team. Captain Rob McGovern, who had been on the trial team for just long enough for us to remember his name before also leaving for reasons unknown to us, stopped in to say hi. Then, we met Captain Kelly Hughes, newly assigned to the team. The smiling face highlighted by vibrant blue eyes and dark hair of the woman who was extending her hand to me were a welcome sight. Since Meg had left the team, we'd hoped for a woman to be assigned to the case again. A woman, we'd thought, would be less restricted in dealing with us on a personal basis, would relate to us better than an all–male team. So we were pleased to meet her, and my first impression of her was reassuring.

Captain John Benson and Major Ruzicka joined us, and we spent a couple hours in the conference room, poring over past and future events. It was a little disconcerting sitting at one end of the oversize table with Siobhan, looking across at the group of attorneys we were trying so hard to believe in. When Siobhan broke down in a rare moment of public tears, it felt as if we were on a stage, and she was in the spotlight. Knowing she felt it, too, and wanting to ease the discomfort, I handed her some tissues and commandeered the floor, asking whatever questions popped into my head and telling tales of Lou until the sniffling subsided and Siobhan cast me a tired smile. The meeting concluded, and the round of handshakes signaled our time to depart.

Mentally and physically exhausted, I opted to turn in early rather than joining Siobhan and her friend at dinner. Instead I downed a pair of sleeping pills and slept the night away.

• • • • •

Life developed a new twist for me. Now, instead of spending the nights alone, Keith came over when the kids were in bed and spent a couple hours hanging out with me. One night, Keith and I were in the kitchen. Busy cleaning up dinner dishes, I didn't realize Keith had wandered to the living room until I heard him say, "Hey buddy, how are you?" and I hurried to the darkened room to see Trevor staring wide-eyed at this unfamiliar giant.

Trevor rarely speaks to anyone he doesn't know unless coerced into doing so. But here, he smiled a cautious little smile at Keith before hugging me good night and returning to bed.

Looking at Keith, I caught a thoughtful expression on his face as he said, "What a cutie." We then begin talking about kids, Keith's former stepchildren, my little guys, our own childhoods, etc. As the hours passed, I discovered an entirely new side to this man. I found myself liking him even more, and the next day I realized I would actually miss him when he left.

The next few months were busy. My real estate license was still current, and Keith asked me to list his house for him. One weekend, we held an open house. Keith's friend Benny, the one who steadfastly refused to wave, was up to help Keith prepare. We'd laughed about the name I'd dubbed him, He Who Never Waves, and come to the point where we could comfortably hang out. Benny asked me what I do for an open house and I'd responded straight-faced that I usually put on a sexy little outfit, cracked open a beer, and lured buyers in. That had flustered him, and he'd walked away unsure if I was serious or not.

The day of the open house, Keith sent Benny on a mission to put lead signs up while I snuck over wearing a hot red outfit I'd picked up for the occasion, cloaked by my long coat as I plowed through the foot of snow between our homes and laughing at the absurdity of this; I would never have done something like this in my other life. I settled at the table and we waited for Benny to return. One look at me and Benny's face was redder than my outfit as we all burst out laughing. It felt good to be able to joke around and laugh again, and I was smiling to myself as I changed into more suitable clothes for the open house.

As the weeks went on, the kids had come to be comfortable with Keith and looked forward to seeing him each day. He, in turn, had grown attached to them and was clearly torn about leaving. The kids started asking Keith why he was leaving; would he call us, talk with us on the computer like Dad did, would he come back? I agonized over allowing all of us to care for him because I knew his departure would create a whole new void in our lives. This was unfair to Keith. Our relationship had deepened beyond friendship, but I knew I was in no way ready to commit to him. I was unable to fall in love the way he deserved a woman to love him, yet I gladly took him up on it when his house sold and he said he'd stay with us.

Throughout all of this, our families had been awaiting charges to be referred against Martinez. Since the trip to DC, we now knew that additional charges were to be brought at a second 32 Hearing. In addition to existing charges, Martinez now faced charges dealing with unlawful disposition of government property, unlawful possession of alcohol, and unlawful possession of a flare gun. Petty charges in normal circumstances, but in this case they contributed to the character of the defendant. We dealt with the unwelcome delay by reminding ourselves it was for a good cause.

A couple of weeks before this hearing, Siobhan received some of the emails she'd requested from Phil's AKO (Army Knowledge Online) account. In these emails were messages from Phil about Martinez, stating that the supply sergeant was a problem and needed to be dealt with. It gave us a new look at what had been going on, and prompted me to request Lou's emails.

The hearing date arrived and I prepared for my first trip to Fort Bragg, NC. We resigned ourselves to traveling from New York to North Carolina for any proceedings when the case had wound up transferred into the hands of the VIII Airborne Corps upon the Corps redeployment to Fort Bragg. How that was worked out was explained to us and still made no sense, but we were forced to accept it.

My first drive to Fort Bragg was a test of my patience, bogged in unrelenting traffic on I-95. I told myself it was just a few times, that we'd get this 32 done, maybe one or two more hearings, and be done with the whole thing within the year. In the meantime, I was grateful Keith had offered to take care of the boys so I could make the roughly 650-mile trip a day early and have a day to myself to unwind.

Phil's sister, Alyssa, and her husband, Michael, arrived with Siobhan a day after me, and we all met with Valerie, the Victim Witness Liaison at Fort Bragg. Valerie's bubbly personality was matched by her bright wardrobe. Every time we saw her over the years, she was decked out in perfectly coordinated, vibrant outfits that were overshadowed only by her smile. Helpless to provide us with the answers we needed, she strove to accommodate any other needs we might have.

The courtroom was double booked, and our hearing was bumped to the conference room. Larger than the makeshift courtroom in Kuwait, it was nonetheless a little too cozy for comfort. The super-size table claimed most of the space, projecting in a line straight up the middle of the room. Chairs were placed for each set of counsel on either side, near the entrance, and the chairs set up for spectators. The IO's chair was at the head of the table, almost across the room, and Martinez's chair was disturbingly close to ours. Whoever had the last seat in our row would be able to lean over and touch him.

A peek at the courtroom we would presumably hold the rest of the hearings and the trial itself in showed a room smaller than I'd imagined. Directly in the doors was the gallery, with padded benches resembling church pews on either side. About seven rows each. It looked like each row would hold up to ten people, if they were all crammed in. In front of the bar on both sides was a table for counsel and the defendant. The government table was on the right, a few feet from the bar separating counsel tables and the courtroom floor from the spectator seats. Our families would sit on this side of the room. The court reporter had a desk and chair for his or her paraphernalia immediately in front of the raised desk and black swivel chair for the judge, and to the right of that was another chair and a microphone in front. To the far right side of the room was the panel box. Two rows of more padded chairs lined up behind long desks. I counted fourteen of those seats.

Assessing the view from our seats, we noticed the gallery was on a small slant, and the view in many places was blocked by large pillars. I imagined Terri Seifert sitting here listening to the trial against the man who murdered her husband, and was renewed with gratefulness that she remained willing to coach me through this process she had endured. Our tour complete, we returned to our hotel to pass the night.

Morning. I was up and nervously watching the clock. My stomach was churning and my palms were cold and clammy. I felt the loneliness of being alone in a hotel room and wished with all my heart that Lou was here. This feeling brought with it a stab of guilt, like I was cheating on Keith by missing Lou.

I was dressed and downstairs early. Saw my in–laws and two of Lou's sisters, Jen and Vicki. This would be an emotional day for them, seeing Martinez in person for the first time.

On hand to assist the families, Meg came down and joined me. One by one we all assembled in the dining room, valiantly trying to choke down the terrible food. The part of me that is compulsively early for everything started alerting me it was time to go. There was quite a crowd to gather for a caravan over and several of us were nowhere near ready. I didn't know most of the people from Phil's side, and I was annoyed to be forced to wait for them.

Finally, we were on our way, and I was feeling bad about my internal temper tantrum. Linda Thorburn had been assigned to work with Meg for this hearing, and she now rode shotgun in Meg's car. Siobhan and I were sitting in the back. We approached the gates and the two of us began discussing the curious abbreviations on our Widow IDs. In one spot were three letters, URW, and we wondered what on earth that meant. As I was thinking it, Siobhan laughed out "You Are Widows." For whatever reason, we both found that to be hysterical and started convulsing in laughter. Linda and Meg exchanged glances and shook their heads.

We arrived at the building and were ushered through security, metal detectors, and into our seats in the conference room. As it turned out, there was no need for me to panic about the time; we spent the next couple of hours stewing while Martinez held the show up. Those of us who'd already had the pleasure of seeing the star of the show in person were impatient and annoyed. For those about to see him for the first time, however, there was the added dread and uncertainty.

The explanation we were given for this delay was vague. Martinez was being difficult about something. We had no way of knowing what was really going on behind the scenes that day. Why the trial team and defense counsel all wore pinched, strained faces more drawn than usual. I attributed my sense of something big happening behind closed doors to an overactive imagination. Surely the trial team would tell us of any important developments. Two and a half years later, I would remember my feeling that day, and wish I had trusted it enough to pursue it then.

Finally, we were told Martinez was on his way up. Colonel Reinert took his place at the head of the room. We all sat and stared at each other until someone walked up to the colonel and spoke quietly to him. He looked at us apologetically and informed us that Martinez was, in fact, not quite on his way yet. I offered to go get him. The colonel smiled.

After another eternity, with little fanfare, defense, Martinez, and his wife joined us. Now that everyone was present, the next logical step would be to begin the proceeding. Instead, defense and prosecution left the room, followed by Colonel Reinert. This left the two families, Martinez, and his wife in the room with a couple of MPs and reporters. We were so close to him that some of us could lean over and touch him. We all sat there, glaring at him and his wife. "Isn't this cozy." I said. My composure was leaving me as I stared at the man who had caused so much damage. I looked at his flat eyes and wondered what Lou thought when he looked at this creature. Many of us were openly contemplating how quickly we would be able to pounce on him and end this. I started talking with my sister–in–law, loudly reminiscing about the day I'd been notified Lou was dead. Others joined in and the topic changed to methods of execution we would prefer to see used on Martinez. The MPs concentrated on the floor and allowed us to needle the defendant. It wasn't much, but it did provide a release. Eventually the others returned and we once again looked expectantly to the front of the room. Wondered what the hell was going on.

Take Two. With no explanation, the previous scene was repeated. We found ourselves once again waiting in close proximity to the person we all hate. This time, though, MPs came and removed Martinez. His wife was left sitting there, the focus of our glares, until she left.

Take Three. This time, when everyone returned, the proceedings finally began. Whatever was happening must have been resolved and have no bearing on the 32 Hearing today.

We started with two of the three witnesses set to testify by phone. The first witness was Sergeant 1st Class Peggy Schumacher. Before she had a chance to be sworn in, defense counsel were on their feet, clamoring to exclude her telephonic testimony. The prosecution admitted the witness was never offered to be put on orders to testify in spite of her stated willingness to do so. Captain Benson explained she "wasn't an important witness" and therefore it wasn't deemed necessary to issue orders to her. Siobhan and I looked at each other, wondering how any witness could be "not important" and if they are, why include them in the first place. Maybe not so uncommon in the legal sense but to us it seemed absurd, and our confidence in the prosecutor wavered. This hearing was not off to an impressive start.

The first witness to actually testify was Sergeant Amy Harlan. As I watched, a cute young woman walked to the witness seat. I recognized her from the hallway. In one of the waiting sessions Vicki and I had searched for some cokes. This woman was sitting in the hallway with a young guy. She smilingly told us where a machine is located and I thanked her. Now she was settled nervously in her seat and began her testimony.

Sergeant Amy Harlan was the supply NCO at FOB Danger. She knew Martinez from February through June, when she saw him almost every day. She spoke of an Iraqi national named Tiger who was friends with Martinez. Once, she witnessed Martinez give some army issued printers to Tiger and ask for a bike or a motorcycle in return. She also accompanied Martinez to the Defense Reutilization and Marketing Office at another base, Anaconda. There, she witnessed Martinez turn in paperwork proclaiming he was turning in equipment that he did not.

In April or May of 2005, Martinez showed Sergeant Harlan a privately owned, 7 millimeter Iraqi pistol. He boasted it was his and she saw him take it from a filing cabinet in the supply room. She also saw him in the supply room with what he told her was alcohol. Martinez spoke to her about selling equipment and a truck to locals, and she saw him with a flare gun and flares.

When defense questioned her, Sergeant Harlan testified that there were signs on the printers saying they were broken. She agreed most people piled stuff up and it is a common procedure to falsify documents when property is lost or unaccounted for. She gave body armor as an example of something she herself falsified paperwork for. In general, she stated, supply sergeants "helped each other out" in these matters.

Defense changed the subject and the witness went with it, testifying that she did not, in fact, smell or taste the purported alcohol. She also said that Iraqi weapons were commonly stored at FOB Danger.

Prosecution took another turn with Sergeant Harlan, and she specified that Martinez told her he received the 7–millimeter from a local. As far as the body armor she spoke of, only the fabric was improperly turned in. When asked who the head of supply was, the witness answered, "Martinez." Defense then made one last point, saying Phil was ultimately responsible for supply. By the end of this testimony, my feelings for defense were subzero and my feelings for this witness were turning unfriendly.

Sergeant Harlan was excused. Passing me on her way out, her light brown hair framing a petite face with downcast eyes, she glanced quickly at me on her way out of the room.

A break was called while attempts were made to get the Iraqi witness on the phone. We gathered outside on the balcony to discuss the morning's events. There was some difficulty getting the witness on the phone due to the delays this morning. We were about to give up when we received word that he was standing by. Court was called to order again.

We heard a heavily accented yet clearly understandable male voice on the line. He unhesitatingly identified himself and said he was calling from a room at Speicher in Iraq. Tiger confirmed that he was alone and not using any notes. Said he lived on FOB Danger and was currently employed as a translator.

The prosecution began to question Tiger, but the witness interrupted to "say hello to my good friend Martinez." There was a moment of silence in the room. We knew from the trial team that this witness was Martinez's friend and accomplice in the transfer of equipment to Iraqis. We'd expected him to sound defensive or surly about being pegged as Martinez's buddy. Martinez slunk down in his chair. Gregory, now a major, and Cipriano each lost more color from their already pallid faces. Prosecution appeared to be biting back smiles, and we were openmouthed in disbelief.

The witness then testified about a time he convoyed to the media station, and asked a Sergeant Gates to give him some printers. Gates refused but Martinez was present and overheard the request. Martinez approached Tiger and offered printers from FOB Danger. Martinez asked about motorcycles as well. Tiger cheerily spoke of going to FOB Danger with his dad and brother in a truck. They backed the truck up to supply and Martinez gave them about twenty printers as well as three or four fax machines belonging to the 42nd Infantry. The equipment bore labels proclaiming them to be property of the army. Tiger testified that Martinez told him to remove the stickers, which he did. He then sold the printers at the general market. Upon request, Tiger also supplied Martinez with alcohol.

When defense took over, Tiger clarified that he asked Sergeant Gates for broken printers and asked Martinez for printers in general. The ones he received from Martinez were either broken or contained no CDs or cables. He stated Martinez offered to buy a motorcycle from him. As Major Gregory attempted to ask the next question, Tiger interrupted again. Witness and counsel engaged in a moment of voice battle, each trying to speak over the other, until Major Gregory, having lost control of his witness, yielded the floor. Still worked up from the verbal scuffle, Tiger loudly apologized to his friend for not getting him the motorcycle he wanted, and wondered aloud if it had been a World War I or World War II motorcycle he'd promised to get.

Defense had no more questions. The witness was thanked and hastily disconnected.

I turned to look at everyone else to see if I imagined or exaggerated in my mind how outlandish this testimony was. All around me, people were shaking their heads in wonder, bewildered by the proceedings so far.

Next up was CID agent Comesanas, telephonically testifying from Connecticut. Agent Comesanas had been a CID investigator for one and a half years, and was employed as a state trooper. On June 8, 2005, he was involved in the murder investigation at FOB Danger. Before I was even notified that Lou was dead, this man was walking around the explosion site.

We listened as Comesanas described searching Martinez's room, finding a flare pistol and about thirteen flares in a plastic bag within a rucksack. The witness was excused, and that was the end of testimony. Defense asked the colonel to delay his findings until such a time that defense was granted a mitigation specialist to work with their team and offer testimony on the defendant's behalf. This was another surprise to us. We'd heard defense make this same request in Kuwait, six months ago. Tasked with digging into the defendant's life, searching for experiences or reasons to excuse his actions, a mitigation specialist could invoke the pity card for Martinez and convince a panel to go easy on him. Regardless of how disgusting it was to us, what turned our stomachs even more was the fact that this six–month–old request was still an issue. A defendant in a capital case is entitled to a mitigation specialist. Proceeding without one is grounds for an appeal. Knowing that, it was unclear to us why the government would withhold the resource. To us, it seemed like a delay that could well have been avoided. It was just another frustration for us, not being privy to the rationale behind decisions like this.

The request was granted and we were sent home to wait. Again.

CHAPTER TEN

A BUMPY NEW LIFE AND THE FLAT TIRES OF JUSTICE

✪ ✪ ✪

The arrival of spring brought with it a familiar sense of fear. I have not figured out why, but each time the season changes, it sends me into anxiety attacks. Another season between myself and Lou. Another sign that this march through time will stop for no one.

I began visiting with Lynda, my friend who runs Equine Rescue. My "blue–collar therapy" there was a great outlet for me. Being with the horses, smelling their scent, and the workout of cleaning so many stalls was a great healer. Deciding to adopt horses of my own, I put in my request and adopted two horses. Lenny, a black Percheron, and Lil Joe, a small black and white paint, became welcome additions to our family, and the kids and I have benefited from the time we spend taking care of them.

The day was drawing near when the sale of Keith's house would be final. It was an anxious period of time for us. Neither one of us had been looking for or expecting to find a new and lasting relationship. He had not been even remotely interested in a nodding acquaintance when I moved in. I had just spent almost eleven years flourishing in a relationship with Lou, and it had been only a year since he was killed. I was emotionally crippled. The person who was able to love so freely and honestly, the person who held so much naïve enthusiasm and threw her entire being into life with careless abandon was gone, my ability to love permanently wounded. But the impending sale of Keith's house meant we had decisions to make.

Both of us would prefer to continue as is for a while. See how it goes, take our time. But neither of us wanted to say good bye. I enjoyed the friendship, and thought I could help him work through his own emotional turmoil as he helped me with mine. Keith was not close to his own family. His mom died in a botched surgical procedure when he was nineteen. He was angry at the world. His past was full of elements I didn't know of, but saw only how bitter he had become as a result. But he was gentle with the kids and strong for me, and I wanted to believe the friendship we had would sustain each of us. After hours of discussing our options, we decided Keith would move in with us.

A few months later I had purchased a new home and we were busy moving again. We were all excited to renovate the tired interior and spend summers enjoying the nearly 4 acres of property with a pool and two ponds. The icing on that cake was that two of my sisters, Janice and Beth, had houses less than 2 miles from our new home. Our kids would ride the school bus together and see each other in school. It was idyllic.

The relationship with Keith was a tough pill for some of the family members to swallow. There was concern about my choice to move in with him. They liked Keith but were slow to trust him, and wondered if I fully appreciated the decision I was making. Initially, doubts about Keith abounded, and my relationship with Lou's family suffered. Accusations flew from some that I was forgetting Lou, allowing his children to forget their dad. Others thought Keith may be preying on my vulnerability. I, in turn, accused them of attempting to hinder my healing and needing to see me as miserable as possible just to verify I had loved Lou. The family that had once been peaceful and supportive of each other now drew lines and chose sides. It was a time of raw and hateful words that served only to unite Keith and me in our attempt to carve some happiness out for ourselves and the boys.

Siobhan and Steve were my sounding boards through that time. If they had doubts about Keith they never voiced them to me. Instead, they offered to listen to my troubles and support me in whatever decisions I made. They believed both families would calm down and we would work our way through this turmoil. And they were right. Eventually, we called a truce. My family accepted Keith after just a short hesitation. It was about a year before the majority of Lou's family agreed Keith had withstood the test of standing by my side and facing my challenges with me. Finally, it seemed as though we had worked through the worst of times, and could look to the future.

●   ●   ●   ●   ●

We had just moved in to the new home when word came that the long awaited arraignment was finally at hand. We expected to be in court at the end of September. On September 27, 2006, we were notified that capital charges had been referred, and an arraignment would arrive after about a month. The time passed quickly enough, as I was immersed in the new house, settling the kids in new schools, and gearing up for a big interview with CNN.

It had been a year since I was interviewed by Soledad O'Brien. She had recently reached out to me to ask about the case and talk about a follow up story. I agreed, and CNN's camera crew arrived early one morning, transforming our kitchen into a TV studio. High power lights, microphones, and cameras dominated the area. It was a long, bizarre day with cameras in our faces. I sat down for an interview with Soledad, and then she interviewed the boys. It was emotional but therapeutic for the three big guys, who needed to feel they were helping me. Keith stayed as far away from the cameras and crew as possible without actually leaving the house. He was uncomfortable with the situation but did his best to be there for me.

After the interview we spent the days renovating the house and catching our breath from the past months of intense emotional duress. But I couldn't rest long. It was soon time for the arraignment. I kissed the kids good bye again and made my way back to Fort Bragg.

In the courtroom, I was ushered into the second row and wound up sitting up against a wall, my view completely blocked. As I sat there wedged up in a makeshift corner, I could hear Lou saying "Nobody puts Baby in a corner." It's one of the movie quotes he enjoyed bringing out on more than one occasion and I had no doubt he'd use it now. The thought brought a smile to my face, along with a sensation of loss. I missed him.

I saw our newly assigned handler, Major Ohlweiler, up front with Valerie. I'd yet to be introduced to Fort Bragg's new Chief of Capital Litigation, but I'd heard whispers that he intended to commandeer all channels of communication between our families and the prosecution team. My in–laws met with him earlier, and he was now walking to me with his hand extended. I was not enthusiastic about the insertion of the Major. I had a good rapport with John Benson and resented being told I'd have to deal with someone else. I returned his handshake, noting the annoyingly artificial smile I'd seen on so many others sent to deal with us, before he scurried to his front–row seat.

Martinez's wife had not appeared today. I was thankful to be spared any more public displays of affection between her and her husband. The back two rows were filled with members of the media. I was glad to see them here, because it meant this case was still deemed newsworthy.

"All rise," boomed from some unseen corner of the room and we all stood as the judge entered. This was our first introduction to Colonel Parrish. I hoped he'd be as likeable as

Colonel Reinert, someone who had little tolerance for any unnecessary antics and kept the proceedings flowing. I couldn't help but compare Colonel Parrish's appearance to Judge Wapner, from the People's Court t.v. show, and Siobhan and I laughed at that later. His white hair, neatly cut but longer than a high and tight, was really the only similarity I could think of between the two, but it didn't matter. It was my first impression and it stuck with me.

The arraignment was unusually concise, and court was soon dismissed. Before retracing our path on I–95, we all huddled in the conference room, where Major Ohlweiler spewed out the customary speech about how motivated the government was, and how the case was in good hands. I studied the midsized Major as he spoke, distracting myself from his words by trying to decide if I'd label his hair color strawberry blond or faded red, and deciding I really didn't care enough to label it anything. I was snapped back to his speech when he mentioned he would be the new conduit for the families and the trial team. He explained how the team was necessarily absorbed in the case, and he felt it was in everyone's best interest for us not to distract them. Throughout his speech, the trial team remained mute, seated behind him.

Any notion that I may have been wrong about the major's intentions vanished. To be fair, I understood how smothering it could be to deal with the mob our families created when we gathered. I knew if we all took to calling John for information he'd never get anything done. But I had been careful with my calls and emails and could honestly say I didn't abuse his willingness to speak with me by flooding his inbox or voice mail. In return, I was rewarded with John's comfortable demeanor and candid responses. With him, I finally felt I was speaking to a human, one who was doing his best not to let the confines of his job prevent him from treating the families with respect, or caring personally about this case and our loss.

Selfish as it is, I hadn't wanted to be involved in any large meetings or have to deal with anyone other than Siobhan and the trial team directly. Instead, that day's meeting was the most disastrous ever to take place with our families.

There were several members of both the Allen and Esposito families attending, in addition to family friends of the Espositos. Emotions were flaring and the meeting soon erupted into a shouting match. An hour or so into this mess I still had asked only a few questions. I was sick and my voice had vanished, so it was a challenge to be heard. Then, with little advance warning, Major O. announced the meeting was over and assured us he'd do what he could to address our concerns. That was it. I was furious at having been thrust into a situation that seemed to be a carefully orchestrated calamity. Against the advice of those who knew us, the meeting was run in a manner sure to cause the reaction that occurred.

After meeting with the media, Siobhan and I returned to the hotel and spent the remainder of the day stewing. The next day, we hit the road home. We were exhausted. Mentally and physically. And this was just the arraignment. Relatively nontraumatic. Knowing this was just the beginning was daunting.

As I pulled into my driveway at about eight P.M. I welcomed the wave of relief washing over me. Leaving the kids for these trips always upset me, and I missed Keith, too. He had the ability to help put things in perspective for me. We'd become closer over the past few months and were now firmly embedded in this relationship.

I walked into the dimly lit house. Soft candlelight flickered from an assortment of candles on every available surface. Keith stood in the middle of the room, the shadows from bouncing flames spilling over his face. I could feel the stress and tension leaving my tight muscles as he held me in a comforting hug, lightly kissing the top of my head and whispering a low, "Welcome Home, Babe" in my ear.

Leading me into the kitchen, Keith stepped back to reveal a trail of Welcome Home Mom! signs leading up the stairs. I followed the signs and the muffled giggles into the room the boys were sleeping in while their bedrooms were being redone. "Mom!!!" they yelled, and then I was drowning in little boys. Arms, legs, heads all crashed together in a wild hug. I dodged an elbow in my face just in time to have a knee thrust into my abdomen as the four boys wrestled one another to hug me. The breath knocked out of me from that knee thrust, I laid down in mock surrender, laughing and relieved to be home with my children. Lou's children. The emotions of the past few days had left me raw and tired. The greeting I just experienced was a soothing balm on fresh wounds. The tears that fell that night were unashamed tears of exhaustion and happiness, as I was newly aware of all that was still good in my life.

● ● ● ● ●

Fall gave way to winter and the holiday season was upon us again. It was our second Christmas without Lou. This year, the widows on the Gold Star Wives site were chattering about a newly founded organization, SnowBall Express. Founded by one man who was driven to comfort families of fallen soldiers, the organization recognized the holiday season as particularly difficult, and was offering to fly our families to California for a few days of festivities.

I agreed with the general consensus that it seemed too enticing to be true. Who would fly families, for free, to California? Who would really pay for our families to stay in hotels, and bus us from one carefully designed event to another? Did people really care about us so much? Or was this just someone trying to exploit the tragic image of war widows and children? Most of the widows opted to pass on the offer, but after endless hours of back and forth discussion, a few of my more daring widow friends and I decided to take a chance and check it out.

Try as I might, I could not convince either Siobhan or Terri to join the adventure. Instead, they wished us well and I promised to tell them all about it. That December, the boys and I boarded an American Airlines Jet with my sister, Beth. The organization behind the event, SnowBall Express allowed her to come assist me with my small children. Trevor was just seven years old. Colin was six. Sean was five and Jeremy was three. It would have been too much for me to navigate crowded airports with the four of them on my own.

We landed in California and were met by people holding welcome signs and beaming smiles at us. Taken to a spacious hotel room and then introduced in person to some of the widows I had only known as online chat buddies. Our kids played together, and could be heard talking about their dads in a way they could not talk to kids who hadn't experienced a similar loss. We met the volunteers behind SnowBall Express and American Airlines. People lined the streets as our buses passed, holding signs reading *Your Dad is My Hero*. Businesses opened their doors to our kids. A day in Disney finished off the trip of red carpet treatment.

It was an emotionally rejuvenating experience that has had a lasting impression on my kids and me. We remain close friends with the other families we met, as well as with many of the volunteers from SnowBall Express and American Airlines. This event has grown and now well over a thousand family members of fallen soldiers board American Airlines charter flights to meet in California or Texas every December. My boys and I have been honored to attend each time, and I would recommend the experience to all eligible families.

That Christmas was easier than the last, as I was carried through on the adrenaline rush of SnowBall Express. The new year rang itself in, and a new season of hearings was upon us as we hoped 2007 would be the year we saw justice.

●　　●　　●　　●　　●

January 8, 2007. We were back in court to hear arguments on three pretrial motions. The defense was requesting an independent criminal investigator, an independent forensic investigator, and access to a CT scan of Martinez's brain. The scan was done in Iraq as part of a sanity board procedure. We took our seats in the now familiar courtroom, but this time Siobhan and I were in the front row.

Martinez was at his table, looking soft and chunky. His two defense attorneys, Major Cipriano and Major Gregory, were at his side. His wife sat across the aisle from us. On our side, Captains John Benson and Adam Siple were joined by yet another new trial team member, the next in an ever–revolving door of faces. Kelly Hughes had opted out and Major MacNeill now made his debut. Colonel Parrish entered and court was called to order. Let the games begin.

In a scene reminiscent of the arguments over a mitigation specialist, defense won their motion for an independent investigator, and I knew we'd be delayed again while that investigator did his job. I wasn't surprised or angry at hearing this. Just defeated. Helpless to stop these people from playing with our lives with their endless delays and games. I couldn't understand why the investigator had not been granted earlier, if it was standard procedure. Why eighteen months into this we were nowhere near a trial.

When court was adjourned, Siobhan and I waited for John Benson to find us. Over strong protest from the Gatekeeper, as we'd dubbed Major Ohlweiler, we had a meeting scheduled with the trial team. The Gatekeeper had informed Valerie there would be no meetings for us except with him, and I'd gone a few rounds over that. It made me like him even less than before.

John appeared and we followed him to his office. We settled in our seats in the sweltering room, where Major Craig MacNeill and Captain Siple joined us. John opened the meeting by asking us to voice our questions and concerns. Siobhan and John had something of an antagonistic relationship. Prior to this meeting I'd asked her to please, please, humor me and phrase any thoughts carefully. If she was annoyed at my request, she didn't let on. Our meeting went smoothly, with the trial team unhurriedly answering all of our questions. We said our good byes and returned to the hotel.

Defense had been unprepared to argue one of the motions that day, and Colonel Parrish had granted them the opportunity to do so on Monday. Which meant we were going to be staying the weekend instead of driving home as planned. Siobhan and I were steaming that night. Colonel Parrish had no problem chastising defense in court for failing to prepare, and warned them he wouldn't tolerate it. But his words were empty; for he'd still allowed them to spend the weekend preparing for a motion they were due to argue that day. We were again the hapless pawns in the game. Left to choose between staying another three days to attend the hearing, or return to our children as we had promised.

The kids were unhappy to hear I was not returning that night. I told myself that one day they would understand and forgive me for this. And I took comfort in knowing they were safe at home with someone they'd come to love. Jeremy and Sean had taken to calling Keith pops. And Keith soaked it up. Trevor and Colin cared for Keith, too. Colin would hold back a little and then hug Keith with all his strength, and tell him he loved him. For the older two boys, it was just a bit too much to differentiate between loving Keith and betraying their "real dad." Keith didn't push it. This was unchartered territory for all of us and he was extremely wary of making mistakes. As was I.

Keith was throwing himself wholeheartedly into the challenging situation. He constantly walked a line between trying to be here for all of us while making it clear he was not trying to replace Lou. He steadily reassured the boys that their dad would have come back to them if he could, and that their dad would always be with them. He took turns between holding the boys when they cried and holding me when the sadness overcame me. It could not be easy for him, as he continued to struggle with his own inner conflicts from a past I knew only pieces of.

Monday morning rolled around wet and dreary, the perfect accessory for our moods. I bumped into Mr. Esposito in the hall. He and Mrs. Esposito arrived after ten last night, having had to drive home to care for Mrs. Esposito's mom over the weekend, and back again for this morning's hearing. Ahead of them, as for all of us, was the day's proceedings and another drive home. We all gathered in the lobby, where we rushed down another cup of coffee before making our way to the base.

Once we were all assembled in the courtroom the defense called their first witness. Eric Lakes, a computer expert from Lexington Kentucky, was testifying telephonically.

Much of his testimony, garble of techno talk, I didn't understand. I am barely computer literate and relied on Lou to talk me through things in that area. There didn't seem too much purpose for this witness other than to open the door for the arguments about defense's perceived unjustly restricted access to the computer files in the case. Major Gregory was doing the speaking for defense but he was almost like a puppet for Major Cipriano. As he had done ever since the first hearing we attended in Kuwait, Major Gregory repeatedly paused and leaned into Major Cipriano. Major Cipriano would then whisper into Major Gregory's ear and, like an obedient child, Major Gregory regurgitated what he'd been told. I'd often wondered about the reason for this. Why didn't Major Cipriano, who seemed to be the brains of the team, do the speaking?

After arguing at length about classified and unclassified information, the location of and access to this information, and various computer issues, this argument was brought to a close. Defense was told to draft an order for the judge to review and sign. Their request would be granted. Another expert would join their team.

Next motion. More call for expert help. Talk of blood spatter patterns, crime scene re–creations, and blast evidence did little to brighten our moods. The harshest evidence that morning was our first glimpse of the Water Palace. Defense pulled an enormous screen TV out and with one click we were looking at a computer–generated image of the palace. Images I'd seen only from the three or four pictures Lou emailed were suddenly rotating before us in 3–D.

We'd heard about the palace before, saw Lou's few pictures through a porthole–shaped window overlooking the lake. But seeing the entire building gave us a new sense of where he'd been, what he'd experienced. I remembered how excited we'd been, talking about the historical movement Lou was taking part in. How he'd wanted to take pictures and document his experience, something to show our grandchildren one day.

FOB Danger sits in Tikrit, Iraq, along the Tigris River. Formerly known as Camp Ironhorse, it is one of Saddam Hussein's former palatial properties. Roughly a thousand acres of land boasts eighteen palaces and 136 buildings, including the Water Palace. Built for Saddam's mother, in 2005 the palace housed about ninety–five soldiers. Phil's office and living quarters occupied a basement corner with windows looking out on the manmade lake as well as the pit area. The night they were killed, Lou and Phil had been sitting at a table directly in front of a window to the pit.

The sunken area called the pit could be accessed from steps to the palace and was lined by a concrete wall on the bank of the lake. What may have served as a relaxing patio if attached to a home or hotel was here just an area strewn with wires seeming to lead anywhere and nowhere. The lights mounted on exterior walls rarely worked. On the night of the murders the pit had been shrouded in darkness.

Overlooking the pit and facing the palace were three trailers. One female shower and two male showers. A unisex port–a–pottie area bordered the road leading past the palace. Turning one way on that road lead to the Motor Pool. Turning the other way led to the D Main, a command center for the FOB.

The land around the palace consisted of desolate dirt colored sand broken up here and there with some palm trees and contrasting sharply with the vibrant blue–green water in the lake. In the distance we could see hints of other buildings. But our focus was on the palace, with its steps on either side and the arched bridges over sparkling water. Interior shots showed extravagantly glittering chandeliers and polished floors.

There was Phil's window. There was the road and there, just across the road, were the port–a–potties where, we were told, Martinez hid and detonated the claymore. Defense argued for the necessary expert to utilize this image to re–create the murders. The expert they had in mind could apply detail like hair color to images of people. If defense won this motion and proceeded with this quest, we would have a front–row view of however many versions of our husbands' murders they chose to throw at us. The prospect was a cruel one.

In the end, as expected, defense was granted their expert. The hearing was over and we returned to the conference room. Everyone was anxious to head home. I was such a jumble; it was impossible to tell which emotion outweighed the others. Lost and sad, missing Lou. Sick with dread at the images we now expected to see at trial. I didn't want to continue reliving those last hours of Lou's life. It was torture. I was waging an internal temper tantrum at the unfairness, wanting to scream with rage and the confusion of all these emotions swirling through me at the same time.

I knew it was best to stay away from any media when I was like this. But interest in this case was waning as it dragged through the system, and we worried it would vanish completely. We were afraid of the military politics involved, and the games being played concerned us. The insertion of the Gatekeeper heightened my fears that things were being kept from us, and the only thing I could think of to improve my chances for getting the answers I needed and the verdict called for was to make sure the entire country was watching this case. I knew that wouldn't guarantee the right outcome, but in the absence of any better ideas, I was going with this one. So while our in–laws made for the interstate, Siobhan and I went downstairs for an interview.

Media turnout was small. One paper and one TV station. Both local. But we used the opportunity the best we could. Siobhan went first and then I was up. Efforts to compose myself failed, and my responses to questions bordered on hostile. "Well I don't exactly get the warm and fuzzies about it" was what came out when I was asked the standard "How do you feel listening to this?" I treated the next question, "Why do you feel such a need to attend every proceeding, why go to such an effort to be here?" with contempt: "That question is asked every time and my answer remains the same. I am going to see this through." I sort of snapped at the reporter. Struggling to calm down, I tried to put in a plug for the trial team, and let the defense team know I wasn't running scared, saying I felt the prosecution made valid arguments and I trusted in them to secure a conviction. A few more questions and we were out of there. I could not leave fast enough, hoping my venom had not alienated the few press members willing to cover this case.

Nerves frayed, emotions racing, the day had come for Siobhan and me to finally lay down our politeness and start bickering like sisters. I was annoyed at her for wanting to stop at Starbucks, for her unwillingness to change out of court clothes in the car, in a parking lot. She was annoyed with my impatience, and for telling her we should just drive through somewhere quickly, suggesting she should consume fast–food slop instead of making her healthy, half–hour Subway stop. We argued over the radio volume, and I told her she was chewing like a pig. Instead of snapping back at me, Siobhan reeled herself in, and calmly told me how annoying I was. We offered each other a forced smile as we finally got on the road.

As we approached DC, I was on the phone. When Siobhan asked me if she should get on 495, I waved my hand at her and said no. I was distracted. And wrong. As a result, we were in the thick of DC rush–hour traffic. And we were not nice to each other. "Why did you tell me not to get on 495?" Siobhan shrieked. "If you didn't have to have Starbucks we would be way ahead of all this traffic!" I hissed back. We spent a few minutes like this; mindless of the reporter I had on speakerphone, before finding our way back to the interstate. Still stuck in the parking lot known as I–95, we nonetheless breathed a little easier, and laughed at ourselves for real, amused now at how mad we'd been. Eventually, we made it home, another trip behind us.

March arrived, and I struggled through the hardest month of the year for me. For the big holidays, I become wrapped up in the boys' enthusiasm and spirit. It is nearly impossible not to find a way to be thankful for the moment, for the blessings I still have. But March, our anniversary month, was all for us. Just Lou and I. Each year, regardless of the fact that we were financially decimated, we would find a way to celebrate. And the anticipation would carry us through the month. The first year in our little trailer, we had a budget of minus ten dollars to party it up. So we cranked the heat, made some frothy, fruity drinks. Put on summer wear and blasted Jimmy Buffet. Voilà. We were in the islands again. We honeymooned all weekend.

Last year I was in Florida with the boys and family members on the trip Lou and I had planned with them. It was sad, but I had countless distractions. This year I had weeks on end of kids with fevers and headaches home from school. The weather was miserable and cold. Mindful of Keith's feelings, I had no safe place to break down and cry, just let it out without feeling guilty about hurting him. Keith did his best to respect what I was going through but felt the stress, too. The first signs of tension appeared in our relationship as he began to wonder if I would ever be free to love him, and I began to further doubt I would be able to heal myself, let alone help him crawl out from his own misery that was starting to re–emerge. It's hard to say which one of us was happier to turn the calendar page to April.

●   ●   ●   ●   ●

April 17, 2007. Another hearing. More motions. The beat went on, steadily drumming but leading nowhere. Two more hearings that year brought more of the same and I could not get the sound of Major Gregory's voice out of my head. What he said in court was never pleasant and often insulting. But the way he said it, his nasally, whining voice droning on, pounding his fist on the lectern, incessantly crying foul, and bemoaning the fate of "Al." "He even *looks* like an Al!" he'd once declared, wrapping his arm around his client's shoulder after listening to testimony about Martinez being thrown in the Detainee Internment Facility (DIF) the night of his arrest. How scared he'd been to have his belt and shoelaces taken from him in the holding cells used for Iraqis awaiting questioning. How his cell was coated in fecal matter, and how he'd been taken to CID offices in handcuffs.

The sad times of Al Martinez being presented to us made a mockery of the suffering he had inflicted, to the point that I thought I could take no more. I'd reached the downside of my cycle, experiencing moments of weakness when I wished it would just stop. I didn't need to spend my life trying to end his anymore. I just wanted him to go away. Throw him in some dungeon somewhere and let him shrivel up, the way I had been shriveling up inside since he killed Lou. I wanted to be free of this cycle and the helplessness it evoked in me. But then time would pass, and I would come out of my funk. The hatred would again well up within me, and I would once more allow it to consume me, living for the day Martinez would die for what he did. It was a vicious, ugly cycle. Unhealthy for my body and soul. But I couldn't escape.

CHAPTER ELEVEN
CREEPING TO TRIAL

✪ ✪ ✪

Two and a half years into this process, we had all lost whatever optimism we'd had about a swift conviction. The defense counsel had delayed time after time, and Colonel Parrish showed no signs of reining them in. The trial team was burnt out; Major Benson, Captain Siple, and Major McNeill emanated doom each time they appeared in court. The Gatekeeper and Staff Judge Advocate (SJA), Colonel Ayres, who were supposed to be overseeing the case, were preparing for deployment to Iraq. No one was keeping an eye on this case other than us.

Things went from bad to worse in the spring of 2008 when a third Article 32 Hearing resulted in severing the charges against Martinez. This meant we now faced two trials. Martinez 1 would address the murder charges. All other charges pertaining to possession of a firearm, possession of alcohol, and unlawful disposition of government property would be addressed in the Martinez 2 trial. Essentially, the third Article 32 undid what the second Article 32 had done. The delay caused by that hearing, which was presented to us as necessary in order to include the lesser charges in the murder trial so as to establish Martinez's poor character, had been for nothing. And when we expressed worry over the severing of the charges, the Gatekeeper assured us we didn't really need them, anyway. It was maddening.

We'd been told the chances of the request to sever being granted were extremely unlikely, and entered into this proceeding thinking its main purpose would be to protect the appellate process. Instead we were blindsided by this hit to the case. The Gatekeeper had nothing to say to me when I asked him what assurance our families could have that the government would get itself together and win. Instead he attempted to placate us with the approach that the second trial would now serve as a backup for the first. If something unimaginable were to happen with the murder trial, at least the additional trial would allow the government to try him on the second set of charges, which are much easier to convict on, and still carry prison time. That line of reasoning did nothing to calm us. Siobhan hired her own attorney to accompany her to hearings and present her with an opinion she could trust about events as they unfolded.

The return home was uneasy, and the ensuing weeks brought intense anxiety about the state of things. I finally wrote a letter appealing to the SJA at Bragg for some intervention. About a week later I received a response.

An email from the Gatekeeper one afternoon in April 2008 announced that he and Colonel Ayres would be conference calling all of us, me, Siobhan, her attorney, and both sets of in–laws, later that afternoon. I threw a quick dinner to the boys, then Keith and I barricaded ourselves in the office while the kids watched a movie downstairs.

One by one we all checked in. I was happily surprised when Meg called in, too. Expecting platitudes and half–truths, I was not surprised when that is what we got. Colonel Ayres launched into a fourth–grade analogy by comparing this case to an Iditarod. He pointed out that this was unlike a marathon and as such the members of the team would become tired throughout the process. He thought we all had the same goals regarding a conviction and sentence because we all knew there were no communists amongst us. He read the families loud and clear that the best has got to be a little bit better. He then told us we'd be meeting two new members of the team, both captains. Returning to the nonsensical Iditarod analogy, he pointed out that adding new members wouldn't do any good if everyone pulled [the sled] in different directions or one dog simply latched on to the back of the sled and did not make it go faster. So they would have to figure out how to manage the team to cross the home stretch.

Pleased with his dumbed–down explanation to the simpletons, Colonel Ayres turned to what would happen next, the March 20 39A regarding autopsy photos and the 404B. The 404B referred to a hearing addressing all uncharged offenses. It was a backdoor method for the government to introduce the misconduct associated with Martinez's illegal possession of alcohol and firearms in spite of those charges having been severed. It spoke to his character, and would defuse defense's anticipated efforts to paint their client as a perfect specimen of a soldier who never strayed from the guidelines. A casual note was made that we were also awaiting rulings on some evidence, including statements made by Martinez to CID in Iraq. But the emphasis of the next hearing would be the 404B uncharged misconduct and the autopsy photos.

Later in the conversation, I told the Gatekeeper duo that, had we been told of the impending supplemental assistance to the government team earlier, we may not have felt compelled to raise such a loud outcry. Especially my letter. Colonel Ayres chuckled at this and said he hoped at least writing the letter was cathartic for me. At that point my blood was boiling so loudly that the throbbing in my head drowned out all else. There was a pensive lapse in the conversation. Either unaware or uncaring about what stupid things he was saying to us, Colonel Ayres continued to heap on the BS. He told us they were concerned we would be upset about new members joining the team because we'd developed an appreciation for John and Adam.

Hearing that, I was done. My voice low, even, in what those who know me recognize as barely contained fury, I emphasized how important it was to us that information not be doled out based on what they believed would or would not upset us. That this entire case was upsetting and we were all fully aware that would not change. That we'd shown we were in this until the end, and deserved the respect of being told the truth. Regardless of how unpleasant it was. The others added their own comments, and I listened as the Gatekeeper and Colonel Ayres concluded the call.

This was Keith's first experience with the people involved and he was stunned at the manner of the call. He told me he now had a greater respect for the stamina it must take for me to deal with all of this. Hearing the kids calling for us, we went to them and hung out together until their bedtime. I tucked them in and tried to forget about the Army for a while.

●   ●   ●   ●   ●

The March 20, 2008, hearing commenced with several changes in the ensemble of players. Colonel Parrish, busy with three capital cases, had opted to step away from ours. Enter Colonel Stephen Henley.

As the U.S. Army Trial's Chief Trial Judge, the man with the expansive legal background was able to appoint himself to replace Colonel Parrish. On paper, his background was impressive: Before landing an assignment as a military judge, the former Special Assistant United States Attorney for the District of Colombia had spent time as a trial counsel attorney, and then as a training officer for the Trial Counsel Assistance Program in Virginia. He'd done a stint at West Point as the Chief of Administrative Law in between assignments in Korea, Germany, and spots in the United States. Now the lure of a high-profile case and the excitement that went with it was impossible for the colonel to resist. He was overdue for some time in the trenches again, needed a break from the administrative role his prominent job cast him in.

Having grown weary of Colonel Parrish's empty warnings to defense counsel about unnecessary delays and antics, we looked at Colonel Henley with renewed optimism. Surely he would be just what we needed to finally get to trial and convict Martinez. I tried to ignore John's prediction that we would hate Henley and wish for Parrish back.

Besides our new judge, we had new members on the prosecution. Lieutenant Colonel Bradley Huestis had arrived from Germany to take the lead role in the trial team. When I met the Liteunant Colonel, I played the same game I played with everyone involved, trying to decide who he resembled enough to be played by in a movie. Decided Tom Hanks would fit the bill. Captains Evan Seamone and Scott Quillan rounded out the new trial team, and John Benson was catching them up on the case to date. All three men came with glowing recommendations from the Gatekeeper duo. Which meant I disbelieved in them from the start. Guilty by association until proven otherwise. But I hoped Captain Seamone's skill was as broad as his shoulders and effusive as his personality. Captain Quillan's eyes seemed to smile along with his mouth as he greeted us, hinting he may be genuine. But the only one I truly believed in was newly–promoted Major Benson, the one original member remaining. The others, I would remain hopeful but undecided about for now.

We began the day with telephonic testimony from a Navy officer, Captain Caruso, in Japan. I was particularly grateful Steve had made the trip to Fort Bragg this time, as the day's testimony was graphic and not easy to hear. For about an hour and a half we had the pleasure of listening to the Chief Deputy Medical examiner give excruciatingly explicit details about autopsy photos: Descriptions of pictures, what they signified, why our side wants to use each picture and why Defense does not. Major Gregory argued that a picture of Lou and Phil's faces should not be used because the pictures show only one side. This would lead the panel to believe both sides of each man's face were equally impacted when in fact each suffered significant injuries to only the side facing the explosion. Such pictures, Gregory argued, would be inflammatory.

While this testimony challenged me to remain quietly seated in spite of the mental images it provoked, Martinez appeared bored. He hunched down, stretched, yawned, and stared into space as if he were wasting his time. I wanted to smack him.

The rest of the day failed to rouse us out of our somber moods, and we sulked through until the end, when Colonel Henley snapped us out of our miserable mind frames with an announcement of a schedule. Deadlines were imposed for panel questionnaires to be submitted, objections to be filed, and a plea to be entered by Martinez. Three 39A's were scheduled, with the last to be held in June. Jury selection, or voir dire, was set for June 24, and case in chief for July 7. Hearing that was a relief—finally a trial date that seemed firm. This was well timed after such a harsh day in court, and I cautiously welcomed the unusual feeling of hope.

Then, in a laidback voice that could have been commenting on something as benign as the weather, Judge Henley ruled to suppress Martinez's statements given to CID in Iraq, as well as the flare guns found in the search of his quarters when Martinez signed a consent to search during that interview. He found the arrest was illegal and as such the statement and flares were inadmissible. That the statement was not crucial enough to the government's case to overlook the official misconduct of the CID agents.

It took a moment for my brain to catch up with what I'd just heard. When the import of his words wound their way through my thought process, all the hope that had just surged within me was banished. I listened with weary resignation as Colonel Huestis asked for and received a thirty–minute recess.

Half an hour later we went back on the record while Lieunant Colonel Huestis asked the judge to reconsider his ruling to suppress the statement and evidence. He argued that, contrary to Colonel Henley's reasoning, Martinez's statement was a crucial part of the government's case. He then went through each of defense's complaints about the statement, and the judge's statements in support of those complaints, and laid out why they did not add up to cause to suppress the statement. As Colonel Huestis spoke, Colonel Henley looked at him with ill–concealed contempt. His glasses perched on the tip of his nose, brow pushed together from his raised eyebrows, lips pursed, he waited out Colonel Huestis's arguments and then dismissed them.

Our initial hope of finding relief with a new judge was fading. While Colonel Henley did push the case through on the court docket, his rulings favored the defense. His approach to the case was in harsh contrast with Colonel Parrish, who showed no predisposition to favor one side over the other in his rulings, yet had allowed defense to waste two years of our lives with endless delays. Colonel Parrish's admonitions to defense each time they were not prepared to proceed were much like a mother scolding a child with his hand in the cookie jar before dinner, and then refilling the cookie jar when the child empties it. Defense had continued eating from the cookie jar until Colonel Henley arrived. The new judge had clamped down that lid but opened the door to the bakery, so to speak. We now had a judge who sped up the schedule but offered shelf upon shelf of goodies to choose from in the process.

Colonel Henley was a man with an agenda. He was determined to wrap this trial up before the end of the year and carry the prestige of such an inflammatory case with him to his next assignment. He was equally determined to preserve his appellate record. Defense knew this and used it to their advantage. Majors Gregory and Cipriano were as cunning as their client. They skillfully identified the new judge's Achilles heel and used it to their advantage. Unlike the prosecution, defense counsel had not changed since the first Article 32 hearing in Kuwait. Majors Cipriano and Gregory's devotion to their client superseded all else, and neither attorney would walk away from this case. The continuity of the defense team was in stark contrast to the prosecution. John Benson was the only member who remained from the first Article 32 hearing. The prosecution team had seen numerous turnovers, and this lack of continuity severely hampered its ability to try this case.

The newly–formed prosecution was now availing themselves of a seventy–two hour window to determine whether or not to pursue an appeal of the judge's ruling. Bottom line was, all proceedings were again on hold until a decision was made. Back into a pit of gloom for us.

A meeting after the hearing outlined what would happen next. Gathered in the conference room with the prosecution, we heard about the appellate process. That it would delay things for at least three months and require a hearing in Arlington, Virginia. The argument would be that Colonel Henley had abused his discretion by suppressing Martinez's statement. This was a gamble. It was sure to infuriate the judge, and ran the risk of provoking him to take it out on the government in court. Rules of conduct aside, beneath that black robe Colonel Henley is a human being, susceptible to the same emotions and ego as the rest of us. A wounded ego and the need to assert his dominance could overshadow his professional obligations. If the appeal was lost, it would serve to validate his wrath and encourage him to continue ruling with his appellate record in the forefront, as opposed to justice. If the appeal was won, he could still take it personally as an affront to his authority and make up for it by coming down harder on the government.

We'd all heard both sides' versions of how Martinez gave a statement to CID in Iraq, but Colonel Huestis gave us a recap now.

Around three P.M. on June 8, Martinez was detained by two MPs and escorted to the Detainee Internment Facility on the FOB. The DIF is normally used to hold Iraqi detainees while pending interrogation. Martinez's belt and shoelaces were confiscated, and he was placed in a cell that purportedly had graffiti and feces stain on the walls. At the time, no confinement order had been completed for him, and CID and the MPs all claimed not to know who ordered him to be taken to the DIF, when CID wanted him at their office for an interview.

Interest in Martinez was based on the statement from Sergeant Wentzel, who saw Martinez in the street in front of the pit outside Phil's basement office immediately after the explosions. Wentzel, as he'd testified in Kuwait at the Article 32 hearing, had heard Lou yelling for help. He didn't know if there would be another explosion and thought it odd for Martinez to be standing there "as if he knew it was over" but pulled Martinez to cover behind a concrete wall. Others had come forward to report having heard Martinez threaten or wish Phil dead in the past few weeks. This was enough to cast him as a suspect, and CID ordered the MPs to bring him to their office.

Instead of escorting Martinez to the CID office, Staff Sergeant Francis Rayne and Sergeant Major Albert Blais handcuffed him and brought him to the DIF. He remained in a holding cell, isolated from the prisoners, for about six hours before Special–Agent–in–Charge Collins learned of his status and ordered the MPs to bring him to the CID office.

Agent Corbett Speciale met Martinez there and ordered his handcuffs removed, but did not return his shoelaces or his belt. Much ado had been made about these items being confiscated. Defense had belabored the point and how traumatic that had been for Martinez, until none of us could hear it without groaning.

Speciale ate dinner with Martinez and swapped supply stories with him until Martinez was feeling better. Around nine P.M. in Iraq it was one P.M. in Milford, and while I was at the elementary school telling Trevor what had happened, Martinez was signing a form consenting to a search of his quarters. He then spent a few hours with Agent Speciale, writing a statement claiming he'd been in the port–a–potties across the street when the explosions happened. Further in that statement, Martinez acknowledged Captain Esposito, "threaten to remove me out of supply and reduce me on rank but I ignored him." His statement was laced with scorn for Phil, talking about how Phil held himself to be better than others and was devoid of respect for lower–ranking enlisted people. At the end of the statement, Martinez addressed his being placed in the DIF. He wrote he was treated, "Like I did something wrong I never in my while life felt this bad, Cid explain what happen it whas (sic) a miscommunication." He went on to stress that the CID agents treated him well, and there were no hard feelings after that.

Defense had successfully argued the arrest was unlawful, and the time Agent Speciale spent eating dinner with Martinez at the CID office had not attenuated that taint. That Martinez was not free to leave, and would have been forcibly restrained if he had attempted to do so. Martinez's original attorney testified about a traumatized Martinez weeping on his shoulder after his experience in the DIF, sobbing how he'd never been so scared in his entire life as that night.

I retreated to a corner of the conference room during the meeting, stifling my urge to scream. Working out the timeline, I flashed back to the day my doorbell rang. While I was being told Lou was dead, CID agents had been combing the crime scene. Others had already swept up debris, and people had been stepping over Lou's blood as it dried and soaked into the floor while I had been lying awake, waiting for Lou to call. By the time Lou's parents arrived to my house, Martinez was in the DIF. While we sat in my home attempting to work through the shock and confusion over what had happened, believing Lou had been killed in his sleep by an Iraqi mortar attack, CID determined it was a claymore, and a homicide. Someone decided to take Martinez to the DIF in handcuffs, and the person who'd inflicted catastrophic harm to Lou and Phil, who'd stood in the street and listened as Lou screamed, who'd been told the Commander and Lou were dead from the attack he'd waged, finally wept. But the tears he'd shed that night were not remorseful ones. He hadn't thrown himself down, admitted what he'd done, and begged for mercy. He'd said he wasn't sorry the Commander was dead, and had gone about his business that day until the MPs had come for him. Then he'd cried. Because he thought he was caught, and because he'd been scared in the DIF. And he was furious with CID for putting him through that.

Agent Speciale had done his best to calm Martinez down. To apologize for the "mistake" and set him at ease. Had thought by having Martinez sign his name to a statement placing himself at the scene, and forgiving CID, that he'd saved the day. But today in court we'd heard otherwise. Colonel Henley had sided with defense and called CID's actions a violation of procedure, blaming the agents for the statement's inadmissibility.

I'd battled with my faith in the trial team over these months. Had lost sleep worrying over the intentions of some of the team members and the Gatekeeper. Worried that we'd been misled about the strength of the case and the chances of winning. But I'd maintained a belief that CID had done a bang–up job on the investigation. I'd heard nothing but good things about the resources poured into the investigation, and the dedication of the agents. Now I'd lost that source of comfort.

Lacking personal knowledge of criminal investigative protocol, and limited to what I'd learned of our case as far as military law, I was at a disadvantage. I was in no position to make an informed decision as to whom to believe. Had Colonel Henley abused his discretion by excluding the statement, or did CID really mess up? Was the prosecution right to appeal the ruling, or would that delay the case unnecessarily—Again? Could the case survive trial without the statement? Who can I trust? Will this ever end? I left that meeting more nervous than ever about our chances of seeing Martinez convicted.

The day's events had proven to be more challenging than we'd anticipated. We were exhausted, beaten down by the cruel twists continually presented. I was lower than I'd been in months. Having a trial date dangled before us, with a newly infused prosecution ready to do battle, only to have it and the statement snatched away was crushing. I'd foolishly allowed myself to inflate my hopes that we'd soon be free of this process. That Martinez would be convicted by the summer's end, and I could truly begin to heal, assess my life and my relationship with Keith, which was floundering. I was paying for that hope now, crashing from my high like a junkie in detox.

After court, Siobhan met with one of the new captains to discuss sentencing testimony. She then left to pick up her daughter, who was staying with Siobhan's friend a couple hours' drive from Fort Bragg. I was worried about her driving that night. Exhaustion drooped her shoulders and her eyes were puffy. But she wanted to get to her daughter, and promised to call me when she arrived. I had a similar meeting scheduled with one of the new guys tomorrow. Steve skipped his flight home to stay with me.

I arrived for the meeting coming off a night of no sleep, eyes swollen from hours of crying. Steve was in protective mode, responding to the damsel–in–distress syndrome I'd slipped back into. My best efforts to dry my tears were not enough, and I lost whatever dignity I'd had when I was unable to speak without sobbing. My voice high–pitched and childlike, I filled in Captain Seamone on life before Lou, with Lou, and after, as Steve handed me tissues and Seamone listened attentively.

Without warning, Captain Quillan rushed into the room. Announced he was busy working on the appeal matter and now had only a few moments before he had to go. It was Good Friday, and he was anxious to return to his wife and children in DC. He paused to answer his phone. "Oh, hi, honey… No, I'm just with some people now. I'll call you back in five minutes… Bye!" and a smile in our direction. I looked at Steve and saw by his clenched jaw and flare in his eyes that he shared my annoyance with Quillan over the insensitive intrusion. He confirmed this with a snide comment to Quillan. I was so tired and so mad I just sat there trying to convince myself not to throw something at him. Captain Seamone chose that moment to tell me I should "have a backup plan in place" in case we lose at trial. I should be prepared to help the kids deal with it if Martinez goes free.

"Are you *serious?!*" I spat out, letting loose the helplessness and rage I'd been swimming in since yesterday. "I don't want to hear another *word* about losing! It will be over *three years* of this hell before we get to trial! You told us the three–month delay would allow time to work new angles. Avoid going to trial unprepared! We've been told to trust you! If this case is lost, I will not hold anyone accountable other than the trial team. And *you guys* better have a backup plan in place for the hell that will break loose if he walks away from my husband's murder!"

Captains Seamone and Quillan stared at me with mouths open, rocked back in their chairs away from my wrath. I was a far cry from the soft-spoken, tired and polite widow who'd been introduced to them three days ago. That day I'd driven straight through the night and directly to Fort Bragg. I'd been rundown and nervous but happy to meet the reinforcements and anticipating good news. Today I was a cornered animal, caught in a trap and snarling at them. Steve was trying to calm me, offering soft words I didn't hear and a warm hand on my arm.

Captain Seamone recovered first, and attempted to convince me he understood why I felt that way but all in all I should consider the validity of it. I'd passed the point of reasoning with anyone, and countered all of his points with furious insults. Steve grew more forceful, taking control of the situation with a raised voice and one more calming touch on his crazed widow friend's arm. Quillan excused himself and practically ran out of the room. His departure defused the tension.

After wrapping up the meeting, Steve and I headed to a small park. We meandered along the river as I fought to stave off the fatigue weighing me down, and I had a few laughs at Steve's expense as he gamely manipulated a slippery hill in his yuppie shoes. But beyond that, I had to admit I was not up for anything else, and we left. En route back to the hotel, we picked up some movies to while away the evening and rest up for the trip home the next day.

The next few weeks I spent in limbo. Incapable of focusing on much, I became distant from Keith as well as the rest of my family and friends. The continued helplessness of the situation had me anxious and despondent. I was resentful at the government for dragging this out. I was furious at the judge for suppressing Martinez's statement, and I had a few questions for CID as to how this case was handled. It was all unraveling, the years of emotions and proceedings I'd survived by telling myself it would all be worth it. Martinez would be convicted and we could find some peace. Now that belief was in jeopardy, and I had nothing to drive me forward. No reason to believe anything I'd been told. No idea who to trust.

I had other problems in addition to concerns about the case. Keith and I were unable to work through the walls that had been constructed in our relationship. I was growing impatient with his bouts of depression. Since he didn't want to tell me about much of his past, I had no means to understand his depression and anger. And while he did his best to fit into the rigors of family life, the confines of such a life smothered him. I was an emotional mess and any energy I had was directed to my kids. I had nothing left to offer the man whose friendship had once been a saving grace for me. I knew he loved me, and the boys. I just didn't know how we were going to be able to continue in our relationship. The next three months crept by, until it was time for the hearing.

●   ●   ●   ●   ●

June 11, 2008, we'd just marked the three–year anniversary of the murders and were in Arlington for the appellate hearing. The trial team was present as spectators. Arguments for both sides would be handled by appellate attorneys.

The small courtroom was packed, with an overflow spilling into the hallway. Our families were in the first two rows behind the bar and the trial team was behind us. Across the aisle were Majors Gregory and Cipriano. Seated next to Major Gregory, in shorts and t–shirt and giggling with her dad was Major Gregory's young daughter.

The three judges took their places in the front of the room and the hearing was called to order. Nothing new was heard in arguments for either side. We sat through the hearing and the after–meeting optimistic that it had gone well, and returned home to wait for the decision.

A few months later we were notified the appeal had been lost. We would proceed to trial without the statement.

CHAPTER TWELVE
VOIR DIRE

✪ ★ ✪

The first week of October 2008, our families were in Fayetteville, North Carolina, once again. This time, though, we were not here for a one or two–day hearing. Now, at last, we were here for the trial. The last item of business to see to before opening statements was to seat a jury.

In the military system a jury is called a panel. The panel selection process varies from the civilian courts. Civilian jury pools are comprised on a lottery basis, with registered voters selected at random. Jury members are susceptible to be selected indefinitely, provided they have not served on a jury in the recent past. When members of the military draw panel duty, they remain eligible for that duty for a specified amount of time.

Prior to voir dire, potential panel member names are presented to the General Court–Martial Convening Authority (GCMA). In the military justice system, the prosecutor does not determine what charges go to trial; instead, that decision is made by the GCMCA, who is usually a general officer and the accused soldier's senior commander. By virtue of his or her status as senior commander, this officer has the authority to refer charges to a general court–martial, and to select the members who sit on the court–martial panel. The GCMCA is also the only individual who can approve or disapprove an offer to plead guilty. The SJA is the legal advisor to the GCMCA. Federal law mandates the general select members best qualified for the duty by reason of age, education, training, experience, length of service, and judicial temperament. These determinations are made without the benefit of interviews or questionnaires. Consequently, the GCMA does not know if a soldier has a bias that could influence his or her attitude toward a case.

In our case, the general did not know one member had a raging bias against CID, or that two of the members were a husband and wife team, both strongly opposed to the death penalty. All he knew was that the names before him were recommended by his subordinates, and there was a high–profile capital case awaiting his stamp of approval of the members before proceeding. The voir dire process is in place to ascertain any member bias that would impair his or her ability to be impartial, and the military judge is responsible for presiding over those proceedings in a just manner. The presumption is that the judge will ensure neither defense nor prosecution stack the deck in its favor. But that presumption does not take Colonel Stephen Henley into account.

Day one brought the first group of potential panel members. Twenty soldiers filed in wearing Class A uniforms and swore an oath. For the past three years, we had assembled in that courtroom, and those chairs had always been vacant and lifeless. Today, they were occupied by members and preceded by a folding table with more chairs set up in front of them. Those, too, were bursting with members. Their presence changed the tone of the gathering. Lent more gravity to it.

The Class A is a dark green formal uniform. It is what the military detail was wearing when they appeared at my front door, and what Frank wore for his CAO duties. Lou wore his Class A when he presented the flag to the new widow, as well as when he received his commission. He was also buried in it. All counsel were similarly adorned. The sight of all those Class A's churned my stomach as I stared at the gathering of members seated behind name cards identifying them.

Prior to appearing in court, each member filled out a questionnaire designed to elicit details of professional and personal experiences as well as any views on the death penalty. In general voir dire, each side, prosecution and defense, would have a turn to question the entire panel with yes–or–no questions.

Each round of the selection more or less followed the same pattern: The members entered and took their seats. Siobhan and I had copied their names in our notes, with diagrams of where each person was sitting. This allowed us to identify and remember that person later. We took copious notes on the questions posed to the panel, as well as the responses. We noted who raised their hands in affirmative responses to questions such as "Have any of you been a victim of a crime before?" and other questions related to the members' personal and professional life experiences. Each person we looked at held the potential to sit on the panel and decide the most important factor in our lives. Since we were not privy to the questionnaires they had filled out, we viewed each member as a candidate for the job and strained to capture all responses.

Once the general voir dire was completed, we had a fairly good idea of which members stood a chance of sitting on the panel and which did not. For example, some members replied in the affirmative when asked if they felt a conviction for premeditated murder warranted an automatic sentence of death. Although the government would have an opportunity to rehabilitate that member, what happened more often than not is that the defense argued to excuse any member who showed a willingness to impose the death penalty, and those who openly stated that it would be their first inclination usually ended up being excused. It didn't matter in most cases if the member, when asked a more thorough question in individual voir dire, stated he or she would look at all the facts before deciding on a sentence.

The defense counsel constructed a crazy concoction of a hypothetical situation and posed it to each member who appeared at all willing to consider the death penalty. By the time Major Cipriano wound his way through a "hypothetical" situation in which the Accused was convicted of premeditated murder, the panel found no cause for mental defects or mitigating circumstances, the case had two victims, "Would you, in that situation, impose the death penalty?" the member was cornered and often had no road to take other than to reply "Yes." If the member argued that he or she needed more information, Major Cipriano would recite the supposed hypothetical again, and badger the member until he received an affirmative response. This happened time and again, over prosecution's objections.

Colonel Henley, though appearing annoyed, allowed the defense to employ this tactic until virtually any member who expressed a hint of being open to the death penalty—regardless of whether that member specified the need for *all* the information as opposed to the rigid, black and white parameters of the hypothetical before coming to such a serious decision—was struck from the pool. In contrast, any member who expressed opposition to the death penalty was spared from the hypothetical—which was in reality the elements in this case, and anything but hypothetical—and gently coaxed through defense's individual voir dire.

To me, a civilian with no law degree or experience apart from this case, Colonel Henley's handling of the process was shockingly in favor of the defense, to the extent that he was jeopardizing a fair trial. Believing that impression was based on ignorance of the law and my emotional bias, I later looked into it, and learned I wasn't necessarily so off base.

Three Supreme Court cases are relied upon to determine case law in the voir dire process. The 1968 *Witherspoon v. Illinois* case established the Witherspoon challenge, also referred to as a death qualifying jury, and favored excluding jurors whose attitude toward the death penalty would hamper their ability to determine a defendant's guilt or innocence.

Building on that now outdated law, in 1985 the Supreme Court decided the case of *Wainwright v. Witt*, which replaced the Witherspoon standard. This standard allotted the judge broader discretion in deciding whether the member's attitude would "prevent or substantially impair" the ability to decide fairly. Whereas the Witherspoon standard allowed the inclusion of a member who expressed the ability to "consider" imposing the death penalty, the judge was given leeway to ascertain the *meaningful* consideration that member would apply. Finally, the 2007 Supreme Court *Uttecht v. Brown* case further refined the approach to selecting a death qualified jury. A juror's statements that he would consider imposing the death penalty and follow the law did not overcome the reasonable inference from his other statements to the contrary, and he would be substantially impaired in deciding fairly in that case.

The last of the two case laws are heavily based on deferring judgment to the judge. The government's interest in having a death–qualified jury is subject to the objectivity and impartiality of the individual judge in each case. There is no mechanism in place for the prosecution to meaningfully challenge a judge's decision. All review and challenges are geared to protect the defendant. Sometimes, these considerations established to preserve fairness are abused. Especially in the case of <u>U.S. v. Martinez</u>.

We watched helplessly as one by one the defense manipulated the process with the judge's permission. Only after a few rounds with different panels did Colonel Henley begin to rein in Major Cipriano. By then, though, the impartiality of the panel had already been compromised by the inclusion of two members who expressed clear opposition to the death penalty. Adding to our concern about these members was the fact that they were husband and wife.

Notwithstanding the marital status of the members, which in itself is alarming, because members are not supposed to discussing the case with each other or with anyone else, was the fact that the Crespo duo openly stated their belief that capital punishment violates their religious, moral, and personal beliefs. Mrs. Major Crespo, as we referred to her, went so far as to state that even if her own son was murdered, she did not think she would be able to support the death penalty for the murderer in that case. As her husband, Mr. Major Crespo, had already been seated on the panel, we felt confident the judge would grant the prosecution's request to dismiss Mrs. Major for cause.

It seemed obvious no husband and wife would be able to resist the temptation to discuss this in the privacy of their own home. The Crespos, upon a second, separate round of individual questions, each altered their reasoning for stating opposition to the death penalty. Earlier, each had stated they held moral and religious views against capital punishment. Now, both stated it was not so much religious or moral views against the death penalty, as much as they felt a life spent in prison was a harsher penalty than being allowed to die. Unless they had each reflected separately and coincidentally arrived at the same place in their hearts, the Crepos had violated the order to not discuss the case and had reached a joint conclusion. Which meant there is no way they would not discuss the case during trial, and thus influence each other's decision. Even if they were able to overcome their personal feelings on the death penalty and consider voting to convict in a capital case, any wavering in that determination could be counterbalanced with the support of the other. The two of them could stand by each other and remain firm in their determination to set the case aside in deference to their own beliefs.

Major Cipriano had scored one victory in seating Mr. Major Crespo by badgering the man relentlessly, with nothing but weak admonitions from the judge, until Mr. Major grudgingly conceded he could "consider" the death penalty if ordered to do so. But this was granted only after stating even if ordered to do so, he could not set aside his beliefs and vote for death. In a capital case a person with such strong feelings has no place on the panel. But Colonel Henley disagreed and ruled that Mr. Major was invited to join the party. This decision flustered the prosecution and upset all of us. Defense was being given permission to stack the deck. None of us feared an impartial panel, believing it would convict. And given the "gates" necessary to pass through to reach a sentence of death, most of us had no illusions of securing a death penalty. The 4 gates, according to the Uniform Code of Military Justice, are:

1. Unanimous findings of guilt of an offense that authorizes the imposition of the death penalty, RCM (Rules for Court Martial) 1004(a)(2);

2. Unanimous findings beyond a reasonable doubt that an aggravating factor exists, RCM 1004(b)(7);

3. Unanimous concurrence that aggravating factors substantially outweigh mitigating factors, RCM 1004(b)(4)(C); and

4. Unanimous vote by the members on the death penalty, RCM 1006(d)(4)(A).

We knew ours was a circumstantial case, making it highly likely one or more members would not vote to convict, thus rendering the sentencing phase noncapital. I was surprised to realize I did not even need to see him die at this point. I was so weary of the process, so beaten by the hatred and the pain, and members like the Crespos had added to my own discomfort with the death penalty. I knew even if the death penalty was imposed, it was not likely to be carried out; the last military execution was in 1961. One death row inmate, Ronald Gray, has been residing on Fort Leavenworth's death row since 1988. It appears the method of execution preferred in the military is to allow inmates to grow old and die a natural death. But what we did not expect was to not even have a fair shot.

When Colonel Henley shot down the prosecution's request to excuse Mrs. Major Crespo for cause, I was so upset I had to leave the courtroom. Once in the hallway, I knew I would not be able to get a grip on myself, so I left Fort Bragg. In my mind, the inclusion of Mr. Major Crespo rendered the case noncapital. I struggled with conflicting emotions over that but retained certainty in a conviction. The addition of Mrs. Major, however, convinced me the conviction itself was now in jeopardy. Colonel Henley had already allowed one other member, Major Scott, to remain on the panel over prosecution's objections. This member was absolutely unyielding in his opposition to capital punishment. He was an imposing figure with his strong build and demeanor. He was not impressed with any of the attorneys from either side, and his belief against the death penalty was something no one could order him to set aside in any circumstance. He gave me the impression of a man who meant business and would squash anyone who attempted to convince him to abandon his beliefs. For the purpose of this case the man terrified me.

The next day we gathered again. At this point each side was allowed one peremptory strike. That is, each side can excuse one panel member of their choice without having to elaborate on cause, with the exception being excusals on the grounds of race or gender. Major Scott was clearly the most poisonous seed on the panel and must go. But this paved the way for the Crespos to remain on the panel. Major Benson, Colonel Huestis, and Captain Seamone assembled the families and asked our opinion on which member to excuse. While the decision was theirs to make regardless of our opinion, our families were heavily involved in this case. The trial team recognized that, and even valued our opinion in some areas. We all agreed Major Scott had to be the one to go. We figured striking one Crespo would be ineffective and possibly even insult the remaining Crespo. One angry Crespo in addition to Scary Scott, as I silently dubbed him, spelled certain disaster. With no Scary Scott and two anti death–penalty Crespos we were still pretty screwed but had at least a remote hope of success. In this case, remote hope was better than no hope. The government bid adieu to Scary Scott and we watched with sadness but not surprise as the defense eliminated Major Claffey, a member whose father had died when he was ten years old, and who had been unable to sit through proceedings without sending sympathetic looks our way.

Twelve members were required to vote and the mandatory fourteen members was designed to avoid a mistrial should we lose any of the twelve during the trial. No matter how many members over twelve sat on the panel, all of them would vote, and all of them would have to vote to convict to have any chance of proceeding to capital sentencing.

Two–thirds of the members voting to convict would send us into sentencing to battle over Life with Parole (LWP) or life in prison without the possibility of parole (LWOP). I was confident we would see Martinez behind bars for the rest of his life if we reached that phase. However, in spite of the certainty of conviction I publicly displayed, I was not at all confident of that outcome. I just didn't want to let defense counsel, the trial team, or pretty much anyone else to know I was shaking in my high heels.

●   ●   ●   ●   ●

On one occasion, we had been chatting and hanging out in the courtroom as we waited for Martinez to be brought back in from a break. I'd been leaning on the bar, facing our seats, in my normal position during breaks, when I felt a presence beside me, on my right. Looking up, I'd been taken aback to see Martinez, uncuffed, standing inches away from me, looking me up and down with an upturned lip—half sneer, half smile. The MPs were just coming through the doorway a full thirty seconds behind him. It had taken every ounce of my willpower not to take my pen and stab it into his neck as the fear that he had been about to do the same thing crossed my mind. It had happened in the Akbar trial. Akbar got hold of some scissors and stabbed an MP in the neck. No reason to think it wouldn't happen here. But instead, I'd stood perfectly still as I met his eyes and locked onto his gaze until the MPs finally reached him and he'd taken his seat.

As he walked away, I realized I'd been holding my breath, and it rushed out of me in a grunting noise as I gripped the bar and tried to slow my racing heart. Gary Rinni, the prosecution's investigator, noticed the encounter and asked me if I was okay. He'd then reported the incident to Heustis, who called Major Cipriano into a corner of the courtroom as the defense returned. There was a heated argument with lots of pointing my way, and then Major Cipriano walked over to me, apologizing if I'd been upset by his client and assuring me it would not happen again. Except it did happen again, during the trial.

More than once, one or another of us had been face–to–face with an unrestrained Martinez. The worst incident took place in the men's room. Lou's dad and Phil's dad were in there when the door swung open and Martinez walked in, right over to them, and proceeded to take care of business with no regard to whose presence he was in. That time there had been an MP present, which is probably the only thing that prevented a physical altercation. Although younger and stronger than either of the dads, Martinez may well have been hard pressed to defend himself against the adrenaline–fueled rage of the two men facing the man they know murdered their sons.

Security around the defendant was surprisingly lax, as these incidents and others displayed. His security escorts were comfortable enough with him to laugh about comments he made about me. One appellate exhibit we learned about after the trial detailed how Martinez mentioned that he thought the blond one was a hot piece, and he'd love to have his way with her (me), and how the escorts had laughed about it with him. Once, he'd been left alone with his wife Tammy in defense counsel's office. She'd emerged a while later, clothing and hair in disarray. The smile on her face was matched by the one on her husband's, who reeked of her perfume. The conjugal visit, noted later in an appellate exhibit, was yet another breach in security.

●   ●   ●   ●   ●

Two and a half weeks and four rounds of voir dire left us with eleven members seated. Panel 5 was called in, and we began the process all over again. I'd sat with forced impassivity for four rounds as Major Cipriano held his hand up, palm in our direction, while he reminded the panel not to consider family members emotions that we are not parties to the case and are irrelevant to the proceedings. Four times I'd sat there and quelled the urge to leap up and scream at this insult. The fifth time, I could not suppress the sneer on my face as I listened to him do it again.

I'd become attuned enough to the nuances of the process to recognize which members posed a threat to us, and which members would be banished by the defense. I watched as Sergeant James Craeger and Sergeant First Class (SFC) Dezeborah Evans went through the gauntlet. Craeger appeared to be willing to impose the death penalty if warranted, but only after considering all the evidence and weighing the decision heavily. Major Cipriano did his best to get rid of him, but knowing we needed to have fourteen members before beginning, and finding no grounds to dismiss him, Colonel Henley allowed him to remain.

Next up was SFC Evans, a demure, soft–spoken African American woman who smiled a lot and had no strong feelings on the death penalty one way or another. Her nervous eyes darted around the room before resting on Colonel Huestis, who offered her a smile and gently asked his questions. Major Cipriano took it easy on her, too, and she passed muster to be welcomed into the flock.

Of most concern to me in this group was SFC Shepard. Reading from his questionnaire, Major Benson asked him to clarify his statement about not liking CID, period. Shepard explained he'd been singled out and framed for an offense by CID years ago and it had taken a great effort to clear his name. He'd felt he was targeted because he was black, and the agents had lied about evidence against him. On top of his hatred for CID, he was vehemently opposed to the death penalty in any case.

Shephard's position on CID and the death penalty presented an insurmountable obstacle to impartiality in a case relying on CID testimony, with the death penalty on the table. He was a dream member for Majors Cipriano and Gregory's client. Predictably, he was exposed to Major Cipriano's relentless rephrasing of the same question until, like the Majors Crespo, he weakly conceded he'd agree to "consider" the death penalty if ordered to do so. He said this with as much conviction as I would if asked if I would ever consider nominating Martinez for sainthood.

Colonel Huestis challenged Shepard's inclusion for cause, citing his strong views against CID and the death penalty. Major Cipriano argued that he'd agreed he could separate his experience with CID from this case, and had also agreed to consider the death penalty. The arguments continued, and under normal circumstances I would not have worried about someone like him being included on this panel. But we were at a critical point: We now had fifteen members seated, one more than the magic number for trial. But each side was due one peremptory strike. We could lose one member and be okay to proceed, but losing two would cause the number to fall below fourteen, and thus require another round of voir dire.

What's more, this fifth panel represented the last remaining members available in the pool. There was no group waiting in the wings to start over with tomorrow if we needed one more member. In that event, things would be delayed for at least two days while another pool of members was rounded up. Colonel Henley had no intention of allowing that to happen, and he overruled the prosecution's attempt to strike Shepard for cause.

Despite having witnessed the inclusion of two married, anti death–penalty members, this ruling still shocked all of us. Could Colonel Henley really believe this member would be impartial? Even Major Cipriano looked surprised, then smug, before reinstating a neutral expression on his face.

Then it was time for peremptory strikes.

The previous occasion for strikes saw the prosecution have first licks. This time, Colonel Henley told Major Cipriano to take the first swing. He did, and one member was removed. We now had fourteen members approved, and in a slow, deliberate tone, Colonel Henley inquired if the prosecution intended to strike a member.

Major Benson rose, knowing the judge expected him to forgo the strike. But the prosecution could not meekly accept Shepard's presence in light of his solid anti death–

penalty and anti–CID feelings. It was through no fault of Major Benson that it had come down to Shepard as the last member needed. He returned Colonel Henley's stare, then moved to exercise the strike against Shepard.

Colonel Henley's face reddened as he looked to Major Cipriano, who was already on his feet objecting to the strike. According to Major Cipriano, Major Benson had not met the criteria set forth in the Batson case, which mandated that a peremptory strike may be exercised for any reason other than race or gender discrimination.

It was a ridiculous argument, accusing Major Benson and the prosecution of prejudice, because they had excluded Major Scott, also African American. He made no mention of the fact that most of the selected members were non–Caucasian, or that he, too, had challenged African American members.

I could barely contain my disbelief when Colonel Henley entertained defense's argument. Even I knew a peremptory strike was untouchable if, as in this case, there was reason aside from race or gender. Now Colonel Henley was openly glaring at Major Benson, daring him to disagree.

Major Benson was in a difficult position. Colonel Henley had established his opinion by asking the prosecution if it was aware that striking this member would bust the panel, dropping the number of members to thirteen, and if they really wanted to do that. The inference was clear; He did not want to start over with round six, and the defense had given him the excuse to keep Shepard. The only thing in the way now was the prosecution's obstinate insistence on exercising the strike—regardless of the fact that defense had issued a strike first, or that the government was entitled to the same, or Shepard was about as biased as a member could be. His mind made up, he ruled with the defense, agreeing on the record that prosecution had failed to prove any motive other than race behind its strike.

A blanket of silence covered the room for a minute, before Major Benson recovered and asked for a recess.

We all retreated to the prosecution's waiting room and the trial team came in behind us, closing the door to the small room that was identical to the defense's next door, with its pinkish color scheme and two lines of chairs facing each other. Some of us had taken to referring to this holding room as the Victim's DIF.

There was no levity in either the families or the trial team today. No smiles or sarcastic comments. We were all in a state of disbelief over what had just happened. Unsure if we had misjudged the latitude of a peremptory strike, we listened as the trial team removed that doubt and assured us it is unheard of to overrule a strike. I asked Major Benson if the judge had essentially stated he was guilty of prejudice, and if he was angry about that. He said it looked that way, and yes, it did make him angry.

It had been a stormy voir dire, marked with several objections by the defense about Colonel Huestis. The first complaint concerned the Colonel leaning back in his chair, showing disrespect for the proceedings and conveying to the panel that defense was not to be taken seriously. Major Gregory kept his eyes on Colonel Huestis for much of the proceedings and would whisper any perceived offense to Major Cipriano, or leap to his feet and call attention to the matter himself.

Colonel Huestis, in return, would roll his eyes at defense's accusations and continue to rock back in his chair. This had gone on for a few days until someone replaced the soft, rockable chairs with rigid wooden ones. Next, the defense made note of Colonel Huestis chuckling in the panel's direction during Major Cipriano's voir dire questions, and his loud comments to fellow trial team members. Colonel Henley chastised Huestis on the record several times, and the defense moved on various occasions to have Colonel Huestis removed from the case.

It had grown increasingly apparent there was personal animosity between defense and Huestis, first noted on the record in pretrial hearings with bickering between the two parties, until Colonel Henley had finally ruled there was to be no communication between Huestis and defense counsel, and any matter requiring discussion between the trial team and defense would be handled by Benson or Seamone. Now in the victim's DIF, Colonel Huestis was steaming along with the rest of us.

Captain Seamone was unusually quiet, deferring to the two senior members of the team as they explained it was within their right to appeal this ruling to a higher court. The words echoed with the taste of the last delay from the appellate process, ending in defeat. Major Benson explained that the judge had again abused his discretion, and his voir dire rulings had no place in the interest of a fair trial. He also said he was prepared to return to the courtroom and take on the judge, insisting Shepard be struck, and knowing he would incur greater wrath for his argument. The possible outcome of starting with round six could be for or against us; there was just as much a chance of having a room full of Shepards and Crespos as there was in seeing any Colonel Michael Evans—a member that defense had fought tooth and nail to remove, for he displayed high intelligence and had deftly outmaneuvered their trap of the hypothetical question, as well as being in favor of the death penalty. He'd also frequently glanced over to us, ignoring defense's admonition to ignore us.

The other possibility to consider, Major Benson continued, was the numbers. We needed only one more member to proceed but could be faced with twenty to choose from. While there is a minimum number needed, there is no maximum. Defense could choose not to object to any of them, and leave us with up to thirty–three panel members who must be convinced to convict, instead of fourteen. As it stood now, prosecution had to convince ten members of Martinez's guilt to proceed to non–capital sentencing, and we all knew that was the best–case scenario with the Crespos on board. If the defense did choose to rack up the numbers, government could be faced with having to convince upwards of twenty–three people to convict, at a minimum, just to proceed to the same place. Counting out three votes we assumed we'd already lost with the Crespos and Shepard that left eleven members who appeared impartial and willing to consider guilt.

It was a gamble, based on the ability to convince ten of those eleven that Martinez is guilty. We were counting on members like Colonel Michael Evans and Sergeant Saunders, a female member who had been the only person to blow up at Major Cipriano when he'd badgered her with his hypothetical. She'd called him out, angrily telling him she knew his hypothetical wasn't a hypothetical at all, but the circumstances of this case. Defense had lobbied hard to excuse her for cause, saying she would be disinclined to believe them because she felt they'd attempted to deceive her. To his credit, Colonel Henley had overruled them, and Saunders had received her party invitation. Members like her, we hoped, would prevail in the mind games that defense would surely employ to establish reasonable doubt. And we tried to keep an open mind about the Crespos, hoping they would at least be able to separate a conviction from a death penalty.

The brief conference ended with the realization that we were in an unwinnable battle this time. We all agreed the lesser of the two evils here would be to swallow this defeat and hope Shepard would not poison any other members with his bias. We returned to the courtroom, Major Benson admitted defeat, and Colonel Henley announced for the record we were prepared to proceed to trial.

CHAPTER THIRTEEN
PROSECUTION'S CASE

✪ ✪ ✪

Wednesday, October 22, was just another day for the rest of the world. But for us it was anything but normal. Three and a half years of angst had culminated in the trial that was beginning in just a few hours. Adding to the enormity of the day for Siobhan and me was our anticipation of taking the stand as the first two witnesses.

Tight faces and grim smiles were the expression of choice for all of us assembled in the victims' DIF that morning. Getting the "All clear" from the MPs, we moved into the hallway, making the two left turns and taking our positions for the first of the last times we would ever have to be here.

"All rise" was bellowed, and the jammed courtroom fell silent. On the right side of the courtroom, the front rows were packed with our family members. The back rows were jammed with media. The front rows on the other side of the room were bursting with MPs. Behind them sat Tamara. Next to her were the mitigation specialist and Martinez's father. Throughout the trial, different members of Martinez's family would take turns accompanying Tamara, who appeared to have been given a makeover. Gone were the sloppy clothes and unkempt appearance from the Article 32 in Kuwait. Newly cut hair farmed a face that had been introduced to makeup. In front of the bar, opposing counsel and the defendant spearheaded the teams. All of us squared off for a fight to the death.

Colonel Henley's black robe wrapped around his legs for a few strides into the room before working free to afford him the dramatic judge entry for this important case. The court reporter we'd spent three years staring at for so many hearings raised her mouthpiece, obscuring half her face, so only her eyes and the tops of her cheeks lent her any expression.

Those eyes locked on mine for a second, and the mouthpiece lifted with her cheeks as she offered an encouraging smile.

A few moments of last–minute bickering about stuff I didn't pay attention to, and "All rise" was again called out. This time, the court officer positioned stage left of the judge opened the door to the deliberation room, and the fourteen panel members entered the scene.

My mouth was dry and my palms clammy as I watched the members move to their assigned seats. Colonel Henley announced we'd be dismissing early to accommodate a panel member. Siobhan and I looked at each other in mutual annoyance.

Colonel Henley addressed the court, his words not penetrating my miffed bubble as I took in the sight of our panel in their Class As, focused on the judge. Sergeant First Class Saunders, whom I'd noticed as she entered had pulled her dark hair into a tight bun that day, was hidden by the top right corner where the panel seats angled into the wall, so only her hands were visible. Sergeant First Class (SFC) Dezeborah Evans was on her right, next to the worrisome SFC Shepard. This member Evans bore no relation to Liteunant Colonel Evans, whom defense waged a relentless yet unsuccessful battle to get rid of. She and Shepherd were leaning towards each other in a picture of comfortable familiarity. Master Sergeant Dugas, on Shepard's right, bore a strong enough resemblance to Cuba Gooding, Jr, that I would keep forgetting his name and refer to him as Cuba. Master Sergeant Keen's almost military version of a Mohawk on his light brown hair, cut sharply to give his face an angled look, sat forward with his hands clasped, eyes on the judge. SFC Creager's face was thoughtful and clean–shaven, blending in with his smooth head which was turned to the judge. Next to him, rounding out the top row, gray–haired SFC Tabler, whose eyes were just as often gazing through his eyeglass lenses at our families as they were to the judge or the witness, smiled and nodded our way before focusing on Colonel Henley.

Closest to our seats, in the front row on the right was Sergeant Major Wilson, one of the female members I didn't know what to make of yet. Mrs. Major Crespo was to her right, her long black hair also confined within a bun today. Next was Lieutenant Colonel Bowsher, the unassuming female member whose soft, honey–colored hair was cut short along her pale complexion and small round glasses. On her right was Colonel Fiorey, the panel forewoman. Probably the shortest of the bunch, Colonel Fiorey wore her almost orange hair in a sharp bun as well. She rarely let her expression waver, keeping her countenance neutral and making it impossible to discern what she was thinking. Over the weeks of testimony, I never saw her glance our way. Lieutenant Colonel Evans was sandwiched between the Crespo husband and Colonel Fiorey. His dark skin would make it impossible to miss his flashing white teeth whenever he'd smile, and he made little to no effort to hide his amused expressions. Mr. Major Crespo had been promoted, and was now Lieutenant Colonel Crespo. But his dark eyes still reflected the defensive posture of his crossed arms and scowling expression that he'd displayed during voir dire, earning him the nickname "Captain Angry." He was the next–to–last member in the front row. Major Burton held the last position in that row. Rounding out the female half of the panel, she was even harder to read than Colonel Fiorey. Her dark skin never reflected the whiteness of her smile, because I never saw her smile. Or scowl. Or flinch. The woman was a study of inscrutability.

Captain Evan Seamone rose and strode deliberately toward the panel, all eyes on him as he rounded his broad shoulders, took a deep breath, and uttered the first words of the court martial. We listened, spellbound, as Evan laid out the case about to be presented. Piece by piece, he walked the panel through the elements that had survived the pretrial process.

Starting with the night of June 7, 2005, he described the sandstorm that kept most people indoors. How inside the Water Palace, Lou and Phil were enjoying the quiet evening with a game of RISK at a table set up next to a window. It was Lou's third night there, and conversation had turned from work to families. While Lou and Phil sat behind a thick blue curtain, a claymore mine was being placed just a few feet from them, on the other side of the window. FRONT TOWARD ENEMY is engraved on these mines, and that night it faced Lou and Phil. At 2200 hours, "the detonation of the mine rocks the building."

Evan's words had captured the room's attention. His flair for the dramatic, matched by his physical size and commanding voice, ensured that attention never wavered from him. Now he raised it up a notch, declaring, "The evidence will show you that this happened by the will of Staff Sergeant Alberto Martinez."

The scene before me was right out of Hollywood, except for the fact that this was no contrived drama. It was as real as the throbbing in my temples, and the sickening taste of bile forcing its way to my mouth as the prosecutor wound his way through that night, and the time preceding it. Unable to convince my hands to grip my pen, I gave up on taking notes, and listened as Evan continued.

We heard about Martinez's "war within a war" against Phil and then Lou. How Lou's "sole job would be to identify all the problems" created by Martinez. Mincing no words, Evan spelled out the kill zone created by the 700 steel ball bearings in a claymore, and how 436 impact points were later mapped out in the room. The rest of the bearings were either recovered from Lou and Phil's bodies or discarded with the furniture before CID halted the cleanup process.

"The evidence will show you," he said, how Martinez plotted in advance to make this seem like an enemy attack. How he threw three grenades away from the palace after detonating the claymore, successfully creating enough confusion to convince those present that night, and the CID agents who responded, that it had been a mortar attack. He bought himself enough time to throw the claymore wire in the lake the palace perched on and cast himself as a lucky soldier who'd narrowly escaped that attack. Further complicating matters were the efforts of the first responders, focused more on trying to save Lou and Phil than preserving the sanctity of the scene.

Backtracking, Evan took his audience to Troy, New York, and the animosity that grew between the commander and the staff sergeant. "The commander's in my shit. The commander's riding my ass." were Martinez's "mantra." The panel listened raptly as the missing sensitive equipment and the ensuing investigation of the $30,000 loss was explained, ending with the dual liability of Phil and Martinez. How Martinez had attempted to weasel a meeting with Major General Taluto, the Division Commander, by pleading with the general's son, Sergeant Taluto, for "five minutes with your father. He has to understand how bad Captain Esposito is. We need to relieve Captain Esposito; I'll do anything for just five minutes."

Evan switched gears with this, detailing the specific threats and insubordinate comments that would be heard through witness testimony. Expanding on earlier statements in his opening, Evan offered quotes like "The f— bastard is trying to ruin my life. I am going to burn him!" and "I hate that Mother F—; I am going to *frag* that Mother F—!" These comments, Evan emphasized, weren't name–calling. They were a promise. And they had elevated to the "formation of a specific intent to kill and consideration of the act intended to bring about death." That equaled intent, and intent is "an element of the crime of premeditated murder."

Some of the panel members had risked glances our way, perhaps noticing our ashen faces or our semi–suppressed sobs as we envisioned the damage done. Some members were looking at Martinez as if attempting to align the complacent, expressionless defendant before them with the offensive murderer he was accused of being.

Evan kept at it, detailing how Martinez had figured out a way to "eliminate both sources of his discontent with three clicks of the clacker," and told of a witness who would testify about seeing Martinez "standing in a manner indicating he came from the direction of the blast"—the same area he'd been seen casing out for weeks prior to the murders—and how the witness would remember thinking it was odd to see Martinez there, not taking cover. That witness, Wentzel, would be testifying about being in the shower trailer across the street from the Water Palace when the blasts occurred, and that some of the walls had collapsed from the explosion.

The second half of Evan's opening statement focused on placing a claymore in Martinez's hands, placing Martinez—through his own words—within thirty to forty feet of the explosions, and hammering in detail after detail to create the unshakable impression that Martinez did it; How he'd asked another soldier to learn Captain Esposito's personal routines and report her findings to him. Martinez was under serious financial pressure; he feared the repercussions of Lou and the Captain examining his misdeeds. He was the only soldier who openly threatened to frag or otherwise harm the commander, who spoke of wanting to *burn* him. He'd used the dust storm to his advantage that night, hiding in its cover. And he'd been the one of just a handful of people who knew Lou and Phil were at that table in those moments. But he was the only one of those people with means and motive to kill.

Evan stressed the fact that Martinez was directly where the blasts occurred, and the only one *not* taking cover. He'd even reported to the clinic the following day, complaining of hearing loss and ringing in his ears—classic symptoms of someone too close to an explosion. And he'd been the only soldier to report with those symptoms.

As Evan spoke, I watched the panel as intently as I could without being too obvious about it. Some of them were leaning forward, some leaning back. A few would look over to us as Evan hit the more sensitive areas. Wrapping up, Evan reiterated how the evidence would prove Martinez was, "the only person who was within claymore detonation range, who had obtained claymores, who also had access to grenades, who promised to frag the same commander who was killed." He assured the panel they would not fall into the same confused state as the first responders, and put them on notice that at the trial's end, the prosecution would be asking them to find the Accused guilty.

It was a strong opening, and an emotional one for us. There was also a level of discomfort, knowing the strangers in the panel box held the power to decide the outcome of this nightmare. Would it be over for us in a few weeks? Would we walk out of here knowing Martinez would be in prison forever? Or would we stagger out of this room, as he is set free? I was convinced I would never recover if he was not convicted.

A short recess, and it was Major Gregory's turn. I tried not to roll my eyes as he began his litany about the evil government conspiring with CID to frame poor Al for the murders. Struggling to appear respectful of his spiel about the investigation that was constructed around his client's presumed guilt, I faltered a moment when Major Gregory declared, "Staff Sergeant Martinez is *innocent* of these charges." John's objection was interrupted by Colonel Henley, who asked the panel to step out of the room before he admonished Major Gregory for this statement. In response to the judge's question pertaining to evidence of another individual committing the murders, Gregory admitted there was none. He then acknowledged the judge's reprimand for stating his client's innocence, and the panel was brought back into the room.

Major Gregory carried on with the opening. As had happened numerous times over the years, I was left with the impression that I'd missed something of significance. John and Heustis had their heads together in a muted conversation, and Colonel Henley's compressed lips conveyed an irritation at Major Gregory beyond the scope of what I thought was simply more melodrama, declaring his client innocent. I chalked it up to another element of the legal world I didn't understand, and refocused on defense's opening statement. Once defense wrapped up, court was dismissed. Having made it through the morning, I returned to my apartment. Siobhan and I hung out for a while, quietly watching the clock until we tried to get some sleep.

•   •   •   •   •

Day two. I watched the clock change from 3:59 A.M. to 4:00 A.M. Figuring that qualified as morning, I ceased battling sleep and shuffled to the kitchen. I stood there in the dark for a moment while I debating turning on the coffeepot or going for a run. Opting for the run, I walked the short distance in the nippy predawn air to the complex fitness room. Pounded out an eight–minute mile—a respectable time for me—and some of my nervous energy before returning to my apartment. Three hours later I reemerged, this time into early morning light. Walked past the building where both sets of in–laws were staying and to Siobhan's building across the parking lot. Mrs. Esposito had come across this place, and had finagled three–month leases for all of us. It was more comfortable than hotel life, and I'd brought enough personal items from home to make it as familiar as possible.

Siobhan answered my knock and I stepped inside, out of the chill. It was another big day. Siobhan would be the first witness, and I would take the stand after her. We were jittery, hepped up on caffeine and adrenaline. We blared the music on the way to the base, bobbing our heads to "Tubthumping" screaming, "I get knocked down, but I get up again, you ain't never gonna keep me down!" and cracking up. Behind us, we saw the mitigation specialist. She was a seemingly nice, professionally demeanored woman we called the Spy because she watched us like a hawk. It would have been hard for her not to notice the flailing heads and hair in the car in front of her as she followed us through the light, into the parking lot. It amused us to wonder what she would think of the widow's head banging their way into court.

This time, our usual reserved parking spots were not waiting for us. The first section of spots was now reserved for the panel. So we parked in the back of the lot and walked to the new security table at the building entrance. Greeting the MPs at the door, we signed in and received our personnel badges. These badges allowed us to skip the sign–in process and go directly to the MP who would wand us. Over the coming weeks, I enjoyed bantering with the MPs, bringing them candy or hot chocolate, and entertaining myself by trying to make them blush with little innuendos. I'd lower my voice and whisper that I knew wanding the widows was a dream come true. One day when Steve had arrived, I winked at the MP and confessed Steve let me go first because he "liked to watch." But my favorite moment with them was when they allowed me to wand Siobhan, and she stood there gamely while I had fun with it. It was decidedly improper behavior, but we all needed to get our kicks where we could. Whatever helped ease the stress even for a moment was worth it.

Today, there was nothing funny except watching each other climb two flights of stairs in our heels. Siobhan maintained her classier than me status today with her demure black cowl–necked sweater that coordinated smartly with a black and beige pleated skirt, resting just above her knees. I felt a little inappropriate next to her in my snug black skirt and red, form fitting cowl–necked sweater, all perched on black, three–inch heels.

The MPs corralled us behind closed doors in our victims' DIF, a sure sign that Martinez was being escorted into the courtroom. A few minutes later everyone but Siobhan and I filed out. Then Siobhan was called in and I spent a half hour alone, increasingly apprehensive since Valerie popped in and mysteriously told me it was crazy in there, but she couldn't tell me why.

I had no idea why Siobhan's testimony, planned to identify Phil from a picture and establish who he was, had turned from a five–minute experience into a half–hour one.

Finally, I was sent for. Walking into the courtroom, this time with the eyes on me, I looked over to Siobhan and noticed how pale she was. Recognized the distressed look on her face. John swore me in as I wondered what had happened during Siobhan's testimony.

My testimony went quickly. I identified Lou as my husband in the picture John published on the screen. Mentioned our four kids. Glared at the defense when the judge asked them if they'd like to question me, and left the stand a moment later when defense declined.

Returning to my seat, I tried to slow my pounding heart while the next witness was called. Siobhan leaned over and whispered that defense had cross–examined her. I couldn't prevent the surprised gasp that was loud enough to draw the attention of a couple of panel members; I had to bite my lip while Siobhan hurriedly whispered a recap of her testimony. About identifying Phil in the picture, and telling of the New Year's day in 2005 when she and baby Madeline had kissed him good bye for the last time. How defense had surprised her with a cross–examination. How everyone had been surprised by Major Cipriano asking pointed questions about the statement Siobhan had given to CID, insisting they investigate everyone. Asked her if Captain Esposito had mentioned feeling concerned for his life, even after she'd explained that he didn't talk about his job with her. I regretted missing her testimony even more as she continued, telling me Heustis had questioned her on redirect, asking if Martinez had ever made contact with her. She'd said not directly, but he had made eye contact with her in the hallways and sent looks she'd deemed threatening. Colonel Henley had then excused the panel, and Siobhan went on to say she knew Martinez had killed her husband; after over three years of listening to testimony and learning facts, there was no doubt in her mind that he did it. The panel had been called back in, and Siobhan was excused. I now understood why I'd felt such tension walking into the room immediately after that.

While Siobhan was filling me in, Major Pat Kern had taken the seat I'd vacated and was recounting his relationship with Lou and Phil from the 101. He mentioned the "Cav Mafia," the nickname commonly applied to members of the 101 who had joined the 42nd, before telling the court he'd been on the FOB that day, working his shift as Chief of Operations. His expression hardening, dark eyes growing darker as he lost himself in the moment, Major Kern remembered how he'd arrived on the scene after Lou and Phil had been evacuated. How he'd noticed the impact patterns were not normal but had been too distraught to think much of it.

Following Major Kern, Command Sergeant Major Fearnside took the stand. After giving some background on the AGR and military technician jobs, he switched to the laid–back atmosphere at the 42nd prior to March 2004. He told of a phone call from Major General Taluto, explaining the 42nd had been selected to join the Operation Iraqi Freedom mission. It had been Fearnside's call about Captain Werzbowski. He'd felt the unit's current command team was "weak, not skilled enough" for the mission, and brought First Sergeant Willsey aboard. He then added he'd felt Werzbowski was "not qualified" and was happy to follow Willsey's suggestion to offer Phil the slot.

On cross–examination, we sat through a repeat of much of the testimony already elicited from the prosecution, and most of us in the room let our attention wander. Some of the panel members used the opportunity to make eye contact with us, or stare at the defendant. Eventually the testimony moved into other areas, and Fearnside was being asked if Phil could have just switched Martinez out of his position if he was a problem. The witness responded slowly, purposefully, as he explained that Phil and Willsey would have wanted to "develop the soldier" instead of foisting him off on another unit.

The witnesses came and went over the following days, some of them offering new insight, and others reaffirming previous testimony. From Major David Palmieri, the 42nd's former Chief of Operations, we heard more about the strain between Martinez and Phil. How Palmieri had personally gone through supply at Drum and saw equipment issued "hundreds of times" with no receipts. How that lax attitude from Martinez had finally been too much for Phil, and that in May 2005 he'd spoken with Phil about the problem. Phil had then told him he was bringing Lou forward to help. Under cross–examination, Palmieri was asked about personal knowledge of Phil's rebuttal to the accountability charges for the missing NVGs, where Phil had laid the blame on Germosen, who'd been standing in for Martinez that night, and on Ash, for being the one to fail to return them. Palmieri said he'd not heard of the rebuttal.

The next witness was a retired National Guard soldier who had been on the FOB during the explosions. It was hard not to find some amusement in the recreation of the witness's movements that night. Evan received permission from Colonel Henley to have the witness jog about the courtroom and dive to the ground, feigning his actions as the explosions hit. According to Mr. McClure's testimony, the explosions occurred one on top of the other, spaced at most by a few seconds. This would be confirmed by some witnesses, and contradicted by the memory of others. Some witnesses accounted for three instead of four explosions. When McClure was cross–examined, the emphasis was switched to Willsey. Defense's strategy relied heavily on creating other suspects and was centered on Willsey. McClure's testimony was our introduction to this strategy. It was unremarkable, and I would notice only in retrospect that it had been a seed planted when the witness was asked about that night. He'd been assigned to guard the office after Lou and Phil were removed, and had let no one in, until Willsey arrived and removed a computer and possibly a safe. McClure also stated Willsey didn't like Phil as a commander. That next seed planted, the witness was excused.

There was a large screen in the courtroom, used to publish pictures for the panel. To familiarize the members with the scene and allow them to follow testimony, various angles of the Water Palace were displayed throughout the trial.

Colonel Robert Crow, the FOB's former Acting Garrison Commander, took the stand, speaking of the force protection order issued on the FOB. Crow told of his Memorial Day weekend visit with Phil, when he'd asked Phil why his office windows had not been sandbagged and boarded up in accordance with the order to protect all ground–floor windows from blast damage. Phil had explained resources and manpower were in short supply, and he'd ordered his windows to be the last on the list, so as to protect his soldiers first. Continuing, Colonel Crow testified that other than the night of the murders, no enemy had managed to infiltrate the walls of the FOB for a direct attack. Lou and Phil had been the only soldiers to die in an attack on the FOB, and the Water Palace had never been hit.

Defense took their turn with Colonel Crow, and turned to the night of the murders. Crow emphasized that he'd authorized the removal of items by Willsey. Moving on to the aftermath of the explosions, we listened as Crow took us through finding legs to what appeared to be a claymore. He described the ball bearings covering the room, and the pockmarks on the walls and ceiling, of calling CID back in after the cleanup had begun.

Each day in court drained us in its own way, and we all welcomed opportunities to find distractions. In our front row seat, I was on the end until Steve arrived, or unless Valerie sat there. On my right was Siobhan, followed by her attorney, Brent. The young associate had proved able to keep up with our bantering, and fit into our mini society well. Rounding out our row was the prosecution's investigator, Gary Rinni. The large man maintained an unassuming presence in his effort not to intrude on our families' personal drama. By the end of the trial, however, he'd joined in the conversation and added to the dynamics of our group. Among us, we noticed our pew had been pushed back from the half wall separating us from the courtroom floor. Brent had been admonished for resting his feet on that wall. When Steve joined us, he, too, had been asked to keep his feet off the wall. And then our seat was farther back, an inch or two each day, until we could no longer reach the wall. In a small protest, we moved the seat forward again, only to arrive one day to find a sign in front of Steve's and Brent's spots, making it clear we were not to rest feet on the wall. Unfortunately, the signs appeared on the morning I'd played a little hookie to spend some time with my kids. Arriving late, I entered a quiet courtroom with testimony in progress. My seatmates gazed expectantly at me, waiting for me to notice the signs. Which I did, and the five of us barely contained grunts of laughter.

The government's endeavor to establish Martinez's absolute guilt in spite of the crippling blows to the case, and defense counsel's merciless drive to impugn Phil's character, CID's tactics, and virtually everyone in the 42nd save for their client, had been a fierce and unrestrained battle from the first words of opening statements. Heustis and both defense attorneys made no attempt to mask their contempt for each other, and their animosity often seeped into the courtroom. More than once, Colonel Henley addressed the men, chastising one or the other for their behavior.

For days the tension had been escalating in the courtroom as we listened to a range of testimony describing mundane facts about jobs and benefits. We all knew it was important to lay out background information, but were impatient to get to the meat of the case. Get it over with. The bickering between opposing counsel was getting on our nerves and some of us began noticing panel members losing patience with the childishness, too.

From Quick Response Force witnesses we heard more about the moments and hours after the explosions. For the first time, the panel heard testimony about entering the pitch–black room, choking on smoke and dust, noticing there was "blood everywhere" as first responders tended first to an unresponsive Phil and then to Lou, who had been "complaining of back pain" as he'd been treated and loaded into the ambulance. I knew that was a toned–down version of what Lou had been saying, and was torn between wanting to know more. How he'd been. Was he screaming? Was he afraid? Was he crying? And then feeling thankful to not have to hear about it. With that glimpse of the reality behind all the legalese and endless procedures, we recessed for the weekend.

Monday morning, day four of the trial, the government began pulling out the bigger witnesses. Finally addressing the heart of things. The first witness in the lineup was David Wentzel, now a retired Noncommissioned Officer. In greater detail than he'd given in Kuwait during the first Article 32 hearing, the 42nd's previous unit drivers training instructor testified about his experiences and interactions with Martinez. It was all new to the panel, but for us the beginning of this witness's testimony held no surprises as he spoke again about Fort Drum and how Martinez had complained about the "by the book" commander. How comments like that escalated in Kuwait and Iraq, into "I can't wait for him to get hit" and "You'll never guess what the f— asshole did" in regard to the missing NVG incident, and having his supply access restricted. I began paying closer attention now; I hadn't been familiar with the last thing Wentzel said and wanted to hear any new details he offered. Martinez "didn't react well" to the action being taken against him by Phil. He "had a lot to lose." It would affect his civilian AGR job.

When he turned to the night of the explosions, Wentzel's staid countenance faltered. In a slightly less steady voice than before, he spoke of a huge explosion rocking the shower trailer (located close to the Water Palace) he'd entered only moments ago. The walls had started coming down around him and he'd run out, across the street to seek shelter from what he'd thought were mortars raining down. With the sound of a smaller explosion, he'd decided to seek "more substantial cover" by running back across the street to the pumphouse, where he settled into a nook and looked out just as another explosion blasted. Then, he saw a soldier in the street, coming from the direction of the blasts. He'd hollered for the soldier, who stopped walking and stood there, head shaking from side to side, shaking from head to toe.

Pausing for a moment—that soldier had not been in the street a moment ago, when he'd run across—Wentzel hollered to the soldier to get down, but the soldier just stood there "as if he knew it was over" instead of following the basic training to seek cover. So Wentzel had abandoned his own cover to run over to the soldier. He recognized Martinez when he reached him and pulled him to cover. With no further explosions coming now, a new sound reached him. Cries for help. And he'd gone toward the cries, intending to help, until he'd been deflected by others already on the scene rendering aid. He and Martinez, who'd followed him into the building, now went their separate ways to their individual rooms.

Wentzel continued, but I couldn't keep up. I was again frozen in time; in my mind I was there, on the street, hearing Lou scream. And I could see Martinez standing there in the swirl of dust and blood and confusion he'd orchestrated, listening to his victim screaming for help. Forcing myself to refocus, I picked my pen back up and resumed note taking.

Wentzel spoke to Martinez three times after that night. Each time left him more nervous than the last, until he'd begun to fear for his own safety. The first time, around June 9, he'd passed Martinez in a hallway. Brushing off Wentzel's greeting, Martinez said he'd heard Wentzel was interviewed by CID and asked how long the interview had gone. Wentzel told him it had run a couple of hours, and Martinez's already strained cordiality now slipped into unmasked anger as he abruptly ended the conversation and walked away.

The second encounter had taken place in Wentzel's classroom. Martinez had entered the room and closed the door behind him, shutting Wentzel in alone with him. Martinez wanted to know what Wentzel had told CID. Uncomfortable with telling him, Wentzel had replied he shouldn't be having this conversation, all the while watching Martinez as his fellow soldier looked around the classroom instead of meeting his gaze. While Martinez had appeared less angry this time, something about his icy demeanor and the way he'd studied the classroom made Wentzel nervous, and then relieved when Martinez blew off his question as mere curiosity, leaving as suddenly as he'd entered.

The third encounter left Wentzel the most unnerved. In his third floor room one day, he'd been startled by Martinez's unexpected appearance. Martinez had never before come up to Wentzel's room. It was out of the way and not on anybody's path unless they had a room near there. Now Martinez said he'd been "in the area and wanted to say hi." He'd then made comments about Wentzel's room, noting, "Boy, there's a lot of concrete over your head." The tone of Martinez's voice, his body language, and the previous encounters all shook Wentzel up. "I'm very scared now. Hand on my weapon watching this guy." Martinez said he wanted to clear his name. Wentzel ushered him out of his room, and returned to CID to report the encounter.

Defense counsel did its best to unpaint the picture Wentzel had just painted. Pointed out that Wentzel, while hearing Martinez say he couldn't wait for Phil to "get hit" had never heard Martinez threaten to kill the commander. That he hadn't considered Martinez's words threatening until after June 8, 2005. Almost sarcastically, counsel asked Wentzel, "If someone told you to do your job but you were not allowed in your office, you may call him an asshole?" Again, minimizing the disrespectful comments repeatedly heard from Martinez. Condoning them as a rational response to an overbearing, out–of–control commander who was relentlessly harassing poor Al. I could feel Siobhan bristling beside me, and again marveled at the strength it took for her to sit here listening to her husband be cast as the real villain. Behind me, Phil's parents and sister could not contain exasperated gasps or grunts whenever a witness badmouthed Phil. Often, one or both of his parents would become so upset, they would walk out of the courtroom. As the trial progressed and Phil was routinely bashed by disgruntled soldiers' testimony and relentless defense counsel, Mr. and Mrs. Esposito's comings and goings no longer drew glances from anyone. It simply became part of the experience.

Major Jason Ward, of the Weapons Intelligence Team, was a segue way witness to CID testimony. Introducing the first precursor of the investigation efforts, the Major told of his small involvement. How he'd been told about the deaths from a mortar attack, and then been greeted at work on June 8 by the Chief of Staff bearing a piece of metal removed from the scene. That he'd thought it looked like a claymore, or some other unidentified weapon, and he'd wanted to look into it so as to prevent a reoccurrence. Returning to the scene with experts from the Explosive Ordnance Division (EOD) he'd taken photos and felt more comfortable determining it was claymore damage.

We were treated to an array of visuals with this witness's testimony. He had a selection of items in evidence containers ranging from wires to claymore fragments, offering our first glimpse of a leg from the murder weapon. It nearly made me sick. The EOD witnesses would later give similar testimony. None of it pleasant, but still, we consoled ourselves with the belief that our suffering, at least in this area, would soon be over when Martinez was convicted.

The first CID witness was the commander of the 366 CID, or the Special Agent in Charge, based at FOB Danger. The only gauge of height I had for this meticulously groomed man came as he passed John en route to the witness stand. He appeared to be close in size to the prosecutor, next to whom I felt like an Amazon. Hunkering down in the witness seat for what he knew would be an extended amount of time, Collins calmly answered Evan's questions and laid out some background information.

While the witness was on FOB Danger between 2004 and 2005, CID investigated over 120 incidents, including one death and one suicide. Prior to June 8, 2005, it was not standard procedure to investigate combat deaths. He'd decided to respond to the call of two combat deaths strictly for a quick "open and close" investigation similar to when a soldier is killed off base in the United States. Taking Agent Speciale with him, Collins dutifully made an appearance at the scene, commented on the tragedy of a mortar happening to land on the windowsill of an occupied office, and left after filling out a minimal amount of paperwork—just a couple more dead soldiers. Nothing noteworthy about that. Shortly after returning to his office, however, he received a call from Colonel Crow telling him to come back. Instead of returning himself, he'd sent two other agents, Fernholz and Comesanos.

Sometime around 11 A.M. Collins returned to the scene and finally realized it was a homicide. It had been thirteen hours since the attack, and several people had begun cleaning up the room. As this witness testified I found myself again mentally replaying the time line. Processing all the people involved, all the events taking place while I had been lying awake in our bedroom waiting for Lou to call that night. Finally rechanneling my attention to the here and now, I tuned back in as Collins explained the thirteen–hour span between crime and investigation did not spell disaster.

Knowing defense intended to put CID's investigation on trial, Evan took his time with this witness, allowing him to lay out exactly what steps were taken to make up for those lost thirteen hours, and the cleanup that had commenced. I kept one eye on the witness and one eye on Shepard in the panel box. Previous testimony had appeared to bore him, but now he was finally paying attention, writing in his notebook and conferring conspiratorially with Dezeborah Evans on his left.

Collins explained how he'd ordered his agents to cease and desist all work on other cases and focus full force on this one. Assigning Fernholz and Comesanos, and Assistant Special Agent in Charge Johnny Belyeu to process the scene, all other agents were tasked with canvas interviews. These interviews were short and sweet, consisting of the following five questions:

1. What was your location on 7 June 2005 at 2200?

2. Did you hear any blasts? (If so) How many?

3. Did you see the blast impacts? (If so) Where?

4. Do you know who had ill feelings for the Commander of HHC 42nd ID?

5. Do you have any information pertaining to the incident under investigation?

Agents were told to follow all leads and keep an open mind. Agent Fernholz was charged with maintaining a case file and CID plan, which Collins reviewed and sometimes added to. A large whiteboard was utilized to update the plan on a daily basis. Of the 256 canvas interviews conducted, about 30–yielded pertinent information to be followed up on with sworn statements and interviews.

The give and take between Collins and Evan had thus far been smooth, allowing testimony to flow freely. Collins, having no problem following Evan through the intricate process, easily followed the next change of direction.

Evan asked about Martinez as a suspect. Staff Sergeant Martinez, Collins said, first appeared on radar the afternoon of June 8, around three PM. when Wentzel had approached Speciale to tell him about seeing Martinez that night. The same day, other agents learned the commander was in the process of disciplining Martinez who, as the supply sergeant, had access to ordnance. Bearing in mind the statistic that two–thirds of homicide victims are killed by someone they know, this information captured attention. Especially Wentzel's statement placing Martinez on the scene. Collins wanted Martinez to be interviewed *now*. He knew the responsible party had intended to get away with the crime by disguising it as a mortar attack. He felt it would better to interview Martinez early, catch him off guard.

Testimony was interrupted when Colonel Henley excused the panel. Outside the presence of the members, Evan was asked why he felt entitled to use Martinez's excluded interview. No ruling had been made to allow the interview into evidence, and by referencing an interview in his testimony, the witness was in danger of mentioning excluded evidence. Captain Evan Seamone, stifling any urge he may have been feeling to argue, assured the judge he would not mention the statement. Members were called back, and testimony resumed.

I tried again to quell my concerns about Shepard, in spite of the scrunched–up face and small nodding of his head as he looked now at the witness. Had the interruption played into his distrust of CID? Did it allow him to justify his paranoia about that organization? Did he think the witness was lying or misleading the court? Realizing it wouldn't do any good to get all worked up about it, I nonetheless mentally berated Colonel Henley again for allowing Shepard to sit on the panel.

Evan asked the witness about the procedures that were followed. Collins walked us all through how a suspect is advised of his rights before speaking with him. Of obtaining necessary consent and authorization before searching any premise, and that these procedures had been followed with Martinez. No mention of Martinez's interview was made, as per the court's orders. Instead, it became the proverbial elephant in the room as Evan and the witness moved to a search of Martinez's workspace and personal quarters on June 8.

Confronting the dicey events leading to Martinez's statement being suppressed, Evan asked Collins to continue relaying what happened next. Collins obliged, and panel members heard for the first time about the confusion involved when the witness was told Martinez had been taken to the DIF He had been "extremely livid" to hear that, Collins said.

Instead of elaborating on what happened next, the matter was dropped. Conspicuously so. Testimony turned to other matters as Collins stated other suspects were being looked into, and that Martinez had been released due to a lack of probable cause to detain him at that time. No mention was made of how he was released. Was he released from the DIF or from CID headquarters? Who released him? The panel had heard Martinez was read his rights, but by whom? When did he sign the consent–to–search form the witness testified about? Was anything found in the search? Presumably not, since no probable cause was found to detain him. As with the illegal transaction of government property to an Iraqi, the panel did not hear about the flares and flare guns, the alcohol, or an Iraqi pistol in Martinez's possession. They did not hear about the statement he voluntarily gave to Agent Speciale after sharing a meal with him, accepting Speciale's apologies on behalf of CID for the episode at the DIF. That he'd been in Phil's office for almost thirty minutes that night discussing an order for a clock with Phil, and stood by while Phil made a call about it. How he'd seen Lou and Ash at the table by the window, with a chair for Phil, playing RISK. How he said he'd left, gone to his room to watch TV for a while before going to put some drinks in his vehicle. He'd stopped at the port–a–potties across the street "to do #2" and the explosions boomed as he was finishing. He'd described how confused he'd been, and disoriented as he stumbled around the street. He hadn't heard any typical "whistle sounds" associated with incoming mortars, or anything else, because he was "taking a poop."

Later in his statement Martinez had written about Phil:

"When I meet the Commander for the first time he express him self (sic) to be much better than me and other people. He never have respect for the lower enlisted people. The

commander also trye (sic) to proved other soldier that they were wrong and he was right knowing that he was wrong. Also the commander accuse me of not keeping track of my property book in fact he was the person who was doing the damage. A few times he verbally threaten me to throw me out of supply for not doing the supply books his way not by the Army way."

Martinez wrote that Phil "threaten to removed me out of supply and reduce me on rank but I ignore him" and that those threats had taken place twice, once at Fort Drum and again, in April on FOB Danger.

None of that equaled a confession. But it corroborated much of CID's actions and beliefs, and would have been a valuable tool in the prosecution's case. Being barred from using the interview and statement would lead to awkward fumbling around the subject with each CID witness on the stand. While we understood the reason for this fumbling, the panel did not. It was clear the panel knew there had been an interview of some kind. And they knew it was being omitted from testimony now. Some of them were shrugging their shoulders at each other. Shepard's already furrowed brow became, if possible, more so. Dezeborah Evans leaned in with her new friend and mimicked his display. I worked hard on appearing unconcerned.

Collins was explaining how at the time Martinez's spaces were being searched, CID had not received consent from any other individual. But he offered half a dozen names of other suspects whose spaces were searched later in the investigation.

By June 12, Collins testified, Martinez was considered **the** suspect. This was based on a number of facts, including: Martinez was on the scene, being disciplined, and had access to ordnance. The commander's room was altered before the blast. The table had been moved next to the window four days before June 7, and only a handful of people knew that. Martinez met with the commander nightly, including that night. Martinez was not only being disciplined, he was about to have an Article 15 levied. Phil was throwing the book at him. Witnesses heard Martinez threatening the commander's life.

While the focus was on Martinez, agents were nonetheless investigating other suspects. Martinez's supply subordinate and close friend Specialist Sherman had been seen with Martinez on April 10. Two witnesses came forward to state Sherman appeared to be serving as a lookout for Martinez as they executed a practice run for some sort of mission at the Water Palace. Martinez had been dressed all in black, including a ski mask over his face. The witnesses had asked Martinez what he was doing, and he'd responded they shouldn't worry about it. A few days later, Martinez ran into the witness again, and asked if the witness could fashion a tool for him. Similar to a screwdriver but thinner and just as strong.

The witness asked him what the tool was for, and Martinez said not to worry about it. The witness had not made any tool for Martinez. Since Sherman was seen on the street near the pit area ten minutes before the explosions, it was possible he was acting as a lookout for his friend, just like their practice run. In his statement, Sherman drew a diagram of where he'd been, smoking his cigarette before heading back inside. Said he passed Martinez on the steps as he was going up into the building and Martinez was going down, out of the building, moments before the blasts.

Collins listed at least three other individuals investigated as suspects, including Lieutenant Luis Badillo, the unit XO. But Badillo was home on leave that night, and the other suspects all had solid alibis. Martinez was the only remaining suspect with means, motive, and opportunity.

Listening to this testimony, I was reminded of the casual references made about Sherman over the years. I'd always had him on a list of things to find out about. Each time I'd asked, my questions had been subtly, or not so subtly, dismissed. Occasional concessions were made, such as, "Yeah, he's dirty, but we can't prove it." And I was supposed to be okay with that. Even though Sherman looked like a good candidate for an accomplice. I made a note now to myself, to ask if he was on the witness list. I was anxious to hear from him.

Evan was wrapping up with Collins. The last portion of a nearly two hour direct examination was spent hammering key facts home: Countless hours were spent on this investigation. Many Requests For Assistance were sent to CID offices in Iraq and stateside, and agents in several offices assisted. Many official crime scene diagrams were done in this case. The diagrams were published and explained to the court.

Finally, after rehashing the care and due diligence with this case, Evan made a stab at discrediting one of defense's strategies, casting Willsey as the real murderer. Disputing defense's assertion of Willsey's guilt, Collins explained that was not out of the ordinary for Willsey to remove computers and equipment from the Captain's office. Willsey was temporarily in charge when Phil and Lou died. With all the people coming in and out of the room, he was responsible for securing the computers and the sensitive information on them.

As Evan thanked Collins and turned him over to the defense, Siobhan and I nodded assurances to each other. We thought Collins had come off as believable and helped lay out the case, in spite of the dangling statement issue. But we were nervous about what Major Gregory would do to him on the stand.

Wasting no time, Major Gregory took his place at the podium, angling it to face the panel members instead of the witness. A minute or two of sorting his notes, steepling his hands to his face and choosing his words, he then opened up on Collins.

Major Gregory's first swing was at the thirteen–hour gap between the blasts and the investigation. "Special Agent Collins, isn't it true that crime scenes need to be secured immediately? In the CID Handbook, doesn't it warn there is only one chance to secure a scene?" The questions were hammered out, stated more than asked. Collins sat up in his seat, on the defensive now, "That's the effort."

Major Gregory turned to questions about CID approaching the scene with a preconceived concept. Then came a series of questions about who was in charge of the investigation, tying into his earlier claims in the opening statement that each time he'd sought to speak to the Agent in Charge, he'd been unable to find any agent willing to assume that title. How CID had toyed with him. Collins maintained a level voice when responding and deflecting the assault, but he shifted in his seat at times, annoyance eking out through his body language.

Major Gregory focused now on the two grenade pins found outside. How they'd been found two days after the explosions, missed in earlier searches. Collins had no answer as to where the pins came from, and said his agents were confident they had not been there when the area was searched.

I stopped taking notes as Major Gregory shot rapid–fire questions and monologues. My wrist was already sore from the furious pace of writing, and I'd heard the next line of questioning so many times I could practically recite the questions and answers along with the attorney and witness: We were back to the DIF, and the CID office, and the great injustices bestowed upon Martinez. And then, Major Gregory threw out a question about Martinez being interrogated until four in the morning. It was a clear reference to the statement, but the prosecution's objection was quashed with a scathing look from Colonel Henley before John had fully risen from his chair. Panel members replayed the confused looks to each other as the elephant returned to the room.

Major Gregory set about attempting to prove the claymore could not have been detonated from the port–a–potties across the street, because the amount of wire recovered did not stretch that far. "CID worked hard on this. The idea that Sergeant Martinez being in the port–a–potty is important to the investigation." Major Gregory continued with his theory that the investigation was tailored to fit Martinez while Collins continued to insist it had not been. This would have been the time for the agent to explain they'd been following up on Martinez's statement. Except he was forbidden from doing so, and Gregory was taking full advantage of the suppressed statement. Using it less as the shield it was supposed to be than as a sword to the heart of CID.

We heard about a boat underneath a bridge near Phil's room that had not been searched. Gregory asked if a claymore wire could reach the palace roof. "I don't know" Collins answered. Gregory pounced on that, and it would become one of his favorite theories, how the roof would be a perfect place for someone to detonate the claymore, and CID had "not bothered" to search up there for a satchel, or grenade spoons, et cetera.

Next, Major Gregory addressed the list of other suspects CID had investigated. One soldier who had been issued a no–contact order by Phil, after arguing with the commander about policies. Another soldier had tried to drive a bus off a cliff, with someone else in it, and so on. Names that Collins had been through with Evan on direct examination were run through again. And again, Collins stated each suspect had been investigated and cleared.

Collins's cross–examination ran for over two and a half hours. It had been an antagonistic exam, as Major Gregory made no pretense of being nice to the witness, and the witness returned the feeling. Under redirect, Evan did his best to clear away the smoke cloud Major Gregory had blown with his multiple unproved theories about CID framing Martinez and all the other suspects who were more likely to have killed Lou and Phil than his client. Of the 3500 soldiers on FOB Danger, 8–10% had been interviewed. That, according to Collins, is a large percentage. Agent Belyeu, who would testify later, was the one who did the tests with the claymore wire. He would answer detailed questions. But Collins stood by the port–a–potty location as logical and open–minded for a test. CID regulations mentioned by Major Gregory are guidelines, not regulations.

Step by step, Evan ticked through Major Gregory's list of CID's alleged misdeeds and had his witness explain the genuine investigative value of these procedures. Finally, he summed it up by asking, "On 8 June no one else was as close to the blasts, who made threatening comments regarding Captain Esposito, and had access to ordnance?" And the witness reaffirmed Martinez was the only individual who fit all those categories.

With the redirect over, it was time for the panel to have its turn. It took more than a few minutes for Colonel Henley to review the stack of questions before allowing both sides of counsel to read them over. Some of the pages were set to the side without passing to counsel. After much conferring, counsel returned to their seats, and Colonel Henley read the questions to Collins.

By the depth and tone of the questions, it was clear Major Gregory had succeeded in clouding the issue for several members. Questions about Wentzel and Willsey. Had *their* rooms been searched? Why not? Collins explained at the time Martinez's rooms were searched, CID had not obtained consent from anyone else, and could not search without consent. Questions touched on topics from the CID handbook, to the claymore wire, to areas of the sidewalk damaged from the blasts, and one question asking what time the interview with Martinez began. The questions reflected a panel that was paying attention, but some who had lost sight of the facts in the smokescreen deployed by defense. Also, one member at least was not ready to forget about the interview. Colonel Henley addressed members on occasion, during their question sessions, with the reminder; "You have all the information on that matter you are to consider." The implication was clear: There are things you are not being told. But the reason was not explained, and this was bothering them.

Prosecution and defense asked a few cleanup questions, and the witness was excused. Court was adjourned for the day, and we were all too happy to get out of there.

●   ●   ●   ●   ●

Major Christopher Himes, an explosives expert with EOD, started us off the next morning. His testimony began with information we'd already heard about the cursory inspection of the scene, and finding no evidence of mortars. About examining the scene and the found fragments, and calling Colonel Crow to tell him it was a homicide. They had confirmed it was a claymore. The cleanup crew had been dismissed and the investigation had begun. Three of the four claymore legs were found inside in the debris, and one grenade spoon was found outside.

John handed a brick–size, rectangular object to Himes, who identified it as a training claymore. Siobhan and I swapped pale–faced looks as we realized this was a model of the murder weapon. We'd only seen pictures before. Himes then described how a claymore emits steel balls similar to .22 bullets and is attached to roughly one hundred feet of wire. The detonation device is called a clacker. The weapon can be prepped in advance, and wire can be wrapped around the body of the mine, so long as the mine is tied off so it does not move away from where it is aimed.

Finishing his brief testimony, the witness explained he'd returned the following day for about one to two hours, and had then departed on leave. That had ended his involvement.

Major Gregory rose for cross–exam, and within three or four questions he began challenging Major Himes's testimony. "Remember when we spoke, you said your team had been there before CID. Your testimony now is that CID was there first?" Major Himes denied ever telling Gregory his team had arrived before CID, and stuck with his testimony. Major Gregory moved on.

"While there, you never told CID it was not indirect fire?" The witness responded that they needed to rule everything out before making any determinations. A few questions later Major Gregory half stated, half asked, "The items moved into piles from people sweeping. If you (EOD) indicated earlier to CID it wasn't indirect fire, no one would have swept up." Major Gregory was building on his theory of an incompetent investigation, and I was continuing my silent prayers that the panel would not buy into it.

The panel's questions were detailed and direct. Did the witness have an opinion as to where the grenades were thrown from? "Hard to determine." After a claymore explodes, will the adapter at the end of the wire remain? "Sometimes," Major Himes responded, before stressing again the extreme danger of being within sixteen meters of the explosion, and for up to three hundred feet, shads will fly. Through questions and answers, including counsel having another shot, the witness testified that a person should be one hundred feet away, under cover, to avoid injury when detonating a claymore. That claymore pellets travel quickly, three to four thousand feet *per second*. I thought Siobhan shuddered with me as we heard that and envisioned our husbands in the path of hundreds of steel balls exploding in at them at that rate.

A couple more questions were asked about the components of a claymore surviving the blast, how any wire not wrapped around the mine would probably be blown into pieces, but not disintegrate, and that a claymore can be set up and detonated within minutes. Major Himes was excused. The bailiff was told to call the next witness, and Special Agent Paul Comesanos was next on the stand.

Agent Comesanos had been sent to the Water Palace the morning of June 8 for the limited purpose of carrying on a Serious Sensitive Incident, or to document a hostile death or deaths. He'd released the scene back to Willsey and returned to his office after taking a series of photos. Those photos were displayed on the screen, and they were not something I'd been prepared to see. As one picture after another of Phil's office flashed on the screen, and we saw Lou's and Phil's blood half–mopped up, next to piles of debris, defense counsel looked back to our families. Checked to see if the pesky victims' families were distracting the panel with our emotional displays. For our part, we all tried to remain impassive. But we hadn't been warned these photos would be shown, and most of them we hadn't seen before. Phil's parents in particular had a hard time with it, and we could hear their groans. I worried we'd all be kicked out, even while part of me was wishing we would be.

The slideshow over, Agent Comesanos resumed explaining the shift from a hostile death to a homicide investigation. Yellow crime scene tape had gone up in place of QRF's red tape. Guards had been posted. The scene was locked down. He detailed collecting wire fragments and the claymore legs, and ensuring the chain of custody was maintained. We saw more photos, this time of the evidence that had been collected.

Next, Agent Comesanos told of Agent Belyeu's methodical and arduous task of stringing up the room. How the agent had stretched hundreds of colored strings from the points of impact on the scene back to the area of detonation in the window. Each string represented a ball bearing bursting from the mine, at the already determined rate of three or four thousand feet per second. Again without warning, another picture was published, and will forever be seared into my memory.

Taken from what looked to be where Lou and Phil were sitting, one picture showed those hundreds of simulated ball bearings hurtling toward the camera. The effect was a graphic visual of what Lou and Phil had been in the path of. The violence and savagery of the claymore's kill zone was impossible to miss, as was the vision of Lou sitting there with his friend, innocently chatting, as he was swept away by the force of the explosion and those steel balls pummeled his body, shredding him.

I didn't know then and I don't know now if I'd have been so overcome with emotion from that one picture, as I was that day had I seen it under other circumstances. Was the combination of the constant stress of the courtroom and the situation, added to the previous surprise of the crime scene pictures a few moments ago, what sent me over the edge with this picture? Regardless of why it affected me so much, I realized I would not be able to hold myself together and had to consciously keep from running as I fled the courtroom. An extended cry and some dry heaves in the bathroom left me looking like a train wreck, and I made some futile efforts with makeup to mask my newly reddened eyes, swollen lids, and pasty complexion before returning to the courtroom just as a break was called.

Back on the record a short while later, Agent Comesanos recalled how the port–a–potties had been moved, and he'd sorted through fecal matter as it was dumped, searching for any evidence that might have been hidden within the disgusting mess. That search hadn't turned up anything, but on top of the shower trailers were three pieces of wire, and on the ground was a plastic canister "consistent with grenades." More plastic pieces and wire fragments were found scattered about. They had drained the entire lake surrounding the palace, and resting on the bottom was the clacker with some wire from the mine. The crime scene had been worked for eight days. The window grate outside the office had

been dusted for prints, since that is where the claymore had been set. But the doorknob
to Phil's office, because of the high traffic it received, had not been printed. Likewise with
the shower trailer. Too many people came into contact with those areas for fingerprints to
be relevant.

When Comesanos was opened up to cross–exam, Major Gregory was ready. Standing
between our families and the courtroom screen, he played a nine and a half–minute video
of the crime scene made by Agent Belyeu. Had we been able to see the screen, we would
have seen footage of the Water Palace as the panel did. Instead, all we saw was Major
Gregory, casually taking swigs from his water bottle as the video played.

With a touch of incredulity in his voice, Major Gregory asked the witness if all 817
photos he took were of the office. "Correct" Comesanos replied. Asked if any photos the
MPs took that night had been forwarded to CID, the witness responded in the affirmative,
and yes, he would be surprised to learn defense had not received any copies, and yes, those
are the only known photos of the scene taken the night it happened.

We recessed early that day, and picked back up the following morning. Agent
Comesanos resumed his spot on the stand and Major Gregory asked about the importance
of fingerprints in an investigation, and determining how much printing was done in this
case. Not enough was Major Gregory's assertion. Along the lines of other suspects, it was
noted the whiteboard in Captain Esposito's office held possibilities, as it listed an A128
assault charge, pending. Agent Comesanos did not know who it referred to. Several names
were offered on Major Gregory's list; Phil had been counseling a handful of soldiers.
Touching on the search of Martinez's quarters, Gregory asked if it had yielded any results.
It had not.

Returning to the theory that Lance Willsey had killed Lou and Phil, Major Gregory
asked about the safe Willsey had removed that night. It had been returned empty. CID
had not printed it, or the doorknob to Phil's office. That little seed planted, he moved on.

The last round of questions had to do with CID isolating Phil's office, rather than the
entire Water Palace. Agent Comesanos explained the office was the crime scene, as opposed
to the entire Water Palace.

On redirect, John sought to clear up any confusion established by Major Gregory's
admittedly ingenious barrage of unrelated facts and people. I knew facts the panel would
not be told yet the man sometimes had me confused. So my concern grew each day that
he would prevail. The fingerprint issue was maddening, but it seemed an effective ploy to
cast doubt on CID's thoroughness. I'd have given about anything to hear one agent had

printed the doorknob to the office so that Major Gregory would have to find some other irrelevant fact to distort. A keybox holding keys to the connexes had been in Martinez's office. Someone could conceivably have popped in and swiped a key. Neither keybox nor keys were printed, but John emphasized the things that *had* been printed: the grenade spoon, the clacker, wire, pieces of the mine.

Next up we heard from EOD again, this time through the testimony of Kevin Fitzgerald. After recapping his role in events we'd already heard, the witness explained how an M67 grenade is detonated. That the spoon falls away from the pressure exerted by the pressure pin, and how two spoons were found about three to four feet apart.

In cross–examination, Major Gregory stuck to his M.O. by immediately attacking the witness, designing his questions to prove overall incompetence by those involved. "Looking back, it was pretty obvious it was a claymore. Because you were looking for indirect fire, you missed that it was a claymore." Addressing the grenades, "And there are too many variables to nail down where the spoons go? And it's possible to have the spoon land at your feet?" Allowing a chuckle to escape as he answered this question, Fitzgerald responded, "Yes, Sir but I would not recommend doing that." This response drew laughs from the courtroom but Major Gregory, unamused, plowed through the rest of his questions and turned to the experiments done by CID with the claymore wire. Once he'd confirmed the 100–103–foot wire just reached the port–a–potty spot, and the experiment was done four times with Agent Belyeu, defense was done with Fitzgerald. After follow up questions by the still–engaged panel and both sides of counsel, the witness stepped down.

Special Agent Miller would be the last witness that day. The CID agent first offered testimony about photographing Lou's and Phil's bodies, and performing vapor tests on them before returning to FOB Danger to assist in the investigation.

After dusting for prints, he'd assisted Collins and Speciale with interviewing Martinez, but did not know Martinez had been in the DIF. Again, the interview with Martinez was alluded to and dropped. Miller had been tasked with interviewing the medics and first responders. As to the investigation, he could only testify the scope and the involvement were large.

Captain Seamone asked about Willsey, and Miller replied he'd heard of possible contention between Phil and Willsey regarding Willsey's weight problems. But Willsey had supplied whereabouts and been accounted for, the weight problem had been cleared up, and he'd been eliminated as a person of interest. That all sounded good, and I sincerely hoped it would be enough to squash Major Gregory's attempts to cast suspicion on Lance Willsey.

Perhaps anticipating defenses cross exam, Evan ran through the list of other suspects again, and this witness corroborated previous testimony that they'd all been investigated and cleared. Court recessed for the day. Agent Miller would finish testifying in the morning.

Before hearing witnesses that Thursday morning, court was called to order and Colonel Henley ruled to allow the diagram Martinez had drawn during his interview. The prosecution was not happy about this, and argued now to keep the diagram excluded, since introducing it at this point would only confuse the panel. Furthermore, since being struck down in the appellate court on the matter, prosecution had restructured its case to adapt to the ruling. Colonel Henley would have none of it. In a voice dripping with disdain, he asked the prosecution if it was now opposed to being granted something it had spent so much time and effort taking to the appellate court? Over prosecution's objections, the diagram was allowed, and the trial team was forced to scramble to right its newly capsized ship.

Colonel Henley called for the panel and soon Miller was back on the stand. Major Gregory wanted to know why no one other than Martinez was tested for gunshot residue, and then rehashed the suspects. I was frustrated listening to this all again, and hoped the panel was, too. Flipping to an empty page in my notebook, I wrote to Siobhan, "Mr. Peacock did it in the library with a candlestick!" and bit my lip as she choked back a laugh.

Our laughter died as Major Gregory mockingly referred to the "CID Reunion" here at trial before rounding off his list of suspects by adding some more names to the cast this time. The panel wasn't laughing. Especially Shepard.

If I'd been concerned before about the level of success Major Gregory accomplished with his Willsey theory, the questions for this witness from the panel had me sick with fear: In his interview, did Willsey indicate he had a strained relationship with Captain Esposito? "No." In hindsight, do you believe the investigation was thorough? "Yes." Do you know why Willsey turned in the safe on 12 June, and not earlier? "No." Who determines a person is no longer of interest? "The Special Agent in Charge." How was Martinez "acting peculiar" as per Wentzel? The questions poured in and we were horrified that the panel seemed to be buying into the defense's conspiracy theory. Evan made a valiant but unsuccessful effort to assuage the doubts voiced by the panel in their questions. Miller testified it was not a big issue for Willsey to remove items from the office. Willsey had become the highest–ranking officer that night, and it was his responsibility to secure items. About Wentzel, the witness emphasized he'd been *very* concerned about Martinez's comments.

But Major Gregory sensed blood in the water, and moved in for another attack. "CID can go back anytime to look at someone as a person of interest? "Yes." Willsey had full access to documents, connexes? "Yes." The witness was excused and a break was called.

We knew CID testimony was the thrust of the prosecution's case. And we hoped the final two agents in the lineup would wipe up the damage Major Gregory had done to it. It would be up to Agents Corbett Speciale and Johnny Belyeu to convince the panel that CID had conducted a thorough investigation, and to trust in their findings that Martinez was guilty. Expert witnesses would testify about grenade fuse particles and components, but none of that would matter if the panel had not believed CID.

Heustis allowed Agent Speciale to ease into the details as he warmed up by explaining his background. The stocky blonde agent followed the same suit and tie dress code as the rest of the agents, and his tie dangled now as he leaned forward as if he could not wait to charge into things.

This is the agent who'd been approached by Wentzel and had interviewed Martinez. With the mention of the interview, we all held our breath. It was always like watching a tight–rope artist wobble across that line up in the air. Would he fall? Was there a net?

It seemed this balancing act would be okay at first. Agent Speciale recounted walking into the interview room and seeing Martinez in cuffs. Ordering the cuffs to be removed and apologizing to Martinez. How he'd called upon his experience in supply to talk about that job with Martinez before advising him of his rights. Martinez had still been pretty upset about the DIF, and Speciale had apologized and talked to him until he'd calmed down.

So far, so good, I thought, as Speciale began telling about the now–allowed diagram Martinez had drawn. While Martinez drew the diagram of the street and trailers outside the palace, he'd been talking about his actions. Speciale was not allowed to mention that. But he did talk about how he'd collected computers, memory sticks, and also the black bag Martinez said he'd had. "Objection! Request a 39A!" flew out of Major Gregory's mouth. The tight–rope act was falling.

Outside the presence of the members, Major Gregory was beside himself with indignance as he moved for a mistrial. Agent Speciale had violated the court's ruling by testifying about the "black bag Sergeant Martinez *said* he had with him."

Heustis argued the comment had been fleeting and the testimony was directly about the black bag, not Martinez's interview. Gregory jumped in and argued it was the second time the witness made the comment, and the two verbally sparred over upcoming witnesses who would be testifying about seeing Martinez with the black bag. Meantime, Agent Special attempted to avoid having a nervous breakdown up in the witness stand, worried he'd inadvertently caused a mistrial.

Colonel Henley listened to the dueling counsel before ruling the witness statement was, "inadvertent due to unfocused trial counsel. A mistrial is not the best case of justice." He warned Agent Speciale this was a caution to him, to be more careful. The members returned, and Colonel Henley instructed them to disregard the witness testimony about the Accused telling him he had a black bag. This caused some of the members to swap confused looks again. Now they had confirmed that Martinez spoke to CID, and they would not be permitted to hear what was said. I crossed my fingers and hoped they would not assume CID was hiding something. We'd already given Shepard more than enough ammunition to support his CID paranoia, and by the way he and Dezeborah Evans had been cozied up in the courtroom and in passing, in the hallways, I was now worried she would be swept up in his fears and bias.

The much–talked–about black bag was admitted into evidence, and Speciale confirmed it was the bag that had been retrieved from the floor of Martinez's office.

Having elicited all the testimony needed from Speciale, Heustis turned him over to defense. Major Gregory spent some time asking questions about what agents were involved with which parts of the investigation, who was in charge, who was the "go to" guy in this case, and so on, before again referring to the "CID reunion" here at trial. Speciale demurred, saying he wouldn't call it that, and Gregory said, "But you saw Agent Fernholz here, waiting to testify." And then he again went into the fingerprinting that had not been done in this case.

The antagonistic question and answer session went on for some time, and eventually landed on Speciale's interview of Sherman. "He was a suspect?" Yes. "Because he associated with Martinez?" Speciale explained Sherman was a suspect because he was on the scene, and Gregory kept at the subject for a few more questions while I wondered if he'd now succeeded in confusing the panel more.

Heustis kept his redirect questions brief, and Major Gregory asked the judge for permission to re–cross–examine the witness. Granted. "Staff Sergeant Martinez opened the door of the port–a–potty on the second explosion?" Speciale responded, "Yes." Gregory continued, "He said he was seeking cover?" The Agent hesitated slightly, still jittery from the earlier slip. "Ultimately he said he was going to jump in the lake." I sat there, bewildered with the rest of the group, as to why Major Gregory was being given the latitude to ask questions like this. Wishing I had a law degree so I would understand the rules. A glance at Steve and Brent revealed equally bewildered expressions as Major Gregory continued asking Speciale to confirm things Martinez had said.

The panel questions indicated a still–present doubt in their minds as to who was a suspect. This time, someone asked why Wentzel had not been considered a suspect. Speciale thought he had been, but was not personally involved in investigating him. It seemed as though Majors Gregory and Cipriano were presenting a brilliant defense. We had one CID agent to go, and as of that moment, the panel was exhibiting signs of not buying into the investigation. Or at least, having doubts about it.

Special Agent Johnny Belyeu was called to the stand later that afternoon, and I paid close attention from the minute he walked through the doors. Underneath the suit and tie, the tight haircut, the outward show of confidence the tanned, wiry agent was nervous. Would he maintain his composure? Would he be convincing enough to allay the uncertainty running rampant in the panel box? Would he be able to undo the confusion spun by the artfully woven web of distorted and irrelevant facts so far? Because if not, if the panel did not believe whatever he was about to testify to, we were in trouble.

Agent Belyeu had been the Assistant Agent in Charge of the investigation. As such, he'd been tasked with proofreading reports and supervising agents in addition to his own investigative duties. The morning of June 8th, 2005, he'd focused on administrative duties while sending agents to investigate what he thought were two combat deaths. He'd spent just a little time at the scene that day, but had spent almost nine hours on the following day, setting up the trajectory strings we'd seen pictures of. Agents had testified to Belyeu's unwavering focus that day, as he'd painstakingly mapped out and strung up what he now told us had been 463 points of impact. The rest of the 700 steel ball bearings "probably went into the furniture or the victims." From this display, it appeared the weapon had been aimed straight into the window.

Evan published a picture the witness identified as a claymore placed in the window. Agent Belyeu explained it would be easy to tie a claymore onto the grate outside the window, and then detailed the extensive and unusual process of draining the lake in search of evidence. Based on the location of the mine, and the grenade spoons found the same distance apart as the blast seats, CID determined it had been possible for one person to carry out the attack. After about an hour and a half of direct testimony, the witness was turned over for cross–examination.

I was expecting Major Gregory to spare no punches with this witness, and I was not disappointed. But my worry about Belyeu crumbling on the stand was unfounded, for he handled himself beautifully. Calmly addressing questions about which agent had been in charge of what aspect of the investigation, and what he'd personally been involved in, Agent Belyeu managed to remain poised even when Major Gregory asked things like why CID had not requested the commander do a Health and Welfare Search of rooms throughout the Water Palace. "Can't the commander order soldiers to allow their quarters to be searched?" Belyeu's explanation that such a directive is a commander's function and not an investigative tool was cut short by Colonel Henley, who excused the members.

When the door closed behind the last member, Colonel Henley slowly and deliberately asked Major Gregory if any evidence obtained from such a directive from the commander, Willsey at that point, would have been subject to objection, as such a search is not an investigative tool? Major Gregory conceded it would be, and Colonel Henley granted the prosecution's request to instruct the panel such a search is not an investigative tool in a CID investigation.

It seemed as though Major Gregory's winning streak with CID had come to an end, and I felt some hope begin to trickle back. At least one of the panel members was now nodding his head in agreement as Agent Belyeu explained why CID could not arbitrarily ask for consent to search quarters "out of the blue." And Major Gregory seemed helpless to stop himself from hammering the witness with more and more questions about various searches CID had not conducted, until Colonel Henley announced it was time to recess for the day. For the first time since we began, we returned to our apartments enjoying the unfamiliar, if tentative, sensation of ending the day on a high note.

Next morning's testimony began on the same note yesterday's had ended. Agent Belyeu remained unruffled and refused to crack under Major Gregory's rehashing of yesterday's questions regarding the search conducted. Today, even Colonel Henley had had enough, and excused the members so he could rein in the proceedings. Advising both sides to pull out the manuals for courts martial, the judge referred to MRE 611, which addresses the repeat of testimony, and questions of which the witness has no knowledge. "Don't do it! Is that clear?" he asked.

Major Gregory refused to accede to the judge. Almost frantically, reminding me of my kids right before they have a total meltdown, Major Gregory replied "No. Sir. Each agent points to the other! This witness and the Special Agent in Charge tried to present the impression that CID was open–minded but the investigation was focused only on Sergeant Martinez."

"Stop!" Colonel Henley had apparently had enough. He advised counsel there was a time and place for arguments in closing statements, and he told the emotional defense attorney to stop asking questions when he has an answer, even if he doesn't like the answer. He was not to attack or impeach unless he had evidence.

I'd be lying if I said I was not enjoying the floor show that morning. It amused me to see Major Gregory scolded like a child, and Siobhan and I were biting back laughs as we wrote notes about his getting a "time out." Slaphappy with stress and fatigue, we struggled to compose ourselves as Colonel Henley advised Major Gregory, "Get a hold of yourself" after the Major's near–whining about this being the biggest case he'd ever had and how he was doing his best, trying not to argue with the witnesses, but he didn't know how else to do this. Asked if he was in control of his emotions, if he needed to sit, and then warned not to say something he'd regret, Major Gregory took a few deep breaths and assured the court he was ready to continue.

Major Gregory moved to the agent's interview with Captain Carl Prober, who had testified at the 32 Hearing in Kuwait. His first few questions drew objections from the prosecution, and he was ordered to move on to different topics. He asked about the diagram Agent Belyeu had shown the witness, prompting another objection from the prosecution. Testimony again came to a halt as the members were excused to allow for arguments. The stop–and–go pattern of the testimony was beginning to have an effect not only on the members but on the witness. Agent Belyeu was fidgeting in his seat, no longer the picture of calm and collected. His responses were adopting a frustrated, defensive tone as the day progressed and the questions did not let up. He was cracking, and I'd seen what Major Gregory did to witnesses once he broke them. I knew we were headed for disaster.

Resuming testimony, Major Gregory did a thorough job of erasing any vestige of CID credibility that may have survived until now. Asking about the diagram, pointing out the M written in, and that it represented Martinez's location, another battle ensued between witness and counsel as Agent Belyeu insisted the M represented the site of the claymore detonation, and Major Gregory insisted it represented Martinez in the porta–potty.

Producing a picture of Agent Belyeu in a chair, holding a clacker with wire stretching from it, Major Gregory asked if this experiment had been done based on Martinez's location that night. Again, Agent Belyeu insisted that experiment had been based not on Martinez's location but on the length of a hundred–foot claymore wire. No, the chair's location and direction it pointed was not intended to simulate the port–a–potty, or Martinez in it. And no, he didn't know which direction the port–a–potty faced.

Major Gregory was in the zone now, and no one was interrupting him. Gathering momentum, he was nothing like the scolded child he'd been earlier during his tantrum. He was again the ruthless individual determined to stop at nothing in his effort to exonerate his client. And he was on a roll.

I watched with a newly infused sense of panic as Agent Belyeu crumbled on the stand. Major Gregory asked more than once about the experiment Agent Belyeu had conducted. Previous testimony had established the port–a–potty location and direction. We all knew it was exactly like the picture we were seeing. That the chair Agent Belyeu sat in was in the same position as the toilets, and where Martinez said he was.

No one likes being lied to or played for a fool. By insisting his experiment had nothing to do with Martinez, Agent Belyeu insulted the intelligence of every member of the panel. And dealt a crippling blow to the credibility of the entire investigation.

There would be nothing unusual about an experiment designed to establish the possibility of Martinez or anyone suspected of the murders. Had the witness testified that this experiment was in fact based on Martinez's location, and followed up with another recap of investigative steps centered on other suspects, or why this particular experiment was run, it would have been just another step in the process. But denying it, and standing by that denial when the tight expressions and shaking heads—even some disbelieving smiles—on the panel members' faces indicated they were not buying his version of the truth, was not a good move. Even members who wanted to believe in CID would have a hard time trusting in this witness right now.

The panel's questions were more an extension of the cross–exam, than general questions. Captain Prober stated he saw a wire? Did he retract that? Did CID determine there was a wire? Where did he say the wire went? One diagram had the detonation point at the port–a–john, where you had the green chair located—Did that represent the port–a–john? Did Martinez's diagram indicate which direction he exited the toilet? One after another the questions poured in, and Agent Belyeu stuck to his testimony about the chair and the experiment. I tried not to slump down in our pew, or project any other outward signs of the raging fear surging through me as I watched the final CID witness of the prosecution's case collapse.

That sensation stayed with me the rest of the day, making it difficult to concentrate on Mrs. Stacey Kerwin as she testified. The weapons armor analysis expert witness spoke about the ball bearings matching a claymore and the grenade fragments that matched an M67. But all I could do was focus on calming my fears and getting through the rest of the long day, until we broke for the weekend. It was Halloween, and I was missing another fun day with my kids to sit here. *For what*, I wondered.

On it went, days blending into each other, and Siobhan and I developed our own routines. I would be on the treadmill around four A.M. and leave a silly note for her to find when she ran at five. We'd meet at her place and drive in together. Steve would usually arrive before Brent, but after the rest of us. I loved the chance to spend time with Steve, as he has a way of making even the most mundane moments enjoyable. In court, he provided answers to my legal questions and comfort during the traumatic testimony. Outside of court, we sampled the area's restaurants, visited state parks, and even played a wild game of Lazer Tag one day that left me laughing harder than I had in months. In mellow moments we'd rent movies, and he got me to church a couple of times. If the boys were visiting, they would alternate between hanging with me and messing around with Steve. An impromptu walk in the park led to a mud fight and then a picnic under the trees. One evening we'd relaxed outside at the apartment complex, joined by my parents, the Espositos, Lou's parents, Doc Sullivan, and Evan. An odd mishmash of people in unusual circumstances, but any casual observer would think nothing of it—just another group of friends and family taking advantage of the weather. But moments of lightness were fleeting. We still had to get through the trial.

With the CID portion of the government's case behind us, I held on to some hope the rest of the witnesses would be strong. Really make it clear why CID had narrowed the search down to Martinez, and overcome any doubts about the likelihood he was innocent.

I opted to spend time with my kids instead of being in court when the expert on grenade fuse particles testified. The crux of that expert witness was establishing particles emitted from the grenade had been indentified on Martinez's bag. Or in it. Seemed inconsequential, as those particles were free–floating all over, and would have turned up on any item that had been in the proximity that night, had CID tested anything else. I knew Major Gregory would point that out, and manage to erase any real value to the testimony. And when I arrived later, I was told that was exactly what had happened.

The next wave of witnesses were those who'd heard Martinez threaten Phil, or witnessed animosity between the two. Leading off this lineup was Sergeant Sartori. She'd see Martinez every day, and he'd greet her by saying "F— frag him." Sartori worked in proximity to the commander, and Martinez asked her to keep track of Phil's movements. When she refused, he then asked her for the keys to the office, explaining he wanted to sabotage data on a computer. He was "very belligerent" about Lou's arrival and told Sartori that Phil had initiated UCMJ action against him, trying to chapter him out and fire him from his AGR job. Seeing how angry Martinez was, Sartori suggested he speak with a JAG officer. And still, she never mentioned this to her commander. Instead, she'd gone to the XO, Luis Badillo.

She'd seen Martinez upstairs, carrying a black bag, at 7:45 the night of June 7. He'd asked her if she was going back down to the office and she'd said no. Later, she'd assisted the first responders at the scene of the explosions. She'd been motivated to speak to CID, she said, because of the hatred she'd seen in Martinez's eyes as he met hers after the explosions.

Major Gregory wasted no time having his way with the sergeant. I'd seen this witness testify at pretrial hearings, and she'd been a disaster. Flighty, giggly, rambling off on tangents. Heustis had done an excellent job with her on direct. Watching that testimony, you'd never recognize her as the same woman. But Major Gregory knew she was and had no problem impeaching her testimony.

Ticking off a list of Sartori's complaints against others—including a sexual complaint against Phil's replacement—Major Gregory delivered his first blow to her credibility in less than ten minutes. He then hammered out a string of questions about the "chaotic" HQ Division. About Ash, "People called him T? It was your opinion you had to do T's work? It was your opinion his relationship with Captain Esposito was inappropriate? They wrestled like kittens? And this weirded you out?" Sartori, a tiny woman to begin with, seemed to shrink in the stand. She cast imploring looks at the prosecution team, begging for rescue from the barrage of questions she could not keep up with. She was intimidated by the situation, by the pace of the questioning, and by the subject matter of the questions. And she wasn't even close to being done. In a small attempt to push back, she clarified Ash and Captain Esposito wrestled "like brothers" instead of kittens, but the next question rolled over her response.

Asked about her CID statement, that she had not mentioned seeing Martinez with a bag that night, Sartori replied she believed she had. Until Major Gregory produced her statement and she was left no choice but to acknowledge he was right. As with Agent Belyeu, being caught in a lie, intentional or otherwise, ruined her credibility. And panel members were openly shaking their heads.

Now that he had the witness under his control, Major Gregory launched the next wave of his attack: the Lance Willsey theory. Throughout the trial he would continue to build on his premise that Willsey was the true culprit. The facts he used and the manner of questions he asked were nonsensical to those of us who had been along for the ride over the years. But to someone who was not privy to suppressed facts and witnesses, and whose only knowledge of the case was through this testimony, it would be easy to let the shenanigans distract from the truth. Especially if a person held biases or beliefs that predisposed them to hear what fit into those beliefs and biases.

Asking a slew of yes–or–no questions, "The first sergeant and Captain Esposito didn't get along? The first sergeant would slam doors in meetings? One time at FOB Danger it got worse?" Major Gregory managed to elicit a picture of an out–of–control, angry and disrespectful Willsey who was acting strange and deliberately confused after the blasts.

Heustis scored a point on redirect by emphasizing that Martinez was the only individual Sartori had heard say he wanted to "frag the f—." But it was a small point, and defense still won that round.

Testimony carried on over the following days and developed a pattern. While the prosecution called one witness after another who'd heard Martinez threaten the commander, the defense used many of those same witnesses to build its own theories about Willsey, and the purportedly slanted CID investigation. One witness spoke of seeing Martinez seeming to case the area for several nights leading up to the murders. Major Gregory used her to establish there was access to the roof and that the access was common knowledge. Major Jude Mulvey heard Martinez speak ill of Phil so often she advised Phil to fix the problems, that the comments made her uncomfortable. But she never specified to Phil the seriousness of what Martinez was saying. Phil never knew that within weeks before June 7, Martinez had ranted to Mulvey that, "You don't know what's going on. He's trying to take my job away. He doesn't know what could happen. He should be scared." Especially disheartening to us was hearing Major Linda Thorburn testify about her friend Phil. Apparently, her friendship with him had not been enough for even her to tell Phil about threats she'd heard Martinez make against him. We felt betrayed by this—especially Siobhan. We had trusted Linda and believed she had Phil's back over there. We'd invited her into our inner circle, unaware she had turned her own back on Phil, or that she would join Taluto's staff when she got home, and terminate contact with us.

I was glad to see the members reacting to that testimony with looks toward the defendant, and raised eyebrows at the threats. Until Major Cipriano got up, explained away all the behavior as the same kind of empty venting anybody else has ever engaged in, and no one looked interested anymore.

The final week of the prosecution's case included witnesses like Sergeant Schumacher, familiar to us from pretrial hearings as the person who'd helped Martinez pass his aptitude tests, and more recognizable names and faces like Specialist Portella and Sergeant Amy Harlan, who'd since married and changed her last name to Loehr.

Sergeant Schumacher expanded on her pretrial testimony with details about a supply unit so dysfunctional she was called upon to give Martinez, his fellow supply member Sergeant Rodriguez, and Badillo an impromptu class on how to run a supply unit. The witness was defensive of Martinez and emphasized that ultimate responsibility was the commander's. She told how he would call or stop in almost daily, and added a touch of scorn to her voice when recalling Phil to be the "most focused commander on the FOB." She then spoke of one argument in particular between Martinez and Phil that got out of hand, each yelling at the other until Rodriguez joined the fray, and finally Badillo stepped in to defuse the situation. She'd been so uncomfortable she'd left. Later, Phil called her to ask about bringing the former supply officer back to replace Martinez. She highly doubted it, she'd said, but recommended to the commander that he should call their superior, Chief Masey, about it. Phil did, and the chief denied the request. Martinez, meanwhile, was growing angrier, and told her he wished the commander was dead.

Schumacher told about another Report of Survey (ROS) that came out after June 8, with the new commander Dominic Oto at the helm. This ROS showed a loss of equipment totaling, "between nine hundred thousand and one–point–one million dollars."

Under cross–exam, the witness relaxed in the stand a little. Her previously tense posture softened as she agreeably answered Major Gregory's questions. The ROS had been conducted after Martinez was in pretrial confinement. Yes, it had been done without the supply sergeant's input. Martinez was always gracious to her, getting her whatever she needed. Yes, Rodriguez also yelled at the commander. No, Martinez never appeared threatening. Theirs was not the only unit that was screwed up, the Massachusetts unit property book was also screwed up. Martinez had approached her for help. She'd referred him to the Inspector General, and then JAG. Yes, he'd called JAG. And finally, she'd seen Martinez a few days after the deaths, and he'd told her CID "was trying to pin it on me."

"Defense counsel pointed out the ROS after the deaths didn't have Sergeant Martinez's assistance?" asked Heustis on redirect. "Right" came from the witness. Heustis dropped his head a fraction, hands at his sides, as he softly said, "But they didn't have Captain Esposito's, either." To which the witness had no choice but to acknowledge that truth, leaving in the air for a moment the vision of all the things Captain Esposito would now never be able to do. It was a powerful moment, albeit brief. And it was the last impression we were left with before court adjourned for the day.

Lieutenant Luis Badillo commandeered the spotlight much of the next day. Having seen him testify in pretrial hearings, we knew what a show he was capable of putting on. Our feelings for this witness were tepid, at best. But it would be more accurate to say we just didn't like him. Any of us. He displayed an arrogance that begged to be knocked down and an air of contempt for Phil's "micromanaging" that infuriated Phil's family. He was prone to rambling outbursts on the stand, even stopping once to inform the judge how he thought things should be done. We knew Evan would have his hands full with this one. And it would be a long day.

Siobhan and I couldn't help rolling our eyes at each other as the man of the hour walked in. Noting his impeccable appearance in suit and tie and how it made his shoulders seem too broad for his head, was juvenile and immature of me. I just couldn't stop the inner giggling at the sight. I had been so stressed for so long it was starting to crack me.

The former executive officer of the 42nd HHC took his seat and recapped Phil's arrival to the unit in May 2004. As the XO explained how he'd educated himself on supply in order to keep up, he confessed his initial impression that Martinez had things under control was inaccurate. Then he'd heard from Martinez that Captain Esposito and First Sergeant Willsey didn't like him, and wanted to remove him. After recalling how he and Martinez actually moved into the supply room for a period to meet the demands of the job, Badillo's thus far controlled countenance showed its first crack.

"Captain Esposito expected us to run full function. That was not possible. There was no help, and constantly increasing work. His expectations were above and beyond the help, experience and knowledge of supply." Badillo seemed helpless to stem the flow of indignities he felt the captain bestowed upon the supply unit. "Captain Esposito became a micromanager" and had pointed out problems in an open forum.

Chronicling the conversations he'd had with Martinez about "Little Mussolini" and "Little Hitler," referring to Phil and Willsey, Badillo's voice wavered with the effort of remaining calm. So far, those of us who had seen him earlier were impressed with Evan's ability to keep this witness under control.

"Things eventually boiled over until we had the whiteboard at Drum" Badillo was saying. Recalling the method an exasperated Phil had resorted to in an effort to keep Martinez focused, the witness told about the board Martinez had to write on each night. On it, he was ordered to outline every moment of the following day, to manage his time more efficiently. "I thought it didn't make sense. Captain Esposito could keep track of Sergeant Martinez by phone." His voice stronger now, hands clenching in front of him, Badillo appeared incredulous again, just thinking about what had transpired.

He and Martinez had gone to Colonel Betor, the Inspector General (IG) on FOB Danger, where Badillo informed the IG this wasn't working. Supply and HQ was all one big dysfunctional family. "This will get worse in Iraq. Someone is going to get hurt." His voice dropping now, Badillo shook his head as he said there was never a successful resolution, and it was so bad he'd told the IG he was ready to resign his commission to get away from the situation.

Suddenly, Badillo changed his tune. Seemed as though he'd received proper acknowledgement for his work when they arrived in Kuwait. "But in Kuwait, Captain Esposito told me he heard what a good job I did, how happy he was with me. I was relieved to finally get praise." He'd had an epiphany of sorts, and now understood the pressure placed on Captain Esposito. He'd then begun acting as a buffer between commander and supply sergeant. He even agreed with Willsey's suggestion to put a guard on Martinez following the May 13 counseling session that had ended with Martinez being given restricted access to the supply room. But Captain Esposito had not thought it was necessary.

Siobhan and I looked at each other then, thinking the same thing: If Phil had known about any of the threats made against him, if *one person* had come forward and reported it, maybe he would have agreed to that guard. But he was unaware Martinez was that angry. He had no idea his supply sergeant was dreaming of his death, threatening to frag him, wishing him dead or asking others to track his movements. So he had no reason to think he was in danger. And even then, while telling his commander he thought a guard was a good idea, Badillo never mentioned *why* he thought so. Never told Phil about the threats he'd heard, or conversations he'd had with his buddy.

The night of that counseling session, after Phil restricted Martinez' supply access, Badillo had seen his friend in the breezeway outside, with "this look on his face" as he stared at the commander's office. They'd walked together and encountered Sergeant Rodriguez, their fellow supply member and Martinez's friend. Badillo attempted to explain to Martinez the reason he was again in trouble was for missing hand receipts. "You reported one hundred percent but that was not accurate." Martinez was angrier than ever, feeling it was the second time he was being blamed for something that was not his fault. Badillo and Rodriguez had begun talking about ways for Martinez to fix this, and Martinez dismissed them, saying, "Don't worry, I'll take care of it."

The following day, Badillo continued, he'd helped his friend move his things to another office, and it had been smooth sailing from there. He'd left for his personal leave ten days later.

Backtracking, Evan asked Badillo how he'd felt that April, when Captain Esposito told him about Lou coming in. He'd welcome Lou on board, he'd said. And made Martinez aware that Lieutenant Allen would be coming to supply. When Martinez asked why, he'd explained, "I was too busy" and that, "I expect you to support Lieutenant Allen." Martinez had wanted to know if Captain Esposito knew Lieutenant Allen. Badillo relayed how Phil and Lou knew each other. "He's probably one of his boys" Martinez had snapped.

Badillo had gone on leave, with some email contact between him and Martinez, as well as Lou and Phil, before the night of June 7. But on June 8, he'd received a call from his father telling him about two deaths, and naming Lieutenant Allen as one of the dead soldiers.

When Major Gregory took over, I inwardly cringed in dread of what could happen if he succeeded in uncorking Badillo's top. He went through background facts about the seeming unnecessary move of replacing Werzbowski with Phil. Got Badillo to admit he himself had referred to Phil as a "lunch money victim," like the kid in school who is bullied out of his lunch money, now in a position of power. That Martinez tried hard, but Captain Esposito pushed him harder. Badillo grudgingly confirmed all the questions posed to him. Until he was asked if he himself, in reference to Phil, had said, "I could f— kill that guy." Badillo adamantly denied ever saying such a thing. He also denied knowing there was a relief for cause process, meaning Phil had initiated steps to remove Badillo from his position, in effect against him.

Returning to his Willsey theory, Major Gregory asked Badillo, "And the first sergeant was angry when he said he'd put your head under the wheel of a truck?" Badillo denied that, too, insisting Willsey had said that to Martinez, and not him.

Major Gregory asked about arguments Badillo had with his commander, and elicited testimony about several occasions Phil and Badillo had argued. That because "sensitive items are the kiss of death for a commander" everyone thought Phil would be relieved of his command due to the ROS accountability. He denied egging Martinez on and agreed it had seemed as though "Captain Esposito was on a vendetta" against Martinez.

I was filled with too many thoughts at once as I watched Badillo step down after over four hours on the stand. This is the guy whose emails to Lou had sounded friendly, and set me at ease about the deployment. I couldn't help but feel that Badillo had set Lou up. It was an epic storm brewing over there, and Lou was eagerly preparing for a mission, knowing even less than Phil about what he was walking into. If Phil was right there, in contact with Martinez and the rest of the 42nd on a daily basis, and had no knowledge of the danger he was in, how could Lou? Why didn't Badillo's emails include any warning to Lou about the volatile situation he was getting himself into? Instead of telling Lou what a fabulous room they would be sharing, maybe he should have given him a heads–up about how unhinged the supply sergeant was. He'd claimed to be a buffer between Phil and Martinez. He knew

Martinez was angrier than ever before, and he would only get angrier once Lou arrived. But he washed his hands of the whole situation and left Lou to figure that out for himself.

I was still lost in thought as the next witness was sworn in, and when next I paid attention James Pounds was on the stand. The former Non–Commissioned Officer In Charge (NCOIC) of the Water Palace had known Martinez since their time in Troy, New York. Martinez had been his supervisor, and they'd had a friendly relationship. Pounds described conversations with Martinez, reminiscing how Martinez spoke of being sabotaged by Ash during the sync meetings. "Haji" as Martinez referred to Ash, was deliberately messing up Martinez's slides for presentations. Pounds had seen Martinez upset on several occasions, much like we'd heard others testify to.

The night of the explosions, he'd been locked down in the building with the rest of its inhabitants. He, Rodriguez, and Martinez had set up folding chairs and sat around cracking jokes.

My recently calmed blood pressure skyrocketed again when I heard about Martinez sitting around *cracking jokes* after killing my husband. Lou wasn't dead yet, but he was nearly dead. And the individual who killed him, who'd first had the pleasure of listening to Lou's screams, was now sitting around laughing as Lou and Phil had their chests cracked open and drew their lasts breaths. It took enormous effort for me to remain quietly in my seat as I sent hateful glares to the defendant.

Specialist Diana Portella took the stand as I was trying to get a grip on myself. Seeing another Martinez minion did little to help. The petite, mournful faced woman began her testimony, much of which was a review of her testimony from a previous hearing. She told of the overworked, underappreciated supply sergeant who was still her friend. How he'd secured the NVG's in Kuwait and left them in the care of another soldier who hadn't wanted to hand them out. But Captain Esposito took them anyway. And the twenty–two NVGs had vanished. Portella said she'd counted them and they were all there after the training exercise that night but had later gone missing. Martinez claimed he'd never received them back. Captain Esposito insisted they'd been returned and Martinez had not hand–receipted them.

Portella's soft voice and reluctant responses altered with the next batch of questions. Still soft but now slightly raised, she told of Captain Esposito ordering her to personally sign for all the equipment and arms in the arms room. She hadn't wanted to accept that amount of responsibility. Sergeant Martinez had agreed it was too much for her. Upon the captain's insistence she'd signed as instructed. Then, unbeknownst to the commander, she'd signed it back to Martinez. Captain Esposito had no idea they were keeping two sets of books. She'd been grateful to Martinez for looking out for her.

Next, Captain Esposito had been anxious to find some missing radios. The joint responsibility for the NVGs was announced while the radios were still missing. Martinez had gleefully anticipated the captain's relief of his command for the missing items. But it hadn't happened. Instead, Martinez had been removed from supply. Been forced to report every night to the commander. He'd told Portella it would affect his job back home. He'd have to find another job.

About a week later, Martinez had alarmed her by asking if she was going to be in the vault, as they referred to the supply room. She hadn't known why he asked her, since he wasn't supposed to be in there anymore without an escort. That was about two weeks before June 7, 2005.

Portella grew increasingly morose as she spoke. At times petulant, she was backed into a corner with no way to circumvent detailing incidents that painted her friend in an unflattering light. Especially as she was asked about the procedure to sign ammunition out. The several-step process would take one and a half hours at best. To hasten things, they'd devised an alternate method using equipment not on the books—a special stash never logged in, originating from the previous unit's leftovers. This stash was kept in connex 10, to which Martinez held a key. Originally there had been no grenades in this stash. Those had arrived later, about two weeks before June 7, 2005.

Martinez told Portella it wasn't necessary to sign for equipment that was not on the books. She'd been relieved. Happily following Martinez's advice, she'd simply handwritten notes on the new ammunition, noting only the grenades, and not the claymores. Captain Esposito had not been informed of this.

Portella spoke about meeting Lou three days prior to June 7, and how everyone knew why he was there. On June 7, she'd been mad at Martinez for leaving a directive that she should be out of supply while the XO was on leave. She'd grudgingly complied with the order to remove her things from supply. And she remembered seeing a set of keys to connex 10 in Martinez's makeshift new office. That night, after Lou and Phil had been evacuated, she'd obeyed the acting commander's order to go to Captain Esposito's office to retrieve Lieutenant Allen's and the captain's weapons. She'd gone to breakfast the following morning "sad and traumatized" where she'd encountered her friend goofing off. He was stacking hot sauce packets in a tower and appeared happier than she'd seen him a while.

Huestis ended his direct examination on that note. Having made it through about an hour of testifying, the witness risked an apprehensive glance at Martinez. He ignored her, and Major Gregory quickly captured her attention.

Focusing the witness on a document he entered into evidence, Gregory asked if it wasn't actually May 7, 2005 when the ammunition was transferred, and not two weeks prior to June 7. Portella confirmed the date as Gregory continued firing questions about the people present when the ammunition was transferred—about five others, including the commanding general's son, Sergeant Taluto. The ammunition had been transferred simply as a means for the 350 to get rid of it, and it had not arrived with any documentation. Martinez had not personally handled any of that transaction. As far as signing those property books back over to himself without the commander's consent or knowledge, Martinez had done that to protect her.

Taking her back to the night of the explosions, Gregory asked what had happened immediately after the blasts. Portella confirmed she and Martinez had gone to look for Rodriguez, who was missing in the chaotic aftermath. She, Martinez, and another soldier had taken a vehicle first to the gym, and then to the Aid station in their search.

My body snapped to attention about thirty seconds before my brain processed what I'd heard. Martinez had gone to the Aid station *while Lou and Phil were there*. I couldn't believe it. First, he'd stood by and listened as Lou screamed in agony and fear, mortally wounded and sitting in the dark after being hurtled across the room from the claymore explosion. The explosion Martinez had caused. I'd had a difficult enough time picturing Martinez enjoying those screams, and now I was confronted with the even worse vision of him strolling into the Aid station while Lou was in the hallway. Alone and slipping away while Phil was being worked on. Had Martinez seen Lou? Maybe spoken to his victim? Taunted him or just assured himself Lou would die? Had he inwardly gloated over his victory as my husband lay helpless before him? It was too much. It seemed too cruel a pleasure to afford him. I wanted to release the bloodcurdling screams of hatred and rage out of my mind, where they were heard only by me. Pictured leaping across that bar, plowing over anyone who stood in my path, until I reached Martinez and beat him to a bloody pulp.

Steve and Siobhan sent me concerned looks, maybe wondering if I was going to do what they knew I was thinking.

The rest of the day crept by as we heard from the now retired Assistant Inspector General, Mr. Landowski (Major), and others in the Inspector General's office, including the big guy himself, Lieutenant Colonel Betor. The cast of that office had combined testimony that recounted Martinez complaining to the office about Phil. He hadn't wanted to lodge an official complaint. He just "wanted someone to know" the commander lost equipment. Martinez had expressed concern to much of the IG staff about losing his job in Iraq and at home. About a commander and first sergeant he was not able to speak with. How Martinez was "a little pissed I spoke to the commander about him." How the staff sergeant had vowed, "I'm not the only one going down on this! I have things on those guys. That's bullshit!" Master Sergeant DiPaola, also from the IG office, spoke with Captain Esposito several nights a week and had discussed the supply problem. That May Captain Esposito had come to DiPaola concerning a "problem with a soldier." Martinez had been incensed when he spoke with DiPaola next, bumping into him in the DFAC, "I can't f— believe you're doing this to me! You're one of them now!" Shocked by the staff sergeant's flushed face and loud outburst, he'd told Martinez to calm down, come to the office. "I've never been talked to like that in my career" he testified. And he never spoke to Martinez again after that day. He'd also not reported Martinez for such blatant disrespect of senior NCO.

Talking about the night of the explosions, DiPaolo broke down in unashamed tears remembering how he'd seen Phil on the floor and not recognized him. How he'd spoken to Lou, attempting to render aid and comfort. How he'd later washed Lou's blood off his hands with baby wipes.

Betor had been the Inspector General on the FOB. He'd been apprised of the supply situation from several people, and he knew Badillo felt micromanaged. While he knew of similar complaints in other units, within this unit the supply company's complaints had stood out from the others. Especially when he, too, had experienced Martinez's rage. "The commander is trying to f— me. You're trying to f— me. You are taking the commander's side!" Betor remembered hearing Martinez say to him. He, in turn, had been "stunned and offended" by the statement. And had also had never filed any charges for disrespecting an officer, in spite of the egregious violation of the policy. Nor had he notified Phil of the level of anger burning in Martinez.

Later in the trial we heard from Sergeant Malinowski, who'd been the administrative clerk in that office. As early as Fort Drum he'd experienced Martinez's anger. Initially Martinez's complaints had been about Willsey, too. Searching his memory, the witness told of Martinez storming into the office, talking about Willsey "He could not work this way. They were driving him crazy. He wanted to file a complaint of harassment. The first sergeant and commander were harassing him. Something had to be done." Sergeant Malinowski remembered how Martinez's hands were shaking that day. In Iraq he'd heard a conversation between Sartori and Martinez that May evening. Malinowski was just a few feet away from Sartori and Martinez when Martinez had screamed about Captain Esposito "Martinez said he was sick of this f— shit. He's (Captain Esposito) constantly f— with my life. Constantly on my ass." At that point Malinowski had said to Martinez that "whatever happened, you can fight it at home." But Martinez was "unraveling, ready to combust." Malinowski had been unprepared for the venom in Martinez' response "He's f— with my life! He's f— with my family! I'm gonna *burn him*!" Malinowski had not mentioned this to Phil. Instead he'd relied on Sartori to calm Martinez down. When next he saw Martinez in the DFAC, he'd been upset to be accused of "working for them." The last incident he remembered, before the night of June 7, he'd been so unnerved by the anger in Martinez's eyes that he'd exited the Humvee they were in. He'd been rattled and uncomfortable enough that he'd felt unsafe riding in the vehicle with Martinez.

The recurring testimony about one soldier after another who'd sensed such menacing levels of anger from Martinez's words and actions that they'd been scared to be around him was mind boggling. Mostly because none of these soldiers had thought to do anything other than protect themselves by keeping their own distance from Martinez. Apparently, it never occurred to anyone to afford the object of Martinez's rage the courtesy of a warning. Sitting there listening to all these missed opportunities to alert Phil, to let him know the threat he faced, I could not prevent the tide of "what ifs" swirling in my mind.

The parade of witnesses continued to testify about threats and rants from Martinez. Statements such as, if Captain Esposito continued coming down hard on him (Martinez) then he would get his, too. Asked about radios for the commander's vehicle. Martinez responded to a major, "F— the commander. He doesn't need a f— radio."

It was a slew of hateful and threatening comments bandied about with impunity. For all the shock each incident generated, still not one person thought to report Martinez. Not even Sergeant Jason Taluto, son of General Taluto. Martinez had attempted to prevail upon his friendship with Sergeant Taluto, "Can you talk to your old man and get him fired? Give me five minutes with your old man." When Sergeant Taluto told Martinez that wasn't possible, Martinez responded with "I hope the motherf— gets killed over there." A shocked Taluto asked Martinez if he really meant it. "Yes I do mean that. I hope that piece of shit dies." Sergeant Taluto never reported this to his commander. If he ever reported it to his father, we haven't heard. General Taluto was not called in the trial. My inquiries about his testifying were met with hems and haws, and some line about a witness with his rank intimidating the panel. No one ever bothered to explain to me why the man Phil reported to on a regular basis had nothing to add to the prosecution's case. I remembered the meeting I'd had with General Taluto that day in Watertown, after Doc Sullivan reviewed Lou's autopsy report with me. The general telling me about an impromptu conversation he'd had with Phil shortly before he was killed. The general was on his way out when Phil arrived. Needing to talk with his superior officer, Phil accompanied the general on a helicopter ride.

General Taluto professed not to remember what it was that Phil had wanted to talk about. Siobhan had been particularly interested to know what they'd discussed. Phil hated to fly and she was convinced he would not volunteer for a helicopter ride without a very good reason. But my questions on that matter were brushed off as insignificant and we still don't know what the two men discussed.

With the sounds of hundreds of unreported threats still ringing in our ears, we watched in uninspired interest as Ash Thimmaiah swore to tell the truth, the whole truth, and nothing but the truth. Appearing only slightly less upset than he had in Kuwait, Phil's close friend and Readiness NCO filled the panel in on his duties on the FOB. Tasked with day–to–day personnel training, logistics, and various company responsibilities, he lived in the Water Palace and he was very familiar with the defendant.

Once they'd walked through the basics, we heard about Lou being the first–ever officer who'd come in to a unit for the sole purpose of overseeing supply. The night of June 7, he'd been playing Risk with Lou and Phil for a couple hours. Stopping at five P.M. for dinner, Lou had then spoken to the boys and me on the video chat. The game resumed at seven–thirty.

Some of the panel members glanced my way as Ash spoke of Lou calling me. I concentrated on my lap as I pictured the last time I'd seen Lou smiling at me, racing to turn the camera off before I did.

Ash was talking now about the evening wearing on, and closing the thick drapes between the table and the window. They'd closed the drapes early that night, wanting to avoid being spotted playing a game. Martinez came in looking for Phil at seven P.M. Ash told him the commander wasn't there, and Martinez left. An hour later the supply sergeant returned. Ash and Lou hung out at the table, chatting while Phil spoke with Martinez. Behind Lou, Martinez could see the whiteboard with *A15,* referring to the Article 15 being filed against him, written on it.

With that night's business over, Phil returned to the game. He and Lou eliminated Ash, who'd then gone out for a smoke. Deciding to take a shower, he'd stopped back in to Phil's office first to use the bathroom en route to the shower trailers. It was nine–thirty when he'd gone outside. He hadn't seen anyone on or near the docked boat by Phil's quarters.

Ash's voice shook now as he said out loud what he was reliving in his mind. Getting out of the shower, starting to get dressed. Being shaken by explosions, how the trailer window blew in. The darkness in the pit area as he'd run out. The screaming he heard from Phil's office.

Siobhan was wringing her hands in her lap much in the way I think Ash would have done if he wasn't trying so hard to appear unemotional. But his voice betrayed him still as he struggled through the rest. Getting to the office. Looking upon the same space he'd occupied less than thirty minutes ago. A place that had been warm, brightly lit, with one old friend and one new one laughingly ganging up on him. It may as well have been a different planet, a different time zone he'd entered after the explosions.

The pitch–black was pierced by the beams of a few flashlights bouncing in quivering hands. He saw Phil on the floor. His mind knew it had to be Phil, because Lou was against the wall. But he couldn't believe the blackened, unconscious and blood–soaked body before him was the same man he'd just been sitting with. The next morning he'd requested to go to Speicher. He wanted to identify Lou's and Phil's bodies. And he'd done so.

It was defense's turn, and Major Gregory swiftly changed the traumatic tone in the room. One after another came the questions as he fell into the hammer pattern that was so effective for him:

"You never liked Sergeant Martinez did you? You felt he never respected you? You felt he was disrespectful? You felt he was disrespectful for calling people by informal names? But you often called him Al?" Ash barely responded before the next question was out of Major Gregory's mouth. He'd been indifferent to Martinez. He had no opinion of Martinez being disrespectful to himself. In certain situations he was disrespectful to others.

Asked about Sergeant Germosen, the soldier who'd been left in charge of the NVGs the night they disappeared, Ash agreed he'd said the soldier had "the IQ of an apple." Major Gregory asked Ash if he knew Captain Esposito blamed him for the NVG loss, and accused him of not properly hand–receipting. Ash replied he knew nothing about any of that. We didn't know, either. It was the first time we'd heard such a thing. And what was the point? Was Major Gregory offering Ash up as a suspect, too?

It seemed that was precisely what was being implied. The next series of questions was more accusations than anything else, "*You* knew the curtains were closed because *you* closed them. *You* told Sartori to leave. *You* knew there were latrines outside but you used the commander's. *You* knew a thick concrete wall separated the office from his latrine." On it went, fast and hard. Questions more like statements designed to show the panel that Ash had means, motive, and opportunity to kill Phil. But no true motive ever presented itself for him to kill Phil, and none at all for him to kill Lou. If the panel was buying this theory, it wasn't evident from their expressions. I held on to the hope that this theory, at least, would not take root.

John cut right to it on redirect. "Any problems with you and Captain Esposito?" "Absolutely not" came the reply. Ash was released as we exhaled a collective breath of relief. It was getting late and there was only one more witness left to finish the week. We were punch–drunk on testimony and trauma when Sergeant Erin Driesen took the stand. Which may account for the record time it took her to earn the nickname, "Nurse Ratchett." She surveyed us as we surveyed her. Brown hair in a harsh bun made her face tight. Light blue eyes met mine briefly, before moving to Heustis as the questions began. We listened as she explained she was a medic and a civilian nurse as we congratulated ourselves on the appropriate nickname for the surly witness. I halfheartedly took notes while I waited to uncover the reason for her dour attitude.

Driesen had almost daily contact with Martinez back at Fort Drum. She thought Captain Esposito didn't always treat Martinez as professionally as he treated the others. She didn't blame Martinez for calling the Captain "Little Hitler." After all, supply was micromanaged more than the other units. One could hardly fault Martinez for "venting" with "I just wish he'd go away. I just wish he'd die. I'm going to kill him."

In Iraq, her friend Martinez was upset to be restricted from supply as if he were a thief. Adding insult to injury the Captain told him he had to move out of Badillo's old office, too. It was being given to Lou. When Martinez asked his commander where he should move to, Captain Esposito said, "It's not my problem." That was the week before June 7. Martinez grew so incensed, and she "was tired of hearing Sergeant Martinez bitch about the commander." She'd recommended that her friend report to the Combat Stress Unit for help with his anger.

Listening to the supply unit groupie talk about her friends in that section, tasting her bitterness for Phil was unpleasant. Hearing what came next made unpleasant testimony seem like a gift.

The night of June 7 she'd answered the Aid Station phone to hear Ash screaming for medics at the Water Palace. She rode in the ambulance with Lou. I jumped to attention when I heard her clinically detached version of that ride. Whereas Doc Sullivan had been unable to mask the emotional effect it had on her to be with Lou, talk to him, and take part in treating him, Nurse Ratchett maintained a levelness in her voice and a blank expression that could just as well have been attached to the face of someone reading a boring textbook. It was a noticeable difference from her tone and demeanor when she'd had talked about her abused friends in the supply section. Knowing she was a good friend of the individual who had killed Lou and Phil, and that she'd been with Lou in the last moments of his life, broiled my insides. I was more grateful than ever that Doc Sullivan had been there, too, and could only hope Lou had focused on her warmth instead of the icy presence of the woman on the witness stand.

The morning after the murders, she'd had lunch with Sherman, Rodriguez, and Martinez. Al had been in a buoyant mood compared to his mood prior to that day, except for his complaints about the ringing in his ears from being too close to the explosions. At her encouragement he'd gone to the Aid Station to have his ears checked out. He'd been the only soldier that day reporting of ringing in his ears. The irony of it continued to pour in. How Martinez's friend and fellow anti–Phil soldier had been in the ambulance with Lou. And how Martinez had returned to the same Aid Station his victims had been taken to as they were dying, because the explosions he'd triggered were bothering his ears. The only polite word for that is audaciousness.

Having earned our hostile glares and utter contempt, the witness offered her friend Martinez a small smile as Major Cipriano began the cross–exam. Martinez got along with his coworkers. They all liked each other. Morale had been fine in the unit until Captain Esposito and Willsey arrived. By bringing in their own people, they'd broken up the cohesion in the unit. But they'd all agreed Al "lacked the balls to stand up to Captain Esposito." As for the commander, he'd been smart but had no social skills with females. That comment went over about as well as one would expect it to with Siobhan. We ended that week with a refreshed hatred for Martinez and the rest of the supply unit.

The last day of the prosecution's case brought with it the hope of hearing something that would offer us the comfort of believing in its presentation of the case. I had a sickening knot in the pit of my stomach when I thought of how it had been going. If I had had to predict the victor in this battle right then, I would have to award it to defense. Majors Gregory and Cipriano may not be very likeable, but they were taking no prisoners in their campaign to save their client.

The morning's witnesses were more of the same, unremarkable in that they added nothing other than more testimony about Phil's unpopularity and tidbits about a ladder leading to the roof, offering the possibility of someone climbing it to access the rooftop. The star of the prosecution's case was Sergeant Amy Loehr, and she was the prosecution's final witness.

The prosecution's final and key witness took the stand unaware of how much we needed her to save the case. Sergeant Amy Loehr, formerly Harlan, was the woman who'd given the claymores to Martinez. I was dreading what ammunition defense counsel had locked and loaded, ready to fire upon her credibility. John had spent countless hours working with Loehr. The petite woman with the demure voice kept her eyes pasted on him as she politely answered the first questions.

Her unit, the 350 PSYOPS, had worked with the 42nd HHC in Iraq. Shortly after the January 2005 arrival of that unit, she and her first sergeant introduced themselves to Martinez and his supply unit, inviting them to monthly barbeques. They'd maintained a friendly relationship until June 2005, when her unit left country.

She'd seen Martinez almost every day between February and June, either at chow or in supply. She'd forged a genuine friendship with him and soon was exposed to his litany of complaints about the commander. It began with the missing equipment, about which he employed volumes of profanity to express his discontent. Martinez's anger became so intense toward the end of her deployment that she'd "sort of felt uncomfortable around him." That May she stopped spending so much time with him. But then she was ordered to reduce her inventory. A final cleaning before heading home. Sergeant Loehr swallowed her discomfort and approached Martinez.

Martinez had come to her supply room and picked out some flares, grenades, claymores, and other items. A few weeks later, she'd packaged and delivered his order personally. None of the equipment was on the books.

Storing the boxes on and under his desk, Martinez thanked her with a humorless smile, assuring her the items would be put to good use. She hadn't seen him again until the morning she left on June 8. He'd not said a proper goodbye to her, and she'd been hurt by his gruff manner.

John finished with his star witness after just thirty minutes. He'd established what was necessary: Martinez had claymores in his possession. Untraceable claymores as well as untraceable fragmentation grenades. He'd established a critical component of the means necessary to convict. If we'd been able to conclude there, without exposing the witness to Major Gregory, we may have been okay. Part of me wanted to leave before he had his way with her. I knew he'd have to tear her to shreds to cast doubt on her testimony. And she was our last shot at a conviction.

"First Sergeant Gates told you to go to the 42nd, bat your eyelashes, and see what you could get?" were the first words from Major Gregory. I'd been right. He was in the zone and was not going to play nice. A downcast Loehr responded, "Yes." And right away lost some respect in the panel box.

Major Gregory, satisfied with his first punch, softened the questions a little, using the same song and dance he had with the others to make it clear Martinez *always* used profanity.

Taking the witness back to her arrival in country, Major Gregory asked about the trip in. Loehr told about stopping at more than one base to both draw and drop equipment en route to FOB Danger. "You got to Danger and fell in on supply, unorganized and uninventoried?" Right, she replied. Correct, there was no paperwork at all. Yes, there were already claymores there. No, she never took inventory or put them on the property books. "You think you had nine or ten claymores." I don't remember. "You remember meeting with defense counsel, us telling you it was a capital case, and it was important to be truthful." "Yes."

My hackles rose when Major Gregory went down the road of truthfulness. What did he have on this witness? Or what was he going to somehow get away with insinuating about her that would destroy her credibility? I was dreading finding out.

Loehr's fragile grasp on her composure was slipping now as Major Gregory continued to ask her about the interview she'd had with him and Major Cipriano. He was trying to get her to commit to how many claymores she'd said were in her unit. She didn't want to commit. She couldn't remember. And she was shrinking in her seat, her voice cracking with tension as she argued with Gregory until the courtroom was cleared. Outside the presence of everyone, the witness would listen to a recording that had been made of that interview. We followed one another out of the room, down the hall to our DIF.

Talk among us was clipped, terse. Loehr struck me as someone who was buckling under the stress of her role in this. I couldn't believe she would have given Martinez claymores and grenades if she'd had any inkling of what he was going to use them for. And yet, like so many others, she'd sensed a real enough threat from him to convince herself she should avoid him. I was powerless to do anything but hope and pray that she would not succumb to Major Gregory's ruthless impeachment tactics.

Reassembling a short while later, a newly assured Major Gregory asked again, "You remember you had about nine to ten claymores?" This time, a dejected Loehr responded yes. And was reluctantly led through the next series of questions outlining the fact she had not inventoried the claymores, she'd packed some in boxes and left four to seven mines on the shelf. Her voice higher now, frustration creeping in, she continued fielding Gregory's accusatory questions. "Now that you've heard your interview, you remember." His implication was plain as day, treating her as a hostile witness caught in a lie. In reality, she tried to explain; she had forgotten the amount of claymores. Referring to a brief interview with a CID agent on June 25, 2005, Gregory pounded out the items she'd stated she gave to her friend. Missing from that list was claymores. "You were aware Sergeant Martinez was accused of using a claymore to kill Captain Esposito? That was a sworn statement?" Major Gregory was on fire, and the witness was flushed with emotion as she answered yes. She was frustrated at the misleading tone of the questions, and continued her desperate glances to John. With no life preserver thrown her way from the prosecution's table, she continued to struggle. No, no one else came to talk to her after that CID agent. At least, not until December 2005, when a prosecutor came and she told him of the claymore. Rushing to get an answer in before the Major could interrupt her again, Loehr gushed out an explanation. The prosecutor asked a specific question, The CID meeting had been brief. She'd been nervous, hadn't gone into specifics.

Loehr fielded the onslaught as best as she could. If Major Gregory had any twinges of conscience he did a beautiful job masking them in his full–on effort to defend his client. Back and forth he went, at once cajoling and derisive, slipping into blatant mockery as he asked her questions calculated to have exactly the effect they were having.

Loehr's voice suggested tears just below the surface as she sought to defend herself from the attack on her character. The panel members sat transfixed by the spectacle before them. Much like being unable to look away from a car accident, we all sat in our rows equally mesmerized and frozen to our seats as the government's witness took the last few blows:

"Sergeant Martinez never asked you for claymores? He said he'd be willing to take them?"

"He *never said* Sgt Loehr can I have a claymore mine! "No." Meek.

"You were afraid of CID." "I'm not afraid." Defiant.

"So you didn't tell CID about the claymores, but you told a noncommissioned officer. And no CID agent ever returned." If possible, the witness would have been in a fetal position, begging for help. Especially when the major delivered the coup de grace:

"Sergeant Loehr you've lied to police officers before." The witness's eyes had just popped out of her head in surprise as John leapt to his feet with an "Objection!" and Colonel Henley glared at the defense counsel before he excused the panel members.

We watched as the panel members' shaking heads disappeared behind their deliberation room door. Prayed to the trial gods that the prosecution would sort this out and the witness would be rehabilitated with the panel. If not, we were doomed. And we knew it.

Major Gregory rushed to defend his accusation by telling the court of an incident five years ago. The sergeant, he claimed, had told a police officer who'd pulled her over that her license was at home. The officer checked and discovered she had a suspended license, at which point he arrested her. A conversation between the judge and the witness revealed Loehr had been young, in college, and made a mistake. But she had not been arrested and there had been no repercussions from the incident. The objection was sustained, but our relief was brief: Colonel Henley refused to allow the prosecution to rehabilitate the witness. Further clarification of the accusation was forbidden. The panel returned and was told to disregard the statement about Loehr lying to the police. But nothing further was offered. The damage was done. Masterfully so. Because panel members were now openly scrunching faces at Sergeant Loehr, sharing whispered comments and head shakes.

John made a last stand on redirect, cutting through the smoke as best as possible.

"Did you deliver claymores and grenades to Sergeant Martinez?"—"Yes."

"Were there also some left over?"—"Yes".

"When did the CID interview occur?"—"25 June 2005."

"How long had you been home?"—"One day."

John walked the witness through the numerous duties she'd been tasked with when unexpectedly approached by CID. How she'd been anxious to get home and noticed the agent "didn't seem to know about the case." That Sergeant Martinez was her friend in Iraq. She didn't know the details, and hadn't thought it was important. The CID agent told her she'd probably not hear back from any agents. She didn't think she'd be getting Martinez in trouble. And finally, she'd made five separate requests to defense counsel to hear the recording of the interview she'd done so long ago. But "they didn't let me."

Loehr's hands were restless in her lap, her voice a margin stronger as she leapt on the opportunity to clear up the CID interview. But her credibility had taken a big hit with the "lying to police" accusation still smoldering in the room. Left unchecked, that doubt grew into a greedy fire that consumed the truth and laid waste to our key witness. The panel smelled it, and wanted some answers.

Questions flew in for the witness. They covered everything from why she'd gone to see Willsey on June 8 (she didn't know), to how long she'd been a supply sergeant prior to June 8 (not long), to how many claymores she'd given Martinez (at least three). Martinez had said these would come into good use as he took the boxes and saw what was in them.

Major Gregory landed a few more scathingly sarcastic questions before freeing Loehr, who all but bolted from the room.

The prosecution announced it had no further witnesses as I tried to find some scrap of positive memory from any of the testimony. Failing to come up with anything of comfort, I resorted to self–assurances that things were not as bad as they seemed. The panel was dismissed, and we all tried not to let our fear show as we exited Fort Bragg.

Lou and me, New Year's eve 1995

*Me, Lou, his parents, Robert and Vivian Allen, Trevor
and Colin at Lou's commissioning ceremony summer 2000*

Phil, Siobhan, and Madeline

Lou about to present a flag to a new widow at her husband's funeral. This picture was taken six months before Lou was killed.

Aerial view of the Water Palace. Phil's office and the pit area are on the left side of this picture, facing the trailers.

Water palace, pit area. Exterior view of Phil's window from the pit area. The claymore was placed in the left window.

View looking through window into Phil's office. The strings represent ball bearings as they exploded inward from the mine.

String trajectory picture. Each string represents a ball bearing. Lou and Phil were seated at a table directly in front of the window when the mine exploded.

Crime scene picture of Phil's office. Impact impressions from ball bearing can be seen on the wall by the whiteboard. A swept up pile of debris partially covers the stain from Lou's dried blood on the floor.

Lou was thrown across the room and landed on the floor by this wall. His blood can be seen on the floor.

United States	)	
	)	Offer to Plead Guilty
v.	)	
	)	3 April 2006
Staff Sergeant Alberto B. Martinez	)	
Headquarters and Headquarters Company	)	
XVIII Airborne Corps	)	
Fort Bragg, North Carolina 28310	)	

1. I, Staff Sergeant Alberto B. Martinez, the accused in the pending court-martial, offer to plead:

To Specification 1 of The Charge: Guilty, except the words "with premeditation"; to the excepted words, Not Guilty.

To Specification 2 of The Charge: Guilty, except the words "with premeditation"; to the excepted words, Not Guilty.

To The Charge: Guilty.

To the Specifications of the Additional Charges and the Additional Charges: Not Guilty.

2. I offer to plead guilty to the Charges and Specifications as stated above provided that the Convening Authority does not refer the court-martial capital; does not approve any sentence in excess of the sentence set forth in Enclosure 1; directs the trial counsel to not prove up the excepted words of the specifications of The Charge; and directs the trial counsel to dismiss the specifications of the Additional Charges and the Additional Charges prior to the announcement of findings by the military judge without prejudice with prejudice to ripen upon announcement of the sentence by the military judge.

3. As part of this offer, I agree:

    a. To enter into a stipulation of fact with the trial counsel setting forth the essential facts and circumstances of the offenses to which I am pleading guilty. I understand that this stipulation may be used by the military judge to determine if I am in fact guilty and will be considered, along with any other evidence presented, in determining a sentence.

    b. To be tried by military judge alone.

    c. To waive the pending Article 32, UCMJ investigation. This waiver is conditioned upon acceptance of this offer and once the military judge accepts my pleas and enters findings, my waiver becomes unconditional.

    d. To not request a mitigation expert at the government's expense.

    e. To not have my trial defense counsel cross-examine the widows of Captain Phillip T. Esposito or First Lieutenant Louis E. Allen should they testify during the pre-sentencing procedure.

First page of the offer to plead guilty (OPG)

I reserve the right to have my trial defense counsel object to the admission of any evidence not otherwise permitted by either the Rules for Court-Martial, the Military Rules of Evidence, or by appropriate judicial precedent.

    f. To a trial date no later than ninety days after the acceptance of this offer by the Convening Authority.

4. I understand that I may request to withdraw from this plea of guilty at any time before my plea is accepted and that if I do so, this agreement is cancelled. I further understand that the government may withdraw from this agreement upon the occurrence of any of the following events:

    a. My failure to agree on the contents of a stipulation of fact with the trial counsel.

    b. My failure to plead guilty as stated above.

    c. My withdrawal from this agreement, for any reason whatsoever, prior to acceptance of my plea of guilty by the military judge.

    d. The military judge refuses to accept my plea of guilty, or, an appellate court sets aside the findings because a plea of guilty entered pursuant to the agreement is found improvident.

5. The government agrees not to prefer additional charges on any other misconduct which I may have committed of which the government is aware at the time the Convening Authority accepts this offer.

6. There are no other promises, conditions, or understanding regarding my offer to plead guilty that are not contained within this offer. This offer to plea originated with me. No person has made any attempt to force or coerce me into making this offer. This offer shall not be affected by consolidation, dismissal, or modification of any specification or charge.

7. I am satisfied with the advice of my trial defense counsel. They have advised me of the meaning and effect of my guilty plea, and I understand the meaning and effect thereof.

ALBERTO B. MARTINEZ   MARC D. A. CIPRIANO   E. JOHN GREGORY
SSG, USA   MAJ, JA USAR   CPT, JA
Accused   Trial Defense Counsel   Senior Defense Counsel

The offer to plead guilty dated 3 April 2006 is (~~accepted~~)/(not accepted).

4 APR 2006

JOHN R. VINES
Lieutenant General, USA
Commanding

2

Second page of the OPG.

United States	)	
	)	Offer to Plead Guilty
v.	)	
	)	Enclosure 1
Staff Sergeant Alberto B. Martinez	)	Quantum
Headquarters and Headquarters Company	)	
XVIII Airborne Corps	)	3 April 2006
Fort Bragg, North Carolina 28310	)	

In exchange for my offer to plead guilty, the Convening Authority agrees:

To disapprove any confinement in excess of life with the possibility for parole.

Any other lawfully imposed punishment may be approved.

ALBERTO B. MARTINEZ
SSG, USA
Accused

MARC D.A. CIPRIANO
MAJ, JA USAR
Trial Defense Counsel

E. JOHN GREGORY
CPT, JA
Senior Defense Counsel

The foregoing is (accepted) (not accepted).

9 APR 2006

JOHN R. VINES
Lieutenant General, USA
Commanding

3

The third page of the OPG.

Alberto Martinez's mug shot.

CHAPTER FOURTEEN
DEFENSE CASE

✪ ✪ ✪

The second half of the show started with a main character for defense. Sergeant Rodriguez is a close friend of Martinez. He'd gotten alone fabulously with his supply sergeant and enjoyed working with him. He was also romantically involved with Nurse Ratchett. The two of them made the most of their required presence in town by frequenting each other's hotel rooms. Now, he easily answered Major Gregory's questions.

Martinez was awkward and didn't join in with jokes on the company commander. For instance, Rodriguez once put training wheels on Captain Esposito's faithfully ridden bike. That was not the kind of relationship his friend had with the captain. Rodriguez had his share of hard times with Captain Esposito, too, he said. He then recounted his version of a time he'd been interrupted by Phil while taking a shower. He stated he was annoyed the captain barged in on him when he was "buttass naked." Stories like that were difficult to swallow, especially since Phil was not here to refute them.

Rodriguez had heard of the "Cav Mafia" comprised of former 101 members. One of those members was Willsey, who was afforded luxuries he chose to share only with fellow Cav Mafia members. Luxuries like the inflatable pool he'd float in while smoking a cigar. Rodriguez had found Willsey in that pool one day upon returning from a convoy. He'd been annoyed at Willsey for pouring water on himself and tuning out the convoy briefing.

Questions were quickly lobbed and answered as Rodriquez explained he'd introduced Martinez to Loehr. He'd never seen the box with claymores, and he continued working in supply after 7 June 2005. At work one day he'd been at a loss how to react when two CID agents came and questioned Sherman for several minutes. Mindless of the small crowd gathered, they'd patted Sherman down and taken him away. Gathering his wits enough to ask when he'd be getting his soldier back, he'd been further put off by the laughing response, "5–10 years."

Between Martinez's first and second arrests, Rodriguez had listened to his friend's complaints about how he was treated. He hadn't thought Martinez appeared any happier than he'd been before the blasts. CID told Rodriguez they found the clacker with Martinez's prints on it, and he'd be going away.

Major Gregory interrupted the witness with feigned surprise as he asked "Are you sure the agents actually told you they had found his prints? What did he tell you about Sergeant Martinez frying? Was there something about the interview that bothered you?" Rodriguez unhesitatingly confirmed he'd been told about the prints, and "your boy is going to fry." Then the agent made a comment that bothered Rodriguez, "First he asked what am I. First I said American. He asked again. I said a soldier. He said, 'You're Puerto Rican, so is Martinez, do you guys stick together?'" I'd become skilled at denying my facial muscles their persistent requests to cringe each time I heard of something damaging about CID. But several panel members were freer with their faces, and their muscles ran away as they heard that.

With more force in his voice than the normally soft–spoken prosecutor had previously employed, John leapt into the cross–exam. Through this exchange we learned Rodriguez was also a former member of the 101. At some point the witness and others had discussed their combined belief that Martinez should switch out of supply. While he believes Martinez can be a supply sergeant, Rodriguez "would have made changes" if he'd been commander. The last was a grudging admission, followed by equally unenthusiastic admissions of comments made by his friend. "I hope he doesn't come back from convoy. I hope he drops dead. I hate that f— guy," were all routinely uttered by Martinez in regard to the captain.

Rodriguez denied ever seeing claymores in Iraq. He, Sherman, and Portella got along well and he was defensive of his friend. Seeing how unhappy Martinez was about Lou's impending arrival, he'd suggested maybe Lou could act as a buffer between Martinez and the captain. Even tried to convince his friend it may be a good thing to have the new lieutenant on board. But Martinez would have none of it, continuing to hope the commander would be relieved for losing NVGs or would die in an explosion. Martinez was still furious at the captain for blaming the loss on him.

Amidst the swirl of rumors after the explosions, word spread that Rodriguez was arrested. In reality he'd been home on leave. Asked if Martinez got along well with the Willsey, the witness pushed a "yes" past his pained expression before his cross exam came to an end.

Almost marching to the lectern before squaring off toward his witness, Major Gregory barely kept from screaming as he asked about the CID agent "trying to get you to say Sergeant Martinez was angry." Rodriguez indignantly recalled he'd been "told I needed to create a bad picture." Another nail in CID's coffin. True or not, it had been hammered in. Major Gregory was methodically burying the Investigative Agency in the minds of panel members, whose questions were extensive and touched on matters like did Captain Esposito ever tell the witness to do something illegal, to questions about Ash and Willsey as soldiers. Mixed in there were inquiries about Martinez but those were more afterthoughts than the main idea. It was not looking good as Rodriguez exited and Mr. James Bennet took the stand.

The scribbled caption "Brokeback Mafia?" on the top of my notebook reflects our desperation to maintain a grasp on sanity. Laughing about something—anything—was our lifeline. And Mr. James Bennet provided plenty of rope for that lifeline.

His gangly frame at half–mast posture, nervous energy all around him, the witness perched in his seat. Eyes wide and shaking with his effort to contain himself, Bennet explained how he'd developed a friendship with Willsey while in the 101. Previous commanders "pretty much gave the first sergeant the keys to the company and he would do his own thing." It had been Willsey who'd asked Bennet to join him in the 42nd to help set up the Family Readiness Group. The FRGs were a critical support to soldiers and their families, and he'd done the same duty for the 101. Bennet had been just one of the 101 guys Willsey recruited for the 42nd.

Bennet became more lively as he warmed up to his time in the spotlight. He was enjoying his opportunity to paint the commander as the new "by the book" commander who took a more hands on role than Willsey was used to. Willsey "had a hard time with that" as well as with the "Dumbass" supply sergeant. Captain Esposito "knew the regulations inside and out. Willsey did not; I had to help him." Rambling on, Bennet mentioned another 101 import, Sergeant First Class Graw. According to Bennett, Graw and Willsey were "best friends, or more." Hence the Brokeback Mafia written on top of my page of notes.

As Bennet told his version of how indispensable he'd been, I focused on not rolling my eyes at his warped sense of self–importance. Having been exposed to his previous testimony at hearings we knew he believed everything he was saying, which made it that much funnier to us. What we worried about was if the panel would take him seriously, assuming Major Gregory managed to work his magic and weave his witness' delusions as fact. So far he was managing to keep a lid on the crazy. His testimony was the next wave in the attack on Willsey.

In Iraq, Bennett heard Willsey make overtly angry comments about Captain Esposito. Specifically, the witness remembered being in the walkway over the water when he'd heard the comments. Willsey's weights were in that walkway area. He'd had them shipped over on the government's dime. After one of the infamous Sync meetings, Bennett heard Willsey fuming, "I hate that f— guy. I'd punch that guy in the face and throw him in the lake!" He'd known Willsey was serious, based on the tone of voice and inability to hide anger well. Another incident standing out in Bennett's memory was a request from Willsey to take him out in the boat on the lake. Willsey planted a glow–in–the–dark mounted pigeon outside the captain's window. The pigeon was mounted on a cross with its wings splayed out, resembling a crucifixion.

Major Gregory asked nothing further about the pigeon, instead leaving that odd tidbit for the panel to file away unexplained. It was another addition to the doubt about Willsey, and prosecution hurried to explain the behavior as a practical joke aimed at Phil and Ash's pigeon hunting on the lake. We hoped it would clear the incident up in the minds of any panel members tempted to use it as another reason to nominate Willsey's odd behavior as signs of being the real killer.

Continuing, Gregory and the witness worked to establish more doubt about Willsey: Bennett had been the one who maintained height and weight records. Captain Esposito implemented a new policy of not awarding honors to any soldier who failed P.T. In Iraq, the Willsey weighed 270 pound plus some. Bennett never saw Willsey take a P.T. test. That question and answer session added to the visual of the portly First Sergeant Willsey as he appeared in court earlier. Several witnesses had been grossly overweight—including General Taluto's son—and the panel had not refrained from expressing disdain for their physical condition through facial expressions or questions about their weight. That Willsey fell into the out–of–shape category did not help our side.

Gregory moved on. Bennett knew the building took a hit that night. He'd been on the roof of the Water Palace before. No, the roof slope is not so steep it would be difficult to throw something from. Watching a muted CID video of the FOB, Bennett narrated his actions during and after the blasts. At this point, he began losing his toehold on the mountain of sanity as he allowed himself to become swept up in re–creating those moments. His voice choppy, changing pitch from high to low, slow to fast in nanoseconds, Bennett recounted running out after the first blast. Hearing two more smaller blasts. DeFranc, another soldier, ran in. Said somebody's out there. The commander is dead. He saw Pounds. Told him to keep DeFranc in. Went outside as DeFranc pushed past him out into the smoke. He went out and yelled, "Is anyone out there. And someone yelled, "No!"

Unsure if we'd been the only ones who caught that, Siobhan and I again smothered laughter at the absurdity of what he'd just said. No one else appeared even remotely amused. Maybe the widows were the ones who'd lost toeholds, I thought. But didn't care. It was still funny.

The hours dragged on along with Bennett's testimony. The two and a half hours of direct had been longer than we anticipated. Now John took his time, too, methodically ticking through his list of topics to neutralize.

Addressing the matter of the roof as a possible location for the murderer to carry out the attacks, Benson elicited facts about the ladder going directly to the roof, and how it did not allow access into the building en route. That the passageway to the roof consisted of catwalks and narrow areas that never saw daylight. Like an obstacle course in the pitch dark. The rooftop was falling apart, strewn with trash and covered in terra cotta tile.

Next on the list was reestablishing animosity between Martinez and Phil. Check. Then the video we'd seen but not heard, of the office and stairs in the Water Palace, leading out to the porta potties through the pit area. This CID video had been used instead of the one narrated by the witness himself, with the assistance of a defense counsel paralegal. Why the switch, we were never told.

Agitated now, Bennett appeared impatient with the prosecution's questions. He'd become less candid in his responses, offering one or two words instead of rambling.

Softening his own tone a notch, the prosecutor's already hushed voice required an effort to hear as he asked the witness "Is it fair to say since coming back the events have been fairly traumatic for you?" Thrown off, Bennett offered a quick "Yes" before confirming he is in counseling and taking medication. Before he could recover, John asked about his CID statement, tripping him up with discrepancies between it and his testimony. It was a nice switch, to see a defense witness come apart on the stand instead of one of the good guys.

Bennet spoke of the large crowd of rubberneckers taking pictures of the bloody scene, and how an NCO would want to clean that up as soon as possible. And then he found his groove again, explaining how he'd known immediately it was a claymore while the experts had not. He'd not pointed it out because CID had been there all night. CID returned, established a sign- in sheet, and interviewed a handful of soldiers. Bennett worked hard to point out that all CID interviews he'd helped get people in for came to a screeching halt once Wentzel spoke with CID. He had no idea why CID stopped the interviews, and no, he had not mentioned Willsey in his own CID interview. My favorite point John worked in was the fallout between Bennett and Willsey. Listening to Bennett describe Willsey as the cause for his failure to get promoted cleared up why Bennett was so eager to distort facts about Willsey. Now all we needed was for the panel to stop asking about him.

Panel questionnaires were reviewed and returned to Henley, who led off the list with a Willsey question. My hope plummeted as it became obvious several members still could not see through defense's smokescreen. Questions about Willsey's weight and access to claymores, his relationship with Martinez and also about the roof meant some members were still open if not receptive to the possibility of the stout first sergeant walking catwalks in the pitch dark to set off the attack from the roof. It was terrifying.

The next ten days in court further revealed the brilliant simplicity of defense counsels' strategy. Hour after hour, day after day we heard witnesses drop nuggets about the ladder leading to the rooftop, and how it would be possible to throw grenades from there. We heard about Martinez's good nature and Willsey's foul one. About the "Good 'Ole Boys" in the Cav Mafia who didn't have to work for their perks and about all the soldiers who were either never interviewed or testified to being coerced into painting a bad picture about Martinez.

The roof theory seemed ridiculous to us: The claymore would have to be dangled from the top of the building all the way down to the recessed pit area outside Phil's window. The wire would have to be tied, while the individual made his way over the planks and down tight chutes with wobbly ladders, in the dark, down into the building. Exited the building and tied the mine to the grate outside Phil's window. Returned to the roof and detonated. Run to the edge of the roof and thrown three grenades—without falling in the dark, in a sandstorm, off the slanted roof, all in a minute or two after detonating the claymore. Then retracted the excess wire and clacker and hurl them into the lake before descending back into the building. Unfortunately, Major Gregory had thrown so many ideas out there it was inevitable for at least one to stick. And it seemed as though the Willsey–from–the–roof theory was a winner. Major Gregory managed to sneak in subtle snippets about his pet theory so often it was almost plausible—even to me. He was the hypnotist dangling the gold watch in front of the panel, and some of them were going under.

As if the direction the trial was headed was not worrisome enough, bickering between Heustis and defense counsel had become a full–blown distraction. The claims from defense that Heustis was playing up to the panel members or making snide comments in and out of court were now too frequent to be funny. Especially when the claims eclipsed testimony, as happened after Sergeant Timothy Olsen testified.

Olsen recalled laughing with other soldiers as they called Ash, Phil, and Willsey "Batman, Robin, and Penguin" when the officers were out of earshot. He allowed himself to feel newly disgusted while he remembered the "stupidest idea they'd ever heard" in regard to Captain Esposito implementing a largely ignored and then rejected helmet policy in the motor pool. Major Gregory worked in his usual morsels about Willsey and the roof before plugging his client's non–violent demeanor. John got in a few good points and the witness was dismissed. It had seemed like the usual testimony and I'd noticed nothing remarkable about it. So the 39A request from Defense surprised me.

The door had barely closed behind the last panel member when Major Gregory began bemoaning Heustis' behavior again. The claim was that when Olsen had been asked if someone Martinez had not particularly liked was still working at the Waterlivet Arsenal, Heustis said to John, "That's because he didn't have access to claymore mines." Gregory and Cipriano held that the comment was loud enough for the panel to hear, and demanded again that Heustis be removed from the case. Which made me think I must be deaf, because I was sitting about six feet from Heustis and John and had not heard a thing. Henley called John to the stand, surprising us all. John refuted defense's claim while keeping a lid on any impulse to join the name–calling and tantrum war between sides. Seemingly unsatisfied, Henley instructed Heustis not to speak at all while in court unless questioning a witness. Heustis was instructed to use notes to communicate with co–counsel and warned this was his last chance. The following day's news coverage of the trial focused not on testimony, or the alarming path we were taking, but on Heustis being scolded in court as the opposing sides acted like children to each other.

Having successfully poured a solid layer of irrelevant facts as well as tales of Martinez's helpful, non–violent behavior, Willsey's gross abuse of power, CID's strong arming witnesses to speak ill of Martinez, and widespread dislike of Captain Esposito, defense was moving in for the kill. So far, some panel members showed they were receptive to defense's theories. While I knew they did not have all the information we did, I was amazed at how gullible some of them were. And frustrated at how the suppressed statement was being used against the government.

Defense started laying the groundwork in their opening that CID fixated on Martinez early on. That by itself was not improper or unexpected. However, not known at the time of the opening was that the defense would attack CID agents for the large number of investigative leads they pursued involving Martinez. The obvious answer was that Martinez made a statement to CID, within twenty–four hours of the murders, where he placed himself at precisely the location where it appeared the murders were committed. He made disparaging comments to a CID agent about his company commander only hours after his death; he showed no signs that he was saddened to know his commander had been killed just a few meters away from him. He told CID that the commander was threatening to take his job away—a concern that CID knew was often repeated to other witnesses. In short CID would have been negligent not to pursue leads concerning Martinez because even at the early stages the evidence was pointing toward him. CID agents had been prevented from explaining all of this. Prohibited from explaining *why* their investigation included a strong interest in Martinez.

Continuing the assault on CID, Defense called more agents to the stand. Special Agent Paul McNelly told of interviewing Harlan on June 25, 2005. He thought he remembered mentioning claymores, but she never said anything about them. He then spoke to Gates, who remembered seeing about five claymores on the FOB, but doubted Harlan would have given one to Martinez.

A 39A interrupted this witness as arguments about Harlan's (Loehr's) credibility ensued. Colonel Henley would have none of it. Listening to a few minutes of arguments, he looked down at counsel and told them neither side can run away from the facts; they are what they are. Continue. I'd noticed the judge was running out of patience, even with defense. The twenty–four hour candy store he'd kept open for defense now appeared to close at midnight. In the back of my mind I wondered what brought about the change, and wished it had come earlier; He almost seemed impartial now.

Gregory got in a few jabs at CID by pointing out no agent ever re–interviewed Harlan. Evan took a shot at undoing the jabs, and the witness was dismissed.

Interspersed with experts on fingerprinting and ammunition we heard from witnesses like Amy Church, Martinez's sister, and soldiers who'd served with Martinez. All of these witnesses fell over themselves describing what a good guy Al is. All I could do was sit quietly and hope the panel didn't believe them. And inwardly fume at Henley's decision to forbid the government from putting rebuttal witnesses on the stand regarding Martinez's angelic personality.

The fingerprint and ammunition experts served their purpose by adding more information than was necessary, thus stoking the fire and creating more smoke to filter. Jack Berens from the Joint Munitions Command in Davenport Iowa offered a lengthy explanation of grenades, spoons, and components. Whittled down, his testimony amounted to his assessment that the spoon numbers from those in this case correlate to about 500 thousand possible grenade lot numbers. Under cross exam, he conceded the lot numbers from this case correspond to a lot issued to Tikrit, Iraq. The lot numbers from the clacker contained one component stored in Tikrit.

Mr. William Doyne was called to the stand, and the certified latent print examiner described the process of fingerprinting methods in enough detail to lull even the most restless infant to sleep. We heard about fifty–nine items he'd been given to process for this case, including one grenade canister with a palm print from someone other than Martinez. And about the sample he'd requested from other individuals, but had never received. Defense's emphasis was on CID not bothering to provide other samples because they were interested only in Martinez, and his prints were not found on any items tested. When Evan had his turn, he was careful to elicit the fact that it is possible for someone to touch an object without leaving a print.

Witnesses filtered in and out, some adding big points and others adding small ones, but all contributing to the classic defense tactic of attacking the investigation, blaming as many other people for the crime as possible, creating a choking smokestorm of irrelevant and manipulated facts to combat their client's guilt. Witnesses were called to cast doubt on other witnesses, or to confirm another witnesses' credibility. And on the final day of defense's case it was impossible to discern what the panel was thinking. We'd heard more than one comparison made about this case to the infamous OJ Simpson case, and the parallels were impossible to ignore. But we fervently hoped the similarities would end with the verdict.

Rebuttal witnesses made their appearances on Monday, November 24, and flowed into a sur–rebuttal portion, wrapping up on the following Monday. It had been a smaller version of the trial, with some new witnesses adding to the litany of threats heard by Martinez, and some all too familiar witnesses like Lance Willsey, who spent hours on the stand as government tried to erase any guilt about him and defense countered with renewed attacks on his credibility.

Tuesday, December 2nd dawned with the biting cold outside not unlike the cold fear coursing through me as I waited in the courtroom for the closing arguments to commence. The panel members had arrived in their Class As today, shirking the comfortable digital uniforms they'd been wearing in honor of the solemnity of the occasion. More representatives of the media were present as well. This was the big stuff—the part that garners long scenes in movies and drives law students forward through the gauntlets of the bar exam. The high drama and passion involved in closing arguments, where each side gasps its last breath into their case, and victims are as unbalanced as they have ever been, knowing they are still helpless to make something right come of whatever tragedy they have endured.

Siobhan and I sat without our usual company of Steve and Brent that day. Steve had to return home and Brent was running late as Colonel Henley addressed the court and read his deliberation instructions to the panel before closing arguments could be heard.

Listening to the long list of charges the panel had the option to convict or acquit on struck a chord of fear off within me. Could they really convict him on something as light as Assault or Battery? Could they possibly find him not guilty of *any* of the charges? And where were the instructions and explanation of the gates necessary to pass through in order for a possible death penalty to enter the picture? Why wasn't Colonel Henley offering this panel the same instructions he'd offered in the Akbar case, making it clear even a unanimous vote to convict did not mean Martinez would be sentenced to death? Did the panel understand how exhaustive a process it was, how much power each of them held to spare his life even if they voted to convict? I waited anxiously for some scrap of information to be offered about that, but it never came. Fifty minutes later John had the floor, and closing statements began.

Watching John take his place at the podium, listening to the man I'd gradually come to respect and like over the years, I fought to contain the swell of emotion threatening to release a new crop of tears as his words rained down over an otherwise still courtroom. Commanding the floor in a way I had not seen him do in these three and a half years, he meticulously spelled out the merits of the prosecution's case.

For more than an hour he took us back through each detail of the case. Differentiated between facts of the investigation pointing towards Martinez, and the smokescreen billowing around those facts. The endless hearings we'd been to, the thousands of miles on I–95, the empty hotel rooms and time away from our kids almost seemed worth it now as we listened to the compelling arguments in support of a guilty verdict.

"Let the smoke dissipate. There's one conclusion left." I hoped the panel was paying attention and listening as intently as they appeared to be. For the closing statement whittled away all the conjecture and contorted facts thrown about by defense.

Pictures of Lou and Phil flashed on the screen, their smiling faces the only testament to their lives, their existence here in the world. The autopsy pictures were redistributed in their booklets to the panel members. During the pathologist's testimony in the first part of trial, we'd been ambushed with 8x10 glossy pictures of our husbands' bodies calculated to be displayed to us after we'd been assured we would not see them. It had been a hellish experience. This time we were spared the sight of pictures. I was still seething at Heustis for setting us up that day, and only the knowledge that he was using us and our reactions for the strength of the case has allowed me to forgive him. But the fact remains that I am now carrying around the picture of Lou's nearly unrecognizable face as he laid on the autopsy table with dried blood and black and purple skin. Of the white bag zipped open revealing his naked body encased within, still bearing medical equipment from efforts to save him. I will carry those images with me forever, along with a level of anger at having that choice I'd consciously made to avoid those pictures taken from me.

John's voice broke through my haze and brought me back to the courtroom. He was wrapping it up and the passion in his voice spilled over into the room, revealing just how much he believed in this case and the years of his own life he'd devoted to it. The Accused is guilty. He'd gone to extraordinary measures to create the illusion of an Iraqi attack. All the evidence in CID's diligent investigation pointed to one man, and that man is Alberto Martinez. I wanted to leap up and hug the prosecutor as he walked back to his seat. But Major Gregory was already in place and ready to go.

Matching John's level of devotion to his case, Major Gregory threw himself into his closing with the unrestrained belief that Al should be acquitted. That CID framed him to meet the needs of the investigation and that only the panel held the power to right this wrong. They alone could undo the harm inflicted by the big bad government and not let Al suffer for one more day.

Openly mocking of prosecution witnesses and mocking the "cute words" used by the prosecutors, it was a no–holds–barred fight to the death, and Major Gregory was giving it his all.

This *is* a process about finding the truth, and not a melodramatic show, he started. The irony of that statement was apparently lost on him; It was *his* histrionics and melodramatic outbursts that had plagued the process these years.

Recapping the weeks of trial, Major Gregory pulled all of his seeds together and displayed a neatly sown row of conjecture and pet theories; CID never investigated this case. Willsey did it. Ash did it. Anyone other than Martinez could have done this, and poor Martinez is the "proverbial low–hanging fruit" the otherwise nice CID agents mistakenly constructed the case around. Again, he took advantage of the agents' discomfort skirting around the suppressed statement by creating the illusion they were hiding something, withholding to protect themselves as opposed to obeying the court's order. A sword, instead of a shield.

Explaining away Martinez's behavior as normal for him—the shifty eyes described by some, as reflecting an immature man who often avoids eye contact. The foul language simply a mark of poor taste. The threats? Mere innocent venting from an unfairly badgered man. The calculating required for this attack was way above Al's abilities. As Gregory described the inferior thought process of his client I recalled one hearing where he'd offered Martinez's kids' unimpressive report cards into evidence, asserting they'd inherited their dad's feeble mind. It had shocked me to see a parent offer his children up like that, and I wondered if his kids knew what their dad had allowed to be said about them in open court, on public record. Not to mention it was such a leap from the truth I don't know how Gregory said it with a straight face. Martinez had outwitted an arson investigation, played puppet master with UPS, and even from his jail cell was drawing elaborate plans for the house he intended to build, the businesses he planned on starting once this pesky trial nonsense was behind him. Now, there was a very real possibility he was about to skate away from two murders, on top of whatever black market dealing he'd never even be charged for.

Caught up in his argument, Gregory could not resist declaring his client did not commit this crime. Crossing over the lines of permissible statements with impunity. Again. An hour and a half after he'd started, Major Gregory asked the panel to "Give Sergeant Martinez the chance he was never provided in life" and find him not guilty. The rows of family members let loose a disgusted moan as we heard that, with the obvious chances Lou and Phil had not been provided leaping into our minds. Listening to the mouthpiece for the killer who'd denied Lou and Phil a chance to live, to defend their own lives, come home to their families, denied us the right to welcome them home and our kids the right to know and grow with their dads, was no easy chore.

It was Heustis' turn now. Prosecution, with the burden of the proof upon it, was granted a rebuttal. "I'm going to frag that Mother F—. Those are the words of the Accused and the evidence shows that's what happened." Heustis was just as forceful and just as determined as anyone else in this battle as he dove right into the brutal reality of this case. Picking through defense's closing and laying bare the gaping holes in their theories, he spent almost an hour spelling out the evidence against Martinez. As he concluded, Siobhan and I nodded our agreement that he'd cleaned up defense's mess. If we were going just on closing arguments, we'd feel confident in the outcome.

It was 3 PM as Colonel Henley read some more deliberation instructions to the panel. Absent again was any mention of the gates to a death penalty. Wrapping up his condensed instructions, he dismissed the panel for the day. We would assemble tomorrow for the deliberation process. The waiting began for what would become the most important two days in our lives since Lou and Phil were murdered.

CHAPTER FIFTEEN
THE VERDICT

✪ ✪ ✪

December 3rd came and went with no verdict. We'd all passed the time at the courthouse in our own ways. We watched movies on Lou's laptop, took walks, stared into space. Conversation varied as much as our moods. Evan began calling us in groups to his office, running his sentencing arguments past us. The air in that building was tense, emotions all over the map as the two families grappled to find a way to pass this endless waiting.

We'd occasionally rush into the courtroom in response to word that we were going on the record, only to learn the panel wanted a break, or the panel was simply reconvening from a break. Each time I would look at the members, desperate for some sign of assurance. But not even Tabler, who'd often openly smiled at us in court, would meet our eyes. Driving back to the apartment that night I fought hard to deny the full blown panic gaining force within me. Something was not right. But my mind would not allow me to confront the unthinkable. I hung out with family, dreaming of the following day and the moment we'd all waited so long to hear the word "Guilty" coming after the premeditated murder charges. The day when Martinez would finally know he'd not gotten away with it. When we knew the government had not let us down, that we would be free to find some peace now, and maybe even happiness one day.

December 4. Today had to be the day. The courthouse was bursting with people that morning. Class As and digital uniforms filled the halls and outnumbered our families. Reporters had turned out in full force. Did they know something we didn't?

My insides were rolling as we hurried back to our seats that day, having heard the panel had questions. What did that mean? Were they close? It had been another long day and the afternoon was wearing on. Would we be sent home again to wait out the night?

225

Addressing the panel's written question, Colonel Henley explained the votes needed to convict. Colonel Fiorey inquired about not having the ten votes to convict on one charge—what then? Henley responded that equaled an acquittal. The entire room froze for a full heartbeat with that exchange. A moment later Colonel Fiorey responded in that case, the path was clear, or something to that effect. I don't remember her exact words because the impression given was that they were about to acquit Martinez. Major Cipriano turned to look directly at me, his shocked expression likely a reflection of mine. Except his was followed by a smile, and mine was followed by the explosion of pain in my chest. I was about to have a panic attack, and barely managed to propel myself out of the room when the panel returned to deliberations.

Back in the Victims' DIF I called Steve to tell him about the panel's question. Tried to keep the panic from my voice as I told him they seem like they want to acquit. Steve did his best to reassure me but it was a lost cause. And then we were aware of a swarm of movement in the halls.

MPs and security guards descended on the scene. Outside, police cruisers patrolled the parking lot. Dogs were brought in and a security check was placed outside the courtroom; the panel had a verdict.

No one smiled. No one spoke, or even breathed too loudly for a few moments as our door was shut by a tight-faced guard who informed us we had to leave all belongings here. Nothing was to be carried into the courtroom for the verdict. We would each have to pass through a wanding station before being permitted to enter the courtroom. Our DIF was jammed with family and friends, and a few reporters we'd come to know. Paul Woolverton of the *Fayetteville Observer* and Estes Thompson of the AP had maintained a friendly yet respectful attitude with all of us. Their need for a story never outweighed their compassion for our families, and we appreciated their dedication to covering the case. Now they tried to melt into the walls of that DIF, intent on not intruding again.

Nervous comments slowly began cropping up as the moments passed and our door did not open. When it finally opened we exited one-by-one and walked to the wanding station, then back into the courtroom. I had not thought it possible to ever feel this level of sick fear swallowing me again as it was in those moments spent entering the courtroom. Seeing the armed guards barricading the bar, arguing with the one who told me I was not allowed in the front row, until he gave in and let me stay. Seeing Siobhan take her seat next to me, watching the rest of the families dragged in, caught in the gravitational pull of dread at what we were most afraid of possibly about to transpire.

The "All Rise" came one last time. The panel would not look at us as we took our seats. Until I caught Tabler shooting a haggard look at us before practically jumping to look away as he accidentally caught my eye. *Oh no oh no oh no oh no oh no* screaming in my head now as I fought to figure out what that meant. Watching the paper handed to Henley, hearing him say it was in order. Seeing Colonel Fiorey square off as she rose to answer "How do you find" on the one count of premeditated murder. The words "Not Guilty" slamming into me and Siobhan half yelled, a high pitched, startled "aaaahhhh!" escaping from her as I struggled to silence the cacophony in my own head while Colonel Fiorey said those words again. Then the panel was turning, double-timing it out of the room as Colonel Henley bound past us, Siobhan yelling, "This is the United States of America" in a voice filled with disbelief that our country's court would fail in such a way.

I didn't understand what happened, even as the panel members were stampeding out of the room and I asked Colonel Henley, "Are they going back in to deliberate?" Much like I'd nearly asked the notification detail if Lou was okay moments after they told me he was dead. A protective mechanism in my brain frantically trying to ward off the damage such a catastrophic event would cause if allowed to filter through my consciousness.

"That's it" Heustis said, more than once as I beseechingly asked him again what now. "That's *it?*" I shrieked out the words as Mrs. Major Crespo made it to her exit door and the moment clicked. "He slaughtered our husbands and *that's it?*" I was out of control. Snapped. Leapt up and leaned over the bar, as I saw John crumple at the table, head in his hands and Majors Gregory and Cipriano cover their client with their own bodies as shields between him and the raging madness pouring from me as I screamed and kicked the bar, "You murdered my husband, you piece of shit!" to Martinez, who was hiding like the coward he is behind his attorneys.

A new level of hatred, of sheer and pure animalistic rage and fury invaded every inch of my body and soul in those moments. I saw now the reason for those guards as even the shock I felt on some plane of my consciousness was not enough to dispel the absolute hatred and raw pain possessing me while Martinez was lead from the room in a sea of soldiers. The look on Cipriano's face had been fear, and the fear had been directed to me. He'd looked convinced he and his client were in mortal danger. And he'd probably been right. There is no doubt in my mind. Had I been provided an opportunity in those moments to kill Martinez myself, I would have taken it. Such was the power of the emotions and the impact of that verdict. It is something I had never felt before, and hope to never feel again. It is representative of all that is evil in this world, and the exact opposite of the person I strive to be. But it was real, and part of me now lives with the knowledge that I possess the capability to feel it.

CHAPTER SIXTEEN

THE AFTERMATH

✪ ✪ ✪

A few minutes later there were just five of us in the courtroom. I'd smacked away Valerie's compassionate arm and my parents and sister had been left with no choice but to leave the room without me. I couldn't walk. I'd collapsed onto the seat screaming and crying. The adrenaline was racing through my veins; I could feel my limbs pulsing with every frenzied beat of my heart. Siobhan and me had instantly resumed the roles we took the first few weeks of the murders. I was the weak one, crumbling in a pitiful display of sobs and snot while she was the picture of composure, dry–eyed and resolutely standing of her own volition. Even reaching out to comfort me, and coax me from my seat, onto my wobbly legs and out of that room. Heustis asked where we'd like to go, and I barely managed to respond, "To your office, please." As with the wake and the funeral, I needed to be away from the gathered crowd of family members. Couldn't be with anyone now as the impact of what had just happened careened through me.

Only vaguely aware of the people staring at me en route downstairs, I tried unsuccessfully to process what had happened. In the office, the door was shut and Siobhan and Brent stood next to me on one side of Heustis' desk. On the other side stood John and Heustis, separated by that desk and looking at me with blank expressions. I was trying to find something to grab on the wall, support myself with. I didn't want to sit; I was too electrified to sit. The level of shock and fear streaming through me, the sheer horror and force of what had just transpired, was equivalent to greeting the notification detail at my door. John and Heustis in their Class As may as well have been the two soldiers urging me to sit down, looking at me expectantly as if I would know what to do with myself.

Unlike when I'd greeted the soldiers that day, though, this time the tears were immediate. While Siobhan stood poised and spoke quietly, asking calm questions and rubbing my back encouragingly, I gave in. Gave up. Just let the past three and a half years wash over me, into me, as I begged the two men to explain this. "Is there any chance he was innocent?" Before I got the question out they were each shaking their heads no. No way, they said. What am I supposed to do now? How do I tell my kids? I promised them it would be OK. What do I tell them? Over and over with the same few questions no one had any answers to, other than that Martinez is guilty. And got away with it. And there was nothing we could do about it.

Heustis told us we could have the office as long as we wanted, and he, Brent, and John stepped out to give Siobhan and me some privacy. We each turned our phones on. She called her parents and I called Keith. I wanted him to keep the kids home from school the next day. Turn off the TV and radio that night. I didn't want them to hear it on the news. I almost fell over when Colin answered. "Hello Mom!" came his voice, barely loud enough to hear over the background noise of the five of them in the kitchen, happily chattering away over dinner. I managed to get out "Hey, Buddy. Can you please put Keith on the phone" and listened as the phone was fumbled into Keith's hands. "Keith" I whispered and sobbed at the same time as I told him what happened. He was at a loss, and I felt the surge of rage return as we spoke; No way was I going to let it end this way.

We kept it short. He agreed to keep the kids home and sequestered from the world until I got back. I got off a text to Steve and Meg: Not Guilty. And that was all I could do. We asked John and Heustis back in. Brent came in, too. John promised me he would be here if we wanted to go over it. If there was anything we needed from him, all we had to do was call. Having heard enough, and had enough, I needed to get out of there. Now. Making my way to the door I grabbed Brent's shoulder, nudging him out of the way "Let me out of here" I pleaded as I got the door open and made my way into the hallway. Siobhan was with me, her arm around my shoulder and guiding me up the flight of stairs to our families. I didn't speak to anyone, including my parents, as I waited for Siobhan to get her things. Jen came over and said she'd drive me back to the apartment. I nodded and the three of us descended the stairs one last time. Reaching the bottom floor, the MPs I'd joked around with stopped talking when they noticed us. I was wailing like a banshee and they all stared at me as I made my way into the dark parking lot. The panel members' spots were empty; they'd all fled the scene within moments of shattering our lives. Back to their families and away from this. In the Crespos' case, they could go home together. Husband and wife could console each other, telling themselves they'd done the right thing as they decimated us and turned their backs on justice out of fear of being compromised in the sensitive area of capital punishment. I wondered if they had any idea what they'd done. How they could live with themselves, seeking solace in each other's arms while sending the rest of us home in agony. And for Siobhan and I, there was no husband to return to. No arms could comfort us the way our husbands' could.

I knew without being told that the Crespos and Shepard were the culprits in this. I would bet my home on Dezeborah Evans aiding them; She'd clearly been infatuated with Shepard, and it was not a stretch to believe she'd gone his way. Those two spent as much time eyeing each other through the trial as they had paid attention to testimony. Except when it came to the CID agents. Then Shepard would focus on the courtroom, shaking his head and raising his eyebrows at the agents, and looking over at Dezeborah with a disgusted expression. That left at least one more member to identify. One more person who had defied logic and common sense, and set Martinez free.

Back at my apartment, I collapsed on my bed and called Steve. At that moment I would have loved to have him there with me. He'd been with me for so much of this, and his was the one set of arms I wanted to be in right now. I didn't pause to ask myself why I wanted him there, and not Keith. But the truth is Keith would be a bundle of fury, lashing out at everyone. And Steve would just hold me and let me cry, which is all I wanted to do. Then he was on the phone, difficult to hear as he was in the midst of a crowded sidewalk. He offered his best, telling me I needed to find a way to live with this and move past it. At which point I realized maybe I was better on my own than with anyone; I didn't need extra anger and I was not ready to hear about accepting this. I hung up and sat for a minute, then joined Jen in the living room. There I called Meg, who offered to drive up from Alabama and be with me. I loved her for that, but told her I'd decided to go home after all.

The boxes we'd just carried in from the car, packed in anticipation of a jubilant ride home that night and then brought back in when I crumbled, were again carried outside and placed in the car. I was now filled with my own defiant fury. No way would I let him get away with this. No way would I let the government walk away without answering for its failure. Colonel Henley needed to be held accountable. The panel members needed to know what they'd done. All the things that had lead up to this moment; the weaknesses, the games, the pride, the mistakes. All of it needed to be examined and recognized. But most of all, I would make him pay.

In those first hours, I was raging with the most intense anger and hatred I have ever experienced, or hope to experience again. Had I encountered either defense attorney, or Martinez, or even Henley, I would have run them down and backed up again to be sure I'd done the trick. Beaming down I–95 in the cover of night, listening to radio reports of the surprise verdict and picturing the rejoicing going on in the Martinez camp, I wanted him dead. But first I wanted him to suffer. And I wanted him to know why he was dying.

Gradually, I began to calm. My foot eased up on the gas pedal, and Jen relaxed her grip from the dashboard. I swapped calls with Siobhan, who was driving home alone. We alternated between vowing revenge and cursing out everyone who had ever lied or failed us before settling into a path of accepting the reality, and working to right as much of it as we could—legally. But the power of those feelings I had for a while that night is something I will never forget. I was now a woman on a mission. I needed to set this right. Do something—anything—to find out what went wrong, and if there was a way to get him for something.

Siobhan and I agreed we would follow up on the second set of charges, the trial we'd been told would act as a backup for this one. Maybe he could be convicted for that stuff. I occasionally slipped back into wanting to see him dead, and wondering how we could make that happen. Then I would be gripped with an overwhelming fear of Martinez: Look what he'd done. How he'd escalated over the years as he continued to get away with his misdeeds, until he'd now been given a free pass on murdering two men. Would he be so incensed at our families for daring to pursue the case that he would feel entitled to exact revenge on us? Was he so warped that he'd want to punish us for his three years in prison, show us he was still untouchable? Because we knew he believed he was—believes he is still—untouchable. He'd had a few worrying moments first in the DIF and on occasion in the courtroom, but he'd won. He'd again proven he was smarter than any system. Better than any man. And what was to stop him now from escalating again?

It was not the most rational fear I'd had but I could not stop from entertaining the thought. And it fueled me to want him dead, because that was the only way I would ever feel safe from him hurting my family again.

We pulled into Jen's driveway around 4 AM. I didn't want to go home until the kids were picked up to go out for the day. I couldn't face them until I figured out what to say, how to handle this. So while Jen built a fire for me, I sat in the early darkness and wrote a final article for the series I'd written during the trial. A couple branches of our local paper had been running these articles, and I'd received a strong response to them. Jen's husband Tom came out to the living room to say hello, and we talked a few minutes. Then as they returned to bed and the fireplace lit up the room, I sat in the glow of their computer and poured out the article. Emailing it to the editor, I stretched my stiff muscles and looked for some more coffee. The sun made its entrance, diminishing the glow from the flames, and I knew it was time to go home.

Condolence calls began rolling in as word of the verdict spread. It was a replay of the days after the murders. Friends and family had no idea how to approach me; I was inconsolable. I'd taken Trevor and Colin aside separately and broke the news to them. Sean and Jeremy were still just 7 and 5 years old, and I'd decided not to have the conversation with them yet. Meantime, Siobhan and I had some decisions to make on how to proceed from here; was there anything we could do about this? Could we get people to care about what had happened? Was it possible to set the record straight and make it known that the military allowed a murderer to go free? Would our husbands remain ineligible for the Purple Heart? We knew none of the questions would be easily answered. The government had no interest in anything other than closing the door on the case and filing it away under the "oops" label. It would be up to us to determine how badly we wanted to follow up on all of this.

The first thing I had to do was return to Fayetteville to pack up my apartment. Siobhan and I had also scheduled a meeting with Lieutenant Colonel Erisman, Chief of the Criminal Law Division at Bragg. Siobhan's attorney agreed to make the trip and sit in on the meeting with us. My parents offered to watch the boys for a few days so Keith could come with me. This would be his first trip to my second home. He'd declined my invitations in the past, and I hadn't wanted to pressure him into more than he'd already had to deal with. Now, he wanted to be there for me and I hoped by experiencing the town, seeing my apartment and going through this part with me, we'd begin to heal the ever–growing rift between us.

I was still a strung out mess, fueled on nerves and anger instead of sleep and food. Packing up the apartment, laughing through new tears at the Trial Survival Kit my sisters had sent with me. The opened items like chocolate and an inflatable stress bat we'd all bopped each other with over the weeks. The bubble bath, pez dispensers, wine, joke books and inspirational mementos mixed in with the still wrapped gifts I'd planned to open during sentencing. Another reminder of the things that will not be.

The day before our meeting with Erisman, word came to me of another mind–blowing piece of information. In April 2006, while we'd been at Bragg for the second 32 Hearing, Martinez and his attorneys had offered a signed guilty plea to the government. In the military system, such a plea cannot be submitted unless the Accused and his attorneys believe they can convince a judge of the defendant's guilt. Essentially, it is a concession of guilt that cannot be explained or excused away as being offered to avoid being railroaded by an imbalanced system or unfair circumstances. The defendant must assert his guilt and the attorney must believe it.

Our families had not been informed of the Offer to Plead Guilty. Instead, Colonel Gade instructed the government to turn it down and keep it quiet. General Vines signed the document rejecting the offer. Spinning back in time to that hearing, I remembered all the stops and starts of that day. How we'd waited impatiently for Martinez to come and then for the hearing to begin. Of the extra strain on the government's faces, and of defense meeting with Steve and me later, attempting to convince me a liaison between defense and the victims was to our benefit. How it would allow us to be informed of things we would otherwise not be informed of, and how the trial counsel had been intrigued to hear this. That I'd scoffed at the notion and trial counsel had not attempted to convince me otherwise. Suddenly it all made sense, and a new feeling of betrayal entered the picture.

After that hearing, Steve approached trial counsel to ask about the possibility of any pleas. He'd been introducing the idea to me slowly, that a plea may be the best way to go in a circumstantial case like this one. But he was told no pleas were on the table now or ever, in spite of the newly rejected and suppressed offer. Accepting the plea would have sent us directly into the penalty phase of a trial. The battle would have been life in prison with or without the possibility of parole. And it would have been over with. Martinez would be in jail for almost a year and a half that December, instead of the free man he is today. We would have been the ones released from this cruel process. Free to return to our lives and put them back together, secure in the comfort that Lou and Phil's deaths were accounted for. We would have maintained faith in our system and the belief that it can work. Instead we were left with one betrayal after another. Individuals whose pride superseded justice and moral decency, who had toyed with our lives and our husband's murders and left us to bear the scars.

I called Siobhan and told her what I'd learned. She shared my outrage as we talked together about where to go from here. We decided to focus our meeting on finding out what the government would do about the second trial—the one we'd been told would act as a backup in just this situation. But I would also ask about the existence of any plea. We knew the government had already washed its hands of us and this case. An official press release quoted Erisman saying the verdict exemplified a system that worked. We'd have preferred to skip this meeting and jump straight to the top, to Major General Curtis Scaparrotti, acting commander of the 18th Airborne Corps. But for now, we had to start with Erisman. Already distrustful of him, I planned on using the plea question as a gauge of his sincerity. Would he acknowledge what I'd learned and trusted to be true—that a plea had been offered and suppressed, and he had received a copy of it the day before? Or would he deny all of it and confirm my lack of trust. Expectations were low as we drove back to Bragg for this meeting less than a week after the verdict.

Seated in his office, Erisman introduced us to Colonel Robinson, the Staff Judge Advocate at Bragg. Formalities out of the way, we asked our questions and they spun their replies. Soft assurances about the government's continued devotion to our families and regret over the verdict were enough to test my patience on a good day. Which this was not. It was made clear that any second trial was improbable. Martinez would be discharged from the military and free to live his life, and we would have to deal with it.

In my best casual, dumb–widow voice I asked a last minute question about any pleas ever being offered. In their best politician voice, each man assured me none had been offered, other than early discussions in 2005. Adopting a confused look, I offered a "Huh, funny. I was told there was a plea, and we were never informed." And was treated to Erisman looking me straight in the eye as he again assured me he had never seen or heard of such an offer. I left the meeting more disgusted than ever.

The drive home was spent largely in silence. Keith and I had run out of things to say to each other. He'd been pinning his hopes on a guilty verdict signaling the end of my obsession with the case and the turmoil in our lives. I was annoyed at him for already asking me if I planned on making this my life's work now—setting things straight if I could, getting the purple heart—when would I focus on him? The answer was clear to me but something I could not yet deal with.

Over the past year Keith and I had lost the ability to be together. The moments of closeness, the feeling that we would make it through this trial and the aftermath, had long since evaporated. Going into the trial things had been almost unbearable between us. Though we put on a good façade for the boys, things had reached a breaking point. Then at Thanksgiving we'd spent a few days at a hotel near Siobhan. Seeing him make that trip with the boys, knowing how much he hated leaving the small–town atmosphere for the busy DC area, touched me. I was reminded of how hard he'd been trying to fit into our lives, how much he loved us. We'd enjoyed a reprieve from our personal conflicts and I'd returned to Fayetteville more optimistic that we'd work it out.

But less than a week after the Thanksgiving break, we'd watched Alberto Martinez walk out of the courtroom a free man. Our relationship took a back seat to my new struggle to overcome the verdict.

One bright escape for Siobhan and me came about two weeks after the verdict. On the day we expected to be in court for sentencing testimony, we were instead on an American Airlines charter flight to California, off for another trip with SnowBall Express. I was thrilled Siobhan decided to come that year. The Board members had gone above and beyond to accommodate us in our unpredictable situation. The timing of the event so soon after the verdict provided exactly the lift we needed to shake off the despair, even for a few days, and newly take stock of our blessings as we approached the holidays.

We each made it through Christmas and turned immediately to our next meeting. Major General Scaparrotti agreed to meet with us—on the condition no attorneys attend—on December 30. Undaunted by the timing, Siobhan and I made the trek again. Endured Colonel Robinson in the room again, as we heard the same party lines we'd heard last time. The one difference being while I could not decide if the general was being untruthful when claiming not to know of a plea, or simply uninformed of it, I did believe he was sincere about his displeasure with the case and sympathetic to our efforts. Even if he had no intention of doing anything about it. The verdict was a done deal. No further charges would be pursued. The Gatekeeper's promise of a second backup trial had been as empty as the rest of the platitudes we'd heard. Colonel Henley, even if he had overstepped propriety—which no one was saying he had—was untouchable. There will be no review of his rulings. He continues to serve as the Chief Trial Judge for the Army.

The ensuing months were a strange combination of pursuing answers and accountability, still enmeshed in the nightmare, and attempting to put our lives together. My email inbox reflected the new twilight zone I'd landed in; Emails to and from family and friends interspersed with those to and from Admiral Mullen, a few panel members who'd responded to my letter to them, a representative from the White House finally offering my kids and I the chance to meet President Bush were just a few examples. The latter was the end result of three years spent asking for this meeting.

Trevor and Colin knew "other kids with dead soldier parents" got to meet the president and could not understand why they were not allowed to. And I had not had the heart to explain to them how my repeated requests had been denied or played with. Like the day my phone rang at 4 PM, and I'd answered to a White House staffer asking me if I wanted to join a group of families in Green Bay Wisconsin at 10 A.M. the following morning to meet the president. And he sounded surprised that I could not get myself and four boys from New York to Green Bay in time. Finally, a sympathetic insider on the staff confessed my request fell under political ones, as opposed to general public ones, due to the sensitivity of the case. But there was no way I was going to get into that with the kids. Instead I'd kept it on my list of things to do, and it paid off. The kids were thrilled to go to the White House for the reception for our families, and the three years were worth their smiles.

The trip to the White House remains fresh in my mind. The biting cold weather, the boys in their suits. The other families milling about the area, taking turns greeting Condoleeza Rice, Dick Cheney, and President Bush. Five-year old Jeremy had been unimpressed with the table full of appetizers, and was happily munching on some chips Lou's sister Laurene had talked a kitchen staffer out of. He didn't know or care who Condoleeza Rice was and he was not about to put a chip down to get his picture taken. When the Secretary of State asked me to tell her about my husband, I avoided the details and just said he died in Iraq. I was making an effort to keep this visit focused on the kids, and didn't want to take a chance on having it marred by the circumstances.

Our turn to meet the President arrived, and after being relieved of all personal items we were escorted to a room where the President was striding forward to meet us, a smile on his face. He was taller than I expected. He ignored my hand and hugged me instead before greeting Lou's parents, sister, and the boys. He then grabbed my hand in both of his and asked me how I was doing. Mindful of the fact that this was not a meeting about my situation, that it was intended for the boys to have this experience, I kept my mouth shut and offered the lie, "I'm well, thanks." Thinking that would suffice, I was surprised when he grabbed my hands firmer, looked directly into my eyes, and asked, "How are you *really* doing?" At which point my control slipped and I snapped, "Oh, well, I'm *really* enjoying my perfect life, thanks for asking."

President Bush, perhaps unaccustomed to people like me talking to him like that, snapped his head up, released my hand, replaced his wide smile with a tight one and ushered us into place for a photo op. I backpedaled in an attempt to ensure the kids' time with him was as long as the time he'd spent with the other families instead of curtailed because I'd insulted him. Standing for the picture I babbled about how great this was for the kids, how long they'd waited. And the President spent a moment with each of them before sending us off without making any further eye contact with me. Last but not least, we met Dick Cheney.

Ruffled by the encounter with the President, I stood back while the boys met the Vice President. But Mr. Cheney drew me in, shook my hand, and asked me how my husband died. So I told him. And said perhaps he'd heard of the case. To that, he cocked his head to the side, smiled in amusement, and chuckled out a, "No, I never heard of it." That annoyed me enough for me to respond, "Really, that's too bad. Being the Vice President you should have heard about such an important case in the military." The words were hardly out of my mouth before Mr. Cheney's palm was in the small of my back, guiding me forward and away from him with a, "Nice to meet you."

The boys enjoyed the visit, but the experience left me feeling the need for a long hot shower.

•   •   •   •   •

Unencumbered by the mandates and repercussions of wearing the uniform, Siobhan and me freely spoke of the case to media and anyone who would listen. And some who wouldn't listen. Lou's family did the same. Even his cousin Mike Allen, serving in Iraq, joined us. Ignoring the risk of any possible repercussions, Mike called Colonel Henley. To his surprise, the judge took the call and listened as Mike told him what a disgrace he is to the case. That our families blame him for the outcome. Colonel Henley entertained the conversation for a few minutes before hanging up. Mike called again. And the colonel answered again. This time Henley stressed the improperness of the call, and ended it more quickly. But the point had been made and Mike became a family legend for his willingness to speak up for what he believed in, even at risk to himself.

Playing around with AKO configurations one day, I took a stab at the military email addresses for the panel members and sent them all an email. Asked them if they thought about Lou and Phil, or our families. If there were any lingering questions or doubts in their minds they would like answers to. I was shocked when a few members responded, sharing their dismay over the verdict. One member told me of sleepless nights and driving home from court that day sobbing at what had transpired. Another offered to continue communicating, and thanked me for reaching out. The verdict was not easy for some of them to digest, either. Siobhan sent her own email and received her own responses. Fairly certain word of this contact would eventually reach up the food chain; we were not surprised when Siobhan's attorney forwarded an email he received from Erisman:

Mrs. Esposito and Mrs. Allen have been e-mailing the panel members requesting information about the trial. Please inform the spouses that the following panel members do not want to be contacted…

I was at once jealous of and sorry for the members who could turn away from this so easily.

•   •   •   •   •

The months passed and our lives passed with them. My personal life spun around as my relationship with Keith met an ugly demise. He moved out in the spring, and it was the boys and I on our own again. I was also beginning my campaign to publicize the trial and what went wrong. Convince the government to award Lou and Phil the Purple Hearts they have been denied. Appearances on news shows and support on Internet blogs and Causes began to grow, and continues to grow still.

The meetings we held, the emails and phone calls with any member of the government we could reach, had been long shots. The Military Awards Division refused to budge on the Purple Heart matter. I'd lobbied the Department of the Army to change the death certificates to "Hostile" death, thus making Lou and Phil eligible for the honor and properly reflecting their deaths. Denied over and over, until my rejection letters expressed a growing exasperation with my continued efforts. Recently, I renewed these efforts and will be campaigning hard to right this wrong.

Stopping short of agreeing with our charges of Colonel Henley sabotaging the case, and the government acting against the interest of justice in suppressing a plea, Admiral Mullen's responses to me began as casual friendly, signing off as "mike" and then changed their tone as he informed me there was nothing he could do.

The military continued to balk at admitting there had been a plea offer. Our direct questions had been met with "We'll look into it." That changed on February 20, 2009. Paul von Zielbauer's front–page story in the NY Times laid to rest any doubt about a suppressed plea. Detailing how the military plea system works, that the defense attorneys may only sign a plea if they believe in their client's guilt, the article revealed that the government withheld this plea offer from our families, and left little room for anyone to doubt Martinez's guilt. A copy of the signed plea was included in an online link to the article.

We heard from our military contacts of an uproar after the article. Officials were seething, wondering how the Times had gotten their hands on a copy of the plea. But the effect was minimal in our world. Media interest drifted to current cases and military courtrooms began hearing the latest soldier–on–soldier homicide cases. A combined nine soldiers had been murdered in those cases. At this writing, each of those cases is wending their way through the pre–trial hearing process. I am in contact with a family of one of the murdered soldiers, and hope to offer them the same support Teri Seifert offers me. We are a small but strong community, those of us military survivors of homicide. And a shooting rampage at Fort Hood expanded that community again. I have not been in touch with any of those families, but would welcome the opportunity.

It will always prove a challenge to find peace with the botched justice in our case. In the government's sweeping it under the rug, out of minds, and refusing to hold anyone accountable. Martinez, we were whispered, is in Puerto Rico enjoying his life. A newspaper there ran a story describing the celebration in his native land, welcoming its vindicated citizen home. A follow up story included pictures of Lou and me, and a copy of the plea. I could only hope that would put an end to his hero status there.

As for the other players in this case, life moved on for all of them. Some have been promoted, including General Taluto. First awarded a position as Adjutant General of the NY National Guard, he was then nominated by President Obama to be the Director of the nation's National Guard. However, Siobhan lobbied members of the Senate to look closely at General Taluto's command of the 42nd and the breakdown in its good order and discipline. Her efforts convinced the Senate to pass her concerns to the nomination committee. The resulting inquiry outlasted General Taluto, who ultimately withdrew his nomination.

Sherman and Rodriguez have not been investigated as accomplices, in spite of the belief they had a hand in the murders or at least knew the truth. Majors Gregory and Cipriano have bragging rights to pulling off what should have been an unwinnable victory.

Few people in the military or political arena are willing to attach their names to our efforts. Happy to express condolences or commiserate with our pain, support often stops when asked to join us, sign a letter to a representative asking to change the death certificates or look into rulings in the case. Initially frustrating to the point of distraction, I've now grown accustomed to this reaction, and am more surprised when someone goes against the norm by paying more than lip service to this case. I remain optimistic about changing the death certificates and seeing Lou and Phil awarded Purple Hearts. I refuse to believe this country will allow their legacy to remain stained by the murders. Eventually I will find those with the courage and integrity to confront the ugly, unpleasant truth in this case instead of hiding from the mistakes.

Lou and Phil were not famous. Our families are just normal families. But the case is bigger than our families. Bigger than people's jobs and egos. It affects each person wearing the uniform. It affects their families and friends, and it affects how our military is perceived by other countries.

Much like our planet's ozone layer protects us all from damaging and even fatal entities, our troops provide a layer of defense for our country. Without people willing to lay their lives on the line, to sacrifice time away from family and home, our country and our way of life would not exist. This line of defense, the people forming that line, deserve to be protected from unnecessary harm. They deserve to have faith in a government that does not hide from embarrassment or deny mistakes, instead of losing faith in a system declaring itself above the responsibility of doing do.

Unless the mistakes in this case are addressed, it will happen again. Our soldiers need to be trained to recognize threats before them, even when originating from an unconventional enemy—our own soldiers. Our military needs to acknowledge what went wrong and make steps to remedy the weaknesses that contributed to this travesty.

This case raised important questions that demand answers: Is the military equipped to handle capital cases? Is the voir dire system flawed? Why were we not told of the plea in April 2006? Did Colonel Henley's professional and personal pride deal fatal blows to the case? Are there other Martinezes out there, serving alongside someone else's husband, father, mother, daughter, or best friend? Will the soldier homicide cases in the system now be watched closer, to ensure the same mistakes are not made? Will the government openly take a position on Martinez's guilt? Will the death certificates be reconciled with the verdict? The questions are endless and the answers are not forthcoming. And they are now a part of my life that I cannot walk away from.

This is not a story with the conventional happy ending. There is no package pretty enough to be wrapped in the neat little bow to leave people feeling warm and fuzzy. Fortunately, most of us have learned to glean happiness in our unconventional existence.

The pain of losing Lou will be with me, and our family, forever. There is no escaping that. The shock and compounded tragedy of the verdict are something I am helpless to change. But along the way I began to recognize the beauty and blessings still present in life. For all the evil I experienced and witnessed, for each person who lied to us or betrayed our trust, there were other people who stepped forward to help. Friends and family who refused to give up on me and strangers willing to speak with us. People came into my life and became part of it. Out of tragedy, there has been triumph. For me, that is my happy ending.

I will carry a love for Lou with me for the rest of my life. I will be grateful each day for the time I had with him, and for the privilege of raising our boys. Some days I'll be caught up in the sadness of just missing him, wanting him here. And I will allow myself to feel that. But I have also opened the door to a new life. One with the chance of new love and happiness. And the boys and I are running through that door.

We'll welcome the future as we mourn for the past. We'll hold on to the good things Lou gave us, and find comfort that he is at peace. But most of all, we will never forget.

P.S:

I encourage everyone who is moved to help to do so. Write your representatives and tell them about this case. Ask them to examine the facts, and help ensure the mistakes are not repeated. Ask them to encourage the military to implement stronger training on how to recognize threats from within. Join my efforts to secure Purple Hearts for Lou and Phil. The Purple Hearts they earned when they died in service to our country. Visit my website at www.unconventionalenemy.com for further information.

Most of all, in spite of your political inclinations or feelings about this war, thank a soldier.

AUTHOR'S NOTE

✪ ✪ ✪

This book began as a journal, meant as a means for me to release the emotions of my situation while also serving as a record of events for my children to read one day. If they have questions about what happened, how we felt at the time, why I was behaving the way I was, or anything else, I hoped they would find those answers in my journal.

As time passed, I shared the journal with close friends and family, who encouraged me to explore possibilities of publishing. Curious about the prospect but not exactly sure what to expect, I dashed off a note to literary agents who wrote and published a book on how to get published. Their book stressed the fact that several of these query letters will be necessary before an author receives a positive response from an agent. Ignoring that note, I sent just the one letter and forgot about it. Much to my surprise, I heard back from the agents, and was soon officially represented.

The journal was to be a book. A memoir of my experience of losing Lou and life surrounding the trial and conviction of the individual who killed him. Yet the acquittal changed everything, including my purpose for writing the book. Much of the original was struck and the book was almost entirely rewritten. The change in focus resulted in my agents' losing interest in my book, and I proceeded alone until Morgan James offered to publish my work.

I have done my best to accurately portray events as they unfolded. Testimony from hearings was able to be based on transcripts. But the government has thus far refused to respond favorably to numerous Freedom of Information Acts (FOIA) requests from Siobhan and me, submitted through Siobhan's attorney, for any audio or written transcript of the actual court martial. Therefore, testimony relayed in my book is based upon extensive notes Siobhan and me took throughout the trial, as well as consults with Captain Steven Raiser, Lieutenant Colonel Meg Foreman, and now–retired Major John Benson.

The glossary was compiled by my good friend Bill Eastwick, who has served our country alongside others, and briefly knew Lou. Bill relied on his own experience as well as assorted Army Field Manuals for his descriptions of terms.

Much of the testimony heard over the years and especially at trial was more upsetting than any of us were prepared for. In addition to details of the attack, Lou's dying moments, and the wounds both men endured, were the countless unreported threats and disparaging remarks made about Phil Esposito. The remarks were malicious in nature and based in incompetence and ignorance rather than fact. That they were used to malign Phil's character with no opportunity afforded for Phil or his family to testify on his behalf was exceptionally painful and further torment for them, as well as insulting to all Phil stood for.

The unreported threats exemplify a breakdown in command and the danger of allowing such threats and behavior to be left unaddressed. It is a situation every soldier, from enlisted all the way up the chain of command, should be aware of and alert for.

General Taluto, as Commanding General of the 42nd ID, never publicly addressed what happened. When promoted to Adjutant General of the NY National Guard, he did not publicly address the murders in his unit, or make an effort to heighten awareness of this threat within the NY National Guard. His expressed concern for our families and respect for Phil failed to transcend into action he could have taken to implement training on a state level. Training that would teach soldiers to recognize threats from within, and prevent the escalation of those threats. It is unlikely he would have done so had his presidential nomination been confirmed and he was in a position to make national changes within the National Guard.

The fratricide cases in the military court today, as well as many past cases, all carry similar warning signs that were left unheeded with disastrous results. If these deaths serve no other purpose, may they at least serve as a wakeup call to the military that there are other enemies in addition to the conventional ones we are taught to fear and hate. In light of these murders and others like it, I can only hope today's leaders recognize the need to train soldiers to recognize and act upon such threats.

Unconventional enemies in our own military, either dangerous before they enlist, or becoming dangerous after enlistment, are a threat to every soldier. It is inevitable that some of these individuals will slip in unnoticed or overlooked. But they do not have to be permitted to escalate unchecked. Recognizing this threat and acting upon it can and will prevent future murders within the military. There is no shame in acknowledging the presence of these individuals. The only shame lies in denying they exist. And it is a fatal mistake to do so.

An effective step in preventing future and current cases to disintegrate in court the way ours did would be to review current practices and study our case. What went wrong can be learned from and should never happen again. Next, the military should allow publicity of the cases. Military court cases should be subject to being broadcast the same as civilian courts are. This case was as inflammatory and disgraceful as the O.J. Simpson case. But the clamp on broadcasting prevented it from being known. I was approached by producers from more than one major news and crime show, only to have them lose interest when they learned cameras were not permitted in the courtroom. I sometimes lose sleep wondering what would have been different if the government had been under the watchful eye of its people, instead of free to run amuck with the case in obscurity.

I would like to stress the fact that I maintain and encourage utmost respect and gratitude to all men and women who serve or have served honorably. My brother and more than one cousin or other family member, as well as close friends of mine, are among that group. Without you, our freedom would be lost.

GLOSSARY

❂ ❂ ❂

Acting Garrison Commander – A Garrison Commander is the person in charge of a facility and all its day-to-day operations. An Acting Garrison Commander is temporarily filling in as Garrison Commander.

Adjutant General (AG) – In the United States, there are three definitions for this term:

The chief administrative officer of the United States Army with the rank of Lieutenant General, who is subordinated to the Army Chief of Staff, and is known as the Assistant Chief of Staff, G–1, or ACS, G–1. He is head of the Adjutant General's Corps, and is responsible for the procedures affecting personnel procurement and for the administration and preservation of records of all army personnel. See List of Adjutant Generals of the U.S. Army.

The chief administrative officer of a major military unit, such as a division, corps, or army. This officer is normally subordinated to the unit Chief of Staff, and is known as the G–1.

The senior military officer and de facto commander of a state's military forces, including the National Guard, the Naval Militia, and any State Defense Forces. He is known as TAG, and is subordinated to the Chief Executive. In 48 states, Puerto Rico, Guam, and the US Virgin Islands, the Adjutant General is appointed by the Governor. The exceptions are Vermont, where the Adjutant General is appointed by the legislature, South Carolina, where they are elected by the voters, and the District of Columbia, where a commanding general is appointed by the President of the United States of America.

ADSW – Active Duty Special Work – A tour of active duty for reserve personnel authorized from military and reserve personnel appropriations for work on active or reserve component programs.

AGR – Active Guard Reserve – Is a United States Army and United States Air Force federal military program which places Army National Guard and Army Reserve soldiers and Air National Guard and Air Force Reserve airmen on federal active duty status to provide full–time support to National Guard and Reserve organizations for the purpose of organizing, administering, recruiting, instructing, or training the Reserve Components.

AHA – Ammunition Holding Area – The area where the ammunition vehicles may be positioned.

AKO – Army Knowledge Online – Provides corporate intranet services to the United States Army, and provides the US Army's single enterprise web portal. AKO provides the Army enterprise with email, directory services, portal, single sign on, blogs, file storage, instant messenger and chat. All members of the Active Duty, National Guard, Reserves, DA Civilian and select contractor workforce have an account which grants access to Army web assets, tools and services worldwide. In addition, retirees and family members are also entitled to accounts.

Article 15 – AKA Non–judicial punishment (NJP) – Refers to certain limited punishments which can be awarded for minor disciplinary offenses by a commanding officer or officer in charge to members of his/her command.

Article 32 Hearing – A proceeding under the United States Uniform Code of Military Justice, similar to that of a preliminary hearing or a grand jury proceeding in civilian law. Its name is derived from UCMJ section VII ("Trial Procedure") Article 32 (10 U.S.C. § 832), which mandates the hearing.

A128 (Article 128) Assault Charge – Refers to an official charge of assault under covered under Article 128 of the UCMJ.

ANCD – Automated Net Control Device – A United States National Security Agency–developed, portable, hand–held fill device, for securely receiving, storing, and transferring data between compatible cryptographic and communications equipment.

Apache Helicopter – AH–64 Apache – A four–blade, twin–engine attack helicopter with reverse–tricycle landing gear arrangement, and tandem cockpit for a crew of two. It is the US Army's primary attack helicopter.

ASVAB – Armed Services Vocational Aptitude Battery – A multiple choice test, administered by the United States Military Entrance Processing Command, used to determine qualification for enlistment in the United States armed forces.

BDU – Battle Dress Uniform – Is the name of the military uniform that the armed forces of the United States have used as their standard uniform for combat situations since September 1981. It became unauthorized for wear in the US Army on April 30, 2008, with the introduction of the Army Combat Uniform (ACU).

Camp Smith – A military installation of the New York Army National Guard in Cortlandt Manor near Peekskill, NY, about 30 miles north of New York City, at the northern border of Westchester County, and consists of 1,900 acres.

CAO – Casualty Assistance Officer – A soldier detailed to help the family of a soldier killed, wounded, or captured in the line of duty.

Cavalry – The U.S. Cavalry is reconnaissance, security and mounted assault. Cavalry has served as a part of the Army force in every war the United States has participated in.

Chief of Staff – The leader of a complex organization, institution, or body of persons, who is the coordinator of the supporting staff or a primary aide to an important individual, such as a Division Commander.

CID – The United States Army Criminal Investigation Command (USACIDC) is a federal law enforcement agency that investigates serious crimes and violations of civilian and military law within the United States Army.

Class A Uniform – The most formal military uniform, typically worn at ceremonies, official receptions, and other special occasions; with order insignias and full size medals.

C4 – Composition C4 is a common variety of the plastic explosive known as Composition C. It is 1.34 times as powerful as TNT.

Claymore Mine – The M18A1 Claymore is a directional anti–personnel mine used by the U.S. military.

CO – Commanding Officer – The officer in command of a military unit. Typically, the commanding officer has ultimate authority over the unit, and is usually given wide latitude to run the unit as he sees fit, within the bounds of military law.

Color Guard – The color guard (where the word "color" here means "flag") carries the National Color and other flags appropriate to its position in the chain of command. The color guard renders honors when the national anthem is played or sung, when passing in review during a parade, or in certain other circumstances.

Company – A military unit, typically consisting of 75–200 soldiers and usually commanded by a Captain. Most companies are formed of three to five platoons although the exact number may vary by country, unit type, and structure.

DCU – Desert Camouflage Uniform – Is the name of the military uniform that the armed forces of the United States have used as their standard uniform for desert combat situations. It became unauthorized for wear in the US Army on April 30, 2008, with the introduction of the Army Combat Uniform (ACU).

Defense Reutilization – Any action that increases the effectiveness of allied forces through more efficient or effective use of defense resources committed to the alliance. Rationalization includes consolidation, reassignment of nation priorities to higher alliance needs, standardization, specialization, mutual support or improved interoperability, and greater cooperation. Rationalization applies to both weapons/materiel resources and non–weapons military matters.

Deployment – The movement of armed forces and their logistical support infrastructure.

DFAC – Dining Facilities Administration Center – A building that serves as both the FOB dining facility, and administration office for the dining facility management.

DIF – Detainee Internment Facility – A United States detention facility that temporarily holds enemy combatants for questioning and in processing, until transportation can be arraigned to bring them to a permanent detention camp. When in a theater of war, a DIF is also used to hold persons suspected of committing a crime who may not be enemy combatants.

Division – A large military unit or formation usually consisting of between 10,000 and 30,000 soldiers. In most armies, a division is composed of several regiments or brigades, and in turn several divisions make up a corps. In most modern militaries, a division tends to be the smallest combined arms unit capable of independent operations; due to its self–sustaining role as a unit with a range of combat troops and suitable combat support forces, which can be divided into various organic combinations.

D–Main – Division Main Headquarters – Refers to the main Headquarters for the 42nd Infantry Division, located at FOB Danger. D–Main was the largest palace on the

FOB, and was the workspace for all of the senior staff and command elements for the division.

Drill – Refers to Reserve or National Guard drill weekend in which training is conducted.

EOD – Explosive Ordnance Disposal – EOD Soldiers are the Army's preeminent tactical and technical explosives experts. They are trained, equipped, and integrated to attack, defeat, and exploit unexploded ordnance, improvised explosive devices, chemical, biological, and nuclear ordnance and Weapons of Mass Destruction.

Family Readiness Group – Within the United States Army, a Family Readiness Group is a command–sponsored organization of family members, volunteers, soldiers and civilian employees associated with a particular unit. They are normally organized at company and battalion levels, and fall under the responsibility of the unit's commanding officer. FRG's are established to provide activities and support to enhance the flow of information, increase the resiliency of unit soldiers and their families, provide practical tools for adjusting to military deployments and separations, and enhance the well–being and esprit de corps within the unit.

FOB – Forward Operating Base – A forward operating base is any secured forward position that is used to support tactical operations. A FOB may or may not contain an airfield, hospital, or other facilities. The base may be used for an extended period of time. FOB's are traditionally supported by main operating bases that are required to provide backup support to them. A FOB also reduces reaction time and increases time on task to forces operating from it.

FOB Anaconda – Now known as Joint Base Balad, it is one of the largest American military bases in Iraq, and was formerly the largest Iraqi air base.

FOB Danger – Home to the 42nd Infantry Division while assigned to the Iraq theater. FOB Danger was located in Tikrit, Iraq before being handed over to the government of Iraq in November 2005.

FOB Speicher – Now known as Contingency Operating Base (COB) Speicher, was captured by 2nd Light Armored Reconnaissance Battalion as part of Task Force Tripoli in 2003. It is named after Scott Speicher, a U.S. Navy pilot who was Killed In Action in Iraq During the 1991 Gulf War when his F/A–18 Hornet was shot down by antiaircraft fire. It was reassigned from a Forward Operating Base to a COB because of its size. Installations are located near Tikrit in northern Iraq, approximately 170 kilometers north of Baghdad and 11 kilometers west of the Tigris River. The airfield is served by two main runways measuring

10,000 and 9,600 feet (2,900 m) long with a shorter runway measuring 7,200–foot (2,200 m). In Operation Iraqi Freedom, it is the location of the headquarters of the United States Forces–North (USF–N, formerly Multinational Division, North, (MND–N)).

Force Protection Order – Force protection consists of those actions to prevent or mitigate hostile actions against DOD personnel (including family members), resources, facilities, and critical information. It coordinates and synchronizes active and passive (offensive and defensive) measures to enable the force to perform while degrading the opportunities for the enemy. Force protection includes air, space, and missile defense; NBC defense; antiterrorism; defensive information operations; and security to operational forces and means. Force protection does not include actions to protect against accidents, weather, and disease. It is the commander's responsibility to ensure that force protection measures are planned for and executed. A force protection order is issued when further measures need to be put in place. For example, unrestricted access to off–post is now restricted due to an increased threat level. Or, free and unrestricted communication to family members is now restricted or unauthorized do to the possibility of the spread of sensitive information.

Form 581 – Refers to DA Form 581, Request for Issue and Turn–In of Ammunition. This form is supposed to be filled out when ammunition is transferred from one soldier, or unit, to another.

Fort Bragg, NC – Fort Bragg is a major United States Army installation, in Cumberland, and Hoke Counties, North Carolina, U.S., mostly in Fayetteville but also partly in the town of Spring Lake. It covers over 251 square miles in four counties, and is home to multiple divisions of the US military, including US Special Forces.

Fort Drum, NY – Fort Drum is a U.S. Army military reservation primarily in Jefferson County, New York, United States. The population was 12,123 at the 2000 census. It is home to the 10th Mountain Division.

Frag – Short for "fragging." The act of attacking a superior officer in one's chain of command with the intent to kill that officer. The term originated in the Vietnam War and was most commonly used to mean assassination of an unpopular officer of one's own fighting unit, occasionally by means of a fragmentation grenade (hence the term) or with firearms.

Health and Welfare Inspection – A health and welfare inspection is an examination of all or part of a unit, organization, installation, aircraft, or vehicle. Commanders may authorize inspections of barracks and work areas to ensure the safety of those facilities and the welfare of the soldiers working and living in them. Health and welfare inspections may include inspections of POVs if the POVs are parked in the unit parking lot normally under the control of that commander. However, commanders DO NOT have authority to conduct inspections or authorize searches in privatized housing or in a soldier's off–post quarters. Therefore, any searches off of the installation must be conducted in conjunction with a valid search warrant. A commander may not use the inspection as a substitute for a lawful search based on probable cause when probable cause does not exist. Administrative inspections are not tools for criminal investigations. For example, if a commander suspects that a soldier possesses illegal drugs in his wall locker but does not have probable cause to conduct a search, the commander may not use a health and welfare inspection as a subterfuge for an improper search of an individual soldier.

HHC – Headquarters and Headquarters Company – A headquarters and headquarters company is a company sized military unit, found at the battalion level and higher. In identifying a specific headquarters unit, it is usually referred to by its abbreviation as an HHC. While a regular line company is formed of three or four platoons, an HHC is made up of the headquarters staff and headquarters support personnel of a battalion, brigade, division, or higher level unit. As these personnel do not fall inside one of the regular line companies of the battalion, brigade, or division, the HHC is the unit to which they are administratively assigned. The typical personnel strength of an average HHC is 80 to 110 personnel.

Honorable Discharge – Service members who meet or exceed the required standards of duty performance and personal conduct, and who complete their tours of duty, normally receive honorable discharges.

HQ – Headquarters – The location where most, if not all, of the important functions of an organization are coordinated.

IG – Inspector General – The Army Inspector General's office investigates allegations of misconduct by Army officials at the rank of colonel or below. Complaints can be filed by soldiers, their family members, retirees, former soldiers or civilians working for the Department of the Army.

Infantry – A unit of soldiers specifically trained for the role of fighting on foot to engage the enemy face to face and have historically borne the brunt of the casualties of combat in wars.

Invitational Travel Orders – Invitational Travel Authorizations (ITA) are government orders that can authorize up to 3 family members of a service member to travel to visit a wounded family member, or attend ceremonies and hearings.

IO – Investigating Officer – The responsibility of an investigating officer is to thoroughly investigate all charges and specifications alleged in the charge sheet(s) during an Article 32(b) Investigation; and, to complete this investigation impartially.

JAG – Judge Advocate General's Corps – The legal branch or specialty of any of the United States Armed Forces. Judge Advocates serve primarily as legal advisors to the command to which they are assigned. In this function, they can also serve as the personal legal advisor to their commander. They also serve as prosecutors for the military when conducting courts–martial. They are charged with both the defense and prosecution of military law as provided in the Uniform Code of Military Justice. Highly experienced officers of the JAG Corps often serve as military judges in courts–martial and courts of inquiry.

Joint Munitions Command – Joint Munitions Command (JMC) is the latest in a series of commands since World War II that have managed the nation's ammunition plants. Since 1973, those commands have been headquartered on Rock Island Arsenal. The headquarters on Rock Island Arsenal is responsible for munitions production and storage facilities in 16 states. JMC employs 20 military, over 5800 civilians and 8300 contractor personnel. Of these approximately 14,000 personnel, 738 work in the headquarters on Rock Island Arsenal. JMC has an annual budget of 1.7 billion dollars. JMC provides bombs and bullets to America's fighting forces—all services, all types of conventional ammo from 500–pound bombs to rifle rounds. JMC manages plants that produce more than 1.6 billion rounds of ammunition annually and the depots that store the nation's ammunition for training and combat. It is responsible for the management and accountability of $26 billion of conventional munitions and stores $39 billion of missiles.

JPED – Joint Personal Effects Depot – The Joint Personal Effects Depot is where all the personal belongings of service members killed and wounded during the Global War On Terrorism are meticulously processed before being returned to their families. It was originally housed at Fort Myer, Va., but was moved to Aberdeen in mid–2003.

Missing Man Fly–By – The missing man formation is an aerial salute performed as part of a flyover of aircraft at a funeral or memorial event, typically in memory of a fallen pilot, but is also commonly used for any fallen service member. The missing man formation is often called "the missing man flyby". The missing man formation varies, using either pull–up, split–off, or empty–position variations. There is an equivalent salute in motor sport.

Mobilization – Mobilization is the act of assembling and making both troops and supplies ready for war.

Mortar – A mortar is a muzzle–loading indirect fire weapon that fires shells at low velocities, short ranges, and high–arcing ballistic trajectories. It typically has a barrel length less than 15 times its caliber.

Mortuary Affairs – Mortuary Affairs is a service within the United States Army Quartermaster Corps tasked with the retrieval, identification, transportation, and burial of deceased American and American–allied military personnel.

Motor Pool – The Motor Pool is an area designated for a unit's vehicles. In most motor pools, the unit mechanics have a shop, and keep inoperative and spare vehicles.

MP – Military Police – An MP is service member in the US Army. The Military Police Corps is the uniformed law enforcement branch of the United States Army. Investigations are conducted by Military Police Investigators or the United States Army Criminal Investigation Command, both of which report to the Provost Marshal General.

MRE 611 – Military Rule of Evidence number 611 in the Manual for Courts Martial covers the mode and order of interrogation and presentation of a witness within a trial. It gives guidelines the defense and prosecution must follow when questioning a witness, and states alternative modes of questioning when a witness' circumstances prevent them from being at the trial, are a child, or whose identity is classified.

M67 Hand Grenade – A fragmentation hand grenade used by the United States Military. The M67 Grenade has a steel sphere body that contains 6.5 ounces of Composition B explosive. The M67 grenade is 14 ounces in total and has a safety clip for ease of manipulation.

NCO – Non–Commissioned Officer – A non–commissioned officer is an enlisted military member holding a position of some degree of authority who has obtained it by promotion from within the non–officer ranks. The non–commissioned officer corps is often referred to as "the backbone" of the armed services, as they are the primary and most visible leaders for most military personnel. Additionally, they are the primary military leaders responsible for executing the military organization's mission, and for training military personnel so they are prepared to execute their missions. NCO training and education typically includes leadership and management as well as service specific and combat training.

Senior NCOs, with their wealth of leadership, mission training and experience, are considered the primary link between the bulk of the enlisted personnel and the officers in any military organization. Their advice and guidance is particularly important for junior officers, who begin their careers in a position of authority but generally lack practical experience.

NCOER – Non–Commissioned Officer Evaluation Report – There are three functions of an NCOER. The first is to provide a soldier with meaningful feedback on what is expected of them, advice on how well they are meeting those expectations, and advice on how to better meet those expectations in the future. The second is to provide a reliable, long–term, cumulative record of performance and potential based on that performance. The third is to provide the Centralized Selection Boards, and NCO promotion boards and other personnel managers sound information to assist in identifying the best qualified enlisted personnel.

NCOIC – Non–Commissioned Officer In Charge – An NCOIC is an NCO who has limited command authority over others in the unit (such as a squad or team leader), or who is placed in charge of a detail (such as a color guard or work detail).

NVG – Night Vision Goggles – NVGs are an optical instrument that allows images to be produced in levels of light approaching total darkness. The term usually refers to a complete unit, including an image intensifier tube, a protective and generally water–resistant housing, and some type of mounting system. Many NVGs also include sacrificial lenses, IR illuminators, and telescopic lenses.

Officer – A US Army Commissioned Officer is a member of the Army who holds a position of authority. Commissioned officers derive authority directly from the President of the United States and, as such, hold a commission charging them with the duties and responsibilities of a specific office or position. Commissioned officers are the only persons able to act as the commanding officer of a unit.

Platoon – A platoon is a military unit typically composed of two to squads and containing 16 to 50 soldiers. Platoons are organized into a company, which typically consists of three to five platoons. A platoon is typically the smallest military unit led by a commissioned officer—the platoon leader or platoon commander, usually a lieutenant. He is usually assisted by a senior non–commissioned officer—the platoon sergeant.

Platoon Leader – A Platoon Leader, sometimes referred to as a Platoon Commander, depending on the type of unit, is a Commissioned Officer placed in command of a platoon, and is assisted by the platoon sergeant, a senior NCO.

PNOK – Primary Next of Kin – For the US Military, the primary next of kin is the person who is contacted in the event of an emergency, and who receives the US flag at the funeral if a service member is killed in action.

Property Book – The property book is a record of the unit's equipment. It keeps track of where, when, and who received the property at the company level—usually supply—and to whom within the company it is currently assigned.

PSYOPS – Psychological Operations – The planned use of propaganda and other psychological actions having the primary purpose of influencing the opinions, emotions, attitudes, and behavior of hostile foreign groups in such a way as to support the achievement of national objectives. The US Army has units specifically geared toward this.

PT Test – Army Physical Fitness Test (APFT) – The Army Physical Fitness Test is designed to test the muscular strength/endurance and cardiovascular respiratory fitness of soldiers in the United States Army. Soldiers are given a score based on their performance in three events consisting of the push–up, sit–up, and a two–mile run.

Purple Heart – The Purple Heart is a United States military decoration awarded in the name of the President to those who have been wounded or killed while serving on or after April 5, 1917 with the U.S. military.

PX – Post Exchange – In the US Army, PX is a common name for a type of retail store operating on US Army installations worldwide. Originally akin to trading posts, they now resemble department stores or strip malls.

QRF – Quick Reaction Force – The QRF is a small team ready to respond to any type of emergency, typically within ten minutes or less, at a moments notice.

Readiness NCO – In most Army National Guard units, the unit Readiness NCO is the senior full–time person in the company. The Readiness NCO typically handles the day–to–day issues within the company, and they also manage the full–time staff to include a Training NCO, Administration NCO, and Supply NCO.

Rear Detachment – The rear detachment operations pick up the home–station daily workload of the deployed unit and provide support for the unit.

Rear Detachment Commander – The RDC is responsible for the administrative operations of the rear detachment, including maintaining command and control, accounting for unit property and equipment, and managing personnel.

Redeployment – The movement of military forces from one theater of operations to another.

ROS – Report of Survey – An instrument for recording circumstances concerning loss, damaged, or destruction of Army property. It serves as, or supports, a voucher for dropping articles from property records on which they are listed. It also serves to determine any question of responsibility (financial or otherwise) for absence or condition of the articles.

Section – A section refers to any organization within a company that is not actually a platoon. For example, supply, the motor pool are considered sections. They do not typically have an officer in charge of each one, and fall into the company headquarters platoon.

STAR Card – The STAR Card is a credit card offered to military personnel and family members through Army and Air Force Exchange Services, also known as AAFES.

SINCGAR – SINCGARS (Single Channel Ground and Airborne Radio System) is a Combat Net Radio (CNR) used by the U.S. Military. The radios are easily maintained, and very secure.

Sync Meeting – A sync meeting is a meeting between the heads of each sections within a military unit, where current information regarding readiness and other information vital to company operations is exchanged and reported to the commander.

SINCGAR – SINCGARS (Single Channel Ground and Airborne Radio System) is a Combat Net Radio (CNR) used by the U.S. Military. The radios are easily maintained, and very secure.

Taps – Taps is played during military flag ceremonies and funerals. The original version of Taps is the traditional instrumental version that most people are familiar with. There have been lyrics added by several different poets over the years.

UCMJ – Uniform Code of Military Justice – The UCMJ is the code of military law that applies to all members of the armed services, home and abroad.

Victim/Witness Liaison – The victim/witness liaison protects the lives and property of members of the military community, and establishes a comprehensive program to provide support and assistance to victims and witnesses of crimes.

Water Palace – Refers to a palace that sits on a small lake on FOB Danger, Tikrit, Iraq.

Weapons Intelligence Team – A WIT can identify any type of weapon, especially explosives, used in an attack. They provide accurate and timely reports on enemy tactical and technical capabilities to command. These reports are used as a tool in command's overall intelligence gathering, and tactical planning.

XO – Executive Officer – XO reports directly to the Company Commander, and supports the CO in any way necessary.

MANY THANKS

✪ ✪ ✪

My thanks to all organizations who support the troops and their families. The organizations below have all directly assisted my family or families I know, and I encourage you to visit their websites for more information:

SnowBall Express: www.snowballexpress.org

TAPS (Tragedy Assistance Program for Survivors): www.taps.org

Families of War Vets: www.familiesofwarvets.org

America Supports You: www.americasupportsyoutexas

The American Fallen Soldiers Project: www.americanfallensoldiers.com

The American Widow Project: www.americanwidowproject.org

The Got Your Back Network: www.gotyourbacknetwork.org

Camp Better America: www.campbetteramerica.com

For further information on the case, our family, and current efforts, visit: www.unconventionalenemy.com

JUST LIKE THAT

Moments I'd only dreamed about
Days I believed I'd never have
Nights beside someone I knew would never leave, You gave all those things to me

Tomorrows taken for granted
Todays spent caught up in
Holdin on holdin tight to the best friend of my life

Then just
Like that
It all disappeared
The life we had
Was it ever really here?
Moments last for hours Nights drag on for years
Wanting you, wanting to, get back the best days of my life

Moments filled with fear
Chased by hours chased by years
Stumbling through, without you, will I ever get it right

See you in our childrens' eyes
Feel you in their hard—earned smiles
Gotta stand Gotta fight
Can't give up on their lives

Then just like that
It all comes crashing back
How we loved
How we laughed
God I want that feeling back
Will I ever live again?

On my knees in the night
Cursing at my life
One more drink still no sleep still can't kill the pain
Pray to God make it stop Let me go And then…
    Mommy please, come to me. I had another dream
    Daddy's here holding you
    Saying you know what to do…
And just
Like that
Was how I got it back
Gonna try Gonna rise Gonna take back my life
Gonna laugh gonna cry 'cause I feel you by my side,
I'm on my way.
Just like that.

BUY A SHARE OF THE FUTURE IN YOUR COMMUNITY

These certificates make great holiday, graduation and birthday gifts that can be personalized with the recipient's name. The cost of one S.H.A.R.E. or one square foot is $54.17. The personalized certificate is suitable for framing and will state the number of shares purchased and the amount of each share, as well as the recipient's name. The home that you participate in "building" will last for many years and will continue to grow in value.

Here is a sample SHARE certificate:

HABITAT FOR HUMANITY

THIS CERTIFIES THAT

YOUR NAME HERE

HAS INVESTED IN A HOME FOR A DESERVING FAMILY

1985-2005

TWENTY YEARS OF BUILDING FUTURES IN OUR
COMMUNITY ONE HOME AT A TIME

1200 SQUARE FOOT HOUSE @ $65,000 = $54.17 PER SQUARE FOOT
This certificate represents a tax deductible donation. It has no cash value.

YES, I WOULD LIKE TO HELP!

I support the work that Habitat for Humanity does and I want to be part of the excitement! As a donor, I will receive periodic updates on your construction activities but, more importantly, I know my gift will help a family in our community realize the dream of homeownership. **I would like to SHARE in your efforts against substandard housing in my community!** *(Please print below)*

PLEASE SEND ME _____ SHARES at $54.17 EACH = $ $_____

In Honor Of: _____

Occasion: (Circle One)   HOLIDAY   BIRTHDAY   ANNIVERSARY

          OTHER: _____

Address of Recipient: _____

Gift From: _____ *Donor Address:* _____

Donor Email: _____

I AM ENCLOSING A CHECK FOR $ $_____ PAYABLE TO HABITAT FOR HUMANITY <u>OR</u> PLEASE CHARGE MY VISA OR MASTERCARD *(CIRCLE ONE)*

Card Number _____ Expiration Date: _____

Name as it appears on Credit Card _____ Charge Amount $ _____

Signature _____

Billing Address _____

Telephone # Day _____ Eve _____

PLEASE NOTE: Your contribution is tax-deductible to the fullest extent allowed by law.
Habitat for Humanity • P.O. Box 1443 • Newport News, VA 23601 • 757-596-5553
www.HelpHabitatforHumanity.org

LaVergne, TN USA
06 October 2010
199892LV00002B/6/P